THE ENCYCLOPEDIA OF
Dance & Ballet

THE ENCYCLOPEDIA OF

Dance & Ballet

EDITED BY MARY CLARKE & DAVID VAUGHAN

PITMAN PUBLISHING

First published 1977

PITMAN PUBLISHING LIMITED
39 Parker Street, London WC2B 5PB

Associated Companies
Copp Clark Ltd, Toronto
Pitman Publishing Co. SA (Pty) Ltd, Johannesburg
Pitman Publishing New Zealand Ltd, Wellington
Pitman Publishing Pty Ltd, Melbourne
Sir Isaac Pitman Ltd, Nairobi

ISBN: 0 273 01088 3

This book was designed and produced by
RAINBIRD REFERENCE BOOKS LTD
36 Park Street,
London W1Y 4DE, England

House Editor: Perry Morley
Assistant Editor: Raymond Kaye
Designer: Karen Bowen
Picture Research: Pat Vaughan

Text filmset by Jolly & Barber Ltd, Rugby, Warwickshire, England
Printed and bound by
Dai Nippon Printing Co. Ltd, Tokyo, Japan

Introduction

The title of this book has been chosen to indicate that the entries are not confined to classical ballet but record also activity in contemporary dance styles. We are concerned, however, only with dance raised to a theatrical level as a performing art in any of the media of the twentieth century. We look back to the major influences but we do not attempt to cover the whole subject of 'dance'. That is something so vast it can never be compressed into a single volume. (Lincoln Kirstein's book *Dance*, New York 1935, and its bibliography, give the best overall picture.) We have not ventured into the fields of primitive, folk, or ritual dance although we acknowledge that theatre dance has always drawn inspiration from other forms.

The length of the entries has been governed by the existence or non-existence of definitive books on their subjects. The classic dance technique is well codified in various books; not so the technique evolved by Martha Graham which has been so influential in the middle part of this century. Graham technique therefore has a longer entry. We have also included articles on peripheral arts, such as mime, which are important to dance but not readily available in condensed form in dance literature. We have noted the contributions of designers in addition to the work of choreographers and musicians.

Books relating to a specific subject are listed under the entry. There is also a general bibliography with explanatory notes.

We are aware of omissions forced upon us by reasons of space but believe the cross-referencing system and the bibliographical material will enable the reader to pursue further studies.

Dance is the most ephemeral of the arts. Film, television, and notation are only now beginning to capture the true quality of stage productions or the dancers' art. Moreover the dancer's performing life is short. Virtuosity has gone by about age 40 although artistry is undimmed. By age 17 or 18 potential talent is usually obvious to teachers and connoisseurs. While this book is in production a young graduate will establish a claim for recognition, a new choreographic talent may emerge.

We acknowledge our debts to such lexicographers of the dance as Anatole Chujoy, P. W. Manchester, G. B. L. Wilson, and Horst Koegler. Our gratitude goes also to our contributors, many of whom gave help and advice beyond their own entries. Our great sorrow was the death in January 1977 of Natalia Roslavleva who completed her Russian entries but did not live to approve our edited and abbreviated versions. Her friend Vera Krasovskaya of Leningrad has answered many queries. We are grateful also to Barbara Newman in New York for editorial assistance.

The staff of Rainbird Reference Books Ltd, who conceived and produced this book, have been meticulous in their scrutiny of entries and queries about inconsistencies. They have refused to allow us to assume any prior knowledge of the subject on the part of the reader and have thus saved us from many imprecise statements. Our thanks above all to Miss Perry Morley for synchronizing the whole operation and for maintaining good humour and patience when confronted with some of the vagaries of the world of dance and ballet.

Mary Clarke and David Vaughan 1977

Contributors

JA Jack Anderson. Associate critic, *Dance Magazine* and associate editor, *Ballet Review* (New York); New York correspondent, *The Dancing Times* (London). He is the author of *Dance* (1974) and many articles, reviews, and broadcasts. Since 1975 he has been a member of the Dance Advisory Panel of the (US) National Endowment for the Arts. Teaches dance history and criticism at university level; broadcasts; co-editor, *Dance Chronicle: Studies in Dance and The Related Arts.*

AC Arturo Castillo. Correspondent for several US publications on Mexican affairs, especially politics and ballet; organizer in Mexico for RAD, 1971–6.

ACy Anthony Crickmay. Photographer who has worked for the RB, Royal Opera, and National Theatre in London, also LFB and LCDT; has also worked for NB of Canada, Australian B., Stuttgart B., and NDT. Photographer of ballet, opera, and drama for *The Times* (London).

CC Clement Crisp. Ballet critic, the *Financial Times* (London); London correspondent, *Les Saisons de la Danse* (Paris); Librarian and Tutor, RAD; Lecturer in Dance at the British campus of New England College. Joint author, with Mary Clarke, of *Ballet: An Illustrated History* (1973), *Making a Ballet* (1974), and *Introducing Ballet* (1976); with Peter Brinson of *Ballet for All* (1970, 1971); with Edward Thorpe of *The Colourful World of Ballet* (1977); edited *Ballerina: Portraits and Impressions of Nadia Nerina* (1975).

KC Kitty Cunningham. Freelance contributor to major US dance periodicals; critic for *Dance and Dancers* (London) from 1971.

MC Mary Clarke. Editor since 1963 of *The Dancing Times* (London) and former London Editor, *Dance News* (New York); author of the standard histories of the Sadler's Wells B. and B. Rambert. She was Associate Editor (to Arnold L. Haskell) for many years on *The Ballet Annual*; author, with Clement Crisp, of *Ballet: An Illustrated History* (1973), *Making a Ballet* (1974), and *Introducing Ballet* (1976).

M-FC Marie-Françoise Christout. Librarian, Bibliothèque Nationale, Paris, specializing in the Départment des Arts du Spectacle. Author of *Le Ballet de Cour de Louis XIV, 1643–1672* (1967), 'The Court Ballet in France 1615–1641' (*Dance Perspectives* No. 20), and *Maurice Béjart* (1976); has contributed to many international periodicals and encyclopedias.

RC Roger Copeland. Teaches courses in history and criticism of dance, film, and drama, Oberlin College, OH; has also taught in the History of Art Department, Yale University; frequent contributor to the *Sunday New York Times*; has also contributed to *Dance Magazine, Dance Scope, The Village Voice,* etc.

SJC Selma Jeanne Cohen. Founding editor of *Dance Perspectives* (New York 1965–76); has taught courses in dance history at university level; editor of *The Modern Dance: Seven Statements of Belief* (1966); *Dance as a Theatre Art* (1974); and author of *Doris Humphrey: An Artist First* (1972).

CD Craig Dodd. After contributing to the *Guardian*, the *New Statesman* and, principally, *The Dancing Times* (London), in 1972 moved into personal management, representing principal dancers from major international companies.

DD David Dougill. Dance critic of the *Sunday Times* (London) from 1975. Research assistant to Richard Buckle.

GD George Dorris. Assistant Professor of English, York College, CUNY; Associate Editor and Music Editor, *Ballet Review* (New York); member of the Board of Dance Perspectives Foundation; co-editor, *Dance Chronicle: Studies in Dance and The Related Arts.*

GPD Gedeon Paul Dienes. Studied dancing at Duncan Academy, Nice and Paris, in the early 1920s; in Budapest graduated in art of movement, National Choreographic Teacher Training College; taught history of dancing and staged dance plays in the 1930s. Now head of library and international department, Hungarian Institute for Culture, Budapest; as a dance critic and historian, has contributed many articles to international periodicals and encyclopedias.

JD Jennifer Dunning. Staff critic, *Dance Magazine* (New York); writes on the arts for the *New York Times.*

JDy Jane Dudley. Director of Graham Studies, LSCD; soloist and member of the Martha Graham Dance Company; artistic director, Batsheva Dance Co., Israel; member, Dudley-Maslow-Bales Dance Trio.

PD Penelope Doob. Associate Professor of English and the Humanities, York University, Toronto, Canada; studied ballet and Graham technique in Boston; writer on dance from 1972.

PME Parmenia Migel (Ekstrom). Dance historian; founded first USA Ballet Guild, and Dance Forum at New School for Social Research, New York. Has lectured at several universities; author, *Titania* (1967), *The Ballerinas, from the Court of Louis XIV to Pavlova* (1972) and of many articles. President, Stravinsky-Diaghilev Foundation; writing full-length biography of Augusta Maywood.

AHG Ann Hutchinson Guest. Leading specialist on dance notation; one of the founders of the Dance Notation Bureau; author of the standard textbook on the Laban method, *Labanotation or Kinetography Laban: System of Analysing or Recording Movement* (1970) and has revived a number of old works from notation. Early career in Broadway musicals; now teaches Labanotation at Goldsmiths' College and at the RAD, of which she is a Governor.

IG Ivor Guest. Writer on the history of ballet and foremost authority on the Romantic period; associate editor, *The Ballet Annual*, 1952–63. Author of many books and several issues of *Dance Perspectives*, including biographies of Fanny Cerrito, Fanny Elssler, Adeline Genée, and Virginia Zucchi. His *The Romantic Ballet in Paris* (1966) is the definitive work; commissioned 1975 by the Paris Opéra to write the official history of its ballet company. Chairman, RAD, from 1969; vice-chairman, British Theatre Museum Association from 1966, and member of the Theatre Museum Advisory Sub-Committee; organized National Book League Exhibition of books on ballet 1957–8.

MG Marina Grut. Producer, choreographer, and teacher; studied at UCTBS as well as in London and Spain; taught ballet history and Spanish dance, UCTBS 1956–75; has produced and choreographed all CAPAB B's major Spanish dance productions; has contributed to many international periodicals and encyclopedias.

ALH Arnold L. Haskell (*see* entry in text)

BH Bengt Häger. Director, Dansmuseet (The Dance Museum), Stockholm, since 1950; member of the Swedish Government Council for Culture, 1969–75; vice president, International Council for Dance, a non-governmental organization within UNESCO, from 1974 when it was founded; founded Swedish High School for Choreographic Art 1963 and remained as Dean when it was renamed the State Dance School, leaving 1971.

DH Dale Harris. Professor of English, Sarah Lawrence College, New York; author, 'Merce Cunningham' and 'Twyla Tharp' in *On Modern Dance* (1977); dance critic and contributing editor, *Saturday Review* (1974); associate editor, *Ballet Review* (New York); contributing editor, *High Fidelity*; contributor of articles and reviews on dance and music to the *Guardian* (Manchester and London), *Atlantic Monthly, New York Sunday Times*, etc.

DHe Doris Hering. Executive Director, (US) National Association for Regional Ballet; critic-at-large for *Dance Magazine* (New York); formerly associate editor and principal critic; Adjunct Associate Professor of Dance History, New York University.

PH Philippa Heale. Australian dancer and dance notator specializing in the dances of Spain (professional name Felisa Victoria). Studied with Mercedes and Albano; at present dancing and researching into dance in Spain.

DJ Deborah Jowitt. Has written a weekly column on dance for *The Village Voice* (New York) from 1967; has contributed articles to many other publications; author, *Dance Beat: Selected Views and Reviews 1967–1976* (1977); also a dancer and choreographer.

SKJ Svend Kragh-Jacobsen. Ballet critic and historian; drama, ballet and film critic, *Nationaltidende* (Copenhagen) from 1936; drama, ballet, and film critic, *Berlingske Tidende* from 1938. His many books include *Ballettens Blomstring* (*Flowering of the Ballet*, 1945), *Margot Lander* (1948); wrote two-thirds of *Den Kongelige Danske Ballet* (*The Royal Danish Ballet*, 1952), which he edited with Torben Krogh; from 1955 editor, *Teater-årbogen* (*Theatre Annual*); has lectured widely and contributed to many international encyclopedias and periodicals.

EK Elizabeth Kendall. Dance critic in New York; writes for *Ballet Review, The New Republic*, the *New York Times*; working on a book about early American modern dance.

JL Joan Lawson. Writer, critic, and dance teacher; author of *A History of Ballet and Its Makers* (1964), *The Teaching of Classical Ballet* (1973), *Teaching Young Dancers: Muscular Co-ordination in Classical Ballet* (1975); on the staff of RBS from 1963; has contributed to many international periodicals and encyclopedias.

JLy John Lanchbery. Studied at the Royal Academy of Music, London; Musical Director, Metropolitan B. 1948–9; SWTB 1951–9; principal conductor RB 1960–72; since then Musical Director, Australian B. Has composed several ballets and made many arrangements including, notably, *La Fille Mal Gardée* (for Ashton). Fellow of the Royal Academy of Music; Bolshoy Theatre Medal.

JUL Juan Ubaldo Lavanga. Dance critic, magazine *Todo la Danza* (*All About Dance*; Buenos Aires).

TL Thomas Leabhart. Studied with Étienne Decroux; founder of Arkansas Mime Theatre; currently director, Wisconsin Mime Theatre; founder and editor of *Mime Journal* and *Mime News*.

DM Don McDonagh. Writes dance criticism for the *New York Times*; an associate editor, *Ballet Review*; contributed American entries to *Ballet for All* (1970, 1971; edited by Peter Brinson and Clement Crisp); author, *The Rise and Fall and Rise of Modern Dance* (1970), *Martha Graham* (1973), and *The Complete Guide to Modern Dance* (1976).

FM Francis Mason. Ballet critic, *The Hudson Review* (New York) 1948–54; former cultural attaché at the US Embassy in London; has collaborated with George Balanchine on *Balanchine's Complete Stories of the Great Ballets* (1954, 1968), *101 Stories of Great Ballets* (1975), and *Balanchine's Book of Ballet* (1977).

JM James Monahan, CBE. Dance critic, the *Guardian* (Manchester and London) from 1935 (now writing as James Kennedy); 1952–72 Controller of European Services of the BBC; author of *Fonteyn: a Study of a Ballerina in her Setting* (1957, 1958) and *The Nature of Ballet* (1976); contributor to *The Ballet Annual, The Dancing Times*, and many other publications. Director, RBS, from 1977.

JMu John Mueller. Teaches dance history at the University of Rochester, NY; writes a monthly column on dance films for *Dance Magazine* (New York); has published an annotated and evaluative directory of dance films.

NM Nathan Mishori. Senior lecturer, Academy of Music, Tel-Aviv University; music and dance critic, *Ha'aretz*; has contributed to many periodicals and to *Grove's Dictionary of Music and Musicians*, 6th edition; closely associated with dance as an accompanist, musical adviser, critic, lecturer, and member of national committees, for 25 years.

PWM P. W. Manchester. Secretary to Marie Rambert 1944–6; editor, *Ballet Today* (London) 1946–51; managing editor, *Dance News* (New York) 1951–69; New York dance critic, *Christian Science Monitor*, 1960–8; Adjunct Professor of Dance, University of Cincinnati, College-Conservatory of Music, since 1969; author *Vic-Wells: a Ballet Progress* (1942); co-editor (with Anatole Chujoy), *Dance Encyclopedia* (1967); lectures widely and broadcasts.

RM Reginald Massey. Indian writer, film maker, critic, and lecturer on the arts, particularly of India, now resident London; co-author with Rina Singha of *Indian Dances: their History and Growth* (1967); co-author with Jamila Massey of *The Music of India* (1976); contributor to *The Dancing*

Times, The Musical Times, and *Music and Musicians*. Fellow of the Royal Society of Arts.

MLN Maria Luisa Noronha. Brazilian dancer; worked with Dalal Achcar from the foundation of B. do Rio de Janeiro, 1956; studied ballet with Maria Makarova and at the London RBS; director, Ballet Dalal Achcar School, and of *Dança* newspaper. Ballet mistress, B. do Rio de Janeiro.

FP Freda Pitt. Freelance ballet critic; ballet critic, *Daily Mail* (London 1955–6, deputy ballet critic, *Daily Mail*, 1958–60); to Milan 1962; in Rome since 1970; Italian correspondent, *The Dancing Times* (London) from 1962; regular contributor to Turin quarterly *Musicalbrandé*; occasional contributor to Rome monthly *Il Dramma*.

JP John Percival. Ballet critic, *The Times* (London); associate editor, *Dance and Dancers*; author, *Modern Ballet* (1970), *The World of Diaghilev* (1971), *Experimental Dance* (1971), and *Nureyev: Aspects of the Dancer* (1975).

JPu Janina Pudełek. Curator of Polish Theatre Museum in Warsaw; ballet historian and critic; studied dance with Leon Woizikowski; author of *Warszawski Balet Romantyczny 1802–1866* (*Romantic Ballet in Warsaw 1802–1866*; 1968) and *Warszawski Balet w II Połowie XIX Wieku* (*Ballet in Warsaw in the Second Half of the 19th century*); and *Warszawski Balet międsy Wojnami 1918–1939* (*Ballet in Warsaw between the Wars 1918–1939*) (the last two in preparation); contributes to many Polish and international periodicals; broadcasts.

AR Allen Robertson. Children's theatre playwright and director; began writing about dance in 1973; dance critic, *Minnesota Daily* (Minneapolis); contributor to *Ballet Review* (New York) and *Dance Magazine*.

KR Kenneth Rowell. Australian painter and stage designer. His works for ballet have included designs for B. Rambert, LFB, RB, RDB, and Australian B. Author, *Stage Design* (1972); lectures widely.

NR Natalia Roslavleva. Writer on ballet; educated University of Moscow and studied at Lunacharsky Choreographic Technicum, Moscow; began writing on ballet in 1943, contributing articles to many Soviet magazines as well as to British, American, and Italian encyclopedias and periodicals; her books include *Maya Plisetskaya* (in English 1956; in Russian, enlarged, 1968), *Angliisky Balet* (*English Ballet*, 1959), *Stanislavski and the Ballet* (in English, 1965), *Era of the Russian Ballet* (in English, 1966), 'Petipa's Family in Europe' in Yuri Slonimsky (ed.), *Marius Petipa, Materiali Vospominaniya Stati* (*Materials, Reminiscences, Letters*) (Leningrad 1971), 'Tikhomirov, his Life, his Work' in *Vassily Dmitrievitch Tikhomirov* (1971), *Maris Liepa* (1976).

NRe Nancy Reynolds. Former dancer with New York City Ballet; editor, art-book publishing house; author of articles on art and dance for magazines and encyclopedias, and of *Repertory in Review: 40 Years of the New York City Ballet* (1977); editor, *American Dance Guild Newsletter*.

AGS Anna Greta Ståhle. Lecturer on dance and Oriental theatre, journalist, critic, and teacher. On staff of *Dagens Nyheter* (Stockholm) 1942–75; theatre editor 1954–66; dance critic 1950–75. Scandinavian correspondent, *Dance News* 1955–75; contributor to American, British, and German ballet encyclopedias; teaches at the Stockholm university and State Dance School; author, *Classical Japanese Theatre* (1976).

JHS James H. Siegelman. Co-author, with Jerry Ames, of *The Book of Tap* (1976).

JS Janet Sinclair. Critic and writer on dance; has written many articles for *Ballet Today* and other British publications, mostly in collaboration with her husband Leo Kersley, a former principal of SWB, now teaching; author, with Kersley, of *A Dictionary of Ballet Terms* (1952).

JSas José Sasportes. Journalist and writer; formerly dance critic for Lisbon newspapers and magazines, Radio Canada (Montreal) and correspondent to *Dance Magazine* (New York). Co-founder, Portuguese Ballet Centre; principal, National Conservatory Dance School, Lisbon; author of 'Feasts and Folias: The Dance in Portugal', *Dance Perspectives*, No. 42 (1971); now at Portuguese Embassy in Rome.

MBS Marcia B. Siegel. Dance critic, *The Hudson Review* and *Soho Weekly News* (New York); two collections of her reviews and articles, are *At the Vanishing Point, A Critic Looks at Dance* (1972) and *Watching The Dance Go By* (1977).

SRS Sally R. Sommer. Dance critic on four Brooklyn newspapers; has contributed many articles on theatre and dance to various journals and book anthologies; Associate Professor of Theater, C.W. Post College; currently writing a book on Loie Fuller.

DV David Vaughan. Associate Editor, *Ballet Review* (New York); Secretary and Archivist, the Cunningham Dance Foundation; studied dance with Marie Rambert and Audrey de Vos in London; won a scholarship to the School of American Ballet, studied there and with Merce Cunningham, Antony Tudor, and Richard Thomas. Co-founder with James Waring of Dance Associates (1951), danced in the companies of Shirley Broughton, Louis Johnson, Katherine Litz, Paul Taylor, Waring, and in U.S. Terpsichore (1974–6), etc. Author, *The Royal Ballet at Covent Garden* (1975), *Lynn Seymour* (1976), and *Frederick Ashton and his Ballets* (1977); a contributor to many periodicals.

GBLW G. B. L. Wilson. Author of *A Dictionary of Ballet* (1957; and subsequent editions); London correspondent, *Dance News* (New York); writer, photographer, and lecturer on ballet, founder of the Association of Ballet Clubs (1947). Adviser on ballet careers to the London RBS from 1967 and hence in close touch with all European opera houses.

KSW Kathrine Sorley Walker. Author of many books on dance and ballet including *Robert Helpmann* (1958), *Eyes on Mime* (1969), *Dance and Its Creators* (1972); edited *Writings on Dance by A. V. Coton 1938–68* (1975); a ballet critic for the *Daily Telegraph* (London) from 1962. Has contributed to many international periodicals and encyclopedias, and written program notes for the Australian B.

MHW Marian Hannah Winter. Writer and lecturer in English and French on dance, circus, early cinema, popular theatre, and fairs. Her books include *Le Théâtre du Merveilleux* (Paris 1962, English translation 1964), and *The Pre-Romantic Ballet* (1974, 1975). In 1974 she was awarded a Guggenheim Fellowship.

Editorial Note

Some points of treatment require explanation:

We have given the titles of all ballets in their original languages, where they were first performed with an English, French, German, Italian, or Spanish title. For those originally with a title in Danish, Polish, Russian, or some other language less commonly known in English-speaking countries, we have used an English title, choosing in most cases a literal translation of the original. In a few instances we have kept to well-known English titles that are not translations of the original (e.g. *Cracow Wedding*). For consistency, we have capitalized titles in all languages as they would be in English.

Dates of works, unless otherwise noted, are those of first stage production. Russian dates are generally given in new style.

Place names are generally given as currently spelled in the country concerned, except for a few cities (Munich, Prague, etc.) where readers will be more familiar with the English rendering; when a city has changed its own name (St Petersburg, Petrograd, Leningrad) we give the form under which it was known at the time. In certain entries, current or historical alternative forms are also given.

All personal names are printed as the owner would spell them, complete with accents. For names transliterated from the Cyrillic script, we have based our system upon that used in *Grove's Dictionary of Music and Musicians*, 6th edition. We have, however, retained the inconsistent but familiar forms in some instances (e.g. Diaghilev, not Dyagilev; Nijinsky, not Nizhinsky; Tchaikovsky, not Chaykovsky). Cross-references within entries are indicated by the use of SMALL CAPITALS.

Abbreviations

ABT, ABTS	American Ballet Theatre (called Ballet Theatre 1939–57; *see* AMERICAN BALLET THEATRE in text), American Ballet Theatre School, New York
acad.	academy (or equivalent in any language)
AL	Alabama
AR	Arkansas
arr.	arranged (by)
AZ	Arizona
B.	Ballet (or equivalent in any language, e.g. Australian B., Berliner B., B. Russes)
b.	born
BAM	Brooklyn Academy of Music, New York
BBC	British Broadcasting Corporation
B. des CE	Ballet des Champs Élysées, Paris
BR	Ballet Rambert, London
B. XXe S.	Ballet du XXe Siècle, Paris
c.	century
c.	costumes (by)
c.	*circa*
CA	California
CAPAB	Cape Performing Arts Board (*see* CAPAB in text)
CBE	Commander of the Order of the British Empire (*see* AWARDS AND DECORATIONS in text)
CC	City Center, New York
CCJB	City Center Joffrey Ballet, New York (since 1976 the Joffrey Ballet)
CG	Covent Garden (Royal Opera House), London
CGOB	Covent Garden Opera Ballet, London
CH	Companion of Honour (*see* AWARDS AND DECORATIONS in text)
ch.	choreographed (by)
co.	company
CO	Colorado
COMPLETE BOOK	C.W. Beaumont, *Complete Book of Ballets* (*see* General Bibliography)
cons.	conservatory (or equivalent in any language)
CT	Connecticut
d.	died
dan.	danced (by), dancers (principals)
DBE	Dame Commander of the Order of the British Empire (*see* AWARDS AND DECORATIONS in text)
DC	District of Columbia
DE	Delaware
dir.	directed (by)
DL	Drury Lane Theatre, London
de Cuevas B.	any of the de Cuevas ballet companies: B. de Cuevas, Grand B. de Cuevas, Grand B. du Marquis de Cuevas, etc. (*see* GRAND BALLET DU MARQUIS DE CUEVAS in text)

DTW Dance Theater Workshop, New York
fest. festival
FL Florida
GA Georgia
IA Iowa
ID Idaho
IL Illinois
IN Indiana
inst. institute (or equivalent in any language)
KA Kansas
KY Kentucky
LA Louisiana
LCDT London Contemporary Dance Theatre
LFB London Festival Ballet, London (originally Festival Ballet, *see* LONDON FESTIVAL BALLET in text)
lib. libretto (by)
LSCD London School of Contemporary Dance
ltg lighting (by)
m. marriage, married
MA Massachusetts
MBE Member of the Order of the British Empire (*see* AWARDS AND DECORATIONS in text)
MD Maryland
ME Maine
Met Metropolitan Opera, New York
MI Michigan
MN Minnesota
MO Missouri
MS Mississippi
MT Montana
mus. music (by)
NAPAC National Performing Arts Council (*see* NAPAC in text)
NB National Ballet (e.g. Dutch NB, NB of Canada)
NBS National Ballet School
NC North Carolina
ND North Dakota
NDT Nederlands Dans Theater
NE Nebraska
NH New Hampshire
NJ New Jersey
NM New Mexico
NOB National Opera Ballet
NT National Theatre (e.g. Prague NT)
NV Nevada
NY New York
NYCB New York City Ballet
NYCC New York City Center
NYST New York State Theater
O. Opera (or equivalent in any language, e.g. Paris O. = Paris Opéra)
OBE Officer of the Order of the British Empire (*see* AWARDS AND DECORATIONS in text)
OBS Opera Ballet School
OC Opéra-Comique, Paris
OH Opera House
OH Ohio
OK Oklahoma
OR Oregon
orch. orchestrated (by)
PA Pennsylvania
PAC-OFS Performing Arts Council of the Orange Free State (*see* PACOFS in text)
PACT Performing Arts Council of the Transvaal (*see* PACT in text)
perf. performance, performed (by)
pub. publication, published (by)
RAD Royal Academy of Dancing, London
RAM Royal Academy of Music, London
RB Royal Ballet, London
RBS Royal Ballet School, London
RDBS Royal Danish Ballet, Copenhagen
RDBS Royal Danish Ballet School, Copenhagen
RFH Royal Festival Hall, London
RI Rhode Island
RSB Royal Swedish Ballet, Stockholm
RSBS Royal Swedish Ballet School, Stockholm
RWB Royal Winnipeg Ballet
S. School (or equivalent in any language)
SAB School of American Ballet, New York
SC South Carolina
Sc. La Scala (T. alla Scala), Milan
sc. scenery (by)
SD South Dakota
SW Sadler's Wells, London
T. theatre (or equivalent in any language, e.g. T. des CE = Théâtre des Champs Élysées; T. Regio = Teatro Regio; T. a. d. Wieden = Theater auf der Wieden)
TN Tennessee
tr. translated (by)
TS Theatre School (e.g. St Petersburg TS)
TX Texas
univ. university (or equivalent in any language)
UCT University of Cape Town (*see* UCT in text)
UT Utah
VA Virginia
VT Vermont
WA Washington
WI Wisconsin
WV West Virginia
WY Wyoming
YM & YWHA Young Men's and Young Women's Hebrew Association, New York

Åkesson, Birgit, b. Malmö, 1908. Swedish dancer and choreographer. Studied with WIGMAN; debut 1934, Paris; toured Europe and USA as soloist. Developed her own style of modern dance. Choreographed for RSB in collaboration with Swedish composers, poets, and painters, ballets incl. SISYPHUS, *Minotaurus*, and *Rites*, and also the dances for Karl-Birger Blomdahl's opera *Aniara*. Cofounder with Bengt Häger (1964) of the Stockholm Choreographic Inst. (now the State Dance S.). Head of the choreographic department until 1968, when she retired to study ritual dances in Africa. AGS

Alain, a simple-minded, wealthy young man, intended husband of LISE in FILLE MAL GARDÉE

Albrecht, GISELLE's lover and betrayer, disguised as peasant Loys in Act I

Albrecht, Angèle, b. Freiburg, 1942. German dancer. Studied in Munich. London RBS 1959, VAN DIJK. Debut Mannheim B. 1960, then Hamburg OB 1961–7 where she specialized in the works of BALANCHINE, van Dijk, and PETIT. B. XXe S. since 1967. Created for BÉJART important roles in MESSE POUR LE TEMPS PRÉSENT, *Baudelaire* (1968), NIJINSKY, CLOWN DE DIEU, *Stimmung* (1972), *Pli selon Pli* (1975). Also dances in Béjart's *Bhakti*, *Roméo et Juliette* (as Mab), NINTH SYMPHONY, *Boléro*, SACRE DU PRINTEMPS. Her original personality is accompanied by brilliant technique and dramatic authority. M-FC

Alder, Alan, b. Canberra, 1937. Australian dancer. Scholarship to London RBS 1957; CGOB 1957–8; RB 1958–63, becoming soloist. Australian B. 1963, principal dancer 1969. An excellent dramatic dancer, who can tackle a virtuoso role (the Jester, CINDERELLA) or a subtle character study (ALAIN). He m. ALDOUS. KSW

Aldous, Lucette, b. Auckland, New Zealand, 1938 (moved to Australia at four months old). Australian dancer. Gained Frances Scully Memorial Scholarship to SWBS 1955. BR 1957–63, ballerina 1958; LFB 1963; RB 1967; Australian B. 1970 (guest artist); from 1971 resident principal ballerina. A vital, technically brilliant classical dancer, capable equally of comedy (KITRI, filmed 1973) and of sensitive lyrical dancing (SYLPHIDE). She m. ALDER. KSW

Aleksidze, Georgi (Gogi), b. Tbilisi [Tiflis], 1941. Soviet dancer and choreographer. From well-known Georgian theatrical family: father, theatrical director Dmitry Aleksidze; aunt, ballerina Irina Aleksidze. Studied Tbilisi and Moscow Choreographic S., graduating from the latter 1960 (MESSERER's class). Danced in Tbilisi T. of O. and B. 1961–2. To Choreographers' faculty, Leningrad Cons., pupil of F. LOPUKHOV. In 1966 showed first choreographic miniatures in new Chamber B. headed by the musician Vitaly Buyanovsky and Kirov dancer Tatiana Bazilevskaya; created three programs, incl. Benjamin Britten's *Metamorphoses*, and showed considerable artistic independence. Invited by Kirov T. for productions of *Oresteia* (mus. Yuri Falik, 1968) and *Scythian Suite* (mus. PROKOFIEV, 1969). Has taught at Leningrad Cons. since 1967. From 1972 artistic director and principal choreographer Tbilisi B., choreographing there *Les Petits Riens*, *Choreographic Fantasies*, *Berikaova* (mus. Bidzina Kvernadze, based on Georgian folk music), a revival of his *Oresteia* and a new version of COPPÉLIA, etc. Documentary film about his work made at Lenfilm studios (*Theme and Variations*, 1971) mainly on his works for Chamber B. NR

Algaroff, Youly, b. Simferopol, 1918. Russian-French dancer. Debut 1937, B. de la Jeunesse. Studied with KNIASEFF. Danced at the O. de Lyon, Nouveaux B. de Monte Carlo 1946–7, B. des CE 1945, 1948–9. Engaged as *étoile*, Paris O. 1952–64. Impresario since 1965. Noble, expressive, he combined elegance and lyricism in works as diverse as GISELLE; LIFAR's *Chota Roustaveli* and OISEAU DE FEU; SYMPHONIE FANTASTIQUE; FORAINS. M-FC

Algeranoff [Essex], Harcourt, b. London, 1903; d. Robinvale, Australia, 1967. English dancer, ballet master, and choreographer. Studied Japanese and Indian dance as well as classical ballet. A. PAVLOVA B. 1921; MARKOVA–DOLIN B. 1935; DE BASIL B. Russes 1936; International B. 1943; Australian Children's T. 1955–7; BOROVANSKY B., ballet master, 1959; Australian B., guest artist, 1962–3. Settled in Mildura, Australia, 1959, and opened studio. A specialist in character and Oriental dance, he created the Astrologer (COQ D'OR) and is particularly associated with the roles of DR COPPÉLIUS and Pierrot (CARNAVAL). Ballets incl. *For Love or Money*. Published *My Years with Pavlova* (London 1957). He m. dancer Claudie Algeranova. KSW

Algues, Les, ballet, 4 scenes, ch. CHARRAT; mus. Guy Bernard; lib./sc. Bertrand Castelli. Paris, T. des CE, 20 Apr 1953; dan. Charrat, Maria Fris, VAN DIJK. A poetic evocation of a madhouse which revealed especially the dramatic power of Charrat and Fris, and the strong personality of van Dijk. M-FC

Alhanko, Anneli, b. Bogotà, Colombia, 1953, of Finnish family, naturalized Swedish. Studied RSBS and abroad. Soloist 1973. Principal dancer 1976. Danced MACMILLAN's JULIET and AURORA. Silver medal, Varna Competition, 1972. Studied in Leningrad together with SEGERSTRÖM 1974; debut in GISELLE with Kirov B. AGS

Allan, Maud, b. Toronto, 1883; d. Los Angeles, CA, 1956. Canadian dancer. Largely self-taught. Regular musical instruction in Berlin combined with her interest in fine art resulted in the development of her own style of dramatic dance. Her most successful vehicle was VISION OF SALOME. Her halter and flowing transparent skirt were considered daring and the climactic moment of the dance when she pressed her lips to the severed head was too powerful for some audiences. To accommodate squeamishness, she sometimes substituted a mimed passage for the conclusion. Her greatest acclaim came in the years before World War I when she toured the world, though she continued to dance until the late 1930s. After retirement, she taught in England. Published *My Life and Dancing* (London and New York 1908). DM

Allard, Marie, b. Marseille, 1742; d. Paris, 1802. French dancer, pupil, partner, and mistress of G. VESTRIS and mother of A. VESTRIS. Debut 1760, Paris O.; retired 1782 when corpulence set in. Appeared in ballets by NOVERRE and Maximilien Gardel. MC

Alonso [Martinez], Alicia, b. Havana, 1917. Cuban dancer. She m. teacher and dancer Fernando Alonso. Studied New York with A. FEDOROVA and VILZAK, and at SAB. Danced in Broadway musicals and in KIRSTEIN's B. Caravan 1939–40. Ballerina of ABT 1941–60, with some interruptions during which she danced with the Pro Arte in Havana (1941–3), with her own co., B. Alicia Alonso (1948 and thereafter), and B. Russe de Monte Carlo (1955–7). During much of this time she formed a legendary partnership with YOUSKEVITCH. Her own co. became the B. de Cuba 1955, and has toured the USSR, China, and Europe. One of the greatest GISELLEs of her generation, her repertory incl. both classic and contemporary ballets – among others *Theme and Variations* (BALANCHINE), UNDERTOW, and FALL RIVER LEGEND. She has also choreographed several ballets and staged *Giselle* (1952) and SLEEPING BEAUTY (1974) for the Paris O. In 1975 she returned to the USA after an absence of several years to dance the *pas de deux* from SWAN LAKE (Act II) in an ABT Gala Performance at NYST. DV
See T. de Gamez, *Alicia Alonso at Home and Abroad* (New York 1971); I. Lidova, 'Alonso', *Les Saisons de la Danse* (Paris, Nov 1970) which contains complete list of roles

Alston, Richard, b. Stoughton, Sussex, 1948. English dancer and choreographer. Educated at Eton. Studied art at Croydon College of Art 1965–7, then dance at LSCD 1967–70. First choreographed for workshop performances at The Place, London, 1968. In 1972 co-founded Strider, a cooperative *avant-garde* dance co. Several of his pieces, incl. some originally made for Strider, have been taken into the repertory of LCDT. Works incl. *Cold* (mus. ADAM, 1971), a contemporary gloss on the theme of GISELLE Act II; *Combines* (mus. Franz Schubert *et al.*, 1972); *Tiger Balm* (1972); *Windhover* (1972); *Headlong* (1973); *Blue Schubert Fragments* (1974); *Soft Verges* (1974–5); *Slow Field* (1975); *0–9* (1975); *Souvenir* (1975); *Edge* (1976). To USA for a year's study 1975. DV

Amati, Olga, b. Milan, 1924. Italian dancer. Sc. BS 1934, principal dancer 1942–56, later teaching at Rome OBS. FP

Amaya, Carmen *see* SPAIN

Amberg, George H., b. Halle an der Saale, Germany, 1901; d. 1971. US citizen from 1946. Stage director, lecturer, photographer, and writer. Curator of Dance Archives, Museum of Modern Art, NY, 1943; later curator of Dept of Theater Arts there until 1948 when the department became a division of the Music Library of the Museum. Univ. lecturer, New York Univ. 1948–52; associate professor, Univ. of Minnesota, Minneapolis, 1952–6; Professor at Univ. of Minnesota and Minneapolis S. of Art 1956–7. Contributor to many distinguished publications. Author of *Ballet in America* (New York 1949, with subsequent editions) and editor of *Art in Modern Ballet* (New York 1946; London 1947). MC

America *see* UNITED STATES OF AMERICA

American Ballet (company) *see* NEW YORK CITY BALLET

American Ballet Caravan *see* NEW YORK CITY BALLET

American Ballet Theatre, co. founded in New York in 1939, under the direction of Richard Pleasant and CHASE. It was then called simply Ballet Theatre (the word 'American' was added in 1957). Its stated aim was to present 'the best that is traditional, the best that is contemporary and, inevitably, the best that is controversial'. Eclecticism, in other words, was proclaimed from the beginning as a positive artistic policy, justified then because the co. was starting almost from scratch, with a nucleus of dancers and a few ballets from the MORDKIN B. (1937–9). FOKINE was invited to stage SYLPHIDES and CARNAVAL, DOLIN mounted GISELLE and SWAN LAKE Act II, new ballets were commissioned from American choreographers like DE MILLE and LORING, and a British contingent consisting of TUDOR and HOWARD was imported to revive pieces originally made for BR and Tudor's London B. After a period of shakedown a basic repertory was assembled that is one of the best in the world. In addition to further revivals, original works were presented by Fokine (*Bluebeard*, 1941; *Russian Soldier*, 1942; *Helen of Troy*, 1942, later revised by LICHINE), BALANCHINE (*Waltz Academy*, 1944; *Theme and Variations*, 1947), Tudor (PILLAR OF FIRE, 1942; ROMEO AND JULIET, 1943; DIM LUSTRE, 1943; UNDERTOW, 1945) and MASSINE (*Aleko*, 1942; MAM'ZELLE ANGOT, 1943).

In its early years, Ballet Theatre drew from the prewar Russian cos for both repertory and personnel:

Left: Maud Allan as she appeared in her dance *Mendelssohn's Spring Song*

Below left: Alicia Alonso in Act II of GISELLE, partnered by BRUHN

Below: American Ballet Theatre's staging of FALL RIVER LEGEND, sc. O. SMITH, with KAYE (right) as the Accused and D. ADAMS as her Mother, who appears to her in a dream sequence after the double murder

for several years its stars were MARKOVA and Dolin; BARONOVA, NEMCHINOVA, RIABOUCHINSKA, TOUMANOVA, EGLEVSKY, LAZOWSKI, Lichine, and YOUSKEVITCH also joined for longer or shorter periods. But the choreographers who gave the co. its unique flavour were the British Tudor and the American ROBBINS, who emerged from the ranks in 1944 to create FANCY FREE, followed by INTERPLAY, 1945, and *Facsimile*, 1946. Tudor and Robbins developed dancers like KAYE, LAING, KRIZA, H. LANG, D. ADAMS, and KIDD, for whom the blend of the classic and contemporary in their ballets seemed a natural form of expression. The co. produced its own classic ballerina in ALONSO.

More than most cos, perhaps, ABT has been plagued by rapid turnover of personnel, the one constant being Chase, who has remained as director (with O. SMITH, since 1946, as co-director). Both Tudor and Robbins broke away; lacking a resident choreographer of any stature, Chase was obliged to shop around for new ballets. MACMILLAN, Herbert Ross, and FELD have all been associated with ABT for brief periods, but very few choreographers have ever made more than two or three ballets for the co.; even Tudor, who has had the most lasting influence on its style, has made only eight in the 36 years – with some interruptions – he has been associated with it. In 1974 he was appointed associate director. The chief exception is de Mille, who has given ABT a dozen ballets since its inception. Until a few years ago it was still true to say that all of the important original ballets in the repertory were made in the first seven years of ABT's existence. This situation was remedied by the addition of LEAVES ARE FADING . . . in 1975 and THARP's *Push Comes to Shove* in 1976.

ABT has continued to pursue its aim of preserving 'the best that is traditional' with productions of August BOURNONVILLE's SYLPHIDE, 1965, the full-length *Swan Lake*, 1967, and *Giselle*, 1968 (both the latter by BLAIR), and MAKAROVA's staging of BAYADÈRE, Act IV, 1974. Less successful were Enrique Martinez's clumsy reworking of COPPÉLIA, 1968, and NUREYEV's considerably amended version of RAYMONDA, 1975. In summer 1976 the co. presented SLEEPING BEAUTY, staged by SKEAPING in the decor and costumes designed for the RB (then SWB) in 1946 by MESSEL.

Ballet Theatre was the first foreign co. to appear at CG after World War II, in the summer of 1946; since then it has made frequent tours of Europe, has twice visited the USSR (1960 and 1966), and is the only major co. to continue the practice of annually touring the USA, coast to coast.

ABT has always drawn its personnel from abroad as well as from the USA: the ranks of principals have included, in addition to those already named, Sonia Arova, BABILÉE, Patricia Bowman, BRUHN, Karen Conrad, DANIELIAN, D'ANTUONO, DENARD, DOUGLAS, FERNANDEZ, FRACCI, GOLLNER, HAYDEN, HIGHTOWER, KIVITT, Ruth Ann Koesun, T. LANDER, Michael Lland, Annabelle Lyon, MARKS, MOYLAN, NAGY, OSATO, PETROFF, Janet Reed, SERRANO, SKIBINE, Maria and Marjorie TALLCHIEF, VERDY, and S. WILSON. In recent years the co. has tended to trade increasingly on the superstar status of such guest artists as Makarova, Nureyev, and BARYSHNIKOV. The public adulation of such dancers has to some extent spilled over on to native artists like BUJONES, C. GREGORY, KIRKLAND, and van HAMEL, but not enough to prevent several defections from the co. DV

See Selma Jeanne Cohen and A. J. Pischl, 'The American Ballet Theatre: 1940–1960', in *Dance Perspectives*, No. 6 (New York 1960)

Amiel, Josette, b. Vanves, 1930. French dancer. Studied with Jeanne Schwarz and VOLININ. Paris OC, then in 1952 went to O., *première danseuse* 1953, *étoile* 1958–71. Created roles in modern works, e.g. LIFAR's *Chemin de Lumière* (1957); LESSON; Juan Giuliano's *Noces de Sang* (1972); and in classical works, e.g. SWAN LAKE, staged BURMEISTER 1961. M-FC

Amodio, Amedeo, b. Milan, 1940. Italian dancer and choreographer. Studied Sc. BS. From Sc. to Rome OH; principal there 1966; then freelanced (Milan, Rome, Menegatti-FRACCI touring co., etc.). Forceful presence and strong technique. FP

Amour et son Amour, L', ballet, 1 act, ch. BABILÉE; mus. César Franck (*Psyché*); c. COCTEAU. Paris, T. des CE, B. des CE, 13 Dec 1948; dan. Babilée, PHILIPPART. Evokes the loves of Eros and Psyche with a youthful freshness. Babilée and Philippart also danced the ballet as guests with ABT. M-FC

Amours de Jupiter, Les, ballet, 5 scenes, ch. PETIT; mus. Jacques Ibert; sc./c. Jean Hugo; lib. KOCHNO, based on Ovid's *Metamorphoses*. Paris, T. des CE, B. des CE, 5 Mar 1946. Petit, as Jupiter, came as Golden Rain to Danae (PHILIPPART), as the Swan to Leda (SKORIK), and the Eagle to Ganymede (PAGAVA). BABILÉE was Mercury and Ana Nevada the faithful Juno. An erotic work with beautiful designs by Hugo, typical of its time in that Ganymede was danced by a girl. MC

Amsterdam Opera Ballet Co. *see* NETHERLANDS

Anastasia, ballet, orig. in 1 act, now in 3, ch. MACMILLAN; mus. Bohuslav Martinů; sc. (film projections of Russian imperial family and Revolution)/ c. Barry Kay. W. Berlin, Deutsche OB, 25 June 1967; dan. SEYMOUR. An extraordinarily dramatic and moving portrayal of the woman Anna Anderson and her fight to be recognized as Anastasia, the youngest daughter of Tsar Nicholas II, believed to have been assassinated with the rest of the Imperial family.

When MacMillan returned to the RB as director he added two preceding acts to give the co. a full-length work of epic proportions. London CG, 22 July 1971; sc./c. Barry Kay; mus. TCHAIKOVSKY (1st Symphony for Act I, 3rd Symphony for Act II); dan. Seymour, BERIOSOVA, RENCHER, SIBLEY, DOWELL. Act I shows the happy family life Anastasia knew in 1914, culminating in the declaration of World War I. Act II is a ballroom scene in 1917 in which the debutante Anastasia realizes the complicated relationships of her parents with characters like Rasputin and KSHESSINSKA. It ends with Revolutionaries sacking the Winter Palace. All these characters and events are recalled in the last act by Anna Anderson. MC

Andersen, Ib, b. Copenhagen, 1954. Danish dancer. Entered RDBS in early 1960s; debut while still a pupil in title role of MONUMENT FOR A DEAD BOY (Copenhagen, T. Royal, 1973). Engaged as dancer with RDB. Several August BOURNONVILLE solos and smaller parts. Romeo in NEUMEIER's production of ROMEO AND JULIET (Copenhagen, Dec 1974); more important parts in ÉTUDES and Ivan in OISEAU DE FEU 1976. SKJ

Andersson, Gerd, b. Stockholm, 1932. Swedish dancer. Studied RSBS. Promoted to principal dancer 1958. Danced classical roles like GISELLE; created main role in ECHOING OF TRUMPETS. Guest artist, PAGE B., NB of Canada, and LFB. AGS

Andreyanova, Elena, b. St Petersburg, 1819; d. Paris, 1857. Russian dancer. Graduated from St Petersburg TS, 1837; danced Bolshoy T., St Petersburg, 1837–55. First Russian GISELLE (18 Dec 1842). Object of much gossip because of the favouritism shown her by the director of the Imperial Ts, Aleksandr Gedeonov, and the notorious affair of a dead cat thrown onto the stage at Moscow, Bolshoy T., 3 Dec 1848, during her guest appearance in PAQUITA. She was equally good in classical and character dances, and an expressive mime. M. PETIPA chose her as his partner for his debut in *Paquita* (1847), and danced MAZILIER's *Le Diable Amoureux* with her (1848). She created roles of Black Fairy in *La Filleule des Fées* (1850), and Countess Berthe in *Le Diable à Quatre* (1850), staged by PERROT in St Petersburg. Danced at Paris (1845 etc.), London (1845, 1852), and Milan (where a special bronze medal was cast in her honour). Studied under BLASIS. Toured Russian provinces 1853–5 with group of Imperial B. dancers with vast repertoire of romantic ballets. In Voronezh showed first production of FOUNTAIN OF BAKHCHISARAY. Retired 1855 to Paris. NR
See Korneyev, 'Two Forgotten Russian Danseuses', in *Annual of the Imperial Theatres*, No. 4 (St Petersburg 1909)

Angiolini, Gaspare (Gasparo), b. Florence, 1731; d. Milan, 1803. Italian dancer and choreographer. Son of Francesco Angiolini, described as 'a man of the theatre', the circumstances of his early training as a dancer have not yet come to light. His first recorded public perfs seem to be at T. San Moisè in Venice, 1746; he appeared with different cos in Venice until 1750. *Primo ballerino* with HILVERDING's co. at the Vienna Hof T. 1754, and married the ballerina Maria Teresa Fogliazzi. He rapidly became Hilverding's favourite pupil and most gifted disciple. When Hilverding left in 1758 for a post in St Petersburg, Angiolini succeeded him as *maître de ballet* in 1759, during the artistically creative years in which Count Giacomo Durazzo was in charge of Vienna's Imperial Theatres. Durazzo brought together the talents of Christoph Willibald Gluck, Raniero di Calzabigi, the librettist (credited by Gluck as the man who evolved the *azione in mimica*), and Angiolini for the creation of the ballet *Le Festin de Pierre ou Don Juan*. The premiere in Oct 1761 was a triumph. Compared to the *Don Juan* libretto the Greek and Roman mythological plots of NOVERRE now seem antiquated, although Noverre's *Letters* which advocated reforms in ballet predated the *Don Juan* premiere. *Don Juan* was Angiolini's most performed ballet but his work influenced many choreographers, most prominent among them GALEOTTI, who established the RDB. When Hilverding, ailing, left St Petersburg, Angiolini succeeded him as Catherine the Great's *maître de ballet* 1766–72. He returned to Vienna as successor to Noverre, then left for a second St Petersburg contract 1776–8. He returned to Italy with a contract for Sc. and in two years as *maître de ballet en chef* choreographed some 25 ballets, including *Demofoonte* (1779), *La Morte di Cleopatra*, and *Solimano* (both 1780). Final Russian contract 1782–7. Returned to Sc. and created another notable series of ballets, among them *Fedra* (1789). He was a talented musician who composed the scores for many of his ballets. On retirement he settled in Milan, whence he was exiled to Cattaro for republican activities in 1799. Released after the Peace of Lunéville in 1801 he returned to Milan, remaining there until his death in 1803. MHW
See Marian Hannah Winter, *The Pre-Romantic Ballet* (London 1974; New York and Toronto 1975)

Anisimova, Nina, b. St Petersburg, 1909. Russian dancer and choreographer. Graduated from Leningrad Choreographic S. 1926, class of Maria Romanova, VAGANOVA, Aleksandr Shiryaev. Character dancer, Maly OB 1926–7; Kirov B. 1927–58. A lively dancer-actress who created Thérèse, the Basque Girl in FLAME OF PARIS; Nastia in VAINONEN's *Partisans' Days* (1937); Aisha in GAYANÉ, which she choreographed for Kirov B. in Perm, 1942, and which remained in the repertoire for many years. Choreographed *Cranes' Song* for Bashkir O. (Ufa, 1944), and for Maly O. *Magic Veil* and a new version of SCHÉHÉRAZADE, etc. Teacher at Ballet Masters' faculty, Leningrad Cons. from 1963. Honoured Artist, RSFSR; Honoured Art Worker, RSFSR; People's Artist, Bashkir ASSR. NR
See M. Frangopulo, *N. Anisimova* (Leningrad 1951)

Left: Apollo, as danced by KENT and D'AMBOISE with NYCB; *below left: Apollon-Musagète* in its original form, 1928, sc./c. André Bauchant, with LIFAR as Apollo leading the Muses towards Olympus at the end of the ballet

Right: L'Après-midi d'un Faune, in its original production, 1912, with NIJINSKY as the Faun, sc./c. BAKST

Anna Karenina, lyrical scenes, 3 acts, ch. PLISETSKAYA, Natalia Ryzhenko, Viktor Smirnov-Golovanov; mus. Rodion Shchedrin; lib. Boris Lvov-Anokhin after novel by Leo Tolstoy; sc. Valery Levental. Moscow, Bolshoy T., 10 June 1972; dan. Plisetskaya alternating with KONDRATIEVA (title role), FADEYECHEV (Karenin), LIEPA (Vronsky). The work concentrates on Anna's personal tragedy. Reproduced with the same choreography, Novosibirsk O. etc.; remains in the repertoire of Moscow, Bolshoy B. Choreographed by PARLIĆ for Belgrade NT. NR

Ansermet, Ernest, b. Vevey, 1883; d. Geneva, 1969. Swiss conductor. A distinguished and able musician, who led the premieres of several DIAGHILEV ballets, among them PARADE; TRICORNE; *Chout* (Paris, 1921; ch. Taddeo Slavinsky and LARIONOV); and NOCES (Paris, 1923; ch. NIJINSKA). Conducted OISEAU DE FEU for RB at CG. DH

Antonio (Ruiz Soler) *see* SPAIN

Apollo (original title, *Apollon-Musagète*), ballet, 2 scenes; lib./mus. STRAVINSKY. (1) Ch. BOLM; sc. Nicholas Remisov; Washington, DC, Library of Congress, 27 Apr 1928; dan. PAGE, Berenice Holmes, Elise Reiman. (2) Ch. BALANCHINE; sc./c. André Bauchant (new c. Gabrielle Chanel 1929). Paris, T. Sarah Bernhardt, 12 June 1928; dan. LIFAR, Alice Nikitina (alternating with A. DANILOVA), TCHERNICHEVA, DUBROVSKA. The birth and youth of Apollo, who instructs the Muses of poetry, mime, and dance, and then departs to join the other gods on Olympus. The ballet that decisively established Balanchine on the path of neoclassicism. Revived by many cos, incl. RDB (sc. Kjeld Abell, 18 June 1931); American B. (sc. Stewart Chaney, NY Met, 27 Apr 1937); Buenos Aires, T. Colón (sc. TCHELITCHEV, 1942); ABT (sc. Eugene Dunkel, c. (Barbara)

Karinska, NY Met, 25 Apr 1943); Paris O. (sc. André Delfau, 5 May 1947); NYCB (NYCC, 15 Nov 1951); RB (sc. John Craxton, CG, 15 Nov 1966). There have been versions by other choreographers incl. MILLOSS and Lifar, but Balanchine's remains definitive. FM/DV

Appalachian Spring, modern dance work, ch. GRAHAM; mus. COPLAND; sc. NOGUCHI; c. Edythe Gilfond; Washington, DC, Library of Congress, 30 Oct 1944; dan. Graham, FONAROFF, P. LANG, Marjorie Mazia, O'DONNELL, YURIKO, CUNNINGHAM, and HAWKINS. A young bride and her husband take possession of their land and future under the watchful eyes of a pioneer woman and revivalist. DM

Appel, Peter, b. Surabaya, Java, 1933. Dutch dancer, teacher, and director. Trained under Karel Shook in Holland; joined Nederlands B. 1953, Dutch NB 1954; soloist 1957; to Basel B. 1962 as principal. Guest ballet master of Raimundo de Larrain's Cendrillon co. in Paris 1963, and of LFB 1964. To Hamburg 1966 as soloist and teacher. Assistant ballet master, Cologne B. 1966 and director 1969–71. A director of the Cologne Dance Acad. from 1971 and of the International Summer Acad. there. To Hamburg B. as teacher, 1976. A fine BLUEBIRD, he has subsequently become an inspiring and popular teacher. GBLW

Après-midi d'un Faune, L', choreographic tableau in 1 act, ch. NIJINSKY; mus. DEBUSSY; sc./c. BAKST. Paris, T. du Châtelet, DIAGHILEV's B. Russes, 29 May 1912; dan. Nijinsky, NELIDOVA. Nijinsky's first and only surviving ballet, in which he made a radical departure from orthodox methods of composition; the dancers moved in two-dimensional profile, flat-footed, turned-in, and the choreography was not tied to the metre of the music. These innovations were of more lasting significance than the scandal provoked at the premiere by the Faun's final masturbatory caressing of a scarf dropped by a startled nymph, a gesture modified at later perfs. Revived BR 1930; BR 24 Apr 1931 by WOIZIKOWSKI; Paris O., revised version by LIFAR, 1936; DE BASIL, 1936; B. Russe de Monte Carlo, 1938; ABT, 1941; Paris O., Nijinsky's choreography revived MASSINE with the help of Romola Nijinsky, in Bakst's decor, 1976. *See also* AFTERNOON OF A FAUN. DV

Archives and Museums. The first important archive specializing in dance was Les Archives Internationales de la Danse, inaugurated in Paris in 1931 by Rolf de Maré, the Swedish art patron and founder of BALLETS SUÉDOIS. In 1950 it was dissolved and its thousands of books and engravings were donated to the Musée de l'Opéra in Paris. The collections from Indonesia and Les Ballets Suédois alone went to Stockholm, there to form a basis for the Dance Museum, opened to the public in 1951. This was the first museum for dance in all its aspects all over the world. It has a large library and its archives include iconographica, films, and videotapes. The Director since its foundation is Bengt Häger. Among the special collections are those relating to dance in India, Indonesia, Thailand, Sri Lanka, China, Japan (costumes, masks, model theatres, accessories, iconographica), DIAGHILEV's B. Russes and his successors (a complete series of some 5,000 programs, 80 costumes etc.), Les Ballets Suédois, the JOOSS archive, and European modern dance. There are 21 Indonesian documentary films made before World War II.

The most comprehensive dance archive in the world is The Dance Collection in the Performing Arts Library at Lincoln Center, NY. Formed in 1947 under the leadership of Genevieve Oswald, its curator ever since, it was first housed in the NY Public Library and moved to its present site in 1965. It contains some 30,000 books, 6,000 prints, 200,000 photographs, 150,000 programs, 60,000 manuscripts, and a great collection of films. The printed catalogue in 11 volumes constitutes a monumental bibliography. Dance in America is especially well covered. Among particular collections are those relating to FORNAROLI, I. DUNCAN (Edward Gordon Craig's letters), Diaghilev material, DENISHAWN archives, the H. HOLM collection, and the ROBBINS film archive.

The LIFAR collection at the Wadsworth Atheneum, Hartford, CT, is the finest collection of designs relating to the Diaghilev B. This was purchased from Lifar in 1933.

Another important American collection is that of the STRAVINSKY-Diaghilev Foundation, of which the President is Parmenia Migel Ekstrom. As the name indicates, the purpose of the Foundation is to preserve and present work by Diaghilev's collaborators. The collection includes some 15,000 documents and autograph letters relating to the B. Russes as well as original designs, posters, programs, books, musical scores, and memorabilia.

The San Francisco Dance Archive opened in 1975 with Russell Hartley as Director.

Major American dance libraries are in the Harvard University T. Collection, Cambridge, MA, mainly a research library; and in the University of Florida, specializing in contemporary dance; and the University of California. In recent years an ever-increasing number of American universities and colleges are adding libraries and collections to their dance departments.

The Musée de l'Opéra in Paris has conscientiously kept material pertaining to its own activities and offers the best facilities for the study of the history of ballet in France from the 17th c. A branch of the Bibliothèque Nationale, it was formed in 1876 and is presently headed by François Lesur and administered by Martine Kahane. Its series of designs and of paintings of ballerinas are outstanding as also are its musical scores. In the permanent exhibition is much of A. PAVLOVA's former property and it has acquired some of KOCHNO's collection of Diaghilev material, including many remarkable photographs.

At the Bibliothèque de l'Arsenal in Paris, in existence since the 18th c., the T. Collections under the direction of Cécile Giteau are rich in ballet material from the 17th and 18th c. to which was added in 1925 the Collection Rondel which includes press cuttings, photographs, posters, and programs, as well as books. Unique is the Collection Farina, the most complete on the art of mime, and some Craig–Duncan correspondence.

The Museo Teatrale alla Scala in Milan was opened in 1913 and in 1958 the library Livia Simoni was added. The Director is Giampiero Tintori. It covers especially ballet in Italy; noteworthy are manuscripts by BLASIS and MANZOTTI, much other material on them and VIGANÒ, Italian librettos, etc.

Of German archives, the Dance Archive in Cologne, founded in 1953 in Hamburg and transferred to Cologne in 1965 at the initiative of Kurt Peters, functions as a centre for research in folk and artistic dance. The Stuttgart B. Co. has purchased the large book collection of Doris Niles and Serge Leslie.

The London Archives of the Dance, founded in 1945, is now part of the T. Museum, administered by the Victoria and Albert Museum, with Alexander Schouvalov as curator. Inaugurated in 1974, the T. Museum is largely a library containing many press cuttings, programs, and music scores and, notably, the Ashley Dukes–RAMBERT collection of Romantic ballet prints. In recent years, some important Diaghilev material has been acquired.

The T. Museum in Copenhagen, founded in 1922 by Robert Neiiendam, now with his daughter-in-law Karen and grandson Klaus in charge, is housed in the charming old court theatre and has much interesting August BOURNONVILLE material, and many photographs and costumes from that time.

Outstanding among private collections is that of DERRA DE MORODA, destined for the Institute of Music Science at the University of Salzburg. Among its 8,000 books are practically complete editions of everything published before the 1850s, some unique. The 2,000 early prints are a very fine selection.

The American collector and donator Edwin Binney 3rd specializes in early lithographs, mainly from the 19th c., of which he has thousands.

The Institute for Research Films (Institut für den Wissenschaftlichen Film) in Göttingen, founded in 1956 under the direction of Gotthard Wolf, contains (lends and sells copies of) the largest existing collection of non-European documentary dance films. Das Deutsche Tanzarchiv (German Dance Archive) beim Institut für Volkskunstforschung in Leipzig, E. Germany, founded by Dr Kurt Petermann in 1957, is publishing a vast bibliography of all books and articles on dance written in German.

Most of the European opera houses have archives relating to their own productions (see BRINSON's *Background to European Ballet* (Leiden 1966) for some indication of their contents). In Russia, the Kirov T. in Leningrad has its own museum and the Bakhrushin T. Museum in Moscow contains much ballet material. BH

Argentina. From 1908, when the present T. Colón in Buenos Aires was built, until 1925, when the opera house established a permanent nucleus of orchestra, opera, and dance cos, there was very little dance activity. However, PREOBRAZHENSKA appeared there in 1912 as Alladine in the opera *Ariane et Barbe Bleu* (by Paul Dukas, directed by Arturo Toscanini), the DIAGHILEV co. appeared there in 1913 and 1917, and A. PAVLOVA also danced there.

In 1925 the direction of the new group of dancers was taken over by BOLM; the first work he staged was COQ D'OR. The first soloists were PAGE, LUDMILA, Aimee Abraamova and, later, VILZAK, A. OBUKHOV, and DUBROVSKA danced there. NIJINSKA and Boris Romanov worked there in the 1920s and early 1930s and in 1931 FOKINE, accompanied by SPESSIVTSEVA and her partner LESTER, came to stage his OISEAU DE FEU. Fokine's assistant, Esmée Bulnes, the celebrated English teacher, stayed on for nearly 20 years in Buenos Aires and is considered the real moulder of Argentina's finest dancers. In 1934 ballets by LIFAR were staged, with the local star RUANOVA dancing principal roles. In 1937 Margarethe Wallmann worked at the Colón; during her stay the leading dancers were Ruanova and SHABELEVSKY. BALANCHINE staged APOLLO 1942 and in 1943 the Colón became the wartime base of DE BASIL's Original B. Russe. In 1947 LICHINE staged some ballets and in 1948–9 MILLOSS worked there. MASSINE was in Buenos Aires intermittently 1948–53 and 1955, staging many of his most famous ballets. T. GSOVSKY, H. ROSEN, CHARRAT, and TUDOR all staged ballets during the 1950s. The 1950s and 1960s were notable for the visits of the DE CUEVAS co. and LFB. With both cos Argentine dancers appeared. J. CARTER has staged many works for the Colón co., incl. his versions of COPPÉLIA, SWAN LAKE, and SLEEPING BEAUTY. In 1971 NUREYEV staged his NUTCRACKER and danced in it with the Colón's principal ballerina FERRI. In 1971 the Colón co. suffered a tragic blow when nine principal dancers incl. the very talented NEGLIA and Norma Fontela were killed in a plane crash. In 1974 LACOTTE staged the first South American SYLPHIDE.

A new group was formed in 1976 and already talented young dancers are emerging. Teachers and choreographers have incl. KNIASEFF, Alexander Minz and Héctor Zaraspe. In 1976 Aleksandr Plisetsky, brother of PLISETSKAYA, was a guest teacher and choreographer. The T. Colón has played host to some of the greatest cos of the world and been visited by innumerable great dancers. The resident co. has toured S. America and in 1968 appeared at the International Dance Fest. in Paris. The theatre has employed designers of the calibre of GONCHAROVA, TCHELITCHEV, and Nicola Benois. *See also* SPAIN. JUL

Argentinita, La (Antonia Mercé) *see* SPAIN

Argentinita, La (Encarnación López Julvez) *see* SPAIN

Ari [Jansson], Carina, b. Stockholm, 1897; d. Buenos Aires, 1970. Swedish dancer and choreographer. Studied RSBS and with FOKINE. Ballerina of B. Suédois 1920–5. Had leading role in LIFAR's *Le Cantique des Cantiques* (mus. Arthur Honegger) at Paris O. 1938; also danced and choreographed for OC. Among her ballets are: *Sous-Marine* (mus. Honegger, Paris OC 1925); *Rayon de Lune* (mus. Gabriel Fauré, Paris O. 1928); *Valses de Brahms* and *Jeux de Couleurs* (mus. Désiré Émile Inghelbrecht, Paris OC 1933); *La Métamorphose d'Éve* (mus. Inghelbrecht, RSB 1936); *Ode à la Rose* (mus. RAVEL and others, RSB 1938). She bequeathed a fortune to a Swedish foundation named after her to be used for grants to dancers; also donated a dance library to the Dance Museum, Stockholm. AGS

Arpino, Gerald, b. Staten Island, NY, 1928. American choreographer. Studied ballet with Mary Ann Wells and modern dance with O'DONNELL and Gertrude Shurr; also at ABTS. Associate Director of CCJB, for which all of his ballets have been made. His works are often controversial and noted for their treatment of contemporary themes and use of *avant-garde*, sometimes rock, music; they include *Viva Vivaldi!* (1965), *Nightwings* (1966), CLOWNS, TRINITY, and KETTENTANZ. DV

Arthur, Charthel, b. Los Angeles, CA, 1946. American dancer. Studied with NIJINSKA and at American B. Center. Principal dancer with CCJB, excelling in both classical and modern repertory. Her roles incl. the title role in PINEAPPLE POLL, Ballerina in PETRUSHKA, Hermia in DREAM, and the Young Girl in GREEN TABLE. DV

Asafyev, Boris (pen name Igor Glyebov), b. St Petersburg, 1884; d. Moscow, 1949. Musicologist and composer. Graduated from St Petersburg Univ. in philology 1908, and then studied composition under Anatoly Lyadov at the St Petersburg Cons. until 1910. Immediately became both rehearsal pianist of the Maryinsky B. and chief music librarian of the Imperial Theatres, which work provided enough practical knowledge of choreography for Asafyev to make his own initial attempts at composing small ballets. In 1906, he invited the student NIJINSKY to choreograph his children's opera *Cendrillon* on amateur artists aged 8–13. From these modest efforts, Asafyev became one of the major figures in the history of Soviet ballet. He composed 28 ballets, based both on Russian classics – FOUNTAIN OF BAKHCHISARAY, PRISONER IN THE CAUCASUS – and on Western literature, e.g. LOST ILLUSIONS. Central to his composing was the theory that every epoch creates its own characteristic music and sound, which then recalls that period throughout time. Thus, his FLAME OF PARIS (1932), a cornerstone of modern Soviet ballet, is founded on songs of the French Revolution, and *Fountain of Bakhchisaray* on musical themes of Aleksandr Pushkin's time. Despite these applications of his theory to ballet music, Asafyev was never able to realize its complete development in symphonic music. People's Artist USSR; Academician. NR
See B. Asafyev, *On Ballet*, introduction by A. N. Dmitriev (Leningrad 1974)

Asakawa, Takako, b. Tokyo. Japanese dancer. Studied at GRAHAM S. and with NEMCHINOVA and Matt Mattox. Debut with Graham Co. 1962. Has also danced with AILEY Dance T. and with the cos of P. LANG, MCKAYLE, FALCO, ROSS, LUBOVITCH, and

Below: Frederick Ashton dancing in the Vic-Wells B.'s production of FAÇADE with (left to right) HELPMANN, June Brae, and Joan Sheldon; *bottom:* Ashton rehearsing FONTEYN and NUREYEV in a revival of his *Birthday Offering*

YURIKO. Has taught and/or choreographed at Jacob's Pillow, Harvard College, the Univ. of Hawaii, Juilliard S., LSCD, the Graham S., and elsewhere. Has danced many leading roles in the Graham repertory incl. the title role in CLYTEMNESTRA, St Joan in *Seraphic Dialogue*, the Girl in Red in DIVERSION OF ANGELS, Medea in *Cave of the Heart*. She m. WALKER. DV

Åsberg, Margaretha, b. Stockholm, 1939. Swedish dancer and choreographer. Studied RSBS, entered the co. 1957. To USA 1962 to study modern dance at Juilliard and GRAHAM schools. Entered the Choreographic Inst., Stockholm, 1967. Choreographed *from one point to any other point* (1968); *Through the Sea, Through the Earth* (mus. Sven-Erik Bäck, 1972); *Dance Suite* (mus. Karl-Birger Blomdahl, 1973). Teaches modern technique at RSBS. AGS

Aschengreen, Erik, b. Copenhagen, 1935. Danish ballet historian and critic. Drama and ballet critic of *Berlingske Tidende* from 1964, and chief ballet critic of that paper's *Weekend-Avisen* from 1975. His books and articles incl.: *Études* (Copenhagen 1970); *Ballet, en Krævende Kunst* (*Ballet, a Demanding Art*, Copenhagen 1972), on H. LANDER; and No. 58 in *Dance Perspectives* series, *The Beautiful Danger: Facets of the Romantic Ballet* (New York 1974), tr. from Danish by Patricia N. McAndrew. Since 1974 he has taught history of ballet at RDBS. He lectures in the USA and Canada. SKJ

Ashbridge, Bryan, b. Wellington, 1926. New Zealand dancer and director. Studied with KIRSOVA and BOROVANSKY, Sydney. Adeline Genée Gold Medal, 1947. London, SWBS, 1947; SWB (RB) 1948–65; principal dancer, 1958; Australian B. 1969, assistant artistic director; associate director 1975. Specialized in TV productions. A stylishly athletic classical dancer, he partnered GREY and BERIOSOVA in SWAN LAKE, GISELLE, and SLEEPING BEAUTY. KSW

Ashmole, David, b. Cottingham, Yorkshire, 1949. English dancer. Studied at Kilburn School, Wellingborough, and RBS. Joined RB 1969, soloist 1972, principal 1975. A well-built dancer of cheerful sturdiness in roles like COLAS, Benvolio (MACMILLAN's ROMEO AND JULIET), and as one of the athletes in BICHES; he can also give a fine account of the princely roles in SWAN LAKE and SLEEPING BEAUTY. A stalwart of the RB. MC

Ashton, Frederick (William Mallandaine), b. Guayaquil, Ecuador, 1904. English dancer and choreographer. After seeing A. PAVLOVA dance in Lima, Peru, 1917, he determined to be a dancer, and began studying with MASSINE in London in the early 1920s. Later studied with RAMBERT, who encouraged him in his first attempts at choreography and danced with him in his first short ballet, TRAGEDY OF

FASHION. Joined RUBINSTEIN's co. in Paris 1928, working under Massine and NIJINSKA. Returned to England 1929 to choreograph for Rambert and the CAMARGO SOCIETY. Many of his early works were strongly influenced by Nijinska, e.g. *Pomona* (1930), but also showed the beginnings of a distinctive personal style, witty, elegant, and lyrical, e.g. FAÇADE (1931), *Les Masques* (1933), and, for the Vic-Wells B., RENDEZVOUS (1933). To USA 1934 to stage the Virgil Thomson–Gertrude Stein opera *Four Saints in Three Acts*. During the 1930s pursued a successful secondary career in the commercial theatre as choreographer of numbers in musical comedy and revue, e.g. *The First Shoot* in Charles B. Cochran's revue *Follow the Sun* (1935).

In 1935 was invited by DE VALOIS to join Vic-Wells B. as dancer and choreographer; began association with FONTEYN who created leading roles in most of his ballets of the next 25 years. His prewar ballets at SW showed increasing authority in working on a larger scale: BAISER DE LA FÉE (1935), *Apparitions* (1936), *Nocturne* (1936), PATINEURS (1937), WEDDING BOUQUET (1937), *Horoscope* (1938). His wartime ballets, *Dante Sonata* (1940), *The Wise Virgins* (1940), *The Wanderer* (1941), and *The Quest* (1943), dealt in various ways with the conflict between good and evil. Served in RAF 1941–5.

In 1946 the SWB moved to CG, where Ashton created his first postwar ballet, SYMPHONIC VARIATIONS (1946), an affirmation of the supremacy of the classic dance, to counteract the increasingly literary tendency of British wartime ballets. From then on the dance element has always been of primary importance in his work: SCÈNES DE BALLET (1948), CINDERELLA (his first 3-act ballet; 1948), *Daphnis and Chloe* (*see* DAPHNIS ET CHLOÉ) (1951), SYLVIA (1952), *Birthday Offering* (1956), ONDINE (1958), all of which continued to provide Fonteyn with her greatest roles outside the classical repertory. Ashton also created ballets around the talents of younger dancers, such as DREAM for SIBLEY and DOWELL (1954); FILLE MAL GARDÉE for NERINA and BLAIR (1960); DEUX PIGEONS for SEYMOUR and GABLE (1961); as well as setting the seal on the partnership of Fonteyn and NUREYEV in MARGUERITE AND ARMAND (1963). In 1963 succeeded de Valois as Director of the co., now called RB, in which capacity he continued to provide works for the repertory, though with less frequency. The two *pas de trois* that comprise MONOTONES (1965 and 1966) are a further distillation of Ashton's classicism in its purest form. ENIGMA VARIATIONS (1968), a series of dance portraits of Elgar, his wife, and his friends, is at the same time in essence a classic ballet.

Ashton retired from the directorship 1970, in which year he choreographed and danced in the film *Tales of Beatrix Potter* (US title: *Peter Rabbit and the Tales of Beatrix Potter*). Since then he has choreographed several *pas de deux*, notably *Thaïs* for Sibley and Dowell (1971) and *The Walk to the Paradise Garden* for PARK and WALL (1972), and for Seymour a solo, *Five Brahms Waltzes in the Manner of Isadora Duncan* (1975–6), based on his memories of I. DUNCAN, whom he saw when a young man and who, like Pavlova, has been a continuing influence on his work. Also in 1976, he choreographed his first full-length ballet since 1970, MONTH IN THE COUNTRY, also for Seymour, which showed that there had been no diminution of his powers in the intervening 'fallow' period.

Although most of his works have been for the co. of which he is now named Founder Choreographer, he has also worked as guest choreographer for various cos, notably B. Russe de Monte Carlo (*Devil's Holiday*, 1939); NYCB (ILLUMINATIONS, 1950 and *Picnic at Tintagel*, 1952); RDB (ROMEO AND JULIET, 1955). Many of his other ballets have gone into repertories of cos all over the world. As a performer, Ashton's greatest successes have been in character roles such as CARABOSSE, Kostchey in OISEAU DE FEU, and opposite HELPMANN as an Ugly Sister in his own *Cinderella*.

Under his directorship, the RB rose to new heights, and the *corps de ballet* became the finest in the world. The first important, and still the greatest, British choreographer, his works have been largely responsible for formulating the native style of classic ballet. CBE 1950; knighted 1962; CH 1970. Hon. Doctor of Music, Oxford, 1976. DV

See David Vaughan, *Frederick Ashton and his Ballets* (London and New York 1977)

Asia. The various dances of the continent of Asia may be divided into two types: the classical forms and the community or folk dances. Even now there exist in the different regions of Asia many varieties of folk dance that can be identified as, for example, seasonal, martial, sacrificial, talismanic, instructional, or celebratory. Here, however, only the artistic or classical dance forms will be dealt with.

The classical styles of the India–Pakistan–Bangladesh subcontinent and those of Sri Lanka (Ceylon) and SE Asia form one corpus. Born as they were out of deep spiritual impulses they still retain, by and large, a particular religious bias. Shiva, the most powerful member of the Hindu *trimurti* (triad) is himself, as Nataraja, the Lord of Dance. He represents the masculine or powerful type of dance known as *tandava*; and his consort Parvati represents the feminine or lyrical type known as *lasya*. According to legend it was Shiva who created heaven and earth when he performed his Dance of Creation.

The earliest book on dance, drama, and music, the *Natya Shastra* of Bharata, is variously dated from the 2nd c. BC to the 3rd c. AD. The work attained the status of holy writ and has for centuries been the manual for dancers, actors, and musicians. In ancient times these three professions were basically the same for stage productions which were mostly in the nature of danced operas.

There are three main components, *natya, nritta*, and *nritya*, which make up the classical dance.

Natya is the dramatic element and is 'a mimicry of the exploits of gods, demons, kings, as well as householders of this world'. Bharata maintains that *natya* will teach and 'give courage, amusement, as well as counsel'.

Nritta is the rhythmic movement of the body in dance. It does not set out to express a mood or sentiment or tell a story. It visualizes and reproduces music and rhythm by means of abstract gestures of the body and hands and by extensive and precise use of footwork. Because it is concerned solely with movement, *nritta* is often termed 'pure dance'.

Nritya is that element of the dance that 'suggests *rasa* (sentiment) and *bhava* (mood)'. Both *rasa* and *bhava* are conveyed through facial expressions and appropriate gestures. The most important book on *nritya* is the *Abhinaya Darpanam* of Nandikeshvara, who is thought to have lived in the 2nd c. AD. There are some differences between Bharata and Nandikeshvara on points of detail but their general approach and philosophy are the same.

Natya and *nritya* employ *abhinaya*, a word that signifies 'a carrying to the spectators'. The practice of *abhinaya* involves four techniques: *angik*, *vachik*, *aharya*, and *satvik*. *Angik abhinaya* is the term used for all gestures of the body. There are, for example, 13 gestures of the head, 36 glances, 7 movements of the eyeballs, 9 of the eyelids, and 7 of the eyebrows. The nose, the cheeks, the lower lip, each have 6 movements and the chin has 7. There are 9 gestures of the neck. The hand gestures, known as *mudras* or *hastas*, are 67 in number. Besides these there are 32 *charis*, which are movements for the foot and include the calf and thigh. The four ideal postures of the body in movement are called *abhanga* (slightly bent), *samabhanga* (equally bent) i.e. equilibrium, *atibhanga* (greatly bent), and *tribhanga* (thrice bent). *Vachik abhinaya* deals with the dancer's use of poetry, song, recitation, music, and rhythm. *Aharya abhinaya* covers the use of costume, make-up, and jewelry, and there are provisions for the appearance of every type of character. *Satvik abhinaya* represents physical manifestations of various mental and emotional states. These include perspiration, change of voice, change of colour, and weeping.

The *Natya Shastra* enumerates eight *rasas*, sentiments or emotional states. These are love, humour, pathos, anger, heroism, terror, disgust, and wonder. Later authorities mention a ninth *rasa*, serenity. Nandikeshvara gives this hint as to how a dancer might attempt to evoke *rasa*:

> Where the hand goes, there also should go the eyes,
> Where the eyes go, there should go the mind.
> Where the mind goes *bhava* should follow,
> And where *bhava* goes, there *rasa* arises.

The solo temple dance of S. India is called *Dasi Attam*. It derives its name from *devadasi*, or dancing girl in the service of the gods. Till recently this dance style was the preserve of the *devadasis* who were attached to S. Indian temples. Nowadays this dance is called *Bharata Natyam* in an attempt to dissociate the art from the temple dancers who had, with the passage of time, become temple prostitutes. However, the name *Bharata Natyam* could apply to any of the major dances of India since it simply means 'dance according to the principles of Bharata'.

Dasi Attam's bold, clear lines and marvellous sculpturesque poses invest it with a classic quality. An important feature of this dance is the interpretation of *padas*, poems, in praise of various deities. *Padas* cover every conceivable aspect of love from the mystic to the profane and are written in Tamil, Telugu, or Sanskrit. The dancer acts out the poem, as it were, and in order to allow the fullest expression the movement of the dance is slow. A balanced combination of all the elements of *Dasi Attam* is seen in the *varnam* where pure dance alternates with expressive dance. This is the most complex item in the performance.

The dedication of girls to temple service was ended in 1930. After that the social stigma attached to the profession of dancing was slowly removed and now girls from the highest Hindu castes avidly learn this dance style.

The home of *Kathakali*, the powerful male dance drama, is Kerala in SW India. The dancer-actors are usually Nayars, that is, members of the martial caste of Kerala. The artists employ the vivid language of gesture and mime, not only to translate the words of the play as they are sung by the musicians standing behind them, but also to create the atmosphere and setting for each scene. Thus by a mere glance and a gesture a dancer transports his audience to a romantic garden where lovers linger by the lotus pool and later into a fearful and bloody battle where the villain is inexorably slain.

The characters in *Kathakali* are always larger than life and the costumes, headdresses, and make-up are therefore highly distinctive.

The *Ramayana* and the *Mahabharata*, the epics of ancient India, provide most of the material for these dance dramas, which depict the heroic deeds of gods and warriors, the treacheries of demonesses, and the baseness of evil men.

Kuchipudi from Andhra and *Bhagvata Mela Nataka* from Tamil Nadu are dance dramas with common origins. In both, the dancer-actors were traditionally men of the Brahmin or priestly caste. In recent years *Kuchipudi* has gained in popularity and women have begun to learn it. They, however, perform only short extracts as solo items.

The *Odissi* dance of Orissa was rediscovered comparatively recently. It provides an interesting example of cultural fusion, for whereas the dance movements show an affinity with the S. Indian *Dasi Attam*, the accompanying music is N. Indian in character. There is evidence of an unbroken tradition of temple dancers in Orissa from the 9th c. AD. The *maharis*, girl dancers, together with their male counterparts, the *gotipuas*, have preserved the art. *Odissi* is lyrical, often sensuous, and takes a large part

Asia. *Right:* Ritha Devi in a *Bharata Natyam* recital; *below:* an early picture of GOPAL dancing on the shore near Bombay

of its subject matter from the Krishna legends.

The Krishna cult also sustains the *Manipuri* dance from NE India. The inhabitants of Manipur, the Meities, are a deeply sensitive and artistic people. By their very isolation from the rest of India they have evolved a unique pattern of life. Here, both the expression and the appreciation of art – and mainly of dance and music – seem to be the focal point in the everyday life of the people. The Meities love to dance. All their joys and sorrows, hopes and aspirations, are interpreted through the dance.

Originally the Meities were followers of a primitive religion with some allegiance to the god Shiva. Then, in the 18th c., they were converted to Vaishnavism which meant the worship of the god Vishnu in his incarnation as Krishna, the Blue God, whose love for the maidens of Vrindaban was symbolic of the love that united God with the human soul. The new religion encouraged music and dance, for Krishna himself was a musician and dancer.

Bhagyachandra, the ruler of Manipur during the latter half of the 18th c., codified the principles and techniques of the dance. The style is today distinguished by its overall stress on the graceful movements of the body. The quality of grace and fluidity has been developed to a degree not found in any of the other classical dances of India. The head, the hands, and the feet move together in perfect harmony and the mood is created by the entire body, without undue emphasis on any one part.

The *Kathak* dance of N. India and Pakistan had its genesis with the *kathaks* or storytellers who disseminated moral and religious instruction in the form of *kathas* or stories. Later they added music, mime, and dance to their repertoire. This style is unique in the sense that it combines Hindu and Muslim influences in perfect harmony. The Hindu elements derive from Aryan and perhaps even pre-Aryan sources, and the Muslim elements come from Arabia, Turkey, Persia, and Central Asia.

The poetry and music of Vaishnavism is deeply embedded in *Kathak* and a constant theme is the love that Radha bore for the god Krishna. During the reign of Akbar the Great, *Kathak* entered its golden era and dancers flocked to the imperial court and to the palaces of the many rajahs and nawabs. The dance was now no longer confined to the myths and legends of Hinduism. The wider repertoire included imperial, social, and contemporary themes. In fact, under rulers less tolerant than Akbar, *Kathak* developed along purely secular lines. The dancers concentrated on brilliant variations of rhythm, the beauty of which was heightened by tantalizing pauses and incredibly fast pirouettes. However, *Kathak* as we know it today is the result of the patronage that it received at the courts of Lucknow and Jaipur during the last century. The Lucknow *gharana* (school) matured into a distinct and individual style largely through the work of the brothers Binda Din and Kalka Prasad who served the last, ill-fated nawab of Avadh.

Thumri andaaz is a unique feature of the *Kathak* dance. In this particular manner of rendering a poem the performer repeatedly sings a single line and interprets it differently each time. The acting thus brings to life metaphors, images, similes, and metaphysical conceits, which are not explicit in the poem.

Among the lesser-known classical styles mention must be made of the *Sattra* of Assam, the *Chhau* masked dance of Seraikilla, and the female solo *Mohini Attam* of Kerala.

India's cultural influence spread, in varying degrees, throughout SE Asia. The *Ramayana* and the *Mahabharata*, already mentioned, form the basis of most of the dance theatre of these countries. The famous dances of Java and Bali are heavily indebted to ancient Indian dance forms and techniques. The Balinese, like the Meities of Manipur, consider dance an important part of life. Children are taught to dance from an early age and the beautiful *Legong* dances are the result of years of arduous training. In Thailand the *Khon* male dances require the use of masks and in Sri Lanka the *Kandyan* dancers use elaborate headdresses. The Indian influence in both is apparent.

The Islamic countries of W. Asia have a rich and living tradition of folk dance. However, the Muslim religion excludes dance as a form of worship and so this art has no place in Islamic religious ritual. This attitude to dance is common to all monotheistic faiths; Islam's sister religions, Judaism and Christianity, have always been suspicious of religious dancing. There are historical reasons for this. The heathen temples of western Asia, North Africa, Greece, Cyprus, and Egypt were centres of prostitution and the dancing girls who served in them were the chief source of revenue for the temple authorities. For Jew, Christian, and Muslim alike this was an intolerable situation and had to be stopped. In the process of proselytization temple dancing was wiped out.

Nevertheless, the Islamic countries do possess a type of sacred dance which is practised by the Sufis who resemble the ascetic Christian monks in many ways but place great emphasis on the realization of the Divine through the medium of poetry, music, and dance. The 13th-c. mystic Jalal-uddin Rumi founded a Sufi brotherhood at Konya in Anatolia and, over the centuries, the members of Rumi's fraternity have developed their dance style. The dance starts with solemn unaccompanied singing in praise of the Prophet; later the atmosphere of reverence and mystery is heightened by the flautists. The sheikh (leader) then strikes the floor and the dervishes (the word derives from a Persian word signifying 'poor') slowly advance round the dance area three times. These rounds represent the three stages towards the Divine: science and knowledge, understanding and vision, and the final union. After divesting themselves of their black cloaks, symbolic of the tomb, the dervishes, with arms outstretched like wings, start whirling slowly. Almost imperceptibly the whirling increases in speed until a trancelike hypnotic state is

Asia. A typically spectacular production by a Chinese dance ensemble in a song and dance pageant, *The East is Red*

achieved. This last movement has a quality of ecstasy, a feeling of fulfilment. Other Sufi orders in the Islamic world perform similar dances.

The classical dance of China, which grew in Peking, was always an integral part of opera. The opera artist, therefore, had to master movement, mime, and the complicated vocabulary of gesture. The art was greatly developed during the last century by Cheng and Chang-keng. In this century the great Mei Lan Fang remoulded and redefined the dance. Now, with the massive resurgence so evident in China, all the arts are being used as weapons of national reconstruction. Dance too is being so used.

The dance theatre of Japan has a long and fascinating history. *Bugaku*, which originated in the 7th c. AD, was first performed for the general public after World War II. Before that it was performed only at the imperial court and at a few exclusive shrines. *Bugaku* has always been semi-religious in intent. With the rise of the *samurai* (warrior) class the *Noh* dance drama took shape. At its zenith it was austere and severe and dealt chiefly with heroic subjects. The principles of the art were laid down by Ze-ami in his famous *Kadensho* which is still the handbook of the *Noh* dancer-actor.

By the 15th c. the merchant class was gaining in riches and power. To amuse them and to get their custom the dancers devised the *Kyogen*, a short satirical piece inserted between two *Noh* plays. The butt of the jokes was always a simple-minded *samurai* and the baiting was done by a clever character of low birth. This was a step towards a popular dance theatre for commoners. However, it was only at the end of the 16th c. that this aim was finally achieved. The credit for this must go to O Kuni of Izumo, a lady of doubtful repute. Her creation, called *Kabuki* ('song and dance'), developed in Osaka and Tokyo and was enthusiastically taken up by women of easy virtue to advertise their charms. So immoral were some of the dance dramas that in 1629 the Shogunate banned the new entertainment. To circumvent the law (the ban only applied to female prostitutes) male dancers adopted the *Kabuki* style, and thus started the profession of the female impersonator or *onna gata*. From early childhood selected boys were trained to specialize in female roles and over the years this became an honoured calling.

By the beginning of the 18th c. the art of *Kabuki* had become well established. Today *Kabuki* has an international reputation, thanks mainly to two powerful dance dramas, namely, *Chushingura* (*The Forty-seven Loyal Samurai*) and *Sumidagawa* (*The Sumida River*). The first is based on historical fact and tells of honour and revenge; the second is the tragedy of a deranged woman's search for her lost son.

Shamanism, Taoism, Confucianism, and Buddhism have influenced the course of Korean dance. It is a highly sophisticated form that depends on the merest hints and suggestive nuances. A favourite religious theme is the dilemma of the monk who wishes to forsake the religious life but who is plainly unprepared and unequipped for the rigours beyond the monastery walls. The *keesaengs*, cultivated courtesans like the *geisha* of Japan, were once numbered among the intellectual elite of the country. Their dance and poetry, veined with pain, nostalgia and delicate imagery, have considerably enriched the culture of the Korean people. RM

See also Bharata, *Natya Shastra*, tr. Manomohan Ghosh (Calcutta 1950); Beryl de Zoete, *The Other Mind* (London 1953); Beryl de Zoete and Walter Spies, *Dance and Drama in Bali* (London 1938; New York 1939); Jane Ellen Harrison, *Ancient Art and Ritual* (London and New York 1913; repr. London 1951); Nandikeshvara, *Abhinaya Darpanam*, tr. Manomohan Ghosh (Calcutta 1934); Curt Sachs, *World History of the Dance* (London 1938); Rina Singha and Reginald Massey, *Indian Dances: their History and Growth* (London and New York 1967); Eiryo Ashihara, *The Japanese Dance* (Tokyo 1964)

Astafyeva [married names Kshessinskaya; Grevs], Serafina, b. St Petersburg, 1876; d. London, 1934. Russian dancer. Graduated into *corps de ballet*, St Petersburg, Maryinsky T., 1895. She m. the celebrated character dancer, Jozef Kshessinsky (KSHESSINSKA's brother) 1896. Promoted to *coryphée* 1903, performing character parts. Her personal dossier in the archives of the Imperial Ts is filled with notes about illnesses and leaves of absence. In 1909, 1910, and 1911 took part in DIAGHILEV ballet seasons. Lived abroad, finally settling in London, where she taught MARKOVA, DOLIN, and FONTEYN (briefly), among others. Diaghilev and A. PAVLOVA both visited her London studio regularly in search of young talent. NR

See Mikhail Borisoglebsky (ed.), *Materials for the History of Russian Ballet*, Vol. II (Leningrad 1939)

Astaire, Fred [Frederick Austerlitz], b. Omaha, NE, 1899. American dancer and choreographer. With very little formal dance training, he and his sister Adèle were launched as a vaudeville child act by their parents 1906, and toured the USA until the 1915–16 season. Their first appearance in musical comedy was in a 1917 show, *Over the Top*, with music by Sigmund Romberg, and they danced together in many musicals and revues both in NY and London until Adèle's retirement on her marriage in 1932. The Gershwins wrote *Lady, Be Good!* (1924) and *Funny Face* (1927) for them; their last show together was *The Band Wagon*, in which Astaire also danced with LOSCH. He appeared in one more stage show, Cole Porter's *Gay Divorce* (1932), in which his partner was Claire Luce.

Astaire's first film appearance was in *Dancing Lady* (1933), in which he did a brief 'guest' stint as Joan Crawford's partner. In the same year he made another film, for RKO-Radio, *Flying Down to Rio*, in which his performance of 'The Carioca' with Ginger Rogers created a sensation. (In 1930, Astaire had choreographed 'Embraceable You' for Rogers in the Broadway musical *Girl Crazy*.) The team of Astaire and

Fred Astaire dancing with Ginger Rogers in the Waltz in *Swing Time*

Rogers became one of the biggest moneymakers of the 1930s; they made eight more films together for RKO: *The Gay Divorcee* (1934), *Roberta* (1935), *Top Hat* (1935), *Follow the Fleet* (1936), *Swing Time* (1936), *Shall We Dance* (1937), *Carefree* (1938), and *The Story of Vernon and Irene Castle* (1939).

Astaire and Rogers danced to the finest popular music of their time, composed for them by the Gershwins, Irving Berlin, and Jerome Kern. Without pretending to be anything but entertainment of the lightest kind, Astaire's dances, all arranged by himself, usually in collaboration with his dance director Hermes Pan, represent the highest choreographic achievement of the cinema.

Although she was nothing like as accomplished technically as Astaire, Rogers was the ideal partner for him; she had an extraordinary plastic ability to mould her body to his, and her outgoing personality complemented his reserve – as CROCE put it, he gave her class, and she gave him sex.

After the inevitable break-up of the team, Astaire made many more movies with many more partners, among them Eleanor Powell (*Broadway Melody of 1940*); Rita Hayworth (*You'll Never Get Rich*, 1941, and *You Were Never Lovelier*, 1942); Judy Garland and Ann Miller (*Easter Parade*, 1948); Vera-Ellen (*Three Little Words*, 1950, and *The Belle of New York*, 1952); Cyd Charisse (*The Band Wagon*, 1953, and *Silk Stockings*, 1957); CARON (*Daddy Long Legs*, 1955); and Audrey Hepburn (*Funny Face*, 1957). But, enjoyable as many of the films were on their own terms, none of these partnerships seemed to have been made in heaven in the same way as that of Astaire and Rogers was – a fact made even more poignantly obvious by the failure of the attempt to reunite them in *The Barkleys of Broadway* in 1949. In the later films Astaire's own solos tended to become more concerned with props and gimmicks – some of them brilliantly executed, as in the number in *Royal Wedding* (1951), where he danced not only on the floor but on the walls and ceiling of his room.

In recent years Astaire has continued to appear in films in acting roles. In 1949 he received a special Academy Award 'for his unique artistry and his contributions to the technique of musical pictures'. The Oscar was presented to him by Ginger Rogers. He is BALANCHINE's favourite male dancer. DV
See Fred Astaire, *Steps in Time* (New York 1959; London 1960); Arlene Croce, *The Fred Astaire and Ginger Rogers Book* (London and New York 1972); Stanley Green and Burt Goldblatt, *Starring Fred Astaire* (London and New York 1974)

Astarte, ballet, ch. JOFFREY; mus. Crome Syrcus; sc. Thomas Skelton; c. Hugh Sherer. NYCC, CCJB, 20 Sept 1967; dan. Trinette Singleton, Maximiliano Zomosa. Astarte is the Phoenician Aphrodite, goddess of fertility and sexual love. The ballet is an audience-participation fantasy, made 'real' by rock music, strobe lighting, and film of the dancers that is reflective of the action. Fascinated by the goddess, a boy in the audience is drawn to the stage, where he joins her in a dance of sensual discovery and submission. FM

As Time Goes By, ballet, ch. THARP; mus. Franz Joseph Haydn; ltg Jennifer Tipton; c. Chester Weinberg. NYCC, CCJB, 24 Oct 1973; dan. Beatriz Rodriguez, Larry Grenier. Set to the 'Farewell' Symphony, this plotless ballet seems to say goodbye to certain pretensions of classic ballet and indicates new directions for dance. FM

Atanasoff, Cyril, b. Puteaux, 1941. French dancer. Studied Paris OBS, PERETTI, 1953. *Corps de ballet* 1957, *premier danseur* 1962, *étoile* 1964. Created roles in BÉJART's DAMNATION DE FAUST, SACRE DU PRINTEMPS, PETIT's NOTRE-DAME DE PARIS. Leading roles in the great classics, SUITE EN BLANC, *Les Mirages* (ch. LIFAR), APRÈS-MIDI D'UN FAUNE. One of the best dancers of his generation. His range of technique and dramatic power enables him to dance with nobility in the classical repertory, and also to perform more human and modern roles by Petit or Béjart. A frequent guest artist with LFB and much in demand for international galas. M-FC
See A.-P. Hersin, 'Cyril Atanasoff', *Les Saisons de la Danse* (Paris, Nov 1968) with list of roles

ATER (Associazione Teatri Emilia-Romagna). Association with headquarters in Bologna (in the Emilia region of Italy) that organizes perfs in a network of cities by touring opera and ballet cos at the historic opera houses – some only recently reopened – of Bologna, Parma, Modena, Reggio Emilia, Piacenza, Cremona, Ferrara, Ravenna, etc. Guest dance cos are frequently from Eastern Europe. FP

Atlanta Ballet *see* REGIONAL BALLET (USA)

At Midnight, ballet, ch. FELD; mus. Gustav Mahler; sc. Leonard Baskin; c. Stanley Simmons. NYST, ABT, 1 Dec 1967; dan. MARKS, SARRY, Terry Orr, C. GREGORY, Feld. Revived Eliot Feld B. 1974. A dramatic ballet about man as passive hero, about loneliness and unachieved joy, performed to four of Mahler's Rückert Songs. Also in repertory of RSB. FM

At the Still Point *see* STILL POINT, THE

Auber, Daniel François Esprit, b. Caen, 1782; d. Paris, 1871. French composer, notably of the comic opera *Fra Diavolo* (Paris 1830) and the grand opera *La Muette de Portici* (Paris 1828; ch. Jean Aumer), whose title character is conceived for a dancer (originally Lise Noblet; later filmed with A. PAVLOVA, 1915). In Auber's opera-ballet *Le Dieu et la Bayadère* (Paris 1830; ch. F. TAGLIONI) M. TAGLIONI scored her first great success. The ballet *Marco Spada* (Paris 1857; ch. MAZILIER) was not an adaptation of Auber's comic opera of the same name but an anthology, made by the composer, of tunes from his various works. Auber's music, effervescent and skilfully made, has been used by various 20th-c. choreographers, among them V. GSOVSKY (*Grand Pas Classique*; Paris 1949) and ASHTON (RENDEZVOUS). DH

Aureole, modern dance work, ch. P. TAYLOR; mus. George Frideric Handel. New London, CT, Palmer Auditorium, Connecticut College, 4 Aug 1962; dan. Taylor, Elizabeth Walton, WAGONER, Sharon Kinney, Renee Kimball. A lyrical work in which flirtatious good humour prevails. In the repertory of many other cos; a favourite of NUREYEV. DMD

Auric, Georges, b. Lodève, Hérault, 1899. French composer, originally influenced by RAVEL, then by SATIE, from whom he derived an admiration for simplicity and wit. Member of Les Six (with MILHAUD, POULENC, Arthur Honegger, Germaine Tailleferre, and Louis Durey), all of whom, save the last, collaborated on *Les Mariés de la Tour Eiffel* (Paris 1921; ch. BÖRLIN) for Ballets Suédois. Wrote three ballets for DIAGHILEV: FÂCHEUX, *Les Matelots* (London 1925; ch. MASSINE), and *La Pastorale* (Paris 1926; ch. BALANCHINE). With nine other composers (incl. Ravel, Poulenc, Milhaud, Jacques Ibert, Albert Roussel, Florent Schmitt) wrote *L'Eventail de Jeanne* (Paris 1929; ch. Yvonne Franck and Alice Bourgat) in which the 10-year-old TOUMANOVA appeared. Auric's other ballets incl. *La Concurrence* (Monte Carlo 1932; ch. Balanchine), and PHÈDRE, in both of which Toumanova starred, and *Bal des Voleurs* (Nervi 1960; ch. Massine). DH

Aurora, Princess, the heroine of SLEEPING BEAUTY

Aurora's Wedding (*Le Mariage d'Aurore*), all that survived from DIAGHILEV's production of *The Sleeping Princess* (*see* SLEEPING BEAUTY). After the London debacle in 1921, he presented at the Paris O., 18 May 1922, a 1-act *divertissement*, consisting of the dances from the last act of M. PETIPA's ballet, with some additions by NIJINSKA; sc. BAKST, some costumes from PAVILLON D'ARMIDE, some additional ones by GONCHAROVA; dan. TREFILOVA and VLADIMIROV. This version, which was very successful, with some alterations, remained a staple item in the repertory of DE BASIL's co. DOLIN staged another production, *Princess Aurora*, for ABT at the NY 44th St T., 26 Nov 1941. All the principal ballerinas of the 1930s and 1940s danced Aurora. Once the SWB had revived the full-length *Sleeping Beauty* and established its popularity, the shorter version disappeared, replaced everywhere by 3-act stagings. The RB on tour in smaller theatres now frequently gives *The Sleeping Beauty* Act III as the final item of a mixed program. MC

Ausdruckstanz (Ger. 'expressive dance'), term used to describe those forms of theatrical dancing which are not based on the technique of the classical or *danse d'école* style. It refers particularly to the 'free' styles of WIGMAN and LABAN, called at the time in English 'Modern Dance'. The German term dates from the 1920s when the style was in full flower in Central Europe, hence it is also known as 'Central European Dancing'. GBLW

Australia. Drama preceded dance into the Australian theatre – a natural state of affairs in a robust pioneering society; but in the 1840s SYLPHIDE was performed in Melbourne, and in 1855 Sydney and Melbourne saw a version of FILLE MAL GARDÉE with a French dancer, Aurelia Dimier, as Lise.

However, it was the visits of GENÉE and, particularly, A. PAVLOVA that aroused the continuing strong minority passion for classical ballet. Genée, with VOLININ and a group called The Imperial Russian B., staged COPPÉLIA and SYLPHIDES in Melbourne, June 1913. Pavlova made her first tour 1926, with NOVIKOV, and her second, with VLADIMIROFF, 1929. Two dancers from the Pavlova B. eventually settled in Australia: ALGERANOFF in Mildura and BOROVANSKY in Melbourne.

In 1934 Victor Dandré directed the Levitoff Russian B., headed by SPESSIVTSEVA and VILZAK, and from this tour Australia gained an eminent teacher, KELLAWAY; and LAKE established a branch of the Cecchetti Society. In 1938 the RAD extended its activities to Australia, appointing Kathleen Danetree, who later settled there, as examiner.

In 1936 J. C. Williamson Theatres Ltd arranged a tour for the DE BASIL B. Russe de Monte Carlo, headed by WOIZIKOWSKI. Further tours, under different titles, took place 1938 and 1939, when the principal dancers numbered all the great names of contemporary Russian ballet.

Overseas ballet cos on tour almost always lose one or two dancers to Australia. KIRSOVA settled in Sydney after the first de Basil tour and opened a studio July 1940. In July 1941 she presented a small co. at the Conservatorium. The Kirsova B., whose repertoire contained many ballets by Kirsova herself, survived until her return to Europe, 1946. Australian dancers with the co. incl. Rachel Cameron, Peggy Sager, Strelsa Heckelman, and Henry Legerton.

In 1939 BOROVANSKY, with his wife Xenia Nikolaeva, opened an academy in Melbourne and presented a group in occasional perfs. This co., originally backed by the Melbourne Ballet Club, turned professional May 1944, sponsored by J. C. Williamson Theatres Ltd. It did not have a continuous performing life, but gave seasons at intervals over the years.

The repertoire was predominantly Russian, but two Australian choreographers, MARTYN and Dorothy Stevenson, worked for the co. Stevenson's *Sea Legend* (Melbourne 1943) was the first all-Australian ballet (mus. Esther Rofe; sc. Alan McCulloch and Jean Oberhansli; revived International B., London, 1948; new sc./c. John Bainbridge). (The first all-Australian ballet with an Australian theme was the Australian B. Society's *Arkaringa*, Melbourne 1946, ch. Philippe Perrottet, mus. Gwendoline Cooper, sc. Russell Hooper.) The Borovansky B. was led by Tamara Tchinarova, but most of the principals were Australian. Apart from Martyn and Stevenson, names to recall from this period incl. Edna Busse, Paul Hammond, and Martin Rubinstein.

By the time Borovansky died suddenly (Dec 1959), a new generation of soloists had emerged, among them GORHAM, M. JONES, WELCH, and Vassilie Trunoff. The final season was directed by VAN PRAAGH, who became founding artistic director of the AUSTRALIAN B., launched Nov 1962.

The Australian dance scene was not limited to the Borovansky B. nor is it now limited to the Australian B. In Nov 1946 the Victorian B. Guild, formed by Martyn for the Melbourne B. Guild, had its inaugural perf. This co. has greatly encouraged Australian dancing, choreography, music, and design. Now called B. Victoria, it acquired Welch as assistant artistic director 1974.

The NTB, Melbourne, formed by the NT Movement of Australia, was directed 1948–51 by GRAEME in association with REID. It ceased its full-time activities in 1955.

In modern dance, BODENWIESER and Margaret Barr played an important part. Bodenwieser, from Vienna, opened a studio in Sydney 1938 and formed the Bodenwieser B., choreographing many works. Her Dance Centre is continued by Margaret Chapple and Keith Bain. Barr, an American born in Bombay, runs the Sydney Dance Drama Group.

Other existing cos incl.: the Dance Co. (NSW), director Graeme Murphy, originally founded 1965 as B. in a Nutshell by MUSITZ, but now a contemporary dance group; the Australian Dance T., Adelaide, founded 1965 by DALMAN, its artistic director until 1975, now directed by Jonathan Taylor; the New Dance T., founded 1968 in Turramurra, NSW, director Ruth Galene; the Sydney City B. Co., director Tanya Pearson, designed to present ballet programs for children, became professional in 1974; the Perth City B., director Diana Waldron; the Queensland B., director Harry Haythorne, founded 1960 by LISNER as the Lisner B. and retitled 1962; the West Australian B., director Robin Haig; the Tasmanian B., director Kenneth Gillespie; the Kolobok Character Dance Co., Melbourne, director Marina Berezowsky, founded 1970; the Dance Concert, Sydney (character dance), director Margaret Walker.

Schools abound in all the States, many with long histories and fine results in the way of professional dancers. Annual open choreographic competitions are held in Sydney under the title Ballet Australia, director Valrene Tweedie. Aboriginal dance and mime have been considerably researched, and occasional small teams of dancers have been presented in theatres. KSW

Australian Ballet, The. The present Australian. B. has its roots in the BOROVANSKY B., which ceased activities early 1961. Borovansky, its founder and director, had died suddenly Dec 1959, and VAN PRAAGH was invited to take over the final season 1960–1. Because of the co.'s popularity and van Praagh's excellent direction, the Australian B. Foundation, established by the Australian Elizabethan T. Trust and J. C. Williamson Theatres Ltd, asked her to become the first artistic director of a new co. to be called the Australian B.

The first perf. took place on 2 Nov 1962, at Her Majesty's T., Sydney, and the ballet was SWAN LAKE, with guest artists Sonia Arova and BRUHN. The co. had strong RB connections. Not only was van Praagh director, but Ray POWELL, initially on leave from the RB, was ballet master. Principal dancers that season incl. M. JONES, GORHAM, and WELCH.

These dancers had been with the Borovansky B., but the repertoire that emerged under van Praagh's direction was quite different from Borovansky's. It incl. works by ASHTON, BALANCHINE, CRANKO, Ray Powell, and REID; and in 1964 HELPMANN's all-Australian ballet *The Display* was premiered with enormous success. Its importance for its time and in its environment should not be underestimated.

Also in 1964 came the opening of the Australian BS, which has been given distinguished guidance by its founder-director, M. SCOTT, who had settled in Australia after the BR tour of 1947–8. From this school have graduated some of the best younger dancers to enter the co., for example ROWE, MEEHAN, and NORMAN. It is a Federal school and auditions for pupils, who join it for a two-year course after their initial training to a high level at other ballet schools all over Australia.

In 1965, the year that Helpmann became co-artistic director of the co. with van Praagh, continuing the RB connection but also, for the first time, bringing an Australian on to the Borovansky–Australian B. directorial scene, the Australian B. made its first overseas tour, taking a small repertoire to the 10th International Festival at Ba'albek, the Commonwealth Arts Festival in Britain, and the 3rd International Festival of Dance at Paris. During the tour, NUREYEV, who has been closely associated with the co. as a valuable guest artist and producer, staged his full-length RAYMONDA for it.

The Australian B. has made consistent and rapid progress. Although removed by distance from the rest of the dance scene, standards have been maintained by the international experience of the directors and regular guest appearances by great dancers from abroad. The repertoire is a wide-ranging one. It incl., apart from the classics, works by FOKINE, MASSINE, Balanchine, Ashton, TUDOR, Helpmann, PETIT, MACMILLAN, Cranko, BUTLER, TETLEY, and MORELAND. Productions have also been adopted from its annual choreographic workshops: Welch's *Othello*, Meehan's *Night Episode*, Julia Cotton's *Super Man*.

Although not designated as such, the Australian B. is in fact a national ballet, with permanent headquarters in Melbourne. Touring, however, is basic to its life – touring the Australian State capitals; country touring, in small sections; and overseas tours. These last have taken them to Canada and S. America (1967); Japan and SE Asia (1968); the USA (1970–1); Singapore and the Philippines (1971); India, E. Europe (incl. Russia), and Great Britain (1973); the USA and Great Britain (1976).

Now an autonomous co. administered by the Australian B. Foundation (chairman, N. R. Seddon, CBE), it receives grants from the Australian Government, the State Governments, and others. It undertakes schools programs, educational TV films and lecture demonstrations, and has an important and excellently run library and dance archives (archivist, Edward Pask) that organize occasional exhibitions.

Van Praagh retired Dec 1974 because of ill-health. From then until June 1976 the Australian B. was directed by Helpmann, with ASHBRIDGE and Ray Powell as associate directors. WOOLLIAMS succeeded Helpmann as artistic director Sept 1976. KSW

Austria. As in Germany, there are ballet cos of varying sizes attached to all the opera houses. In the smaller ones the dancers appear in operas and operettas as required, namely in Baden bei Wien, Graz, Innsbruck, Klagenfurt, Linz, Salzburg, St Pölten. The main centre has always been VIENNA. MC

Avant-garde dance. Avant-garde dance in the USA during the 1960s and early 1970s stemmed largely from CUNNINGHAM and the Cunningham-related explorations that took place at Judson Church in New York. Like most advanced art movements, experimental dance has worked outside the more conventional theatres, gathering small audiences with a taste for its unusual presentations. Given the realities of production and subsidy in this period, however, many avant-gardists have performed in unexpectedly prominent theatres and to audiences that might not ordinarily have sought out their work. Some, like THARP, have choreographed successfully for major ballet cos. At the same time, experimental ideas of some potency have petered out, perhaps before their full import has been developed. Compared to the revolutionary dance that came out of Cunningham and Judson, experimental dance in 1975 was less daring, less shocking, more refined and polished, and – partly due to more knowledgeable audiences – more accessible.

Working out of the philosophy of CAGE, Cunningham applied the devices of indeterminacy and its by-products to his own choreography (*see* MUSIC FOR BALLET). He never dispensed with dance technique, though, and as strange as his work may feel to modern dance or ballet audiences, it maintains much of the traditional appearance of dance. He kept the rhythm and placing, the self-contained performance attitude that is found in any stage dancing.

Avant-garde dance. *Left:* The Trisha Brown Dance Company in *Locus* with (left to right) Elizabeth Garrett and T. BROWN; *right:* Grand Union, a New York-based dance company derived from RAINER's group

Cunningham's principal innovations arose from his approach to the choreographic process. In reaction against the authoritarian role traditionally played by the ballet or modern dance choreographer, Cunningham wanted to make a form of dance that would not be a projection of his own psychological states and attitudes, or a product of his ability to work out steps based on some music or a story. He rejected the romantic view that the artist is possessed of unusual, perhaps even supernatural gifts and a corresponding licence to impress his personality upon his audience and his collaborators. Cunningham had danced for five years with GRAHAM, and his denial of these concepts probably reflected impatience with Graham's dominance in all phases of her choreography, from subject matter and content to stage and costume design to the very personal movement style she imposed on her dancers. But, as an extremely reticent and private personality, Cunningham could also have been seeking alternatives to the 19th-c. assumption that the artist is trying to bare his soul through self-expression. The concentration on form and process that came out of this denial of the godlike artist allies Cunningham to 20th-c. painting, literature, and music, where the same evolution has occurred.

Cunningham found his objectivity in the use of chance operations. By tossing coins or dice, or employing other devices, he determined and recorded on complicated charts the sequence and much of the character of the movement – its duration, focus, location in the performing area, and any of several other variables. Having structured movement in this way, rather than adhering to kinetic or theatrical phrasing, he seemed to have destroyed its ordinary connectedness, its logic. Any movement could follow any other movement, any body part succeed any other body part, within the anatomical capability of the dancer. In disrupting movement's 'natural' sequence, Cunningham gave a more equal value to each part of the movement. The dancer was both more exposed and freer to bring his or her individual quality to the act of dancing.

The corollaries to this great discovery extend into many areas of composition and performance. If the dancer's body does not have to maintain certain predetermined phrasing, positions, preparations, completions, then virtually any sequence of movement could be considered dance. If any part of a phrase could be emphasized, then any dancer could be important, any part of the stage could be enlivened by dance activity. Cunningham's dance is multi-focused. He does not rely on the conventional stage hierarchies and areas of action to draw the audience's attention. Entrances and exits are not always announced. Several people may be doing several different things simultaneously, with no indication as to which one is going to influence the rest of the dance and which one will have a minor role or disappear.

A Cunningham dance has no plot or thematic development, or if it has, these are not intended for the audience's benefit. The dancing is what is important, in its moment-to-moment occurrence, unhampered by literary or musical references. Cunningham's movement has no responsibility except to move. The other elements of his stage works are independently conceived and created, and, except for happening in the same space and time and usually being technically compatible enough not to get in each other's way, music, decor, lights and other effects make their own artistic statements. The audience can experience them separately or synthesize the elements for itself.

The most immediate outgrowth of this opening up of the theatre event to many unrelated activities occurring simultaneously was the 'happenings' of the late 1950s to early 1960s. Perhaps because they were non-repeatable and essentially unstructured, the happenings never became a major outlet for the creative ideas of dancers.

Beginning in 1960, almost 10 years after Cunningham's first chance dance, *Sixteen Dances for Soloist and Company of Three* (1951), Robert Dunn began teaching a composition course at the Cunningham studio. Dunn was also fascinated with the ideas of Cage, and, since he was not running a performing dance co., he and the artists who worked with him over the next four years were able to carry Cage's theories further than Cunningham cared to do. Dunn's workshops concerned themselves with exploring new ways of making dances. Many of his students were painters, but their lack of dance training did not constitute a handicap. In that permissive atmosphere, dance movement and non-dance movement were acceptable. Chance and other compositional techniques were employed. Props could enter into the work; the rules of games or the attitudes of sports could affect the structure. The works were planned for performing in studios or other open spaces, not proscenium theatres. Dunn refused to act as a dogmatic evaluator-teacher, but all the participants discussed each other's works, with special attention to the means each person had used to compose.

In 1962 members of Dunn's workshop began giving concerts at Judson Church in downtown NY, and continued to present their efforts as a loosely organized group, the Judson Dance Theater. Some of the choreographers who worked at Judson in the earliest years, before its creative energies settled down and grew less radical, were RAINER, PAXTON, FORTI, Deborah Hay, WARING, T. BROWN, and Judith Dunn. Events at Judson tended to be extreme – often surrealistic, mysterious, or deliberately shocking. With the exception of Jill Johnston of the *Village Voice* and, briefly, Allen Hughes of the *New York Times*, critics stayed away or, when they came, did not understand. But the Judson audience was loyal, and dance was done at the church for the next ten years.

Although NY has always been the centre for the performing of experimental dance, California and, by extension, the Far East provided a quite different but important source of inspiration. In San Francisco HALPRIN was working towards an improvisational theatre with her Dancers' Workshop. During the early Judson period, Rainer, T. Brown, Forti, and others studied with Halprin, learning to move according to the internal rhythms and connections that were to be discovered through an almost mystical communion with the dancer's own body.

Halprin's own work led to community workshops and the development of life ceremonies that were carried out more as therapy than as performance. But Forti and others pursued the body-level implications they had found in Halprin. Movement was minimal, development slow. The forced dynamics and cerebral developments of Western music and dance were exchanged for an Eastern aesthetic, where through repetition and sustained energy the dancer made contact with cosmic, enduring forces. Drugs helped some of these experimentalists to open their consciousness to non-Western modes of perception.

Since the mid-1960s most of the avant-garde dance in NY has emerged from one or another combination of the influences just mentioned, plus the added technical resource of 'mixed media' and the greater possibilities offered by performing space without the restriction of a proscenium. The focus of many experimentalists' work has shifted considerably over the period. Since they were not interested in developing permanent repertory works, they could go on to new concerns once they felt they had grappled successfully with one set of problems. Some of the most pervasive features of experimental work have been the use of 'natural' or non-dance movement, the development of new and personal yet depersonalized theatrical images, and the exploration of compositional structures that may intentionally be made apparent to the audience.

Rainer, Paxton, Hay, and CHILDS were among the Judson dancers who were fascinated by the way people looked doing simple activities like walking, running, and sitting. If different types of people could execute these actions together, then differences in the movement caused by body type, personality, and other factors would be evident. Rainer especially worked to strip away performing artifice from the movement – the dynamic modifications and distortions that made movement exciting but, she felt, less genuine. She tried for a neutral kind of dynamic, even in movement that was not simple. Her *Trio A* (1966) was performed by dancers and non-dancers, some of them learning the dance in performance. Rainer was interested in what she called rehearsal behaviour as a means of allowing the performers to be more spontaneous in their reactions. She gave the dancers who worked with her a variety of choices and learning situations to cope with, and the most successful of these semi-improvised pieces, *Continuous Project Altered Daily* (1969–70), became the last she did with this group. She decided that a director-choreographer interfered with the working out of the improvisational process. The group stayed together, as the Grand Union, its improvisation becoming more theatrical, more entertaining, with heavy use of ad-libbed and recorded words and music, dance, games, and dramatic skits.

Trisha Brown has followed several lines of development suggested by 'natural' movement. Her *Leaning Duets* and *Falling Duets* of the 1968–71 period posed various sets of rules within which the dancers tested each other's strength, supporting power, and ability to coordinate actions. *Walking on the Wall* (1970) was the most spectacular in a group of studies in which Brown placed the performer in a distorted, even deranged relationship to the environment. Hanging perpendicular to a wall in a harness, the performers attempted to move with the same ease as they would standing upright on the ground. A series of *Accumulating Pieces* that she began in 1971 tried ways of building movement sequences one gesture at a time by adding the new gesture without a break on to the previous chain.

With these pieces Brown became more interested in compositional structure, and her *Roof Piece* (1973) had 15 dancers stationed on the tops of buildings, picking up and relaying a continuous sequence of movement down the line. Her 1975 quartet, *Locus*, presented movement that was somewhat more decorative but that still gave equal importance to each gesture. The work took a semi-fugal form, with all the performers focusing into different parts of the space. Although there may be theatrical imagery implicit in her work, Trisha Brown minimizes this by avoiding costume, special lighting effects, or any deliberate performing artifice.

TAKEI is one of several choreographers who have allowed the metaphorical inferences of simple but intense movement to assume some importance in the dance. Her monumental ten-part work *Light* (1969–76) has sections of almost pure movement, such as one person rocking more and more violently back and forth on her back, or one person squatting and staring into a pool of light while others, blindfolded, test their agility in the space; simple movement sequences repeated with small variations until they seem to stand for much larger ideas, such as the repeated image of a woman and two men hanging onto each other until they fall, then pulling themselves up, hanging together, and falling again; and games structures with an improvised solution, as when a group moves until told to freeze, then continues to move again but with the requirement that the dancers remember the frozen posture so they can create it again on command. The sections of *Light* were unified by the use of similar costumes and properties, and also by the repetition of images such as the planting of rice, the carrying of packs on the dancers' backs, and the symbolic use of light and colour.

Soloist William Dunas's work has evolved gradually from the creation of characters and emotional states through the use of very intense, sometimes violent physical activity, to the presentation of very dispassionate musical, verbal, and movement material that, in combination, directs the observer's attention to social or political injustices. Since his first dance, *Gap* (1968), however, Dunas has always made use of repetitious, highly controlled movement, whether non-dance activity as in his early pieces, or the stripped-down, almost sketchy balletic fragments of recent years.

MONK and R. WILSON have gone even further in the direction of creating theatrical images, with movement assuming an almost illustrative role in the total staged spectacle. Monk's highly original and virtuoso vocal accompaniments are an added element to a theatre that seems fabricated and abstracted totally out of her own mind and experience. Wilson's epic works are filled with stunning visual effects as well as apparently unrelated incident that comes from material contributed and developed by the members of his own school and co. Both Wilson and Monk seem to be creating essentially literary forms that have to be materialized in front of an audience. The dance world is no longer sure whether they still belong to it.

KING also has a strong literary sense. In fact, he is a serious intellectual with a desire to communicate philosophical ideas. His work is often a combination of complicated, punning texts that are spoken live or as taped accompaniment; films, tableaux, or theatrical skits with considerable realistic detail; and his own very skilful, fast, and sinuous dancing.

Although she was initially concerned with reactivating movement by stripping away its theatrical elements, Rainer also was interested in composition. In fact, she seems to be the most direct source of the cerebral early compositional techniques of Tharp. Tharp's fluid, eventful dancing style and her interest in creating popular works superseded the stringent inventiveness of her composing process during the mid-1970s, but Rainer has continued to move away from choreography or even dance. Her latest works incorporated larger and larger amounts of film, until live performers did not appear in them at all. Rainer seems, like Dunas, bent on objectivizing experience, not the experience of a society but of a particular woman, perhaps herself. She does this by removing events from 'real' contexts and putting them into literary, cinematic, or other narrative forms.

L. DEAN has approached the question of objectivity from another tack, that of repetitious, non-melodic music. Keeping her movement very simple – walking, jumping, and spinning – Dean has developed group structures that are often based on the African-derived music of Steve Reich. Rhythm and form are the striking elements of her dance, but underlying her impersonal structures are the ancient and universal experiences of social community and spiritual communion. Since the appearances in the USA of the Whirling Dervishes of Turkey in 1972, many dancers have studied the Sufi and incorporated spinning in their work. The spiritualism and the semi-ecstatic state induced by spinning have become another means to extend dance into new areas of composition and expression. MBS

See Carolyn Brown, 'McLuhan and the Dance', *Ballet Review*, Vol. 1, No. 4 (New York 1966); 'On Chance', *Ballet Review*, Vol. 2, No. 2 (New York 1968); 'The Perils of Dance in the Colleges', *Ballet Review*, Vol. 3, No. 6 (New York 1971); John Cage, *Silence* (Middletown, CT, 1961); Simone Forti, *Handbook in Motion* (Halifax, NS, 1974); Jill Johnston, *Marmalade Me* (New York 1971); Yvonne Rainer, *Work 1961–73* (Halifax, NS, 1974); Marcia Siegel, *At the Vanishing Point* (New York 1972); *Ballet Review*, Vol. 1, No. 6 (New York 1967) (Judson issue: a symposium); 'Time to Walk in Space', *Dance Perspectives*, No. 34 (New York 1968) (symposium on Merce Cunningham)

Aveline, Albert, b. Paris, 1883; d. Asnières, 1968. French dancer, choreographer, and teacher. Paris OBS 1894; *danseur étoile* 1908, left 1934. *Maître de ballet*, teacher, then director of the OBS. For a long time partner of ZAMBELLI, notably in SYLVIA (1920), *Cydalise et le Chèvrepied* (1923), and various works of MÉRANTE, KHLUSTIN, STAATS. He staged elegant and graceful works like *La Grisi* (1935), *Elvire* (1937), *Les Santons* (1938), *Le Festin de l'Araignée* (1939), *Jeux d'Enfants* (1941), *La Grande Jatte* (1950), the Prologue in INDES GALANTES (1952). His dry manner and rigorous professional integrity have contributed towards maintaining the French school and to revitalizing masculine dance. M-FC

Awards and Decorations. Nearly every country honours distinguished figures in the world of dance, as in the other arts. By far the most confusing awards are those conferred by the British and the Soviet authorities, because of the abbreviations.

In Britain names of artists, together with those of other civilians, are put forward to the Government and the actual decorations presented by the monarch (or a member of the Royal Family), nearly always at Buckingham Palace. Titles are not hereditary. Nearly all the dance awards come under the most recent 'order', The Most Excellent Order of the British Empire, for which both men and women are eligible. There are five classes (listed in descending order): for men, Knights Grand Cross (GBE), Knights Commanders (KBE), Commanders (CBE), Officers (OBE), and Members (MBE); for women, Dames Grand Cross (GBE), Dames Commanders (DBE), Commanders (CBE), Officers (OBE), and Members (MBE). A lower rank in an order is automatically absorbed in a higher one. In addition to these, two very distinguished orders are conferred in the field of the arts: Order of Merit (OM), limited to 24 members, and Order of the Companions of Honour (CH), limited to 65 members. ASHTON (in 1970) was the first person from the world of dance to receive a CH. Simple knighthoods may also be awarded to men, as well as GBEs and KBEs. Knights are addressed as 'Sir' with one forename (e.g. Sir Frederick Ashton); women who have received the GBE or DBE are addressed as 'Dame' with one forename (e.g. Dame Marie RAMBERT).

In other European countries similar orders exist, e.g. in France, where artists may be made members of the Légion d'Honneur. The classes in this, in descending order of importance, are *Grand Croix*, *Grand Officier*, *Commandeur*, *Officier*, and *Chevalier*.

In the USSR the highest award to a civilian is Hero of Socialist Labour, held in ballet only by ULANOVA. The highest national exclusively artistic title is People's Artist of the USSR. Next, in descending order, comes People's Artist of any of the 15 constituent republics of the Soviet Union, e.g. the Russian Soviet Federated Socialist Republic (the huge RSFSR which itself comprises 14 autonomous republics or ASSRs), the Ukrainian SSR, the Georgian SSR, the Latvian SSR, etc. Thus LIEPA, for example, holds the titles of People's Artist of the Latvian SSR, whence he comes, and of the RSFSR, where he works. Next comes the title Honoured (sometimes translated as 'Merited') Artist of any of the 15 constituent republics; this may also be granted by an autonomous republic. The title Honoured Worker in the Arts is usually conferred when the recipient has already retired from the stage to teach, advise, or produce. Thus KOREN's distinctions incl. Honoured Worker in the Arts of the N. Osetian ASSR, where he assisted in the preparation of its national arts fests. Similar awards are made in other E. European countries, e.g. Hungary, where the titles Eminent Artist and Merited Artist of the Hungarian People's Republic have been conferred on outstanding artists since 1950.

There are also countless awards made by dance organizations, treasured and merited by the recipients but mostly of local interest. MC/NR

B

Babilée [Gutman], Jean, b. Paris, 1923. French dancer and choreographer. Studied Paris OBS, KNIASEFF, VOLININ, V. GSOVSKY. Debut 1941, Cannes. *Étoile*, B. des CE, 1945, ABT 1950–2, Paris O. 1952. Guest artist, B. de R. Petit, CHARRAT, Milan Sc., Berlin 1953–7. Founded his own co. 1955–7. Co-director, B. du Rhin 1972–3. Unforgettable BLUEBIRD and SPECTRE DE LA ROSE, created Joker in Charrat's *Jeu de Cartes* (*see* CARD GAME); also principal roles in JEUNE HOMME ET LA MORT; LICHINE's *La Rencontre* and *La Création* 1948; BÉJART's *La Reine Verte* 1956; LAZZINI's *Prodigal Son* 1967. Choreographed AMOUR ET SON AMOUR, *Till Eulenspiegel* (1949), BALANCE À TROIS. Has acted on stage and in films. Has feline magnetism, exceptional dancing, and a technique transformed by intelligent and sensitivity. He m. PHILIPPART; one daughter, Isabelle Babilée, a dancer with B. XXe S. M-FC

Jean Babilée rehearsing for the role of the Joker, which he created in CHARRAT's *Jeu de Cartes* with the B. des CE

Baiser de la Fée, Le (*The Fairy's Kiss*), allegorical ballet, 4 tableaux, lib. STRAVINSKY, after Hans Christian Andersen's *The Ice Maiden*; mus. Stravinsky, 'inspired by the muse of TCHAIKOVSKY'. (1) Ch. NIJINSKA; sc. BENOIS. Paris O., RUBINSTEIN's Co., 27 Nov 1928; dan. Rubinstein, SCHOLLAR, VILZAK. Revived T. Colón, Buenos Aires, 1932. (2) Ch. ASHTON; sc. FEDOROVITCH. London, SW, Vic-Wells B., 26 Nov 1935; dan. Pearl Argyle, FONTEYN, TURNER. The Bride was the first major role created by Ashton for Fonteyn. (3) Ch. BALANCHINE; sc. Alice Halicka. NY Met, ABT, 27 Apr 1937; dan. Kathryn Mullowney, Gisella Caccialanza, DOLLAR. Revived NY Met, B. Russe de Monte Carlo, 10 Apr 1940; Paris O., 2 July 1947; NYCC, NYCB, 28 Nov 1950; Milan, Sc., 1953. (4) Ch. MACMILLAN; sc. Kenneth Rowell. London, CG, RB, 12 Apr 1960; dan. BERIOSOVA, SEYMOUR, MACLEARY. The score continues to attract choreographers.

Stravinsky saw the story of a fairy who claims a child with her magic kiss and then returns years later to carry him off to eternal life as an allegory of the life of Tchaikovsky, similarly claimed by his muse and destined for eternal fame. DV

Baker, Josephine, b. St Louis, MO, 1906; d. Paris, 1975. American dancer and singer. Danced in the chorus of the black revue *Shuffle Along* and at the Cotton Club in Harlem before going to Paris in *La Revue Nègre*, 1925, where she remained, except for occasional trips to the USA and a sojourn in North Africa during World War II. Starred in annual revues at the Folies-Bergère and Casino de Paris throughout the 1930s. Studied ballet with BALANCHINE, who later choreographed dances for her. In the Ziegfeld Follies in New York, 1936. She was one of the first international stars to prove, as Janet Flanner wrote in *Paris Was Yesterday*, that 'black was beautiful'. In the last year of her life she made successful appearances at the Palace in NY and at the London Palladium. DV

Bakhrushin, Yuri, b. Moscow, 1896; d. Moscow, 1973. Soviet ballet historian and critic. Son of founder of Aleksey Bakhrushin State T. Museum, member of its Scientific Council. Taught, Moscow Choreographic S. and GITIS. Author of *A. A. Gorsky* (Moscow 1946); 'Ballet of the Bolshoy Theatre' in *Bolshoy Theatre* (Moscow 1948); *History of Russian Ballet*, a textbook for choreographic schools (Moscow 1965, 2nd edition 1973) and many articles. NR

Bakst, Léon, b. Grodno, 1866; d. Paris, 1924. Russian painter and stage designer whose work for DIAGHILEV's B. Russes revolutionized both stage design and fashion with its extravagant use of glorious colour. His range was fantastic; associated with such spectacles as SCHÉHÉRAZADE, DAPHNIS ET CHLOÉ, FEMMES DE BONNE HUMEUR, and *The Sleeping Princess* (*see* SLEEPING BEAUTY) he also designed the delicate, virginal setting for SPECTRE DE LA ROSE. MC

Balance à Trois, ballet, 1 scene, ch. BABILÉE; mus. Jean-Michel Damase; sc. Tom Keogh. Monte Carlo, B. de Jean Babilée, 25 Apr 1955; dan. Babilée, KALIOUJNY, CHAUVIRÉ. The rivalry of two athletes for one girl at practice in a gymnasium. Lighthearted and with some dazzling choreography. M-FC

Balanchine, George [Georgi Balanchivadze], b. St Petersburg, 1904. Russian dancer, choreographer, and ballet master. Most prolific and arguably most influential ballet choreographer of the 20th c. Associated principally with NEW YORK CITY BALLET and its predecessor cos (artistic director since 1934); ballet master, DIAGHILEV's B. Russes, 1924–9; ballet master, B. Russe de Monte Carlo, 1944–5; created works for Paris OB, ABT, B. Russe de Monte Carlo, his own co., Les Ballets 1933, RDB and Buenos Aires B.; created dances for opera, Broadway musicals (*On Your Toes*, 1936, and others), film (*Goldwyn Follies*, 1938, and others), TV (*Noah and the Flood*, mus. STRAVINSKY; sc. TER-ARUTUNIAN, 1962).

Studied piano from the age of five; accepted by the Imperial BS, St Petersburg, 1914, where his principal teachers were P. GERDT and Samuel Andreyanov. Graduated with honours 1921; joined *corps de ballet* and entered the Petrograd Cons. of Music to study theory and piano. Probably received the most thorough musical education of any choreographer; has been called by Stravinsky and others a supreme musician. An outstanding feature of his choreography is its musicality; he was also often far in advance of his time in his selection of scores (*Opus 34*, Arnold Schönberg, 1954; IVESIANA, Charles Ives, 1954; AGON, Stravinsky, 1957; EPISODES, Anton (von) Webern, 1959; *Movements for Piano and Orchestra* (*see* MOVEMENTS), Stravinsky, 1963; *Metastaseis and Pithoprakta*, Yannis Xenakis, 1968). His collaboration with Stravinsky over more than 50 years produced some 26 works, among them some of his undisputed masterpieces (APOLLO; ORPHEUS; *Firebird* (*see* OISEAU DE FEU); *Agon*; *Movements*; DUO CONCERTANT, VIOLIN CONCERTO).

In 1923 Balanchine formed a group of 15 dancers to present experimental works, called 'Evenings of the Young Ballet' (to music of Frédéric Chopin, RAVEL, Stravinsky, MILHAUD, and others). A second 'Evening', without music, although admired by his contemporaries, was denounced by the Maryinsky T., and soon (1924) Balanchine left Russia for good. He later said that while still in Russia his major influences were M. PETIPA, FOKINE, and GOLEIZOVSKY; the last two (Fokine particularly in CHOPINIANA) had the rare distinction at the time of using concert music and discarding plot – two later hallmarks of Balanchine's work.

In 1924, in France, he became Diaghilev's principal choreographer, creating *Le Chant du Rossignol* (mus. Stravinsky; sc. Henri Matisse), *Barabau* (mus. Vittorio Rieti; sc. Maurice Utrillo), both 1925; *La Pastorale* (mus. AURIC; sc. Pedro Pruna), *Jack in the Box* (mus. SATIE; sc. DERAIN), *The Triumph of Neptune* (mus. BERNERS; sc. Aleksandr Shervashidze), all 1926; *La Chatte* (mus. SAUGUET; sc. Naum Gabo and Antoine Pevsner), 1927; *Les Dieux Mendiants* (mus. George Frideric Handel; sc. BAKST), 1928; *Le Bal* (mus. Rieti; sc./c. CHIRICO),

Josephine Baker as she appeared at the Folies-Bergère

1929; and two of his most important works, PRODIGAL SON and *Apollo*, in which he first revealed his creed of classicism. Taking classical technique as his base, Balanchine subjected it to various inversions, 'distortions', reaccentuations, and unexpected sequences of steps, which resulted in a greater dynamism of movement at the expense of traditional classroom correctness. He continued this tendency throughout his career (it is the most outstanding feature of his work), further and further extending the vocabulary. His rigorous pure-dance approach caused his ballets to be criticized as mechanical, gymnastic, and soulless by some, however. Important offspring of *Apollo*'s 'quirky' classicism incl. FOUR TEMPERAMENTS and more distantly, *Agon*.

For the B. Russe de Monte Carlo, Balanchine created (1932) *La Concurrence* (mus. AURIC; sc. Derain) and the atmospheric *Cotillon* (mus. Emmanuel Chabrier; sc. BÉRARD), the latter notable for its presentation of TOUMANOVA, in which Balanchine revealed his sensitivity to the feelings of an adolescent girl. He became known for his response to the female body ('Ballet is a woman', he has often said) and for his ability to bring out special qualities of specific dancers, extending them beyond themselves. Among the ballerinas for whom he made particularly individual roles are A. DANILOVA, MARIE-JEANNE, Maria TALLCHIEF, LECLERCQ, KENT, and FARRELL. His abortive co., Les Ballets 1933, left little lasting effect, the six ballets which he created for it being, from all reports, principally in the '*étonne-moi*' tradition of Diaghilev (*Songes*, mus. Milhaud; sc. Derain; *Mozartiana*, mus. TCHAIKOVSKY; sc. Bérard; SEVEN DEADLY SINS; *Errante*, mus. Franz Schubert; sc. TCHELITCHEV; *Fastes*, mus. Sauguet, sc. Derain; *Les Valses de Beethoven*, sc./c. TERRY); it was pivotal, however, for bringing him into contact with a young American visionary, KIRSTEIN.

Kirstein's idea was to develop a ballet co. in America, at the time a highly optimistic dream. However, Balanchine accepted his invitation to found and head a school in NY: SAB, which, opened Jan 1934, has since developed into one of the foremost in the nation. Within six months, using mostly students, he created his magnificent ensemble ballet SERENADE, which was not, in the traditional manner, a series of set pieces for soloists with the ensemble decorating the stage, but a continuously flowing dance fabric with each member of the group having an individual role. This was a definitive manifestation of his artistic beliefs: primacy of dance (usually plotless but not necessarily themeless or without emotion), use of distinguished music (and, when less than the best, suiting the dance style to the music at hand), full use of a large ensemble; dislike of stars, particularly of the visiting guest artist variety; little if anything of costumes and decor.

Until NYCB's establishment on a permanent basis (1948), Balanchine, with Kirstein, ran various small, unstable cos (American B., American B. Caravan, B. Society) and choreographed works for more august organizations: B. Russe de Monte Carlo (DANSES CONCERTANTES, *Night Shadow* (*see* SONNAMBULA)); ABT (*Theme and Variations*, mus. Tchaikovsky; sc. Woodman Thompson, 1947); and Paris O. (PALAIS DE CRISTAL). From 1948, with the constant backing of Kirstein, he was occupied almost exclusively with NYCB, for which he has created some 90 works.

Roughly speaking, his ballets may be divided into the following (often overlapping) categories: 'Balanchine classical': *Apollo*; CONCERTO BAROCCO; BALLET IMPERIAL; *Four Temperaments*; *Palais de Cristal*; *Theme and Variations*; *Agon*; *Divertimento from* BAISER DE LA FÉE, mus. Stravinsky; sc./c. (Barbara) Karinska, 1972; TOMBEAU DE COUPERIN; 'traditional': SWAN LAKE (Act II), sc. BEATON, 1951; NUTCRACKER; sc. Horace Armistead, 1954; MIDSUMMER NIGHT'S DREAM; HARLEQUINADE; romantic: *Serenade*; VALSE; LIEBESLIEDER WALZER;

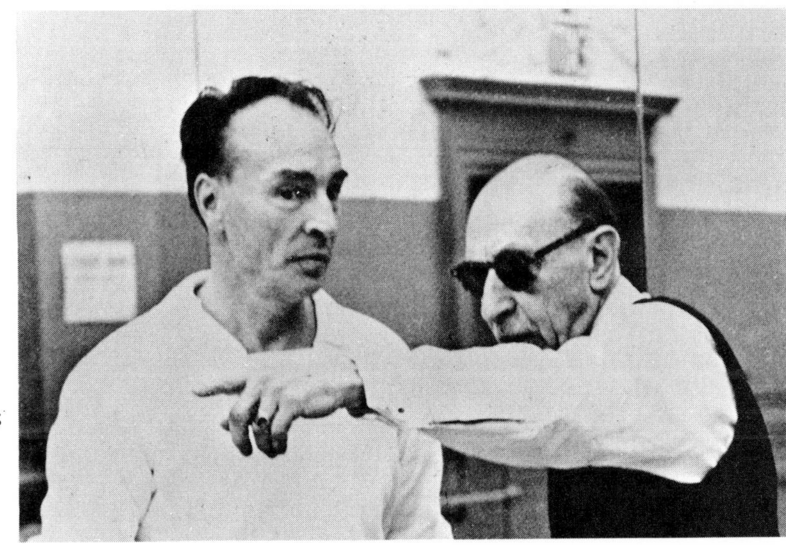

Left: George Balanchine and ROBBINS rehearsing their Beggars' Dance which they performed in their joint production of PULCINELLA (1972) for the NYCB's Stravinsky Festival; *right:* Balanchine with STRAVINSKY, with whom he collaborated closely from the time of APOLLO until the composer's death

Brahms-Schoenberg Quartet, c. (Barbara) Karinska; sc. Peter Harvey, 1966; *Duo Concertant*; avant-garde: *Apollo*; *Four Temperaments*; *Ivesiana*; *Agon*; *Episodes, Movements*; SYMPHONY IN THREE MOVEMENTS; *Violin Concerto*; dramatic: PRODIGAL SON: *Baiser de la Fée*; *Sonnambula*; *Orpheus*; DON QUIXOTE. This listing does not incl. the numerous 'occasional' pieces in a more or less classical style (*pas de deux, divertissements*, etc.) and the full-co. popular ballets that he is known to whip up when necessary in a day's or a week's time. He also responds to bigger challenges such as those set by the Stravinsky Fest. of 1972 and the creation of *Union Jack*, comissioned to celebrate the US Bicentennial 1976. NRe

See George Balanchine, 'Notes on Choreography' in *Dance Index*, No. 4 (New York, Feb–Mar 1945); *Complete Stories of the Great Ballets*, ed. Francis Mason (New York 1954); rev. ed., *New Complete Stories of the Great Ballets* (New York 1968); Yuri Slonimsky, 'Balanchine: The Early Years', tr. John Andrews, in *Ballet Review*, Vol. 5, No. 3 (New York 1976); Bernard Taper, *Balanchine* (New York 1963; London 1964; rev. ed. New York 1974)

Balasaraswati, Srimati T., b. Madras, 1919. The most celebrated dancer of India, the last of the *devadasis*. Born into a family of dancers and musicians; her teachers were Kandappa, Gauri Ammal, Chinayya Naidu, and Lakshmi Narayana Shastri. She has performed and danced in the West since 1961; besides many tours throughout Europe and the USA, she has been a resident teacher at Wesleyan Univ. (1962 and 1968), Univ. of California at Los Angeles (1968), California Inst. of the Arts (1972), and the Center for Asian Studies, Univ. of Washington, Seattle (1968 and 1973). Still unrivalled in the expressive aspects of *Dasi Attam*, she has received many awards in India; in 1976 a full-length film on her artistry was directed by Satyajit Ray. RM

Balashova, Aleksandra, b. Moscow, 1887. Russian dancer. Graduated from Moscow TS 1905; debut at 19 as Tsar-Maiden in HUMPBACKED HORSE, 3 Sept 1906. Facially beautiful and dramatically expressive, she was versatile in any genre and a typical GORSKY ballerina, neglecting correctness of style for picturesque expressiveness. Nevertheless she danced all the ballerina roles, e.g. AURORA, Medora (CORSAIRE), KITRI, SWANILDA, RAYMONDA, Nikia (BAYADÈRE), ODETTE-ODILE. Excelled in *demi-caractère* roles and recital items, usually performed with great success with permanent partner, MORDKIN. Promoted officially to ballerina position, 1915. Last role in Moscow, Bolshoy T., *Danse de Salomé* (ch. Gorsky; mus. Richard Strauss, Jan 1921). Went abroad summer 1921. Her mansion at Prechistenka 20, given to her by millionaire Ushkov (later her husband) accommodated the I. DUNCAN S. in Moscow. Danced Paris O. (LISE), also Russian O., Paris. Gave recital at Femina T. with Viktor Smoltsov from Bolshoy T. 1922. Revived FILLE MAL GARDÉE (mus. Peter Ludwig Hertel) for DE CUEVAS B. 1946–7, for Strasbourg B. 1966, playing WIDOW SIMONE, and in Yugoslavia. Abandoned active dancing 1931; taught for many years. NR

Bales, William, b. Carnegie, PA, 1910. American dancer. A featured performer with the HUMPHREY-WEIDMAN Co. Studied Bennington College Summer S. of The Dance; returned to teach there. With DUDLEY and MASLOW formed the Dudley-Maslow-Bales Trio, 1942–54, for which he created many works. Ceased active performing and choreographing in the early 1950s and concentrated on teaching. First head of the dance department on the State Univ. of NY campus at Purchase. Retired from that post 1975 but continues to teach. DM

Ballet. A form of theatrical entertainment in which a strict dance technique, called the *danse d'école* (the classical school), evolved over the past five centuries, is united with music, decor, and costume to create works of dramatic, lyric, or pure dance interest. Strictly, the word ballet should relate only to works in the classic style but in recent years, with the increasing cross-fertilization of classical ballet and freer contemporary techniques, it has come to be used to describe almost any theatrical dance arrangement.

Ballet traces its history from the Renaissance spectacles which combined music, singing, poetry, dancing and decoration – an amalgamation of all the arts. From Italy it moved to France and found its apogee in the BALLET DE COUR, especially under Louis XIV. Then it entered the professional theatre and the dancing masters of the 18th c., WEAVER, NOVERRE, ANGIOLINI, and HILVERDING, gradually established it as entertainment in its own right. By the early 19th c. BLASIS had codified technique and by the Romantic era ballet had arrived in much the form we know. Later, it flowered in Russia and was then revitalized in the West by DIAGHILEV. By the middle of the 20th c. what had been a diversion for the nobility had become popular worldwide. *See also* MUSIC FOR BALLET; OPERA, BALLET IN; OPÉRA-BALLET; and articles on individual countries. MC

Ballet Caravan *see* NEW YORK CITY BALLET

Ballet Club, The. An association of people who were interested in and sympathetic to the work of RAMBERT and her choreographers and dancers and who, for a small subscription, were entitled to attend Sunday night perfs at the little Mercury T., London. It was founded autumn 1930 by Rambert, her husband Ashley Dukes, and Arnold Haskell; the membership was a roster of great names in the arts. Not to be confused with the ballet clubs of today which are essentially groups of ballet lovers who invite guest lecturers and, mistakenly, put on perfs of amateur ballet. Ballet is such a demanding technical skill that it cannot be presented at an amateur level. *See* BALLET RAMBERT. MC

Ballet Comique de la Reine. Lavish court spectacle with music, singing, and dancing. Staged by Balthasar de Beaujoyeux; mus. Lambert de Beaulieu and Jacques Salmon; sc. Jacques Patin. Paris, Palais Bourbon, 15 Oct 1581. Usually referred to as the first 'ballet' not only on account of its success but because a lavishly illustrated description was published and widely distributed. (A facsimile was issued in Turin 1962.) Unquestionably a seminal work, but there had been many similar court spectacles before it. *See* BALLET DE COUR. MC

ballet de cour. A formal entertainment which incl. music, dance, and verse performed by members of the royal courts of Europe. Developing from the noble entertainments of the Italian Renaissance, it flourished particularly in France from the middle of the 16th c. and reached its apogee during the early years of Louis XIV's reign a century later. Often political in inspiration, the *ballet de cour* could serve as a celebration of some great event or, as in the early *Ballet des Polonais*, Paris, 19 Aug 1573, and the BALLET COMIQUE DE LA REINE, could offer a very clear message to its viewers, a message of power: the BALLET DE LA NUIT, in which the young Louis XIV appeared as the Sun, affirmed to a still disturbed aristocracy the absolute royal authority. With Louis's decision to give up dancing the *ballet de cour* lost its royal impetus and in 1671, with the founding of the ACADÉMIE ROYALE DE MUSIQUE, ballet became a matter for professional performers. MC
See Marie-Françoise Christout, *Le Ballet de Cour de Louis XIV, 1643–1672* (Paris 1967); Margaret MacGowan, *L'Art du Ballet de Cour en France 1581–1643* (Paris 1963); Henry Prunières, *Le Ballet de Cour en France avant Benserade et Lully* (Paris 1914); Roy Strong, *Splendour at Court; Renaissance Spectacle and Illusion* (London 1973); As *Splendor at Court; Renaissance Spectacle and the Theater of Power* (Boston 1973)

Ballet de la Nuit, Le, court ballet, with magnificent designs by the Italian artist Giacomo Torelli. Paris, Salle du Petit Bourbon, Louvre, 23 Feb 1653. Lasting over 12 hours and with 43 different *entrées*, it depicted the events of the night in terms of both ordinary people and mythology, culminating in the arrival of Dawn (Aurora) and the Rising Sun, who was accompanied by happy spirits and praised by all the virtues. Louis XIV, aged 14, appeared as the Sun; it was from this ballet that he earned his title of 'Le Roi Soleil'. *See* BALLET DE COUR. MC
See Lincoln Kirstein, *Movement and Metaphor* (New York 1970; London 1971)

Ballet du XXe Siècle *see* BÉJART

Ballet For All *see* ROYAL BALLET

Ballet Imperial, classic ballet, ch. BALANCHINE; mus. TCHAIKOVSKY; sc./c. Mstislav Dobuzhinsky. NY, Hunter College Playhouse, American B. Caravan, 29 May 1941; dan. MARIE-JEANNE, Gisella Caccialanza, DOLLAR. Revived London, CG, RB, 5 Apr 1950; sc./c. BERMAN; dan. FONTEYN, SOMES, GREY. NYST, NYCB, sc. TER-ARUTUNIAN, 15 Oct 1964; dan. FARRELL, NEARY, D'AMBOISE. A plotless ballet in the language and style of the great Russian Imperial T. of St Petersburg, this work extends the old vocabulary to initiate the contemporary audience. By the early 1970s Balanchine had discarded any suggestion of a St Petersburg setting (the Berman set was by far the greatest) and insisted on the ballet being danced in simple tunics instead of in the short classical tutus for which the women's choreography had been designed. The men's elegant tunics were changed to near practice wear. Consequently the title became meaningless; he changed it to *Tchaikovsky Concerto No. 2*. FM/MC

Left: Ballet de cour. A typical example of a court ballet, given at Versailles in 1668. Note that the performance was directed towards 'the Presence', the royal family and their guests, who are seated in the centre. Other spectators were placed on the two sides of the palace hall.

Below: Ballet Imperial, as danced by the RB at CG in 1950, sc./c. Eugene Berman, dan. FONTEYN and SOMES

Ballet International. British-based international touring co. founded Feb 1976 with backing from Performing Arts Council of the Orange Free State (PACOFS), S. Africa. Director, Max Martin, artistic director Larry Long, artistic adviser Ben Stevenson, musical director André Presser. First performance Welkom, Transvaal, Oppenheimer T., 30 Sept 1976. Repertoire incl. full-length classics staged by Stevenson and modern works. Among principal dancers were FULTON, RADIUS, EBBELAAR, with NAGY, SAMSOVA, and PROKOVSKY as guests. MC

Ballet International (NY) *see* GRAND BALLET DU MARQUIS DE CUEVAS

Ballet National des Jeunesses Musicales de France *see* LACOTTE

Balletomane, Balletomania. The word *balletomane* was first used in Russia early in the 19th c. It signifies a ballet enthusiast. Its French form (cf. *mélomane*) shows that it must have originated among the St Petersburg court circles whose members were *abonnés* of the Maryinsky T. and who have been caricatured looking at their favourite ballerinas through opera glasses, seeing the dancer rather than the ballet. The St Petersburg balletomanes were essentially partisan, highly critical of technique and rejoicing when KSHESSINSKA became the first Russian to emulate the Italians by performing 32 *fouettés*. The balletomanes reached the heights or depths of their mania when M. TAGLIONI danced in St Petersburg during three seasons, 1837–9. Tradition has it that her admirers at a banquet given in her honour drank a soup made of her shoes.

In later days the word took on a less extreme meaning that would have been better expressed by balletophile: lover and something of an expert. Many distinguished critics described themselves as balleto-

Balletomania, as depicted in Gustav Doré's 'La Fosse aux Lions'

manes, among them the scholarly SLONIMSKY and Akim Volyinsky who took classes at an advanced age in order to understand the difficulties of the art. The word balletomania was introduced into the English language by HASKELL's *Balletomania, The Story of an Obsession* (London and New York 1934), which described, with only the faintest touch of irony, his state of mind and that of a vastly increasing public for DE BASIL's B. Russe de Monte Carlo with its famous baby ballerinas, BARONOVA, RIABOUCHINSKA, and TOUMANOVA. ALH

Ballet Rambert (BR), England's oldest ballet co. It dates its origin from the creation of TRAGEDY OF FASHION. 'The Marie Rambert Dancers' gave occasional performances in new ballets (mostly by ASHTON) but the first full-length program was a matinée, also at the Lyric T., 25 Feb 1930. This was followed by short seasons at the same theatre in June–July and at Christmas of that year with KARSAVINA and WOIZIKOWSKI as guest artists. In autumn 1930 the BALLET CLUB was formed, based on the Mercury T. in W. London (bought by RAMBERT's husband Ashley Dukes 1927). Everything produced at this tiny theatre had to be conceived in terms of exquisitely proportioned 'chamber ballet'. The fact that Rambert's school and studio were in the same building gave ideal opportunities for choreographic experiment and she had exceptionally gifted pupils from the beginning. Her co. appeared in West End theatres and outside London during the 1930s but it was at the Mercury that the creative work was done. Ashton was the first choreographer to emerge. He was followed by TUDOR, HOWARD, GORE, and STAFF. The dancers from Rambert's studio included Pearl Argyle, Diana Gould, Prudence Hyman, Maude LLOYD, William Chappell (also a gifted designer), TURNER, and LAING. MARKOVA was ballerina at the Ballet Club for four years. Among dancers who appeared there – all of them for love rather than money – were FONTEYN, HELPMANN, DE MILLE, and Kyra Nijinsky. VAN PRAAGH joined the co. in 1933. Early in 1940 BR became associated with the Arts Theatre Club in London and gave seasons there. In June 1940 it united with the London B. as the Rambert-London B.

In Sept 1941 the Arts Theatre Club discontinued its ballet activities and legal complications forced the co. to disband. It was re-formed in Mar 1943 as the B. Rambert under the auspices of what is now the Arts Council of GB and toured wartime factories and camps as well as giving London seasons. The principal dancers included GILMOUR, Gore, and GRAEME. On 11 July 1946 the co. staged its first full-length classical ballet, GISELLE (designed by Hugh Stevenson), which captured the true Romantic style and was to influence many subsequent British stagings of the work. In 1947–8 BR, headed by its founder and with a co. of 36, which incl. Belinda Wright and GILPIN, toured Australia and New Zealand with enormous artistic success. They returned, however, in financial straits and without some of their dancers (Gilmour for one) who decided to settle in Australia. HINTON succeeded Gilmour as principal dancer and was in turn succeeded by ALDOUS.

In 1955 David Ellis (Rambert's son-in-law) became her associate director and touring became widespread. B. Rambert had outgrown the Mercury and had no London home, although it gave regular seasons at Sadler's Wells T. China was visited in 1957 and the Jacob's Pillow Dance Fest. 1959. During the 1950s there had been a dearth of new choreographic talent within the co. (rectified by the emergence of MORRICE with his first ballet in 1958) and the demands of audiences outside London for the traditional fare of full-length classics led the directors to rely more and more on revivals of works like COPPÉLIA, SYLPHIDE (a delightful restaging in 1960 by E. M. von ROSEN), and DON QUIXOTE. The crippling costs of mounting such productions became, eventually, unendurable. A change had to be made and in 1966 David Ellis resigned. The last perf. by the 'old-style' B. Rambert was on 2 July 1966 but by 18 July 1966 it had been re-formed with Morrice as Rambert's co-director.

Largely inspired by the example of Holland's NDT, the co. was restyled as a smaller group of soloists ready to work in both the classical and contemporary dance styles. Since then the output of new ballets and the mounting of existing works (notably by TETLEY and SOKOLOW) has been prodigious – 50 productions in the first 10 years. From within the co. choreography has come from CHESWORTH, Jonathan Taylor, Joseph Scoglio, and BRUCE. The original image of creativity has been regained and new audiences reached by willingness to perform on open stages such as the Young Vic in London. Invitations have come from important festivals abroad.

Since Apr 1971 the co. has had its own premises at 94 Chiswick High Road, London, where dancers, administration, workshop, and wardrobe work together. Morrice resigned in 1974 from the joint responsibilities of direction and choreography. He was succeeded by Chesworth as Director and Bruce as associate director. MC

See also Arnold Haskell, *The Marie Rambert Ballet* (London 1930); Lionel Bradley, *Sixteen Years of Ballet Rambert* (London 1946); Mary Clarke, *Dancers of Mercury* (London 1962); Clement Crisp, Anya Sainsbury, and Peter Williams, eds, *Fifty Years of Ballet Rambert* (London 1976); the Co.'s loose-leaf brochure of new ballets, updated at regular intervals

Ballet Russe de Monte Carlo (the DE BASIL, R. BLUM and Sergei Denham cos). In 1931 two independent organizations were formed in an attempt to continue the work of DIAGHILEV: at Monte Carlo, R. Blum directed the B. de l'O. de Monte Carlo, and in Paris de Basil joined forces with Prince A. Zeretelli to present l'O. Russe à Paris. In the summer of 1931 the latter co. gave a very successful season of opera and ballet at the Lyceum T., London. Among the dancers were DUBROVSKA, WOIZIKOWSKI, NEMCHINOVA, and A. OBUKHOV; among the ballets PETRUSHKA, PRINCE IGOR. Soon Blum and de Basil joined forces in Monte Carlo as the 'René Blum and Colonel de Basil B. Russes de Monte-Carlo'. Basically, Blum provided the artistic taste and contacts and de Basil the business acumen. They engaged the best of Diaghilev's former collaborators, notably the choreographers BALANCHINE (initially *maître de ballet*) and MASSINE, and his *régisseur* GRIGORIEV to re-stage the old ballets. Woizikowski, SHABELEVSKY, LICHINE and EGLEVSKY were among the principal male dancers, and from the Paris studios of PREOBRAZHENSKA and KSHESSINSKA were recruited BARONOVA, TOUMANOVA, and RIABOUCHINSKA, who became known as the 'baby ballerinas' and, in addition to their great gifts, provided valuable fodder

Top: Ballet Rambert in the 1930s: Maude LLOYD and LESTER in DARK ELEGIES; *above:* Ballet Rambert in 1969: in EMBRACE TIGER AND RETURN TO MOUNTAIN with Lenny Westerdijk and Bob Smith, Gayrie MacSween and Peter Curtis

Ballet Russe de Monte Carlo's staging of BALANCHINE's *La Concurrence*, 1932, sc./c. DERAIN

for the press. For the 1932 Monte Carlo season Balanchine choreographed *La Concurrence*, a comic, *demi-caractère* ballet, and *Cotillon*, strange and poetic. Massine choreographed *Jeux d'Enfants* to show off the virtuosity of the young dancers. He succeeded Balanchine as *maître de ballet* at the end of 1932 when Balanchine left to form his own co., Les Ballets 1933. In 1933 Massine revived BEAU DANUBE and choreographed his first symphonic ballet, PRÉSAGES. The co. appeared in London as the B. Russes de Monte Carlo. By then A. DANILOVA, TCHERNICHEVA, and VERCHININA had joined them. They opened at the old Alhambra T., 4 July 1933 with a program made up of SYLPHIDES, *Les Présages*, and *Le Beau Danube* and were a smash hit. The season announced for three weeks lasted four months. It was followed by a short provincial tour and then impresario Sol Hurok booked them for New York where they opened 21 Dec 1933 at the St James T. A tour followed. The pattern was set: the base was Monte Carlo, capital cities starved of ballet welcomed the co. enthusiastically, and touring, especially in the USA, won a new audience for ballet. Arnold Haskell published his best-selling book, *Balletomania* (London and New York 1934). Ballet, which during the Diaghilev era had been for an elitist audience, became popular.

Blum withdrew from management in 1934 (when the co. began to be billed as the 'B. Russes du Col. W. de Basil'), remaining as artistic director until 1936 when he left the co. He then formed his own group, the 'René Blum B. de Monte-Carlo', to give the annual season in Monte Carlo. FOKINE was appointed *maître de ballet*. This co. appeared in England during the summer of 1936, giving a season at the Alhambra T., London, from 15 May. To a repertory of familiar works Fokine added new creations: ÉPREUVE D'AMOUR and *Don Juan* (1936). In addition, the co. gave a 3-act COPPÉLIA (ch. Nicholas Zverev) and a full-length NUTCRACKER (ch. Boris Romanov). The co. travelled to S. Africa Sept 1936 and returned to Britain early 1937, appearing in Manchester and Glasgow, then in Monte Carlo, Paris, back to London, where it presented Fokine's *Les Éléments* (1937) and *Les Elfes* (1937), and again appeared outside central London. This was the co. with which Massine joined forces after his break with de Basil.

In 1936 de Basil established a second co., headed by Woizikowski, to undertake a tour of Australia and New Zealand. It was largely composed of members of the B. de Léon Woizikowski (founded by Woizikowski in 1935) and its separate life only lasted until the middle of 1937.

Meanwhile friction was growing between de Basil and Massine and their respective supporters. Litigation started in 1936 and lasted until 1938 and was concerned primarily with Massine's rights to the ballets he had made originally for the Diaghilev co. especially BOUTIQUE FANTASQUE and TRICORNE (to which he won the rights). For the London season in 1937, Lichine became co. choreographer and Fokine was called in to stage his own ballets. Massine's contract expired and he gave his last performance with the co. 31 Jan 1938 in Oakland, CA, amid scenes of much emotion on the part of the dancers.

De Basil opened a season at London CG 20 June 1938. Because of the lawsuit, he temporarily resigned direction of his co., which was taken over by a triumvirate made up of Victor Dandré, German Sevastianov and W. G. Perkins (as 'Educational Ballets Ltd'), with Fokine as choreographer. The co. was headed by Baronova, Riabouchinska and Lichine and presented simply as 'Russian Ballet'. (Massine by this time had joined forces with Blum and their B. Russe de Monte Carlo opened at the T. Royal, Drury Lane, 12 July 1938. The seasons overlapped and Londoners spent a happy summer running between the two theatres to see their favourite artists.)

'The Educational B. Ltd's CG Russian B.' (as it was now known) toured in Australasia 1938–9, with DOLIN among the dancers, and reopened at CG 19 June 1939. At the end of that season, de Basil became chairman and managing director of Educational B. Ltd and the co. adopted the name by which it is now best known internationally, the Original B. Russe. World War II began as they started another Australasian tour, which continued until Sept 1940. In 1940–1 Hurok managed both the B. Russe de Monte Carlo and the Original B. Russe. The long two-month season of de Basil's Original B. Russe in NY City which began 6 Nov 1940 was preceded (14 Oct–3 Nov) by a season by the B. Russe de Monte Carlo at the same theatre (51st St T.). The Original B. Russe followed its New York season by a tour which ended in Havana, Cuba, Mar 1941, when some of the dancers went on strike for payment of salaries and Hurok withdrew as impresario. Reorganized, they toured S. America (using the T. Colón, Buenos Aires, as their base) for the rest of World War II and some of the dancers settled there (notably Verchinina). A season in NY Sept–Oct 1946 (with DE CUEVAS as artistic director) was followed by a long, and largely unsuccessful US tour, then an equally unsuccessful season at CG in summer 1947. There was only one further attempt to resuscitate the co. (by George Kirsta and the Grigorievs) in England during the winter of 1951–2 after de Basil's death in Paris 27 July 1951.

When Massine left de Basil in 1938 he returned to Blum and Monte Carlo. His business partner was a US corporation, World Art Inc. (subsequently changed to Universal Art, Inc.). The corporation incl. Julius Fleischmann, of the Cincinnati Yeast Fleischmanns (president) and Sergei Denham, a NY financier. In Feb 1938 Danilova, Toumanova, Eleanora Marra, Roland Guerard, Marc Platoff, George Zoritch, and other dancers left de Basil to join Massine. Hurok agreed to book the co. for US touring and NY seasons. Efrem Kurtz became musical director and MARKOVA, LIFAR, KRASSOVSKA, YOUSKEVITCH, and FRANKLIN all joined. There was talk of a merger with de Basil but it never happened, largely as a result of the 1938 lawsuit. When the B. Russe de Monte Carlo returned to the USA (its first NY season was 12–30 Oct 1938 at the Met) it was strengthened further by SLAVENSKA and Eglevsky. They toured the USA successfully (another London season at CG scheduled for Sept 1939 was cancelled by World War II) but at the end of the 1941–2 season, which had brought the premiere of RODEO but the departure of Massine, the contract with Hurok ended. The co. signed with Columbia Concerts, Inc. but the association lasted only one year. In 1943–4 David Libidins, formerly co. manager, took over the booking direction until autumn 1948 when the 10th anniversary of this co. was celebrated with a gala at the NY Met. By that time it was a non-profit organization headed by its director, Denham, and it is usually referred to now in the USA as 'the Denham co.' although the formal title remained B. Russe de Monte Carlo until its demise. Until 1950 the co. toured the USA and gave NY seasons. Danilova and Franklin were the stars, but other important soloists were DANIELIAN, Ruthanna Boris, MOYLAN, and Nina Novak. The repertory relied heavily on past successes. Massine's last important creations were *Nobilissima Visione* (1938), *Bacchanale* (1939), *Rouge et Noir* (1939), and *Harold in Italy* (1954). Balanchine worked with the co. 1944–6, choreographing DANSES CONCERTANTES and *Night Shadow* (*see* SONNAMBULA), and, with the assistance of Danilova, a 3-act RAYMONDA, but no outstanding choreographic talent emerged from within. In 1957 the B. Russe de Monte Carlo had its first NY season in seven years, with ALONSO and Youskevitch as guests. Then it toured sporadically until it faded away in 1962. However, the foundation retains a NY office to look after its assets. Two colour films were made in Hollywood in 1941 by Warner Bros., Massine's *The Gay Parisian* (GAIETÉ PARISIENNE) and *Spanish Fiesta* (*Capriccio Espagnole*). They still earn royalties.

The B. Russe de Monte Carlo cos did vital work in bridging the period between the death of Diaghilev and the emergence of national cos in the West, such as Britain's RB and, in the USA, ABT and the NYCB. World War II (and the death of Blum) broke the link with Monte Carlo. Most of the former B. Russe dancers settled in the USA and today are teaching and active in regional ballet cos. KSW/MC

Ballets de la Jeunesse, co. founded in Paris by EGOROVA, Jean-Louis Vaudoyer and F. Barette,

The Ballets de Paris staging of CROQUEUSE DE DIAMANTS with JEANMAIRE in the title role

1937. It lasted only a year but launched the careers of e.g. SKIBINE, ALGAROFF, Geneviève Moulin, and BARTHOLIN. M-FC

Ballets de l'Etoile *see* BÉJART

Ballets de Monte-Carlo *see* BALLET RUSSE DE MONTE CARLO

Ballets de Paris, French co. founded by PETIT after his departure from the BALLETS DES CHAMPS-ÉLYSÉES. It began at the T. Marigny, 21 May 1948, and asserted itself quickly as the reflection of the brilliant and very Parisian personality of its creator. He surrounded himself by dancers of quality, such as CHARRAT, JEANMAIRE, SKOURATOFF, MARCHAND, MISKOVITCH and, as guest artist, FONTEYN, for whom he staged DEMOISELLES DE LA NUIT. In 1948 Charrat choreographed for the co. *La Femme et son Ombre* and *'Adame Miroir,* and MASSINE revived BEAU DANUBE. The following year was marked by the creation of CARMEN and DOLLAR choreographed *Le Combat.* A tour took the co. to Britain, then to the USA. In 1950 Petit created CROQUEUSE DE DIAMANTS, then was invited to film in the USA, and dissolved the co. He reconstituted it in an ephemeral fashion for different revivals according to his personal engagements. In 1953, during a season at the T. de l'Empire, and afterwards on tour in London, he presented LOUP, *Deuil en 24 Heures, Ciné-Bijou,* and *Lady in the Ice* (lib. Orson Welles); dan. VERDY, SOMBERT, Marchand, George Reich, PERRAULT, José Ferran. In Dec 1955, he presented *La Chambre* and *Les Belles Damnées* at the T. des CE with Veronika Mlakar, T. BEAUMONT, and Buzz Miller. At the T. de l'Alhambra he choreographed in Feb 1958 several ballets for Jeanmaire, Mlakar, Nicole Amigues, and Dirk Sanders, then *Cyrano de Bergerac* (17 Apr 1959). The B. de Paris could be said to have been revived as the B. Roland Petit, which staged *L'Éloge de la Folie* (ch. Petit after Erasmus), T. des CE, 1966. After that Petit devoted himself to his work as director of the Paris Casino, then as director of the B. de Marseille, which could be regarded as another revival of the B. de Paris, although that title has ceased to exist. M-FC

Ballets des Champs-Élysées, a shortlived but very influential French co. presented by Roger Eudes, director of the T. des CE, from 12 Oct 1945 until 1950. It grew out of dance recitals organized by the French critic Irène Lidova at the T. Sarah Bernhardt, Paris, in 1944 to give opportunities to young rebels from the Paris O. to create ballets of their own. The first choreographers were PETIT and CHARRAT; the pianist Jean-Michel Damase, then aged 16, and the impresario for the group Claude Giraud, aged 20. The first perf. was at the T. des CE, 2 Mar 1945, and its success caused Eudes to give them the theatre as its home. Among the dancers were Petit, JEANMAIRE, PAGAVA, PHILIPPART, SKORIK, ALGAROFF, PERRAULT, and VYROUBOVA. The unique quality of the co. was that from the beginning it had the support, encouragement, and participation of DIAGHILEV's former associates, COCTEAU, KOCHNO, and BÉRARD, who ensured an extraordinarily high artistic standard. The co. was the first from France to visit London after World War II; it opened 9 Apr 1946 at the Adelphi T. and caused a furore by the beauty of its decors, the originality of its choreography and the strength of its male dancers. After Petit left in 1948, BABILÉE created his first ballets and new works by LICHINE were staged. The death of Bérard, who had designed many lovely works, seemed to sound the death knell of the co. Skorik left in 1950; the co., having lost its ballerina, disbanded. MC

Ballet Society *see* New York City Ballet

Ballets Russes (Diaghilev's) *see* Diaghilev

Ballets Suédois, a co. founded by the Swedish art patron Rolf de Maré (1888–1964). It gave its first perf. Paris, T. des CE, 25 Oct 1920. The principal dancer and choreographer was Börlin; for him de Maré commissioned scores and decors from the foremost composers and artists, among them Milhaud, Arthur Honegger, Poulenc, Auric, Chirico (before his work was used by Diaghilev) and Fernand Léger, who designed Milhaud's *La Création du Monde*, a Negro ballet ch. Börlin (Paris, T. des CE, B. Suédois, 25 Oct 1923). The co. toured Europe and the USA but was disbanded 1925. De Maré placed the designs he had commissioned in the Archives Internationales de la Danse in Paris (which he founded 1931) and they are now in the Dance Museum, Stockholm. De Maré was as much in advance of his time as Diaghilev but none of the ballets he presented survived. MC
See Rolf de Maré (ed.), *Les Ballets Suédois dans l'Art Contemporain* (Paris 1931); tr. into Swedish as *Svenska Balett*, with foreword by Bengt Häger (Stockholm 1947)

Ballet Tacoma *see* Regional Ballet (USA)

Ballet Theatre *see* American Ballet Theatre

Ballet-Théâtre Contemporain. French co. founded 1968 under the patronage of the Ministry of Cultural Affairs, directed by Jean-Albert Cartier, with Adret as choreographer. At first at the Maison de la Culture at Amiens, then transferred to Angers 1972, it has a repertory of works using exclusively modern scores and decors in a spirit that attempts to recall that of Diaghilev. The accent is on collaboration between composers, painters or sculptors, and choreographers, who are as diverse as Blaska, Descombey, Lubovitch, Neumeier, Dirk Sanders, Butler, Sanasardo. The co. toured widely throughout the world and incl. among its soloists Martine Parmain, Muriel Belmondo, Marchand, Juan Giuliano, James Urbain, Magdalena Popa, Rhodes. The remarkable quality of its designers and dancers has sometimes eclipsed the choreography. M-FC

Ballet West of Salt Lake City *see* Regional Ballet (USA) and Universities, Dance in (USA)

Ballroom dancing. Social dancing usually performed today by couples in dance halls, night clubs, and at balls and social gatherings. 'Modern' ballroom dances are the Waltz, Foxtrot, Tango and Quickstep; the so-called Latin American dances (because of their origins) are Rumba, Samba, Paso Doble, and Cha Cha Cha. These dances have been codified by the Official Board of Ballroom Dancing in Britain (formed 1929 at the instigation of Richardson) and, sometimes joined by Viennese Waltz and Jive, are danced in ballroom championships now popular throughout the world. The original 'English style' of performing the modern dances is now known as the International style. Championship ballroom dancing is almost as far from ordinary social dancing as is ballet; the techniques are highly complex and when performed by great dancers thrilling to watch. At social occasions, much simpler techniques are employed and every age has its 'craze' dances, from Charleston in the 1920s to Rock 'n' Roll in the 1940s, Twist in the late 1950s. In the championship field the British supremacy is now hotly contended by couples from Germany, Australia, and Japan. MC

Ballroom dancing at its most elegant: Vernon and Irene Castle dancing the Maxixe, *c.* 1914

Balon, Jean, b. Paris, 1676; d. Paris, 1739. French dancer. Son of Paris O. dancer François Balon. He danced with such early ballerinas of the Paris O. as Marie-Thérèse Perdou de Subligny (1666–1736) and Françoise Prévost (1680–1741). He appeared with Prévost in a scene mimed to music, from Pierre Corneille's tragedy *Horace*, presented by the Duchesse du Maine at the Château de Sceaux in 1714, a precursor of the *ballet d'action*. He was noted especially for his lightness and a legend arose that the technical term *ballon* derived from his name (sometimes spelled that way). This is not true; the term (lit. 'ball') simply means 'bounciness'. MC

Balustrade *see* VIOLIN CONCERTO

Barbay, Ferenc, b. Miskolc, 1943. Hungarian dancer. Pupil of Hedvig Hidas, Budapest Inst. of B. and of LEPESHINSKAYA. Joined Hungarian NB 1967. Debut in SPARTACUS (ch. SEREGI). Guest artist, Munich B., 1969; joined that co. as a principal 1970, dancing in FILLE MAL GARDÉE (ch. ASHTON) and *Casanova in London* (ch. CHARRAT), etc. A very virile and athletic performer. Bronze Medal, Varna Competition, 1968. GBLW

Irina Baronova as she appeared in BALANCHINE's *Cotillon*, 1932, c. BÉRARD

Barbieri, Margaret, b. Durban, 1947. S. African dancer, niece of CECCHETTI. Early training at Mannin-Sutton S., Durban, then RBS, London, from 1963. Joined touring section of RB 1965, danced her first (fragmentary) GISELLE with Ballet For All 1967, and danced the full ballet with the touring section at CG 1968. Promoted to principal status 1970 (after she had danced her first AURORA on tour 25 Nov 1969), she epitomizes the Romantic ideal of a ballerina: pale, with dark hair and large dark eyes. Yet her 1965 graduation perf. with RBS was the gipsy girl in DEUX PIGEONS and she possesses considerable dramatic power, best used in HERMANAS. MC

Bari, Tania, b. Rotterdam, 1936. Dutch dancer. Studied with KISS, JOOSS, V. GSOVSKY, MESSERER. B. de l'Étoile 1955; BT de Maurice BÉJART 1958; B. XXe S. 1960. Created principal roles in Béjart's SONATE À TROIS (1957); *Orphée* (1958); SACRE DU PRINTEMPS (1959), *Contes d'Hoffmann* (1961); NINTH SYMPHONY; *Mathilde* (1965); *Bhakti* (1968); *Les Vainqueurs* (1969). Primarily associated with Béjart's work, she brings to it lyrical intensity, feminine intuition, and poetic presence. M-FC
See L. Rossel,'Tania Bari', *Les Saisons de la Danse* (Paris, summer 1971) with list of roles

Baronova, Irina, b. Petrograd, 1919. Russian dancer whose career was entirely outside Russia, her parents emigrating to Paris when she was a child. Studied there with PREOBRAZHENSKA, soloist at Paris O. 1930, T. Mogador 1931. Discovered by BALANCHINE at 'Preo's' studio and engaged for the new B. Russe de Monte Carlo 1932, becoming one of its three 'baby ballerinas'. Created many important roles while still in her early teens, notably the young lover in PRÉSAGES, the Top in MASSINE's *Jeux d'Enfants*, the scene-stealing midinette in BEAU DANUBE, and an important role in CHOREARTIUM. Ballerina ABT 1941–2, she danced with various cos and groups in USA during the 1940s. She made two films *Florian* (MGM, 1939) and *Yolanda* (Mexico, 1942) and in 1946 danced the ballerina in a play based on Caryl Brahms's novel *A Bullet in the Ballet* in England. A dancer of beauty, warmth, musicality, and a remarkable range from the pure classicism of AURORA's WEDDING to the lyricism of SPECTRE DE LA ROSE and SYLPHIDES, and the most enchanting comedy. She m. first German Sevastianov, executive secretary of B. Russe de Monte Carlo, then Cecil Tennant 1946 when she retired from the stage. On Tennant's death (1969) she left England to live on the Continent. A member (at FONTEYN's invitation) of England's RAD she served on its Technical Committee while resident in England. In 1976 she resumed teaching master classes for summer schools and special courses. MC

Barra, Ray [Raymond Barallobre], b. San Francisco, 1930. American dancer and ballet master. Pupil of L. and W. CHRISTENSEN, and VOLKOVA. Debut 1949, San Francisco B., soloist 1953. To ABT 1953 as soloist; principal dancer, Stuttgart B. 1959–60. Stopped dancing 1966 after an injury and became ballet master, Stuttgart. To Deutsche O., W. Berlin, 1966, as assistant to the director (MACMILLAN); to Frankfurt 1970 as assistant to NEUMEIER; went with him in the same capacity to Hamburg B. 1973–6. In Stuttgart he created roles in BERIOZOFF's *Nutcracker* (1959), ULBRICH's *Romeo and Juliet* (1959), also in CRANKO's ROMEO AND JULIET and ONEGIN (title role), and HERMANAS. A fine dancer cut off in his prime, he became an equally successful ballet master and teacher. GBLW

Bart, Patrice, b. Paris, 1945. French dancer. Studied Paris OBS; *corps de ballet* 1959; R. BLUM Prize 1963; *premier danseur* 1968; *étoile* 1972. Guest artist, RWB. Destined by his physique, *ballon,* and *brio* to *demi-caractère* roles, he nevertheless excels as the BLUEBIRD, and shines in the classical repertory. Joined LFB as a guest principal, 1970. Gold Medal, Moscow, 1969. M-FC

Bartholin, Birger, b. Odense, 1900. Danish dancer, choreographer, and teacher. Early studies in Denmark, then with LEGAT and VOLININ in Paris, where in 1928 he joined the co. of RUBINSTEIN. Danced mostly in France with the cos of R. BLUM, KNIASEFF and NEMCHINOVA-A. OBUKHOV, but also appeared in a Charles B. Cochran revue in London. For the B. de la Jeunesse in Paris 1937 he choreographed *Classical Symphony* (mus. PROKOFIEV) and *Romeo and Juliet* (mus. TCHAIKOVSKY), works later taken into the repertory of the RDB. Ballet master, Helsinki, 1954; Oslo 1955. Now teaches in Copenhagen (his own school) and directs successful international ballet seminars, since 1963. MC

Bartók, Béla, b. Nagyszentmiklós, Hungary (now Sannicolau Mare, Romania), 1881; d. New York, 1945. Hungarian composer, who wrote only two ballet scores, WOODEN PRINCE and MIRACULOUS MANDARIN, neither of which has ever been staged with enduring success. The former score was rejected by DIAGHILEV as 'false modernism'; the latter is a masterpiece of music that continues to attract choreographers. Many ballets have been made to existing Bartók music, e.g. Herbert Ross's *Caprichos* (New York 1950) to *Contrasts for Violin, Clarinet and Piano.* DH

Baryshnikov, Mikhail, b. Riga, 1948. Latvian dancer. Began studies in Riga, then became a pupil of PUSHKIN in Leningrad. Joined Kirov B. as soloist 1966; won gold medal, Varna Competition, same year and another gold medal Moscow, 1969. YACOBSON choreographed the solo dance *Vestris* for him and he created the title role in SERGEYEV's HAMLET.

Above: Mikhail Baryshnikov dancing his Act III variation in SWAN LAKE with the RB; *below:* Baryshnikov in the role he created in THARP's *Push Comes to Shove,* ABT, New York, 9 Jan 1976

Batsheva Dance Company in *Sin Lieth at the Door*, ch. Moshe Efrati, sc. Dani Karavan, c. Linda Hodes, dan. Rina Schoenfeld

Decided to leave USSR for the West, summer 1974, while on tour in Canada as a guest artist with a group from the Bolshoy B. Joined ABT; has also appeared as guest artist with Paris OB, RB, etc. A phenomenally gifted virtuoso whose totally original combinations of jumping and turning steps defy description. His classical roles incl. ALBRECHT, JAMES, Solor (BAYADÈRE), SIEGFRIED. His main reason for leaving the USSR was the desire to dance in a more extensive repertory, especially of modern ballets. Since arriving in the West he has danced in PATINEURS, *Theme and Variations* (ch. BALANCHINE), JEUNE HOMME ET LA MORT, SHADOWPLAY, and ROMEO AND JULIET (ch. MACMILLAN). In 1976 THARP choreographed *Push Comes to Shove* for him. Debut as choreographer with his own version of NUTCRACKER, Washington, DC, ABT, 21 Dec 1976. DV
See Baryshnikov at Work: Mikhail Baryshnikov Discusses his Roles, photographs by Martha Swope, text ed. Charles Engell France (New York 1976; London 1977)

Basilio, the hero in DON QUIXOTE

Bat Dor Dance Company (Tel Aviv, Israel) founded by Bat Sheva de Rothschild, 1968, created a new arena for young talents. With Jeannette Ordman as its artistic director and prima ballerina this co. has constructed a specifically contemporary repertoire based on classical techniques. Eighty-two works (13 Israeli) incl. 49 world premieres, by 29 choreographers (7 Israelis) have earned Bat Dor a place of its own. It has toured Europe four times, the Far East (1972), S. America (1973), and S. Africa (1976). Bat Dor's school, with some 600 students, directed by Ordman and founded by Rothschild in 1967, is an important contribution to the dance in Israel. NM

Batsheva Dance Company (Tel Aviv, Israel) was founded in 1964 by Bat Sheva de Rothschild. With GRAHAM as artistic adviser and contributor of eight works incl. a world premiere (*Dream*, 1974), with other works by some of the best modern choreographers and the supervision of Ruth Harris, DUDLEY, and others, this first fully subsidized Israeli modern dance co. wrote a brilliant new page in the dance history of the country. Batsheva's serious repertoire – 83 works (56 world premieres) by 32 choreographers (10 Israelis) – and the marked individual qualities of the dancer-choreographers Rena Gluck, Moshe Efrati, Ehud Ben David, Rehamim Ron, and the unique Rina Schoenfeld and others, won critical and public acclaim in Israel, Europe (seven tours 1967–75), and the USA (1970, 1972). Since Apr 1975, Batsheva (artistic director Kaj Lothmann, *see* SELLING) is supported by the government and by the America–Israel Cultural Foundation; Batsheva 2, a workshop for young choreographers and dancers, was established Apr 1976. NM

Bausch, Pina, b. Solingen, 1940. German dancer, choreographer, and director. Studied at the Folkwang S., and danced for its group and in the NY Met. Choreographed many successful ballets in the Central European style; appointed director of the Wuppertal B. 1974. GBLW

Bayadère, La (*Bayaderka*), ballet, 4 acts, ch. M. PETIPA; mus. MINKUS; lib. Sergey Khudekov; sc. Ivan Andreyev, Mikhail Bocharov, Piotr Lambin, Andrey Roller, Matvey Shishkov, Heinrich Wagner. St Petersburg, Maryinsky T., 4 Feb 1877 (OS 23 Jan 1877); dan. VAZEM, IVANOV, JOHANSSON. The tragic love of a warrior (Solor) for a temple dancer (Nikia). Authoritatively revived by VAGANOVA, Kirov T., 13 Dec 1932; ch. since revised by CHABUKIANI and others. Act IV, 'The Kingdom of the Shades', with its audacious opening *défilé* of the *corps de ballet* down a

repertory, sometimes cut and altered but always in the old master's style. As choreographer, he left only minor dances and the ballet LITTLE MERMAID. Responsible for Danish version of COPPÉLIA (1896), which contains far more character dances, especially in the last act, than other versions. For many years he had a private dancing school in Copenhagen. SKJ

Bedells, Phyllis, b. Bristol, 1893. English dancer and teacher. Debut 1906, Prince of Wales T., London, in *Alice in Wonderland.* In 1914 succeeded KYASHT as prima ballerina at the Empire T., London, for three years the first English dancer to hold such a position. Danced mostly in opera ballets and revues with NOVIKOV and DOLIN. Participated in early attempts to form a national British ballet. Vice-chairman of the RAD and since her retirement from the stage in 1935 an outstanding teacher. Still active as an examiner for the RAD. Her daughter Jean (b. 1924) danced with the SWTB as a soloist and then ballet mistress, now teaches at RBS. Her granddaughter Anne Bedells, trained RBS, is in LFB. MC
See autobiography, *My Dancing Days* (London 1954)

Béjart [Berger], Maurice, b. Marseille, 1927. French dancer and choreographer. Son of the philosopher Gaston Berger. Studied with EGOROVA and VOLKOVA; danced with various classical and modern European cos. Founded B. Romantiques 1953, renamed the B. de l'Étoile 1954, with the critic Jean Laurent, and then the BT de Maurice Béjart 1957 with Henriques Pimental. For Belgian TV and in Paris, Geneva, and Berlin, the co. performed such original works as *Symphonie pour un Homme Seul* (mus. Pierre Henry and P. Schaeffer), *Prométhée* (mus. Maurice Ohana), *Haut Voltage* (mus. Henry), SONATE À TROIS, and *Orphée* (mus. Henry). Following the success of his SACRE DU PRINTEMPS (1959), commissioned by Maurice Huisman, director of the T. Royal de la Monnaie, Brussels, and which won the Prix de l'Université de la Danse and of the Critique dramatique et musicale, this co. dissolved and the B. XXe S. emerged (1960), based on the T. Royal de la Monnaie.

Through ballets like *Boléro* (1960; mus. RAVEL), *Bacchanale de Tannhäuser* (1961; mus. Richard Wagner), *Noces* (1962; mus. STRAVINSKY), this co. became the ideal instrument for Béjart's eclectic explorations of dance. It presented pure dance, as in *Suite Viennoise* (1962; mus. Arnold Schönberg, Alban Berg, Anton (von) Webern); total spectacle with lyrics, as in *Contes d'Hoffmann* (1961); dramatic pieces, e.g. *La Reine Verte* (Paris, T. Hébertot, 1963); and triumphant realizations of orchestral masterpieces, e.g. NINTH SYMPHONY and DAMNATION DE FAUST. *Roméo et Juliette* (1966; mus. Hector Berlioz). Received the Prix de la Fraternité 1966 from the movement against racism and for peace, while such works as *Traviata* (mus. Giuseppe Verdi), *Erotica* (mus. Tadeusz Baird) and *Variations pour une Porte et un Soupir* (mus. Henry) were considered scandalous.

Among other works *Serait-ce la Mort?* (1970; mus. Richard Strauss) and NIJINSKY, CLOWN DE DIEU toured Britain and the USA, where critics were often reserved or even abusive, but the public enthusiastic.

With such exceptional dancers as BORTOLUZZI, GIELGUD, ALBRECHT, LOMMEL and DONN, NYCB's FARRELL and guests incl. NUREYEV, ALONSO, and PLISETSKAYA, the co. presented *Baudelaire* and *Stimmung* (1972), *Le Marteau sans Maître* and *Golestan* (1973), *Trionfi de Pétrarque* (1974). NOTRE FAUST, *Héliogabale* and *Molière Imaginaire* (1976) are more recent investigations of music, paradox, emotional shock and dance stretched often outrageously to serve communication.

Béjart shared the Erasmus Prize in 1974 with DE VALOIS, organized the first Venice Festival of the Dance (1975) and founded MUDRA in 1970 in Brussels, a European centre for research into spectacle and production.

His Ballet du XXe Siècle has appeared in theatres, circuses, stadia, universities, temples, and public squares. Its teachers have incl. MESSERER and V. GSOVSKY. It has danced the works of MASSINE, DOLIN, and CHARRAT. But essentially it is an instrument created by and for Béjart to encourage and explore the use of dance as universal expression. M-FC
See M.-F. Christout, *Béjart* (Paris 1972); *Les Saisons de la Danse* (Paris, May 1968, Jan 1970 supplement) for list of roles

Belda, Patrick, b. 1943; d. Brussels, 1967. French dancer and choreographer. Debut in BÉJART's *Voyage au Coeur d'un Enfant* (1955); from that time until his death in a car accident stayed with Béjart's co. where he created principal roles for Béjart in *Pulcinella, L'Étranger, Quatre Fils Aymon, Renard, Les Oiseaux, Variations pour une Porte et un Soupir, Cygne*, and *Roméo et Juliette* (as Mercutio). Staged with Béjart *Divertissement* (1961); then alone *Pierre et le Loup* and *Jeux* (1965). Imbued with artistic intelligence, humour, and a subtle sense of the rapport between dance and music. M-FC

Belgium. The scene is dominated by BÉJART, but there are ballet cos in Antwerp (B. van Vlaanderen or B. of Flanders) and Charleroi (B. de Wallonie) which receive state support and serve, respectively, the north (i.e. Flemish) and the south (Walloon) of the country. Both have good schools and present an international repertory of classics and modern works. In 1976 both cos were granted the 'royal' prefix by King Baudouin. MC

Belle au Bois Dormant, La *see* SLEEPING BEAUTY

Belsky, Igor, b. Leningrad, 1925. Soviet dancer and choreographer. Graduated from Leningrad Choreographic S. 1943. Actors' Faculty, GITIS, 1957. One of the leading character dancers and dance-actors, Kirov T. 1943–63. Created title role SHURALE, Severyan (STONE FLOWER), Mako (PATH OF THUNDER), Petro (TARAS BULBA), etc. Other roles: Ostap (*Taras Bulba*; F. LOPUKHOV version), Nur-Ali (FOUNTAIN OF BAKHCHISARAY), Lie-Shang-Foo (RED POPPY), Tybalt (L. LAVROVSKY's ROMEO AND JULIET), etc. and character dances in the classical repertoire. Chief choreographer, Maly OB 1962–73. Teacher at Ballet masters' Faculty, Leningrad Cons. 1962–4 and from 1966. From 1973 director, Kirov B. His COAST OF HOPE was a milestone in the successful choreographic solution of a contemporary theme in Soviet ballet; also LENINGRAD SYMPHONY. At Maly O. he choreographed HUMPBACKED HORSE, *Eleventh Symphony* (mus. Dmitri Shostakovich, 1966), *Gadfly* (1967), his own version of NUTCRACKER (1969). People's Artist, RSFSR. He m. dancer Lyudmila Alekseyev. NR
See I. Belsky, 'A Choreographer's Notes' in *Soviet Music*, No. 3 (Leningrad 1964)

Benesh, Rudolf *see* CHOREOLOGY, DANCE NOTATION

Bennington *see* UNIVERSITIES, DANCE IN (USA)

Benois, Alexandre, b. St Petersburg, 1870; d. Paris, 1960. Russian painter, designer, and writer. He did much to formulate the artistic taste of DIAGHILEV and was artistic director of his co. until a quarrel (1911) about the 'authorship' of PETRUSHKA, his masterpiece. A man of wide culture, he excelled in historically accurate but delicate and charming stage settings, e.g. PAVILLON D'ARMIDE, NUTCRACKER. From 1905 he lived in Paris, his spiritual home. His son Nicola Benois (b. St Petersburg, 1902) became chief designer at Sc., working mostly on operas. His niece, Nadia Benois (Peter Ustinov's mother) lived in England and designed for BR, notably TUDOR's *The Descent of Hebe,* DARK ELEGIES, and HOWARD's *Lady into Fox.* MC
See A. Benois, *Reminiscences of the Russian Ballet*, tr. Mary Britnieva (London 1941); *Memoirs*, tr. Moura Budberg (London 1960)

Bérard, Christian, b. Paris, 1902; d. Paris, 1949. French designer of the utmost simplicity and exquisite taste with a rare gift for evoking atmosphere. Often worked with KOCHNO; his first major ballet was BALANCHINE's haunting *Cotillon* (B. Russe de Monte Carlo, 1932). Designed SYMPHONIE FANTASTIQUE, with its striking scarlet ballroom scene and white costumes, and FORAINS in which with two poles, a length of cloth and an old cart he created the world of strolling players. MC

Berg, Bernd, b. E. Prussia, 1943. German dancer. Pupil of BISCHOFF in E. Berlin; joined the E. Berlin B. 1963. Left for the West 1963. Joined Stuttgart B. 1964, soloist 1967, created roles in many CRANKO ballets. To London 1975 to teach at The Place. Joined SWRB 1976. GBLW

Bergsma, Deanne, b. Pretoria, 1941. S. African dancer. Studied with STURMAN and London RBS, joining RB 1959. Made an enormous hit as the one girl in Ray POWELL's workshop ballet *One in Five* (London, 12 June 1960) which first exploited her gift for comedy, later to shine in BICHES and WEDDING BOUQUET. A tall elegant dancer, she excels both in the modern repertory and classical ballets. Dances ODETTE-ODILE, a charming LILAC FAIRY and an authoritative, smooth-*bourrée*ing MYRTHA. Created Lady Mary Lygon in ENIGMA VARIATIONS. MC

Colour Plates. Facing page: The dancer Giovanna Baccelli, painting by Thomas Gainsborough, 1782
Overleaf left: Costume for Franz in COPPÉLIA, by Alfred Albert, 1870 (Franz was then played by a woman);
right: Set model for *Coppélia* designed by Édouard Despléschin, 1875

Coppelia
Ballet 3 tableaux
St. Léon
2
Frantz
Mlle Fiocre
Alf Albert
1870

Madame Taglioni
A. E. CHALON R.A.
J. S. TEMPLETON
V.A.M.

Beriosova, Svetlana, b. Kaunas, Lithuania, 1932. British dancer, daughter of BERIOZOFF. Trained by her father, and by the VILZAK-SCHOLLAR school in New York. Debut 1941 as CLARA with B. Russe de Monte Carlo. Danced with Ottawa B. 1947 and the same year with de Cuevas B. Ballerina Metropolitan B. 1947; created many roles, notably 'heartbreak' girl in DESIGNS WITH STRINGS. To SWTB 1950 and SWB 1952 as soloist; ballerina 1955. An enchanting SWANILDA, radiant AURORA, and supreme ODETTE-ODILE of her generation, she also created major roles in CRANKO's PRINCE OF THE PAGODAS and *Antigone* (1959), in MACMILLAN's BAISER DE LA FÉE and ASHTON's *Persephone* (1961) in which her musical French voice was ideally used. She danced the Hostess in BICHES when the RB revived the ballet 1964 and the Bride in NOCES (1966). In ENIGMA VARIATIONS she created the role of Lady Elgar, a warm and mature character. In ANASTASIA (1971 version) she created the Tsarina part, again a rounded portrait. In these two roles she established a new image of a ballerina, an actress-dancer playing a real character. She appeared in several plays before retiring from the ballet stage in 1975 to devote herself to welfare work and teaching. MC

Beriozoff, Nicholas, b. Kaunas, Lithuania, 1906. Russian dancer and *maître de ballet*. Studied in Czechoslovakia and danced with Prague OB and NB in Kaunas before joining R. BLUM co. in Monte Carlo, 1935, where he learned the FOKINE repertory. Worked at the Sc., with LFB, in Stuttgart, Helsinki, and Zürich 1964–71 where he staged the classical repertory. Now freelancing. Revived COQ D'OR for LFB 1976. Father of BERIOSOVA. MC

Berlin. The first opera house (of the Duke of Brandenburg) opened in 1742 and its first ballet master was Michel Poitier (1742–3) who was followed by Bartholomé Lany (1743–7). La Barbarina danced there 1744–8 and NOVERRE was engaged for a short time in 1744. Étienne Lauchery was ballet master 1787–1812 (among his ballets was Giacomo Meyerbeer's *The Fisherman and the Milkmaid*, 1810). In 1832 the ELSSLER sisters appeared there and in the same year M. TAGLIONI in SYLPHIDE (after her success in Paris). P. TAGLIONI was ballet master 1856–83 and this was a very active period (he staged a *Coppélia* in 1881). At the end of

Colour Plate: M. TAGLIONI as SYLPHIDE, colour lithograph by J. S. Templeton after A. E. Chalon, *c.* 1846

Above: Igor Belsky discussing his new ballet *Icarus* with BARYSHNIKOV in Leningrad, 1973

Below: Svetlana Beriosova as the Tsarina in ANASTASIA

the 19th c. Antonietta dell'Era was prima ballerina. I. DUNCAN made her first appearance in Berlin 1903 and the DIAGHILEV B. in 1910. In 1912 the Charlottenburg OH (later the Städtische O.) opened.

After World War II, ballet in W. Berlin was based at the T. des Westens, then in the Städtische O. until the rebuilt Deutsche O., W. Berlin, opened in 1961 in Charlottenburg. Recent ballet masters have been Jens Keith 1945–9, BLANK 1949–57, T. GSOVSKY 1957–66 (from 1961 with the assistance of REINHOLM), MACMILLAN 1966–9, then Reinholm (in 1971–2 with TARAS also). In E. Berlin the ballet is centred on the Staats O., from 1955 under GRUBER. Also in E. Berlin is the Komische O. made famous by the directorship and opera productions of Walter Felsenstein; opened 1947, its most famous ballet master in recent years is SCHILLING from 1965. GBLW

Natalia Bessmertnova of the Bolshoy B. as Leyly in GOLEIZOVSKY's *Leyly and Medzhnun*, a role which she created

Berliner Ballett. A co. formed by T. GSOVSKY in 1955 for the Berlin Fest. Week, presenting ballets choreographed by herself. For it she choreographed *Labyrinth* (mus. Klaus Sonnenburg), *Signale* (mus. Giselher Klebe), *Souvenirs* (mus. Jacques Offenbach), and *Ballade* (mus. Ernö Dohnányi). Among her dancers were DEEGE, KÖLLER, REINHOLM. The co. persisted after the Fest. for five years and was the main vehicle for Gsovsky's choreography; among her creations were *Das Tor* (mus. Heinz Friedrich Hartig), *Kain und Abel* (mus. Peter Sandloff), *La Dame aux Camélias* (mus. SAUGUET), *Hamlet, The Moor of Venice*, etc. The co. toured in Germany and abroad; among later dancers were SKORIK, Helge Sommerkamp, CHAUVIRÉ, CADZOW, and FERRI. When the new Deutsche O. building was opened (1961), Gsovsky became director of ballet, the co. becoming the touring group of the house. GBLW

Berman, Eugene, b. St Petersburg, 1899; d. New York, 1972. Russian painter and designer; resident USA from 1937, US citizen from 1945. Designer of many ballets, a master at creating Renaissance style and splendour for the contemporary stage. Among his finest productions are *Devil's Holiday* (1939) for ASHTON; ROMEO AND JULIET for TUDOR; BALLET IMPERIAL for the SWTB (an evocation of Imperial Russia); and the *commedia dell'arte* fantasies of PULCINELLA for BALANCHINE/ROBBINS (1972). MC
See George Amberg, *The Theatre of Eugene Berman* (New York 1947)

Berners, Lord (Gerald Tyrwhitt-Wilson), b. Bridgnorth, Shropshire, 1883; d. Faringdon, Berkshire, 1950. English composer, painter, writer, and diplomat. Largely self-taught as a musician, Berners embraced the anti-heroic, parodistic ideals of post-Debussy French music. His ballet scores, *The Triumph of Neptune* (London 1926; ch. BALANCHINE), for DIAGHILEV; WEDDING BOUQUET; *Cupid and Psyche* (London 1939; ch. ASHTON), and *Les Sirènes* (London 1946; ch. Ashton), all for SWB, are marked by geniality as well as wit. He also wrote *Luna Park* (London, 1930 for Charles B. Cochran's Revue; ch. Balanchine), the music for which was later used by Ashton for *Foyer de Danse* (London 1932). DH

Besobrazova, Marika, b. Yalta, 1918. Russian dancer and teacher. Studied with SEDOVA, EGOROVA, V. GSOVSKY. B. Russe de Monte Carlo 1935. Directed her own co. in Cannes 1940–3. Teacher, de Cuevas B. 1947–8, B. des CE 1949–50. Opened school in Monte Carlo 1949. Directed B. du Centenaire de Monte Carlo 1966, Monte Carlo OB 1967. Guest teacher Rome O. 1965–9, Paris O. 1970, Copenhagen, Zürich, Stuttgart. Most contemporary French soloists have been her pupils. On 3 May 1976 her École de Danse Classique gained official recognition and became the Académie de Danse Classique Princesse Grace. Housed in the Villa Casa Mia, it offers full education. M-FC/MC

Bessmertnova, Natalia, b. Moscow, 1941. Soviet dancer. Graduated Moscow Choreographic S. 1962, class of GOLOVKINA, with unprecedented five-plus mark. Accepted into Bolshoy T. as soloist, dancing CHOPINIANA (Mazurka and seventh Waltz); noted for fragile beauty of line, musicality, and fine lyricism On her first tour to USA and Canada in spring 1962, danced secondary roles but invariably attracted attention by striking resemblance to both A. PAVLOVA and SPESSIVTSEVA, with her waif-like beauty. At her debut in GISELLE (1963) at Bolshoy T. she revealed individual qualities auguring growth into one of the best Giselles of the century. Ethereal, elegant dancing veiled by intangible inner mystery conceals refined technique developed under the guidance of SEMYONOVA, her teacher and coach in the first years at the Bolshoy. She dances all classical ballets: SWAN LAKE (especially new version ch. GRIGOROVICH), SLEEPING BEAUTY, DON QUIXOTE, in which her KITRI is translated into a figure from a Goya painting. She was flawless as the Girl in SPECTRE DE LA ROSE, revived by LIEPA, 1966. She also excels in contemporary choreography, creating Leyly in *Leyly and Medzhnun* (1964, ch. GOLEIZOVSKY), Shirien (LEGEND OF LOVE, Moscow version), and PHRYGIA. L. LAVROVSKY said she would make a remarkable JULIET but did not live to see her in his ballet. Her talents achieved full flowering as Tsarina Anastasia in IVAN THE TERRIBLE. Gold Medal, Varna, 1965. People's Artist, RSFSR. She m. Grigorovich. NR
See N. Avaliani and L. Zhdanov, tr. N. Ward, *Bolshoi's Young Dancers* (Moscow and London 1975)

Bessmertnova, Tatyana, b. Moscow, 1947. Soviet dancer, sister of N. BESSMERTNOVA. Graduated Moscow Choreographic S. 1967. Classical and *demi-caractère* soloist. Danced MYRTHA, three swans and Spanish Bride (SWAN LAKE), Street Dancer and variations (DON QUIXOTE). An ebullient dancer of great beauty. She m. Mikhail GABOVICH junior. NR

Bessy, Claude, b. Paris, 1932. French dancer and choreographer. Entered Paris OBS 1942; *première danseuse* 1952; *étoile* 1956. Created leading roles in LIFAR's *Noces Fantastiques* (1955), CRANKO's *La Belle Hélène* (1955), H. ROSEN's *La Dame à la Licorne* (1959), Gene Kelly's *Pas de Dieux* (1960), DESCOMBEY's *Coppélia* (1966), etc. Choreographed *Studio 60*, *Play-Bach*. Many TV appearances. In Gene Kelly's film, *Invitation to the Dance* (1953). Guest artist ABT and Bolshoy B. Director, Paris OB 1970, then in 1971 Paris OBS. Published *Danseuse Étoile* 1971. Gifted with sensuous beauty, she combined great technical skill, energy, and ambition. M-FC
See A.-P. Hersin, 'Bessy', *Les Saisons de la Danse* (Paris, Mar 1969) with list of roles

Bettis, Valerie, b. Houston, TX, 1920. American dancer, actress, and choreographer. Studied in Houston and with H. HOLM at Bennington Summer S. of the Dance. Danced in first perf. of Holm's TREND (1937), and in her co., 1938–9. Began her own concert career in 1941, creating her best-known solo *The Desperate Heart* in 1943. Formed her own co. in 1944, for which she choreographed *Yerma* (after Federico García Lorca, 1946), and *As I Lay Dying* (after William Faulkner, 1948). Danced and choreographed in Broadway revues and Hollywood films. Choreographed *Virginia Sampler* for B. Russe de Monte Carlo (1947); *A Streetcar Named Desire*, after Tennessee Williams, for the SLAVENSKA-FRANKLIN Co. (1952; revived by ABT, 1954); *Early Voyagers* for the NB, Washington, DC (1963). Staged movement and performed in *Ulysses in Nighttown*, after James Joyce, NY and London (1958). Her most recent work is *Echoes of Spoonriver*, based on the poems of Edgar Lee Masters, presented by the Valerie Bettis T./Dance Co., 1976. DV

Bey [Müller], Hannelore, b. Leipzig, 1941. German dancer. Pupil of Gret Palucca's school in Dresden; joined the Dresden B. 1961. Studied Leningrad; became a principal dancer of the Komische O., E. Berlin, 1966, and created roles in many of SCHILLING's ballets. Bronze Medal, Varna 1968; diploma, 1969 Moscow Competition. GBLW

Bharata Natyam *see* ASIA

Biagi, Vittorio, b. Viareggio, 1941. Italian dancer and choreographer. Studied with DELL'ARA, MESSERER, Tatyana Grantseva. Soloist Milan Sc. 1958–60; B. XXe S. 1961–6, where he created role in *Bacchanale de Tannhäuser* (1961), *Divertimento* (1962) and NINTH SYMPHONY for BÉJART; choreographed *Jazz Impression* (1964), *L'Après-midi d'un Faune* (1964). B. Paris OC, 1966–8; danced in GRADUATION BALL, LESSON; choreographed *L'Enfant et les Sortilèges* (1967), *Platée* (1968); at the Lyon Fest. 1969 choreographed *Requiem de Berlioz*. Artistic director, Lyon OB from 1969, has staged there his versions of *Romeo and Juliet*, *Symphonie Fantastique*, *Passion selon*

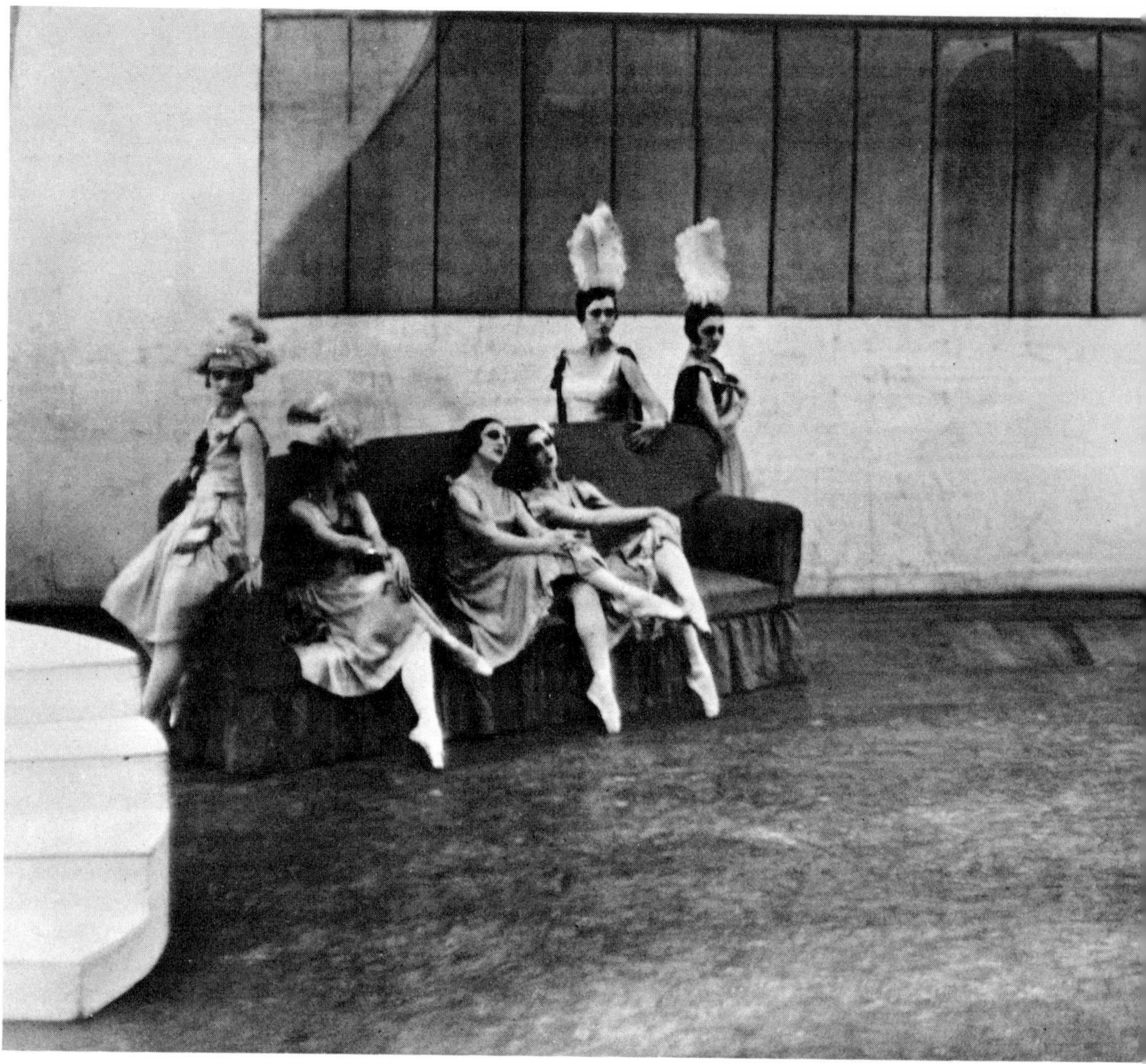

Les Biches, as danced by the Diaghilev B., London, 1928, sc./c. Marie Laurencin. LIFAR and Alice Nikitina (right) as the Athlete and the Girl in Blue; among the girls on the sofa are DUBROVSKA and A. DANILOVA (centre, seated) and (far left) DE VALOIS. Described by its choreographer as a modern SYLPHIDES, the ballet depicts a group of 1920s 'bright young things' at a fashionable house party.

Saint-Jean, Alexandre Nevsky, Hommage à Callot, Sacre du Printemps, 7 Études sur des Thèmes de Paul Klee, Venise Secrète. Endowed with a sure technique and dramatic presence, his best choreography is in narrative ballets such as *Alexandre Nevsky* and *Romeo et Juliette*. M-FC

Bias, Fanny, b. 1789; d. Paris, 1825. French dancer. Her career was almost entirely at the Paris O. but she danced in London at the King's T. in 1821 and Thomas Moore wrote a poem about her. The theatre manager John Ebers described her 'beautiful little half steps, which more than any other, correspond to the epithet "twinkling"'. She was one of the first dancers to use the full *pointe* and there is a lithograph after F. Waldeck (1821) of her standing on toe in which she looks agonized.

Although not a great beauty, she was a great favourite with the public; the artist obviously did not do her justice. MC

Biches, Les, ballet with songs, ch. NIJINSKA; mus. POULENC; sc. Marie Laurencin. T. de Monte Carlo, DIAGHILEV's B. Russes, 6 Jan 1924; dan. NEMCHINOVA, Nijinska, TCHERNICHEVA, L. SOKOLOVA, VILZAK, WOIZIKOWSKI, Nicholas Zverev. Revived by MARKOVA–DOLIN B. 1937, de Cuevas B. 1947, RB 1964. DV

Big City, ballet, 3 scenes, ch./lib. JOOSS; mus. Alexander Tansman; c. Hein Heckroth. Cologne OH, Jooss B., 21 Nov 1932; NYCC, CCJB, 28 Feb 1975; staged Anna Markard; c./ltg Hermann Markard recreated Ray Diffen and Jennifer Tipton. Said to be the first ballet to take up social criticism, it depicts the loneliness of city people. Revived Wuppertal Dance T. (1974). Original German title *Grossstadt 1926*. FM

Bije [Bye], Willy de la, b. Leiden, 1934. Dutch dancer. Classical ballerina (the first Dutch GISELLE) with the Nederlands B.; joined NDT as a founder member 1959, and proved herself equally distinguished in the interpretation of modern works. Created many roles incl. leading parts in TETLEY's *Sargasso, The Anatomy Lesson*, and *Circles*; HARKARVY's *Recital for Cello and Eight Dancers*; and van MANEN's *Variomatic*. Now a teacher and ballet mistress in Australia with her husband FLIER. JP

Billy the Kid, ballet, 1 act, ch. LORING; mus. COPLAND; lib. KIRSTEIN; sc./c. Jared French. Chicago O., B. Caravan, 16 Oct 1938; dan. Loring, MARIE-JEANNE, L. CHRISTENSEN, BOLENDER. The first great American ballet on an American subject, it depicts the legend of the desperado who in real life killed 21 men. The narrative is treated in the framework of the American westward expansion. Revived Chicago O., ABT, 8 Dec 1940; dan. Loring, ALONSO, Richard Reed, David Nillo. The role of Billy was most frequently danced by and closely associated with KRIZA. FM/MC

Birmingham Ballet *see* REGIONAL BALLET (USA)

Bischoff, Egon, b. Gotha, 1934. German dancer and teacher. Studied at Gret Palucca's S. in Dresden, Leningrad; soloist at Staats O., E. Berlin. Now a ballet master and teacher, E. Berlin Staats OBS GBLW

Bittnerówna, Barbara, b. Lwów, 1924. Polish dancer. Prima ballerina of ballet co. in Poznań 1946–9; in Bytom 1949–51; in Warsaw 1951–5; at the Operetta, Warsaw, since 1966. First Polish ZAREMA and JULIET, she also danced SWANILDA, the Bride in HIGHLANDERS, and ZOBEIDE; created many roles in Polish ballets. A perfect actress, with a strong stage personality and dramatic power. For many years she gave recitals of small, well-composed dances with her partner GRUCA. Danced all over Europe. On BBC TV, July 1958; toured Britain Oct–Dec 1958. JPu

Bix Pieces, The, ballet, ch. THARP; mus. Bix Beiderbecke; c. Kermit Love. Paris, IX International Fest. of Dance, 2 Nov 1971; dan. Tharp, RUDNER, Rose Marie WRIGHT, Isabel Garcia-Lorca, RINKER. A loving look at 1920s and 1930s jazz, and a study of balletic and modern dance movement. DM

Bjørn [Larsen], Dinna, b. Copenhagen, 1947. Danish dancer and choreographer. Daughter of N. B. LARSEN. Studied with Edite Frandsen. Debut as Columbine in pantomime at Tivoli 1962. Entered RDB 1964; engaged as ballet dancer 1966; debut in AFTERNOON OF A FAUN. Bronze Medal, Varna Competition, 1968, with *pas de deux* from FLOWER FESTIVAL AT GENZANO. Danced SYLPHIDE 1971. Choreographic debut 1970 with *8 plus 1* for RDB; also choreographed *Anatomic Safari*, Danish B. Acad., 1971, and *The Butterfly Mask*, RDB 1975. Among her bigger parts are Masha (NUTCRACKER) and roles in KERMIS AT BRUGES and FAR FROM DENMARK. SKJ

The Black Crook chorus as they appeared at Niblo's Garden, New York, 1866

Bjørnsson, Fredbjørn, b. Copenhagen, 1926. Danish dancer, choreographer, and teacher. Entered RDBS 1935; solo dancer with co. 1949. Youthful *demi-caractère* roles early in his career. Among his best parts: First Cadet (GRADUATION BALL), FRANZ, Rageneau (PETIT's *Cyrano de Bergerac*); and such August BOURNONVILLE roles as Eskimo (FAR FROM DENMARK), Carelis (KERMIS AT BRUGES), and Gennaro (NAPOLI). He advanced to older character parts, bringing his original talent for mime to the Teacher (LESSON), DR COPPÉLIUS, and the General (*Graduation Ball*). Debut as choreographer with *Behind the Curtain*, 1954, followed by several minor works for the Copenhagen Royal T. and Danish TV. Danced with SAND's group in guest perfs at Jacob's Pillow. Now specializes in teaching Bournonville-style technique at RDBS and international seminars, especially in the USA. He m. K. RALOV. SKJ

Black Crook, The, American theatrical extravaganza, director David Costa. NY, Niblo's Garden, 12 Sept 1866; dan. Marie Bonfanti, Rita Sangalli. It ran for 16 months. Revivals and touring versions continued until 1903 in rapid succession and the production is said to have created the basis for American music hall and vaudeville. The work was presented by the impresario William Wheatley, who acquired some lavish settings and costumes imported from Europe and built the show around them. The plot was a highly complicated one on Faustian lines about an alchemist who promised to deliver to Satan one soul for every year of his life. When *The Black Crook* ended its first run, Wheatley followed it with a similar show, *The White Fawn*. A burlesque revival of *The Black Crook* ch. DE MILLE, in a theatre–beer hall, Hoboken, NJ, 1929; dan. de Mille, Warren Leonard, Bentley Stone. New Yorkers flocked to the show, partly for its own sake, partly for the illegal beer (prohibition was in full force). MC

See G. Freeley, 'The Black Crook and The White Fawn', *Dance Index*, Vol. IV, No. 1 (New York)

Black Queen, the evil victor in CHECKMATE

Black Swan, The. The *grand pas de deux* danced by ODILE and SIEGFRIED in the M. PETIPA SWAN LAKE. So named because it became traditional to dress the sorceress Odile in black in contrast to ODETTE, the white swan queen. A remarkable display of virtuosity, incl. the famous 32 *fouettés* for the ballerina.

A popular item, it is often danced by star dancers at galas. MC

Blair [Butterworth], David, b. Halifax, Yorkshire, 1932; d. London, 1976. English dancer. Joined SWS 1946 and SWTB 1947 where he created important roles in CRANKO's PINEAPPLE POLL and *Harlequin in April* (1951). To SWB at CG 1953, principal 1955. His early partnership in the big classical ballets was with FIFIELD, then with NERINA, and briefly with FONTEYN, a partnership ended by the arrival of NUREYEV in the West. Danced all the major classic roles with flair and brilliance, but his greatest achievements were in *demi-caractère* parts, which called not only on his prodigious technique but also his ebullience of personality, his *panache*, his gift of comedy. He created many roles for Cranko but his supreme achievement was the creation of COLAS, in which role he gave his farewell perf. at CG in 1968. Another notable creation was Mercutio in MACMILLAN's ROMEO AND JULIET. He staged SWAN LAKE in Atlanta, GA, 1956, worked with American regional ballets and staged both the full-length *Swan Lake* and GISELLE for ABT. His death, from a heart attack, came only a few months before he was due to take up the post of director of the Norwegian NB. CBE 1964. He m. LANE; father of twin daughters. MC

Blank, Gustav, b. Altenbögge, 1908. German dancer and teacher. Studied with LABAN, JOOSS at the Folkwang S., Essen, and under EDOUARDOVA and T. GSOVSKY. At the Staats OB, Berlin, 1933–49; ballet master, Städtische T., W. Berlin, 1949–57. Ballet master, Hamburg 1957–62; since 1962 has been teacher and professor at the Munich BS; also has his own school there. One of the greatest of German teachers, he trained many of the present leading dancers in Germany, incl. BREUER and BOSL. Has also choreographed. GBLW

Blasis, Carlo, b. Naples, *c.* 1797; d. Cernobbio, 1878. Italian dancer, choreographer, teacher and, above all, codifier of technique. He lived much of his early life in France, studying with DAUBERVAL in Bordeaux (where he would have learned about NOVERRE's theories and Dauberval's practice of them) and with GARDEL in Paris. Returned to Italy 1817 to work with VIGANÒ and in 1820 wrote his first technical primer, *An Elementary Treatise upon the Theory and Practice of the Art of Dancing* (reprinted New York 1944). He was dancer and choreographer at the King's T., London, 1826–30 during which time he published *The Code of Terpsichore* (London 1828), invaluable both as a manual for dancers and a guide about technique at that time. He became principal dancer at Sc. and in 1837, when injury stopped him dancing, took over its school where his teaching won world renown. His pupils were to spread the influence of the Italian school, notably to Russia, and from Blasis's work stems the whole classical vocabulary of today. He was a man of wide culture, called by one of his contemporaries 'a universal genius'. He invented the position we call the *attitude* (*see* Glossary of Technical Terms). He was also a choreographer, working in the cities of Milan, Venice, London, and Warsaw. MC

Blaska, Félix, b. Gomel, USSR, 1941. French dancer and choreographer. Studied Paris Cons. under Yves Brieux. Danced de Cuevas B. 1960; *Zizi Jeanmaire* revue, Rome; B. de RP 1961–9. Founded his own co. 1969 at the Fest. Châtillon des Arts, approved by the Ministry for Cultural Affairs, and set up in 1973 at the Grenoble Maison de la Culture. For it he choreographed *Sensemaya*; *Electro-Bach* (1969); *Ballet pour Tam-Tam et Percussions* (1970); *Sonate pour Deux Pianos et Percussions* (1971); *Improvisions* (1975). He also staged *Deuxième Concerto* (1970) at the Marseille O.; *Poème Electronique* and *Arcana*, Paris O. (1973). More interested in the abstract than in telling a story. M-FC

Bliss, Sir Arthur, b. London, 1891; d. London, 1975. English composer, whose ballet scores are more notable for their sound craftsmanship than their individuality, though Bliss's orchestration is sometimes highly effective. His ballets, all for SWB, are CHECKMATE, MIRACLE IN THE GORBALS and *Adam Zero* (London 1946; ch. HELPMANN). DH

Bluebird, *pas de deux* in the *divertissement* in the last act of SLEEPING BEAUTY wedding festivities. In the series of danced fairy tales featured in the original production, the Bluebird represented a kindly visitor to the imprisoned Princess Florine and the man's role is characterized by its airborne quality, quick beating of the feet, and fluttering of the hands and arms. The woman's dance is delicate and very feminine. Legend and princess are long forgotten and the dance is admired for its brilliant choreographic structure alone. It follows the formula of all classic *pas de deux* of its era. MC

Blue Skater, the principal male role in PATINEURS, so described because the original costume was blue.

Blues Suite, modern dance work, ch. AILEY; mus. Pasquita Anderson, José Ricci; sc./c. Geoffrey Holder. New York, YM-YWHA, 92nd Street, Ailey Dance T., 30 Mar 1958. The joys of sporting life portrayed in a series of episodes taking place in a bordello, concluding with the mournful sound of a train whistle in the night and reproachful church bells at dawn. Frequently performed with Brother John Sellers as singer. DM

Blum, Anthony, b. Mobile, AL. American dancer. Studied at SAB. Joined NYCB 1958. First principal role was in CUNNINGHAM's revised version of his SUMMERSPACE for that co. in 1966. Created roles in BALANCHINE's DON QUIXOTE and *Tchaikovsky Suite No. 3* (1970), and in DANCES AT A GATHERING (1969), IN THE NIGHT (1970), and GOLDBERG VARIATIONS (1971). DV

Blum, René, b. Paris, 1878; d. Auschwitz concentration camp, 1942. French impresario. Appointed in 1929 by the Société des Bains de Mer de Monaco after DIAGHILEV's death to direct a co. that became (1931) the B. de l'O. de Monte Carlo. He had already established his Monte Carlo OB when joined by DE BASIL (*see* BALLET RUSSE DE MONTE CARLO). He was a man of culture and taste, and probably the greatest benefactor of ballet, both in artistic guidance and total personal involvement in the work of his cos, during the 1930s. A modest man, he shunned the limelight. His memoirs were in the hands of a Paris publisher when the Germans occupied France and the manuscript was lost. MC

Bodenwieser, Gertrud, b. Vienna, 1886; d. Sydney, 1959. Austrian dancer, teacher, and choreographer. Instructor of Dance, Vienna State Acad. of Music and Dramatic Art, 1919; professor, 1926. Director, Tanzgruppe Bodenwieser, formed to develop her own Modern Dance style. Emigrated to Sydney, Australia, 1938. Founded the Bodenwieser B. and choreographed many works, incl. *The Pilgrimage of Truth*, *Life of the Insects*, *Errand into the Maze*. Her Dance Centre is now directed by Margaret Chapple and Keith Bain. KSW

Bogatyrev, Aleksandr, b. Tallinn, 1949. Soviet dancer. Studied Tallinn Choreographic S., acquitted himself so well at rally of all schools in Moscow (1965) that Moscow Choreographic S. wanted to complete his education. Joined Bolshoy B., Moscow, 1969. Rapidly progressed, as true *danseur noble* much needed after FADEYECHEV's retirement. Excellent line, poise, acting ability, good technique, and dependable partner. Dances classical roles, also Ferhad (LEGEND OF LOVE) with an admirable grasp of the Oriental style of the last. Partnered N. PAVLOVA for her debut in GISELLE, Bolshoy T. He m. Galina Kravchenko, character dancer, Bolshoy *corps de ballet*. NR
See N. Avaliani and L. Zhdanov, tr. N. Ward, *Bolshoi's Young Dancers* (Moscow and London 1975)

Bogdanova, Nadezhda, b. Moscow, 1836; d. St Petersburg, 1897. Russian dancer. Daughter of dancer and teacher Konstantin Bogdanov (*c.* 1809–77) and Tatyana Karpakova (1814–42). Trained in father's private school, participated in provincial tours of the family, dancing SYLPHIDE at 12 with her father as JAMES. To Paris with family 1850, performing in French provinces on the way. Attracted attention of Nestor Roqueplan, director of Paris O., and SAINT-LÉON; debut in *La Vivandière* (ch. Saint-Léon) at Paris O. where she was principal dancer 1851–5, returning for a brief span 1865. Studied under French teachers. Ethereal, swift, lyrical dancer, especially outstanding in title roles of GISELLE, *La Sylphide*, ESMERALDA.

She returned to Russia, dancing in St Petersburg and Moscow, frequently with her brother Nikolay, who developed strong technique in Paris and was soloist of St Petersburg B. 1861–82, partnering VAZEM and other ballerinas. Though Bogdanova had 42 curtain calls upon debut in *Giselle* (Bolshoy T., St Petersburg, 2 Nov 1856), and considerable success in ballets by PERROT and Saint-Léon, she lost favour with the directorship of the Imperial Ts; from 1864 was forced to dance in Warsaw, Vienna, Budapest, and Berlin, exerting a beneficial influence on local dancers. Retired Warsaw 1867 when she was at the height of her powers. NR
See Ivor Guest, *The Ballet of the Second Empire* (*1847–1858*, London 1955; *1858–1870*, London 1953); *The Artistic Family of Bogdanovs* (St Petersburg 1856)

Bogomolova, Lyudmila, b. Moscow, 1932. Soviet dancer. Studied Moscow, Bolshoy S. with Maria Khozhukova (as a member of the experimental class for late starters); graduated into the Bolshoy B. 1951, where she danced Olia in LITTLE STORK, KITRI, the Mistress of the Copper Mountain in STONE FLOWER, etc. During the first Bolshoy B. season in London (1956) danced the 'peasant' *pas de deux* in GISELLE with YEVDOKIMOV and appeared in MESSERER's *Spring Waters*. Created the Feather in LIEUTENANT KIJË. JS

Above: Adolph Bolm as Pierrot in CARNAVAL, CG, 1913

Right: The Bolshoy Ballet as they appeared in Act II of GISELLE at their first appearance in the West, CG, 1956. Their dance of the Wilis at that time caused a sensation

Bolender, Todd, b. Canton, OH, 1919. American dancer and choreographer. Studied with Chester Hale and VILZAK and at SAB. Danced with B. Caravan, Littlefield B., ABT, B. Russe de Monte Carlo, and in musicals. Danced and choreographed for B. Society, which became NYCB, and later ROBBINS's Ballets: USA. Created roles in many BALANCHINE ballets, notably FOUR TEMPERAMENTS (Phlegmatic), AGON, BOURRÉE FANTASQUE, IVESIANA; and in Robbins's *Age of Anxiety* (1950), *The Pied Piper* (1951), *Fanfare* (1953), CONCERT. Ballets incl. *Mother Goose Suite* (1943), *Souvenirs* (1955), STILL POINT. Director of ballet at Cologne 1963–6, Frankfurt 1966–9. Has choreographed for NY Met O. and Broadway musicals. Now teaches. DV

Bolm, Adolph, b. St Petersburg, 1884; d. Hollywood, 1951. Russian dancer and choreographer. Trained in Imperial S., St Petersburg, graduating 1903 and becoming a soloist at the Maryinsky T. 1910. Organized and danced in A. PAVLOVA's first tours abroad. Joined DIAGHILEV's B. Russes 1909 and created Chief Warrior in PRINCE IGOR and Pierrot in CARNAVAL. Resigned from Maryinsky 1911 and danced for Diaghilev until the second USA tour of the co. 1916, when he decided to settle in the USA. He founded his B. Intime with which he was later to do pioneer work in films. Worked with the Chicago Grand OB and became principal dancer of Chicago Civic O. In 1924 helped establish the Chicago Allied Arts Inc. to produce modern American ballets. In 1928 choreographed *Apollon-Musagète,* commissioned by Elizabeth Sprague Coolidge. He staged some of the old FOKINE ballets at T. Colón, Buenos Aires, and then moved to Hollywood where he worked in films. In 1932 he staged his *Ballet Mécanique,* to the music of Aleksandr Mossolov's *The Iron Foundry,* at the Hollywood Bowl. In 1933 he joined the San Francisco O. Co. as choreographer and ballet master and established a school. In 1939 he returned to NY to join ABT and choreographed PETER AND THE WOLF which stayed in the repertory many years. He worked with the co. until 1945 when he returned to Hollywood to teach and work on his memoirs until he died. He created in 1929 the first dance film synchronized to orchestral music, the *Danse Macabre* of Camille Saint-Saëns. MC

Bolshoy Ballet. The co. based on the Bolshoy T. and its school in Moscow, which since 1956 has toured worldwide to show its prowess. Its genealogy can be traced from 1776, when ballets began to be staged regularly at the theatre (*see* RUSSIA) but the present co. is essentially a Soviet creation.

At the Revolution in 1917, GORSKY was in charge of the co. and he remained in this position until his death in 1924. During this period the co. was largely dependent for its dancers on survivors from the pre-Revolutionary period, since the Bolshoy S. was not functioning fully until 1920. Leading dancers incl.

GELTSER, MORDKIN and FEDOROVA, MESSERER, MOISEYEV, GABOVICH, and TIKHOMIROV, supplemented in 1930 by SEMYONOVA and YERMOLAYEV from Leningrad. Tikhomirov choreographed RED POPPY, described by SLONIMSKY (*The Bolshoy Ballet*, Moscow 1956) as 'the first successful attempt to render a modern theme on the ballet stage'. The rest of the repertory consisted almost exclusively of reproductions of the classic works of M. PETIPA, IVANOV, and Gorsky.

In 1936 the Leningrad choreographer ZAKHAROV joined the co., staging his FOUNTAIN OF BAKHCHISARAY and producing a new version of PRISONER OF THE CAUCASUS; dancers at his disposal were augmented by GUSEV, LEPESHINSKAYA, KONDRATOV, Georgi Farmanyantz, the superb character dancer RADUNSKY, and GOLOVKINA. Most major works produced at the Bolshoy during this period were revivals or versions of ballets already produced in Leningrad, a tendency that continued after World War II, when the Leningrad choreographers L. LAVROVSKY and GRIGOROVICH were transferred to Moscow. GOLEIZOVSKY, who studied in Leningrad, had returned to Moscow 1909, but most of his work in Moscow was connected with his own private school and co. (the Chamber B.) which caused much interest and controversy in Moscow and Leningrad. He did not succeed as a choreographer at the Bolshoy until the end of his life with *Scriabiniana* (1962) and *Leyly and Medzhnun* (1964). Radunsky, in collaboration with Lev Pospekhin and Nikolay Popko, produced LITTLE STORK and SVETLANA, and also in 1960 a very successful new version of HUMPBACKED HORSE.

When the Germans invaded Russia in 1941, the Bolshoy B. was moved to Kuibyshev; groups toured where possible to entertain the troops. The return of the co. to Moscow at the end of the war and the permanent secondment of ULANOVA and Lavrovsky to the Bolshoy initiated a period in which the Lavrovsky ballets ROMEO AND JULIET, RAYMONDA and *Red Poppy*, Zakharov's CINDERELLA and *Fountain of Bakhchisaray*, LAURENCIA, FLAME OF PARIS, SHURALE, and the old classics GISELLE, SWAN LAKE, NUTCRACKER and SLEEPING BEAUTY all received fresh impetus from the new generation of dancers emerging from the Bolshoy S. in support of Ulanova and Lepeshinskaya: STRUCHKOVA, PLISETSKAYA, BOGOMOLOVA, TIMOFEYEVA, KARELSKAYA, FADEYECHEV, Boris Khokhlov, and LEVASHOV; and the still younger generation: MAXIMOVA, N. BESSMERTNOVA, SOROKINA, M. LAVROVSKY, VASILIEV, etc.

The Bolshoy B. made its first major visit to the West in 1956: its London debut with *Romeo and Juliet* was an instant success, its presentation of *Giselle* with Ulanova and Fadeyechev being immediately acclaimed in its production by L. Lavrovsky as the finest extant. (This production was fortunately preserved on film, albeit incomplete.) Since then it has appeared all over the world, touring with both large and small groups, but a fairly conventional repertory. Several 1-act ballets have been produced with varying success, by L. Lavrovsky, LAPAURI and Olga Tarasova, KASATKINA and VASILYOV, and Messerer, whose *Ballet School* (1962), a cascade of virtuosity, is one of the most successful works presented by the Bolshoy B. abroad. In 1976 the co. was directed by Grigorovich, who has produced a series of full-length works in Moscow incl. STONE FLOWER, LEGEND OF LOVE, and SPARTACUS, also reworkings of *Nutcracker* and *Swan Lake*. In most of these ballets the leading female role has been danced by his wife, N. Bessmertnova.

To some purists, both in the USSR and outside, the Bolshoy style is still regarded as slightly provincial. However, few styles of dancing in the world today can, with such apparent technical ease, produce such an immediate atmosphere of excitement and passionate conviction and sustain it for extended periods. JS

See Yuri Slonimsky, *The Bolshoy Ballet* (Moscow 1956, 1963); Natalia Roslavleva, *Era of the Russian Ballet* (London and New York 1966); *Segodnia Na Szene Bolshogo Teatra* (*Today on the Stage of The Bolshoy Theatre*, Moscow 1976); N. Avaliani and L. Zhdanov, tr. N. Ward, *Bolshoi's Young Dancers* (Moscow and London 1975)

Boniuszko, Alicja, b. Miadzioł (Vilno [Wilno; Vilnyus] dept, now USSR), 1937. Polish dancer. Since 1956 prima ballerina of the Gdańsk ballet co. Dancer of versatile personality who created many roles in Polish ballets based on modern dance devised especially for her. Other roles include ODETTE, JULIET, CINDERELLA, the Bride in HIGHLANDERS, the Girl in MIRACULOUS MANDARIN. Toured in USSR, USA, Brazil, France, Britain and elsewhere. JPu

Bonnefous, Jean-Pierre, b. Bourg-en-Bresse, 1943. French dancer. Studied at Paris OBS, joining the co. in 1960. Guest artist with Frankfurt B.; Kirov and Bolshoy B. 1965 and 1966; Sc. 1968 and 1969. Danced in ballets by BALANCHINE in both Paris and Berlin, and in 1970 was invited to join NYCB, where he dances leading roles in ORPHEUS, AGON, VALSE, WHO CARES?, VIOLIN CONCERTO, DANCES AT A GATHERING, etc. He m. MCBRIDE. DV

See J.-C. Diénis, 'Jean-Pierre Bonnefous,' *Les Saisons de la Danse* (Paris, Oct 1970)

Borchsenius [Jørgensen], Valborg, b. Copenhagen, 1872; d. Copenhagen, 1949. Danish dancer and producer. Entered Royal TBS 1879; in first year was one of Nora's children in the first perf. of Henrik Ibsen's *A Doll's House* there. Debut 1891 as SYLPHIDE (ch. August BOURNONVILLE). Soloist 1895; partnered BECK in all main parts in the Bournonville repertoire. Teacher at the ballet school, where she continued to work after her retirement from the stage 1918. In the 1930s and 1940s assisted H. LANDER in restaging Bournonville works, where her impeccable memory and sharp sense of style and nuance revealed the true wealth of the Bournonville inheritance. She not only helped in the restaging but taught the next generation how to present the ballets in the correct style. A notable pupil was BRENAA. SKJ

Borg, Conny, b. Stockholm, 1938. Swedish dancer, choreographer, and ballet director. Studied at RSBS, Stockholm. Principal dancer 1963. Ballet director of Stora T., Gothenburg, 1967–70. Founded New Swedish B. with GADD 1970, toured Paris and London. Ballet director of Malmö T. 1972. Choreographed *Ritornell* (mus. Ingvar Lidholm), and versions of ROMEO AND JULIET, *Soirée Musicale*, SWAN LAKE, NUTCRACKER, and CINDERELLA. AGS

Börlin, Jean, b. Härnösand, 1893; d. New York, 1930. Swedish dancer and choreographer. Pupil of RSBS and member of the co. Left 1918 to study with FOKINE. Leading dancer and sole choreographer of BALLETS SUÉDOIS 1920–5. Among his ballets were *Nuit de Saint-Jean, Les Mariés de la Tour d'Eiffel, Maison des Fous, La Création du Monde,* and *Relâche.* AGS

Bornhausen, Angelika, b. Sondershausen, 1944. German dancer. Pupil of BLANK and APPEL in Hamburg. Joined Hamburg B. 1963; Cologne 1966–70 (dancing GISELLE). Guest ballerina NB of Canada 1970. Ballerina Zürich B. 1972–4. To Hamburg 1975. GBLW

Borovansky, Edouard, b. Přerov [Prerau], 1902; d. Sydney, 1959. Czech dancer, director, and choreographer. Prague NTS. Prague NT 1926, character soloist. A. Pavlova B. 1926. B. Russe de Monte Carlo (de Basil) 1932. Established dance academy, Melbourne, 1939, with his wife Xenia Nikolaeva, and the Borovansky B. 1942 (which became professional, May 1944). A vital force for ballet in Australia, Borovansky produced dancers of strong technique and lively personality. He is associated with roles such as King Dodon (COQ D'OR); his best-remembered ballet is *Terra Australis* (mus. Esther Rofe; sc. William Constable). KSW

Borowska, Irina, b. Buenos Aires, 1928. Argentine dancer of Polish parents (US citizen since 1964). Trained by Michel Borowski, Esmée Bulnes, and SHABELEVSKY she first made her name as the Gloveseller in GAIETÉ PARISIENNE. After reaching ballerina status at T. Colón, joined B. Russe de Monte Carlo as ballerina 1954 and was ballerina with LFB 1961–6 when she m. MUSIL and settled in Vienna where she now teaches. JUL

Bortoluzzi, Paolo, b. Genoa, 1938. Italian dancer and choreographer. Studied with DELL'ARA, KISS, V. GSOVSKY, MESSERER. Danced in MASSINE's co. Nervi Fest. 1957. B. XXe S. 1960–72, creating roles in many of BÉJART's works. After leaving that co. continued to dance Béjart's choreography as guest artist with numerous cos (notably roles created for him, e.g. *Nomos Alpha* (1969) and LIEDER EINES FAHRENDEN GESELLEN, with NUREYEV), also classical roles at Milan Sc., frequently as partner of FRACCI; Düsseldorf O.; Hamburg O.; Geneva Grand T.; ABT; etc. Elegant and precise, he has an exceptionally pure technique, a sense of humour, and a theatrical radiance which Béjart has fully exploited. Combines Latin subtlety with virile brilliance. M-FC/FP
See L. Rossel, 'Paolo Bortoluzzi', *Les Saisons de la Danse* (Paris, Aug 1969) with list of roles.

Bosch, Aurora, b. Havana, *c.* 1940. Cuban dancer. Studied with ALONSO, danced in San Francisco and Los Angeles; joined NB of Cuba 1959, soloist 1962, prima ballerina 1967, now ballet mistress. Silver medal, Varna Competition, 1965; gold medal, Varna, 1966; gold medal, Mexico, 1971. Tall and dark, with a lyrical pure style, excels in the Prelude in SYLPHIDES, ideal MYRTHA with quiet regal presence. MC

Bosl, Heinz, b. Baden-Baden, 1946; d. Munich, 1975. German dancer. Pupil of Munich BS from 1955, under DE LUTRY, BLANK, etc. Joined Munich B. 1962 becoming soloist 1965, and creating many important roles, incl. ALAIN. He often partnered FONTEYN, in Berlin and the USA 1973, and first danced in London 1974. He was tall with an engaging stage presence. His death from leukaemia was a sad loss to ballet. GBLW

Boston Ballet, US ballet co. of Boston, MA, founded by E. Virginia Williams, the Boston teacher and choreographer who remains its artistic director. It began in 1958 as the New England Civic B., a non-professional group drawn from students of Williams's Boston S. of B. Appearing in five successive regional ballet festivals, the co. was noticed by BALANCHINE who, with W. McNeil Lowry, director of arts and humanities for the Ford Foundation, was making a survey of American schools and cos. Upon their recommendation, a Ford Foundation grant was awarded in 1963 which enabled the co., now called the Boston B., to become fully professional in the 1964–5 season. In 1967 the Boston B. made its NY City debut at Hunter College Playhouse. Balanchine served as artistic adviser to the new co., allowing it to dance many of his works, incl. APOLLO, *Symphony in C* (*see* PALAIS DE CRISTAL), *Allegro Brillante*, CONCERTO BAROCCO, PRODIGAL SON, and SERENADE. Samuel Kurkjian, Ron Cunningham, Alfonso Figueroa, and Lorenzo Monreal have served as resident choreographers. The co.'s world premieres incl. SOKOLOW's *Time Plus Six* (mus. Teo Macero, 1966), TARAS's *Dolly Suite* (mus. Gabriel Fauré, 1971), FALCO's *The Gamete Garden* (mus. Michael Kamen, 1971), and DE MILLE's *Summer* (mus. Franz Schubert, 1975). In stressing diversity of repertoire, the co. has also given perfs of such ballet and modern dance works as RODEO; CUNNINGHAM's SUMMERSPACE and *Winterbranch*; ROAD OF THE PHOEBE SNOW, GRADUATION BALL; and MEDEA. Classics presented incl. NAPOLI, Act III (staged by BRENAA), SWAN LAKE, Act II, GISELLE (staged by Dimitri Romanoff), COPPÉLIA (staged by Williams), and an annual Christmas NUTCRACKER (staged by Williams). Boston B. has toured the USA regularly, since 1972 under the auspices of the National Endowment for the Arts Coordinated Touring Residency Program. JA

Bourmeister, Wladimir *see* BURMEISTER, Vladimir

Bournonville, Antoine, b. Lyon, 1760; d. Fredensborg (Denmark), 1843. French dancer and later ballet master in Denmark. Danced in NOVERRE's ballets in Vienna and was a popular soloist in Paris and London. Engaged for the Swedish O., Stockholm, by Gustaf III in 1782. Stayed in Copenhagen after guest perfs at Royal T. 1792, where he was soloist and – after GALEOTTI's death – ballet master until 1823. His works were without importance or originality, but he was an elegant dancer and mime. Taught his son, and successor, August BOURNONVILLE. SKJ
See 'Antoine Bournonville's Diaries from 1892', ed. and tr. from French into Danish by Julius Clausen, into English by Leslie Getz, in 2 parts, in *Ballet Review*, Vol. 2, No. 6; Vol. 3, No. 1 (New York 1969)

Bournonville, August, b. Copenhagen, 1805; d. Copenhagen, 1879. Danish dancer, choreographer, and ballet master. Entered RDBS as child; debut 12 Oct 1813 in an important child part in the first ballet with a Scandinavian theme, *Lagertha* (ch. GALEOTTI). In Paris with his father, Antoine BOURNONVILLE, 1820; pupil of A. VESTRIS 1824–9. Debut Paris O. 1826. With French troupe in London at King's T. 1828. Returned to Copenhagen 1828; after guest performances was engaged to Royal T. as dancer, choreographer, and teacher/ballet master (*see* DENMARK). Until 1848 he was the theatre's brilliant soloist, but at the same time he educated new principal dancers and was creating his own repertoire. First ballet still extant was his version of F. TAGLIONI's SYLPHIDE, in which his pupil GRAHN won fame in the title role. His repertory of more than 50 ballets and *divertissements*, given (to 1975) more than 3,000 times by the RDB in Copenhagen and on tours, was strongly influenced by his early years in Paris, where romantic ballet began. He danced in his Parisian years with M. TAGLIONI, who was always his ballet ideal, but his personal development in choreography gave his romantic repertory a more *petit-bourgeois* horizon, creating a warm and charming atmosphere in his ballets, which had a wide variety of themes, often with a national flavour: Italian, Flemish, Spanish, Norwegian, and, of course, Danish. Today about a dozen of his ballets are still performed and, when well done, are the gems of the Danish repertoire. Among the best are NAPOLI, CONSERVATORY, KERMIS AT BRUGES, FOLK LEGEND, FLOWER FESTIVAL AT GENZANO, FAR FROM DENMARK, VENTANA, and KING'S VOLUNTEERS OF AMAGER. Other important works are: *Festen in Albano* (*Festival in Albano*, 1839), celebrating the Danish sculptor Bertel Thorvaldsen, *Toreadoren* (*The Toreador*, 1840), *Brudefœrden i Hardanger* (*The Wedding at Hardanger*, 1853), and *Thrymskviden* (1868), one of his most ambitious works, taking its theme from Norse mythology.

Apart from two periods Bournonville worked in Copenhagen: he tried unsuccessfully to get his ballets known internationally when he was ballet master in Vienna (1855–6) and *Intendant* at the Stockholm O. (1861–4), where he had nothing to do with Swedish ballet, but introduced an important new style in opera and drama production. He was the leading man in Danish ballet, praised by Denmark's foremost personalities in the art world, proud to be named a 'ballet-poet' by Adam Oehlenschläger, Denmark's most important romantic poet, and friend of writer Hans Christian Andersen (who met the singer Jenny Lind in Bournonville's house). Today Bournonville's works are produced all over the world, the only vehicle for the classical French style of A. Vestris. He also left his memoirs, *Mit Theaterliv* (*My Theatre Life*; Copenhagen 1848–78; tr. Patricia N. McAndrew (Middletown, CT, 1977) and minor publications. SKJ
See Lillian Moore, *Bournonville's London Spring* (New York 1965)

Bourrée Fantasque, ballet, 3 parts, ch. BALANCHINE; mus. Emmanuel Chabrier; c. (Barbara) Karinska; ltg ROSENTHAL. NYCC, NYCB, 1 Dec 1949; dan. LECLERCQ, ROBBINS, Maria TALLCHIEF, MAGALLANES, Janet Reed, Herbert Bliss. Revived London RFH, LFB, 18 Aug 1960; dan. Marylyn Burr, Belinda Wright, FERRI. Also in repertory of RDB. A plotless ballet that shifts from comedy to romance to festivity in character and tempo. FM

Boutique Fantasque, La (*The Fantastic Toyshop*), ballet, 1 act, ch. MASSINE; mus. Gioacchino Rossini, orch. Ottorino Respighi; sc./c. DERAIN. London, Alhambra T., DIAGHILEV's B. Russes, 5 June 1919; dan. CECCHETTI, L. LOPUKHOVA, Massine, IDZIKOWSKI, GRIGORIEV, L. SOKOLOVA. Diaghilev commissioned the designs originally from BAKST but disliked and rejected them. His choice of Derain as the ideal designer marked an important step in bringing pure painting into the theatre. The period is the 1860s and the setting a sunny clime. One of Massine's happiest inventions, about a toyshop in which the dolls come to life during the night and next morning prevent the planned separation of two toy Can-Can dancers who have been sold to different customers (*see* COMPLETE BOOK). The ballet abounds in typically Massine cameo roles, ranging from the dazzling technique of the 'Snob' and the naughty

La Boutique Fantasque, as danced by the Diaghilev B. in London with IDZIKOWSKI as the Snob and LIFAR (left) as the Shopkeeper's Assistant

American boy to the stout and wealthy Russian merchant. Revived by Massine many times for many cos, incl. B. Russe de Monte Carlo, ABT, and RB. Massine has never been surpassed as the male Can-Can dancer. Among Lopukhova's successors A. DANILOVA was outstanding. The RB revival at CG, 27 Feb 1947, was a triumph for Massine, less so for the co. He revived it again for the RB touring co., Stratford upon Avon, 31 Jan 1968; dan. WELLS and EMBLEN (in the Can Can) with much greater success and the ballet, with its well-known score, became again a favourite with audiences. MC
See Cyril W. Beaumont, *The Diaghilev Ballet in London* (London 1940); Leonid Massine, *My Life in Ballet* (London and New York 1968)

Bovt, Violetta, b. Los Angeles, 1927. Soviet dancer. Her parents, Americans of Russian extraction, settled in the USSR in the 1930s. Studied Bolshoy TS 1935–44, graduating from class of Maria Kozhukhova. To Stanislavsky and Nemirovich-Danchenko TB 1944 as soloist; debut as Anne Page in BURMEISTER's *Merry Wives of Windsor*. A technically strong dancer, she was equally good in lyrical and dramatic roles, but especially notable as a heroic character such as Lola in Sergey Vasilenko's ballet of same title. Created ODETTE-ODILE in Burmeister's version of SWAN LAKE. Danced CRANKO's *pas de deux* for Tatyana and Onegin (ONEGIN) at her 'creative evening' with great success. Appeared with her co. in Paris, Milan, Tokyo, and elsewhere. People's Artist, USSR. NR
See G. Granovskaya, *Violetta Bovt* (Moscow 1972)

Bozzacchi, Giuseppina, b. Milan, 1853; d. Paris, 1870. Italian dancer. Early studies at Sc., then (thanks to the patronage of the ballerina Amina Boschetti) to the Paris O. where in 1869 she was chosen to create the role of SWANILDA which she did with great success in 1870 at the age of 16. She danced the role only 18 times, falling ill during the Siege of Paris in the Franco-Prussian war and dying on her 17th birthday. DELIBES played the organ at her funeral, which was attended by many of the artists who had worked with her at the O. MC
See Ivor Guest, *The Ballet of the Second Empire, 1858–1870* (London 1953) and *Two Coppelias* (London 1970)

Bradley, Buddy, b. Harrisburg, PA; d. New York, 1972. American choreographer. Began teaching at Billy Pierce's school in NY, staged musical numbers for Ziegfeld, George White, Earl Carroll, and for Lew Leslie's *Blackbirds*, with which he went to London. Remained in London, opening a successful school and staging numbers for revues produced by Charles B. Cochran and others, many of which had ballets by ASHTON, with whom he collaborated on a jazz ballet, *High Yellow*, for the CAMARGO SOCIETY, 1932. He worked with many American and British musical comedy stars. Returned to NY in the late 1960s. DV

Brazil. Although many Italian and French dancers visited Brazil in the 19th c., and others such as MASSINE and SEDOVA later went there especially to perform in opera seasons, it was not until 1927 that ballet in Brazil really made a start with the invitation to a former A. PAVLOVA dancer, Maria Olenewa, to organize a *corps de ballet* in the T. Municipal do Rio de Janeiro. As there were ballet schools already in existence, such as the one headed by Pierre Michailowsky and Vera Grabinska, Mme Olenewa did not take long to prepare a good Brazilian co. that soon was performing in all the opera seasons, and then, a few years later, giving complete ballet programs.

In 1934, a season was organized to reopen the remodelled T. Municipal, with LIFAR and three of his dancers as guest artists, and the newly formed *corps de ballet*. The co.'s first official season was in 1939 under the direction of the guest choreographer

Vaslav Veltchek. Guest artists were Juliana Yanakieva and Thomas Armour, from the OC, Paris. In 1943 Veltchek, who had been in São Paulo for three years organizing a co. there, returned to Rio to organize another season, this time exclusively with Brazilian artists. It was then that the talented choreographer Yuco Lindenberg appeared who later was given the direction of the co. In 1945 there was another important season, with SCHWEZOFF as artistic director, when the most famous Brazilian-born ballerinas appeared, including Edith Pudelko, ROSANOVA, Tamara Capeller, and Vilma Lemos Cunha.

After that the Rio ballet went through a period of decline and continued only thanks to the perseverance of Lindenberg, who many times promoted perfs, paying the dancers out of his own pocket so as to enable the co. to go on. He died in 1947 and VERCHININA replaced him but was not allowed a free hand in the running of the co.

In 1950, LESKOVA, who had left the B. Russe de Monte Carlo to stay in Brazil, was engaged as ballet mistress, choreographer, and dancer for the T. Municipal. She staged all the classics, invited in many choreographers like Massine, Vaslav Veltchek, DOLLAR, H. LANDER, Schwezoff, and Eugenia Feodorova, and promoted many ballet seasons for the co. in Rio.

The biggest problem with ballet in Brazil has always been the lack of continuity in the work and administrative difficulties within the government-subsidized theatre.

Outside the official theatre there have been a few private ballet cos and organized movements, e.g. B. da Juventude, founded 1947, under the direction of Schwezoff and Carlos Leite; B. Society, founded 1949, directed by Leskova; Conjunto Coreografico Brasileiro, a co. organized by Veltchek with children of 11 to 13 years old, founded 1947; B. do Rio de Janeiro, founded 1956 by ACHCAR, who had as its first guest artists Daphne Dale and Nicolas Polajenko, and then in 1960 arranged the first appearance in Brazil of FONTEYN and SOMES; Companhia Nacional de B., organized by Murillo Miranda in 1966 with Gloria Contreras and MITCHELL as artistic directors; Companhia Brasileira de B., set up by the shipping magnate Paulo Ferraz in 1968 with Mitchell as choreographer and teacher; and lately the Grupo Construção de Dança Teatral, directed by Gerry Maretsky, in the style of NIKOLAIS, in 1976.

In São Paulo ballet was first organized under the direction of Veltchek in 1940, creating a school and a *corps de ballet* for the T. Municipal. When Veltchek returned to Rio, Maria Olenewa went to São Paulo. After she left, Marilia Franco replaced her and is still in charge of the official ballet school.

Most important in the development of ballet in São Paulo was the foundation of the 4th Centenary B. Co., in 1953, under the direction of MILLOSS. The co. opened in Rio in 1954 performing a repertoire of Brazilian ballets, using themes, music, and scenery from the greatest contemporary artists.

The B. Stagium, founded and directed by Marika Gidali and Decio Otero, is the most important ballet co. in São Paulo, performing all over Brazil and in France and the USA, with a repertoire of Brazilian modern ballets.

There are also small ballet groups in other cities of Brazil such as Salvador, Belo Horizonte, Porto Alegre, Recife, Curitiba, and Fortaleza, all founded and maintained by pioneer teachers who are trying successfully to educate the populace towards a taste for classical dancing.

There have been various endeavours in the folklore field since 1930 by dance groups such as Eros Volusia, Felicitas, Mercedes Batista, and Brasiliana.

All the important international cos have visited Brazil and consequently greatly influenced the development of ballet there. Dancers from some of these cos have decided to stay in Brazil as teachers. Maria Olenewa and Maria Makarova have been the most influential teachers in the history of Brazilian ballet. MLN

Brenaa, Hans, b. Copenhagen, 1910. Danish dancer and producer. Entered RDBS 1919; soloist 1943. Debut 1928; danced in classical Danish and international repertory. Guest artist with various European cos; studied with EGOROVA in Paris, leading to his production of AURORA'S WEDDING for RDB 1949. Retired from dancing 1955; from then on specialized in producing August BOURNONVILLE's ballets in Denmark and elsewhere. Guest producer in Europe and USA in the 1960s and 1970s. SKJ

Bretus, Mária, b. Cegléd, 1943. Hungarian dancer. Graduated from State B. Institute 1960 and became soloist at Pécs NT. Studied in Leningrad under DUDINSKAYA 1968–9. A dynamic personality with a wide range of expression, she has danced all major roles in the Pécs repertoire, incl. *The Ballad of Horror* (1961), *Spider's Web* (1962), MIRACULOUS MANDARIN (1965), *Descent to Hell* (1968), *The Pawn Has Flown* (1971), *Sonata* (1972), SACRE DU PRINTEMPS (1972), *Faust Symphony* (1973), and *Monsieur Molière* (1975), all in ECK's choreography. Took part in all the co.'s tours abroad. Liszt Prize 1964, Merited Artist 1972. GPD

Breuer, Peter, b. Tegernsee, 1946. German dancer. Pupil of BLANK. Joined Munich B. 1961; to Düsseldorf 1963; soloist 1965. Guest artist, LFB, 1969–73; now permanent guest artist but retains links with Düsseldorf. Handsome and romantic, he dances all the major classical roles but also enjoys working in the contemporary idiom, for instance in ballets by WALTER and BÉJART. MC

Brianza, Carlotta, b. Milan, 1867; d. Paris, 1930. Italian dancer. Pupil of BLASIS. Not only a ballerina in Milan but also an influential guest artist in St Petersburg, bringing to that city her Italian virtuosity of technique and creating the role of AURORA. She toured the USA 1883. St Petersburg debut 1887 at the Arcadia T. (summer) followed by Maryinsky debut 1889 in TULIP OF HAARLEM. Left Russia 1891 to dance and then teach in Italy and Paris. Danced at Paris OC, 1903–4 in operas *Lakmé* and *Manon*, both choreographed by Mariquita. DIAGHILEV brought her out of retirement to appear as CARABOSSE in his 1921 production of *The Sleeping Princess* (*see* SLEEPING BEAUTY), a sentimental acknowledgment of ballet's debt to the Maryinsky and M. PETIPA. Little is known about her last years. MC

Brinson, Peter, b. Llandudno, 1923. Welsh writer and dance educator. Scriptwriter and Research Director, London Film Centre, 1948–53, at same time writing freelance on cinema and, increasingly, on dance. Wrote, organized, and appeared in the 3-D dance film *The Black Swan* 1952 and edited A. PAVLOVA film 1954. Contributor to *The Times* publications since 1952. Freelance 1953–64 working for TV cultural programs on dance subjects and writing a number of books (listed below). In 1964 founded the RB's B. For All, building, developing, and creating all its productions until appointed Director, UK and British Commonwealth Branch of the Calouste Gulbenkian Foundation of whose Dance Program he is chairman. (He continues to write B. For All's scripts.) Chairman of UK National Study of Dance Education and of Dance Panel, Council for National Academic Awards. Visiting lecturer and adjunct professor in dance, York Univ., Toronto, 1970–5. Brinson's concern throughout his career has been to win recognition of the importance of dance in academic circles. Author of *The Choreographic Art* (with VAN PRAAGH, London 1963), *The Polite World* (with Joan Wildeblood, London and New York 1965), *Background to European Ballet* (Leiden 1966), *Ballet for All* (with Clement Crisp, London 1970; new ed. Newton Abbot 1971). MC

Bristol Concert Ballet *see* REGIONAL BALLET (USA)

Britain. State recognition of dance and ballet in Britain came late – in 1939 with the founding of the Council for the Encouragement of Music and the Arts, now the Arts Council. Royal patronage was not granted until *after* a national ballet had been established. The pattern is very different from the rest of Europe where nearly every country had its royal theatre in which dance as well as drama and opera could flourish. At the court of King James I, the English masque reached its highest achievements but these were mainly in the writings of Ben Jonson and the designs of Inigo Jones; the dance content was slight. English dancers and dancing masters made important contributions in the 18th and 19th centuries and London became a centre of ballet, but everything was achieved without Royal bounty or state aid.

The first English name of significance in the history of ballet is WEAVER. SALLÉ appeared in London as a child 1716–17 and at CG 1734. Other French dancers who made ballet popular in London in the 18th c. – at the King's T. or Drury Lane – were A. VESTRIS and NOVERRE. (An English dancer, Simon Slingsby, in the 1780s, had achieved sufficient prowess to arouse the jealousy of Vestris and was probably the first English dancer to win fame at the Paris O.) DIDELOT was principal choreographer at the King's T. 1796–1800. During LUMLEY's association (1836–58) with the King's T., later renamed Her Majesty's, PERROT and all the famous ballerinas of the Romantic era worked and danced in London, to the delight of Queen Victoria. Later in the 19th c. ballet was found mostly in the music-hall theatres such as the Alhambra and the Empire, Leicester Square. Many fine dancers, notably GENÉE, appeared there. In 1911, preceded by other Russian dancers, such as PREOBRAZHENSKA, A. PAVLOVA, and KARSAVINA, who had danced in London with small groups, DIAGHILEV brought his B. Russes to CG. It had a devoted public in London until the end. Meanwhile English dancers were joining the troupes of both Diaghilev (L. SOKOLOVA was the first) and Pavlova and during the 1920s there were many attempts to establish a native co. These culminated in the work of RAMBERT, DE VALOIS, and the CAMARGO SOCIETY. Today the major cos are the ROYAL BALLET, BALLET RAMBERT, LONDON FESTIVAL BALLET, SCOTTISH BALLET, and the LONDON CONTEMPORARY DANCE THEATRE. There are several vocational schools offering academic tuition as well as dance and theatre training (in addition to the RBS) and a great many teachers of dancing, most of them members of the RAD, the Imperial Society of Teachers of Dancing, and other bodies that watch over standards.

London and other cities play host to visiting dance troupes from all over the world. The London audience prides itself on knowledgeability (especially in the classical field); many daily papers and periodicals regularly carry serious dance criticism. MC

Broadway, Dance on *see* MUSICALS

Bronze Horseman, The (*Medniy Vsadnik*), ballet, 4 acts and 10 scenes, ch. ZAKHAROV; mus. GLIÈRE; lib. Pyotr Abolimov; sc. Mikhail Bobyshov. Leningrad, Kirov T., 14 Mar 1949; dan. SERGEYEV (Evgeny), DUDINSKAYA (Parasha). Moscow, Bolshoy T., same choreography, 27 Mar 1949; dan. GABOVICH and ULANOVA. Based on Aleksandr Pushkin's poem of the same title about a poor petty official bereft of his beloved during the 1824 flood at St Petersburg. Evgeny loses his reason and believes that the famous Falconet statue of Peter the Great is pursuing him. The decor recreated old St Petersburg. NR
See N. Roslavleva, 'How a Ballet is Made' in *Ballet Today*, Nos 22, 23 (Moscow 1950); Rostislav Zakharov, *Iskusstvo Baletmeistera* (*The Choreographer's Art*) (Moscow 1954)

Brown [Rice], Carolyn, b. Fitchburg, MA, 1927. American dancer and choreographer. Principal dancer with CUNNINGHAM Dance Co. 1953–73, during which time she danced in 40 Cunningham works. One of the finest dancers of her generation, notable for her effortless technique, purity of line, and exquisite phrasing. She also created a role in CAGE's *Theatre Piece* (1960) and, on *pointe*, in Robert Rauschenberg's first dance work, *Pelican* (1963). Her own choreographic works incl. *Balloon* for the 1st New York T. Rally (1965); *Car Lot* for Manhattan Fest. B. (1968); *As I Remember It*, a solo in homage to SHAWN, performed by the choreographer at Jacob's Pillow (1972); *Bunkered for a Bogie* for Among Co. (1972); *Port de Bras for Referees* for New England Dinosaur (1973); and *House Party* for Among Co. (1973–4). She is the author of several articles on dance. DV

Brown, Trisha, b. Aberdeen, WA, 1936. American dancer and choreographer. Received BA in Dance from Mills College, Oakland, CA. A founding member of Judson Dance T. 1962, and of Grand Union, an improvisational dance co., 1970. Formed her own co. 1970. Her work incl. experiments in 'anti-gravity and ordinary movement in extraordinary circumstances'. *See* AVANT-GARDE DANCE. DV

Bruce, Christopher, b. Leicester, 1945. English dancer and choreographer. Trained at the RAMBERT S. and joined BR 1963. When the co. re-formed in 1966 he danced Pierrot in PIERROT LUNAIRE and made an instant impression as a dancer of immense dramatic as well as physical gifts. Created many roles in the co.'s new repertory and choreographed *There Was a Time,* FOR THOSE WHO DIE AS CATTLE, *Ancient Voices of Children*, and many other works. His ballet *Wings,* made for Tanz Forum in Cologne, was later mounted by Rambert and staged in Basel. *There Was a Time* is also in the Munich B. repertory. In 1974 he created his first work for the London RB, *Unfamiliar Playground.* He was awarded the first *Evening Standard* Ballet Award in 1974 for his contribution as both performer and creator. MC

Bruel, Michel, b. Sète, 1941. French dancer. Studied with LAZZINI. Marseille OB 1958–64; *étoile* 1960–4. Then guest artist, notably the partner of HIGHTOWER, VYROUBOVA, Sonia Arova, and SOMBERT, after which he joined Lazzini's T. Français de la Danse 1969, and B. du Rhin 1972. Danced with ALONSO in SWAN LAKE 1970. A good partner, attracted by the contemporary repertory. M-FC

Bruhn, Erik, b. Copenhagen, 1928. Danish dancer. Studied at RDBS, joined co. 1947. Danced in London with the Metropolitan B. 1947; continued to perform as guest artist with many cos, especially ABT (from 1949 to the present), NYCB, RB, Australian B., RSB, NB of Canada, etc. One of the great male dancers of his generation, he was the partner, while with ABT, first of MARKOVA, then of FRACCI. His perfs in such ballets as MISS JULIE and CARMEN were remarkable for the strength and subtlety of their characterization. Director of RSB 1967–72, then temporarily retired from dancing. For NB of Canada staged August BOURNONVILLE's SYLPHIDE (1964), and his own versions of SWAN LAKE (1966), and COPPÉLIA (1975), having been appointed artistic adviser to the co. Returned to the stage first in such roles as MADGE and DR COPPÉLIUS, then with ABT, 1975–6, danced Abdul-rakhman (Abdérâne) in NUREYEV's RAYMONDA, Claudius in NEUMEIER's *Hamlet-Connotations*, The Man She Must Marry in

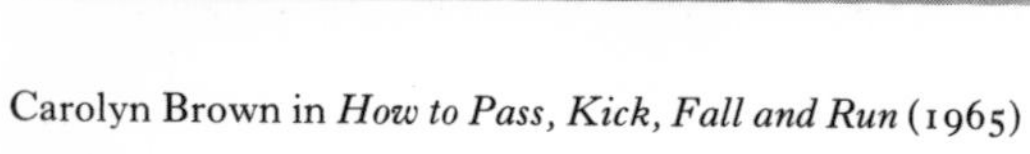

Carolyn Brown in *How to Pass, Kick, Fall and Run* (1965)

Erik Bruhn as James in SYLPHIDE

JARDIN AUX LILAS, PETRUSHKA, etc. Author of *Bournonville and Ballet Technique* (with MOORE, London and New York 1961), and 'Beyond Technique', *Dance Perspectives,* No. 36 (New York 1968). DV
See I. Lidova, 'Erik Bruhn', *Les Saisons de la Danse* (Paris, Oct 1969) with list of roles

Buckle, Richard, b. Warcop, Westmorland, 1916. English writer, critic, and organizer of exhibitions. His addiction to ballet began in 1933 when he read Romola Nijinsky's biography of her husband and the first ballet he saw was GISELLE with MARKOVA at SW. In 1939 he founded his own magazine, *Ballet*, of which two numbers were published before World War II. After war service Buckle restarted the magazine in 1946 and continued to edit it until it was forced into liquidation in 1952. The magazine had an enormous influence and formed the taste of the ballet public. Buckle used the finest writers, photographers, and artists, and enlivened the magazine through the ebullience of his own personality – adventurous, cultured, and witty. Ballet critic of the *Observer* newspaper 1948–55 and of the *Sunday Times* (Who's Who) 1959–75. In 1954, to commemorate the 25th anniversary of DIAGHILEV's death, he organized an exhibition, first at the Edinburgh Fest., then in London, which was innovatory in that he employed a group of artists to design each section. He subsequently wrote a book about it, *In Search of Diaghilev* (London 1955; New York 1956). His other great exhibition was on Shakespeare, at Stratford upon Avon, 1964, to mark the 400th anniversary the poet's birth. His method, 'assailing the visitors' senses, using light, sound, changing scales and levels, smell and surprise' and again employing a galaxy of artists to work with him, was on a Diaghilevian scale. His books incl. *Modern Ballet Design* (London and New York 1955); the editing of L. SOKOLOVA's memoirs *Dancing for Diaghilev* (London 1960; New York 1961), the monumental *Nijinsky* (London and New York 1971) and *Diaghilev* (London and New York 1977). MC
See autobiography: *The Adventures of a Ballet Critic* (London 1953)

Bugaku, ballet, ch. BALANCHINE; mus. Toshiro Mayuzumi; sc./ltg David Hays; c. (Barbara) Karinska. NYCC, NYCB, 30 Mar 1963; dan. KENT, VILLELLA. Revived DTH 1975; dan. ABARCA, PERRY. A dance to music in the style of *Bugaku*, the Japanese court music, the ballet celebrates the love of a young couple in ritual fashion. FM

Bujones, Fernando, b. Miami, FL, 1955. American dancer of Cuban parentage. Studied with ALONSO in Havana and at SAB. Danced with EGLEVSKY B. before joining ABT 1972. Gold Medal, Varna Competition 1974. Dances leading roles in both classical and modern ballets, incl. SWAN LAKE, BAYADÈRE, UNDERTOW, and FANCY FREE. DV

Burmeister, Vladimir, b. Vitebsk, 1904; d. Moscow, 1971. Soviet dancer and choreographer. Son of TCHAIKOVSKY's grandniece. Studied ballet department, Lunacharsky T. Technicum 1925–9 and at the same time made professional appearances. From 1930 in Moscow Art T. of B., headed by KRIGER, which merged with Stanislavsky and Nemirovich-Danchenko Lyric T. Artistic director of ballet, Stanislavsky and Nemirovich-Danchenko T. 1941–60, 1963–71. Choreographed *The Merry Wives of Windsor* (mus. Viktor Oransky and Ivan Kurilov, 1942), *Lola* (mus. Sergey Vasilenko, 1943), *Esmeralda* (1950), *Jeanne d'Arc* (mus. Nikolay Peiko, 1957), etc. His most important staging is SWAN LAKE (1953) to Tchaikovsky's autograph score (but with Act II intact as by IVANOV) and prologue to main swan theme, shown at Paris O. 1956 on the first tour of an entire Soviet ballet co. Choreographed this version at Paris O. (with Act II by himself) 1960, SNOW MAIDEN for LFB 1961, repeating it for Stanislavsky B. 1963. Always interested in *plastique* as means of expression, he choreographed dances to Sergey Rakhmaninov's and GLAZUNOV's music for the I. DUNCAN Studio in Moscow (1946–7), using Duncan barefoot dance idiom. People's Artist, RSFSR. He m. dancer Antonina Krupenina. NR

Burra, Edward, b. London, 1905; d. Rye, Sussex, 1976. English painter of landscapes, figure and still lifes in watercolour, frequently on a large scale and with macabre overtones. Designed *Rio Grande* (ch. ASHTON) 1931, *Barabau* (DE VALOIS) 1936, MIRACLE IN THE GORBALS, *Don Juan* (Ashton) 1948 and DON QUIXOTE (de Valois) 1950; David Paltenghi's *Canterbury Prologue* 1951. CBE 1971. MC

Butler, John, b. Memphis, TN, 1920. American dancer and choreographer. Trained at GRAHAM S. and SAB. Member of Graham co. 1945–55, also dancing in musicals and TV. Choreography for Gian-Carlo Menotti's opera *The Consul* (Philadelphia and New York 1950). Founded his own co. 1955 and took it to Spoleto but disbanded it after a few years to freelance. Choreographed world premiere of Menotti's *The Unicorn, the Gorgon and the Manticore* (1957), later taken into repertory of NYCB. Dance director, Spoleto Fest. 1958 where his own co. presented several new works, again in 1959. Choreographed CARMINA BURANA for NYC O. Co. 1959 and for NDT 1962, and Pennsylvania B. 1966. For NDT also choreographed his version of Menotti's *Sebastian,* 22 Oct 1963, and staged it for HARKNESS B. 1966. His *Portrait of Billie* (choreographed for DE LAVALLADE and himself, 1961) was taken into the AILEY Co.'s repertory 1974. Choreographed *pas de deux, Medea,* for FRACCI and BARYSHNIKOV, Spoleto 1975; taken into ABT repertory 1976. Choreographer of many TV and ice shows. His blending of contemporary and classic styles and strong sense of theatre have brought him success not only in the USA and Europe but also with the Australian B. MC

C

Cadzow, Joan, b. Melbourne, 1929. Australian dancer. Studied Melbourne; to London on scholarship from RAD 1948. Studied at RBS; joined SWTB 1949. To Paris 1952 and danced in recitals with CHAUVIRÉ and joined B. de l'Étoile there 1954–5. Became member of T. GSOVSKY's Berliner Ballett and also danced with the Dutch NB. Ballerina of the ballets in Frankfurt and W. Berlin simultaneously 1960–6 (under T. Gsovsky) and from 1966 the ballerina of the Deutsche O. am Rhein at Düsseldorf, dancing the chief roles in SWAN LAKE, GISELLE, SLEEPING BEAUTY, etc. Guest ballerina of many European opera houses. A fine exponent of the English school of classical dancing, with a pure line and impressive personality. GBLW

La Camargo, painting by Nicolas Lancret in an imaginary fanciful setting. The painting does, however, depict the charm of her costume and the shortened skirt which revealed her pretty ankles.

Cage, The, ballet, 1 act, ch. ROBBINS; mus. STRAVINSKY; c. Ruth Sobotka; ltg ROSENTHAL. NYCC, NYCB, 14 June 1951; dan. KAYE, Yvonne Mounsey, MAGALLANES, Michael Maule. A group of vicious and steely-legged insect women induct a novice into the rites of mating and mate-slaying. FM/DJ

Cage, John, b. Los Angeles, CA, 1912. American composer, student of Henry Cowell and Arnold Schönberg, who has made a radical break with the course of Western music by discarding such elements as harmony, received structures and traditional instrumentation in favour of electronic sounds, tape, chance methods, indeterminacy – a never-ending succession of experiments. In 1942 Cage began his long, fruitful association with CUNNINGHAM, with whom he evolved a new and influential aesthetic, in which dance and music are independent though simultaneous entities. Cage has also written for other choreographers, especially Jean Erdman (e.g., *Daughters of the Lonesome Isle,* 1945). Van MANEN has used his music: *Solo for Voice I* (1968) and *The Perilous Night* for TWILIGHT. DH
See 'John Cage' in a Symposium on Composer/Choreographer, *Dance Perspectives*, No. 16 (New York 1963)

Camargo, Marie-Anne de Cupis de, b. Brussels, 1710; d. Paris, 1770. French dancer. Daughter and pupil of Ferdinand Joseph de Cupis, Italian aristocrat who was dancing master in Brussels, Camargo became the first ballerina of the Paris O. to develop a dazzling technique. A child prodigy, she went to Paris at 10, accompanied by her father, for a season of special classes with Françoise Prévost and then joined the Brussels O. She adopted her maternal grandmother's name for her debut at the Paris O., 5 May 1726, in *Les Caractères de la Danse*, an occasion that created a sensation, as did her sudden improvised solo one night when a male dancer failed to appear for his *entrée*. In autumn 1727 began the celebrated rivalry with SALLÉ which lasted eight years, with journalists and public making great cause of Camargo's brilliant technique versus Sallé's poetic grace. Her lover,

Louis de Bourbon, Comte de Clermont, in 1735 persuaded her to retire to a country château during his absence at the front as Lieutenant-General of the King's armies. She returned to the stage in 1741 and, except for the brief appearances of Marianne Cochois (Sallé's cousin) and Barbara Campanini, she remained for another 10 years the undisputed star of the Paris O., featured in 78 ballets there and at court. Her dancing was admired by Voltaire and NOVERRE. She added to her fame by shortening her skirts (to just above the ankle) so that the public could observe her technical feats (she was the first woman to perform the *entrechat quatre*). She was portrayed by leading painters, incl. Nicolas Lancret, Jean-Marc Nattier, and Maurice-Quentin de LaTour; M. PETIPA, in 1872, choreographed *Camargo* in her honour; and in the 20th c. her name was given to the CAMARGO SOCIETY as well as to several dishes created by the great French chef Escoffier. PME
See Parmenia Migel, *The Ballerinas from the Court of Louis XIV to Pavlova* (New York 1972)

Camargo Society, The, 'for the production of ballet', was formed in London in 1930, partly to fill the gap left by the disbanding of the B. Russes after DIAGHILEV's death, and, more important, to play a part in the establishment of British ballet, by encouraging native dancers and choreographers. The project was initially planned by HASKELL and RICHARDSON; the chairman was Edwin Evans and the secretary M. Montagu-Nathan, and there were committees dealing with the various component arts of ballet, headed by such people as L. LOPUKHOVA (Choreography), Haskell (Art), Evans (Music). Many leaders of fashionable and intellectual society were among the subscribers. The first perf. took place on 19 Oct 1930, when the program incl. DE VALOIS's *Danse Sacrée et Danse Profane* and ASHTON's *Pomona*. At subsequent perfs there were further new ballets by both choreographers, incl. de Valois's *La Création du Monde* and JOB, and Ashton's FAÇADE, *The Lord of Burleigh, Rio Grande*, and *High Yellow* (in collaboration with BRADLEY), as well as revivals of GISELLE and SWAN LAKE Act II. Guest artists included Lopukhova, LUDMILA, MARKOVA, SPESSIVTSEVA, and DOLIN. The directors followed Diaghilev's principles of artistic collaboration, commissioning decors and drop curtains from distinguished painters of the day such as John Armstrong, Vanessa Bell, BURRA, Edmond Dulac, Duncan Grant, and Augustus John, who was to have designed *Pomona* (he was unable to fulfil the commission, and the ballet was designed by John Banting). In 1932 the Society gave a two-week season at the Savoy T. and in 1933 two gala perfs at CG, but thereafter its activities came to an end and the small funds remaining, and many of the ballets that had been created, were handed over to the Vic-Wells B. DV

Canada, National Ballet of, Toronto-based co. but tours Canada extensively. Founded 1951 by FRANCA on the recommendation of DE VALOIS, and subsidized by the Canada Council and the Ontario Arts Council. Artistic directors have been Franca (1951–74), David Haber (1974), and GRANT (from July 1976); music director and conductor since 1951, George Crum; ballet mistress, OLIPHANT, more recently Joanne Nisbet (since 1962) and ballet master David Scott (since 1963); resident producer, BRUHN. The co. now numbers over 60 dancers, principals being Vanessa Harwood, Mary Jago, KAIN, Nadia Potts, TENNANT, Frank Augustyn, Stephen Jefferies, Tomas Schramek, Sergiu Stefanschi, and Hazaros Surmeyan. Most co. dancers have trained at the NBS, founded 1959 by Franca and Oliphant (still its director and principal); consequently the co. has a distinctive and somewhat eclectic style, combining an English precision in legs and feet with a more ample Russian-inspired upper body and arms.

Guided from its beginnings by Franca's insistence on the classics as a necessary basis for any ballet repertoire, the co. mounts the major full-length ballets, often in updated versions: the Franca–M. PETIPA NUTCRACKER (1964), the Bruhn–August BOURNONVILLE SYLPHIDE (1964), Bruhn's controversial SWAN LAKE (1966), Peter Wright's GISELLE (1970), the NUREYEV–Petipa SLEEPING BEAUTY (1973), Bruhn's COPPÉLIA (1975). The development of a Canadian contemporary repertoire has also been stressed. Frequent choreographic workshops are presented to encourage and identify co. talent, and several promising Canadian choreographers are emerging. Other contemporary works offered incl. CRANKO's ROMEO AND JULIET; PETIT's *Kraanerg* (commissioned by the co.) and LOUP; KETTENTANZ; NEUMEIER's *Don Juan*; and FILLE MAL GARDÉE. In recent years the co. has toured widely in N. America, Europe, and Japan, establishing an international reputation. Guest artists have incl. SEYMOUR, FARRELL, MARTINS, MADSEN, KEHLET, BUJONES, and BARYSHNIKOV. Associated with the co. on a continuing basis have been Bruhn and Nureyev, whose impact on the co.'s dancers, repertoire, and reputation has been considerable. The co. has also made films for TV, produced by Norman Campbell: *Romeo and Juliet* (Prix René Barthélémy 1966), Franca's *Cinderella* (Emmy Award 1970), and *Sleeping Beauty* (Emmy Award 1973). PD
For other Canadian cos *see* GRANDS BALLETS CANADIENS, ROYAL WINNIPEG BALLET

Canfield, modern dance work, ch. CUNNINGHAM; mus. Pauline Oliveros; sc. Robert Morris. Rochester, NY, Nazareth College, 4 Mar 1969; dan. Cunningham, C. BROWN, Sandra Neels, SETTERFIELD, HARPER, HAYMAN-CHAFFEY, SLAYTON, Chase Robinson, Mel Wong. The full-length work is a *tour de force* of energy exchanges, fragmentary alliances, and brilliant ensemble work. DM

CAPAB Ballet Co., founded in Cape Town, S. Africa, in 1963 through an agreement between the

Cape Performing Arts Board, the Univ. of Cape Town B. co., and the HOWES Trust; the first professional ballet co. in Cape Town, and, founded on the non-professional UCT BALLET CO., the oldest co. in S. Africa. Apart from touring extensively through S. Africa, Rhodesia, and Namibia (SW Africa), the 60-strong co., led by SPIRA, performs four seasons a year in Cape Town, four in the large Nico Malan OH, and one in Maynardville open-air theatre. Administration and rehearsal premises are shared with the UCTBS.

The co. has in its repertoire the main classics as well as ballets by CRANKO, RODRIGUES, STAFF, POOLE, DE VALOIS, August BOURNONVILLE, JOOSS, and many others. Guest artists incl. FONTEYN, LABIS, VLASSI, BORTOLUZZI, and FRACCI. The two main designers have been Stephen de Villiers and Peter Cazalet. Resident choreographers have been Gary Burne, Staff, and Veronica Paeper. The first director was Howes, succeeded by Poole 1969. MG

Caprices de Cupidon *see* WHIMS OF CUPID

Carabosse, the wicked fairy of SLEEPING BEAUTY

Caracole *see* DIVERTIMENTO NO. 15

Card Game (*Card Party*; *Jeu de Cartes*), ballet, 3 'deals', ch. BALANCHINE; mus. STRAVINSKY; lib. Stravinsky and M. Malaiev; sc./c. Irene Sharaff. As *Card Party*, NY Met, American B., 27 Apr 1937; dan. DOLLAR (the Joker). The music was commissioned for Balanchine; Stravinsky, a keen poker player, wrote it as a balletic joke upon the irruptions of the Joker into the game. Revived as *Poker Game*, B. Russe de Monte Carlo, 1940; dan. FRANKLIN; revised version NYCC, NYCB, 15 Feb 1951; dan. BOLENDER.

New version (*Jeu de Cartes*) ch. CHARRAT, sc./c. Jean Hugo, Paris, T. des CE, B. des CE, 12 Oct 1945; dan. BABILÉE; new version ch. CRANKO; sc./c. Dorothea Zippel. Stuttgart, Stuttgart B., 22 Jan 1965; dan. MADSEN. Revived London, CG, RB, 18 Feb 1966; dan. GABLE. MC

Cardús, Ana, b. Mexico City, 1941. Mexican dancer. First danced with B. Concierto de México 1956; became soloist of de Cuevas B. 1960. Joint principal (with HAYDÉE) of Stuttgart B. 1962–7, creating Olga in ONEGIN. Ballerina of Cologne B. 1967–71. Danced in Italy 1971–2 and joined Hanover B. 1974 as principal. GBLW

Carmen, (1) ballet, 5 scenes, ch. PETIT; mus. Georges Bizet; sc./c. Antoni Clavé. London, Prince's (now Shaftesbury) T., B. de Paris, 21 Feb 1949; dan. JEANMAIRE, Petit, PERRAULT. The ballet is based on Bizet's opera and the music mangled from his score. Undeniably effective theatre, the first perf. caused a sensation. Clavé's brilliantly simple settings and audacious costumes combined with Petit's sometimes erotic choreography won glowing notices even from those who resisted the musical arrangement. Petit created Don José, Perrault the conceited (and very funny) Escamillo. The ballet has been preserved on film (*Black Tights*, 1960) and is in the repertory of the RDB, revived Copenhagen, 15 Jan 1960, dan. SIMONE, F. FLINDT, KRONSTAM.

(2) ballet, ch./lib. CRANKO; mus. Bizet arr. Wolfgang Fortner and W. Steinbrenner. Stuttgart, Staats T., 28 Feb 1971; dan. HAYDÉE. Cranko's program note said he was 'fascinated by the destiny and suffering of a woman from an outlawed community living in a society hidebound by convention. Carmen is a gypsy and everyone else is Spanish. I see her relationship with Don José as her way of showing revenge toward a society into which it is her wish to be accepted . . .'. Other choreographers have used this story, incl. M. PETIPA, GOLEIZOVSKY, PAGE, and Alberto Alonso. MC

Carmina Burana, ballet, ch. Inge Hertling, mus. Carl Orff's cantata of the same name; sc. Ludwig Sievert. Frankfurt, 8 June 1937. A chorus (on or off stage) sings the bawdy, medieval dog-Latin lyrics, while the dancers act them on stage. Other choreographers have been Lizzie Maudrik (Berlin, Staats O., 1941), HANKA (Milan 1942), WIGMAN (Leipzig 1943), H. ROSEN (Bavarian Staats O., 1959), BUTLER (NY City OB 1959; revived NDT 1962, Pennsylvania B. 1966, AILEY CC Dance T. 1973); DARRELL (W. Berlin, Deutsche O., 1968), and Gerhard Bohner (Cologne 1970). GBLW

Carnaval, Le, ballet, 1 act, ch./lib. FOKINE; mus. Robert Schumann's piano pieces of the same name, orch. GLAZUNOV, Nikolay Rimsky-Korsakov, Anatole Lyadov, Aleksandr Tcherepnin; sc./c. BAKST. St Petersburg, Pavlov Hall, 5 Mar 1910, at a charity ball, with dancers from the Imperial B. (who had to appear anonymously because of Maryinsky regulations) and the actor-director Vsevolod Meyerhold as Pierrot. First staged (in the form now known) Berlin, T. des Westens, DIAGHILEV's B. Russes, 20 May 1910; dan. L. LOPUKHOVA, Leonid Leontiev. A charming series of dances by Columbine, Harlequin, the hapless Pierrot, dreamy Chiarina, and fluttering Papillon, in a simple setting and costumes suggesting the Viennese Biedermeyer period of 1840. In Paris and London KARSAVINA and NIJINSKY danced Columbine and Harlequin; BOLM was a fine Pierrot. Repeatedly revived, the ballet pleases mildly but has lost the enchantment of the first staging. MC *See* Richard Buckle, *Nijinsky* (London and New York 1971)

Caroline, the heroine of JARDIN AUX LILAS

Caron, Leslie, b. Paris, 1931. French dancer and actress. Studied Paris Cons. with Jane Schwartz. Joined B. des CE 1948. Created principal roles in LICHINE's *La Rencontre* and *La Création*. Appeared

Left: Carmen, as staged by the B. de Paris (1949) with JEANMAIRE as Carmen, PETIT as Don José and HAMILTON as a thief; sc./c. CLAVÉ

Below: Le Carnaval, as revived by the SWB in the original set and costumes by BAKST; M. SHEARER as Chiarina

in Vincente Minnelli's film *An American in Paris*, with Gene Kelly (1951) and in Charles Walters's *Lili* (1953). Joined B. de Paris and danced PETIT's *Belle au Bois Dormant* (1954). Returned to Hollywood; appeared in more films, notably *Daddy Long Legs* (dir. Jean Negulesco) opposite ASTAIRE (1954), *Gigi* (dir. Minnelli, 1958), *Fanny* (dir. Joshua Logan, 1961). She eventually gave up dancing for an acting career both on stage and in films. DV/M-FC

Carter, Alan, b. London, 1920. English dancer and choreographer. Studied ASTAFYEVA, LEGAT, and Conti S., London, joined Vic-Wells B. 1937, soloist 1938–41 creating principal role in ASHTON's *Harlequin in the Street* (1938). After World War II service, returned to SWTB and choreographed *The Catch* (1946). Ballet master for films *The Red Shoes* (1948, dir. Michael Powell), *Tales of Hoffmann* (1951, dir. Powell), and *Invitation to the Dance* (1953, dir. Gene Kelly). Directed the St James's B., London 1948–50 and was ballet master at the Empire Cinema, London, 1951–3. Director of Munich B. 1954–9; choreographed new versions of MIRACULOUS MANDARIN, PRINCE OF THE PAGODAS, and ONDINE. Subsequently worked in Wuppertal, Istanbul, Helsinki, and Iceland. In 1976 became artistic co-director (with Felicity Gray) at Elmhurst BS, Camberley, Surrey. He m. dancer Julia Murthwaite. MC

Carter, Jack, b. Shrivenham, Berkshire, 1923. English choreographer. Studied SWBS, VOLKOVA, and Anna Northcote, and with PREOBRAZHENSKA in Paris. Danced with LAKE's co., Original B. Russe, BR, and LFB. In Amsterdam 1954–7 working with B. der Lage Landen for whom he did much choreography, notably his best-known work, WITCH BOY. Staged full-length SWAN LAKE at T. Colón, Buenos Aires, 28 May 1963, using complete score of 1877 Moscow creation. Resident choreographer LFB 1966–70, mounting *Swan Lake* 1966 and COPPÉLIA 1968. For

Western TB choreographed *Cage of God* (1967; mus. Alan Rawsthorne), subsequently staged by Cologne B. and B. van Vlaanderen (B. of Flanders), Antwerp. Worked for some years in Japan and on return to England choreographed *Three Dances to Japanese Music* (1973) for Scottish B. and *Shukumei* (1975) for RB. Also for RB, *Lulu* (1976), based on the play by Frank Wedekind. MC

Carter, William, b. Durante, OK. American dancer. Studied with MARACCI, later at SAB; also Spanish dance with Manolo Vargas. Danced with ABT 1957–9, NYCB 1959–61 (created role in LIEBESLIEDER WALZER, opposite D. ADAMS). Co-founder of First Chamber Dance Quartet 1961. Returned to ABT 1969. A rare example of a dancer equally at home in ballet and modern dance, he divides his time between ABT and, since 1972, the GRAHAM Dance Co., dancing leading roles in most of her repertory. Has also danced as guest artist with Maria Alba's Spanish B. and in P. LANG's *The Possessed* (1975). DV

Carzou, Jean, b. Aleppo, 1907. French theatrical designer. His first work for ballet was the Inca scene in the 1952 revival of INDES GALANTES. His half-romantic, half-fantastic style is typified by his use of spike-like patterns. His forest setting for LOUP was a sensational piece of design. He later designed GISELLE for the Paris O. in 1954, breaking away from convention but producing designs of startling beauty. MC

Casado, Germinal, b. Casablanca, 1934. French-Spanish dancer and designer. Studied with Nicholas Zverev and V. GSOVSKY. Wuppertal B., de Cuevas B., B.-T. de BÉJART; B. XXe S. 1960. Created roles in Béjart's *Orphée*, *Violetta*, SACRE DU PRINTEMPS, *Suite Viennoise*, *À la Recherche de Don Juan*, *Mathilde*, NINTH SYMPHONY, *Cygne*, *Roméo et Juliette* (Tybalt), *Bhakti*. Notable designs incl. decor for Béjart's *Contes d'Hoffmann*, *Bhakti*, etc. at T. Royal de la Monnaie, Brussels, and at the Paris O. DAMNATION DE FAUST and *Renard*, and at the Odéon *La Tentation de Saint-Antoine*. Artist gifted with a powerful dramatic personality. From early 1970s freelance director of plays and musicals. M-FC

Casse Noisette *see* NUTCRACKER

Catarina, ou La Fille du Bandit (*Caterina, or the Bandit's Daughter*), ballet, 3 acts and 5 scenes, ch./lib. PERROT; mus. PUGNI; sc. Charles Marshall. London, Her Majesty's T., 3 Mar 1846; dan. GRAHN, Perrot. Staged Milan Sc., 9 Jan 1847; dan. ELSSLER, and St Petersburg, 16 Nov 1849, also with Elssler. The ballet had an extremely involved plot (*see* COMPLETE BOOK) but provided a brilliant and effective role for the ballerina as the youthful leader of a band of robbers. The story is said to be based on an incident in the life of the Italian painter Salvator Rosa (1615–73). It remained popular in Russia for many years and was a favourite vehicle with ballerinas throughout the 19th c. MC

Catulli Carmina, ballet, ch. T. GSOVSKY; mus. Carl Orff's cantata of the same name; sc. Max Elten; c. Helene Schmidt. Leipzig, 6 Nov 1943. To the lyrics of Catullus. Later versions ch. WIGMAN (1955), HANKA (1957), H. ROSEN (1959), BUTLER (1964), DARRELL (1968), and Gerhard Bohner (1970). GBLW

Cecchetti, Enrico, b. Rome (in a theatre), 1850; d. Milan, 1928. Italian dancer, son of two dancers, and one of the greatest teachers in ballet history. Studied with LEPRI in Florence. First stage appearance at age 5 in Genoa. Debut Milan Sc. 1870, then toured Europe as *premier danseur*; St Petersburg debut 1887. His brilliant technique amazed the Russians and occasioned his appointment in 1890 as second ballet master to the Imperial Ts and in 1892 as instructor at the Imperial S. Created roles of BLUEBIRD and CARABOSSE, testimony to his virtuosity and mimetic gifts. While at the Maryinsky T. he created some choreography, notably refurbishing COPPÉLIA in 1894, but his chief claim to fame lies in his extraordinary gifts as a teacher: his pupils incl. A. PAVLOVA, KARSAVINA, NIJINSKY. Ballet master, Imperial S., Warsaw, 1902; in 1905 returned to Italy, then to Russia, opening a private school in St Petersburg and devoting much time to private work with Pavlova. In 1909 he became the official teacher for DIAGHILEV's B. Russes and created roles with that co., notably the Charlatan in PETRUSHKA and the Astrologer in COQ D'OR. In 1918 he and his wife Giuseppina opened a school in London where his pupils incl. nearly every famous dancer of the time. He returned to Italy in 1923; became ballet master at Milan Sc. in 1925, continuing to give occasional classes to the Diaghilev B. During the run of the Diaghilev *Sleeping Princess* in London, he celebrated his golden jubilee on the stage by performing the role of Carabosse for one performance and made his last stage appearance in 1926 as the Charlatan in *Petrushka* in Milan. In London C. BEAUMONT initiated the formation of a Cecchetti Society in 1922 to perpetuate his teaching methods. At Beaumont's instigation *A Manual of the Theory and Practice of Classical Theatrical Dancing – méthode Cecchetti* (London 1922; rev. ed. 1940; New York 1975) was published, in which Beaumont collaborated with IDZIKOWSKI. MC/CC
See C. W. Beaumont, *Enrico Cecchetti* (London 1929); V. Celli, 'Enrico Cecchetti', *Dance Index*, Vol. 5, No. 7 (New York, 1946); 'Letters from the Maestro: Enrico Cecchetti to Gisella Caccialanza', *Dance Perspectives*, No. 45 (New York, July 1946)

Cell, ballet, 1 act, ch. COHAN, mus. Ronald Lloyd; sc. Norberto Chiesa. London, The Place, 11 Sept 1969. An abstract treatment of the theme of society's hemming in of the individual. Its six dancers move within an area enclosed by walls; a man apparently dead is subjected to the intrusion of press photographers; at the end the hero is seen trying to demolish a wall in a flickering strobe light. Created for the opening season of LCDT with Robert POWELL in the leading part, in the repertory ever since – one of the group's strongest dramatic works. JP

Cendrillon *see* CINDERELLA

Central European Style *see* MODERN DANCE

Cerrito, Fanny, b. Naples, 1817; d. Paris, 1909. Italian ballerina and choreographer of the Romantic period. Debut 1832, T. del Fondo, Naples, in Giovanni Galzerani's *L'Oroscopo*. She quickly gained a reputation in Italy and Austria, and in 1838 first danced at Sc., where she came to the notice of BLASIS, who described her as '*la volupté ingénue*'. Engaged at Her Majesty's T., London 1840, where she danced for many seasons and became a special favourite. Her creations in London incl. Antonio Guerra's *Le Lac des Fées* (1840), *Alma* (1842), a joint production by André-Jean-Jacques Deshayes, PERROT, and herself with, as its highlight, the *pas de fascination*; and among the ballets by Perrot, ONDINE (1843), *Lalla Rookh* (1846), and all four of his multi-star *divertissements*. She m. SAINT-LÉON 1845, her regular partner since 1843. Both were engaged at the Paris O. 1847, appearing in a series of ballets choreographed by Saint-Léon. The marriage and the partnership broke up in 1851 when Cerrito became the mistress of the Marques de Bedmar, by whom she had a daughter.

She remained at the O. until 1854, creating the title roles in MAZILIER's *Orfa* (1852) and her own ballet, *Gemma* (1854; lib. GAUTIER; mus. Nicolò Gabrielli). She was engaged in Russia for the seasons of 1855–6 and 1856–7, appearing in Perrot's *Armida* (1855) at the Bolshoy T., St Petersburg, and taking part in the celebrations organized for Alexander II's coronation in Moscow in 1856. During a perf. in Moscow she was struck by a piece of falling scenery, an accident said to have been a factor in her decision to retire. She appeared at CG 1855, and 1856–7 at the Lyceum T., where the Royal Italian O. had taken refuge after CG had been destroyed by fire. Retired 1857. Died in Paris within a few days of the opening of the first season in that city of the DIAGHILEV B. Russes 1909. IG

See Ivor Guest, *Fanny Cerrito* (London 1956; rev. ed. London 1974)

Chabukiani, Vakhtang, b. Tbilisi [Tiflis], 1910. Soviet *premier danseur* and choreographer. Born into a large, poor family, he began making toys at the age of nine. When he delivered some for a Christmas party at Maria Perrini's ballet studio, the only one at that time in Tbilisi, she, seeing his great interest in dance, took him as a scholarship pupil and he remained with her until 1924, receiving a firm foundation in the Italian technique. However, a tour of former Maryin-

Vakhtang Chabukiani as Solor in BAYADÈRE at Leningrad, *c.* 1935

sky dancers LYUKOM and Boris Shavrov showed him that the purest classical training was then in Leningrad. In autumn 1926, he arrived there, penniless, only to find that he was much too old for the Choreographic Technicum (the former Maryinsky S.), but he was accepted for an evening course and then transferred to the regular daytime school, passing the entire syllabus of professional and academic education within three years. His exceptional physique, virility, temperament, magnetic personality, and will power helped him to achieve virtually impossible goals, and in 1929 he joined the State T. of O. and B. (later called the Kirov). In his first season he danced the important role of the Winter Bird (ICE MAIDEN), the classical *pas de trois* in SWAN LAKE, and towards the end of the first season he was given the role of SIEGFRIED, colouring it with energy and temperament, unusual for the classical academic part. Within two years he had become Kirov B.'s recognized *premier danseur* and was soon known all over the country as one of the leading classical dancers.

His prodigious technique played an outstanding role in the formation of the style of male dancing in Soviet ballet. He danced all the major classical roles and, most important, created innumerable roles in Soviet ballets of the 1930s, incl. Vaslav (FOUNTAIN OF BAKHCHISARAY), and Actaeon in VAGANOVA's famous *divertissement* in *Esmeralda*, still danced as a concert piece. He was the *premier danseur* in LOST ILLUSIONS; the Marseillais Jerome in FLAME OF PARIS; Kerim in *Partisan Days* (ch. VAINONEN).

Always interested in dramatic expression, he began creating his own works, at first concert pieces for himself, e.g. *Dance of Fire*. His first big ballet was HEART OF THE HILLS, in which he wedded classical and Georgian dance, placing the Georgian maidens on *pointe*. In LAURENCIA he danced the hero, Frondozo, making the role a true fusion of dancing and acting.

At the beginning of World War II he moved to Tbilisi, where he became principal dancer, teacher, and choreographer, Paliashvili T. of O. and B. Here he choreographed many outstanding national ballets, dancing leading roles in most of them. His greatest success during his Georgian period was OTHELLO, for which he was awarded the Lenin Prize. At the height of his career he also appeared in films, incl. *Masters of the Georgian Ballet*, and with DUDINSKAYA in a documentary of the *pas de deux* from BAYADÈRE. He created his own versions of his parts in *La Bayadère* and CORSAIRE which have now entered the standard male repertory. In 1934 Chabukiani and VECHESLOVA became the first Soviet dancers to tour the USA, giving some 30 perfs. In 1972 he was replaced by ALEKSIDZE as chief choreographer, Paliashvili T., and now holds the post of artistic director, Tbilisi Choreographic S. Lenin and State Prizes; People's Artist, USSR. NR
See Vera Krasovskaya, *Vakhtang Chabukiani* (Moscow 1956; 2nd ed. 1960)

Chansons (Chant) du Compagnon Errant, Le *see* LIEDER EINES FAHRENDEN GESELLEN

Chappell, Annette, b. Liverpool, 1929. English dancer and teacher. Pupil of Judith Espinosa; danced with BR 1944–9, becoming a principal. Danced in musicals 1949–55. Ballerina, Munich B. from 1955; later taught at Munich BS. A teacher from 1970, CRANKO S., Stuttgart. GBLW

Charlip, Remy, b. Brooklyn, NY, 1929. American dancer, designer, choreographer, director, author, and illustrator. Danced with and designed costumes for CUNNINGHAM Dance Co., 1951–61. Founder member of The Paper Bag Players. His choreography incl. *April* and *December* for Judson Dance T. (1964–5); MEDITATION (1966–8); *Differences* for CCJB (1968); *Dance* for LCDT (1972); *Quick Change Artists* and *The Movable Workshop* for Scottish T.B. (1973); *Mad River* for LCDT (1974); *The Woolloomooloo Cuddle* for Dance Co. (New South Wales), 1976. Several of these works, drawing on the results of his experiments in directing for children's theatre and for the NT of the Deaf, were created cooperatively with the dancers, who contributed words and movement derived from their own experience. For several years he taught a 'Workshop in Making Things Up', at Sarah Lawrence College, Bronxville, NY. He has written and/or illustrated 23 books for children. DV

Charrat, Janine, b. Grenoble, 1924. French dancer and choreographer. Studied with Jeanne Ronsay, EGOROVA, VOLININ. Debut in film, *La Mort du Cygne*, 1937. Recitals with PETIT 1941–4. Choreographed *Jeu de Cartes* (*see* CARD GAME), *'Adame Miroir*, B. de Paris, 1948, *La Femme et son Ombre*, B. de Paris, 1949; *Abraxas*, W. Berlin 1949. Guest artist de Cuevas B. Founded her own co. (B. Janine Charrat, later called B. de France) 1951 and produced *Le Massacre des Amazones*, ALGUES, both 1953. She has also choreographed ballets for Milan Sc., de Cuevas B., B. XXe S., Grand T., Geneva, Vienna, and Munich. A sensitive and passionate dancer, she possesses poetic lyricism. Seen at her finest in *Les Algues*, in which she created the role of the pathetic, mad heroine. Badly burned in the early 1960s during TV filming of *Les Algues* but made a remarkable recovery. She tries energetically to keep alive her own co., which is a faithful instrument of her creative taste. Now teaches in Paris. Officer of Arts and Letters. *Officier*, Légion d'Honneur. M-FC
See I. Lidova, 'Janine Charrat', *Les Saisons de la Danse* (Paris, Aug 1970) with list of roles

Chase, Lucia [Mrs Thomas Ewing], b. Waterbury, CT, 1907. American dancer, founder, and director of ABT. Studied with FOKINE, NIJINSKA, and MORDKIN; ballerina of the Mordkin B. (1938–9), which formed the nucleus of ABT when it was founded in 1940. With Mordkin, she danced such ballerina roles as GISELLE and FILLE MAL GARDÉE; in ABT she has been identified with such dramatic roles as the Nurse in TUDOR'S ROMEO AND JULIET, the oldest sister in PILLAR OF FIRE, and the Stepmother in FALL RIVER LEGEND, all of which she created. Over a period of 35 years, she has devoted most of her time and the greater part of her personal fortune to keeping ABT going, often in very difficult circumstances. DV

Chaussat, Geneviève, b. Mexico City, 1941. Swiss dancer. Pupil of BESOBRAZOVA and GOLOVINE. Danced in the Nice B. and in Golovine's ballet in Geneva. From 1968 a soloist (and later principal) of the Munich B. To Düsseldorf 1975 as principal. GBLW

Chauviré, Yvette, b. Paris, 1917. French dancer and teacher. Paris OBS; studied with KNIASEFF and V. GSOVSKY; *étoile* 1941. Quickly noticed by LIFAR, who entrusted her with major roles in *Le Roi Nu, David Triomphant*, then *Alexandre le Grand* (1937). Starred in film, *La Mort du Cygne* (1937). Created the role of the lady in CHEVALIER ET LA DAMOISELLE; *Istar*, solo of 18 minutes which gained her the title of *étoile*; Lifar's *Joan de Zarisse* (*see* JOAN VON ZARISSA); *Les Animaux Modèles* (1942), SUITE EN BLANC (1943). Left the O. with Lifar. Nouveau B. de Monte Carlo 1946, where she created roles in DRAMMA PER MUSICA, *Chota Roustaveli, Nautéos* (1947). Returned to the O. and created *Mirages*, one of her longest-lasting roles. Lifar produced *L'Écuyère* as a showpiece for her tours. Left the O. 1949, returned there 1953 and created roles in *La Belle Hélène* for CRANKO (1955); H. LANDER'S *Concerto aux Étoiles* (1956); PÉRI (1957); DOLIN'S PAS DE QUATRE (1959); *La Dame aux Camélias* (1960); and at Monte Carlo BABILÉE'S BALANCE À TROIS (1955). Has danced in the classic repertory both in France and round the world, incl. SLEEPING BEAUTY (with London RB at CG 1958) and GISELLE, of which she presented a remarkable and richly expressive interpretation. Guest artist Milan Sc., RB, Bolshoy B., Berlin, New York. Farewell to the Paris O. in *Giselle*, 20 Nov 1972. Nominated artistic and technical adviser, Paris OBS, 1963. Has directed the International Acad. of the Dance in Paris since 1970. Produced *La Péri* (1955), *Arabesque* (1957). Published *Je Suis Ballerine* (*I am a Ballerina*), Paris 1960. The greatest French dancer of her time, combining grace, a moving lyricism, and technical mastery. Her genius bloomed in the neoclassicism of her master Lifar and in the classical repertory. *Officier*, Légion d'Honneur, 1964; later *Commandeur*. M-FC
See 'Yvette Chauviré', *Les Saisons de la Danse* (Paris, Feb 1968)

Checkmate, ballet, 1 scene and a prologue, ch. DE VALOIS; lib./mus. Sir Arthur Bliss; sc./c. Edward McKnight Kauffer. Paris, T. des CE, Vic-Wells B., 15 June 1937; dan. June Brae, TURNER, MAY,

Yvette Chauviré, supreme French classical ballerina of her generation (signed photo). At the height of her fame she was affectionately known in Paris as 'la Chauviré nationale'.

Left: Giorgio de' Chirico's setting for *Le Bal*, Diaghilev's B. Russes, 1929

Right: Choreartium, as staged by the B. Russe de Monte Carlo, 1933. Danced to Brahms's Fourth Symphony, it was the most controversial of MASSINE's symphonic ballets.

HELPMANN, LONDON, SWT, SWB, 5 Oct 1937. Revived and redesigned by McKnight Kauffer, CG, SWB, 18 Nov 1947. The prologue shows Love and Death at a chessboard; Love backs the Red Knight to win, Death the Black Queen. The Black Queen wins the love of the Red Knight, and when victory is in his grasp his love prevents him from 'killing'; the Black Queen immediately stabs him in the back. The Red King, old and feeble, the last remaining Red piece, makes one final gesture of defiance before the Black Queen's warriors kill him and Death is victorious. No dancer-mime has ever rivalled Helpmann's performance as the Red King. The Black Queen has had many fine interpreters from the glamorous Brae to LYNNE, GREY, GIELGUD, and MAKAROVA. Turner's stamina sustained the (too long) Mazurka in which the Red Knight expresses his love. Ironically NUREYEV found the choreography and the length of the dance too difficult. Now in repertory of SWRB. MC

Chesworth, John, b. Manchester, 1930. English dancer, choreographer, and director. Joined BR after demobilization from RAF 1952; a late starter and therefore danced only character roles. A latecomer also to choreography, his first work was *Time Base* (1966) and that year he was appointed assistant to the directors of the reformed BR. Appeared effectively in several MORRICE ballets. Associate director, BR, 1970, director 1975. In 1972 supervised *Ad Hoc*, an 'instant' ballet with a different theme and cast at each perf. Has staged his *Pawn to King 5* (London, BR, 4 Dec 1968) for cos in Vienna and Lisbon. MC

Chevalier et la Damoiselle, Le, ballet, 2 acts, ch. LIFAR; mus. Philippe Gaubert; sc./c. Adolphe-Mouron Cassandre. Paris O., 2 July 1941; dan. Lifar, SCHWARTZ, PERETTI. In this medieval legend, a knight delivers a graceful doe from enchantment through his love and turns her back into a woman. M-FC

Childs, Lucinda, b. New York City, 1940. American dancer. Studied with H. HOLM, CUNNINGHAM. Danced in various contemporary dance cos and Judson Dance T., 1962–6. Formed her own co. 1973. Her recent work has been in the area of 'conceptual' dance, concerned with sometimes infinitesimal variations within a rigorously controlled compositional structure. *See* AVANT-GARDE DANCE. DV

Chimera Foundation for Dance, Inc., The *see* NIKOLAIS

China *see* ASIA

Chirico, Giorgio de', b. Volo, Greece, 1888. Italian painter and designer. In Paris 1911–15, met PICASSO and other *avant-garde* painters of the period; in 1925 he was in contact with the Surrealists there. His settings for ballets portray fantastic architectural visions and often include a horse. First ballet GIARA for B. Suédois, then BALANCHINE's *Le Bal* for DIAGHILEV (1929). Designed for the Paris O. 1938 and, for DE BASIL, LICHINE's *Protée* (1938). In recent years worked mostly in Italy for Milan Sc. and Maggio Musicale Fiorentino. MC

Chloé, heroine of DAPHNIS ET CHLOÉ

Cholewicka, Helena, b. Warsaw, 1848; d. Nice, 1883. Polish dancer. Pupil of M. TAGLIONI. *Prima ballerina assoluta*, Warsaw B. 1872–82. Danced in Naples (won gold medal there) and in Vienna 1873. Danced GISELLE and CATARINA. Created title role in *Mélusine* (ch. Adolf Sonnenfeld), Jadwiga (PAN TWARDOWSKI) and other Polish ballets. JPU

Chopiniana. Original title of SYLPHIDES. It was used by A. PAVLOVA for her co.'s version and is still used in the USSR. *Les Sylphides* was revived under this title by A. DANILOVA, NY, State T., NYCB, 20

Jan 1972, to piano only; danced to horror of purists in simple tunics and not Romantic skirts. MC
See Dale Harris, '*Chopiniana*', *Ballet Review*, Vol. 4, No. 2 (New York 1972)

Choreartium, choreographic symphony, ch. MASSINE; mus. Johannes Brahms (Symphony No. 4, in E minor); sc./c. Konstantin Tereshkovich and Eugène Lourié. London, Alhambra T., B. Russe de Monte Carlo (de Basil), 24 Oct 1933; dan. BARONOVA, LICHINE, ZORINA, VERCHININA, A. DANILOVA, SHABELEVSKY, RIABOUCHINSKA, JASIŃSKI, PETROFF. Massine's second symphonic ballet, and the only one without literary or allegorical content. Revived 1953 for a short-lived co. formed by Massine for the Nervi Fest., Genoa. DV

Choreography. The word 'choreography' is a compound of the Greek for 'dance' and 'write'. For the father figure of classical ballet, NOVERRE, late in the 18th c., the word still meant just that: to write down the steps of a dance. Nowadays the term applied to the writing down of steps is DANCE NOTATION, and choreography has come to mean 'the composition of dance', whether the steps are written down or not. The distinction is more than a purist's nicety, for dance, it has been said, 'has no score'. That difference between composing music and composing dance is no longer quite so generally operative as it used to be, but it is still highly relevant. A composer of music usually writes it down. Of course he need not do so: traditional tunes can pass unwritten from generation to generation. But usually the composer writes it down, in a language, a notation, that is universally intelligible; he composes in terms of sound but the link between the sound and its notation is so close as to make them (for the trained musician) scarcely separable. Not so the choreographer. Evidently it has never been entirely true that 'dance has no score'; there have been forms of dance notation at least since the time of the 14th-c. dancing master Domenico of Piacenza: after all, the fact that in the 18th c. choreography still meant 'writing down the steps' shows that the steps were sometimes written down. But not, as music was and is, in a generally intelligible and accepted form. Nowadays two rival forms of dance notation (Labanotation and CHOREOLOGY) have many practitioners and dance is nearer to having a score than it ever was previously; but it is not there yet. Choreographers may be glad of an amanuensis to write down their work, in one or other form, since their work is more likely to be preserved thereby than by a haphazard dependence on their own and their dancers' memories; but even now the best of them may know nothing about dance notation; they compose not in its terms but in those of mobile human bodies (much more difficult to 'write down' than the sound of music). The word 'choreography' in its post-Noverre sense, used to apply only to the composition of ballet; now it covers the composition of every kind of theatrical dance and, indeed, dance that is not theatrical at all. It must also be taken to cover mime since the borderline between dance and mime is blurred.

So choreography, though its literal meaning is clear, has, in practice, been a variable term. Correspondingly, the choreographer's function, though also clear in its literal meaning, has been variable too. Theatrical dance – ballet, pre-eminently, but other kinds as well – is interrelated with music, stage design, and costume. The choreographer belongs to a partnership. Since the choreography distinguishes a 'dance show' from every other kind of theatrical entertainment it might seem that the choreographer, using his instruments (the bodies of his dancers), must be the dominant partner. Often he is; but sometimes he is dominated by his instrument – a live dancer being less biddable than, for example, a violin; or he may be the servant of his music or, less likely, of his designs. He may draw his inspiration from music or a painting or a story or politics or philosophy or a wish to please a dancer; and in all this he is like any other creative artist. He may work in only one dance idiom or, as happens increasingly now, in a mixture of idioms. He tends to be in charge of whatever dance co. he belongs to – an executive role that has nothing to do with choreography but follows from his rarity value. For good choreographers, being the rarest creatures in a world of dance, which has vastly expanded, tend to rule the roost.

To give a few contemporary examples of some of these numerous variables: BALANCHINE, most famous of living choreographers, inexorably dominates his dancers – they are as nearly his passive instruments as may be – and pays minimal attention to his designer partner, but he would certainly not claim domination over STRAVINSKY in their famous collaboration. ASHTON, even more musical than Balanchine, gives very free rein to his dancers' personalities. The versatile ROBBINS works in jazz and modernism in the GRAHAM mode as well as in the classical idiom. Ashton largely improvises; DE VALOIS planned her ballets exactly. De Valois, Ashton, Balanchine, MACMILLAN, CRANKO, Graham, and many other choreographers have run cos. Choreography is very variously produced; choreographers take on much besides choreography.

Choreography, like musical composition, can be taught – up to a point. Instruction in dance history (in the theories, for instance, of Noverre, BLASIS, M. PETIPA, FOKINE) and in methods of putting steps together is obviously useful to the potential dance composer. In fact choreography has till recently been very little taught. Now, when the shortage of choreographers is everywhere evident, more is being done about it as a specific subject for dance pupils. It is in the curricula of some dance schools; there has been a school of choreography, still the only one of its kind, in Moscow since 1946; ballet and other cos encourage 'workshop demonstrations' by their aspiring choreographers. Yet it remains generally, and wastefully, true that choreographers are dancers who show some special taste for 'making' as distinct from 'performing' – and who teach themselves. All choreographers are, or have been, dancers; some, like MASSINE, excellent, others, like Balanchine, mediocre. They are like composers whose whole instruction has been in playing an instrument; the rest they must do for themselves. JM

See P. van Praagh and P. Brinson, *The Choreographic Art* (London and New York 1963); L. Kirstein, 'Choreography: Materials and Structure' in *Movement and Metaphor* (New York 1970; London 1971); Mary Clarke and Clement Crisp, *Making a Ballet* (London and New York 1975)

Choreology. The copyright term for the system of dance notation invented by Rudolf and Joan Benesh, first called Benesh notation. The Institute of Choreology in London (director Monica Parker) trains choreologists who can record all forms of movement but the system has proved most valuable in writing down ballets. Many classical cos have a qualified choreologist on their staff and if an existing ballet is being mounted for another co. it is usual for the choreologist to teach the steps first and for the choreographer then to give the final polish to the production. *See also* DANCE NOTATION. MC

See Rudolf and Joan Benesh, *An Introduction to Benesh Notation* (London 1956)

Christensen, Harold, b. Brigham City, UT, 1904. American dancer and teacher, brother of L. and W. CHRISTENSEN. Director, San Francisco BS. DV

Christensen, Lew, b. Brigham City, UT, 1908. American dancer and choreographer. Brother of H. and W. CHRISTENSEN; m. ballerina Gisella Caccialanza. Studied at SAB; danced in American B. (title role in APOLLO, etc.); B. Caravan, for which he choreographed *Pocahontas* (1936), *Filling Station* (1938), etc.; B. Society. Ballet master of NYCB until 1955 when he became director and choreographer of San Francisco B., for which he has choreographed many ballets (*see* REGIONAL BALLET, USA). DV

Christensen, Willam, b. Brigham City, UT, 1902. American dancer and choreographer, brother of the above. Studied with FOKINE and NOVIKOV. Founded San Francisco B. 1938, for which he choreographed many works. In 1951 became professor at University of Utah and in 1952 founded the Utah B., which in 1968 became B. West. DV

Chryst, Gary, b. La Jolla, CA, 1949. American dancer. Studied at High School of Performing Arts, NY, and American B. Center. First performed as a modern dancer, then joined CCJB 1968. A brilliant character dancer whose roles incl. PETRUSHKA, PULCINELLA, the Chinese Conjuror in PARADE, the Profiteer in GREEN TABLE, the Poor Young Man in BIG CITY, solo in DEUCE COUPE II. DV

Chujoy, Anatole, b. Riga, 1894; d. New York, 1969. US citizen from 1931. Latvian author, editor and lexicographer of the dance. Graduate Law School, University of Petrograd, 1918. A passionate balletomane in Russia (he worshipped KARSAVINA), he devoted his life in the USA to promoting interest in and knowledge of ballet. Author of innumerable articles, he was co-founder and editor of *Dance Magazine* 1937–41, then left to found his own monthly newspaper *Dance News*, which he edited from 1942 until his death (although in his last years he was totally dependent on his close associate P. W. Manchester). Chujoy's personality was reflected as strongly in his *Dance News* as was that of Harold Ross in *The New Yorker*. He knew every dancer in NY and most in America. *Dance News* contained serious reviews and historical material, and through its pages Chujoy publicized and encouraged the whole Regional B. development in the USA. His *Dance*

Encyclopedia (New York 1949) was the first of its kind in English: he wryly described it as 'How to Lose Friends and Antagonize People'. The 1967 edition was revised and enlarged in collaboration with P. W. Manchester. Author of *The Symphonic Ballet* (New York 1937), *The New York City Ballet* (New York 1953), translator of the first English edition of VAGANOVA's *Fundamentals of the Classic Dance* (New York 1946), and editor of FOKINE's *Memoirs of a Ballet Master* (London and Boston 1961). He served on several important committees and his life was entirely devoted to dance. Typically, when the ballet-shoe maker Ben Sommers (a close friend) invaded his office with a dramatic account of the Japanese attack on Pearl Harbor, Chujoy said wearily 'Ben, what has this to do with the dance?' The dance library at the University of Cincinnati is named after him. MC

Cincinnati Ballet *see* REGIONAL BALLET (USA); UNIVERSITIES, DANCE IN (USA)

Cinderella. Many ballets have been based on the fairy story by Charles Perrault, of which the most notable are: (1) *Cendrillon*, ch. François Decombe Albert; mus. Fernando Sor. London, King's T., 26 Mar 1822; dan. Maria Mercandotti; (2) ch. IVANOV and CECCHETTI and possibly M. PETIPA; mus. Boris Schell; lib. Lydia Pashkova; sc. Henrykh Levogt, Matvey Shishkov, Mikhail Bocharov. St Petersburg, Maryinsky T., 1/13 Dec 1893; dan. LEGNANI (her debut at Maryinsky), P. GERDT; (3) ch./sc./c. HOWARD; mus. Carl Maria von Weber; London, Mercury T., 6 Jan 1935; dan. Pearl Argyle, ASHTON, Howard, Elizabeth Schooling. A miniature but imaginative version. The wigs and make-ups devised by Howard for the Ugly Sisters remained in Ashton's memory and he modelled the characters in his own version on hers, playing the meek sister invented by Howard; (4) *Cendrillon*, ch./lib. FOKINE; mus. Frédéric d'Erlanger; sc./c. GONCHAROVA. London, CG, Original B. Russe (de Basil), 19 July

Left: Cinderella as staged by the Bolshoy B., ch. ZAKHAROV; STRUCHKOVA in the title role in the ballroom scene; *below:* ASHTON's version of the same ballet for RB at CG, with Ashton (left) and HELPMANN as the Ugly Sisters on their return from the ball, and FONTEYN as Cinderella

1938; dan. RIABOUCHINSKA, PETROFF. (5) *Zolushka*, ch. ZAKHAROV; mus. PROKOFIEV; lib. Nikolay Volkov; sc. Pyotr Williams. Moscow, Bolshoy B., 21 Nov 1945; dan. LEPESHINSKAYA, GABOVICH. (6) *Zolushka*, ch. SERGEYEV; mus. Prokofiev; lib. Volkov; sc. Boris Erdman. Leningrad, Kirov B., 8 Apr 1946; dan. DUDINSKAYA, Sergeyev. (7) ch./lib. ASHTON; mus. Prokofiev; sc./c. Jean-Denis Malclès. London, CG, SWTB, 23 Dec 1948; dan. M. SHEARER, SOMES, Ashton, HELPMANN. Revived CG, RB, 23 Dec 1965; sc./c. Henry Bardon and WALKER; dan. FONTEYN, BLAIR, Ashton, Helpmann. Revived Australian B. 1972. Ashton omitted the extended *divertissement* depicting the Prince's travels in search of the owner of the glass slipper which began Act III in both Soviet versions. DV/MC

Cinema, Dance in the *see* FILMS, DANCE IN

City Center Joffrey Ballet *see* JOFFREY BALLET

Clara, the child who dreams the NUTCRACKER ballet

Classical Ballet Training. The classic dance technique, evolved over the past 300 years, is the most demanding of all forms of Western dance. Based on principles laid down by the early dancing masters like BEAUCHAMP and WEAVER, developed over succeeding years, codified by BLASIS, and brought to perfection by the Imperial Russian B. at the end of the 19th c., it is an entirely logical system of movement that aims to achieve the maximum control and mobility of the dancer's body. The great difference from other forms of dance is that the classical style is based on a 90° turn-out from the hip socket. This not only gives the legs the greatest possible flexibility but greatly enhances beauty of line in positions like *arabesque* and *attitude*. It has to be achieved gradually over the years of a dancer's training and must always be from the hip, never the knee,

Classical dancers must start young (age 10 or 11) before ligaments become set; the most vital element in their training is correct stance and distribution of weight. Unless this is watched constantly by the teacher, injury, even deformity, can occur. It is impossible to learn classical ballet technique from a book; only a professionally qualified teacher can guide dancers, who must practise every day from joining a ballet school until the end of their careers. (Before a perf. a dancer will always do a 'warm up', a short class to ensure the body is ready for the demands that will be made upon it.)

The system of training in state schools throughout the world is very similar to that described in USSR, BALLET TRAINING IN. The formation of a class is designed to ensure that no part of the vocabulary of steps is neglected. Classes last from one to two hours and begin with exercises at the barre. Small and large *pliés* are practised in all five positions to relax or stretch the leg muscles while keeping the torso straight and still. They are followed by other exercises such as *battements* and *ronds de jambes*, all done first to one side then to the other. The barre exercises are the foundation for all the steps that will follow. Special attention is paid to feet and legs but *ports de bras* are also incl. using the arms and body in co-ordination. The barre work is followed by practice in the centre of the studio, where the same exercises are repeated, followed by slow *adage* and progressing to the more difficult combinations of *pirouettes* and jumps. At the end of the class the girls change their shoes for *pointe* work. *Pas de deux* classes in partnering are not attempted until towards the end of the training. JL
See L. Kirstein and M. Stuart, ill. Dyer, *The Classic Ballet* (New York 1952); A. J. Vaganova, *Osnovy Klassicheskogo Tanza* (*Fundamentals of the Classic Dance*, Leningrad 1934); tr. A. Chujoy as *Basic Principles of Classical Ballet, Russian Ballet Technique*, ed. P. van Praagh (New York 1946; London 1948; revised edition, New York 1969)

Coast of Hope, the Soviet fishermen's dance of friendship from Act I, as staged by the Leningrad State Kirov B.

Clauss, Heinz, b. Esslingen, 1933. German dancer and teacher. Pupil of Robert Mayer in Stuttgart and KISS in Paris. In 1951 joined Stuttgart B. as student and was in the co. until he became a soloist in Zürich B., 1957. Soloist and principal in Hamburg B. 1959–67; returned to Stuttgart as a principal, where he created roles in many CRANKO ballets and was a famous ONEGIN. In Hamburg he danced APOLLO under BALANCHINE's direction, one of his outstanding roles which he subsequently staged and danced in many countries. One of Germany's greatest dancers; also teaches for Stuttgart B. Became director, Cranko S., Stuttgart, 1976, on WOOLLIAMS's departure. Has also staged Balanchine ballets in Oslo, Stockholm, Stuttgart, etc. GBLW

Clavé, Antoni, b. Barcelona, 1913. Spanish decorator and illustrator whose designs embody the Catalan spirit in a highly dramatic and witty style. Designed Ana Nevada's *Los Caprichos* for the B. des CE (1946) and caused a sensation with his brilliantly theatrical CARMEN (1949). Designed PETIT's *Ballabile* for the London RB at CG (1950), *Revanche* for PAGE (Chicago 1952), and *Deuil en 24 Heures* for Petit (Paris 1953). Clavé has designed for opera and the theatre, but in recent years has devoted himself mostly to easel painting. MC

Clowns, The, ballet, ch. ARPINO; mus. Hershy Kay; c. Edith Lutyens Bel Geddes; ltg Thomas Skelton. NYCC, CCJB, 28 Feb 1968; dan. Robert Blankshine, Frank Bays, Erika Goodman, Maximiliano Zomosa. A group of modern *commedia dell'arte* characters are transposed to a world of 21st-c. terror. FM

Clustine, Ivan *see* KHLUSTIN

Clytemnestra, modern dance work, 3 acts, ch. GRAHAM; mus. Halim El-Dabh; sc. NOGUCHI; c. Graham, MCGEHEE. NY, Adelphi T., 1 Apr 1958; dan. Graham, P. TAYLOR, YURIKO, McGehee, TURNEY, WINTER, ROSS. Clytemnestra, a dishonoured shade in Hades, reviews her life in memory, and achieves peace when she acknowledges the guilt of her own lustful desires and actions. Based on Aeschylus' *Oresteia*. DM

Coast of Hope (*Bereg Nadezhdy*), ballet, 3 acts, ch. BELSKY; mus. Andrey Petrov; sc. Valery Dorrer. Leningrad, Kirov T., 16 June 1959; dan. MAKAROV (the Fisherman), OSIPENKO (his Beloved). Poetical lib. by SLONIMSKY uses dancing Seagulls to symbolize the home country for the Fisherman when he is wrecked on a strange shore and withstands all trials. Belsky's choreography concentrates on classical dance, slightly tempered by movements drawn from sport or everyday life. One of the first successful Soviet ballets on a contemporary theme. Also known as *Shore of Hope*. NR

Cocteau, Jean, b. Maisons-Laffitte, 1889; d. Milly-la-Forêt, 1963. French poet, writer, artist, and film director, author of the scenarios for many ballets. Entered the DIAGHILEV circle from the first Paris season 1909 and devised ballets for him, also for BÖRLIN in the 1920s. With KOCHNO and BÉRARD helped the young B. des CE of PETIT in 1945 to recapture some of the qualities of Diaghilev's B. Russes. Gave his blessing to and drew the catalogue portrait for BUCKLE's Diaghilev Exhibition in England 1954. Has left brilliant descriptions of the Diaghilev seasons in his memoirs and made innumerable sketches and caricatures of the Diaghilev entourage. MC
See F. Steegmuller, *Cocteau* (Boston 1970)

Coe, Kelvin, b. Melbourne, 1946. Australian dancer. Studied with REID. Australian B. 1962–73 (principal dancer, 1969) and from 1974. Studied with R.

FRANCHETTI, Paris, 1970. Silver medallist, 2nd International B. Competition, Moscow, 1973. LFB 1974, principal dancer. A classical virtuoso with a fine sense of character (BASILIO), The Caricaturist (MAM'ZELLE ANGOT), Lensky (ONEGIN), and an admirable partner. KSW

Cohan, Robert, b. New York, 1925. American dancer, choreographer, and director. Began to dance after World War II service in US Navy. Studied at GRAHAM S., joined her co. in 1946 and later became one of her regular partners. Taught dancing between his theatre engagements, and formed his own group. To London 1967 as director initially of the LSCD and from 1969 of LCDT (also at first its leading male dancer). Has choreographed many works for the co., among which the most important are CELL, STAGES, *People Alone* (1972), *Waterless Method of Swimming Instruction* (1974). Even his best works are notable for skilful and imaginative production more than their dance content. His outstanding achievement has been the founding and rapid development of the first Graham-style co. in Europe. JP

Cohen, Ze'eva, b. Tel Aviv, 1940. Israeli dancer and choreographer. Studied first in Israel then in NY at Juilliard S. Danced in the cos of SOKOLOW, P. LANG, DANCE THEATER WORKSHOP, etc. In 1971 she initiated her repertory of solo dances by herself and others, incl. Sokolow, Margalit Oved, PEREZ, J. DUNCAN, and WARING, with which she has toured all over the USA, in many countries in Europe, and Israel. DV

Colas, the young farmer hero of FILLE MAL GARDÉE

Cole, Jack Ewing, b. New Brunswick, NJ, 1913; d. Los Angeles, CA, 1974. American dancer. Studied in NY with DENIS and SHAWN at their DENISHAWN S. Toured with Denishawn co. and Shawn's Men Dancers for several years; later with the HUMPHREY-WEIDMAN co. before starting an independent career. Strongly influenced by jazz music and combined it with Hindu gesture he had learned at Denishawn to create *Hindu Serenade* for the 'Ziegfeld Follies of 1942'. Worked on Broadway, in nightclubs, and in film musicals; created a concert group in Los Angeles from studio dancers on the Columbia Pictures lot. DM

Coleman, Michael, b. Beacontree, Essex, 1940. English dancer. Trained RBS, joined touring co. 1959 and RB CG co. 1961, principal dancer by 1968. A virtuoso (BAYADÈRE, BLUEBIRD) and an engaging *demi-caractère* dancer (DANCES AT A GATHERING, COLAS, Mercutio in MACMILLAN's ROMEO AND JULIET), with a gift of unaffected cheerfulness on stage. He gave a dazzling performance as Jeremy Fisher in ASHTON's film *Tales of Beatrix Potter*, 1970 (US title: *Peter Rabbit and the Tales of Beatrix Potter*). MC

Collier, Lesley, b. Orpington, Kent, 1947. English dancer. Studied at RBS. Danced leading role in DEUX PIGEONS at her graduation performance 1965; joined RB same year. First solo roles were in the BLUEBIRD and GISELLE 'Peasant' *pas de deux*. She won plaudits for her performances in variations (of which like VAGANOVA, she became 'the queen'). Since then she has danced the ballerina roles in FILLE MAL GARDÉE, ANASTASIA, MACMILLAN's ROMEO AND JULIET, SWAN LAKE, NUTCRACKER, *Giselle*, and SLEEPING BEAUTY. A dancer of rare musicality. MC

Cologne. The International Summer Academy of the Dance was founded in Krefeld in 1957 under the direction of WENDEL and Heinz Laurenzen, with 174 students. Moved in 1961 to Cologne; held there every July in the Mungersdorf Sports Stadium, with distinguished teachers from all over the world participating, and about 500 students. It has become one of the most important summer courses for dance. Laurenzen continues to direct, with APPEL. GBLW

Michael Coleman as Jeremy Fisher in *Tales of Beatrix Potter*

Colombo, Vera, b. Milan, 1931. Italian dancer. At Sc. from 1949, prima ballerina from 1954 until her retirement in 1975. Wide range of roles, classical and neoclassical. FP

Concert, The, charade, 1 act, ch. ROBBINS; mus. Frédéric Chopin, partly orch. H. Kay; c. Irene Sharaff. NYCC, NYCB, 6 Mar 1956; dan. LECLERCQ, BOLENDER. Revised for Spoleto Fest. 1958; sc. Saul Steinberg. Revived London, CG, RB, 4 Mar 1975; sc. Edward Gorey; dan. SEYMOUR, PARKINSON, COLEMAN. Subtitled 'The Perils of Everybody', an immensely deft Thurberesque comedy ballet, presenting a group of music lovers indulging in the fantasies which some Chopin piano music arouses in them. FM/DJ

Concerto, ballet, 3 movements, ch. MACMILLAN; mus. Dmitri Shostakovich (Second Piano Concerto); sc./c. ROSE. W. Berlin, Deutsche OB, 30 Nov 1966. Revived NY, ABT, 18 Mar 1967; and CG, RB, 26 May 1967. A plotless ballet of pure dance closely matching a dancer or group of dancers to the piano and others to the full orchestra. The second movement is a lyric *pas de deux* often danced at galas. MC

Concerto Barocco, ballet, ch. BALANCHINE; mus. Johann Sebastian Bach; sc./c. BERMAN. NY, Hunter College T., ABT, 29 May 1940; dan. MARIE-JEANNE, Mary Jane Shea, DOLLAR. A plotless ballet to the Concerto in D Minor for Two Violins. Balanchine typically soon discarded the Berman costumes and the ballet is given today in his favourite black-and-white practice clothes. In many repertories, particularly well danced by Pennsylvania B. and DTH. FM

Concerto for Flute and Harp, ballet, ch. CRANKO; mus. Wolfgang Amadeus Mozart. Stuttgart B., 26 Mar 1966; dan. CARDÚS, Ilse Wiedmann, CRAGUN, BERG. An abstract ballet of great beauty and intricacy. Originally *Konzert für Flöte und Harfe*, also called *Mozart Concerto*. GBLW

Concerto in G, ballet, ch. ROBBINS; mus. RAVEL; sc./c. TER-ARUTUNIAN; ltg Ronald Bates. NYST, NYCB, 14 May 1975; dan. FARRELL, MARTINS. A plotless ballet to Ravel's Piano Concerto with certain effects borrowed from jazz. Later called simply *In G Major*. FM

Conducting. The first and most obvious task of the conductor working with a dance or ballet co. is to learn his score so thoroughly that, apart from the minimum leads to his orchestra essential for the performance, he can watch the dancers the whole time they are on stage. At its lowest value, this at least gives the dancers a sense of confidence in the positive nature of the music's contribution to the overall performance (even though, as LAMBERT once confessed, the conductor may, while watching the dancers, be worrying about the deputy trombone player and how he's going to sight-read the tricky passage coming up). In any event the conductor can be of assistance to a dancer, or even more to an ensemble, by making sure that he is seen by them and cueing them. Dancers are not taught like opera singers to watch a conductor out of the corner of one eye. (They should be.) Also important in any kind of narrative ballet, and even in many abstract ones, is that the orchestra, through the conductor and his link with the stage, should enhance the dramatic and emotional aspects of the work.

Most important is the setting and adjusting of the tempos of the music, and here undoubtedly a conductor for ballet needs a more finely calibrated sense of pace than his opera or concert counterpart. In any ballet score there are passages in which the conductor can set his own tempo without over-much reference to the dancers. Strangely enough, the better the quality of the music the more he can be left so to do, for it is generally the more mundane scores (e.g. MINKUS, PUGNI, and DRIGO) in which the greatest care has to be taken to 'follow the dancers'. This is principally for two reasons: first, that good music so often dictates its own correct tempo whereas the lesser stuff sounds equally right (or wrong!) at a wider variety of speeds. Secondly, mundane music seems to be more thickly choreographed than its better-quality counterpart. Choreographers tend after all to treat good music with respect (BÉJART is a law unto himself) and there is little likelihood of a version of, say, NOCES or DAPHNIS ET CHLOÉ in which the accelerator or the brake has to be applied as in ESMERALDA or CORSAIRE. A contemporary symphony (by HENZE) served recently as the musical inspiration of a fine ballet and in this the choreographer wisely designated only certain key moments where the music had briefly to be married to specific dance action. For the conductor this combined all the freedom of performing the symphony as it should be with some of the thrill of precision timing as in motion-picture music.

Regrettably, even during the best of the classical ballet scores there are times when major tempo adjustments seem necessary to accommodate dancers or new choreographic versions. In the case of the latter, the conductor should be on hand in the early stages of the ballet's creation to guide the choreographer away from the temptation of mangling music to fit new ideas. Where dancers are concerned, they have at times to be accompanied with as much loving care as a soloist in a difficult concerto. No one would dream of dictating to a ballerina, for any so-called musical reason, the speed of her *fouetté* music in Act III of SWAN LAKE, for this is a case where she needs all the help the conductor can give her by producing a tempo to fit her steps like an immaculately tailored garment. (This is not a good time for her to see her conductor's head buried in the score.) But even here great care is needed in the conductor's treatment of the dancer, for no one dancer is like another: some like to be coaxed, some led, some need to be encouraged, some practically forced to their optimum speed. Dancers have the hardest and the shortest profession in the performing arts and conductors should study every one with whom he works to find out what makes them dance, how they want to dance, and how they should. When NERINA danced as a guest with the Bolshoy their great conductor, FAIER, then nearly blind, asked the ballerina to take him right through the version she was going to dance so that he would know precisely what she would be doing and what help she needed from him.

Conductors need to spend much time in the classroom; not only should they attend piano rehearsals of a new work but they should also learn basic principles of dance technique. During the notoriously difficult *fouettés*, for example, you learn to watch not only the vertical leg to synchronize the strong musical beat with the heel on the floor but also the 'whipping' leg for signs of tiredness. When learning a role for the first time, dancers will always practise steps at a speed slower than they may ultimately achieve. If the conductor fails to appear until the final rehearsal the dancer may well be shocked at hearing the music ruthlessly taken at a 'decent' tempo and the conductor consequently persuaded to adopt a dreary pace in performance. Also, and this is a point forgotten by many, to match only the steps of a dancer is like reciting poetry in a well-timed monotone: the conductor must learn also how a dancer phrases, and dancers in turn need to feel the natural phrasing of the music. Sometimes a dancer, thinking an adjustment of tempo is necessary and asking for one, needs only for the music to be subtly phrased.

Attendance in the studio also enables the conductor to give guidance to the rehearsal pianist. Minor dangers can be averted in this way: for example, the end of Aurora's last act solo in SLEEPING BEAUTY poses a problem to many pianists, consisting as it does of chords jumped from high up to low down on the piano. No musician likes to play wrong notes, and in this instance the pianist may be tempted to make a slight *rallentando* so as to reach the last chord securely. Left unnoticed, this may produce the request at the stage (orchestral) rehearsal of 'oh, I'm used to a hold-up there, may I have one please?' Any such *rallentando* as requested would rob the ending of its crisp effectiveness, choreographically as well as musically.

Most important are the stage and piano rehearsals at which the pianist watches not the dancers but the conductor who has then to find for himself the right balance of tempo between the needs of the dance and of the music. What finally remains is to rehearse the orchestra with the nuances that will be expected in performance and to present the score as a vital work of theatre and as satisfying, convincing music. JLy

For entries on individual conductors who have contributed to the art of ballet *see* ANSERMET, FAIER, IRVING, LAMBERT, MONTEUX, SIMONOV

Connecticut College *see* UNIVERSITIES, DANCE IN

Connor, Laura, b. Portsmouth, 1946. English dancer. Studied locally with Mavis Butler, then RBS. Joined RB 1965, soloist 1970, principal 1973. A blonde and charming dancer, she epitomizes the English style of dancing and has a range from LISE to BAYADÈRE in ballerina roles. Notable also in DANCES AT A GATHERING. MC

Conseil International de la Danse (CIDD), the International Council for Dance, non-governmental organization attached to UNESCO, started 1973, based at UNESCO, Paris. President Jooss, general secretary Susana Frugone, with 5 vice-presidents for 5 continents: Bengt Häger (Europe), N'Sougan Agblemagnon (Africa), Kumudini Lakhia (Asia), Francis Francis (North America), Josephina Lavalle (Latin America). A forum for exchange of information, research etc. Organized the Fest. for Filmatic Dance, Stockholm 1975, biennial Fest. for Classical Indian Dance in India from 1976. Research programs on dance notation and legislation for choreographers' author's rights. BH

Conservatory, The (*Konservatoriet*), ballet, ch. August BOURNONVILLE; mus. Holger Paulli. Copenhagen, RDB, 6 May 1849. Originally subtitled *A Proposal by Advertisement*, it was last performed in its entirety 1934. The first-act-only version, entitled *The Dancing School of the Conservatory (Danseskolen af Konservatoriet)* and internationally performed (incl. CCJB, 20 Feb 1969; also in repertoires of Australian B. and LFB), shows a typical Bournonville class in which he pays affectionate homage to his teacher A. VESTRIS. SKJ

Contemporary Dance, the name now favoured by GRAHAM and her disciples instead of MODERN DANCE. MC

Contraction and Release *see* GRAHAM TECHNIQUE

Copland, Aaron, b. Brooklyn, NY, 1900. American composer. Studied with Nadia Boulanger and through her was greatly influenced by STRAVINSKY, especially in matters of textural clarity and rhythmic vitality. His absolute music has often been used for dance: his *Music for the Theatre* for *Time Table* (NY 1941; ch. TUDOR), his *Piano Sonata* for *Day on Earth* (NY 1947; ch. HUMPHREY), his *Concerto for Clarinet* for *The Pied Piper* (NY 1951; ch. ROBBINS). Copland's dance scores, which often make highly effective use of American folk songs, traditional hymns, etc., incl. *Hear Ye! Hear Ye!* (Chicago 1934; ch. PAGE), BILLY THE KID, RODEO, APPALACHIAN SPRING, and *Ballet in Seven Movements* (Munich 1963; ch. H. ROSEN). DH

Coppélia, ou La Fille aux Yeux d'Émail (*Coppélia, or the Girl with Enamel Eyes*), ballet, 3 acts, ch.

SAINT-LÉON; mus. DELIBES; lib. Charles Nuitter and Saint-Léon; sc. Charles Cambon, Édouard Despléchin, Antoine Lavastre; c. Alfred Albert. Paris O., 25 May 1870; dan. BOZZACCHI, FIOCRE, François Édouard Dauty. The story, significantly concerned with 'real' people rather than sprites and Wilis (Romanticism by now was dead), is about an old toy-maker, Dr Coppélius, whose prize creation is the doll Coppélia, who is so lifelike that two young lovers are fooled into thinking her real (*see* COMPLETE BOOK).

Typical of the period, Franz was originally played by a luscious ballerina – a tradition that lasted at the Paris O. until the middle of the 20th c. An innovation was the introduction of national dances, e.g. the Hungarian Czárdás in Act I. Little remains of Saint-Léon's choreography and the best-known version danced today stems from a production by M. PETIPA, IVANOV, and CECCHETTI, St Petersburg 1884, brought to the West by SERGUEEFF. This version, in which Franz is danced by a man, is in the repertory of the RB. There have been countless stagings. A. DANILOVA revived it, with revisions by BALANCHINE, for NYCB, Saratoga Springs, 17 July 1974; sc. TER-ARUTUNIAN. The story makes effective theatre but the great glory of the ballet is the score, one of Delibes's happiest compositions, which was to inspire TCHAIKOVSKY. MC

See Ivor Guest, *The Ballet of the Second Empire, 1858–1870* (London 1953); *Two Coppelias* (London 1970)

Coq d'Or, Le (*The Golden Cockerel*), opera-ballet, 3 scenes with prologue and epilogue; ch./prod. FOKINE; mus. Nikolay Rimsky-Korsakov (from his opera of the same name); lib. Vladimir Belsky; sc./c. GONCHAROV. Paris O., DIAGHILEV's B. Russes, 24 May 1914; dan. KARSAVINA (Queen of Shemakhan), Alexis Bulgakov (King Dodon), CECCHETTI (Astrologer). In this production the singers were ranged in tiers on either side of the stage and sang the 'action' while the dancers depicted it. A Russian fairy story, based on Aleksandr Pushkin's poem, the work was a sensation in 1914 because of the unusual treatment, the brilliant colours of the designs based on Russian folk art, and the ingenious mixture of dance and mime, especially in the scenes between the beautiful Queen and the aged King. Revived without singers by Fokine for DE BASIL 1937 with BARONOVA as the Queen and RIABOUCHINSKA especially effective as the Golden Cockerel (not a dance role in the original version). This version was revived by BERIOZOFF for LFB, 6 May 1976. Original Russian title *Zolotoy Petushok*. MC

See COMPLETE BOOK

Coralli [Peracini], Jean, b. Paris, 1779; d. Paris, 1854. French dancer and choreographer of Bolognese ancestry. Studied Paris O., debut 1802. First choreography in Vienna then worked in Milan, Lisbon, and Marseille. Ballet master, T. de la Porte-Saint-Martin, Paris, 1825; in 1831 choreographer, Paris O. where he produced, among many other ballets, *Le Diable Boiteux* (1836), *La Tarentule* (1839), GISELLE (1841; with PERROT), and PÉRI (1843). His last ballet was *Ozai ou l'Insulaire* (1847) with a score by Casimir Gide and scenery by the veteran Pierre Ciceri (1782–1868). It was based on a 'noble savage' fantasy but failed to please. It marked the end of the great days of the Romantic ballet. MC

See Ivor Guest, *The Romantic Ballet in Paris* (London and Middletown, CT, 1966)

Corkle, Francesca, b. Seattle, WA, 1952. American dancer. Studied at her mother's school and at American B. Center. Joined CCJB 1968. A brilliant *demi-caractère* dancer whose roles incl. Pimpinella in PULCINELLA, Street Dancer in PETRUSHKA, and solos in both KETTENTANZ and CONSERVATORY. DV

Le Coq d'Or as revived by LFB, 1976, with RUANNE as the Queen of Shemakhan and Donald Barclay as King Dodon

Le Corsaire, as danced by GELTSER and TIKHOMIROV in GORSKY's Moscow version

Corsaire, Le, ballet, 2 acts, ch. François Decombe Albert; mus. Nicholas Bochsa. London, King's T., 29 June 1837; revived, with WEBSTER, London, T. Royal, Drury Lane, 20 Sept 1844. Twelve years later came MAZILIER's version: ballet pantomime, 3 acts, 5 scenes; mus. ADAM; sc. Édouard Desplèchin, Charles Cambon, Joseph Thierry, machines Sacré; lib. H. Vernoy de Saint-Georges and Mazilier. Paris O., 23 Jan 1856. Based on Lord Byron's poem *The Corsair*, *Le Corsaire* has a complicated plot in which the hero Conrad, the Pirate, saves the heroine Medora (created by ROSATI) from a lascivious Pasha. The lovers even survive a spectacular shipwreck while making their escape (*see* COMPLETE BOOK). The ballet has been popular in Russia. PERROT's version (4 acts, 5 scenes; mus. Adam and PUGNI; St Petersburg, Bolshoy T., 12 Jan 1858; dan. Ekaterina Friedberg as Medora, M. PETIPA as Conrad) stayed close to Mazilier, but had an interpolated *pas d'esclave*, choreographed by Petipa with music by Prince Peter von Oldenburg. Petipa revived it, 13 Dec 1868, in a new version for his wife, Marie Petipa, as Medora, with an elaborate *pas d'action* 'Le Jardin Animé' to DELIBES's music (for two ballerinas and large female *corps de ballet*). He revived it again, 1899, with Waltz and Adagio to music by DRIGO; the interpolated *pas de deux* for LEGNANI is often danced as a concert number but the male dancer today usually eclipses the ballerina. Especially notable was GORSKY's attempt to create a heroic spectacle, bringing it closer to Byron, with interpolated music by Frédéric Chopin to give Conrad (TIKHOMIROV) and Medora (GELTSER) a love duet lacking in other versions. Costumes and, in part, the choreography, showed I. DUNCAN influence in this enduringly successful production (Moscow, Bolshoy T., 1912). Later revivals: GUSEV, Leningrad, Maly T., 1955, to new lib. by SLONIMSKY and for Novosibirsk O., 1962, with Petipa ensembles restored; Nina Grishina's production for Stanislavsky B., 1957, had action mainly in dance with LIEPA in title role; SERGEYEV's version, Kirov T., 1974, incl. 'Le Jardin Animé' and the *pas d'esclave* but had the dance element heightened for Conrad and other male roles. NR

Cosi, Liliana, b. Milan, 1941. Italian dancer. Trained at Sc. BS 1950–8, and Bolshoy. Principal dancer Sc., appointed *prima ballerina assoluta* 1975. Frequent recital appearances N. Italian provinces, also Russian tours. Guest artist LFB 1971. At her best in SWAN LAKE with NUREYEV 1974, also earlier SLEEPING BEAUTY and GISELLE (1970). Memorable JULIET (CRANKO) 1971 (with FASCILLA); *Giselle* with KELLY, Sc. 1972. EXCELSIOR, etc. with Marinel Stefanescu 1975. FP

Costume *see* DESIGN

Coton, A. V. [Edward Haddakin], b. York, 1906; d. London, 1969. English writer and critic of the dance. At first a merchant seaman and policeman; began writing ballet criticism in 1935 and was active in management of TUDOR's London B. by 1938. World War II service in Light Rescue Division in London, saving many people in the air raids. Published during war years mimeographed journal *Dance Chronicle* which was fiercely 'anti-Establishment' and throughout his life helped and encouraged countless young people, both writers and dancers. A controversial figure but important catalyst. London correspondent, *Dance News*, NY, 1943–56, dance critic, *Daily Telegraph*, London, 1954–69. Author of *A Prejudice for Ballet* (London 1938), *The New Ballet: Kurt Jooss and His Work* (London 1946). A collection of his *Writings on Dance 1938–68* has been published (London 1975), selected and edited by Kathrine Sorley Walker and his widow, Lilian Haddakin. MC

Cracow Wedding (*Wesele w Ojcowie*), ballet, 1 act, ch. Julia Mierzyńska and Louis Thierry; mus. Karol Kurpiński and Józef Damse after melodies by Jan Stefani from the Polish opera *Cracoviennes and Highlanders* (1794). Warsaw, B. Kudlicz, 14 Mar 1823. Main characters: the Bride, the Bridegroom, their Parents, the Best Man, the Bridesmaid, the Organist. Folk wedding from the Cracow region, based on folk customs and dances. The oldest Polish ballet still staged. On a European tour the Polish NB danced a version ch. NIJINSKA, London, CG, Dec 1937. The Anglo-Polish B. (a short-lived co. in England during World War II) gave a 1-act version ch. Czesław Konarski, London, Apollo T., 2 Dec 1940. JPu

Cragun, Richard, b. Sacramento, CA, 1944. American dancer. Studied with Barbara Briggs and at Banff S. of Fine Arts in Canada with G. LLOYD, Betty Farrally; also at London RBS. Joined Stuttgart B. 1962, becoming soloist and then principal, partnering Haydée. Guest artist, Berlin, 1964 and Boston, MA, 1968. Partnered Fonteyn in RB touring co. Created many roles in Cranko's ballets, incl. Petruchio in his Taming of the Shrew, 1969. Guest artist with ABT 1976. GBLW

Cramér, Ivo, b. Gothenburg, 1921. Swedish dancer, choreographer, and ballet director. Pupil of Cullberg, Leeder. Founded Svenska Dans T. with Cullberg 1946. Ballet master of Verde Gaio Co., Lisbon, 1948, Ny Norsk B., Oslo, 1952. Founded Cramér B. for Riks T. 1967; left 1975 to become ballet director of RSB. Cramér is a lyrical choreographer often inspired by religious themes and folklore. Prodigal Son (1957) for RSB combines these sources. He has created ballets for children, some for perf. by the pupils of RSBS. The perf. of *Our Lord*, one of the ballets he has choreographed for churches, has become a Christmas tradition at the Skeppsholmskyrkan, Stockholm. He has also directed opera, operetta, and musicals. AGS

Cranko, John, b. Rustenburg, Transvaal, 1927; d. 1973 (during the flight home to Stuttgart from NY). S. African dancer and choreographer, architect of the Stuttgart B. Early training with Sturman, then to Cape Town Univ. BS where he created his first ballet, *A Soldier's Tale* (1942), mus. Stravinsky but using his own story. He choreographed two short works for the UCTB. but in 1946 went to England to study at the SWS and did not work again in S. Africa. He appeared with the SWB at CG 1947 but his gifts as a choreographer had already been recognized by de Valois (he staged *Children's Corner* to Debussy's music for a club perf.) and he was given opportunities to create for the SWTB.

His first big success was Pineapple Poll, quickly followed by the poetic *Harlequin in April* (1951). For the SWB at CG he choreographed the comic *Bonne Bouche* (1952) and the full-length Prince of the Pagodas. He worked for the NYCB, the Paris OB and at the Sc., Milan and in 1955 had a remarkable success in London with his revue *Cranks*. A cool

Above: John Cranko rehearsing Lorrayne and Sibley of the RB at CG, 1966, in his *Brandenburg Nos 2 and 4*

Right: Richard Cragun as Petruchio in Taming of the Shrew

reception for his ballet *Antigone* for the RB at CG (1959), the comparative failure of *New Cranks* (1960) and a disastrous musical, *Keep Your Hair On,* disenchanted him with the London scene and in 1961 he accepted the *Intendant* Walter Erich Schäfer's invitation to direct the STUTTGART B. With HAYDÉE as his ballerina and a devoted team of dancers he built it from a provincial troupe into one of the best-loved cos in the world. His productions of ROMEO AND JULIET, ONEGIN and TAMING OF THE SHREW were but three of the cascade of ballets that poured from him. He spent all his time in the theatre with the dancers, either in rehearsal or in the canteen, and out of this camaraderie grew a co. spirit rare in the world and so strong that it was able to withstand his death.

As a child, Cranko had his own toy theatre and took part in family theatricals. It was a sense of theatre that uniquely characterized his work. His range was from the romantic to the tragic and he had a marvellous gift for comedy. In addition to staging his own ballets, he invited MACMILLAN to work in Stuttgart and it was for that co. that MacMillan created his LIED VON DER ERDE. Cranko's early death shocked the whole ballet world. The school in Stuttgart has been named after him, John Cranko-Schule (Ballettschule des Württembergischen Staatstheaters); a ballet studio in SWT also bears his name. MC

See Walter Erich Schäfer, *Bühne eines Lebens* (Stuttgart 1975); the section of his memoirs relating to Cranko tr. into English by Jean Wallis, published in six instalments, *The Dancing Times* (London May–Oct 1976); Madeline Winkler-Betzendahl and Zoe Dominic, *John Cranko und das Stuttgart Ballett* (Pfullingen 1969; revised with photographs 1975); H. Koegler, 'John Cranko', *Les Saisons de la Danse* (Paris, Mar 1972) with list of ballets and activities

Craske, Margaret, b. 1898. British dancer and teacher. Danced briefly with DIAGHILEV Co. and in various small British cos in the 1920s. A pupil of CECCHETTI, she taught his method in London throughout the 1930s and also expounded it in two authoritative textbooks, *The Theory and Practice of Allegro in Classical Ballet* (with BEAUMONT, London 1930) and *The Theory and Practice of Advanced Allegro in Classical Ballet* (with DERRA DE MORODA, London 1956). Invited to USA in 1946 as ballet mistress of ABT and remained there to teach at NY Met OBS until the old house closed in 1966, when the school ceased to function, and for many summers at Jacob's Pillow Fest. Now teaches at Manhattan S. of Dance. DV

Crassus, the debauched Roman general who defeats SPARTACUS

Créatures de Prométhée, Les (LIFAR) *see* GESCHÖPFE DES PROMETHEUS

Creatures of Prometheus, The (ASHTON and DE VALOIS) *see* GESCHÖPFE DES PROMETHEUS

Crimson Sails (or *Red Sails*; *Alye Parusa*), ballet, 3 acts, prologue and epilogue, ch. Nikolay Popko, Lev Pospekhin, and RADUNSKY; mus. Vladimir Yurovsky; lib. A. Talanov from a story by Alexander Green (Aleksandr Grinevsky); sc./c. Pyotr Williams, Kuibyshev, Bolshoy B., 30 Dec 1942; dan. TIKHOMIRNOVA, PREOBRAZHENSKY, MESSERER, Radunsky. A girl dreams that some day a boat with crimson sails will come to her fishing village and its captain will bring her happiness. A young sailor, learning of her dreams, turns the legend into reality: he comes to fetch her in a boat with crimson sails and they depart for a happy life. New production ch. Yulamey Scott and Yuri Papko, mus. arr. composer's son Mikhail Yurovsky, and some changes in the dramatic sequences, Kuibyshev T. of O. and B., 29 Dec 1975. NR

Croce, Arlene, b. Providence, RI. The most influential and perceptive American writer on dance since DENBY; editor of the periodical *Ballet Review*, critic for *The New Yorker*, and author of *The Fred Astaire and Ginger Rogers Book* (London and New York 1972). DV

Cropley, Eileen, b. London, 1932. British dancer. Studied ballet in London, and modern dance with LEEDER, and at GRAHAM S. Joined P. TAYLOR Dance Co. 1966 (one of the first British dancers to succeed in American contemporary dance), and has danced in most of his works since then. DV

Croqueuse de Diamants, La (*The Diamond Cruncher*), ballet, 4 scenes, ch. PETIT; mus. Jean-Michel Damase; lib. Petit and Alfred Adam; sc./c. Georges Wakhevitch. Paris, T. Marigny, B. de Paris, 25 Sept 1950; dan. JEANMAIRE, Petit. Aided by accomplices (one danced notably by G. HAMILTON), a diamond-eating, voluptuous woman gangster seduces a young market gardener in Les Halles in Paris. Early example of Jeanmaire's later cabaret style, using a mixture of song and dance. The ballet is on film, in *Black Tights* (1960). M-FC

Cuba. Although a *corps de ballet* of sorts was assembled when ELSSLER danced in Havana 1841, there was no real ballet tradition until ALONSO founded her own co. 1948. It took the name B. de Cuba in 1955 and is now the B. Nacional de Cuba. It has toured in E. Europe and in 1966 danced at the Paris International Fest. The repertory incl. the classics, which are well done, especially GISELLE, and contemporary works by the resident choreographers Alberto Alonso, Alicia Alonso, Gustavo Herrera, Alberto Mendez, and Iván Tenorio. International fests have been organized in Havana from 1971 with many guest stars from the USA, Europe, and the USSR. The school, directed by Fernando and Alicia Alonso until they separated in the 1970s, has produced some excellent dancers, incl. Loipa Araújo, Aurora Bosch, Marta García, Josefina Méndes, Mirta

Plá, and Jorge Esquivel. The Cubans have done consistently well in the Varna Competitions. Alicia Alonso is now director general and prima ballerina. F. Alonso teaches in Camaguey. There is also now a B. de Camaguey and a modern dance co. MC
See Arnold L. Haskell, *Balletomane at Large* (London 1972)

Cuevas *see* DE CUEVAS

Cullberg, Birgit, b. Nyköping, 1908. Swedish dancer and choreographer. Studied at Dartington Hall, England, with JOOSS. Appeared as soloist and with small group in satirical and humorous dances. Founded with CRAMÉR Svenska Dansteatern 1946 and toured the Continent. Choreographed MISS JULIE for Riks T. 1950 and was invited to stage the ballet at the Royal T. She was resident choreographer there 1952–7. MEDEA is from this period. She left the theatre to freelance. Choreographed *The Moon Reindeer* for RDB 1957. To USA 1958 as guest choreographer, and *Lady from the Sea* was presented by ABT 1960. She worked for many other countries and then returned to Sweden to found her own co., the Cullberg B., for Riks T. 1967. For her dancers, with her son EK as leading artist, a series of new ballets was composed: *Dionysos*, *Fedra*, *Eurydice is Dead*, *Romeo and Juliet*, and *Revolt*. She has choreographed for TV and won a Prix d'Italia. Cullberg's field is strong dance drama with roles of psychological depth. Her style is based on classical and modern movements. AGS
See I. Lidova, 'Birgit Cullberg', *Les Saisons de la Danse* (Paris, May 1972)

Cunningham, Merce, b. Centralia, WA, 1919. American dancer and choreographer. First formal training in dance and theatre at Cornish S., Seattle. After studying in the Bennington Summer S. of Dance in Oakland, CA, 1939, he was invited by GRAHAM to join her co., and remained as a soloist until 1945, creating leading roles in LETTER TO THE WORLD, APPALACHIAN SPRING, etc. First independent concerts given jointly with ERDMAN and FONAROFF, 1942, incl. a solo, *Totem Ancestor*, with music by CAGE, Cunningham's musical collaborator throughout his career. Cunningham continued to give solo concerts with Cage in NY and across the USA during the next 10 years, and also began to choreograph group works, incl. *The Seasons* (1947; mus. Cage), commissioned by KIRSTEIN for B. Society, *16 Dances for Soloist and Company of Three* (1951), *Noces* (1952), usually for an *ad hoc* co. of dancers. In summer 1949 Cunningham and Cage visited Paris and performed there with LECLERCQ and Betty Nichols. Cunningham was on the faculty of SAB 1948–51; he has been a guest teacher at universities all over the USA, and opened his own studio in NY 1959.

The first performance of Merce Cunningham and Dance Co., which incl. C. BROWN, FARBER,

Merce Cunningham in his *Antic Meet*. The chair was an integral part of the costume and the choreography.

Le Cygne. Above: A. PAVLOVA, for whom the dance was created; *below:* ULANOVA's interpretation

CHARLIP, and P. TAYLOR, took place at Black Mountain College, NC, summer 1953; the first NY season followed in December. Cunningham has to date choreographed some 60 works for his co., incl. *Septet* (1953), *Minutiae* (1954), *Suite for Five* (1956), *Nocturnes* (1956), *Antic Meet* (1958), SUMMERSPACE (1958), *Rune* (1959), *Crises* (1960), *Aeon* (1961), *Story* (1963), *Winterbranch* (1964), *Variations V* (1965), *How to Pass, Kick, Fall, and Run* (1965), *Place* (1966), *Scramble* (1967), RAINFOREST (1968), *Walkaround Time* (1968), CANFIELD (1969), *Tread* (1970), *Second Hand* (1970), *Signals* (1970), *Landrover* (1972), *Changing Steps* (1973), *Sounddance* (1974), *Westbeth*, a video piece (1974), *Rebus* (1975), *Torse* (1976), *Squaregame* (1976). With and without his co., Cunningham has toured the USA, Europe, Latin America, and the Far East. His ballet *Summerspace* has also been in the repertory of NYCB (1966), the CULLBERG B. (1967), and, together with *Winterbranch*, the Boston B. (1974). In 1972 the Fest. de l'Automne in Paris commissioned *Un Jour ou Deux* from Cunningham, Cage, and Jasper Johns for the Paris OB.

From the beginning Cunningham has affirmed the right of dance to be its own subject matter, rejecting the literary and psychological preoccupations of Graham, and has asserted the independence of dance from musical accompaniment, the only connection being that they happen at the same time. Through his choreography and his teaching, Cunningham has been a major influence on younger choreographers (*see* AVANT-GARDE DANCE).

In addition to his continuing association with Cage and his frequent use of SATIE's music, Cunningham's work has consistently involved the collaboration of contemporary composers, incl. David Behrman, Earle Brown, Toshi Ichiyanagi, Gordon Mumma, Conlon Nancarrow, David Tudor, and Christian Wolff, and painters, incl. Marcel Duchamp, Jasper Johns, Mark Lancaster, Richard Lippold, Robert Morris, NOGUCHI, Robert Rauschenberg, Frank Stella, and Andy Warhol. DV

See Merce Cunningham, *Changes: Notes on Choreography* (New York 1968); James Klosty, *Merce Cunningham* (New York 1975)

Cuoco, Joyce, b. Boston, MA, 1953. American dancer. A child prodigy, learning and dancing jazz, tap, ballet, etc.; in 1963–4 was CLARA with Boston B. Danced in TV shows, and at Radio City Music Hall, NY – a virtuosa of the pirouette. Studied with RIABOUCHINSKA and LICHINE; taken by CRANKO into the Stuttgart B. 1970 where she became a principal and was soon dancing all the leading roles. Joined Munich B. as ballerina 1976. GBLW

Currier [Miller], Ruth, b. Ashland, OR, 1926. American dancer. Joined LIMÓN Co. 1949. Most important influence was HUMPHREY, whose creative assistant she was 1952–8. She completed *Brandenburg Concerto No. 4* after Humphrey's death. Began her

Czechoslovakia. Josef Svoboda's setting for the crypt scene of Miroslav Kura's version of *Romeo and Juliet*, Prague NT, 1971

own creative career 1955 with *The Antagonists*, which remains one of her finest pieces. After Limón's death she assumed leadership of the co., creating new works for it and reviving dances from the Limón and Humphrey repertory. DM

Curtis, Paul *see* MIME

Cygne, Le (*The Dying Swan*), solo dance, ch. FOKINE; mus. Camille Saint-Saëns from *Le Carnaval des Animaux*; c. BAKST. St Petersburg, Maryinsky T., 22 Dec 1907 (as part of a charity concert); dan. A. PAVLOVA. Original Russian title *Umirayushtshi Lebedy*. The dance, a very simple one based on *pas de bourrée*, became Pavlova's most famous role.

Many other ballerinas have given their interpretations; according to Arnold L. Haskell the only one comparable to Pavlova in expressiveness was that of ULANOVA. Part of Pavlova's perf. and the whole of Ulanova's are preserved on film. Pavlova's costume is now in the Museum of London. MC

Czechoslovakia. A ballet co. was attached to the Prague NT in 1862, with Wenzel Reisinger as ballet master, but it was not until 1907 that his successor Achille Viscusi staged the full-length SWAN LAKE there. Czech dancers who won international repute were Ivo Váňa Psota (with DE BASIL), BOROVANSKY, and Sacha Machov, who staged the dances in Bedřich Smetana's opera *The Bartered Bride* for London's SWO 1946. Psota was ballet master intermittently in Brno, 1936–52, and it was there that he choreographed the first production of PROKOFIEV'S ROMEO AND JULIET. His Juliet was Zora Semberová, who, after World War II became one of the principal teachers in the Prague State BS. Other pupils of Psota were Miroslav Kura, Olga Skalová, and Vlastimil Jílek. There were only private ballet schools or schools in the theatres until after World War II, since when Russian influence has been strong. There are today state schools in Prague, Brno and Bratislava, and also 'city schools' in cities with theatres. Several state and municipal theatres have ballet cos attached. The principal teachers in Prague have been Dr Marion Tymichová and Olga Aleksandrovna Ilyina (from Moscow) and Aleksandr Bregvadze (from Leningrad). There is constant interchange between Russian teachers working in Czechoslovakia and Czech teachers going to Russia to study. Also Czech dancers are invited to study in Russia, notably Ruzena Mazalovă and Jiří Blažek. The repertory also reflects Soviet taste; GRIGOROVICH staged his LEGEND OF LOVE in Prague, 1963. Czech dancers have had few opportunities to dance in the West but Marta Drottnerová and Blažek danced at a gala in London 1963 and Czech dancers are beginning to make an impression in international competitions (two awards at the 1976 Prix de Lausanne). The former dancer and teacher Stanislas Buzek, who trained Vlastimil Harapes, Bohůmil Reisner, Jozka Šklenar, and KLOS, is now teaching in Düsseldorf. MC
See L. Schmidová, *Ceskoslovenský Balet* (Prague 1962)

Czobel, Lisa, b. Bamberg, 1906. German-Hungarian dancer. Pupil of Berthe Trümpy S. in Berlin and of PREOBRAZHENSKA and EGOROVA. Joined Folkwang S. Essen, 1930 and created Young Girl in GREEN TABLE 1932. Soloist in Bern 1940–4, Basel 1946–7, taught in USA and toured with SCHOOP 1945–6. Soloist in Heidelberg 1950 and Cologne 1951–6. She danced at Jacob's Pillow 1965. A distinguished dancer of the Central European style. GBLW

D

Dalcroze, Emil Jaques [Émile Jaques-Dalcroze], b. Vienna, 1865; d. Geneva, 1950. Swiss composer and teacher, a pupil of DELIBES and Anton Bruckner. While a professor at the Geneva Cons. he invented a system of training later known as 'Dalcroze Eurhythmics', designed to help students develop a sense of rhythm by translating sound into physical movement. He believed that the ear could more easily assimilate the pattern of a phrase of music, and eventually a whole piece, if the body reproduced it. The system was as valuable to dancers and actors as to musicians and has had great influence in the theatre. It is taught today at centres all over the world. In 1910 Dalcroze set up a college in Hellerau, near Dresden, Germany (where DIAGHILEV recognized the virtues of the system and engaged RAMBERT, who was a student there). Others to profit from the teaching of Dalcroze were WIGMAN, H. HOLM, SHANKAR and JOOSS. Dalcroze continued to teach in Geneva until his death. In 1920 the Hellerau S. was moved to Austria where Dr Ernst Ferand and Mrs Christine Baer-Frissell founded the Hellerau-Laxenburg S. near Vienna. It trained some 3,000 pupils before being closed in 1938 after the Nazi *Anschluss*. Ferand then left for the USA where he lectured widely. MC
See E. Jaques-Dalcroze, *Le Rythme, la Musique et l'Éducation* (Neuchâtel 1920), tr. Harold F. Rubinstein, *Rhythm, Music and Education* (London 1921); *Eurhythmics, Art and Education,* tr. Frederick Rothwell (London 1930), also written in French but translated into many languages

Dale [Bolam], Margaret, b. Newcastle-on-Tyne, 1922. English dancer, choreographer, TV producer, film maker. Studied with Nellie Potts (Newcastle); entered SWBS (now RBS) 1937. Debut as the Child in *Le Roi Nu*, 1938 (ch. DE VALOIS). Soloist 1942; danced SWANILDA, SUGAR PLUM FAIRY, and many character roles. Choreographed *The Great Detective* for SWTB 1953, and six ballets for BBC TV 1951–5. In 1954 left RB to join the BBC as producer: responsible for more than 100 productions, directing as well as producing. Won the Society of Film and TV Arts Award 1969. Her work falls into two categories: (1) electronic TV studio productions (1954–68) which consisted of dance and ballet cos presented on TV, incl. many visiting cos from abroad; ballets staged for TV, notably condensations for the small screen of the major classics, and TV creations, such as *Ballet Class* (1964); (2) films (1967–76), incl. *Cranko's Castle* (about CRANKO and the Stuttgart B., 1967), *Ballet by the Black Sea* (the fourth Varna Competition, 1968), *A Mirror from India* (about a theatre school, Ahmedabad, N. India, 1971), *Rambert Remembers* (1970), *Anna Pavlova* (1970), *The Kabuki Theatre of Japan* (1972), *Gene Kelly* (1974). Left BBC TV 1976 to succeed Grant Strate as Associate Professor and Chairman of the Department of Dance, York Univ., Ontario, Canada. MC

Dallas Civic Ballet, Dallas Metropolitan Ballet *see* REGIONAL BALLET (USA)

Dalman, Elizabeth Cameron, b. Adelaide. Australian dancer, choreographer, and director. Studied classical ballet and modern dance, the latter at the Folkwang S., Essen, and with Elio Pomare and NIKOLAIS. Founder and artistic director, Australian Dance T., Adelaide, 1965–75. Pomare Dance Co., guest artist. Taught at International S. of Dance, NY, and in the Netherlands. Her ballets incl. *Release of an Oath* and *Leaving*. KSW

D'Amboise, Jacques, b. Dedham, MA, 1934. American dancer and choreographer. Studied with Maria Swoboda and at SAB. Joined NYCB 1950. First major created role was Tristram in ASHTON's *Picnic at Tintagel* (1952). Subsequently danced many leading roles, both classic (APOLLO, etc.), and *demi-caractère* (L. CHRISTENSEN's *Filling Station*). Partnered FARRELL in many ballets created for her by BALANCHINE, incl. MOVEMENTS. Has choreographed several ballets for NYCB, incl. *Irish Fantasy* (1964), *Tchaikovsky Suite No. 2* (1969). Also danced leading roles in several films, notably Stanley Donen's *Seven Brides for Seven Brothers* (1954) and Henry King's *Carousel* (1956). DV

Damnation de Faust, La, ballet, ch. BÉJART; mus. Hector Berlioz; sc./c. CASADO. Paris O., 13 Mar 1964; dan. VLASSI (Marguerite), BONNEFOUS (Faust). Dance takes an essential place in this version of Berlioz's work, which has a double cast of singers and dancers for the principal roles. M-FC

Dance Collections *see* ARCHIVES

Dance notation, the recording of movement through symbols on paper, has a history extending back to the late 15th c. when letter abbreviations for the well-known steps were used: R for reverence; s – single; d – double, etc. Two early works using this method were the late 15th-c. *L'art et instruction de bien danser (The Art and Instruction of Good Dancing)* and *The Dance Book of Margaret of Austria* (*c.* 1460). Descriptions of how the steps should be performed were given in books by leading dancing masters of the 16th and 17th c., the most famous such book being Thoinot Arbeau's *Orchésographie* (Langres 1588; tr. BEAUMONT, London 1925). The first fully fledged system, *Chorégraphie, ou l'Art de Décrire la Danse (Choreography, or the Art of Describing Dance)*, first

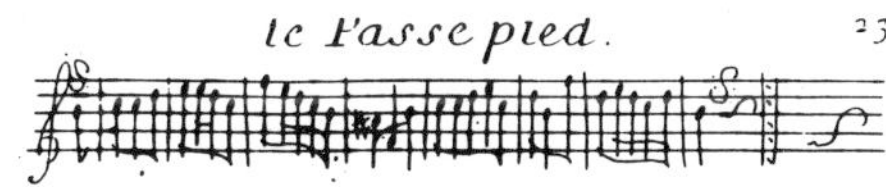

published in Paris, 1700, and credited to Raoul Feuillet (though almost certainly originated by BEAUCHAMP) was so successful that regular publication of collected dances and translation of the textbook into English (WEAVER, 1706) and other European languages provided a dance literature read and practised by the nobility and educated classes. Feuillet's system, based on the device of track drawings, depicted the path across the floor on which were added signs for step direction, turns, beats, and other intricate footwork to be performed. The system was widely used throughout the 18th c., particularly to record social dances, but it fell into disuse when the French Revolution destroyed the social structure of the old regime and classical ballet technique was transformed to meet the needs of theatrical performance.

Visual representation of movement through drawing small stick figures, a device ever popular as a memory aid, first appeared in SAINT-LÉON's *Sténochorégraphie,* Paris 1852. It is interesting to note that Saint-Léon stylized his figures to a greater extent than did Friedrich Albert Zorn, dancing master in Odessa, whose book *Grammatik der Tanzkunst (Grammar of the Art of Dancing)*, Leipzig 1887, was in fact a text on how to dance rather than just an exposition of a system of notation. In 1905 Zorn's book was published in English in Boston, MA, where it was heralded by an American association of dancing masters.

After the rich legacy of the Feuillet system, subsequent methods provided little recorded choreography until the advent of the music note system of Vladimir Stepanov, a ballet dancer at the Maryinsky T., St Petersburg. His book, *Alphabet des Mouvements du Corps Humain*, Paris 1892 (*Alphabet of Movements of the Human Body*, tr. R. Lister, Cambridge 1958), introduced an anatomical analysis of movement, the notes being placed on a three-section, modified music staff, signs for flexion, rotation, abduction, etc., being added to the notes. After Stepanov's early death, a Russian edition of the book was published in 1899 by GORSKY. Adopted into the curriculum of the Imperial BS, the system was used to record 30 ballets from the repertoire of the early 20th c. The resulting manuscripts were used years later by SERGUEEFF in reconstructing works for the Vic-Wells B. and other cos.

The need to record any form of movement rather than one particular style gave rise in the 20th c. to systems based on abstract symbols. Two systems appeared in 1928, both by individuals interested in movement in its widest range. Margaret Morris's book *Notation of Movement*, London 1928, reflects her involvement with physiotherapy as well as dance, individual symbols being provided for each

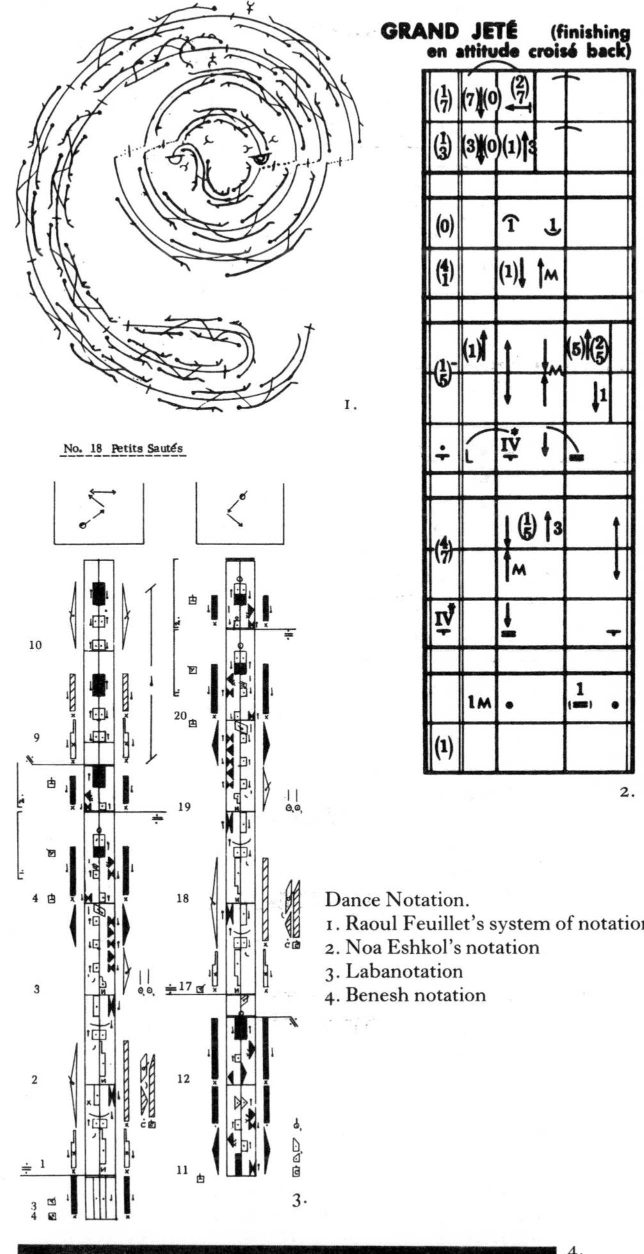

Dance Notation.
1. Raoul Feuillet's system of notation
2. Noa Eshkol's notation
3. Labanotation
4. Benesh notation

anatomical possibility. LABAN's book, *Schrifttanz (Written Dance)*, Vienna 1928, sparked the enthusiasm of many who subsequently contributed to developing his system to a high level. The basic spatial description of movement provided symbols pictorially representing the directions used, these being placed in the appropriate columns of a vertical staff representing the body. Laban's great innovation was the indication of duration of movement through the length of the symbols, timing being thus completely flexible as well as an integral part of the system. The vertical staff allowed for continuous indication of movement without a break. Fine distinctions were developed in recording quality of movement (ebb and flow of energy), known as 'Effort', while 'Motif Writing' evolved as a freer, more general indication of basic movement concepts. The Laban system is today generally accepted by scholars as the most precise method of recording movement, and there is a large and growing literature of published works, from textbooks in several languages to educational material and dance scores.

From 1931 to the present day systems based on existing devices have continued to appear. Both Pierre Conté (*Écriture*, Paris 1931) and NIKOLAIS (*Choroscript*, New York 1948) used music notes, Nikolais's being a modification of the Laban system, also using a vertical staff. A highly abstracted stick-figure system, based on visual representation of movement, was evolved by Rudolf Benesh, an artist, and his wife Joan, a dancer in the RB. First developed as a shorthand for ballet, it was adopted by the RB and has since been used by ballet cos around the world. Published in *An Introduction to Benesh Dance Notation* (London 1956) and later called CHOREOLOGY, the system was further developed and adapted to serve other styles of dance and recording in other movement fields. Drawing what he sees, the writer places the indications of position and the movement lines on a five-line music staff, a notational square on this staff providing a matrix representing the body. Special signs are used to indicate the missing third dimension and specific timing is shown by signs entered above the five-line staff.

The desire to compose dances in terms of intervals of specific types of motion led Noa Eshkol and Abraham Wachmann to devise a mathematical system based on the anatomical fact that all movement is circular by nature. Using signs for vertical, horizontal, and rotary motion, degrees of change are indicated by numerals, a fact that makes this system attractive to computer programmers. The 17-column, horizontal staff representing the body is divided into regular intervals to indicate regular beats (intervals) of time. The original book, Eshkol's *Movement Notation* (London 1958), has been followed by a series of publications featuring different forms of movement and dance styles.

The Laban, Benesh, and Eshkol systems have each established centres of training. AHG

Dances at a Gathering, ballet, ch. ROBBINS; mus. Frédéric Chopin; c. Joe Eula; ltg Thomas Skelton. NYST, NYCB, 8 May 1969; dan. KENT, Sara Leland, MAZZO, MCBRIDE, VERDY, A. BLUM, John Clifford, Robert Maiorano, John Prinz, VILLELLA; pianist Gordon Boelzner. Revived London, CG, RB, 19 Oct 1970. A ballet for 10 dancers to a selection of Chopin piano music. Robbins says: 'There are no stories . . . no plots and no roles. The dancers are themselves dancing with each other to that music in that space.' FM

Dances Before the Wall, modern dance work, ch. WARING; mus. Franz Schubert, Horace Sprott, Louis Armstrong, Bunk Johnson, New Orleans Wanderers, Olivier Messiaen, Doc Bagby, J.-P. RAMEAU, Charlie Gracie, Wolfgang Amadeus Mozart, Gustav Mahler, Fanny Brice, mechanical piano, CAGE, SATIE, and STRAVINSKY; c. Waring; sc. Julian Beck. NY, Henry Street Settlement Playhouse, 30 Mar 1958; dan. Toby Armour, GORDON, Fred Herko, Timothy LaFarge, Ruth Meyer, Judy Ratner, SETTERFIELD, Waring, and Vincent Warren. A full-length work in which objective time is suspended and the spectator enters into a dreamlike state as a series of mysterious, poetic, or funny dances unfolds before him. DM

Dance Theater Workshop, an experimental arts organization in the form of a non-profit membership corporation, founded in 1965 by two dancers from SOKOLOW's co., J. DUNCAN and Jack Moore. The original purpose of DTW was to invite and commission young choreographers working in new forms of dance, to create new works. DTW provided the space, the audience, and services such as mailing, publicity, and guidance. Projects in the first year included a studio series, a subscription series, an ethnic dance series, and master classes. Activity has increased. The list of choreographers who have shown works in DTW series includes most of those active in the modern dance field today, both *avant-garde* and commercial. In its modest loft headquarters on W. 20th St, the organization has actually produced 460 works by 140 choreographers over the past 10 years. DTW has also been active in dance education, and has offered classes in technique, composition, improvisation, pedagogy, stage lighting, tap dance, dance for children, and even economic survival tactics – a spectrum of creative workshops unavailable at any other school in NY. Sokolow has taught a choreography workshop, KONER an 'elements of performing' course, Marcia Siegel and Deborah Jowitt a critics' workshop.

A dance publication, *Eddy*, emerged in 1974 with DTW's help. Small teams of DTW staff have done residencies in colleges and community centres both in the USA and abroad. In 1974 DTW inaugurated a series of special events called 'Tangents' (films, speakers, and panels), arranged in cooperation with NY Univ. EK

Appointed to Dutch NB's artistic staff 1965; co-director 1968; sole artistic director since 1971.

Van Dantzig has mainly worked with modern music (incl. *musique concrète* and electronic music) and for design he has most often turned to SCHAYK. Occasionally a strong social theme appears in his ballets, as in *Painted Birds* (mus. Niccolò Castiglioni and Johann Sebastian Bach, 1971) which reflected on the dangers of pollution, using filmed images as well as dance; and even his most abstract ballets, such as *Moments* (mus. Anton von Webern, 1968) or *Ginastera* (1976), have emotional implications. He has staged many of his ballets for other cos and created *The Ropes of Time* (1970) for NUREYEV with the RB at CG. Other notable creations include *Jungle* (1961), *Epitaph* (1969), *On the Way* (1970), *Après-Visage* (1972), *Ramifications* (1973), and *Blown in a Gentle Wind* (1975). JP

Daphnis et Chloé, ballet, 3 scenes; ch./lib. FOKINE; mus. RAVEL; sc./c. BAKST. Paris, T. du Châtelet, B. Russes (DIAGHILEV), 8 June 1912; dan. KARSAVINA, NIJINSKY, BOLM. Fokine had submitted a lib. after a pastoral by the Greek author Longus to the Director of the Imperial Ts, St Petersburg, 1904, along with his proposals for choreographic reforms. When finally realized, his ballet was overshadowed by the production the same season of the more radical, and scandalous, APRÈS-MIDI D'UN FAUNE. Ravel's score was not matched by choreography of comparable quality until ASHTON made his version, *Daphnis and Chloe*, London, CG, SWTB, 5 Apr 1951; sc./c. John Craxton; dan. FONTEYN, SOMES, FIELD. The score is irresistible to choreographers. DV

Dark Elegies, ballet, 2 scenes, ch./lib. TUDOR; mus. Gustav Mahler *(Kindertotenlieder*, or *Songs on the Death of Children)*; sc./c. Nadia Benois. London, Duchess T., BR, 19 Feb 1937; dan. Maude LLOYD, VAN PRAAGH, DE MILLE, GORE, LAING. Revived NY, ABT, 24 Jan 1940, also NB of Canada 1956, RSB 1963. The mourning of the people of a fishing village for the loss of their children in a disaster. Mahler's songs are sung from the stage by a singer dressed in the same sombre clothes as the parents. The first scene is of anguish, the second a quiet dance of resignation. Tudor's choreographic vocabulary fused the expressionistic techniques of the 1930s and the classical school. MC

Darrell, Peter, b. Richmond, Surrey, 1929. English dancer and choreographer. Trained at SWBS, graduating to SWTB 1946–7. Thereafter he appeared in musicals, and with various ballet cos, incl. LFB and the Malmö B., Sweden. During the early 1950s he choreographed his first ballets for Ballet Workshop at the Mercury T., London. In 1957 WEST and Darrell decided to form a co. – WESTERN THEATRE BALLET – which was to prove one of the most venturesome in Britain. The positive choreographic image of Western TB was established in the many ballets that Darrell created for the co. After West's death in a climbing accident, Darrell was obliged to assume sole directorship of Western TB.

For the first, 1957, season by Western TB, Darrell had produced a characteristic ballet, PRISONERS. Thereafter his ballets could be seen to reflect many of the current social considerations and theatrical trends: *Mods and Rockers* (mus. The Beatles; 1963) charted the social *mores* of urban young. JEUX (1963) updated NIJINSKY's trio of tennis players to make a teasing mystery piece; *Home* (mus. BARTÓK; 1965) dealt with a girl's stay in a mental home. In 1966 Darrell staged the most ambitious undertaking of his career: the 2-act *Sun into Darkness* (mus. Malcolm Williamson), based on a theme by the playwright David Rudkin, which recounted barbaric rituals in a Cornish village. In 1969, just as Western TB was to move to Glasgow, Darrell mounted his second full-length ballet: *Beauty and the Beast* (mus. Thea Musgrave), and with the co. established in Scotland, the 3-act *Tales of Hoffmann* (1972) and the 2-act *Mary, Queen of Scots* (1976) with a score commissioned from John McCabe.

As choreographer Darrell has a sharply theatrical skill – as director he has encouraged an increasingly

Daphnis et Chloé as danced by FOKINE and Vera Fokina

wide choice of repertory, inviting GORE, F. FLINDT, J. CARTER, MACMILLAN, and van DANTZIG among others, to create for the Scottish B. (as the co. is now known). He has ensured too that experiment and versatility are not neglected. He has made intelligent reworkings of GISELLE and NUTCRACKER for his co., and acquired authentic versions of August BOURNONVILLE's SYLPHIDE and VENTANA. CC

Darsonval, Lycette, b. Coutances, 1912. French dancer and teacher. Sister of PERRAULT. Paris OBS 1925, pupil of ZAMBELLI, AVELINE and ROUSANNE. *Corps de ballet* 1930, left 1932 but returned 1936, *étoile* 1940. Toured widely in France and abroad but essentially a Paris O. dancer. Created principal roles in Aveline's *Elvire* (1937) and *Sylvia* (1941); also in LIFAR's *David Triomphant* (1937), *Oriane et le Prince d'Amour* (1938), *Joan de Zarisse* (1942), SUITE EN BLANC, and PHÈDRE; also danced GISELLE. Director, Paris OBS, 1957–9. Director, B. de Nice, 1962. Teacher at Nice Cons. A powerful dancer of great authority on stage. Légion d'Honneur 1959. M-FC

Dasi Attam *see* ASIA

Dauberval [Bercher], Jean, b. Montpellier, 1742; d. Tours, 1806. French dancer and choreographer. Studied with NOVERRE (whose theories he later implemented); debut Paris O. 1761; principal dancer 1770, assistant *maître de ballet* (to Auguste Vestris and later Maximilien Gardel) 1773–83; then retired on a pension. A fine dancer but chiefly celebrated for his direction of the ballet at the Grand T., Bordeaux 1785–90, where he staged the first production of FILLE MAL GARDÉE 1789 with his wife Mlle Théodore (Marie-Madeleine Crespé) as Lise. Among other ballets staged there was his *Le Page Inconstant*, a version of Pierre-Augustin Caron de Beaumarchais's *The Marriage of Figaro*. MC

Davies, Dudley, b. Springs, Transvaal, 1928. S. African dancer and director. Trained by Arnold Dover, Cecily Robinson, and HOWES. Danced with Johannesburg TB, UCT B. and SWTB. With wife, MILLER, returned to S. Africa 1956 to join the staff of the UCTBS. To Johannesburg 1963; produced COPPÉLIA for Johannesburg City B. Made principal of the co.'s school, worked with the newly formed B. Transvaal, collaborated with PACT B.'s first season. Appointed director, Orange Free State B. Group (later PACOFS B. Co.) 1964; director, NAPAC B., Durban, 1968. Known for his radio program *Curtain up on Ballet* and lecture demonstrations. Has produced for UCT, PACOFS, and NAPAC cos. MG

Davies, Siobhan, b. London, 1950. English dancer and choreographer. Studied LSCD; while still a student danced in the first season of LCDT, of which she later became the leading woman dancer and an associate choreographer. Also danced 1971 with the RB's Ballet For All. Her first ballet was *Relay* (1972), followed by *Pilot* and *The Calm* (1974), and *Diary* (1975), marked by individual use of movement. JP

Daydé, Liane, b. Paris, 1932. French dancer. Studied Paris OBS; pupil of ZAMBELLI. *Corps de ballet* 1948, *première danseuse* 1949; *étoile* 1951–9. Created leading roles in LIFAR's *Blanche-Neige* (1951), *Fourberies* (1952), H. ROSEN's *La Dame à la Licorne* (1959), etc. Danced GISELLE, COPPÉLIA, SUITE EN BLANC at Paris O.; SLEEPING BEAUTY with de Cuevas B.; international guest artist Milan Sc., LFB, and in the USSR. Many tours with RENAULT, at the head of the Grand B. Classique de France. M. impresario Claude Giraud. Combines youthful grace, technical ease, charm and *coquetterie*. M-FC

Dayton Ballet *see* REGIONAL BALLET (USA)

Dean, Beth, b. Denver, CO. American dancer, choreographer, and critic. Studied with STAATS and LEGAT. Settled in Australia 1947. With her husband, Victor Carell, has done considerable fieldwork on aboriginal and ethnic dance. Ballet critic, *Sydney Morning Herald*. Her best-known ballet is *Corroboree* (mus. John Antill) staged for the Royal tour of Queen Elizabeth II, 1954. Published *Dust for the Dancers* (with Victor Carell, Sydney 1955); *Softly, Wild Drums* (London 1958). KSW

Dean, Laura, b. Staten Island, NY, 1945. American dancer and choreographer. Studied with HOVING and at High S. of Performing Arts and SAB; later with SANASARDO, GRAHAM, and CUNNINGHAM. Debut with P. TAYLOR Dance Co., 1965; also danced with Sanasardo and KING. Began to choreograph in 1967. Since 1968 she has worked with spinning, steady pulse, repetitive movement, and geometric patterns; in contrast to other *avant-garde* choreographers who have proclaimed the independence of dance from musical accompaniment, Dean has affirmed their identity, especially in her collaborations with the composer Steve Reich (notably DRUMMING); in *Song* (1976) the dancers actually vocalized as they danced. DV

de Basil, Colonel W. [Vasily Grigorievich Voskresensky], b. Kaunas, 1888; d. Paris, 1951. Russian ballet impresario. After army service in Russia, began his theatrical career in Paris in 1925 at a concert agency, then as assistant (1930–1) to Prince Zeretilli,

Colour Plates. Facing page: CECCHETTI, a caricature by LEGAT depicting him as a grasshopper (note the *pochette*, which dancing masters at the time used to play for their own classes).

Overleaf: Design by BENOIS for Scene I of PAVILLON D'ARMIDE, 1909 (watercolour)

— Бр. Н. и С. Легатъ —

Les Ballets Russes
Programme Officiel
édité par
" Comoedia Illustré "
M. MICHEL FOKINE, Directeur chorégraphique des Ballets Russes
et Mme VERA FOKINA, dans "Schéhérazade"
Valentine Gross

running an itinerant opera co., L'Opéra Russe à Paris. In 1931 learned that R. BLUM was forming a ballet co. in Monte Carlo, made his way there, and in 1932 was accepted as co-director of the B. Russe de Monte Carlo. When MASSINE left in 1938, de Basil lost many dancers but kept much of the repertory. He continued to direct his co. under several names, the most frequently used being Original B. Russe, from 1939 until it disbanded in 1948. A colourful character and shrewd publicist, his chief contribution was to make ballet popular. He m. dancer Olga Morosova. *See* BALLET RUSSE DE MONTE CARLO. MC

de Beaumont, Étienne (Comte), b. Paris, 1883; d. Paris, 1956. French painter and patron of the ballet. In 1924 presented a season, Soirées de Paris, that attempted to emulate DIAGHILEV's style of artistic collaboration. Ballets by MASSINE were presented (incl. BEAU DANUBE and *Mercure*; the latter went into the Diaghilev repertory), and COCTEAU's adaptation of William Shakespeare's play *Roméo et Juliette*. Designed several ballets, incl. *Le Beau Danube* (costumes), *Scuola di Ballo* (ch. Massine, 1933), and GAIETÉ PARISIENNE. DV

Debussy, (Achille) Claude, b. St-Germain-en-Laye, 1862; d. Paris, 1918. French composer. Commissioned by DIAGHILEV to write his only completed ballet score, JEUX, remarkably rich and sensuous music, though NIJINSKY's ballet was not the success his APRÈS-MIDI D'UN FAUNE, to Debussy's voluptuous tone poem, had been. ROBBINS has effectively applied this latter music to a different scenario under the title AFTERNOON OF A FAUN. DH

Decor *see* DESIGN

Decroux, Étienne *see* MIME

de Cuevas, Marquis George (eighth Marquis de Piedrablanca de Guana de Cuevas), b. Chile, 1886; d. Cannes, France, 1961. American patron of the arts (Spanish father, Danish mother, US citizen from 1940); director, GRAND BALLET DU MARQUIS DE CUEVAS. M. Margaret Strong, grand-daughter of multi-millionaire John D. Rockefeller. Sponsored Masterpieces of Works of Art exhibition at NY World's Fair 1939–40. Founded Ballet International (NY). A colourful figure in all senses of the word, he organized some fantastic costume balls as well as pouring his considerable private fortune into his ballet co. MC

Deege, Gisela, b. Berlin, 1928. German dancer. Studied with T. GSOVSKY; debut Leipzig 1943. With Staats OB, E. Berlin, 1947–50; B. of W. Berlin, becoming principal dancer, 1956–65, creating leading roles in many of Gsovsky's ballets. One of Germany's most important post-World-War II ballerinas. GBLW

De Jong, Bettie, b. Sumatra, Indonesia. Dutch dancer. Studied in Holland and in NY at GRAHAM S. Performed with cos of Graham, P. LANG, HOVING, and, since 1962, P. TAYLOR. Her imposing presence lends a chilling power to the role of the automaton in Taylor's *Big Bertha*. DV

De Lavallade, Carmen, b. Los Angeles, CA, 1931. American dancer and actress. She m. G. HOLDER. Studied with HORTON and became soloist in his co. To NY in 1954 to dance in the Broadway musical *House of Flowers* (ch. Herbert Ross), opposite AILEY. Danced in NY Met OB, 1955–6, in Giuseppe Verdi's opera, *Aïda*, etc., and with NY City O. in BUTLER's CARMINA BURANA, 1959. Joined Ailey's co. 1962; guest artist with ABT (1965), and many modern dance cos.

In recent years she has been chiefly associated with the Yale (University) Repertory T., as teacher and performer. DV

Delibes, (Clément Philibert) Léo, b. St-Germain-du-Val, Sarthe, 1836; d. Paris, 1891. French composer, student of ADAM at Paris Cons. Delibes's first ballet commission was a collaboration with MINKUS on the score of *La Source* (Paris 1866; ch. SAINT-LÉON), so successful that he was then asked to compose a *Pas des Fleurs* (Paris 1867; ch. MAZILIER) for insertion into Act II of CORSAIRE. This led to COPPÉLIA and his final ballet SYLVIA, these being among the masterpieces of ballet music for inventiveness, charm, atmosphere and brilliance of orchestration. TCHAIKOVSKY's SLEEPING BEAUTY and NUTCRACKER were influenced by Delibes, whom he much admired. Distinguished versions of Delibes's ballets incl. ASHTON's *Sylvia* and BALANCHINE's *La Source* (New York 1969). According to Balanchine, Delibes and Tchaikovsky are together as responsible 'for what is traditionally known as classical ballet as its choreographers and dancers' (*Complete Stories of the Great Ballets*, NY 1954). DH

Dell'Ara, Ugo, b. Rome, 1920. Italian dancer and choreographer. Studied Rome OS. Ballet master at various Italian opera houses, incl. Milan Sc. Since 1965 director of ballet co. and school, T. Massimo, Palermo. Choreographed revival of EXCELSIOR (Florence 1967), dancing role of Obscurantism. Choreographed *Laudes Evangelii* (mus. Valentino Bucchi), Florence 1975, dancing role of Christ. Guest at Florence and Rome 1976. FP

Colour Plate: FOKINE and Vera Fokina in SCHÉHÉRAZADE, design by Valentine Gross for cover of souvenir program, Diaghilev's Ballets Russes, 1914

de Lutry, Michel, b. France, 1924. French dancer and teacher. Studied with EGOROVA. Principal dancer at T. du Châtelet, Paris. To England 1946 after resistance fighting during World War II. Joined International B., London; also danced on TV. Ballet master, T. am Gärtnerplatz, Munich, 1958–60; Zürich, 1960–3; Dortmund, 1963–6; principal of the school at Bavarian Staats O., Munich, 1966–75. He m. dancer Domini Callaghan. Co-director, ballet department, Munich State Acad. of Music 1975. GBLW

de Mille, Agnes, b. New York, 1909. American dancer and choreographer. Graduated from University of California. Studied with Theodore Kosloff, Winifred Edwards, and RAMBERT. Gave concerts in London and danced in DARK ELEGIES (1937) and JUDGMENT OF PARIS (1938). Choreographed dances in a revival of BLACK CROOK (1929), *Nymph Errant* (London 1933), and George Cukor's film *Romeo and Juliet* (1936); for ABT, *Black Ritual* (1940), *Three Virgins and a Devil* (1941; an earlier version of which, completed by TUDOR, had been featured in a London revue, 1934); for B. Jooss, *Drums Sound in Hackensack* (1941); for B. Russe de Monte Carlo, RODEO (1942; revived ABT, 1950); for ABT, FALL RIVER LEGEND (1948), etc. A leading figure in the 'reform' of American musical comedy, she choreographed *Oklahoma!* (1943), *Carousel* (1945), *Brigadoon* (1947), *Gentlemen Prefer Blondes* (1949), and many others (*see* MUSICALS). Author of three volumes of autobiography: *Dance to the Piper* (London 1951; Boston 1952; paperback, New York 1964); *And Promenade Home* (Boston 1958; London 1959); *Speak to Me, Dance with Me* (Boston 1973); and of *The Book of the Dance* (New York 1963; London 1964) etc. Formed a co., Heritage Dance T., at the NC S. of the Arts, 1973, which toured the USA. DV

Demoiselles de la Nuit, Les, ballet, 3 scenes, ch. PETIT; mus. FRANÇAIX; lib. Jean Anouilh; sc/c. Léonor Fini. Paris, T. Marigny, B. de Paris, 21 May 1948; dan. FONTEYN, Petit, HAMILTON. A young man falls in love with a beautiful white cat, Agathe, who has assumed half-human form, and takes her home but her desire for freedom is greater than her love. He follows her in a dramatic flight across the rooftops of Paris. Both fall to death but are thus united. Fini designed some of the fantastic cat masks, for which she has become celebrated. Fonteyn created Agathe as a guest with the B. de Paris; the role was then danced by MARCHAND who also danced it when revived ABT with KRIZA as the young man, NY Met, 13 Apr 1951. MC

Denard, Michaël, b. Dresden, Germany, 1944. French dancer. Pupil of KALIOUJNY, R. FRANCHETTI, and others. Joined Paris OB 1965; *premier danseur* 1969; *étoile* 1971; danced principal roles in a variety of ballets incl. OISEAU DE FEU (ch. BÉJART), LACOTTE's reconstruction of SYLPHIDE, and CUNNINGHAM's *Un Jour ou Deux*. Regular guest artist 1971–5 with ABT, dancing such roles as ALBRECHT, JAMES, SIEGFRIED, the Lover in JARDIN AUX LILAS, and APOLLO. DV
See A.-P. Hersin, 'Michaël Denard', *Les Saisons de la Danse* (Paris, Nov 1974)

Denby, Edwin, b. Tientsin, China, 1903. American poet and critic, and formerly a dancer in both Europe and the USA, 1929–35. Critic of *Modern Music* 1936–42, and of the *New York Herald Tribune* 1942–5; these reviews were collected in *Looking at the Dance* (London 1944; New York 1949), and, together with a further collection, *Dancers Buildings and People in the Streets* (New York 1965), constitute the most important and profound dance writing of modern times. An important influence on younger writers and dancers. He has, in recent years, appeared in theatre pieces by R. WILSON. His *Collected Poems* were published in New York in 1975. DV

Denham co., Sergei Denham *see* BALLET RUSSE DE MONTE CARLO

Denishawn, the school and co. of ST DENIS and SHAWN, from which most American modern dance stems. The school was founded in Los Angeles 1915, the year after the marriage of the two dancers, from whose names it took its title. Both already had distinguished careers as solo dancers. The Denishawn S. taught all forms of dance, incl. Oriental, primitive, and German modern dance, and from the original studio spread throughout the USA. The Denishawn dancers toured widely until Shawn and St Denis separated 1932; their 1925–6 tour of the Orient enabled them to add to the repertory a number of dances learned in India and Japan. From the Denishawn Co. came GRAHAM, Jack Cole, HUMPHREY, WEIDMAN, and many others. The Dance Collection of the NY Public Library has an enormous collection of Denishawn memorabilia. The Joyce Trisler Danscompany presented a season at the T. of the Riverside Church, NY, 4–7 Nov 1976, called 'The Spirit of Denishawn', consisting of works originally choreographed by St Denis, Shawn and Humphrey from *c.* 1920, reproduced by Klarna Pinska, for many years the principal teacher at the NY Denishawn S. MC
See Christena L. Schlundt, *The Professional Appearances of Ruth St Denis and Ted Shawn: a chronology and an index of dances, 1906–32* (New York 1962); Jane Sherman, *Soaring: The Diary and Letters of a Denishawn Dancer in the Far East, 1925–1926* (Middletown, CT, 1976)

Denmark. Ballet in Denmark has the same roots as ballet in other countries. First came the court ballets, under French influence, but with Danish periods under Frederik II (1559–88), Christian IV (1588–1648), and culminating at the court of Frederik III

Left: Denishawn. St Denis and Shawn in *Xochitl* (*Teltec Legend*), a typically 'ethnic' number

(1648–70), whose wife, the German-born queen Sophie Amalie, was a keen supporter of these ballets and danced in some herself. When the first Danish-language theatre, Comediehuset (The Comedy House), opened in Lille Grønnegade, Copenhagen, 1722, ballet was associated with the plays, for example, as an interlude in Ludvig Holberg's *Maskeraden.* Throughout the theatre's existence (1722–8) ballet was always performed by foreign dancers. In 1728, after Comediehuset had gone bankrupt, Landé tried unsuccessfully to form his own co. there, before going to Russia.

In Denmark ballet reappeared with the opening of the Royal T. in Copenhagen on 18 Dec 1748, which since then has had an unbroken tradition as a theatre for the three arts of drama, ballet, and opera. The original theatre, in the square called Kongens Nytorv, rebuilt several times, stood until 1874. The Gamle Scene (Old Stage) opened 15 Oct 1874, and the Ny Scene (New Stage), on the other side of the street with a connecting bridge backstage, opened in Aug 1931. Ballet is performed on both stages, which are the same size so productions can be transferred with ease. The RDB is legally bound to perform also in theatres outside Copenhagen.

During the first generation at the Royal T. there were various foreign ballet masters and the repertory consisted mainly of small pieces and *entrées.* With the arrival of Galeotti, ballet flourished in Denmark for the first time. He created soloists as well as a *corps de ballet* and a repertory of more than 50 ballets and minor *divertissements* of his own, with plots ranging from Shakespeare's *Romeo and Juliet* and *Macbeth* to Voltaire and Jean-François Marmontel. During his time at the RDB his ballets were performed over 2,000 times, but only one, Whims of Cupid, has survived and is still in the RDB's repertory.

After Galeotti, Antoine Bournonville became ballet master 1816–23, and ballet in Denmark declined. His son, August Bournonville, returned

Denmark. The Royal Danish Ballet's production of Young Man Must Marry with Mette Hønningen as the Goddess-Bride and Eliasen as the Young Man

from studying in Paris and took over the direction of the RDB. From 1829 to 1848 he fulfilled all three functions of his position: as a brilliant soloist with French virtuosity, a creative and imaginative choreographer, and a teacher and organizer; his influence on Danish ballet reached far beyond his own time. His control was absolute for almost 50 years (1829–75) and in the few periods when he was away his pupils adhered to his principles. His repertory of more than 50 ballets and minor works was influenced by his early years in Paris, where Romantic ballet began.

After Bournonville's death, ballet in Denmark again deteriorated, and only the efforts of BECK, ballet master 1894–1915, saved the more important Bournonville ballets (with Beck and BORCHSENIUS in the main parts). Neither were pupils of Bournonville but the old master was in the theatre at Beck's debut (1879) a couple of nights before his death. When Beck retired, Danish ballet again went into an artistic decline, trying to live on the Bournonville inheritance and unsuccessful attempts to bring new trends to Denmark, e.g. visits by FOKINE and BALANCHINE, who worked with RDB 1925 and 1930–1.

Under H. LANDER, Beck's pupil, Danish ballet flourished for the third time. Ballet master 1932–51, Lander began, like his predecessors, in the triple position of dancer, choreographer, and teacher/organizer. He gave up dancing rather early, except for a very few character parts, to concentrate on creating dancers and repertory. Successful in his aim to make Danish ballet internationally recognized and to create a special repertory of his own, he also created soloists, the greatest being his second wife M. LANDER. He broke away from the old Bournonville regime by introducing classes in the neo-Russian classical style, and creating in different idioms ballets to international scores from RAVEL's *Bolero* and *La Valse* to Paul Dukas's *L'Apprenti Sorcier* and Ludwig van Beethoven's *Quasi una Fantasia*. When Lander had the co. he wanted, he returned to Danish and international 'classicism', recreating a series of Bournonville ballets, from SYLPHIDE and NAPOLI to FOLK LEGEND and FAR FROM DENMARK. He also used Danish composers; his collaboration with Knudåge Riisager was especially successful, resulting in QARRTSILUNI and ÉTUDES. Lander left Denmark 1951 to pursue an international career in Paris, but returned several times to the Royal T. as a guest artist. Between 1951 and 1966 two of his pupils, N. B. LARSEN and F. SCHAUFUSS, were ballet masters, Larsen 1951–6 and 1960–6 and Schaufuss 1956–9. As Lander in his time had had guest choreographers such as VOLININ and MASSINE, they built their repertory on their own minor works and those of guest choreographers such as Balanchine, LICHINE, ASHTON (who created the first ROMEO AND JULIET to PROKOFIEV's music in the West, Copenhagen 1955, dan. VANGSAAE and KRONSTAM), CULLBERG, TARAS, PETIT, ROBBINS, MACMILLAN, CRANKO, and RODRIGUES. The young Danish choreographer E. HOLM made his debut 1964 with *Tropismer*.

In 1966 F. FLINDT returned from France to become ballet master at the RDB. His first 10 years have followed the usual Danish pattern with himself as dancer (less and less active), choreographer, and organizer. His own repertory has dominated and has given Danish ballet a new young audience due to the 'modern' trend of his creations. He has also had great success with his own versions of such classics as SWAN LAKE and NUTCRACKER, and has retained a certain number of Bournonville ballets in the repertory, mostly produced by BRENAA. Above all Flindt has brought 'modern dance' to Denmark and made the new free styles popular with Danish audiences as well as giving Danish dancers the opportunity to develop in this idiom. Among his guest choreographers have been P. TAYLOR with AUREOLE, TETLEY with PIERROT LUNAIRE, LIMÓN with MOOR'S PAVANE, BLASKA, VAN DANTZIG, LOUIS, and NEUMEIER with his *Romeo and Juliet*. Apart from these, some of the old choreographers have returned; for example, Petit and Cullberg. Young Danish choreographers such as E. Holm, JACOBSEN, BJØRN, and Hans Jacob Kølgaard have been given opportunities to show their abilities.

During the post-World War II period the RDB at long last had the chance to tour the world. The entire co. has visited Britain, the USA, USSR, France, Germany, Italy, Sweden, and other countries, and smaller groups from the RDB have visited Hong Kong, Jacob's Pillow in the USA, and South America. Soloists from RDB who have gained international fame incl. T. LANDER, BRUHN, KEHLET, MARTINS and P. SCHAUFUSS.

The old theatre lives up to its responsibility to keep classical ballet alive and to give a place to the new. Its ballet school, more than 200 years old, where children enter young and may stay for a life-time if they are talented, is still a breeding place for the art of ballet, which in Denmark has been completely dominated by the RDB, although small cos and private enterprises have been formed, up to the present with only brief success. SKJ

See S. Kragh-Jacobsen and Torben Krogh (eds), *Den Kongelige Danske Ballet* (Copenhagen 1952)

Derain, André, b. Châtou, 1880; d. Chambourcy, 1954. French painter and designer, one of the 'Fauves' group at the beginning of this century. Invited by DIAGHILEV to design BOUTIQUE FANTASQUE (1919) he showed an amazing and immediate understanding of linking costume design to his settings. Subsequently designed for Diaghilev *Jack in the Box* (1926), BALANCHINE's *La Concurrence* for B. Russe de Monte Carlo (1932) and *Songes* for Les Ballets 1933, ÉPREUVE D'AMOUR, and MAM'ZELLE ANGOT for SWB at CG 1947. Also worked with PETIT and for the OC. MC

Derman, Vergie, b. Johannesburg, 1942. S. African dancer. Studied London RBS (RAD scholarship); joined RB 1962. A favourite dancer of MACMILLAN, who made many roles for her, ranging from the ragtime ÉLITE SYNCOPATIONS to the Japanese puppet dance in *Rituals*. Tall and blonde, she is inevitably cast in such roles as LILAC FAIRY and a leading swan in SWAN LAKE. Successful debut as ODETTE-ODILE 1975; outstanding imperious perf. as Bathilde (GISELLE). MC

Derra de Moroda, Friderica, b. Pozsony [Bratislava], 1897, of Greek and Hungarian parentage; British subject from 1936. Dancer, teacher, and historian. Studied at Munich OBS, with Flora Jungmann, also with Wilhelm Kopp and Else Bergmann (later wife of KRÖLLER). To London 1913 to appear in music halls and pantomime. Studied with CECCHETTI and received his diploma 1923. With CRASKE and LAKE was his assistant, preparing newcomers. Founder member of the Cecchetti Society. With Craske and BEAUMONT revised the Cecchetti *Manual* 1932 and, also with Craske, wrote *The Theory and Practice of Advanced Allegro in Classical Ballet* (published by Beaumont, London 1956). Arranged dances for Glyndebourne and Sadler's Wells. Taught at Mozarteum Summer S., Salzburg, 1933–8. During World War II, in spite of her British nationality, invited by Heinz Tietjen, director of the Berlin Staats O., to found the KDF BALLETT. With the closing of the theatres, was interned at Tettnang. In 1945 returned to Salzburg where she settled, founded a school and taught until 1967. Now fully occupied with her library and dance archive. Ring of honour, town of Salzburg. OBE 1974. Honorary Doctor, Univ. of Salzburg, 1977. MC

Descombey, Michel, b. Bois-Colombe, 1930. French dancer and choreographer. Studied Paris OBS and with EGOROVA. *Corps de ballet* 1947, *premier danseur* 1959. *Maître de ballet* 1963–9. Choreographed *Frères Humains* (1958), *Pour Piccolo et Mandoline* (1963) and other ballets for OC; *Symphonie Concertante* (1962), *But* (1963), etc. for Paris O.; and *Déserts* (1968), *Violostries* (1969), and *Hymnen* (1970) for BT Contemporain. *Maître de ballet*, Zürich, 1971–3; choreographed *Miraculous Mandarin* (1971); in Tokyo, *Mandala* (1970). He chooses composers and designers with taste, and endeavours to communicate contemporary trends. M-FC

Design for dance and ballet. The stage designer is now accepted as one whose special skills contribute – in varying degrees – to the forging of a theatre work, but in the history of the theatre he is a comparative newcomer. His ancestry is among the artists, architects, and artisans who created the settings and costumes for the elaborate masques, music dramas, and court entertainments which originated in Italy and France in the 15th–16th c. Fortunately we have valuable records of the period in the form of etchings, paintings, and drawings and can attempt to conjure up a picture of the magnificence of the settings and costumes designed for the aristocrats and other performers taking part. The designs by Jean Bérain (1638–1711), for instance, illustrate the superbly elegant style of the costumes – many of which were fantastic adaptations of court dress. Ballets at this time were given at court (with additional decorations) or, sometimes, in the open air, but with the emergence of stages framed by a proscenium arch they were to be seen in a new context.

Artists and architects were found to transform the stage into appropriate settings but gradually the idea grew of the designer as a theatre specialist. Even so, the arts of painting and architecture continued to be the inspiration of all scenic design. The Bibienas, a remarkable Italian family of stage designers, produced settings of great architectural splendour, which also exploited perspective in a manner so dazzling it would have turned the head of many a Renaissance painter. It is worth noting that this same obsession with perspective ('false' perspective as it became rather aptly termed) became a staple of much theatre design in the 19th c. Frequently effective, it also led to optical muddles in which the performer was submerged.

Major aesthetic and pictorial changes came to stage design in the early 19th c. when the wave of Romanticism swept away the neoclassical in favour of a gentle and poetic naturalism. Although this period saw much that was charmingly conceived and free of visual incongruities, as the century progressed a great deal of stage design degenerated into essays in the opulently vulgar – a reflection of bourgeois tastes.

The first reaction to the settings embodying a form of laborious naturalism came, around 1890, from a group of Russian artists and writers whose passionate belief in the theatre as a serious art form led them to the conviction that stereotyped and dramatically irrelevant settings should be replaced by simplified and, essentially, more unified, integrated design. It was, they felt, time that settings should be not merely a background to the action but interpret the nature and meaning of the play, opera, or ballet concerned. Ironically, it was not to conventional stage designers they turned to bring this about, but to the easel painters among their contemporaries who shared their ideals. The experiments that followed greatly impressed DIAGHILEV, who was to become the 20th c.'s key figure in establishing the importance of design in modern ballet production. That the decors created for Diaghilev's B. Russes played a vital part in the co.'s success is indisputable and so much have we come to take for granted his concept of a perfectly balanced harmony between the components of dance, music, and art that it may seem superfluous to reaffirm the significance of his vision and achievement. And yet, in any survey of contemporary ballet design, it is necessary to recall the principles of aesthetic unity which were the basis of Diaghilev's (and of course his collaborators') profoundly important contribution to the development of ballet production and design.

Design. A working sketch by PICASSO for the decor of TRICORNE

Today's choreographer planning a new ballet will have in mind from the outset a carefully calculated balance between all the elements to ensure a finished work of stylistic homogeneity. In this, he will rely to a large extent on his designer to give the work a stamp of visual purpose free of incongruities and anachronisms. At the time of Diaghilev's now celebrated entry on to the stage of Russian ballet this was not the customary practice. Haphazard in the extreme were the methods of theatre production in general. Differences of style and taste became all too apparent when a lack of co-ordination existed between choreographer, composer, and designer. In a single production several designers might be involved and, even worse, scene painters employed to design settings and costumiers the costumes. Not infrequently, leading dancers performed in costumes of their own choosing (a practice, alas, not altogether unknown today!). This lack of overall supervision was bad enough but the further criticism must be added that – cast in the over-ornate, opulent style of the late 19th c. – the designs tended to be aesthetically arid.

In retrospect, Diaghilev's innovations seem a miraculously simple expedient. Mediocre – and in certain cases banal – settings and costumes of the Tsarist theatres were replaced by decors created by the most *avant-garde* and theatre-motivated artists of the day, highly imaginative designs that combined a vivid sense of colour with a deeply felt Russian imagery. Nicolas Roerich, GOLOVINE, Konstantin Korovin, LARIONOV, GONCHAROVA, BENOIS, and BAKST were among the designers who contributed to the realization of this totally new concept in stage design. The idea of treating the area and volume of the stage (framed by the proscenium arch) as a vast painter's canvas was a bold restatement of much earlier scenic traditions. Decors of such visual eloquence astonished audiences conditioned to inexpressive scenic styles. Diaghilev's reliance on *painters* to provide designs for his ballets continued when, in the second phase of his activities as an entrepreneur with the co. based in W. Europe, the École de Paris provided him with some of his most noted collaborators. PICASSO, Henri Matisse, Georges Braque, DERAIN, Marie Laurencin, Naum Gabo and Antoine Pevsner, Juan Gris, Robert and Sonia Delaunay, and CHIRICO, and many others provided designs that contributed largely to the interest generated by his productions. The already long list of established easel painters enlisted as designers for the ballet theatre grew when, following Diaghilev's death in 1929, DE BASIL and R. BLUM formed the B. Russe cos. and, in turn, commissioned decors from many painters incl. André Masson, Raoul Dufy, Derain, and Joan Miró. To this list must be added the name of BÉRARD, who was less a painter than a stage designer blessed with a remarkable instinct concerning the visual interpretation of a subject. It is interesting to note that one of today's most celebrated choreographers, BALANCHINE, at first followed the practice in having a number of his early works designed by painters (Georges Rouault, TCHELITCHEV, André Bauchant, Chirico) but in the great corpus of work on which his reputation is based rejected the use of scenery in favour of simple drapes or cyclorama. This unexpected tactic was born, initially, of economic necessity in that Balanchine preferred to choreograph continuously rather than limit his creative drive to the funds available for full-scale productions involving expensive scenery and costumes. It has remained a source of speculation whether, sympathetically designed, these might not be even greater theatre works.

Towards the end of the Diaghilev epoch it became apparent that a constant striving for pictorial originality and novelty was leading to a serious dramatic imbalance, in which the choreography and dancing were in danger of becoming subservient to the designs. The cardinal rule that ballet – as indeed *all* theatre – is a composite art was being overlooked.

The inevitable reaction to this fatal tendency was the concept of minimal design. What was happening on the ballet stage was not an isolated phenomenon in the theatre. Although the painterly style of design so closely associated with ballet had, to some extent, influenced the staging of plays, by far the greater part of design to be seen in the dramatic theatre belonged to the Constructivist/Realist mould. Settings were often reduced to a few practical and meaningful pieces – a form of scenic shorthand. If ballet designers and choreographers were casting an eye towards the dramatic stage it is probable that both branches of the theatre profited, in turn, from this cross-fertilization of ideas. Dance cos in America were among the first to experiment with simplified scenic forms and the dance dramas designed by NOGUCHI for GRAHAM's co. are a notable example. In these works the use of a few imaginative (and beautifully made) props and sculpted forms proved to be both highly evocative and indispensable to the choreography. The costumes devised for these and other Graham ballets are also models of their kind seeking, as they do, to give an added fluidity and sense of drama to the dancers' movements. (Many were designed by Graham herself.)

No less important than the search for new design techniques has been the development of lighting. So eloquent and self-sufficient can this on occasion prove to be that other scenic ingredients become superfluous.

Although the paring down of both scenery and costumes can produce a purity of style, in unimaginative hands this form of staging can appear visually negative and barren. Truly expressive simplicity is immensely difficult to achieve. Fortunately, certain cos maintain a more positive and interesting link with the arts of painting and sculpture while remaining aware of the need to strike a balance between choreography and design.

In America, CUNNINGHAM has found in the designs of Jasper Johns and Robert Rauschenberg (among others) counterparts to his choreographic inventions. The NDT has very successfully drawn on the work of painters and sculptors, incl. Takis and William Katz. The French BT Contemporain has consistently given to its productions a relevance to the world of contemporary art by commissioning decors from e.g. César, Victor Vasarely, Claude Visieux, Alexander Calder, Bernard Flamonger, and Tuan.

In contrast to all this, the re-emergence of the full-length ballet as a staple in the repertoire of the larger ballet cos has not always led to particularly distinguished design. Many of these works being 19th-c. classics, too many productions seek not the masterly re-thinking of, say, Bakst's designs for Diaghilev's 1921 production of *Sleeping Princess* (*see* SLEEPING BEAUTY) but an insipid pastiche of period style. In British ballet such designers as HURRY, Lila de Nobili, PIPER, and GEORGIADIS have – in their various ways – found imaginative solutions to the problem.

The time span of what might be considered modern ballet design is relatively short, some 50 or 60 years, but a seemingly endless variety of ballet and modern dance productions have been crowded into this period – and continue to proliferate. Mention must be made of the great importance of design and lighting in works created for the cos of JOOSS, DE CUEVAS, and PETIT (for whom the painter CLAVÉ mounted a number of original and brilliant ballets, including CARMEN); the contribution made by British designers during the formative years of British ballet when such names as Rex Whistler, FEDOROVITCH, MESSEL, and BEATON became associated with the ballet theatre. The personality of a particular co. (RB, SWTB, and BR in England, ABT, NYCB, and CCJB in the USA) derives not only from its choreographers, composers, and dancers but also from the visual stamp given by its designers.

In designing a ballet or dance work two main requirements present themselves: the main area of the stage floor must – with few exceptions – be left free for dancing and the costumes must not impede but, rather, stress the line of the dancers' movements. The designer must have a basic understanding of rhythm and form and an awareness of the evocative power of colour harmonies, intuition (to understand the mysterious laws that make an idea 'work' in the theatre), and an acceptance of the limited role played in being one of a number of collaborators.

Usually a choreographer with a theme or subject in mind approaches a designer and invites him to work on the project. The choreographer may or may not have a preconceived idea of the form the design should take. Out of discussions and listening to the musical score certain fundamental characteristics of the mood, shape, and dramatic texture of the work begin to emerge. At this stage the designer may wish to develop his ideas in the form of a scenic model, two-dimensional designs, and costume sketches. Alternatively (though time rarely allows such a luxury) he may evolve the setting and design the costumes only after he has been able to see at least part of the work in rehearsal. The majority of contemporary ballets fall into the 1-act category and for a designer this is – by comparison with plays and operas involving often complex scene changes and large costume plots – an ideal framework for expressive design. In these relatively short, 20- to 45-minute works, the designer must convey to the audience sensations that will heighten their appreciation.

The scenic and costume designs approved, they are passed to the various theatre workshops concerned. Given today's scenic techniques, which often make use of materials – metals, fibreglass, polystyrene etc. – once alien to the stage, the making of a stage setting may require the services of a custom engineer, metal workers, sculptors, and other specialists, as much as the stage carpenter and scene painter.

At the same time that work is being put in hand in the scenic department, discussions will be going on in the costume wardrobe or at the costumiers. Dancers' costumes being so crucial to their performance, much thought must be given to the most suitable materials to be used in their making. As dancers express themselves through the movement of their bodies, two of the qualities most often sought for in the fabrics used in the costumes are lightness and movement potential. In this respect, certain materials have a natural life of their own, where others – useful in other ways – appear dead and static. Of course, dancers' costumes cannot always appear to be an extension of their movements (tutus are an example, although they flatter the classical dancer in a special way) but when this is possible it greatly enhances the dancers' expressiveness.

In both scenic and costume workshops the designer must be continually available to guide the technicians interpreting the designs. Without personal supervision it is highly improbable that the finished settings and costumes will be as intended.

There is one axiom in all stage design: when the ensemble is seen on the stage for the first time the designer must be flexible with regard to his contribution and be prepared to make necessary adjustments to the designs. Inflexibility or unwillingness to compromise might well prove fatal to the success of the work. Experience shows that the chemistry of creation in the theatre is both mysterious and elusive. The most carefully calculated and prepared plans do not always produce the expected results. Seen for the first time at a rehearsal that incl. the scenery and costumes, a ballet nearly always presents unexpected surprises. This is the time (but with the crucially tight rehearsal schedules, the stage itself or the dancers may not be available) for minor and even major alterations and adjustments if the work is to bind into a convincing whole. Miscalculations are not necessarily the result of ineptitude on the part of a ballet's choreographer, composer, or designer, but are merely the price of an adventurous attempt to create something new.

Designing for ballet affords a real and unique satisfaction. The abstract and poetic nature of the medium combined with the dedicated and helpful character of so many choreographers and dancers make it one of the stage designer's most rewarding experiences. KR

Designs With Strings, ballet, 1 act, ch. TARAS; mus. TCHAIKOVSKY; sc./c. George Kirsta. Edinburgh, Metropolitan B., 6 Feb 1948; dan. Sonia Arova, BERIOSOVA, FRANCA, Delysia Blake, BRUHN, and David Adams. Revived NY, Center T., ABT, 25 Apr 1950; c. Irene Sharaff. A ballet for six, two boys and four girls, to the second movement of Tchaikovsky's Trio in A minor. The work has also been performed as *Design With Strings*, and in France as *Dessins pour Six*. FM

Désiré, Prince (or Prince Florimund), the hero of SLEEPING BEAUTY

Desormière, Roger, b. Vichy, 1898; d. Paris, 1963. French conductor. With B. Suédois 1924–5 and DIAGHILEV 1925–9; conducted the premieres of many important works with both these cos. DH

Dessins pour Six *see* DESIGNS WITH STRINGS

Deuce Coupe, ballet, 1 act, ch. THARP; mus. Beach Boys, arr. with variations David Horowitz; c. Scott Barrie; sc. United Graffiti Artists; ltg Jennifer Tipton. Chicago, IL, Auditorium T., 8 Feb 1973; dan. Tharp, RUDNER, Rose Marie WRIGHT, Isabel Garcia-Lorca, RINKER, Nina Wiener, and dancers of CCJB. The interpenetration of two styles of movement, modern and classical, with hilarious confrontations. A *Leitmotiv* is the balletic vocabulary performed correctly by one dancer throughout the confrontations.

Deuce Coupe II, described by the choreographer as a 'remodelled version of *Deuce Coupe* made to be performed by CCJB', without Tharp's own dancers, was first performed St Louis, MO, 1 Feb 1975; sc. James Rosenquist; c. Scott Barrie. DM

Deux Pigeons, Les, ballet, 3 acts, ch. MÉRANTE; lib. Henry Régnier and Mérante; mus. André Messager; sc. Auguste-Alfred Rubé, Émile Chaperon, Antoine Lavastre; c. Charles Bianchini. Paris O., 18 Oct 1886; dan. Rosita Mauri, Marie Sanlaville, Mélaine Hirsch, Mérante. Remained in repertory of O., with the hero, Pépio, being danced *en travesti* until taken by PERETTI in 1942. New version by AVELINE, 1952. First London production, CG, 21 June 1906, ch. François Ambroisiny. Based on a fable by La Fontaine, the ballet tells of a young man who leaves his fiancée to follow a seductive gypsy, but returns home when he learns where his heart truly belongs. ASHTON's version for London RB is in two acts, with simplified story: CG, 14 Feb 1961; sc./c. Jacques Dupont; dan. SEYMOUR, GABLE, Elizabeth Anderton. Now called *The Two Pigeons*. Also in repertory of the Australian B. DV

de Valois, Ninette [Edris Stannus], b. Baltiboys, Co. Wicklow, 1898. Irish dancer, choreographer, and administrator. Studied under ESPINOSA, LEGAT, and CECCHETTI; first performed in Lyceum (London) pantomime; principal dancer Beecham O. Co. 1918; danced with MASSINE's and L. LOPUKHOVA's cos 1922; soloist in DIAGHILEV's B. Russes 1923–5. Founded her own school in London, the Acad. of Choreographic Art, 1926; the same year met L. BAYLIS, which led to the founding of the Vic-Wells B., later called SWTB, of which she was director 1931–63 (*see also under* ROYAL BALLET). She m. Dr Arthur Connell 1935. After 1963 she was an active adviser to the RBS, of which she is a life governor. Only at the age of 73 did she retire altogether from her official duties, and she continued to preside over revivals of her own ballets, notably CHECKMATE, 1975.

In her day she was a fine *demi-caractère* dancer; also

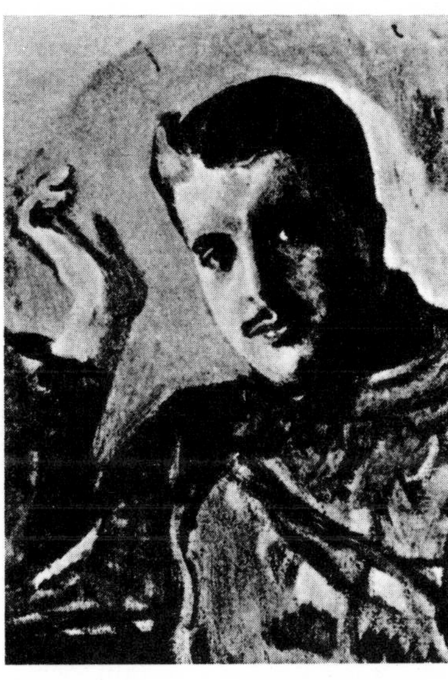

Far left: Dame Ninette de Valois, founder of the Royal Ballet
Left: Sergey Diaghilev, detail of a portrait by Valentin Serov

a highly efficient choreographer, as shown by the longevity of JOB, RAKE'S PROGRESS, and *Checkmate*. She always planned her works exactly; in this respect an apt pupil of Diaghilev, she made many of her ballets in close collaboration with distinguished composers and designers. But her dancing and her choreography were subservient to her main purpose, that of creating Britain's national ballet, which she pursued with self-denying steadfastness. She ceased dancing with her co. when she decided that it no longer needed her as a dancer; having provided it with its first home-made choreography, in order to proclaim that it was no mere museum of the classics but a new, distinctively British force in ballet, she was happy to hand over the main choreographic task to ASHTON and, thereafter, to relegate her own choreographic contribution to 'a supporting role'. She was without vanity and with a far-sighted vision, and had the dynamic energy to make that vision come true; highly intelligent, arbitrary, incalculable, autocratic (an ordinary administrator's nightmare), exceptionally kind, absurdly vague, sensible and forthright, fiery and humorous, and irresistibly persuasive, not by logic but by force of character and by her total integrity. She was almost ascetic in her disdain of personal profit. It would be hard to say whether affection or awe predominated in the feelings of her dancers towards her, but to all of them she was, and is, 'Madam'; every program of the two cos names her 'Founder of the Royal Ballet'. Was also responsible for founding the NB of TURKEY and instrumental in the early planning of the NBs in CANADA and IRAN. Awarded CBE 1947; DBE 1951. Honorary degrees from the universities of Oxford, London, Dublin, Reading, Sheffield, and Aberdeen. *Chevalier*, Légion d'Honneur. Erasmus Prize 1974. JM
See N. de Valois, *Invitation to the Ballet* (London 1937; New York 1938); *Come Dance With Me* (London 1957; Cleveland 1958); *Step by Step* (London 1977)

Diaghilev, Sergey Pavlovich, b. Perm, 1872; d. Venice, 1929. Russian founder and director, Les Ballets Russes de Serge de Diaghilev, 1909–29. Son of cavalry officer, in family with passion for music. Studied law and (for a while) musical composition in St Petersburg. Self-taught scholar of painting. In 1898, with group incl. BENOIS and BAKST, founded art review *Mir Iskusstva* ('The World of Art'), which ran till 1904. Assistant to the Director of Imperial Ts 1899–1901; and with *Mir Iskusstva* group arranged exhibitions of painting in St Petersburg. In 1905, Diaghilev mounted exhibition of 3,000 historical portraits at Tauride Palace; and 1906 took lavish exhibition of two centuries of Russian painting to Petit Palais, Paris.

In 1907 presented five concerts of Russian composers at Paris O. Their success brought him back to Paris in 1908 with his production (first outside Russia) of Modest Petrovich Musorgsky's *Boris Godunov*, with Fyodor Ivanovich Shalyapin and Imperial Ts singers. This and subsequent seasons lost Diaghilev money, but his artistic triumphs gained him enthusiastic and influential patrons, whose timely interventions would make possible the remarkable 20-year history of his ballet co.

Though he had regarded opera as the superior art, Diaghilev turned to the ballet for several reasons: the involvement of his colleagues Benois and Bakst; his enthusiasm for FOKINE, who rebelled against the stagnant stereotypes of the then Russian ballet; and his love for the phenomenal young dancer NIJINSKY. On 19 May 1909, at the specially redecorated T. du Châtelet, Paris, Diaghilev presented his Russian ballet co. for the first time, with A. PAVLOVA, KARSAVINA, Nijinsky, and BOLM leading dancers on summer leave from St Petersburg and Moscow. The splendour and novelty of the productions, the virtuosity and sensitivity of the dancers, captivated Paris each year until the war, as they did, from 1911, London and most European capitals. In 1911

Diaghilev formed his own permanent co., enticing many dancers (notably Nijinsky) to leave the Imperial Ts for good.

Diaghilev's culture and adventurous taste coloured all his productions. But his genius, and his unique contribution to the history of ballet in the West, lay in persuading eminent painters and composers to work for the B. Russes, and in discovering and nurturing significant new talents in all the arts. Though he put on productions of the classics (GISELLE and SWAN LAKE), the early repertory largely comprised the 1-act dramatic works by Fokine, Benois, and Bakst, to Russian – and later French – music. Bakst's brilliant designs for *Cléopâtre*, SCHÉHÉRAZADE, *Le Dieu Bleu*, and *Thamar* inspired a new movement of exoticism not only in stage decor but in *haute couture* and interior decoration. OISEAU DE FEU, PETRUSHKA, and DAPHNIS ET CHLOÉ were among Diaghilev's first, and greatest, commissioned scores.

After Fokine, Diaghilev *created* choreographers, and sought to extend the ballet's boundaries beyond the colourful Russian spectacle he had made it, assimilating the most experimental elements in contemporary European art. In 1912–13 Nijinsky, with Diaghilev's encouragement, invented a completely new, stylized form of movement in APRÈS-MIDI D'UN FAUNE, and again – to even more controversial effect – for STRAVINSKY's cataclysmic score (probably Diaghilev's most important commission), SACRE DU PRINTEMPS. Nijinsky left the co. after the N. and S. American tours of 1916–17. During the insecure war years Diaghilev recruited a new generation of dancers (some non-Russian), and cultivated as Nijinsky's successor MASSINE, who developed a new vein, the comedy of manners, in his choreography, with works such as FEMMES DE BONNE HUMEUR, BOUTIQUE FANTASQUE, and TRICORNE. The Russian *rayonnist* painters GONCHAROVA and LARIONOV designed several new works for this 'middle period'; but after the cubist PARADE of 1917, devised by PICASSO, COCTEAU, SATIE, and Massine, Diaghilev turned more to modern European (usually French) painters and composers. In the co.'s second decade POULENC, AURIC, MILHAUD, Vittorio Rieti, Vladimir Dukelsky, Nikolay Nabokov, PROKOFIEV, Stravinsky, LAMBERT and BERNERS produced scores, while Picasso, Henri Matisse, Juan Gris, Georges Braque, Henri Laurens, Coco Chanel, Pedro Pruna, Maurice Utrillo, DERAIN, Max Ernst, Joan Miró, André Bauchant, Georges Yakoulov, TCHELITCHEV, Naum Gabo and Antoine Pevsner, CHIRICO and Georges Rouault contributed designs. NIJINSKA, who succeeded Massine as choreographer, composed several witty works (BICHES, FÂCHEUX, and TRAIN BLEU among them), and NOCES to Stravinsky's music. Diaghilev's last major choreographer was BALANCHINE, whose two most important ballets were to music by Stravinsky (*Apollon-Musagète, see* APOLLO) and Prokofiev (FILS PRODIGUE).

In 1921 the enterprise had faced ruin with the commercial failure of Bakst's resplendent production of the Tchaikovsky *Sleeping Princess* in London; but the next year Diaghilev secured, for the first time, a permanent base for his co. at the Monte Carlo Casino; and the B. Russes survived until Diaghilev's death in 1929, when it disbanded. Though the repertory was perpetuated for a time in the R. BLUM and DE BASIL cos, Diaghilev's true legacy lies in the later work of his choreographers and dancers, dispersed throughout Europe, Britain, and the USA, many of whom started schools, and some of whom founded national ballet cos. The long list incl. Fokine, Massine, Balanchine, and Nijinska; ASTAFYEVA, Bolm, A. DANILOVA, DE VALOIS, DOLIN, GRIGORIEV, IDZIKOWSKI, Karsavina, KOCHNO, LIFAR, L. LOPUKHOVA, MARKOVA, RAMBERT, SCHOLLAR, L. SOKOLOVA, TCHERNICHEVA, VILZAK, WOIZIKOWSKI, and Nicholas Zverev.

Of the works produced by the Diaghilev B., 1909–29, many survive today in the repertories of major ballet cos. In addition, of scores commissioned by him, several masterpieces have outlived their original choreography (though they have been reinterpreted by later choreographers), notably *Daphnis et Chloé*, JEUX, and Stravinsky's *Sacre du Printemps* and *Le Rossignol*. Designs, costumes and curtains from the co.'s 20 years are now in many theatre museum collections. DD

See Richard Buckle, *Diaghilev* (London 1977); Arnold L. Haskell, with Walter Nouvel, *Diaghileff: His Artistic and Private Life* (London and New York 1935, paperback, Harmondsworth, 1960); Serge L. Grigoriev, *The Diaghilev Ballet, 1909–1929* (London 1953, paperback, Harmondsworth, 1960); Boris Kochno, *Diaghilev and the Ballets Russes* (New York 1970; London 1971); S. Lifar, *Serge de Diaghilew* (Paris 1954); Nesta Macdonald, *Diaghilev Observed by Critics in England and the United States, 1911–1929* (London and New York 1975)

Didelot, Charles Louis Frédéric, b. Stockholm, 1767; d. Kiev, 1837. French dancer, choreographer, and teacher, an important figure in the development of Russian ballet. Son of Charles Didelot, a choreographer and first dancer at the Royal Swedish T., studied first with his father, then at the Paris O. Studied with DAUBERVAL, NOVERRE and A. VESTRIS, debut Paris O. (he had first danced in public aged 12) 1790 where he danced with GUIMARD. Subsequently to London where he staged his most famous ballet *Zephyr and Flora*, King's T., 7 July 1796, in which he introduced 'flying ballet' (on wires) and is credited with innovations in costume and the use of flesh-coloured tights for women. From 1801 to 1811 he was choreographer of the Imperial B., St Petersburg. Worked in London and Paris 1811–16, then returned to Russia where he lived for the rest of his life. He staged some 50 ballets, notable for their plots, e.g. *Apollo and Daphne, Paul and Virginia*; the poet Aleksandr Pushkin said that there was more poetry in Didelot's ballets than in the entire French literature of the time. His greatest contribution to

Russian ballet, however, was in his reformation of the teaching in the St Petersburg S., bringing to it the best of the French training he had learned from Vestris. He m. Rose Paul (or Pohl; d. 1803), then Rose Colinette, a French dancer, in Russia, 1807. MC
See Natalia Roslavleva, *Era of the Russian Ballet* (London 1966); Marian Hannah Winter, *The Pre-Romantic Ballet* (London 1974; New York 1975); M. G. Swift, *A Loftier Flight* (Middletown, CT, 1974)

Die im Schatten Leben (*Eaters of Darkness*), ballet, 1 act, ch. GORE; mus. Benjamin Britten (*Variations on a theme of Frank Bridge*); sc./c. Hein Heckroth. Frankfurt, Frankfurt B., 29 Jan 1958; dan. HINTON. A sane woman confined to a lunatic asylum becomes insane herself. Revived Edinburgh Fest., Gore's London B., 14 Aug 1961; retained its theatrical power although danced in silence (because of a musicians' dispute). Revived Manchester, Northern Dance T., 1976; dan. Hinton. One of Gore's most powerful ballets with a superb role for the woman. MC

Differences *see* MEDITATION

Dijk [Dyk], Peter van, b. Bremen, 1929. German dancer and choreographer. Studied with T. GSOVSKY, KNIASEFF, and LIFAR. Joined W. Berlin Staats OB, 1946, W. Berlin Städtische OB, 1950. Director, Wiesbaden B., 1951; danced in CHARRAT's co. 1952–4. Appointed *premier danseur étoile*, Paris O., 1955, the first German dancer to be so honoured. Became director, Hamburg B., 1962, and Hanover B. 1973. From 1974 he has been director, B. du Rhin, Strasbourg, which moved to Mulhouse Feb 1977. Among his ballets are *Pelléas et Mélisande* (1952; mus. Arnold Schönberg); *Unfinished Symphony* (1957; mus. Franz Schubert); *La Peau de Chagrin* (1960; mus. SEMYONOV). Berlin Critics' Prize, 1958; Prix Nijinsky, 1959. GBLW
See J. Dorvane, 'Peter Van Dyk', *Les Saisons de la Danse* (Paris, Jan 1969)

Dilley [Lloyd], Barbara, b. Princeton, NJ, 1938. American dancer. First studied with Audrey Estey in Princeton, later with CUNNINGHAM. Danced in his co., 1963–8. Founder member of Judson DT and of Grand Union, an improvisational dance theatre, 1970. Further experiments in improvisation with The Natural History of the American Dancer: Lesser Known Species, 1970–3. *See* AVANT-GARDE DANCE. DV

Dim Lustre, ballet, ch. TUDOR; mus. Richard Strauss; sc./c. Motley. NY Met, ABT, 20 Oct 1943; dan. KAYE, LAING. The scene is a ballroom where a man and a woman, recalling other loves, decide to part. The ballet, set to the Burleske in D minor for Piano and Orchestra, stops time to flashback to the past. Revived NYST, NYCB, 6 May 1964. FM

Diversion of Angels, modern dance work, ch. GRAHAM; mus. Norman Dello Joio; sc. NOGUCHI; c. Graham; ltg ROSENTHAL. New London, CT, Palmer Auditorium, Connecticut College, 13 Aug 1948. For the first performance only the work was titled *Wilderness Stair: Diversion of Angels*. The scenery was not used after the first perf. 'A lyric work about the loveliness of youth, the . . . quick joy and quick sadness of being in love for the first time' (program note). MC

Divertimento No. 15, ballet, 1 act, ch. BALANCHINE; mus. Wolfgang Amadeus Mozart (Divertimento No. 15 in B Flat Major, K. 287); sc. James Stewart Morcom; c. (Barbara) Karinska. NYST, NYCB, 19 Dec 1956 (previewed Mozart Fest., Stratford, CT, 31 May 1956). A revised version of a ballet called *Caracole* (ch. Balanchine, NYCC, NYCB, 19 Feb 1952) to the same music but discarding its BÉRARD costumes (which were from *Mozartiana*).

Divertimento No. 15 (II), ch. Balanchine; sc. David Hays; c. Karinska. NYST, NYCB, 27 Apr 1966. Another revision of the same work: a plotless work of pure dance in which Balanchine retained some choreography from the earlier versions but, typically, added and revised on each occasion. MC

Dr Coppélius, the old toymaker in COPPÉLIA

Dokoudovsky, Vladimir, b. Monte Carlo, 1922. Russian dancer. Studied with PREOBRAZHENSKA. Danced with NIJINSKA's Polish B. 1937, B. Russe de Monte Carlo 1938 and 1951. MORDKIN B. and ABT 1939–40. Original B. Russe 1942–52. Now teaches in NY. He m. dancer Nina Stroganova. DV

Dolgushin, Nikita, b. Leningrad, 1938. Soviet dancer and choreographer. Graduated from Vaganova S. 1959; in Kirov B. until 1961; *premier danseur* Novosibirsk B. 1961–7 under GUSEV; created Prince in CINDERELLA and Romeo in ROMEO AND JULIET (both in VINOGRADOV's original versions), Ferhad in LEGEND OF LOVE, staged GRIGOROVICH in Novosibirsk. Renowned for refinement, reserved elegance and expressiveness of dancing. Has great following in Moscow where he has repeatedly appeared in recitals, for which GOLEIZOVSKY choreographed *Lisztiana* and *Prelude* (mus. Johann Sebastian Bach). *Premier danseur* in MOISEYEV's Young B. 1967–8. From Oct 1968 *premier danseur* Maly OB, Leningrad, creating FRANZ and COLAS in Vinogradov's versions of COPPÉLIA and FILLE MAL GARDÉE, and Prince Igor in YAROSLAVNA, and choreographing *Concert in White*, *Hamlet*, *Meditations* and *Mozartiana* (mus. TCHAIKOVSKY). Guest artist at Kirov T. as ALBRECHT, and in the title role of HAMLET (version ch. SERGEYEV). Danced in London 1963, Paris 1967, and Australia. People's Artist, RSFSR, 1977. Gold Medal, Varna, 1964. NR

Dolin, Anton [Sydney Francis Patrick Chippendall Healey-Kay], b. Slinfold, Sussex, 1904. English dancer, choreographer, director, and writer, of Irish descent and temperament. Studied with Grace and Lillie Cone in Brighton as a child, then with ASTAFYEVA where DIAGHILEV saw him. Engaged as a page in *The Sleeping Princess* 1921 (under the name Patrikieeff). Joined Diaghilev's B. Russes as soloist, debut 1 Jan 1924 in Monte Carlo. Was with the co. 1924–5 then again 1928–9. TRAIN BLEU was created for him. With WOIZIKOWSKI created one of the evil companions in FILS PRODIGUE; danced many leading roles including BLUEBIRD, the Moor in PETRUSHKA, Harlequin in CARNAVAL. Appeared in revues, etc., and in 1927–8 founded ballet group with NEMCHINOVA. In 1930 helped in founding of CAMARGO SOCIETY in England, created role of Satan in JOB. Danced ALBRECHT to SPESSIVTSEVA's GISELLE in Camargo Society's summer season 1932. Principal dancer, Vic-Wells B. dancing *Giselle* with MARKOVA 1934. In 1935, with Markova, founded the Markova–Dolin B. which until 1938 toured widely in Great Britain. To Australia 1939 with Original B. Russe, then joined ABT from its inception, not only dancing principal roles but staging many of the classics and choreographing his version of the PAS DE QUATRE (1941), which he has since staged all over the world. Extensive touring with Markova. Returned to England 1948 as guest with RB, dancing DON QUIXOTE *pas de deux* with Markova at a gala perf., 20 May and subsequently the classical ballets with her and assuming again the role of Satan. In 1949 formed a group to appear with Markova and himself in large arenas, which eventually became LONDON FESTIVAL BALLET; he remained as artistic director and principal dancer until 1961. Director, Rome OB, 1962–4. Has since freelanced, staging his two most popular ballets, Pas de Quatre and a male counterpart, *Variations for Four* (1957), in many countries. The first English male dancer of the 20th c. to win world acclaim; one of the greatest partners in classic ballet, presenting his ballerinas with exemplary care and pride. Author of three volumes of autobiography: *Divertissement* (London 1931), *Ballet Go Round* (London 1938), and *Autobiography* (London 1960). Also of *Pas de Deux: The Art of Partnering* (New York 1949; London 1950); *Alicia Markova: Her Life and Art* (London and New York 1953) and *The Sleeping Ballerina* (London 1966), about Spessivtseva. MC

Dollar, William, b. St Louis, MO, 1907. American dancer, choreographer, and teacher. Studied with FOKINE, MORDKIN, BALANCHINE, VLADIMIROFF, VOLININ. Danced with American B., B. Caravan, ABT, B. Society, and in musicals and films. One of the first American classic male dancers, he created roles in Balanchine ballets from SERENADE (1934) to FOUR TEMPERAMENTS (1946). Began to choreograph for B. Caravan 1936, staged ballet for the Ford Pavilion at the NY World's Fair 1940. Most of his ballets show the influence of Balanchine, with the exception of JEUX, an interesting attempt to extrapolate the style of NIJINSKY's original from its iconography. *Le Combat*, first given in 1949 by PETIT's B. de Paris, survives in many repertories despite universal critical disapproval. Other works incl. *Five Gifts* (1943), and *Constantia* (1944). Has worked as ballet master, teacher, and choreographer in Europe, Iran, South America, and all over the USA. DV

Donn, Jorge, b. Buenos Aires, 1947. Argentine dancer. Studied with KISS, HIGHTOWER, Tatiana Grantseva. B. XXe S. 1964; soloist 1965. Created roles in many BÉJART works, notably in NIJINSKY, CLOWN DE DIEU, *L'Ange Heurtebise* (1972), *Le Marteau sans Maître* (1973), *Golestan* (1973), *I Trionfi* (1974), *Ce que l'Amour Me Dit* (1974), *Acqua Alta* (1975). In three films made by Béjart: *Le Danseur, Bhakti,* and *Je Suis Né à Venise.* A lyrical dancer, with true star quality, he concentrates on Béjart's work, of which he faithfully expresses the essence. M-FC
See A.-P. Hersin, 'Jorge Donn', *Les Saisons de la Danse* (Paris, Feb 1974)

Don Quixote, ballet, 4 acts, 8 scenes, with a prologue; ch./lib. M. PETIPA after Miguel de Cervantes' novel of same title, using inserted story about Quiteria (Kitri) and Basilio; mus. MINKUS. Moscow, Bolshoy T., 26 Dec 1869; dan. Wilhelm Vanner (title role), Anna Sobeshchanskaya (Kitri), Sergey Sokilov (Basilio), Vasily Geltser (Sancho Panza), Leon Espinosa (Harlequin). Treated as robust comedy with character dances. Revived St Petersburg, Bolshoy T., 9 Nov 1871 in a new version *à grand spectacle*, with added Act V of 3 scenes (mus. Minkus), with numerous classical ensembles, especially 'Don Quixote's Dream', where Kitri (dan. Aleksandra Vergina) appeared in the guise of Don Quixote's beloved Dulcinea, surrounded by a large female *corps de ballet* and cupids. STUKOLKIN danced the title role; IVANOV was Basilio; P. GERDT partnered the ballerina in an elaborate *grand pas*, of which the *pas de deux* has been performed all over the world as a virtuoso piece.

New version, ch. GORSKY; sc. Konstantin Korovin and Aleksandr Golovin. Moscow, Bolshoy T., 6 Dec 1900. Greatly influenced by the methods of the new Moscow Art T. and of Konstantin Stanislavsky, Gorsky had asked for new decor and costumes and gave each member of the crowd scenes a 'task', thus developing, especially in Act I, a vivid and realistic portrait of Spain. He created contrapuntal movement for the *corps de ballet* and broke the sequence of the traditional *pas de deux* by composing dramatic duets that grew originally from the action. This version was transferred to St Petersburg, Maryinsky T., 20 Jan 1902, in spite of angry attacks from critics who were interested only in Petipa's style.

New version, ch. Gorsky, Moscow, Bolshoy T. 1906–35. Revived 1940 with some additional dances by ZAKHAROV and, 1942, by GOLEIZOVSKY. Still in repertoire of Bolshoy and Kirov Ts and innumerable OHs throughout the USSR. Young choreographers (e.g. Igor Chernyshov in Odessa) show a tendency towards eliminating all mimed action, thus destroying the special charm of Gorsky's creation. NR

Another version, ballet, 3 acts, ch. BALANCHINE; mus. Nicolas Nabokov; sc./c. Esteban Francés. NYST, NYCB, 28 May 1965 (preview 27 May); dan. Richard Rapp, FARRELL, Deni Lamont, M. PAUL. A complete reworking of the Cervantes story by Balanchine, who danced the Don at the preview. The score was commissioned. NUREYEV produced a version (after Petipa) Vienna 1966, Australian B. 1970, filmed in collaboration with HELPMANN, completed 8 Dec 1972, released 1973. The Cervantes novel has been used by many choreographers from HILVERDING onwards. MC

Doubrovska, Felia *see* DUBROVSKA

Douglas, Scott, b. El Paso, TX, 1927. American dancer. After service in US Navy, began studies with ST DENIS and HORTON, Los Angeles, then began ballet training with W. CHRISTENSEN in San Francisco. Joined San Francisco B. 1948, ABT 1950–62. Danced both classic and character roles, notably in SYLPHIDES, FANCY FREE, BILLY THE KID, PATINEURS, PILLAR OF FIRE, BALANCHINE's *Theme and Variations,* RODEO. Toured with ROBBINS's Ballets: USA 1961; Dutch NB 1963; returned to ABT 1964. Artistic Director of NDT 1969–70. Returned to ABT again as ballet master 1973. DV

Dove, Ulysses, b. Jonesville, SC, 1947. BA in dance, Bennington College. Also studied ballet with Alfredo Corvino, modern dance with GRAHAM, LIMÓN, and CUNNINGHAM, in whose co. he danced 1970–3, creating roles in Cunningham's *Tread, Second Hand, Landrover,* etc. Joined AILEY CC Dance T., 1973, where he soon became a principal. DV

Dowell, Anthony, b. London, 1943. English dancer. Pupil of the Hampshire S., London, and RBS. Joined CG OB 1960 and RB 1961, quickly becoming a soloist and then principal dancer. The finest classical male dancer in the RB and, indeed, one of the finest in the world, he first captured attention when dancing a solo from NAPOLI. He progressed to all the leading classical roles, in which he is suitably noble and romantic, but he also gives a vigorous and endearing performance as COLAS. ASHTON gave him his first created role with Oberon in DREAM and TUDOR cast him as the Boy with Matted Hair in SHADOWPLAY. He also created the character of Troyte in ENIGMA VARIATIONS, with a dazzling variation. His partnership with SIBLEY is celebrated and they were both awarded the CBE in 1973. BBC Television presented a documentary film about Dowell on 21 Oct 1976. MC
See Nicholas Dromgoole (text) and Leslie Spatt (photos), *Sibley and Dowell* (London and New York 1976)

Above: Anton Dolin, as Satan in JOB

Below: Anthony Dowell in AFTERNOON OF A FAUN

Doyle, Desmond, b. Cape Town, 1932. S. African dancer. Pupil of HOWES and a member of the Cape Town University B. Joined London RB 1951. Soloist 1953 and ballet master 1970–5. Now freelancing and guest appearances with the RB. Made his reputation as a remarkable actor-dancer when he created the role of the husband in INVITATION. His other major creation with the RB (a role in which he has never been surpassed) was that of Tybalt in MACMILLAN's ROMEO AND JULIET. MC

Dózsa, Imre, b. Budapest, 1941. Hungarian dancer. Graduated from State B. Inst. 1959; danced principal part in *Bihari's Song* (ch. Ernő Váshegyi); solo dancer 1964; studied Leningrad 1967. *Danseur noble* in the purest classical style as well as in modern works. Danced main roles in all the major classics, also ROMEO AND JULIET (ch. L. LAVROVSKY), OISEAU DE FEU (both FOKINE's 1966, and BÉJART's 1973), FOUNTAIN OF BAKHCHISARAY, SPARTACUS, WOODEN PRINCE (ch. SEREGI), and COPPÉLIA. Roles incl. Amyntas in SYLVIA (1972), the chosen youth in SACRE DU PRINTEMPS, title part of SPECTRE DE LA ROSE (1975), and the Artist in Seregi's *The Cedar Tree* (1975). Permanent guest of RSB since 1971. Liszt Prize 1966. Merited Artist 1973. He m. SZUMRÁK. GPD

Dramma per Musica, ballet, 1 act, ch. LIFAR; mus. Johann Sebastian Bach; sc./c. Adolphe-Mouron Cassandre. Monte Carlo, Nouveau B. de Monte Carlo, 2 May 1946; dan. CHAUVIRÉ, KALIOUJNY, B. TRAILINE. This work in grand classical style was revived Paris O. 28 June 1950 by VYROUBOVA and Lifar without Cassandre's decor. Set to Bach's 'Coffee Cantata'; the plot tells what happens when a gentleman is away hunting, having left his young wife alone with her admirers. MC

Draper, Paul, b. Florence, Italy, 1909. American dancer. Nephew of monologue artist Ruth Draper; m. Heidi Vosseler (an original member of BALANCHINE's American B.). Debut as tap dancer in London 1932, with very little formal training. Studied SAB and incorporated ballet technique into his tap routines, arranging numbers to music of Johann Sebastian Bach, François Couperin, and other classical composers; his *Sonata for Tap Dancer* was without music. For many years he performed jointly with Larry Adler, the harmonica virtuoso. Appeared in film of William Saroyan's *The Time of Your Life* (1948). Now teaches in USA. DV

Dream, The, ballet, 1 act, adapted from *A Midsummer Night's Dream* by William Shakespeare, ch. ASHTON; mus. Felix Mendelssohn, arr. John Lanchbery; sc. Henry Bardon; c. David Walker. London, CG, RB, 2 Apr 1964, as part of a program for Shakespeare's 400th anniversary; dan. SIBLEY, DOWELL, K. MARTIN, GRANT. Oberon was Dowell's first created role, and the ballet set the seal on his partnership with Sibley. Revived by touring co. of RB 1966, sc./c. Peter Farmer. Also by Australian B. 1969, CC JB 1973, RSB 1975. *See also* MIDSUMMER NIGHT'S DREAM. DV

Drigo, Riccardo, b. Padua, 1846; d. Padua, 1930. Italian composer and conductor. As conductor at the Maryinsky T., St Petersburg, from 1881 on, he led the premieres there of SLEEPING BEAUTY (1890) and NUTCRACKER (1892), also of the revised SWAN LAKE (1895), in which he made severe cuts. His ballets for the Maryinsky incl. *The Enchanted Forest* (1887; ch. IVANOV), *The Talisman* (1889; ch. M. PETIPA), *The Magic Flute* (1893; ch. Ivanov), *The Awakening of Flora* (1894; ch. Petipa and Ivanov), and MILLIONS D'ARLEQUIN. For Moscow, on the occasion of Emperor Nicholas II's coronation, he wrote *The Pearl* (1896; ch. Petipa). Drigo often edited and amended older ballets. In 1886 he added music to CORSAIRE, in 1889 to SYLPHIDE, in 1892 to ESMERALDA. DH

Drosselmeyer, the old family friend who gives CLARA the NUTCRACKER

Drottnerová, Marta, b. Gottwaldov, 1941. Czech dancer. Studied in Ostrava and with P. GERDT in Moscow; debut in STONE FLOWER 1957. Joined Prague NT 1959; now ballerina there. Silver medal, Varna Competition, 1964; gold medal, Varna 1966. She m. dancer and choreographer Jiří Blažek. A classical dancer with great dramatic gifts. MC

Drottningholm. The Court Theatre, designed by Carl Fredrik Adelcrantz and built 1766, is situated near the Swedish castle of Drottningholm. Operas and ballets were given there every summer until King Gustaf III was shot at the masked ball in the Royal Opera House, Stockholm, in 1792. After a long period of neglect, the theatre, with stage machinery and about 30 original 18th-c. sets, was found to be intact and was restored in 1921, and summer seasons started again on 19 Aug 1922 with a program of arias by Christoph Willibald Gluck and rococo dances. The RSB danced minor works there until a ballet repertory was built by SKEAPING, using original steps and patterns, and themes with Swedish connections. Her *Cupid out of his Humour* (1956) was staged for the state visit of Queen Elizabeth II, followed by *Atis and Camilla*, *The Return of Spring*, *The New Narcisse*, *The Fishermen*, and *La Dansomanie*. AGS

Drumming, modern dance work, ch. L. DEAN; mus. Steve Reich. NY, BAM, 3 Apr 1975; dan. Dean, Joan Durkee, Susan Griss, Greta Holby, Diane Johnson, Kathy Kramer, Dee McCandless. The vocabulary of simple repetitive steps such as the hop, a circling run, or simple bouncing in place has a hypnotic fascination. DM

Drzewiecki, Conrad, b. Poznań, 1926. Polish dancer, choreographer, and teacher. Principal of

Poznań B. 1950–8; danced abroad, in T. d'Art du B., de Cuevas B., etc. 1958–63; Director of Poznań B. 1963–73; since 1973 Director of Polish DT and State BS in Poznań. Danced *Till Eulenspiegel*, VON ROTHBART, Polovtsian Chief in *Polovtsian Dances*, the Devil in PAN TWARDOWSKI, created roles in several Polish ballets. As choreographer he prefers short ballets, mostly to contemporary music. Major works for Poznań OH and Polish DT; *Adagietto* (mus. Gustav Mahler's 5th Symphony); *Divertimento* (mus. BARTÓK); *Variations 4:4* (mus. Franciszek Woźniak); *Epitaphium for Don Juan* (mus. a collage of Spanish music); MIRACULOUS MANDARIN (for Komische O., E. Berlin); and BICHES. Has choreographed several ballet films, e.g. *The Plays* (mus. Johann Sebastian Bach and Eugeniusz Rudnik; Prix Italia 1970). Has collaborated with Paris TV, Dutch NB, Komische O., E. Berlin, etc. and taught at Juilliard S., NY. JPU

Dubrovska, Felia [Felizata Dluzhnevska], b. 1896. Russian dancer and teacher. Graduated from Imperial S., St Petersburg, 1913, joined Maryinsky B. Left Russia after revolution and made her way to Paris, joined DIAGHILEV 1920. Danced in SLEEPING BEAUTY 1921, created leading roles in NOCES (1923), ODE (1928), *Apollon-Musagète* (1928; *see* APOLLO), *Le Bal* (1929), *Le Fils Prodigue* (*see* PRODIGAL SON) 1929. After Diaghilev's death joined A. PAVLOVA's co.; later danced in Paris with LIFAR and in BALANCHINE's production of *Orfée aux Enfers* (mus. Jacques Offenbach, 1932), and with revived B. Russe de Monte Carlo, 1932. Moved to New York with her husband, VLADIMIROFF, when he joined faculty of SAB 1934, and temporarily retired from stage, returning as soloist with NY Met OB, 1938–9. Since then she has herself taught at SAB. DV

Dudinskaya, Natalia, b. Kharkov, 1912. Soviet dancer. Early studies in Kharkov with her mother Natalia Tagliori. To Petrograd 1923; entered Choreographic S. Graduated 1931. One of VAGANOVA's favourite pupils and disciples. Danced CORSAIRE *pas de deux* with SERGEYEV for graduation perf. Solo parts in classical ballets from first season. With the virtuosity of a Vaganova ballerina, she had impeccable technique, purity of line, and outstanding elevation as ODETTE-ODILE, Nikia (BAYADÈRE), AURORA, RAYMONDA; also a feeling for romantic style as GISELLE. She played a most important role during the 1930s–1950s, dancing, in addition to the classical repertory, the new ballets of that period. Created many roles, being particularly outstanding in the heroic title role of LAURENCIA (ch. CHABUKIANI, her first partner), the title role of GAYANÉ, Parasha (BRONZE HORSEMAN), CINDERELLA (Sergeyev version), Sari (PATH OF THUNDER), and Suimbike (SHURALE). She alternated Coralie in LOST ILLUSIONS and Mireille de Poitier in FLAME OF PARIS with ULANOVA. Evacuated to Perm in World War II, she started dancing with Sergeyev, who became her partner and husband. Together they formed one of the outstanding partnerships in the art of ballet, creating many new productions. She danced CARABOSSE in Sergeyev's film of SLEEPING BEAUTY (1964). Conducted *classe de perfectionnement*, Kirov, 1951–70. Retired from active dancing 1961. Teaches at Vaganova S. People's Artist, USSR. NR
See A. J. Vaganova, 'N. Dudinskaya: unforgettable lessons' in *Volume of Materials and Memoirs* (Leningrad 1958); G. Kremshevskaya, *Natalia Dudinskaya* (Leningrad and Moscow 1964)

Dudley, Jane, b. New York, 1912. American dancer. Studied WIGMAN S., NY, 1930–4; member, GRAHAM Co., 1935–46; soloist and guest artist with that co. 1953–4. For 20 years from 1938 she assisted Graham at the Neighborhood Playhouse S. of the T., also teaching at Graham's studio. In 1942 she formed the Dudley–MASLOW–BALES Dance Trio (she was both soloist and choreographer), which performed in NY and toured the USA until 1954; *Dance Observer* sponsored its debut perf. As part of this trio she was a charter member with Graham, HUMPHREY, LIMÓN, and HORST of the New London (CT) Summer S., performing and teaching there 1948–53. Other teaching activities incl.: faculty member, Teachers' College, Columbia Univ., summer school and winter session, 1956–64; faculty member, dance department, Bennington College, VT, where she taught technique and composition, 1966–7.

Director of New Dance Group Studio, 1950–66; artistic director of Israel's Batsheva Dance Co., preparing it for and directing it on its first two European tours, 1968–9; director from 1970 of Graham studies, LSCD. DM

Duet for One Person, modern dance work, ch. Beverly Schmidt; mus. Henry Purcell, Philip Corner, Malcolm Goldstein; sc. Mario Jorrin (film) after an idea by Roberts Blossom. NY, T. of the Second City, 27 May 1963; dan. Schmidt. A graceful dancer in a studio is shown in a filmed rehearsal studio. The live performer develops in three episodes from an awkward beginner to an accomplished dancer, who, it might be inferred, was herself idealized right from the beginning. DM

Dulcinea, DON QUIXOTE's romanticized heroine

Dumilâtre, Adèle, b. Paris, 1821; d. Paris, 1909. French dancer. Debut Paris O. 1840; created role of Queen of the Wilis (GISELLE) the following year. Also danced title role in SYLPHIDE 1841 and in 1842 understudied GRISI in *La Jolie Fille de Gand* (ch. François Decombe Albert). Her elder sister Sophie was also a dancer. Adèle was described as a beauty and Sophie as plain. Adèle also danced in London and Milan with success but left the stage 1848. MC

Duncan, Isadora [Dora Angela], b. San Francisco, CA, 1877; d. Nice, France, 1927. American pioneer of

Isadora Duncan in the garden of her school, Paris, 1919

'free' dance. Her first inspiration was the natural movement of waves and trees. Rebelled against stereotyped conventions of ballet (both in USA and USSR), with what she considered its contortions of the body and restrictive costume. She danced in filmy shifts, barelegged and barefoot, which added a sensational element to her reputation.

She left with her family in 1899 for London, was acclaimed in artistic circles, and discovered in the Greek sculptures of the British Museum her ideal, the beauty of simple, flowing movement reflecting the rhythms of nature and capable of expressing all emotions. Now danced only to music of great composers, particularly Beethoven, Chopin, Schubert. At her first appearances in Europe (1900–2), she triumphed in Paris, Budapest, Vienna, Munich, Berlin, often discoursing from the stage on the nature of her art.

Two of her principles, opposed to the tenets of classical ballet and to have a profound effect on the development of modern dance, were (a) that the solar plexus was 'the crater of motor power, the unity from which all diversities of movements are born'; (b) that the rhythms of dance, like all movement on earth, were determined by either resistance or yielding to the pull of gravity. In so far as her performances (though carefully prepared for) were improvisatory, relying largely on her personal magnetism and emotional response to music, her art could not survive her. Thus her influence on dance would be through later choreographers who assimilated her ideas into a system that could be taught.

In 1903–4 Isadora visited Greece, danced in *Tannhäuser* at Bayreuth (at Cosima Wagner's invitation), and with her sister Elizabeth founded a school for 40 children at Grünewald, near Berlin. On her first appearance in Russia (Hall of Nobles, St Petersburg, 26 Dec 1904), she was much admired by Konstantin Stanislavsky, DIAGHILEV, and FOKINE, already planning ballets that rebelled against prevailing conventions of music and costume. Isadora's performance to music not written specifically for dancing encouraged the climate in which Diaghilev and Fokine created their new ballets for the West.

Her passion and her personal tragedies coloured her dancing. Defiant of social as of ballet conventions, she had tempestuous love affairs: with her kindred spirit, the stage designer Edward Gordon Craig, and with the millionaire Paris Singer, who bought her the Hôtel Bellevue, Paris, for a studio, and who would often rescue her financially in later years. Teaching was left to others as she struggled to support the school from the proceeds of her dancing while also squandering them on lavish living. Her school moved to Paris 1908, was evacuated briefly to NY 1914, then returned via Switzerland to Paris where it disbanded after the sale of the Bellevue in 1919. Throughout her travels (she appeared in Denmark, Egypt, and S. America, as well as returning several times to Russia, to the USA for seasons at the NY Met (1908) and the Century T. (1914), and to Greece in 1920) she tried continually to found a school with civic backing, but met with constant rebuffs.

In 1921 the Soviet Government invited her to Moscow to start a school. Her pupils made their debut with Isadora at the Bolshoy T. Still short of money, she left her adopted daughter Irma Duncan in charge, and set off in 1922 for the USA with her husband, the young peasant poet Sergei Essenine. On this disastrous tour for Sol Hurok, the pair behaved outrageously and were suspected of Bolshevism. Back in Russia in 1923, Essenine left her, went mad, and committed suicide (1925). Isadora, the spirit of revolution, clad in scarlet and dancing the *Internationale* or the *Marseillaise*, both shocked and enthralled. She composed two dances for Lenin's funeral, and made a tour of the Ukraine, distributing her earnings to the poor. In 1924, in poverty, she left Russia for good.

In 1925 she sold her house at Neuilly and settled in Nice, where to raise money she began her famous autobiography *My Life*. She gave occasional performances, one of which was to COCTEAU reading his own poems. Though middle-aged and dissipated, she could still move audiences, even with heroic, static poses as in the *Marche Slave*. (Some, though, like BALANCHINE, who saw her in 1922, thought she had become grotesque.) She gave her last recital at the T. Mogador, Paris, in July 1927. Shortly afterwards, in Nice, she was killed instantly when her scarf caught in the wheel of her open car. She was buried at Père Lachaise cemetery, Paris.

Among the celebrated items in Isadora's repertory were works danced to the music of Johannes Brahms, Frédéric Chopin, Felix Mendelssohn, Johann Strauss, TCHAIKOVSKY, Christoph Willibald Gluck, Richard Wagner, Ludwig van Beethoven, César Franck, Franz Schubert, and Franz Liszt. Impressions of her dancing may be gained from the drawings of Gordon Craig, José Clara, Antoine Bourdelle, Maurice Denis, Abraham Walkowitz, and

André Dunoyer de Segonzac, and from the photographs of Edward Steichen. DD
See Isadora Duncan, *My Life* (New York 1927; London 1928; repr. New York 1966; London 1968); Victor Seroff, *The Real Isadora* (New York 1971; London 1972); Allan Ross Macdougall, *Isadora: A Revolutionary in Art and Love* (Edinburgh and New York 1960); Francis Steegmuller, *Your Isadora* (New York and London 1974); Ilya Ilyitch Schneider, *Isadora Duncan, The Russian Years*, tr. David Magarshack (London 1968)

Duncan, Jeff, b. Cisco, TX, 1930. American dancer and choreographer. Studied modern dance, ballet, and jazz. Danced in Broadway musicals and with the cos of LIMÓN, SOKOLOW, and others. Created roles in Sokolow's ROOMS and *Lyric Suite*. Founder and artistic director of DANCE THEATER WORKSHOP 1965, and of Jeff Duncan Dance Repertory Co., 1975. His works incl. *Three Fictitious Games* (mus. POULENC, 1957), *Winesburg Portraits* (mus. traditional, 1963), *Resonances* (mus. Pierre Henry, 1969), *View* (mus. Andrew Rudin, 1973), *Bach 5th Clavier Concerto* (1975). DV

Dunham, Katherine, b. Chicago, IL, 1912. American dancer and choreographer. M.A. and Ph.B. in anthropology, University of Chicago. Established first school in Chicago 1931. Research in Caribbean, 1937–8. Returned to Chicago and worked with PAGE in Federal T. Project. Director of Labor Stage, NY 1939. First NY concert of own choreography, Feb 1940. With her co. danced in Broadway musical *Cabin in the Sky* (ch. and dir. BALANCHINE, 1940), and in Hollywood films, notably *Stormy Weather* (1943; dir. William Le Bacon). Toured USA and later Europe with her dance revues *Carib Song*, *Bal Nègre*, *Caribbean Rhapsody*, and later *Bamboche*, which incl. full-scale ballets based on her ethnological researches, such as RITES DE PASSAGE, *Chôros* (1943), *L'Ag' Ya* (1944), and *Shango* (1945), as well as numbers based on popular dance forms, all with scenery and costumes by her husband, John Pratt. Opened school in NY, teaching a technique combining elements of classic ballet, modern and Afro-Cuban dance. Lived for several years in Haiti, wrote book on its dances, another on a field trip to Jamaica, *Katherine Dunham's Journey to Accompong* (New York 1946), and a volume of autobiography, *A Touch of Innocence* (London and New York 1959). Choreographed dances in Giuseppe Verdi's opera *Aïda* for NY Met, 1963. Now directs Performing Arts Training Center at Univ. of Southern Illinois, East Saint Louis, IL. Her works are no longer in any active repertory, except *Chôros*, revived AILEY CC Dance T. DV
See Richard Buckle (with Roger Wood), *Katherine Dunham: her Dancers, Singers, Musicians* (London 1949)

Dunn, Douglas, b. Palo Alto, CA, 1942. American dancer and choreographer. Studied with CUNNINGHAM. Danced with RAINER and Group, 1968–70, Cunningham and Dance Co., 1969–73, Grand Union (a collaboration of individual artists), from 1970. Has made collaborative works with RUDNER, GORDON, and others, and presented works of his own incl. two full-length solos, *Time Out* (1973), *Gestures in Red* (1975), and a group work, *Lazy Madge* (1976). See AVANT-GARDE DANCE. DV

Duo Concertant, ballet, ch. BALANCHINE; mus. STRAVINSKY; ltg Ronald Bates. NYST, NYCB, 22 June 1972; dan. MAZZO, MARTINS. A *pas de deux* without a story, to Stravinsky's five-part duo for piano and violin, played on stage. FM

Duport, Louis Antoine, b. Paris, 1786; d. Paris, 1853. French dancer; rival of A. VESTRIS at the Paris O. Danced in Russia 1808–12, achieving spectacular success in ballets by DIDELOT (he is mentioned in Lev Tolstoy's novel *War and Peace*). Having made a fortune, he retired early. A contemporary was a Louis Duport whose career was in America: it is unlikely that they were the same person. MC
See Lillian Moore, 'The Duport Mystery', *Dance Perspectives*, No. 7 (New York 1960)

Duvernay, Pauline, b. Paris, 1813; d. Lynford, Norfolk, England, 1894. French dancer. Studied with A. VESTRIS and F. TAGLIONI. Debut Paris O. 1831; London debut T. Royal, Drury Lane, 13 Feb 1833 in Jean Aumer's *The Sleeping Beauty*. A great beauty, she not only rivalled M. TAGLIONI, who was jealous of her, but enjoyed great success in ELSSLER's famous Cachucha dance. A favourite in Paris and London, she retired in 1837, after a tempestuous love affair. In 1845 she m. a wealthy Englishman, Lyne Stephens, who left her an estate, Lynford Hall, in Norfolk and a fortune. She built a chapel there where masses are still said for her. MC
See Ivor Guest, *The Romantic Ballet in England* (London 1954)

Dying Swan, The *see* CYGNE

Dyk, van *see* DIJK, VAN

Dynalix, Paulette, b. Grenoble, 1917. French dancer noted for her sensitive portrayals. Entered Paris OBS 1928, where she studied under ZAMBELLI. Entered O. Co. 1931, rising to *première danseuse* 1943. Danced role of GISELLE 1936, being the youngest dancer to have done so at the O. Among the roles she created were the Moon in LIFAR's *Les Mirages* (1947), Adah in *Lucifer* (with choreography by Lifar; 1948), Hérodiade in AVELINE's version of *La Tragédie de Salomé* (1954), and many more roles. After retiring as a dancer in 1957 she taught at the Paris OBS and privately. In 1967 visited London to produce extracts from the traditional version of COPPÉLIA for Ballet For All, producing a fuller version 1970 to celebrate the centenary of the ballet. IG

Wayne Eagling of the RB as Romeo in MacMillan's Romeo and Juliet

E

Eagling, Wayne, b. Montreal, 1950. Canadian dancer. Studied with Patricia Webster and then RBS. Joined RB 1969, soloist 1972, principal 1975. A dancer of extraordinary suppleness and great gifts, he has danced triumphantly as MacMillan's Romeo and has created roles in his *Triad* (1972) and *Rituals* (1975). One of the brightest hopes of the RB, outstanding in every role. MC

Eaters of Darkness *see* Die im Schatten Leben

Ebbelaar, Han, b. Hoorn, 1943. Dutch dancer. From age 14 studied with Max Dooyes. Joined NDT 1959, a founder member, and worked with Harkarvy. Strongly influenced by van Manen. Danced with ABT 1969–70 when he returned to Holland as principal dancer with Dutch NB. Has danced classical roles, Balanchine ballets (Episodes, Agon) and important parts in works by van Dantzig and van Manen. He m. Radius 1963, with whom he has danced at many gala perfs. Honoured (with his wife) by Queen Juliana of the Netherlands Apr 1975 for services to ballet. Joined B. International 1976. MC

Echoing of Trumpets (*Ekon av Trumpeter*), ballet, 1 act, ch./lib. Tudor, mus. Bohuslav Martinů (*Fantaisies Symphoniques*); sc./c. Birger Bergling. Stockholm, Royal T., RSB, 28 Sept 1963; dan. Andersson, Svante Lindberg. Tudor's first creation for RSB and his return to a work about human suffering after a long fallow period. Inspired by incidents in Poland in World War II. The dance style is classical but with folk-dance elements. Revived NY Met OB 1966, ABT 1968, LFB at London Coliseum, 27 Apr 1973. MacMillan used the same music for the third act of his Anastasia. MC

Eck, Imre, b. Budapest, 1930. Hungarian dancer and choreographer. Nádasi's pupil; dancer 1947, soloist 1950. Staged his first ballet, *Csongor and Tünde* (mus. Leó Weiner) 1959, followed by six more in the Budapest O. incl. Sacre du Printemps (1963), Bartók's *Music for Strings, Percussion and Celesta* (1965) etc. Organized new co. in the Pécs NT 1960, with graduates from the State B. Institute. In his first 14 ballets (1961–2) he outlined neatly his style and message in anti-war ballets, e.g. *As Commanded* (mus. Viliam Bukovy, 1962), ballets about youth, e.g. *Variations on an Encounter* (mus. Tihamér Vujicsics, 1961), and *Spider's Web* (mus. László Gulyás, 1962), humorous works, e.g. *Overture* (mus. Gioacchino Rossini, 1962), and in abstract studies, e.g. *Etudes in Blue* (mus. Antonio Vivaldi, 1964). In 1965 he produced his versions of Bartók's ballets incl. Miraculous Mandarin and his *Concerto* in an evening 'Homage to Bartók' and started his series of miniatures incl. *Passacaglia* (mus. Emil Petrovics). His *Don Juan* (mus. Christoph Willibald Gluck, 1966), *Descent to Hell* (mus. Franz Schubert and exotic folklore, 1968), and *Lulu* (mus. Alban Berg, 1967) are action ballets. His 'Hungarian period' brought 12 1-act ballets, incl. *Summer Evening* (mus. Zoltán Kodály, 1970); *Hungarian Dolls* (mus. Weiner, 1971). Staged Franz Liszt's *Faust Symphony* (1973). 'Brooding' (1976) consists of eight music-less miniature dancing and pantomime scenes. He has choreographed *Ondine* (mus. HENZE, 1969) for Belgrade O.; *Tempest* (mus. Jean Sibelius, 1974) and *Kalevala* (1976), in Helsinki. Also in 1976 he produced a two-act ballet to Giuseppe Verdi's *Requiem* under the same title. With about 70 ballets to his credit, he has combined various styles of dance: classical, modern, jazz, and acrobatics; invariably an outstanding composer of *pas de deux*. Liszt Prize, 1962; Merited Artist, 1970. GPD

Edouardova [Eduardova], Eugenia, b. St Petersburg, 1882; d. New York, 1960. Russian character dancer and teacher. Graduated from St Petersburg TS into *corps de ballet* 1901. From 1907 often danced abroad, had success in A. PAVLOVA's co. Became interested in GORSKY's experiments, went to Moscow, Bolshoy T., for two months, 1910; commended by Gorsky. Known as an elegant performer of character dances. Danced successfully in the classical repertoire but less successful in *demi-caractère* part of Street Dancer (DON QUIXOTE) at ebb of career at the Maryinsky T., 1916. Retired 1917; to Berlin where she opened her own school; to Paris 1938, NY 1947. NR

Educational Ballets Ltd *see* BALLET RUSSE DE MONTE CARLO

Edwards, Leslie, b. Teddington, Middlesex, 1916. English dancer, teacher, director of RB Choreographic Group, and ballet master to the Royal O., CG. Studied with RAMBERT, also CRASKE, IDZIKOWSKI, and VOLKOVA. Joined SWB 1933 but then danced with BR 1935–7 when he returned to SWB. Always an elegant stylist, he found a new career as a character dancer-actor when he created the role of the Beggar in MIRACLE IN THE GORBALS. His gallery of famous roles (more than 50) continues until today and incl. Catalabutte, the Master of Ceremonies, in SLEEPING BEAUTY which he played 1946–68. Assumed role of the King in that ballet 1968. Another superb creation was the rich farmer Thomas in FILLE MAL GARDÉE. OBE 1975. MC

Eglevsky, André, b. Moscow, 1917. Russian dancer. He m. dancer Leda Anchutina. Studied Paris with EGOROVA, VOLININ, KSHESSINSKA, London with LEGAT. Debut, DE BASIL's B. Russe de Monte Carlo, 1932; danced with WOIZIKOWSKI's co. 1935, R. BLUM's B. de Monte Carlo 1936. Settled in USA 1937, danced with American B. 1937–8, B. Russe de Monte Carlo 1938–42, ABT 1942–3, 1945, B. International NY, 1944, for which he choreographed *Colloque Sentimental* (sc. Salvador Dali), Original B. Russe 1946–7, de Cuevas B. 1947–50, NYCB 1951–8. Created roles in ÉPREUVE D'AMOUR (1936), MAM'ZELLE ANGOT (1943), BALANCHINE's *Scotch Symphony* (1952), etc.; also danced classical repertory and a variety of roles ranging from the GOLDEN SLAVE to APOLLO. After leaving NYCB he taught at SAB, opened his own school and formed a co. in Massapequa, Long Island. His daughter, Marina Eglevsky, is a dancer. DV

Egorova, Lyubov (Princess Trubetskoy), b. St Petersburg, 1880; d. Paris, 1972. Russian dancer. Graduated St Petersburg TS 1898; pupil of CECCHETTI, also continued under VAZEM, Anna Johansson. Starting as *coryphée*, she slowly advanced, being a lyrical dancer endowed with softness and cantilena typical of the Russian school as opposed to the extrovert virtuosity then popular. Danced title role in M. PETIPA's *Blue Dahlia* (1905); MYRTHA (1907); RAYMONDA (1910); debut as AURORA as late as 1911; ODETTE-ODILE (because of her style of dancing excelling in Odette, 1913). Promoted to ballerina 1914. Her GISELLE (1914) compared favourably to that of A. PAVLOVA. Farewell perf., Maryinsky, 22 Jan 1917 in SWAN LAKE. Danced Aurora in DIAGHILEV's 1921 *Sleeping Princess* (*see* SLEEPING BEAUTY) and 1923–68 taught in Paris. In 1937 she formed a small co., Les B. de la Jeunesse, to show the prowess of her pupils. NR
See V. Krasovskaya, *Russian Ballet Theatre of the Beginning of the 20th Century*, Vol. 2, *Dancers* (Leningrad 1972)

Ek, Niklas, b. Stockholm, 1943. Swedish dancer. Son of CULLBERG. Studied with Donya Feuer, Juliet Fisher, and Lilian Karina, with CUNNINGHAM in New York. Leading soloist when the Cullberg B. was founded 1966. Joined B. XXe S. 1972 and became soloist, dancing leading parts in BÉJART's repertory. Returned to the Cullberg B. 1975. A modern dancer with a strong personality. AGS

Eliasen, Johnny, b. Copenhagen, 1949. Danish dancer. Entered RDBS 1956; with Scandinavian B. 1964–5; RDB 1966; soloist 1972. Debut 1967, Copenhagen, as Brighella (PIERROT LUNAIRE). Has danced a wide repertory, both *demi-caractère* and *sérieux*, from FRANZ to Tybalt (NEUMEIER's ROMEO AND JULIET), Gennaro (NAPOLI) and the 'heros' in F. FLINDT's *Trio* (1973) and TRIUMPH OF DEATH. SKJ

Élite Syncopations, ballet, 1 act, ch. MACMILLAN; mus. Scott Joplin, Scott Hayden, Paul Pratt, James Scott, Joseph F. Lamb, Max Morath, Donald Ashwander, Robert Hampton; c. Ian Spurling. London, CG, RB, 7 Oct 1974; dan. PARK, MASON, COLEMAN, WALL, DERMAN, SLEEP, KELLY. The (ragtime) band is on stage. A series of brilliantly choreographed dances, many of them very funny. The ballet found little favour with the critics, who objected especially to the outrageous costumes and lack of feeling for the underlying sadness of much of

Fanny Elssler dancing *The Cracovienne*, wearing a typically Romantic representation of Polish costume

the music, but was an immense popular success not only in London but also in NY. It was televised from the Big Top when the RB danced there in Battersea Park, London, 1975 and won more admirers. The success has been largely due to the dazzling perfs by the entire cast. MC

Elssler, Fanny, b. Gumpendorf, 1810; d. Vienna, 1884. Austrian dancer. Represented the 'earthly' side of Romanticism and was specially noted for her dramatic skill. Daughter of Johann Florian Elssler, Joseph Haydn's copyist and valet. Entered the Vienna Hof O. as a child, studied under Jean Aumer; stage debut 1818. In Naples 1825–7; resumed career in Vienna, rising to playing leading parts and becoming the intimate friend of the publicist, Baron von Gentz. Engagements in Berlin 1830 and 1831–2, and London 1833 and 1834, added to her reputation, and Dr Véron, director of the Paris O., engaged her to provide a counter-attraction to M. TAGLIONI. She studied further under A. VESTRIS; Paris debut 1834 in CORALLI's *La Tempête*. At the O. until 1840, shining alongside Taglioni, with whom a rivalry was successfully stimulated. GAUTIER conveyed the contrast in their styles by calling Elssler a 'pagan' and Taglioni a 'Christian' ballerina. Among the ballets she appeared in at the O. were Coralli's *Le Diable Boiteux* (1836) in which she danced her celebrated Cachucha (a stylized Spanish classical dance which she made famous), MAZILIER's *La Gipsy* (1839) with its Cracovienne, and Coralli's *La Tarentule* (1840) with its Tarantella.

To USA 1840; as the first Romantic ballerina to appear there, she had extraordinary triumphs in NY, Boston, Philadelphia, Washington, Charleston, New Orleans, and other cities. Tempted by the fortune she was making, she deliberately overstayed her leave from the O., was sued for damages, and never danced in Paris again. Her adventures in the USA were vividly chronicled in letters sent to her family by her cousin, Katti Prinster. In Washington she met the President, and the House of Representatives could not always muster a quorum when she was dancing. She also danced in Havana 1841 and 1842.

To Europe 1842; appeared in several ballets produced in London by PERROT, incl. GISELLE and ESMERALDA. It was at this point in her career that her dramatic gifts were fully developed, and her interpretation of Giselle became the model for the future rather than the more danced rendering of GRISI. Perrot created two ballets for her at Sc.: *Odetta* (1847) and *Faust* (1848). The first night of *Faust*, on the eve of revolution, developed into a riot, of which Elssler, as an Austrian, was a victim. She left Milan at once, never to dance there again. Her last and perhaps greatest triumphs took place in Russia: St Petersburg 1848–9 and 1849–50, Moscow 1850 and 1850–1. She danced in public for the last time in Vienna 1851. IG

See Ivor Guest, *Fanny Elssler, The Pagan Ballerina* (London 1970); Allison Delarue (ed.), *Fanny Elssler in America* (New York 1976)

Elvin [Prokhorova], Violetta, b. Moscow, 1924. Graduated from Bolshoy S., Moscow, 1942; ballerina Tashkent 1943 during wartime evacuation. Soloist with Bolshoy B. 1944. She m. English writer Harold Elvin and arrived in England 1945. Joined SWB; debut in BLUEBIRD *pas de deux* on second night of SWB's first CG season; the first opportunity for Londoners to become acquainted with the Soviet style. Worked closely with her compatriot VOLKOVA, teacher and friend. With the SWB danced all the great ballerina roles and created for ASHTON the seductress Lykanion in *Daphnis and Chloe* (*see* DAPHNIS ET CHLOÉ), Water in the 1953 Coronation ballet *Homage to the Queen* and for HOWARD character of La Favorita in *Venezia* 1953. Guest appearances notably at Sc. 1952. Farewell perf. at CG, 23 June 1956, as AURORA while still at the height of her career as a dancer. Unforgettable in the SWB revival of TRICORNE as the Miller's Wife, a most glamorous ballerina. Now resident in Italy, m. to Fernando Savaressi; mother of one son. MC

Emblen, Ronald, b. Port Said, Egypt, 1933. English dancer and teacher. Studied with Anna Northcote, VOLKOVA and at RBS. Danced with various cos, notably LFB, until joining RB touring section as soloist, 1962, becoming principal 1964. At first a nimble *demi-caractère* dancer, he soon established himself as a remarkable mime with a wonderful gift for comedy. Celebrated roles incl. WIDOW SIMONE, the Tutor in SWAN LAKE, and DR COPPÉLIUS. Joined teaching staff of RBS 1975 but continued to appear with the RB. MC

Embrace Tiger and Return to Mountain, modern dance work, 1 act, ch. TETLEY; mus. Morton Subotnick (*Silver Apples of the Moon*, 1967); sc./c. N. BAYLIS; ltg John B. Read. London, Jeannetta

Cochrane T., BR, 21 Nov 1968. Tetley based his ballet, to an electronic score, on *T'ai-Chi*, a system of shadow boxing developed by the Chinese in the 6th c. Also in repertories of RSB, NDT, and FELD B. MC

Enchanted Prince *see* PRINCE OF THE PAGODAS

Enigma Variations (*My Friends Pictured Within*), ballet, ch. ASHTON; mus. Edward Elgar; sc./c. Julia Trevelyan Oman. London, CG, RB, 25 Oct 1968; dan. RENCHER, BERIOSOVA, DOYLE, SIBLEY, DOWELL, GRANT, SHAW, BERGSMA. A series of portraits of the composer, his wife and friends; the ballet is also a meditation on friendship and the loneliness of the artist. An earlier, plotless ballet to the same music was choreographed by STAFF, for TUDOR's London B., 1940. DV

Enters, Angna (Anita), b. New York, 1907. American dancer-mime. Her training began with social dance and continued at a professional level when Michio Ito invited her to be his partner. First program of her solos, which were character vignettes, 1924; *Moyen Age* (1926), the most noted, remained in her repertory until shortly before she retired. A screenwriter in the 1940s, she subsequently produced two volumes of autobiography, a novel, and a treatise on mime. She designed her own costumes and held exhibitions of her paintings. She was, in her stage work, a composer of dramatic portraits. DM

Episodes, ballet, part 1, ch. GRAHAM; mus. Anton (von) Webern (*Passaglia*, Op. 1; *Six Pieces for Orchestra*, Op. 6); sc. David Hays; c. (Barbara) Karinska; part 2, ch. BALANCHINE; mus. Webern (Symphony, Op. 21; Five Pieces, Op. 10; Concerto, Op. 24; Variations for Orchestra, Op. 30; 'Ricercata for Six Voices from Bach's *Musical Offering*'); sc. Hays; c. Karinska. NYCC, NYCB, 14 May 1959; dan. Graham, ROSS, S. WILSON, MCGEHEE, WINTER, Linda Hodes, VERDY, Jonathan Watts, D. ADAMS, D'AMBOISE, P. TAYLOR, HAYDEN, MONCION. The Graham part on Mary Queen of Scots was in period costume; the Balanchine part in practice dress. FM

Épreuve d'Amour, L', ballet, 1 act, ch. FOKINE; mus. attributed to Wolfgang Amadeus Mozart (composed for a carnival 1791; discovered 1928 in Graz, Austria); lib. Fokine and DERAIN; sc./c. Derain. Monte Carlo, R. BLUM's B. Russe de Monte Carlo, 4 Apr 1936; dan. NEMCHINOVA, EGLEVSKY, KIRSOVA, A. OBUKHOV. A charming piece of *chinoiserie* about the triumph of true love over money. One of the happiest inventions of Fokine's later years. Revived Helsinki, Finnish NB, 22 Mar 1956 by George Gé, after Fokine's original. MC

Erdman, Jean, b. Honolulu, Hawaii. American dancer and choreographer. Studied with GRAHAM at the Bennington College Summer S. of The Dance; invited to join her co. 1938. Danced many roles, among them the noteworthy One Who Speaks in LETTER TO THE WORLD, which she continues to perform as guest artist. Her own first works were collaborative pieces with CUNNINGHAM, also a member of the Graham Dance Co. She established her own concert group 1944 and is best known for *The Coach With the Six Insides* (1962), an adaptation of James Joyce's *Finnegans Wake*, shown all over the world. She has pursued an interest in collaborative productions in which dance, music, scenic effects, and the spoken word are balanced. In 1976 she created a new major theatre piece, *Gauguin in Tahiti*, first performed by her co., T. of the Open Eye, in Honolulu. DM

La Esmeralda, as danced by GRISI

Erler, Stefan, b. Breslau, 1944. German dancer. Pupil of the Munich S., joined Munich B. 1962; soloist 1965, creating roles in many of CRANKO's ballets. GBLW

Eshkol, Noa *see* DANCE NOTATION

Esmeralda, La, ballet, 3 acts, 5 scenes, ch./lib. PERROT based on Victor Hugo's novel *Notre-Dame de Paris*; mus. PUGNI; sc. William Grieve, machinery D. Sloman; c. Mme Copère. London, Her Majesty's T., 9 Mar 1844; dan. GRISI (Esmeralda), Perrot (Gringoire), Antoine Louis Coulon (Quasimodo). A version of Perrot's ballet was staged by the Monplaisir B. Co., NY, on 18 Sept 1848. Revived St Petersburg, Imperial B., 2 Jan 1849; dan. ELSSLER, Perrot, Peter Didier. Revived by M. PETIPA in St Petersburg 1886, additional mus. DRIGO. Esmeralda was KSHESSINSKA's favourite role (she brought her pet goat on stage). New version ch./lib. TIKHOMIROV and BURMEISTER, mus. GLIÈRE and S. Vasilienko, Moscow Stanislavsky and Nemirovich-Danchenko T., 14 Oct 1950. New version, London, RFH, LFB,

ch. Beriozoff, 14 July 1954 (after a try-out in Barcelona); dan. Krassovska, Gilpin, Keith Beckett; mus. arr. Geoffrey Corbett; sc./c. Nicola Benois. A ballet based on the same story was staged by Antonio Monticioni at Milan Sc. 1839. *See also* Notre-Dame de Paris. MC
See Complete Book

Espinosa, Édouard, b. Moscow, 1871; d. Worthing, Sussex, 1950. English dancer and producer of Spanish extraction. His father Léon (b. The Hague, 1825; d. London, 1903) had been a dancer who trained (and danced) at the Paris O. and had a colourful career, being captured by Indians on tour in the USA in 1850. In 1865 he appeared in Isler's Gardens, Moscow, with such success that he was taken into the Bolshoy T. and stayed seven years. Returned to London 1872 and opened a school. Édouard had a long career as a dancer and as a producer of spectacular entertainments and arranger of dances in plays – he worked for Sir Henry Irving. His most lasting influence was as a teacher; de Valois was one of his pupils. Much concerned with the low standard of ballet teaching in Britain, he persuaded Richardson in 1920 to set up what is now the RAD. In 1930, he created his own teachers' organization, the British B. Organization, directed since his death by his son Edward Kelland Espinosa (b. London, 1906). His three sisters were also teachers: Judith (1876–1949), Lea (1883–1966), and Ray (1885–1934), known as Mme Ravodna. MC

Études, ballet, 1 act, ch. H. Lander; mus. Carl Czerny arr. Knudåge Riisager; sc./c. Erik Nordgren. Copenhagen, RDB (as *Étude*), 15 Jan 1948; dan. M. Lander, Brenaa, Jensen. With some alterations, Copenhagen, RDB, 18 Feb 1951. Final version, produced H. Lander, Paris O., 19 Nov 1952. A ballet of mounting technical excitement based on the shape of a ballet class. The best-known Danish work in the international repertory, produced by Lander all over the world, frequently with his wife T. Lander as the ballerina and, after his death, as producer; notable productions London, LFB, 8 Aug 1955; NY, ABT, 5 Oct 1961; also Amsterdam, Helsinki, Munich, Cologne, Hamburg, Vienna, Gothenburg, Budapest. A special version designed for television was produced H. Lander, Copenhagen 1969; dan. T. Lander, Bruhn, F. Flindt, and Kronstam. SKJ

Evdokimova, Eva, b. Geneva, 1948. American dancer, Bulgarian father, Canadian mother. Studied Munich OBS 1956–9; RBS 1959–65. With RDB 1966–9; in 1969 to Deutsche O., W. Berlin. Danced her first Giselle there 1970, coached by Chauviré. In 1970 also worked with Kirov B., under Dudinskaya. Guest with many cos in Europe but since 1971 has danced most frequently with LFB. A dancer of exquisite lightness and fragility, as delightful in August Bournonville (Flower Festival at Genzano) as in *Giselle* or Sleeping Beauty. Danced Aurora in the first perf. of Nureyev's production of *The Sleeping Beauty* with LFB 1975. Prize at Varna, 1968; at Moscow, 1969; Gold medal, Varna, 1970. MC

Excelsior, ballet, 2 acts, ch. Manzotti; mus. Romualdo Marenco; sc. Alfredo Edel. Milan, Sc., 11 Jan 1881; dan. Bice Vergani, Rosina Viale, Carlo Montanara. Manzotti's most successful spectacular ballet, in 12 scenes full of scenic tricks. The work celebrates man's technological progress. The music is largely made up of mazurkas, marches, etc. Revived Maggio Musicale Fiorentino (T. Comunale, Florence) 27 June 1967; ch. Dell'Ara; mus. revised Fiorenzo Carpi; sc./c. Giulio Coltellacci; dan. Tcherina, Fracci, Labis, Dell'Ara. Also at Sc., Sept 1974–Feb 1975; dan. Fracci, then Cosi; Bortoluzzi, then Marinel Stefanescu; Elettra Morini, Dell'Ara. Also in repertoire of Colla Marionettes. FP

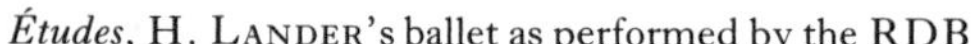
Études, H. Lander's ballet as performed by the RDB

F

Façade, ballet, 1 act, ch. ASHTON; mus. William Walton, originally written as a setting to poems by Edith Sitwell; sc. John Armstrong. London, Cambridge T., Camargo Society, 26 Apr 1931; dan. L. LOPUKHOVA, MARKOVA, Ashton, Prudence Hyman, Maude LLOYD, TUDOR, William Chappell, GORE, Pearl Argyle, GOULD. Went almost immediately into repertory of BR, and of Vic-Wells B. 1935; revised and redesigned 1940. Still in the RB repertory; revived by many others incl. JOFFREY and the Australian B. A series of comedy dances satirizing folk and popular dance forms, one of the wittiest and most enduring of Ashton's ballets. DV

Fâcheux, Les, (1) *comédie-ballet*, ch./mus. BEAUCHAMP; lib. Molière. Vaux-le-Vicomte, 17 Aug 1661, at a fête for Louis XIV; repeated later at Fontainebleau. Spoken comedy and ballet were united to evoke the troubles of the lover Eraste. Said to be Molière's first *comédie-ballet*, it was a seminal work of the BALLET DE COUR and a direct forerunner of NOVERRE's *ballet d'action*. M-FC
(2) ballet, ch. NIJINSKA; lib. KOCHNO; mus. AURIC; sc./c. Georges Braque. Monte Carlo, B. Russes (DIAGHILEV's), 19 Jan 1924; dan. DOLIN, WOIZIKOWSKI, TCHERNICHEVA. Based on the theme of Molière's work, celebrated chiefly for the beauty of Braque's designs and Dolin's dancing on *pointe* as The Dandy. MASSINE choreographed a new version for the co., Monte Carlo, 3 May 1927, and danced in it himself. It was not a success. MC

Fadeyechev, Nikolay, b. Moscow, 1933. Soviet dancer. Graduated from Bolshoy TS 1952, in Bolshoy B. until 1974. *Premier danseur noble*, perfect Romantic-classical dancer of Russian school. First danced SWAN LAKE 1953, GISELLE 1956, became PLISETSKAYA's permanent partner. Danced ALBRECHT to NERINA's Giselle on BBC TV 23 Nov 1958. Danced Romeo 1960. Created Danila in STONE FLOWER (Moscow version), Don José in CARMEN (ch. Alberto Alonso) with Plisetskaya in title role, Karenin in ANNA KARENINA. Presently teaches Choreographers' Faculty, GITIS. People's Artist, RSFSR. NR

Faier, Yuri, b. 1890; d. Moscow, 1971. Russian conductor. At Bolshoy, Moscow, since 1923, appearing with the B. co. in London 1956 and NY 1959, in both of which cities, though his eyesight was too poor for him to see the stage clearly, he made a great impression for his sensitive support of the dancers. Recorded a memorable GISELLE. DH

Faison, George, b. Washington, DC, 1945. American dancer and choreographer. Originally interested in drama, then studied dance at Jones-Haywood S. of B., Washington; scholarship at Harkness BS; studied modern dance with Thelma Hill and D. WILLIAMS, James Truitte and L. JOHNSON. Invited to join AILEY Dance T., where he remained for three years. His interest in stage and costume design led him to redesign the costumes for BLUES SUITE. Formed his own co., the George Faison Universal Dance Experience, 1971; created *Poppy*, a full-length collection of dances about drug abuse. His flamboyant and at times naïve sensibility has a theatrical resonance as his award-winning choreography for the Broadway musical *The Wiz* (1975) attests. DM

Falco, Louis, b. New York. American modern dance choreographer and dancer. Studied ABTS, and the American B. Center (school of the CCJB), and with GRAHAM, LIMÓN, and WEIDMAN. Joined the Limón Dance Co. 1960, forming his own co., Louis Falco and Featured Dancers, 1967, and began to choreograph. He has used decors by such artists as Robert Indiana and Marisol (M. Escobar). His work is in the repertories of NDT, BR, and Boston B. He has staged opera and musicals. In 1971, his work, hitherto lyrically abstract, took on a theatrical quality with the use of spoken dialogue and dramatic props and situations; the dance element has been reduced. JD

Falla, Manuel de, b. Cádiz, 1876; d. Alta Gracia, Argentina, 1946. Spanish composer. His two ballets are *El Amor Brujo* (Madrid 1915; ch. Pastora Imperio) and TRICORNE, the latter written for DIAGHILEV and an enduringly lively score. DH

Fallis, Barbara, b. Denver, CO, 1924. American dancer and teacher. Studied at Vic-Wells S. and appeared with co. 1938–40. Danced with ABT 1941–9, B. ALONSO 1949–52, NYCB 1953–8. Roles incl. Calliope in APOLLO, Dance Impromptu in GRADUATION BALL, AURORA, and MYRTHA. A dancer of great musicality. With her husband Richard Thomas she now directs the NY S. of B. and its co., U.S. Terpsichore. Their son Richard is an actor, their daughter Bronwyn a dancer. DV

Fall River Legend, ballet, 8 scenes with prologue, ch. DE MILLE; mus. Morton Gould; sc. O. SMITH; c. Miles White. NY Met, ABT, 22 Apr 1948; dan. ALONSO, KRIZA, D. ADAMS. The story derives from the fate of Lizzie Borden, who in 1892 'took an axe and gave her mother forty whacks; when she saw what she had done, she gave her father forty-one!' FM

Fancy Free, ballet, 1 act, ch./lib. ROBBINS; mus. Leonard Bernstein; sc. O. SMITH; c. Kermit Love. NY Met, ABT, 18 Apr 1944; dan. KRIZA, H. LANG,

Robbins, Muriel Bentley, Janet Reed, Shirley Eckl. The American character ballet *par excellence*, Robbins's first ballet and immediate success shows what happens to three sailors on a hot summer night in NY during World War II, the two girls they meet, the ensuing competition, the tough good humour of wartime comradeship. A seminal work, its mix of old and new dance has widely influenced developments in the US theatre and ballet. FM
See George Amberg, *Ballet in America* (New York 1949) in which Robbins's detailed scenario is reproduced; reprinted in Selma Jeanne Cohen, *Dance as a Theatre Art* (New York 1974)

Farber, Viola, b. Heidelberg, Germany, 1931. American modern dance choreographer, dancer, and teacher. Studied music at American University, Washington DC, and dance with LITZ, Alfredo Corvino, and CRASKE. Attended Black Mountain College, NC, 1953, where she became an original member of the CUNNINGHAM Dance Co. With Cunningham until 1965; with P. TAYLOR in 1953 (as his mother in *Jack and the Beanstalk*) and with Litz several years later (as a vampire in *Dracula*). She formed her own co. 1968. Her works are performed by the Repertory Dance T. of Utah and the Nancy Hauser Dance Co. She m. SLAYTON 1971. They were awarded the Ninth International Dance Fest. (Paris) gold medal for expression and creativity 1971. She began to choreograph 1965. Her repertory of some 40 works is characterized by demanding, fragmented movement, chance order, humour and, in her solos, a dramatic sense of personality. Among her best-known works are *Survey* (1971; mus. David Tudor), *Mildred* (1971; mus. Carl Czerny), *Notebook* (1968; mus. Farber), *Route Six* (1972; mus. Longines Radio Favorites transcript), and *Dune* (1972; mus. Alvin Lucier). JD

Fancy Free, with (left to right) Eric Braun, KRIZA, Enrique Martinez and Christine Mayer

Farewell *see* LIED VON DER ERDE

Far From Denmark (*Fjernt fra Danmark*), vaudeville-ballet, 2 acts, ch./lib. August BOURNONVILLE; mus. Josef Glæser, Louis Moreau Gottschalk, Hans Christian Lumbye, Édouard Dupuy, and Andreas Frederik Lincke. Copenhagen, RDB, 20 Apr 1860. Still in the repertory. A young Argentine lady enchants a Danish lieutenant during a carnival held on board his ship on a visit to Buenos Aires. SKJ

Farrell, Suzanne, b. Cincinnati, OH, 1945. American dancer. Studied SAB. Joined NYCB 1961, dancing her first solo role in SERENADE 1962. BALANCHINE created many roles for her, incl. DULCINEA. Left the co. 1968, danced with B. XXe S. 1970–4. Returned to NYCB 1974, assuming both old and new roles, notably in Balanchine's *Chaconne* (1976), with a maturity and technical authority that make her more than ever the perfect interpreter of Balanchine's works. DV
See N. Goldner and A.-P. Hersin, 'Suzanne Farrell', *Les Saisons de la Danse* (Paris, Dec 1975) with list of roles

Farron, Julia, b. London, 1922. English dancer and teacher. Studied with Grace Cone and then Vic-Wells (later SW) BS. Joined SWB 1936; created role of Pépé the little dog in WEDDING BOUQUET 1937. A delightful classical dancer of great charm, she developed into a fine actress. One of her best roles was the nasty sister, Belle Epine, in CRANKO's PRINCE OF THE PAGODAS which she created. After a brief spell in retirement, 1961, she returned to RB 1964 to become a valued teacher at the RBS and to play character roles at CG, notably Lady Capulet in MACMILLAN's ROMEO AND JULIET, another major creation. She m. RODRIGUES. MC

Fascilla, Roberto, b. Milan, 1937. Italian dancer and choreographer. Sc. BS 1948–56. First soloist, then principal (1964). Appointed *primo ballerino assoluto* 1975. Danced in most ballets given at Sc. during that period. Exceptionally reliable partner and good actor.

Choreographed for Menegatti-FRACCI touring co., incl. reduced versions of COPPÉLIA and ROMEO AND JULIET (Turin, Sept 1975). FP

Fedorova, Aleksandra, b. St Petersburg, 1884; d. New York, 1972. Russian dancer and teacher. Graduated 1902 into *corps de ballet*, Maryinsky T.; by 1904 was second soloist. Elegant, ethereal dancer. Appeared in Troitsky T. of Miniatures, owned 1914–17 by her husband Aleksandr Fokine, brother of M. FOKINE. While in Maryinsky co. often neglected her duties and dismissed 1922 when co. reduced staff. Departed with her son Leon Fokine to Riga; became prominent teacher in Latvia and Lithuania, bringing ideas from the Russian school and exerting influence in the formation of national ballet cos in these republics until her departure to the USA 1937, where she taught until an advanced age. NR

Fedorova, Sophia, b. Moscow, 1879; d. Paris, 1963. Russian dancer. From a coppersmith's family and said to be of gypsy origin, a striking dark beauty. Her mother, widowed early, placed her three children (Sophia, Olga and Mikhail) in the Moscow TS. Sophia graduated into the *corps de ballet* in 1899, acquiring the name 'Fedorova II' (because of another, obscure dancer, Fedorova I, who had graduated earlier). Her first opportunity came in Dec 1900 when she replaced GELTSER in DON QUIXOTE with great success.

With the Street Dancer (Act I of the same ballet) and other parts, GORSKY began moulding Fedorova into an outstanding theatrical personality, capable of completely identifying herself with any role. She became his devoted disciple, and her Gypsy dance in HUMPBACKED HORSE, which he especially created for her, was charged with deep emotion. He began to create entire ballets for her. She created the slave Khita to A. PAVLOVA's Bint-Anta in Gorsky's version of FILLE DU PHARAON. She was a charming LISE with MORDKIN as COLAS. In spite of her fear of the classical repertory, which sprang from rather weak technique, Gorsky visualized Fedorova in classical parts. He therefore tailored GISELLE especially to suit her, omitting most of M. PETIPA's dances in Act I and turning the act into a series of village revels. The title role, having been created by KARALLI in 1907, was first danced by Fedorova with great nervous strain in 1913. A year later, she refused to dance any classical parts whatever, and gradually ceased attending classes and rehearsals. Her final contract with the Imperial Ts expired 1 Sept 1917; although she was still considered a member of the co., continued absence from the theatre caused her salary to be discontinued in Dec 1918. In January 1919, she presented the theatre with a doctor's certificate stating that she had suffered for years from progressive acute neurasthenia. In the same year, she moved to Petrograd with her husband, Pyotr Oleinin (a singer and opera director) and, upon his death in 1922, settled in Paris, spending the 1925–6 season in Pavlova's co.

Sophia Fedorova as Ta-Hor in *Cléopâtre*

Fedorova's association with DIAGHILEV's B. Russes began during its first Paris season (1909), when she triumphed in the Polovtsian Dances from PRINCE IGOR (she danced it as late as 1928). She danced many roles in the Diaghilev repertory, incl. Ta-Hor in *Cléopâtre*, replacing Pavlova. Following total nervous collapse in 1930, she lived in obscurity.

Olga, Sophia's sister, b. 1882 and known as Fedorova III, graduated from the Moscow TS 1900 and occupied the position of character dancer at the Bolshoy T. She was as attractive and temperamental as Sophia, but lacked her extraordinary personality. Olga moved to the Maryinsky B. 1909, where she was character soloist, and danced there until 1924.

Their brother, Mikhail (dates unknown) also graduated from Moscow TS and danced with Diaghilev's B. Russes. NR

See S. Grigorov, *Fedorova II, An Essay* (Moscow 1914); V. Krasovskaya, *Russian Ballet Theatre of the Beginning of the 20th Century*, Vol. 2, *Dancers* (Leningrad 1972)

Fedorovitch, Sophie, b. Minsk, 1893; d. London, 1953. Russian-born designer who settled in London in 1920, became a British subject and one of England's foremost theatrical designers. Her lifelong friendship with ASHTON (whom she met through RAMBERT) led to the creation of many exquisite works, among them *Les Masques* (1933), *Nocturne* (1936), *Horoscope* (1938), *Dante Sonata* (1940) and, supremely, SYMPHONIC VARIATIONS (1946). She also designed FÊTE ÉTRANGE for HOWARD. Fedorovitch, like BÉRARD, used the minimum of design to achieve maximum effect and supervised the making of all costumes. She had a unique understanding of the necessity for a dancer to be able to move freely, no matter how decorative a costume. She was working on Howard's *Veneziana* at the time of her tragic death (from the fumes of a faulty gas pipe) for the SWB, to which she was an artistic adviser. MC

Feld, Eliot, b. Brooklyn, NY, 1942. American choreographer and dancer. Studied at SAB, NY High S. of Performing Arts, New Dance Group, and with Richard Thomas. Danced with NYCB as child in NUTCRACKER, then with P. LANG, MASLOW, and MCKAYLE cos, Broadway and film versions of *West Side Story* and TV. Joined ABT (1963–8), choreographing *Harbinger* (mus. PROKOFIEV, 1967) and AT MIDNIGHT. Roles incl. Third Sailor (FANCY FREE), and Billy (BILLY THE KID). In 1968 choreographed *Meadow Lark* (mus. Franz Joseph Haydn) for Royal Winnipeg B. Formed American B. Co. (1969–71) as resident co. at BAM, a small co. with a diversified repertoire. Choreographed INTERMEZZO, *Early Songs* (mus. Richard Strauss, 1970), *The Consort* (mus. John Dowland, Thomas Morley, *et al.*, 1970), *Theatre* (mus. R. Strauss, 1970) and *The Gods Amused* (mus. DEBUSSY, 1971). The repertoire incl. revivals of CARNAVAL, ROSS's *Caprichos* and *The Maids*, and McKayle's *Games*. He rejoined ABT (1971–2), choreographing *Eccentrique* and *A Soldier's Tale* (both mus. STRAVINSKY, 1972) and dancing PETRUSHKA. Choreographed *Winter's Court* (mus. Elizabethan lute songs, 1972) for RDB and *Jive* (mus. Morton Gould, 1973) for CCJB. Formed Eliot Feld B. 1974, a chamber co. resident at the NY Shakespeare Festival Public T., choreographing *The Tzaddik* (mus. COPLAND, 1974), *Sephardic Song* (mus. traditional, 1974) and *The Real McCoy* (mus. George Gershwin, 1974). The repertoire also incl. EMBRACE TIGER. Feld's style combines an athletic neoclassicism with influences from modern dance and jazz. His ballets incl. lyric abstractions, introspective dramas, satires, and meditations on Jewish themes. The music is frequently piano or vocal chamber music in live performance. GD

Femmes de Bonne Humeur, Les (*The Good-Humoured Ladies*), ballet, 1 act, ch. MASSINE; mus. Domenico Scarlatti, arr. Vincenzo Tommasini; sc./c. BAKST. Rome, T. Costanza, DIAGHILEV's B. Russes, 12 Apr 1917; dan. L. LOPUKHOVA, TCHERNICHEVA, Massine, IDZIKOWSKI, WOIZIKOWSKI, E. and Giuseppina CECCHETTI. Based on Carlo Goldoni's comedy *Le Donne di Buon Umore*, the ballet had a highly complicated plot of disguises and mistaken identities with young love in the end triumphing over crabbed age.

The heroine Mariuccia was one of Lopukhova's greatest roles and A. DANILOVA had a success in it with DE BASIL's B. Russe de Monte Carlo. Revived DE CUEVAS; sc. Derain; London, CG, 7 July 1949; Paris, OC; sc. André Masson, 1952. Revived by Massine, CG, RB, 11 July 1962; dan. SIBLEY (Mariuccia), L. SOKOLOVA (the Marquise). Its life in the RB repertory was short.

The highly stylized make-ups for the principal characters, which were also devised by Bakst, are illustrated in KOCHNO's book *Le Ballet* (Paris 1954). MC

See COMPLETE BOOK

Fernandez, Royes, b. New Orleans, LA, 1929. American dancer. Studied with A. DANILOVA and Vincenzo Celli. Debut with Original B. Russe 1946; MARKOVA–DOLIN co. 1947–8; B. ALONSO 1948–50 and 1952–4; ABT 1950–3; BOROVANSKY B. 1954–6; rejoined ABT 1957 and became its leading *danseur noble*. As well as the classic repertory he has danced APOLLO, *Theme and Variations* (BALANCHINE), ÉTUDES, and, with FONTEYN on her 1963 world tour, SYMPHONIC VARIATIONS. He has also partnered Alonso, T. LANDER, SLAVENSKA. Now teaches at State University of NY at Purchase. DV

Ferri, Olga, b. Buenos Aires, 1928. Pupil of Esmée Bulnes; studied in Paris with V. GSOVSKY and Nicholas Zverev. During the 1950s she progressed from soloist rank to prima ballerina at the T. Colón, Buenos Aires. Guest artist with Les Étoiles de Paris with MISKOVITCH, also with Munich and W. Berlin cos. Danced with LFB 1960 and 1963 in ballerina roles, notably GISELLE. Starred in J. CARTER's TV film *The Life and Loves of Fanny Elssler* (Belgium 1961). Although she has danced frequently with regional cos in the USA she remains the pride of the Colón. Her repertory incl. SWAN LAKE. Has danced with NUREYEV in Argentina and Brazil in SYLPHIDES and APOLLO. Opened a school in Buenos Aires 1971. JUL

Festival Ballet *see* LONDON FESTIVAL BALLET

Fête Étrange, La, ballet, 2 scenes, ch. HOWARD; mus. Gabriel Fauré (six piano pieces and two songs, *Mandoline* and *Soir*); lib. Ronald Crichton; sc./c. FEDOROVITCH. London, Arts T., London B., 23 May 1940; dan. Maude LLOYD, STAFF, David Paltenghi. Revived SWTB (orch. Lennox Berkeley) 25 Mar 1947; dan. June Brae, Donald Britton, Anthony Burke. CG (re-orch. Guy Warrack), RB, 11 Dec 1958; dan. BERIOSOVA, TRECU. Revived Norwich, T. Royal, Scottish B., 30 Sept 1971; RBS student perfs, summer 1973; Leicester, Haymarket T., RB, 29 Jan 1974. Crichton, who also selected the music in collaboration with Howard, based his story on an episode from Alain Fournier's novel, *Le Grand Meaulnes*. A country boy stumbles upon an engagement party and unwittingly, by falling in love with the young *châtelaine*, disturbs the equanimity of the occasion. A sensitive, understated work with the central theme expressed through a series of *pas de trois*. Exquisitely designed, a wintry landscape which transforms to an indoor scene, all the colour being in the costumes. Howard's masterpiece. MC

Fewster, Barbara. English dancer and teacher, principal of RBS since 1968. Early studies Wessex S., Bournemouth, then SWS. A founder member of SWTB 1946, assistant ballet mistress 1947 and ballet mistress 1951–4. Toured USA with Old Vic production of Shakespeare's *A Midsummer Night's Dream* 1954–5. Joined staff of RBS 1955, deputy principal to MORETON 1967. Not only a fine teacher but has photographic memory of choreography, invaluable in staging ballets from the RB's early repertory for RBS perfs and other cos. Chairman of judges, Prix de Lausanne 1975, 1976. MC

Fialka, Ladislav *see* MIME

Field [Greenfield], John, b. Doncaster, Yorkshire, 1921. English dancer and teacher. Trained at Elliott-Clarke S., Liverpool; debut with Liverpool B. Club; joined Vic-Wells B. 1939. Career interrupted by World War II service but returned to SWB and became a principal dancer, taking most of the major classical roles and frequently partnering GREY. Retired from dancing 1956 when he took over the direction of the touring RB. He built this co. up to almost equal status with that of CG, became an assistant director of the RB and in 1970 was appointed joint director with MACMILLAN. Disagreements about policy led to his resignation early in the 1970–1 season. To Sc. as director of the ballet, Oct 1971, but, like many before him, was constantly frustrated by the domination of the opera co. there. In 1975 returned to England as artistic director of the RAD; the following summer became its director. Noted, as a director of ballet cos, for developing talent among his dancers and winning their respect and loyalty, Field is an extrovert character, easy talker, and excellent spokesman for ballet in the world of education. He m. former dancer Anne Heaton. MC

Field of Tulips *see* TULIP OF HAARLEM

Fifield, Elaine, b. Sydney, 1930. Australian dancer. Scully-BOROVANSKY S. RAD Scholarship 1945, to SWBS. SWTB 1947, becoming principal dancer. RB 1954–7, ballerina. Borovansky B., 1957–9. Has appeared with the Australian B. at intervals since 1964. Her classical dancing is characterized by a delicate sense of comedy (Poll in PINEAPPLE POLL) (created) or Columbine (CARNAVAL)). Created title role in ASHTON's *Madame Chrysanthème*. Published *In My Shoes* (London 1967). KSW

Fille du Pharaon, La, ballet, 3 acts, 7 scenes with prologue and epilogue, ch. M. PETIPA; mus. PUGNI; lib. H. Vernoy de Saint-Georges. St Petersburg, Bolshoy T., 30 Jan 1862; dan. ROSATI, Nicholas Goltz, Petipa, IVANOV. Inspired by GAUTIER's *Le Roman de la Momie*, an improbable story about an Englishman, Lord Wilson, who, under the influence of opium while touring Egypt, dreams of the beautiful Princess Aspiccia (a mummy who comes to life) and of his wooing of her. In his dream he is transformed into an Egyptian, Ta-Hor, and saves her from the King of Nubia. The ballet was made for Rosati's farewell and earned Petipa the post of second ballet master of the Imperial Ts. The original version lasted nearly four hours and required nearly 400 dancers and extras – an example of the prodigality of the Tsar towards his ballet. Aspiccia was a favourite role with Imperial ballerinas. Original Russian title *Doch Faraona*. MC
See COMPLETE BOOK

Fille Mal Gardée, La, *or Vain Precautions*, ballet, 2 acts, ch./lib. DAUBERVAL; mus. unknown composer. Bordeaux, Grand T., 1 July 1789, under the title *Le Ballet de la Paille*; dan. Mlle Théodore (Dauberval's wife). One of the first ballets to deal with everyday contemporary life, it tells how Lise and her lover Colas outwit her mother's plans to marry her off to the half-witted son of a rich landowner. The title by which the ballet is now known was first used when Dauberval revived it at the Pantheon T., London, 30 Apr 1791, again with Théodore, partnered by DIDELOT; the cast also incl. VIGANÒ and his wife Maria Medina. Paris, T. de la Porte-St-Martin, 13 Oct 1803; ch. Eugène Hus, after the original. Never

La Fille Mal Gardée, Act I, as revived by GORSKY, at the Bolshoy T., Moscow, *c.* 1920; Anastasia Abramova as Lise

long out of the repertory in London or Paris, also presented in many other European cities.

Revived by Jean Aumer, Paris O., 17 Nov 1828, when it acquired a new score by Louis Joseph Ferdinand Hérold, to which was added a *pas de deux* on themes by Gaetano Donizetti when ELSSLER danced it, 15 Sept 1837. Again given a new score, by Peter Ludwig Hertel, for the revival by P. TAGLIONI at Königliche O., Berlin, 7 Nov 1864. This was basically the score used by M. PETIPA and IVANOV at the Bolshoy T., St Petersburg, 27 Dec 1885; dan. ZUCCHI and P. GERDT, and in most subsequent revivals, e.g. those by GORSKY, Moscow 1901, by A. PAVLOVA's co., London 1912, by L. LAVROVSKY, Leningrad 1937, by NIJINSKA for ABT, New York 1940, by BALASHOVA for Nouveau B. de Monte Carlo, Monte Carlo 1946. An entirely new version was presented by RB, CG, 28 Jan 1960; ch. ASHTON, mus. adapted by John Lanchbery mostly from Hérold's 1828 score; sc./c. Osbert Lancaster; dan. NERINA, BLAIR, HOLDEN, GRANT. This version, one of Ashton's masterpieces, incl. some traditional material provided by KARSAVINA and dating back at least to the time of Zucchi, notably Lise's mime scene in Act II which Pavlova also used to perform. Revived RDB 1964; Australian B. 1967; PACT B., Johannesburg 1969; Hungarian State B. 1971; Munich 1971; RSB 1972; Ankara 1973; Zurich 1974; Toronto NB of Canada, 1976; etc. DV

See Ivor Guest (ed.), 'La Fille Mal Gardée', *Dancing Times* (London 1960); John Lanchbery and Ivor Guest, 'The Scores of *La Fille Mal Gardée*', *Theatre Research*, Vol. III, Nos 1, 2, 3 (London 1961)

Film, Dance on. Dance films can be used to preserve choreography and definitive perfs; they can bring the best dance to areas where major cos rarely tour; since they can be scheduled to the viewer's needs and can be easily replayed, they can be a tremendous aid in the study and the teaching of dance as a coherent art; and they can become a unique art form themselves.

Although dance people often seem aware of these advantages, important perfs and choreography none the less have often been permitted to vanish without being filmed. For example, there appears to be no film record of the dancing of NIJINSKY, I. DUNCAN, or KARSAVINA and only hasty glimpses of A. PAVLOVA or WIGMAN exist. Major works from the 1930s, 1940s, and 1950s by such choreographers as BALANCHINE and GRAHAM are represented, if at all, only by snippets in silent films taken by amateurs.

There are several reasons for this situation. Filming takes time and money, commodities precious to the barely solvent dance co. that always seems to be rushing off to the next engagement. It is also a complex medium outside the experience of most dancers and choreographers who are orientated to the live theatre. In addition, unless the filming is handled with considerable expertise there is almost inevitably some loss in transferring the rectangular, three-dimensional, theatrical art of dance into the tri-angular, two-dimensional world of the camera. Other objections incl. the arduousness of the filming process, the absence of a stimulus from a live audience, poor pay, the fear that films will misrepresent the art and drive away the audience (or seduce it from live performance), and a concern that films will allow competitors to steal choreography.

It is useful to distinguish between three kinds of dance films: record films, films for theatrical presentation, and 'cine-dance'.

Record films. Filming for record purposes involves the least commitment and expense. A single camera is mounted at the back of the theatre or performing space and turned on to record a continuous or nearly continuous perf. Sometimes a modest amount of editing is done – there may be more than one take, or perspectives from other camera positions may be cut in – but the purpose is simply to obtain a perf. record that can be used for future reference or revivals.

Major perfs in the Soviet Union have been routinely filmed in this way for years. This is the case not only for the Soviet cos, but also for visiting ones so that, ironically, some important Western choreography and performances are preserved only on films held within Soviet archives.

Western choreographers and dance cos have, from time to time, managed to record their repertory on film. MASSINE has created a collection of silent films of his works which are used for revivals. The then-current repertory of the Graham co. was filmed in the mid-1960s, that of the CUNNINGHAM co. was videotaped in the early 1970s – but only after dozens of important works by these two artists had been allowed to fall out of repertory.

An important systematic effort to create and collect record films was begun in the 1960s by the Dance Collection of the NY Public Library. Professional record films of dozens of dance works are made every year and prints are deposited at the Dance Collection where they can be seen only with the permission of the choreographer. Among the films on deposit are works performed by ABT, NYCB, CCJB, and the Graham and AILEY dance cos.

Dance films for theatrical presentation. Some films have attempted to translate theatrical dance to the screen in presentations suitable for general, as well as specialist, audiences. They range from full-blown features to 16mm art films made on minimum budgets. The most satisfying dance films of this sort characteristically let the dance work speak as much as possible for itself and seek to keep the camera work and editing as unobtrusive as possible.

A superb early example of this is a 1934 filming of HUMPHREY's *Air for the G-String* which blends a respect for the choreography with some tasteful close-ups of Humphrey's own sensuous performance. A contrast would be two 1941 Hollywood shorts of works by Massine, GAIETÉ PARISIENNE and *Capriccio Espagnole*, in which the viewer is bewildered by a phantasmagoria of cuts, angles, takes, and gimmicks.

Except for a few examples like these, stage dance

filmed for theatrical purposes became a serious commodity only in the 1950s, and only to a limited degree then. In Britain Paul Czinner produced two feature-length films that gave audiences a view of the Bolshoy (with ULANOVA) and the RB (with FONTEYN). Some material also began to come out of the USSR incl. a film of Ulanova in L. LAVROVSKY's ROMEO AND JULIET. In the USA Graham filmed her APPALACHIAN SPRING and NIGHT JOURNEY and created the popular film *A Dancer's World*.

Film productions like these continued in later years. Among them are an Australian DON QUIXOTE (with NUREYEV), a Kirov SLEEPING BEAUTY and SWAN LAKE, two features and ENIGMA VARIATIONS by the RB, documentaries on various dancers, cos, and choreographers, and a filming in Germany in 1973 of 15 Balanchine works as danced by NYCB.

Cine-dance. A related approach to dance on film is the combination of special cinema or video techniques with choreography to result in a unique assemblage. Leaders in this area incl. the Canadian Norman McLaren with his films *Pas de Deux* and *Ballet Adagio*, and CULLBERG with her imaginative use of the TV technique, chroma-key. JMu
See also TELEVISION

Films, Dance in. When still photographs were first set in motion and the movies were born, in the last decade of the 19th c., any kind of movement was their raw material, and naturally this incl. dancing. Many early films record fragments of ethnic or theatrical dance, though the choice of subject was too haphazard to ensure that very much of it was of great historical importance. As films grew longer and capable of telling more complicated stories, dance continued to have a place in feature films. D. W. Griffith, in particular, was keenly aware of the power of dance to heighten the emotion or enhance the lyricism of a scene. Most of his actresses were dancers – Carol Dempster, for instance, had been in the DENISHAWN co. (so had Louise Brooks, though not a Griffith player). The dancers in the Babylon sequence of *Intolerance* (1914) may in fact be ST DENIS and SHAWN themselves. Dance was also a way of depicting sexuality without giving offence, as in Rudolph Valentino's famous tango in *The Four Horsemen of the Apocalypse* (Rex Ingram, 1921) and Joan Crawford's provocative Charleston in *Our Dancing Daughters* (Harry Beaumont, 1928).

With the coming of sound, the musical film became a possibility. The first were all-star revues, collections of musical numbers staged like their theatrical equivalents and photographed by a stationary camera, just as most early 'talkies' were photographed stage plays. The film musical as an independent form came into being through the work of two men whose approach to cinema was diametrically opposed, ASTAIRE and Busby Berkeley. The best numbers in the films Astaire made with Ginger Rogers (b. 1911) were usually shot in two or three continuous takes, without fancy angles or editing, often on simple sets.

Films, Dance in. *Above:* A typical Busby Berkeley number from *Dames*; *below: The Red Shoes*, with M. SHEARER and HELPMANN

Berkeley (1895–1976) was a Broadway hoofer who went to Hollywood in 1930 and, in a series of films made for Warner Brothers, perfected a kind of spectacular routine that used all the cinematic resources spurned by Astaire – intricate camera movements, optical effects, montage – with a minimum of actual dancing: his choreography was for the camera itself, and although he staged scenes for backstage musicals like *42nd Street*, *Footlight Parade* (both Lloyd Bacon, 1933), and the *Gold Diggers* series, they usually took place on sets that no theatre could possibly accommodate. Significantly, his favourite heroine, Ruby Keeler (b. 1909), was an indifferent dancer.

Popular musicals were also made in Britain during the 1930s, but although they could boast one great dancing star in Jessie Matthews (b. 1907), they were hardly innovative in cinematic terms. In Hollywood, great individual dancers like Bill ('Bojangles') Robinson (1878–1949) and DRAPER made occasional screen appearances, and there were a few attempts at screen ballet. Since BALANCHINE happened to be married to Vera Zorina at the time, he did a certain amount of choreography for the movies she made, but only *The Goldwyn Follies* (George Marshall, 1938) was of more than ephemeral interest. The most popularly successful ballet film was *The Red Shoes* (Michael Powell and Emeric Pressburger, 1948), which made an international star of M. SHEARER. The ballet sequences, choreographed by HELPMANN, are unadulterated *Kitsch*.

After Astaire and Berkeley, the most important innovator in screen dancing is Gene Kelly (b. 1912), who went to Hollywood from Broadway following his success in the title role of *Pal Joey* (1940). It was not until *Cover Girl* (Charles Vidor, 1944) that he was able to put some of his ideas into practice, in his famous 'alter ego' dance. In 1949 he made *Take Me Out to the Ball Game*, directed by Berkeley, but with dances by Kelly and his habitual assistant, Stanley Donen; later in the same year they co-directed a film of their own, *On the Town*, from ROBBINS's stage musical (derived from FANCY FREE). The film broke new ground with exhilarating numbers filmed on location all over Manhattan. Less successful was the big 'ballet' but this unfortunately was the element that assumed increasing importance in subsequent films: *An American in Paris* (Vincente Minnelli, 1951), *Singin' in the Rain* (Kelly–Donen, 1952), *It's Always Fair Weather* (Kelly–Donen, 1955), and, most disastrously, Kelly's *Invitation to the Dance*, consisting of three 'ballets' whose pretentiousness was such that the film, made in 1954, was not released for two years, and then as unobtrusively as possible.

The advent of CinemaScope in the early 1950s put an end to the fluency of camera movement and variety of rhythm in cutting that were the properly 'cinematic' qualities of earlier musicals. Screen adaptations of stage musicals like *Oklahoma!* (Fred Zinnemann, 1955) and *Guys and Dolls* (Joseph L. Mankiewicz, 1955) were inflated and unwieldy. There were a few exceptions like Robbins's own film (with Robert Wise) of *West Side Story* (1961), at least in the opening sequence, shot on location. Donen, working on his own, tried to introduce new concepts in *Seven Brides for Seven Brothers* (1954), *Funny Face* (1957), and *The Pajama Game* (1957), with some success though with inevitable compromises. In the last-named, and in the musical version of *My Sister Eileen* (Richard Quine, 1955), Bob Fosse's choreography was refreshingly witty and unpretentious, but his later work as director, *Sweet Charity* (1968) and *Cabaret* (1972), possesses none of these qualities. The great days of the film musical would seem to be over, mostly because every successful film has to be a 'blockbuster' in scale. DV

See E. Kendall, 'Lo! The Entertainers: D. W. Griffith and Dance', *Ballet Review*, Vol. 5, No. 2 (New York 1975–6)

Fils Prodigue, Le *see* PRODIGAL SON

Finland. The Finnish OB was founded in Helsinki [Helsingfors] in 1921 when the Finnish O. gained its own permanent building soon after the proclamation of independence. The director, Edvard Fazer, had worked with the St Petersburg Imperial B. and continued its classic traditions in Helsinki. He engaged George Gé (a pupil of LEGAT) as first ballet master and the first perf. in Oct 1922 was SWAN LAKE, which is still the greatest favourite and has been performed more than 500 times. To the St Petersburg repertory were added the masterpieces of FOKINE. Gé left in 1934 to join R. BLUM's co., taking with him the leading dancers Lucia Nifontova and Arvo Martikainen. He was succeeded by Alexander Saxelin, a Russian character dancer who had also studied in St Petersburg. The first Finnish choreographer was Irja Koskinen. Gé returned to Finland in 1955 (bringing with him ÉPREUVE D'AMOUR) and worked as ballet master to the Finnish OB until his death in 1962. He was succeeded by BERIOZOFF, who staged ESMERALDA for the ballerina Maj-Lis Rajala, his own version of SLEEPING BEAUTY, and a new staging of SACRE DU PRINTEMPS. In 1970 the Finnish choreographer Elsa Sylvestersson became ballet master and in 1974 Johani Raiskinen became director, with Konstantin Damianov as ballet master. The repertory incl. such Soviet ballets as FOUNTAIN OF BAKHCHISARAY and STONE FLOWER (staged, respectively, by ZAKHAROV and L. LAVROVSKY) as well as works by native choreographers on Finnish themes and often using music by Jean Sibelius. Doris Laine became prima ballerina in 1956; principal dancers incl. Leo Ahonen, Klaus Salin, Margaretha von Bahr, Ulrika Hallberg, Marianna Rumjantseva, Jarmo Rastas, Aku Ahjolinna, Arja Nieminen, and Juhani Teräsvuori.

In 1976 the co. consisted of 8 female and 8 male soloists and a *corps de ballet* of 21 female and 19 male dancers. The principal choreographers are Sylverstersson and Heikki Värtsi (also a dancer). The director of the OBS is Marita Ståhlberg. The co. has toured widely and has special affiliations with the RSB. MC

Fiocre, Eugénie, b. Paris, 1845; d. 1908. French dancer, principal at Paris O. 1864–75. A luscious lady, she excelled in *travesti* roles and created FRANZ. Jean Baptiste Carpeaux (1827–75) made a handsome bust of her and Émile Marcelin an amusing but delightful caricature. Edgar Degas (1834–1917) painted her in SAINT-LÉON's ballet *La Source*. MC

Flame of Paris (*Plamya Parizha*; although this ballet is often called *Flames of Paris* in English, the Russian is *Flame*), ballet, 4 acts, 6 scenes, ch. VAINONEN; mus. ASAFYEV, based on songs of the French Revolution, with backstage choir; lib. Nikolay Volkov, Vladimir Dmitriev; advising *régisseur* Sergey Radlov; sc. Dmitriev. Leningrad, State Academic T. of O. and B. (GATOB), 6 Nov 1932. Impressive epic, using national dances as means of characterization; especially impressive scene of the storming of the Tuileries by the Marseillais, shown in Moscow separately 6 Nov 1932; dan. YERMOLAYEV (Jerome), LEPESHINSKAYA (Jeanne). Entire ballet staged Moscow, Bolshoy T., 6 June 1933; dan. CHABUKIANI (Jerome), JORDAN (Jeanne), ANISIMOVA (Thérèse, the Basque heroine), ULANOVA (Mireille de Poitiers, an actress who joined the revolutionaries. *Pas de deux* from last act, *grand divertissement* modelled on open-air celebrations in the style of the painter Jacques-Louis David, often danced as virtuoso piece. Staged by Vainonen in Budapest, copied elsewhere; also filmed as part of the Soviet *Trio Ballet* (1953). NR

Flickers, modern dance work, ch./sc. WEIDMAN; mus. Lionel Nowak; lib. Alan Porter and Weidman. NY, Humphrey–Weidman Studio, 27 Dec 1941; dan. Weidman, HUMPHREY, LITZ. An endearing presentation of the days of silent films complete with choppy movement. The sections incl. the foreclosed mortgage, the vamp, and the sheikh. DM

Flier, Jaap, b. Scheveningen, 1934. Dutch dancer, choreographer, and ballet director. Danced the classic repertory with Nederlands B. and created his first ballet for them (*The Trial*, 1955). A founder member of DT, creating many leading parts incl. TETLEY's *The Anatomy Lesson* made specially for him. His ballets for NDT incl. *Nouvelles Aventures* (mus. György Ligeti, 1969) and *Hi-kyo* (mus. Kazuo Fukoshima, 1971). Artistic director 1970. Now working as director of the Dance Co. (New South Wales), Sydney, with his wife BIJE. The first dancer to be made Knight, Order of Orange Nassau (1968). JP

Flindt, Flemming, b. Copenhagen, 1936. Danish dancer, choreographer, and ballet director. Entered RDBS 1946; ballet dancer 1953; soloist RDB 1957. Left RDB 1960 after several guest appearances at Jacob's Pillow, LFB, and BR. From 1961 *étoile* at Paris O. During 1960s guest dancer all over the world with different cos. Director, RDB, 1966–78. First choreography LESSON, followed by YOUNG MAN MUST MARRY, *The Three Musketeers* (*De Tre Musketerer*, 1966), *Gala Variations* (1967), *Tango Chikane* (1967), TRIUMPH OF DEATH, *Felix Luna* (1973), *Trio* (1973), *Dreamland* (1974), and others. Also produced in Denmark classics from SWAN LAKE and NUTCRACKER to MIRACULOUS MANDARIN. SKJ
See E. Aschengreen, 'Flemming Flindt', *Les Saisons de la Danse* (Paris, Dec 1970)

Flemming Flindt as the mad Dancing Master and ØSTERGAARD as the Pupil in LESSON

Flindt [Gelker], Vivi, b. Copenhagen, 1943. Danish dancer. Entered RDBS 1951; *coryphée* 1961; soloist 1967. Debut as MISS JULIE 1965. Has danced many parts in both classical and modern style, at her best in the modern repertoire such as AUREOLE and MOOR'S PAVANE. Created important parts in her husband's (F. FLINDT) works, incl. MIRACULOUS MANDARIN and TRIUMPH OF DEATH. Among classic roles are several August BOURNONVILLE ones. From 1975 ballet instructor, RDB. SKJ

Florimund, Prince (or Prince Désiré), the hero of SLEEPING BEAUTY

Flower Festival at Genzano, The (*Blomsterfesten i Genzano*), ballet, 1 act, ch. August BOURNONVILLE; mus. Edvard Helsted and Holger Simon Paulli. Copenhagen, RDB, 19 Dec 1858. The ballet was last given in full in 1930. The great *pas de deux* was inserted by H. LANDER in his 1-act version of NAPOLI for LFB, 30 Aug 1954, and has ever since been a popular number for star dancers; it is a brilliant example of the Bournonville style. SKJ

Fokine, Mikhail, b. St Petersburg, 1880; d. New York, 1942. Russian dancer, teacher, and choreographer. Entered the Imperial TS 1889, graduating into Maryinsky co. 1898 with rank of soloist. Began to teach in Imperial S. 1902. First choreography 1905, *Acis and Galatea*, staged for a pupils' perf. In 1907 choreographed CYGNE for A. PAVLOVA and PAVILLON D'ARMIDE for the Imperial T. In 1908 invited by DIAGHILEV to produce ballets for his 1909 Paris season; worked with Diaghilev until 1913, creating works incl. SYLPHIDES, CARNAVAL, SPECTRE DE LA ROSE, PRINCE IGOR, SCHÉHÉRAZADE, OISEAU DE FEU, PETRUSHKA, and DAPHNIS ET CHLOÉ. At the start of World War I returned to Russia where he choreographed six works for the Maryinsky, the last being the dances for a revival of Mikhail Glinka's opera *Ruslan and Lyudmila* (1917). Left Russia for Sweden (where he had already worked) 1918; eventually settled in New York in the early 1920s. Travelled widely staging his famous ballets and producing new ones. Towards the end of his life he worked for the DE BASIL B. Russe de Monte Carlo, creating notably ÉPREUVE D'AMOUR, also *Don Juan* (1936), and *Les Éléments* (1937). His last important work was for ABT for whom, in addition to staging *Les Sylphides*, *Petrushka*, and other early works, he choreographed the comedy ballet *Bluebeard* (1941), *Russian Soldier* (1942) and the first drafting of *Helen of Troy* on which he was working when he died.

Fokine's influence on the course of ballet in this century and its consequent transformation from a pretty entertainment to a potent art force is summarized in his Five Principles, published in a letter to the London *Times* 6 July 1914. His total refusal to compromise for reasons of expediency brought him, like many other reformers, much personal unhappiness and frustration as is evident from his autobiography. He m. dancer Vera Fokina; their son Vitale was also a dancer and teacher. JS

See Cyril W. Beaumont, *Michel Fokine and his Ballets* (London 1945); M. Fokine (tr. Vitale Fokine, ed. Anatole Chujoy), *Fokine, Memoirs of a Ballet Master* (New York 1961; enlarged and revised edition, ed. Yuri Slonimsky, Leningrad 1962; contains much material from archives found in Leningrad, with complete list of Fokine's roles and ballets); *see also* complete documentation in *Les Saisons de la Danse* (Paris, Feb 1973)

Folk Dance. Dances created spontaneously by a people to express the characteristics of their temperament and environment. In some countries, especially the less urbanized ones, they are a part of community life. In others, they have been expertly but somewhat artificially re-created. There has been a growing tendency in recent years for governments to recognize the propagandist and tourist attraction of translating colourful or ritualistic folk dance into theatre. Inevitably, in making the transition, authenticity suffers. Genuine folk dance has, however, been used with taste in ballets, e.g. in COPPÉLIA, CRACOW WEDDING and ASHTON'S FILLE MAL GARDÉE, and has been the source for many social dances, for example the Polka and the Rumba. MC

Folk Legend, A, *or A Folk Tale* (*Et Folkesagn*), ballet, 3 acts, ch. August BOURNONVILLE; mus. Johann Peter Emilius Hartmann and Niels Wilhelm Gade. Copenhagen, RDB, 20 Mar 1854. Still performed in Copenhagen. A medieval story about a changeling, Hilda (the human child) and Birthe (the troll child) and a young nobleman Ove, who loses his mind in the Dance of the Elves (influenced by GISELLE). In the end the lovers are united to the Bridal Waltz (still the most popular wedding music in Denmark). SKJ

Folkwangschule, a theatrical training school founded by the City of Essen, in 1927, at which all forms of theatrical art are taught. JOOSS was director of dance; he was joined there by LEEDER, Frederic (Fritz) Cohen, the composer, and others, who in 1929 formed a Folkwang B. (Folkwang Tanzbühne). Their ballets later formed the repertoire of the B. Jooss. Teachers of classical ballet at the S. incl. Cleo Nordi, Audrey Harman, and WOOLLIAMS. In 1968 ZÜLLIG became director. GBLW

Fonaroff, Nina, b. New York, 1914. American dancer. Studied both dance and graphic design. Her most influential teacher was GRAHAM, who invited her to join her co. 1937. Her involvement as a teacher began almost concurrently with her performing career and she was assistant to HORST in his composition course for 15 years. Most widely known for her early solo *Little Theodolina* (1942) and the duet *Mr Puppet* (1947), the latter selected by MARKOVA and DOLIN for inclusion in one of their tours. Among her teaching posts have been the Neighborhood Playhouse, NY, the Graham S. of Contemporary Dance, and LSCD, where she specializes in dance composition. DM

Fonteyn, Margot [Margaret Hookham], b. Reigate, Surrey, 1919. British dancer. Her mother is half-Brazilian, her father a mining engineer; she had a vagrant childhood (China, N. America). Her childhood ballet teachers were Hilda Bosustov, GONCHAROV, and, in London, ASTAFYEVA. Joined Vic-Wells BS and co. 1934. Progress in the infant co. was quick: from her first role as a Snowflake in NUTCRACKER, to the young Tregennis in DE VALOIS's *The Haunted Ballroom* (her first solo role) and, in 1935, to be heiress-designate to MARKOVA as ballerina. By 1939 she had danced GISELLE, ODETTE-ODILE, and AURORA; and, in *Nocturne*, *Apparitions*, and other works, the fruitful association between ASHTON as choreographer and Fonteyn as dancer was under way. She shared the co.'s fortunes during World War II; until 1959 (when she loosened her connection with the RB, as the co. was now known, by becoming a guest artist) she was the jewel for which the rest of the co. was the setting. This was the period during which her dancing came to its peak; it was then that she acquired her distinctive and memorable mastery of the classics (SLEEPING BEAUTY was her 'signature' classic but she first achieved greatness in SWAN LAKE). In SYMPHONIC VARIATIONS, *Daphnis and Chloe* (*see* DAPHNIS ET CHLOÉ) and ONDINE Ashton's choreography and her dancing proclaimed, supremely, the British style of ballet. By 1960 retirement seemed near – she was then over 40, a ripe age for a ballerina – but NUREYEV provided a partner who matched her in international fame and gave her a new lease of life. As globetrotting ballerina, partnered at first by Nureyev and later by many others, she began, in effect, a new career, which continued beyond her 58th year.

Fonteyn has captivated audiences the world over not by pyrotechnical brilliance but by the less gaudy virtues of musicality and line, by the exquisite proportions of her physique (for ballet) and, especially, by the seemingly effortless projection of her natural, warm personality across the footlights. Others, as she has readily admitted, could perform feats of virtuosity that were beyond her; but she has won affection as they have not, to become the most famous ballerina of all. In 1956 she m. Panamanian politician Roberto Arias, who, 10 years later, was left almost totally paralysed by the shots of a would-be assassin. CBE 1950; DBE 1956. JM
See M. Fonteyn, *Margot Fonteyn* (London 1975; New York 1976); James Monahan, *Fonteyn: A Study of a Ballerina in Her Setting* (London 1957; New York 1958); Keith Money, *The Art of Margot Fonteyn* (London 1965; New York 1966); *Fonteyn: The Making of a Legend* (London 1973; New York 1974)

Forains, Les, ballet, ch. PETIT; mus. SAUGUET; sc./c. BÉRARD; lib. KOCHNO. Paris, T. des CE, B. des CE, 2 Mar 1945; dan. VYROUBOVA, Petit, PAGAVA. A sad little tale of a troupe of strolling players who set up their circus, give a perf. (a clown, Siamese twins, a conjuror, a virtuoso ballerina), only to find when they take round the hat that their audience has melted away. *Les Forains* epitomized the ideals of the B. des CE; it did not survive. MC

Fornaroli, Cia, b. Milan, 1888; d. New York, 1954. Italian dancer and teacher. Studied Milan Sc. BS under CECCHETTI, of whom she was a favourite pupil. Ballerina, NY Met OB, 1910–13; prima ballerina, Sc. 1918–32. In charge of the ballet school 1928–33, removed by the Fascist administration. She m. Walter Toscanini, son of the conductor Arturo Toscanini. Taught in NY after removal from Sc. Generally considered the outstanding Italian ballerina of her generation. After her death Toscanini gave a large Fornaroli archive to the Museum of the Performing Arts, Lincoln Center, NY. FP

for these who die as cattle, modern dance work, 1 act, ch. BRUCE; no mus.; lib./c. N. BAYLIS. London, Young Vic. T., BR, 9 Mar 1972; dan. Bruce, Sandra Craig. The title is a quotation from the poet Wilfred Owen and the work is concerned with the horror of war and death. Especially effective on an open or thrust stage. MC

Forti, Simone, b. Florence, Italy, 1935. American dancer. Taught by HALPRIN in San Francisco, also studied with CUNNINGHAM. She was attracted immediately to *avant-garde* dance activity and began to show her work first in 1960 in NY, where she was living with her husband Robert Morris. She was active in 'happenings' with her second husband Robert Whitman. Her interest has always centred on the idea of process rather than end product in designing her dances. She is intrigued with the idea of any movement being dance movement if properly set, and has often worked with non-technically trained persons. DM

Fountain of Bakhchisaray, The (*Bakhchisarayskiy Fontan*), ballet, 4 acts with prologue and epilogue, ch. ZAKHAROV; mus. ASAFYEV (deliberately using musical references to Aleksandr Pushkin's time, e.g. Maria's principal theme is a *Nocturne* by John Field); lib. Nikolay Volkov, based on Pushkin's poem of the same title; sc. Valentina Khodasevich; advising *régisseur* Sergey Radlov. Leningrad, Kirov T., 28 Sept 1934; dan. ULANOVA (Maria), SERGEYEV (Vaslav), Mikhail Dudko (Girey), JORDAN (Zarema, alternating with VECHESLOVA). Staged Moscow, Stanislavsky-Nemirovich-Danchenko T., same ch. and sc., 20 Apr 1935; also Bolshoy T., 11 June 1936. Staged Budapest, Helsinki, Belgrade and many O. and BTs in USSR. This ballet launched the use of literary themes in Soviet ballet, applied Konstantin Stanislavsky's system to dance characterizations, and exercised influence on dramatic ballets of the 1930s. It gave Ulanova her first great created role. NR
See Rostislav Zakharov, *Iskusstvo Baletmeistera* (*The Choreographer's Art*) (Moscow 1954); Natalia Roslavleva, 'Stanislavsky and the Ballet', *Dance Perspectives* No. 23 (New York 1965)

Four Temperaments, The, ballet, 5 parts, ch. BALANCHINE; mus. HINDEMITH; sc./c. Kurt Seligmann; ltg ROSENTHAL. NY Central High School of Needle Trades, Ballet Society, 20 Nov 1946; dan. Gisella Caccialanza, LECLERCQ, MOYLAN, Elise Reiman, Beatrice Tompkins, BOLENDER, L. CHRISTENSEN, Fred Danieli, DOLLAR, José Martinez, MONCION. A series of variations on the ancient idea that the human organism is made up of four humours or temperaments – melancholic, sanguinic, phlegmatic, and choleric. Revived London CG, RB, 25 Jan 1973; SWT, SWRB, 4 Oct 1976. In repertoires of many cos. Now danced in practice clothes. Revised for NYCB without decor 1951. FM

Fracci, Carla, b. Milan, 1936. Italian dancer. Sc. BS 1946–54. Resident dancer at Sc. until 1963. The first

20th-c. Italian ballerina to win an international reputation, a guest artist at opera houses all over Italy as well as with many foreign cos, incl. LFB (1959), RB (1963), and, particularly, ABT. Her most famous role is GISELLE, which she has danced with large number of partners, incl. NUREYEV, VASILIEV, KRONSTAM, LABIS, PISTONI, BORTOLUZZI, BARYSHNIKOV, and, above all, BRUHN, with whom she filmed the work in BLAIR's production. Other roles incl. SYLPHIDE, SWANILDA, JULIET, 'Civilization' in EXCELSIOR, also leading roles in many ballets by Pistoni and Loris Gai. From late 1960s also toured Italy frequently at head of small co. directed by her husband, Beppe Menegatti. FP
See I. Lidova, 'Carla Fracci', *Les Saisons de la Danse* (Paris, June 1972) with list of roles

Franca, Celia, b. London, 1921. English, now Canadian, dancer and choreographer. Studied at RAD with IDZIKOWSKI, TUDOR, RAMBERT. Joined BR 1937, SWB 1941, creating Queen Gertrude in HELPMANN's HAMLET, the Prostitute in MIRACLE IN THE GORBALS, etc. Ballet mistress and dancer with Metropolitan B. 1947–9. Founded NB of Canada 1951, acting as principal until 1959 and as Artistic Director until 1974. Choreographed NUTCRACKER (1964), CINDERELLA (1968), etc. Officer, Order of Canada, 1967. PD

Françaix, Jean, b. Le Mans, 1912. French composer, student of Nadia Boulanger. His elegant, lightweight ballets incl. *Beach* (Monte Carlo 1933; ch. MASSINE), *Le Roi Nu* (Paris 1936; ch. LIFAR) and *Les Demoiselles de la Nuit* (Paris 1948; ch. PETIT). Françaix orchestrated various pieces by Luigi Boccherini (1743–1805) for the ballet *Scuola di Ballo* (Monte Carlo 1933; ch. Massine). DH

France. The art of ballet owes its origins to France, to the BALLET DE COUR and then to the Académie Royale de Musique, the PARIS OPÉRA, and its school of dance. All the greatest dancers and ballet masters of the 16th and 17th c. were associated with the PARIS OB. In the 18th c. the travels of NOVERRE to Marseille and to Lyon and DAUBERVAL's work in Bordeaux testify to the spread of ballet to other cities during the reign of Louis XV. The Paris O., however, was pre-eminent in attracting both dancers and choreographers until the middle of the 19th c. The great days of the Romantic period ended in 1863 with the death of Emma Livry, M. TAGLIONI's pupil and natural successor. Fine dancers continued to be produced by the school, as they have been to this day, but the ballets became less interesting; it was as if the soul had gone out of French ballet. The last triumph was COPPÉLIA before, crushed by the aftermath of the Franco–Prussian War, the Paris OB sank into decline. It could in no way compete with DIAGHILEV's B. Russes which 1909–29 (with the exception of the war years) gave regular seasons in Paris. The Diaghilev example prompted Jacques Rouché, Director of the Paris O. from 1914, to present ballets by composers such as Paul Dukas, RAVEL, and Vincent d'Indy and to begin to bring the Paris OB back to life. He invited great Russians such as FOKINE, A. PAVLOVA, and SPESSIVTSEVA to work there and then LIFAR. Lifar won a new public and revitalized the co. Above all, to the fury of the *abonnés*, he turned off the house lights during perfs, raising them only during intermissions, and he closed to the public the Foyer de la Danse, where so many liaisons between *abonnés* and dancers had been formed in the history of the Paris O. The years immediately following World War II brought a remarkable flowering of young talent in B. des CE and in the cos of PETIT, CHARRAT, and others. The DE CUEVAS B. with its galaxy of international stars was based on Paris. The Paris O. in 1947 was forced to recall Lifar to direct the ballet co. which he did for the next 10 years, succeeded in turn by SKIBINE, DESCOMBEY, TARAS, and R. FRANCHETTI. None of these directors possessed Lifar's gifts for inspiring a co. or creating a repertory and some of the best dancers sought careers elsewhere. Choreographers like BÉJART, Petit, BALANCHINE, and ROBBINS in the classical idiom, and CUNNINGHAM, Carolyn Carlson, and TETLEY in the modern idiom were invited to stage works during the 1970s. VERDY assumed the direction in Jan 1977. Throughout its history the Opéra-Comique engaged many celebrated dancers and choreographers and in recent years has staged more adventurous work by choreographers like Roger Quinault, Constantine Tcherkas, Charrat, and F. FLINDT.

The spirit of national individualism, token of vitality but also of dispersal, has since 1950 resulted in various shortlived cos built around such artists as BABILÉE, MISKOVITCH, LACOTTE, and TCHERINA. Béjart, although based in Brussels, is very popular throughout France. In 1968 André Malraux set up the first of the *maisons de la culture* to bring together the various arts and the BT Contemporain, first in Amiens then Angers, found an image more exciting than anything then happening in Paris. Decentralization was officially encouraged; Petit worked in Marseille, BIAGI in Lyon, BLASKA in Grenoble, and VAN DIJK in Alsace. Also active are the T. du Silence of Jacques Garnier and Brigitte Lefevre, and Les B. Anne Béranger. The old partiality for dancing has not been lost in France and still flourishes today. M-FC/MC

Franchetti, Jean-Pierre, b. Paris, 1944. French dancer. Studied with his father, R. FRANCHETTI. *Corps de ballet*, Paris O.; *premier danseur* 1968; *étoile* 1971. Dances both noble and character roles in classic and modern repertory. Has an elegant physique but somewhat lacks stage personality. M-FC

Franchetti, Raymond, b. Aubervilliers, 1912. French dancer and teacher. Studied RICAUX. B. de la Jeunesse 1937; B. de Monte Carlo 1938, 1943–45; Nouveau B. de Monte Carlo 1946; Paris O. 1947.

Premier danseur de caractère; teacher, Paris OBS 1963. Taught privately in Paris. Director of dance, O., 1971–6. Guest teacher, London RB. Faithful to traditions of the French school, his teaching is appreciated by many pupils. Father of J.-P. FRANCHETTI. M-FC

Franklin, Frederic, b. Liverpool, 1914. English dancer. Studied with Shelagh Elliott-Clarke in Liverpool, then in London with LEGAT and KYASHT, in Paris with EGOROVA. Debut 1931, Casino de Paris, with the famous music-hall star Mistinguett. Danced in London musicals, MARKOVA–DOLIN B. 1935–7, B. Russe de Monte Carlo 1938–49 and 1954–6. As guest artist, partnered A. DANILOVA with SWB, CG, 1949. With SLAVENSKA formed Slavenska-Franklin B., 1951. Danced a wide variety of roles incl. ALBRECHT, GOLDEN SLAVE, FRANZ, Poet in SONNAMBULA, Champion Roper in RODEO; partnered many great ballerinas. His legendary memory has enabled him to restage many works incl. BALANCHINE's BALLET IMPERIAL and *Pas de Dix*, and several classics. Director of Washington (Civic) B. 1959–60 and then of NB of Washington 1962–74. Since then he has been artistic director of both Pittsburgh BT and PAGE's Chicago B. DV

Franz, the fiancé of Swanilda in COPPÉLIA

Fränzl, Willy, b. Vienna, 1898. Austrian dancer and ballet master. Joined Vienna Staats OB 1914, soloist 1921, principal 1938. Director of its S. 1931–62; 1935–62 ballet master and jealous custodian of tradition and the old repertory. MC

French, Ruth, b. London, 1906. English dancer and teacher. Studied with KHLUSTIN and became a principal dancer with A. PAVLOVA's co. Her strong technique and experience were great assets to the young Vic-Wells B. Her career was mostly in revues and musicals. An outstanding teacher, she is one of the most respected examiners of the RAD. MC

Frey, Frank, b. Munich, 1947. German dancer. Trained at the Munich Staats OBS and under BLANK; joined the Wuppertal B. 1964. He subsequently danced in the Basel and Zürich ballets and joined the Deutsche O., W. Berlin 1967 as soloist, creating many roles, notably in MACMILLAN's *Cain and Abel* and *Olympiad* (both 1968). GBLW

Friendly Hearts *see* LITTLE STORK

Fukagawa, Hideo, b. Nagoya, 1949. Japanese dancer. Studied with Minora Ochi in Tokyo and Jürgen Schneider in E. Berlin. Bronze Medal, Varna Competition, 1965; joined Komische OB, E. Berlin 1969. Silver Medal, Moscow International Competition, 1969; Silver Medal, Varna, 1970; joined Stuttgart B. 1971, Munich B. 1973, as soloist. Frequent guest appearances. GBLW

Fuller, Loie [Mary Louise], b. Fullersberg, IL, 1862; d. Paris, 1928. Self-taught, she worked 1865–91 as an actress, playwright, singer, dancer, producer in American theatre. Choreographed *Serpentine Dance* 1891; arriving in Paris 1892, she received immediate critical and popular acclaim. Accepted by the Symbolists, Impressionists, and Art Nouveau movement as a revolutionary in art, she became the first American dancer honoured as the originator of a modern dance form. In her dances, light and colour were thrown on masses of silk. Costumed in hundreds of yards of diaphanous silk, dancing on a darkened stage stripped of decor, bathed in the powerful glow of multi-directioned, multi-coloured lights, she seemed suspended in space. Choreographing for body and silk, she caused delicate ripples or sculpted huge configurations, representing natural forms: *Butterfly* (1892), *Clouds* (1893), *Lily*, and *Fire* (1895). Airy, silken forms changed in harmony with the lights as colour washed in an iridescent flow across the surface of the silk. From 1900, her choreography evolved

Loie Fuller depicted in a gilt-bronze lamp by Raoul Larch, an interesting example of her influence upon fashion in the Art Nouveau Period

from solo to group works, the silks expanded from costumes to scenography, her lantern slides, lighting effects, and stuffs creating mysterious landscapes: *Bottom of the Sea* (1906), *Ballet of Light* (1908). In 1921 she choreographed a series of shadow dances, phantasmagoric images evocative of visions. She and her school frequently performed outside where moonlight, sunlight, and wind became the special effects of her dances. Choreographed 130 dances 1892–1928; in 1908 founded a school; made two experimental films; wrote an autobiography; was painted, sculpted by many artists, incl. Toulouse-Lautrec, Auguste Rodin and Pierre Roche; honoured by French scientists for artistic contributions to lighting theories; managed first Continental tours of I. DUNCAN, ALLAN; invented and patented costume designs, light machines, stage devices; had a theatre built for her; co-founded two museums in USA; had an extraordinary political career; toured and performed until 1925. SRS
See Loie Fuller, *Quinze Ans de ma Vie* (Paris 1908), translated as *Fifteen Years of a Dancer's Life* (London and Boston 1913, New York 1976); Sally R. Sommer, 'Loie Fuller', *The Drama Review* (Mar 1975)

Fülöp, Viktor, b. Budapest, 1929. Hungarian dancer, ballet master, and choreographer. Became NÁDASI's pupil 1937, danced his first principal role in WOODEN PRINCE (1947) and PETRUSHKA (1948). A powerful artistic personality with a wide gamut of expression from *danseur noble* to character dances, he performed all the main roles of the Budapest O. in post-World War II years, incl. Philippe in FLAME OF PARIS, GIREY, the title role in MIRACULOUS MANDARIN, ALBRECHT, SIEGFRIED, etc. Choreographed *Mario and the Magician* (1964; mus. István Láng) and *Gayané Suite* (1968). Several study periods in USSR. Liszt Prize, 1960; Kossuth Prize, 1962; Merited Artist, 1968; Eminent Artist, 1971. GPD

Fulton, Gaye, b. Manchester, 1939. English dancer. Studied Cone-Ripman S., London; joined LFB 1958, immediately noticed for the delicacy and charm of her dancing. Soloist 1960. Principal dancer 1964–6 in Zürich, where she danced all the main classical roles. Guest with Washington NB 1970; LFB 1970–1, rejoined 1972. She m. Swiss conductor Karl Anton Rickenbacher. Credits the greatest influence and help in her career to BURMEISTER with whom she worked on his revival of SNOW MAIDEN for LFB 1961. Joined B. International 1976. MC

Furtwängler, Gise, b. Berlin, 1917. German dancer and ballet mistress. Pupil of TERPIS and Tamara Rauser in Berlin. Danced in cabaret in Berlin and in the cos in Königsberg and Wuppertal. In 1944 ballet mistress in Wuppertal and then of Bonn and Heidelberg and was a dancer in the Komische O., E. Berlin. Ballet mistress, Oberhausen 1961–4; Münster 1964–6; Cologne 1966–9; Krefeld 1971–4; Hanover 1974–6. Choreographed many ballets. GBLW

Gable, Christopher, b. London, 1940. English dancer and actor. Studied London RBS; joined RB 1957, becoming, in the touring co., very quickly a soloist then principal. Created the Cousin in INVITATION; then the Young Man in ASHTON's *The Two Pigeons* (*see* DEUX PIGEONS). Both roles used with enormous effect his handsome looks and his youth. An outstanding COLAS. Transferred to the RB at CG in 1963 where MACMILLAN created the role of ROMEO for him (although NUREYEV danced the premiere). Gable was the undoubted male star of his generation with the RB. In 1967, plagued with minor injuries, he left ballet, studied acting and scored a remarkable success as Eric Fenby in Ken Russell's BBC TV film *Delius*. One of the few dancers to make the transition from silent dance/acting to the spoken word. MC

Gabovich, Mikhail, b. Moscow, 1905; d. Moscow, 1965. Soviet dancer. Graduated Bolshoy TS, class of GORSKY and TIKHOMIROV. Soloist, Bolshoy T. since 1924. *Premier danseur* famed for dramatic gifts and characterizations. Created, among other roles, the Actor (FLAME OF PARIS; Moscow version), Vladimir (PRISONER OF THE CAUCASUS), Prince (CINDERELLA; Moscow version); Evgeny (BRONZE HORSEMAN), and especially ROMEO in L. LAVROVSKY's 1945 production in which he partnered ULANOVA for many years. Taught at Bolshoy BS from 1951, artistic director 1954–8.

On retirement wrote excellent analytical ballet criticism and a book, *Soul-inspired Flight* (Moscow 1965, pub. posthumously). People's Artist, RSFSR; two State Prizes.

His son Mikhail, b. 1948, soloist Bolshoy B. since 1967, inherited his dramatic gift and noble appearance; dances Paris and Romeo (ROMEO AND JULIET), CRASSUS, Evil Genius and SIEGFRIED in GRIGOROVICH's version of SWAN LAKE. He m. T. BESSMERTNOVA. NR

Vincenzo Galeotti's WHIMS OF CUPID, as danced by the RDB in the 1950s; KARSTENS and Jan Holme in the Quaker Dance

Gadd, Ulf, b. Gothenburg, 1943. Swedish dancer and choreographer. Studied in Gothenburg with Mila Gardemeister, joined RSB 1960, soloist 1965. Danced with Harkness B. 1967–8. To Stora T., Gothenburg, 1968. Choreographed MIRACULOUS MANDARIN (1970) and founded with BORG the New Swedish B. as a touring co. Staged *Miraculous Mandarin* for this co., the RSB 1971, ABT 1972, and Deutsche O., W. Berlin. Director, Gothenburg B., 1976. Among his ballets are *Tratto*, *Gemini Suite*, *Orpheus*, and *Kalevala*. AGS

Gades, Antonio *see* SPAIN

Gaieté Parisienne, ballet, 1 act, ch. MASSINE. lib./sc./c. DE BEAUMONT; mus. Jacques Offenbach, arr. Manuel Rosenthal. T. de Monte Carlo, B. Russe de Monte Carlo, 5 Apr 1938; dan. Nina Tarakanova, Massine, FRANKLIN, YOUSKEVITCH. Life in a fashionable Parisian café in the 1890s. Tarakanova's role of the Glove Seller was later taken by, and will always be associated with, A. DANILOVA. Revived by many cos incl. ABT 1970, LFB 1973. Filmed by Warner Bros with B. Russe de Monte Carlo as *The Gay Parisian,* 1941. DV

Gala Performance, ballet, 1 act, 2 scenes, ch. TUDOR; mus. PROKOFIEV (1st Movement of 3rd Piano Concerto, and Classical Symphony); sc./c. Hugh Stevenson. London, Toynbee Hall, London B., 5 Dec 1938; dan. VAN PRAAGH, Maude LLOYD, G. LARSEN, Tudor, LAING. In repertory of BR since 28 June 1940; revived NY, Majestic T., ABT, 11 Feb 1941, new sc./c. Nicolas de Molas. Also in repertory of RSB. A burlesque of a late 19th-c. ballet gala, at first backstage, then the gala itself with three rival ballerinas, La Reine de la Danse from Moscow, La Déesse de la Danse from Milan, and La Fille de Terpsichore from Paris, all vying for attention. The ballerina from Milan has the noblest choreography, the Parisian dancer is all fluffy femininity. The ballet is most successful when danced 'deadpan'; if dancers indulge in too much byplay, it becomes a burlesque even of itself. MC

Galeotti, Vincenzo, b. Florence, 1733; d. Copenhagen, 1816. Italian dancer, student of ANGIOLINI. Featured dancer at T. San Moisè 1759; by 1765 choreographer and first dancer with own co. at T. San Benedetto, Venice. Worked as choreographer in Milan and Turin and 1769–70 at King's T., London. Engaged by Royal T., Copenhagen, 1775; worked there until knighted and retired from stage 1812. He took with him to Copenhagen a considerable Angiolini inheritance but subsequently developed a more personal style, and introduced Scandinavian and Romantic themes. His ballet WHIMS OF CUPID is still, in a somewhat revised form, in the repertory. He m. Antonia Guidi, formerly a dancer with NOVERRE's co. in Stuttgart. *See* DENMARK. MC
See S. Kragh-Jacobsen and T. Krogh (eds), *Den Kongelige Danske Ballet* (*The Royal Danish Ballet*) (Copenhagen 1952).

Ganio, Denys, b. Villeneuve-lès-Avignon, 25 Apr 1950. French dancer. Studied Paris OBS 1962, *corps de ballet* 1965–8. Engaged by HIGHTOWER as soloist at Cannes, then at B. de Marseille by PETIT, for whom he created roles in *Allumez les Étoiles* 1972, *Les Intermittences du Cœur* 1974 and danced in revivals of many of Petit's ballets. Guest artist, Frankfurt O. Exceptionally well-proportioned, he possesses smooth technique and dramatic sense. M-FC

Gardel, Pierre, b. Nancy, 1758; d. Paris, 1840. Member of a noted Lorraine family of musicians and dancers, son of Claude Gardel, assistant *maître de ballet* at the Palatinate Court of Stanislas I of Poland, younger brother of Maximilien Gardel, first dancer and later *maître de ballet en chef* of the Paris O. Pierre

Gardel entered the O.'s École de Danse as a child, and became a gifted performer in the difficult but limited genre of noble dance; he made a lifelong defence of it against the incursions of *demi-caractère* dancing to which it eventually ceded. When Marie Antoinette imposed NOVERRE as *maître de ballet en chef* at the Paris O., 1776, bypassing Maximilien Gardel who had hierarchic rights, the Gardel clan was active in the cabals that eventually wearied Noverre into demanding his retirement in 1780. Maximilien Gardel finally gained the post of *maître de ballet en chef*, and on his death in 1787 was succeeded by Pierre. When the French Revolution placed the Paris O. under the jurisdiction of the Comité de Salut Public, Pierre Gardel was favoured by the authorities and was responsible for dances in the great Revolutionary fêtes devised by the painter Jacques-Louis David. He continued in favour with Napoleon, who strengthened the O.'s monopoly on ballet by closing its rivals, the Boulevard theatres (1807). Under the Restoration he pleased Louis XVIII and retained autocratic control of the O. ballet until his retirement in 1829. His wife, Marie Miller Gardel, was one of his most gifted interpreters. His ballets *Psyché* (1790, mus. Ernst Ludwig, known as Miller), *Télémaque dans l'Ile de Calypso* (1790, mus. Miller), *La Dansomanie* (1800, mus. Étienne Méhul), and *Paul et Virginie* (1806, mus. Rodolphe Kreutzer) not only had unprecedented long runs at the Paris O. – although Gardel's control of programming doubtless accounted for many of these perfs – but *Psyché* and *La Dansomanie* were popular in the European repertory. Gardel was gifted in the creation of *divertissements*, but his ruthless exclusion of young rival choreographers from the Paris O., and from Paris itself when possible, eventually left the ballerinas unprepared for the great roles of Romantic ballet at its advent. MHW
See M. H. Winter, *The Pre-Romantic Ballet* (London 1974; New York and Toronto 1975)

Gaskell, Sonia, b. Kiev, 1904; d. Paris, 1974. Russian dancer, teacher and administrator. Started teaching in Paris in 1936 after a peripatetic career as a dancer (briefly with DIAGHILEV); in 1939 moved to Holland where she did her most important work. Formed her own group, B. Recital, after World War II. From 1955 Director of Nederlands B. at The Hague; set up its school. Artistic Director of Dutch NB 1961–8, instrumental in staging a vast classic repertory. MC

GATOB (*Gosudarstveny Akademichesky Teatr Operi i Baleta*), the State Academic T. for O. and B., the name of the Maryinsky T., St Petersburg (Petrograd) from the 1917 October Revolution until it was renamed the Kirov T. in 1935. *See* KIROV BALLET

Gautier, Théophile, b. Tarbes, 1811; d. Neuilly, 1872. French poet, writer, and critic, a passionate devotee of the Romantic ballet and especially of GRISI for whom he devised the role of GISELLE. His affection was not returned and he m. her sister Ernesta although he died with Carlotta's name on his lips. His reviews were collected and translated into English by BEAUMONT (London 1932) as *The Romantic Ballet as seen by Théophile Gautier*. MC
See also Deirdre Priddin, *The Art of the Dance in French Literature* (London 1952); E. Binney 3rd, *Les Ballets de Théophile Gautier* (Paris 1965)

Gayané (*Gayaneh*), ballet, 4 acts, 6 scenes, ch. ANISIMOVA; mus. KHACHATURIAN; lib. Konstantin Derzhavin; sc. Natan Altman; c. Tatyana Bruni. Perm O., Kirov B., 9 Dec 1942; revived Leningrad, Kirov T., 19 Feb 1945; dan. DUDINSKAYA, Feya Balabina, SERGEYEV, Nikolay Zubkovsky. An Armenian story of love and war; well-known extracts are the *Sabre Dance* from Act IV and a *pas de deux* which became a favourite item in FONTEYN's repertoire. New version ch. Anisimova, Leningrad, Kirov T., 13 June 1952; sc. Valery Dorrer. Also staged with Anisimova's choreography at Sverdlovsk (1943), Erevan (1947). New choreography Sergey

Ekaterina Geltser as Aurora in SLEEPING BEAUTY

Sergeyev, Kiev, 1958; Nina Danilova, Kuibyshev 1952. Often revised. Many choreographers in E. Europe have used the colourful music. Some of it was used in PRISONER OF THE CAUCASUS. JS/NR

Geltser, Ekaterina, b. Moscow, 1876; d. Moscow, 1962. Russian dancer. The daughter of a mime and *régisseur*, Vasily Geltser. Studied Moscow, Bolshoy S., from 1884, joining the Bolshoy B. 1894. In 1896 studied in St Petersburg with JOHANSSON and M. PETIPA. Roles incl. ESMERALDA, ODETTE-ODILE, AURORA, RAYMONDA, and SWANILDA; created title role in GORSKY's *Salaambô*, 1910, and Tao-Hoa in RED POPPY; also appeared in the second season of DIAGHILEV's B. Russes, Paris, 1910, dancing SYLPHIDES. Danced with MORDKIN's co. in USA 1910–11 and appeared at Alhambra T., London, 1911 with TIKHOMIROV but preferred to tour her own country, traversing it many times. She had a magnetic stage personality. Retired 1935 but appeared in war-time recitals (1944), dancing the Mazurka and Polonaise with incomparable artistry. She m. Tikhomirov. People's Artist, USSR, 1925. JS/NR
See O. Martynova, *Ekaterina Geltser* (Moscow 1965)

Adeline Genée in *The Dryad*, 1907

Gemini, ballet, ch. TETLEY; mus. HENZE (Symphony No. 3); sc./c. N. BAYLIS. Newtown, Sydney, Elizabethan T., Australian B. (for whom it was commissioned), 6 Apr 1973; dan. ROWE, Alida Chase, MEEHAN and NORMAN. A pure dance work for two pairs of identically costumed dancers. Revived Stuttgart B. 1974, ABT 1975, SWRB 1977. KSW

Genée, Dame Adeline [Anina Margarete Jensen], b. Hinnerup, Århus, 1878; d. Esher, Surrey, England, 1970. Danish dancer. Trained by her uncle Alexander Genée and his wife, the Hungarian Antonia Zimmerman who were both pupils of M. PETIPA and JOHANSSON. Debut at age 10 in Christiania (now Oslo) dancing a Polka. Accompanied her uncle on his travels, and in Munich on 21 Nov 1896 made her debut in COPPÉLIA, her most famous role. London debut at the Empire T., 22 Nov 1897; engaged for a few weeks but stayed as principal dancer for 10 years. Her repertoire was innocuous and charming; although endowed with strong technique she was admired mostly for her porcelain beauty. *Coppélia* was revived for her (the first 2 acts only) on 14 May 1906. US debut Philadelphia, 20 Jan 1908 at Chestnut Street OH followed by NY debut 28 Jan 1908; several US tours. Toured Australia and New Zealand 1913. Official 'farewell' London season, Coliseum 9 May 1914, but further seasons followed until 1917. Last public appearance in *The Love Song* (a suite of dances arr. Genée, inspired by a painting by Arthur Devis) 2 Feb 1933 partnered by DOLIN, also at the Coliseum. Founder-president of the RAD until 1954. DBE 1950. Also honoured by the Danish Government. She m. Frank S. N. Isitt (d. 1939) and thereafter used the name of Genée-Isitt. MC
See Ivor Guest, *Adeline Genée: A Lifetime of Ballet under Six Reigns* (London 1958)

Geologists, The (*Geologi*), also known as *Heroic Poem*, ballet, 1 act, ch./lib. KASATKINA and VASILYOV; mus. Nikolay Karetnikov; sc. E. Sternberg. Moscow, Bolshoy T., 26 Jan 1964; remains in repertoire. Gave SOROKINA and VLADIMIROV their first created roles as the two heroic young geologists (caught in a taiga fire, the girl saves a badly burned comrade); acclaimed as one of the best works on a contemporary theme. NR
See Natalia Roslavleva, 'Heroic Geologists' in *The Dancing Times* (London 1964)

Georgi, Yvonne, b. Leipzig, 1903; d. Hanover, 1975. German dancer, teacher, choreographer, and director. Pupil of DALCROZE, WIGMAN, and ROUSANNE. Debut Leipzig 1923; soloist in JOOSS's Münster B. 1924. Became ballet mistress at Gera 1925 and began her choreographic work. Partnered KREUTZBERG and toured the world with him (in the

USA 1928). Worked with V. GSOVSKY in Hanover 1932–6. During World War II she had her own co. in the Netherlands and in 1950 choreographed for Ludwig Berger's film *Ballerina* (dan. VERDY). Ballet mistress, Düsseldorf 1951–4 and Hanover 1954–70 where she choreographed many ballets and introduced some classical ballets at the time when Germany was turning away from Wigman-style works. Her *Elektronisches Ballet* (1957) used electronic music. GBLW
See H. Koegler, *Yvonne Georgi* (Velber 1963)

Georgiadis, Nicholas, b. Athens, 1925. Greek painter and designer. Resident London, where he completed his studies. Works in close sympathy with MACMILLAN, their first collaboration being DANSES CONCERTANTES. His superb setting for MacMillan's *Noctambules*, RB at CG 1956, revealed a designer of major importance with a love of glowing, Byzantine colour. A master of the large-scale, opera-house spectacular he has also designed sparser works such as HERMANAS. MC

Gerdt, Elizaveta, b. St Petersburg, 1891; d. Moscow, 1975. Soviet dancer and teacher. Graduated from St Petersburg TS 1908, class of FOKINE. The year before graduation she created Armide in production of *The Animated Gobelins* (a scene from future PAVILLON D'ARMIDE) partnered by NIJINSKY. Also danced second version of CHOPINIANA (later known as SYLPHIDES) with him for graduation perf. 6 Apr 1908. From 1913 first soloist Maryinsky T., in State T. of O and B. 1917–28; from 1919 ballerina. She inherited from her father P. GERDT softness, nobility, and grace. From 1917 danced entire classical repertoire. Created principal parts in Soviet ballets, *Red Whirlwind* and *Pulcinella* (both ch. F. LOPUKHOV). Outstanding teacher, who exerted considerable influence on the formation of the style of her pupils: SHELEST, STRUCHKOVA, PLISETSKAYA, MAXIMOVA, and BOVT. Leningrad Choreographic S. 1928–34; Moscow 1936–60; from 1960 *classe de perfectionnement* Bolshoy T. Retired 1971 after her 80th anniversary. Honoured Art Worker, RSFSR. NR
See A. Volynsky, 'Lily of Ballet' in *Life of Art* No. 19 (Petrograd 1923); R. Struchkova, 'Remarkable teacher of classical dance' in *Teatr* No. 12 (Moscow 1963)

Gerdt, Pavel, b. St Petersburg, 1844; d. Vommala, Finland, 1917. Russian dancer, teacher, and choreographer. Graduated St Petersburg TS 1864, class of M. PETIPA and JOHANSSON. Started dancing at Maryinsky T. at 16, soloist 1860–1916. Impeccable nobility and grace, good mime. Created SIEGFRIED, Prince DÉSIRÉ, ABDÉRÂME; danced all other classical roles. Taught at St Petersburg 1880–1904, forming A. PAVLOVA, KARSAVINA, E. GERDT, to some extent VAGANOVA and FOKINE. Choreographed *False Dryads* (1899) for Pavlova's graduation, SYLVIA (with IVANOV), etc. NR

Germany. Although the duchies, principalities, and little kingdoms that constituted the old Germany became united in the time of Bismarck, there is still no German national ballet but a great number (over 60) of cos situated in the many opera houses of separate and rival cities throughout the land. The prime purpose of these groups is to appear in the operas and operettas, but in the medium and larger houses they give regular perfs of ballets (*Ballettabenden*). The ballet master selects his dancers each season, offering a one-year contract, and choreographs the ballets (or calls in an occasional guest choreographer). Because these ballets are for the most part seen only by the local inhabitants, little attempt is made to build up a repertoire or evolve a distinctive style, for in any case the ballet master moves on to another city after about three years, and the ballets are discarded. There are two exceptions to this rule: the STUTTGART B. and the ballet in Düsseldorf which has retained its ballet master, WALTER, since 1964 and achieved a distinctive style and repertoire.

From the middle of the 18th c. the ballets were like those in most of the European opera houses – classical and narrative, strongly influenced by the Paris O. However, after World War I the strong German feeling for 'modern dance' (*see* AUSDRUCKSTANZ) led to a change and the opera houses appointed ballet masters who practised this style. This persisted until after World War II when the classical influence of SWB (later RB), DE CUEVAS B. and others led German opera houses to engage some classical ballet masters from abroad. A. CARTER went to Munich 1954, BERIOZOFF to Stuttgart 1957, and in 1961 GEORGI, with great perception, invited ADAMA to become her assistant and to stage some classical ballets. Throughout all these changes T. GSOVSKY in Berlin was choreographing ballets in both classical and modern styles (she was trained in both) according to the mood of the moment. One by one the opera houses introduced classical ballets and, since the German teaching of this style was very limited, engaged many dancers from Britain and the USA to fill the cos. This trend appeared to reach its climax in about 1971 when the old German penchant for introverted and intense styles reasserted itself and the 'modern dance' began to return – first in Cologne (the Tanz-Forum group) and later in Wuppertal and Darmstadt. American choreographers, e.g. TETLEY and BUTLER and German exponents, e.g. Helmuth Baumann, began to find favour. By the mid-1970s NEUMEIER, first in Frankfurt and then in Hamburg, had devised ballets on ingenious and obscure intellectual themes danced by classical dancers.

In E. Berlin and in the German Democratic Republic, the influence of the USSR, with its classical and propaganda ballets and famous teachers from Moscow and Leningrad, has predominated since World War II. GBLW

Geschöpfe des Prometheus, Die (*The Creatures of Prometheus*), ballet, ch./lib. VIGANÒ; mus. Ludwig van Beethoven; sc. Cassentini, Viganò. As *Gli Uomini di Prometeo*, Vienna, Burg T., 28 Mar 1801. Prometheus as the creator of mankind. Beethoven's noble score has proved impervious to choreographic treatment, even when the original libretto, stilted and static, has been ignored. Among those who have made the attempt are LIFAR (*Les Créatures de Prométhée*, Paris O., 1929), DE VALOIS (*Prometheus*, Vic-Wells B., 1936), ASHTON (RB, 1970). DV

Giara, La (*The Jar*), 1-act ballet, ch. BÖRLIN; mùs. Alfredo Casella; sc. CHIRICO. (As *la Jarre*), Paris, T. des CE, B. Suédois, 1924. Based on a comic short story by Luigi Pirandello, set in Sicily. Many choreographers have used the score, and the story, incl. DE VALOIS (1934), NOVARO, NIJINSKA, and MILLOSS. FP

Gielgud, Maina, b. London, 1945. English dancer. Niece of the actor Sir John Gielgud. Started training at Hampshire S., London, then with many distinguished teachers of whom the most influential was probably HIGHTOWER. Has danced with innumerable cos, notably B. XXe S. 1967–71. A strong dancer with a powerful personality, she excels in BÉJART choreography and in such roles as the BLACK QUEEN and the Siren in PRODIGAL SON, both of which she has danced with the RB in London and on tour. Ballerina with LFB since 1972; guest perfs all over the world. MC
See P. Combescat, 'Maina Gielgud', *Les Saisons de la Danse* (Paris, Jan 1969)

Gilmour, Sally, b. Malaya, 1921. To London 1930 to study with KARSAVINA, then RAMBERT, eventually joining BR with which she made her career. In 1939 created leading role in HOWARD's *Lady into Fox*, an immediate triumph. A dancer of fey delicacy and a superb actress, she shone in both JARDIN AUX LILAS (as Caroline) and in DARK ELEGIES. In 1946 danced full-length GISELLE. Other created roles were an adorable Duck in STAFF's PETER AND THE WOLF, a dramatic solo in *Confessional* (1941, based on Robert Browning's poem; ch. GORE), and Tulip in Howard's *The Sailor's Return* (1947). In 1953 m. and went to live in Australia where she worked for RAD. Returned to London 1972. A fine example of Rambert's ability to develop artistry and rate it above technique. MC

Gilpin, John, b. Southsea, 1930. English actor, dancer, and teacher. Studied Cone-Ripman S., London, then RAMBERT S. (after success as child actor). Joined BR 1945, quickly becoming principal dancer and toured Australia with them. In 1949 joined PETIT's B. de Paris, creating leading role in ASHTON's *Le Rève de Léonor*. In 1950 joined LFB and became its greatest star, inheriting classical roles from DOLIN, dancing SPECTRE DE LA ROSE, and also the Hussar in BEAU DANUBE. Partnered many great dancers from the B. Russe cos of the 1930s, incl. A.

John Gilpin in the title role of WITCH BOY

DANILOVA and RIABOUCHINSKA. Assistant artistic director, LFB 1959, artistic director 1962; in 1969 became guest artist but resigned 1970. Guest artist with RB at CG 1961 (debut there in PATINEURS) and 1963 when he danced the Prince in SLEEPING BEAUTY. A virtuoso dancer, the most dazzling of his generation in England, he made the principal role in H. LANDER's ÉTUDES his own. Injury and ill health shortened his dancing career and he turned to teaching. Toured the world with LFB; most impresarios insisted on his presence before booking the co. MC
See I. Lidova, 'John Gilpin', *Les Saisons de la Danse* (Paris, Dec 1972) with list of roles

Girey, the Khan in FOUNTAIN OF BAKHCHISARAY

Giselle, ou Les Wilis, romantic ballet, 2 acts, ch. CORALLI and PERROT; mus. ADAM (except for the Peasant *pas de deux* by Friedrich Burgmüller); lib. GAUTIER, H. Vernoy de St Georges, and Coralli; sc. Pierre-Luc-Charles Ciceri; c. Paul Lormier. Paris O., 28 June 1841; dan. GRISI, L. PETIPA, DUMILÂTRE. Giselle, a young peasant girl, goes mad with grief and dies when she discovers that her supposed peasant lover, Loys, is in fact a nobleman, Count Albrecht, already betrothed. In Act II, the Wilis, led by their Queen, Myrtha, attempt to dance Albrecht to his death but Giselle, now herself a Wili, saves him.

Gautier's first libretto was inspired by Heinrich Heine's account of the old German legend of the Wilis, 'maidens who have died before their wedding day, because of faithless lovers', who return at night to take vengeance on any man who strays into their domain. He worked closely with the very experienced St Georges and the other collaborators to produce the most famous and enduring ballet of the Romantic period. Although Perrot's name did not appear on the official program, it is generally thought that he arranged all Giselle's dances for Grisi, especially the

sustained, poetic *pas de deux* of Act II. Coralli probably arranged the ensembles. Adam's music, composed in a week, was ideal for the subject and was an early example of the use of *Leitmotiv* in ballet.

The ballet was an immediate and enormous success. Its fame spread quickly. Perrot staged it in London, 12 May 1842, dancing Albrecht to Grisi's Giselle. The first US production was in Boston, 1 Jan 1846; dan. LEE, G. W. SMITH. Perrot produced it in St Petersburg 1848 with ELSSLER and M. PETIPA in the leading roles, and again in 1850 in St Petersburg with Grisi. M. Petipa kept the ballet alive in the Russian repertory throughout his long reign, while it slipped into oblivion elsewhere; he integrated the developments in dance technique that occurred towards the end of the 19th c., especially greater use of pointe work, but preserved the essence of the ballet. A waltz in E major in Act I and other additions to the music were made during this period. In 1910 DIAGHILEV brought it to Paris, later to London, with KARSAVINA and NIJINSKY. A. PAVLOVA also danced it during the 1911 London season but the public preferred Diaghilev's more exotic offerings. Revived Paris O., 26 Nov 1924, for SPESSIVTSEVA's debut there (with AVELINE) and stayed in the repertory. The B. Russe cos of the 1930s ensured its world fame; nearly every classical co. today dances it. The first British production to be staged from SERGUEEFF's notes of the St Petersburg version was for the CAMARGO SOCIETY, 24 June 1932 with Spessivtseva and DOLIN. The Vic-Wells B. staged it 1 Jan 1934 with MARKOVA and Dolin; it has been in the RB repertory ever since in various productions.

Impossible to list all the ballerinas who have illuminated the role: supreme in our time have been those already mentioned, and ULANOVA, FONTEYN, CHAUVIRÉ, ALONSO, MAXIMOVA, MAKAROVA. Ulanova's perf. is on film (Bolshoy 1956). MC

See Cyril W. Beaumont, *The Ballet Called Giselle* (London 1944); Ivor Guest, *The Romantic Ballet in Paris* (London and Middletown, CT, 1966); S. Lifar, *Giselle* (Paris 1942)

Giselle. P. WRIGHT's production for the RB at CG

GITIS, initials of Gosudarstveni Institut Teatralnovo Iskusstva (State Inst. of T. Art), Moscow, an inst. of higher education dating from 1878, when a musical-dramatic school was founded. By 1886 it was run under the auspices of the Moscow Philharmonic Society. It now trains actors, theatrical directors, theatre historians, and choreographers.

The choreographers' faculty was founded 1946; the course is five years; only students with full choreographic education and two years' practical experience of opera and ballet or folk-dance ensemble are accepted. In 1957 a pedagogical division was organized, with a course of four and a half years, providing theoretical and practical knowledge of the Soviet method of ballet education in 19 State ballet schools (called 'choreographic schools') of the USSR. Choreographers with GITIS diplomas head ballet cos all over the country. The Chair of Choreography is held by ZAKHAROV. Olga Tarasova is Dean of the choreographers' faculty.

A choreographers' faculty, now headed by GUSEV, was founded at the Leningrad Cons. 1962. NR

Glazunov, Aleksandr Konstantinovich, b. St Petersburg, 1865; d. Paris, 1936. Russian composer, pupil of Nikolay Rimsky-Korsakov, a youthful prodigy who wrote his First Symphony at 16. A brilliant orchestrator and sound melodist. The first of his three ballets, all choreographed by M. PETIPA, was the 3-act RAYMONDA, a continuation of the style of TCHAIKOVSKY's SLEEPING BEAUTY, but in a more heroic, and occasionally more stolid, vein. His other ballets were *Les Ruses d'Amour* and *Les Saisons* (both St Petersburg 1900), both melodious and graceful. ASHTON's *Birthday Offering* (London 1956) is set to a selection of his orchestral music. DH

Glière, Reinhold, b. Kiev, 1875; d. Moscow, 1956. Soviet composer, conductor, and professor. Graduated 1900 from Moscow Cons. where classes in

composition, harmony, polyphony and violin firmly linked his own composing to the traditions of Russian classical symphonic music. His first ballet, *Crisis*, (1912; ch. GORSKY) was performed by a studio of 'free dance'. It was followed some years later by *Cleopatra* (1926; after Aleksandr Pushkin's *Egyptian Nights*), composed for the Musical Studio of the Moscow Art T. His outstanding ballet was RED POPPY. Other ballets were *The Comedians* (1931; after Lope de Vega's *Fuenteovejuna*), BRONZE HORSEMAN, and *Taras Bulba* (composed 1951–2, unperf.) Doctor of Arts, People's Artist of the USSR. NR
See S. Katonova, *Ballets of R. M. Glière* (Moscow 1960)

Glushkovsky, Adam, b. St Petersburg, 1793; d. Moscow, 1860. Russian dancer, teacher, and choreographer. Pupil and ward of DIDELOT. Graduated 1809; occupied a leading position in St Petersburg ballet, successfully rivalling even DUPORT. Transferred to Moscow 1812, remaining at the Bolshoy T. until 1839 as *premier danseur*, head of the school and principal choreographer. Following a serious injury, which halted his performing career, he devoted himself to teaching and choreography, and in 1812 saved the Moscow BS from destruction by evacuating it two days before the French invaded the city.

Besides staging many of Didelot's ballets at the Bolshoy, Glushkovsky created works of his own. His *Ruslan and Lyudmila* (1821), though dramatically weak, marked the first use of Aleksandr Pushkin's work for a ballet, and directly influenced Didelot's PRISONER OF THE CAUCASUS (1823), also inspired by Pushkin. His contribution to the development of Russian ballet cannot be over-emphasized. NR
See A. Glushkovsky, *Reminiscences of a Balletmaster (Vospominania Baletmeistera)*, ed. Yuri Slonimsky (Moscow and Leningrad 1940)

Godfrey, Louis, b. Johannesburg, 1930. S. African dancer. Studied with STURMAN and Ivy Conmee in Johannesburg, and with VOLKOVA in London. Danced in musicals in S. Africa and England, and with MARKOVA and DOLIN's group 1949. With LFB 1950–64, becoming soloist and then principal dancer. Ballet master of PACT B. 1970, and 1973 together with his wife SCHULTZE, artistic director. MG

Godunov, Aleksandr, b. Riga, 1950. Soviet dancer. Graduated from Riga BS 1967, danced three years in MOISEYEV's Young B. From 1971 at Bolshoy T. Lyrical, tall dancer with excellent elevation. Has virtuosity in technique, especially in turns. Debut in CHOPINIANA, followed by SWAN LAKE (GRIGOROVICH version), BASILIO. Became PLISETSKAYA's partner when FADEYECHEV retired. Danced José to her Carmen with great success (Alberto Alonso's CARMEN). Gold medal, Moscow, 1973. NR

Goldberg Variations, ballet, ch. ROBBINS; mus. Johann Sebastian Bach; c. Joe Eula; ltg Thomas Skelton. NYST, NYCB, 27 May 1971. A plotless ballet performed to the aria and 30 variations of Bach's keyboard masterpiece. FM

Golden Age, The (*Zolotoy Vek*), ballet, 3 acts, 5 scenes, ch. VAINONEN, YACOBSON, and Vladimir Chesnokov; mus. Dmitri Shostakovich; lib. A. V. Ivanovsky; sc./c. V. M. Khodasevich. Leningrad, State Acad. T. of O. and B., 26 Oct 1930; dan. ULANOVA, CHABUKIANI. The lib. (about a fight between Fascists and a Soviet football team) won a prize in a competition for ballets with Soviet themes. Out of the repertory since the following season, chiefly remembered as being Shostakovich's first ballet score, still in the concert repertory. JS
See COMPLETE BOOK

Golden Cockerel, The *see* COQ D'OR

Golden Slave, the principal role in SCHÉHÉRAZADE

Goleizovsky, Kasyan, b. Hradec Králové [Königgrätz], Bohemia, 1892; d. Moscow, 1970. Russian dancer and choreographer. Studied Moscow, and from 1907 at the Maryinsky S., St Petersburg; graduated into the co. 1909, transferring to the Bolshoy B. 1910. Strongly influenced by the work of FOKINE and GORSKY; produced several plays, operettas, and dances for Nikita Balieff's revue *La Chauve Souris*. After the 1917 Revolution, directed a private ballet studio where experimental choreography was created. Much of his choreography of the 1920s was very beautiful and at the time undeservedly criticized simply because it was innovative. Works incl. a version of the *Polovtsian Dances* from PRINCE IGOR (1933), in the repertoire for many years; *Scriabiniana* (1962), a solo from which helped VASILIEV gain his gold medal and grand prize at the First Varna Competition, 1964; and *Leyli and Medzhnun* (mus. Sergey Balasanian, 1964). He m. Bolshoy B. soloist Vera Vasilieva. Honoured Artist, Byelorussian SSR; Honoured Art Worker, Lithuanian SSR. JS/NR
See K. Goleizovsky, *Images of Folk Choreography* (Moscow 1964); E. Surits, 'The Beginning of the Way' in *Soviet Ballet Theatre, 1917–1929* (Moscow 1976); Mikhail Mikhailov, 'Kasyan Yaroslavich Goleizovsky' in *Muzika i choreografia sovremennogo baleta* (Leningrad 1974)

Gollner, Nana, b. El Paso, TX, 1920. American dancer. Studied with Theodore Kosloff. Debut in Max Reinhardt's production of *A Midsummer Night's Dream* (Los Angeles 1934). Danced with American B. 1935, B. Russe de Monte Carlo (DE BASIL) 1935–6, B. de Monte Carlo (R. BLUM) 1936–7, ABT 1939–41, 1943–6, and 1947–50, Original B. Russe 1941–3, International B., London, 1947. A ballerina of striking beauty of line, she danced mostly classic roles, but created Medusa in UNDERTOW. Now teaching in California. She m. PETROFF. DV

Golovine, Serge, b. Monaco, 1924. French dancer, choreographer, and teacher. Studied with SEDOVA, RICAUX, ZAMBELLI, PREOBRAZHENSKA, VOLININ. *Corps de ballet*, Monte Carlo O. 1941, *premier danseur* 1944, *étoile* 1945. *Corps de ballet*, Paris O. 1946. Engaged as soloist, de Cuevas B. 1949; *étoile* 1950. Danced notably in PIÈGE DE LUMIÈRE, revivals of SPECTRE DE LA ROSE, PETRUSHKA, SYLPHIDE, SLEEPING BEAUTY, NOIR ET BLANC, SYLPHIDES; choreographed *Feu Rouge, Feu Vert* (1953), *La Mort de Narcisse* (1958). Founded his own co. 1962; Artistic Director, B. du Grand T., Geneva, 1964–8, staging various works. Started a school in Geneva 1969. Taught in Paris 1971. Revived *Petrushka*, Toulouse 1973, produced on TV with NUREYEV, and finally at the Paris O. where he gave his farewell perf. in the principal role, Apr 1976. Gifted with exceptional *ballon* and with a very pure classical style. His sister Solange Golovina, and brothers Jean Golovine and George Goviloff are also dancers. M-FC
See I. Lidova, 'Serge Golovine', *Les Saisons de la Danse* (Paris, Apr 1976) with list of roles

Golovkina, Sofia, b. Moscow, 1915. Soviet dancer and teacher. Graduated Bolshoy TS, class of Aleksandr Chekrygin. Bolshoy T. 1933–59. Classical ballerina with a pure style and strong technique, especially good as AURORA, Nikia (BAYADÈRE) and LISE (GORSKY version). From 1960 director and teacher, Moscow Choreographic Academic S. Taught N. BESSMERTNOVA. People's Artist, USSR. NR

Goncharova, Natalia, b. near Moscow, 1881; d. Paris, 1962. Russian painter and designer, who lived in Paris. Encouraged by LARIONOV (whom she later m.) to paint in *rayonnist* style, then abstract and cubist. Also described as a 'Moscow futurist'. Her decors for DIAGHILEV ranged from the riot of colour for COQ D'OR to the extreme simplicity of NOCES. Also designed FOKINE's *Cendrillon* (*see* CINDERELLA, London, DE BASIL) 1938. Re-created her 1926 designs for OISEAU DE FEU for the RB in 1954. MC

Good-Humoured Ladies, The *see* FEMMES DE BONNE HUMEUR

Gopal, Ram, b. Bangalore, 1920. Indian dancer and teacher. Studied *Kathakali*, *Bharata Natya*, *Manipuri* and *Kathak* styles with India's greatest teachers and in 1935 opened his own school in Bangalore (SARABHAI was one of his pupils). To Europe 1938; London debut with own co. 1939. A dancer of extraordinary beauty, Gopal did more than any other person to explain and introduce Indian dancing in the West. He has toured throughout the world, a lucid talker as well as a brilliant performer. MC
See Ram Gopal, *Rhythm in the Heavens, An Autobiography* (London 1957); Ram Gopal and Sarosh Dadachanji, *Indian Dancing* (London 1951); Kay Ambrose, with an introduction by Ram Gopal, *Classical Dances and Costumes of India* (London 1950)

Gordeyev, Vyacheslav, b. Moscow, 1948. Soviet dancer. Graduated from Moscow Choreographic S. 1969, class of Pyotr Pestov. In third year with the Bolshoy danced Prince in NUTCRACKER (GRIGOROVICH version). Virile, with strong technique and unbounded energy, by performing the title role in SPARTACUS, has proved himself a valuable dance actor. Gold medal, International B. Competition, Moscow, 1973, partnering N. PAVLOVA, his wife. NR

Gordon, David, b. Brooklyn, NY, 1936. American dancer and choreographer. Studied with WARING and CUNNINGHAM. Danced with Waring's co. 1958–62, RAINER Dance Co. 1966–70. Founder member of Judson Dance T. 1962, and of the cooperative improvisational dance theatre co. Grand Union 1970. Formed his own co. 1974. He m. SETTERFIELD. Works incl. *Mannequin Dance* (1962), *Random Breakfast* (1963), *Sleepwalking* (1971), *The Matter* (1972), *Chair* (1974), *One Act Play* (1974), *Times Four* (1975), and *Personal Inventory* (1976). *See* AVANT-GARDE DANCE. DV

Gore, Walter, b. Waterside, Scotland, 1910. Scottish dancer, choreographer, and director. Studied dance and drama at Italia Conti S., then ballet with MASSINE. Joined BR for its first season 1930; spent most of the next 20 years with that co., interrupted by a season with the Vic-Wells B. (1935–6), work in musicals, and war service. A fine character dancer, he excelled in dramatic and especially in comic roles. Directed cos in Australia (1955–6), Frankfurt (1957–9), Lisbon (1965–9), and Augsburg (1971–2); also twice formed and directed his own independent co., first the Walter Gore B. (1953–5) and later the London B. (1961–3). Both toured widely and achieved a degree of success without any subsidy, an unusual achievement in that period. His works incl. *Valse Finale* (1938), *Confessional* (a duet with GILMOUR to Robert Browning's poem, 1941) and *Simple Symphony* (1944). He made a series of works with notable dramatic roles for his wife, HINTON; outstanding were *Winter Night* and *Antonia* (both 1948), and later *The Magical Being,* DIE IM SCHATTEN LEBEN, and NIGHT AND SILENCE (all 1958). Gore has worked for cos all over the world, staging original works and reviving ballets made for Hinton. Several of his ballets, e.g. STREET GAMES and *Die im Schatten Leben,* entered the repertories of Scottish B. and Northern Dance T. JP

Gorham, Kathleen, b. Sydney, 1932. Australian dancer and teacher. Studied with Lorraine Norton and KELLAWAY. BOROVANSKY B. 1947; BR 1948; SWBS 1949; SWTB 1951–2; B. de Paris 1949; DE CUEVAS B. 1953. Borovansky B. 1954, principal dancer. Australian B. 1962–6, principal ballerina. Currently co-director, NT BS, Melbourne. A strongly dramatic dancer whose expressive talent was exploited in HELPMANN's ballets, *The Display* and *Yūgen*. OBE 1968. KSW

Gorsky, Aleksandr, b. St Petersburg, 1871; d. Moscow, 1924. Russian dancer, choreographer, and teacher. Graduated into the *corps de ballet* from St Petersburg TS 1889; *premier danseur* 1900, performing classical, character, and mime roles. A man of many talents who read widely, studied music, and attended evening classes at the Acad. of Arts, he was entrusted by GLAZUNOV with conducting orchestral rehearsals of his ballets. Gorsky's expertise in Vladimir Stepanov's dance notation, used for recording M. PETIPA's ballets, led to his being sent to Moscow in 1898 where he staged SLEEPING BEAUTY in three weeks. While there, his friend the singer Fyodor Shalyapin (Chaliapin) introduced him to Konstantin Stanislavsky's Art T., just opened, and the thriving Private Russian Opera of Savva Mamontov where a new style of decor was evolving from the painters Konstantin Korovin, Mikhail Vrubel, Viktor Vasnetsov, and others. Gorsky reluctantly left to return to St Petersburg's routine, but in 1900 gladly accepted the commission to stage RAYMONDA at the Bolshoy T., Moscow. Late that year, his transfer to Moscow was made permanent and he was named *régisseur* of ballet, a post meant to prevent any private achievement on his part.

The activity in Moscow had inspired Gorsky; his choreographic debut took place on 6 Dec 1900 with a new production of DON QUIXOTE, which represented a major reform in ballet. His ideas were enthusiastically received by young dancers, led by ROSLAVLEVA and MORDKIN, and by the Moscow audiences which had come to accept and support fine acting and dramatic content in dance. He demanded intensive research and the highest artistic standards. Even DIAGHILEV noticed him; only World War I prevented him from choreographing a ballet commissioned by Diaghilev, *Red Masks* (mus. Nikolay Cherepnin). A dedicated follower of I. DUNCAN from her first appearance, Gorsky applied her idiom to his work; his new version of CORSAIRE contained a duet for TIKHOMIROV and GELTSER wearing a Greek *chiton*. He was always eager to create new forms while staging the old classical ballets, and his contribution to the Bolshoy B. cannot be over-estimated. He continued to teach at the Bolshoy S. after 1917; with Tikhomirov was instrumental in its reopening 1920. NR

See Natalia Roslavleva, *Era of the Russian Ballet* (London and New York 1966)

Goryanka (*Mountain Girl*), ballet, 3 acts, ch./lib. VINOGRADOV, after poem of same title by the Daghestan poet, Rassul Gamzatov; mus. Murad Kazhlayev; sc. Marina Sokolova. Leningrad, Kirov T., 20 Mar 1968; dan. KOMLEVA. A girl from a Daghestan mountain village, where old customs and traditions remain strong, refuses to marry the man to whom she has been pledged in wedlock at infancy. She escapes to enter a medical college, but is tracked down and stabbed by the abandoned bridegroom. For the successful creation of the first ballet to a Daghestan theme, Vinogradov, Kazhlayev, and the creators of the principal roles were awarded State Prize of the RSFSR 1971 and title of Honoured Artist of the Daghestan ASSR. Also produced Varna 1973 (ch. Asen Gavrilov; sc. Angel Atanasov). NR

See V. Vanslow, 'A Mountain Legend' in *Soviet Music Magazine*, No. 6 (Moscow 1968)

Goslar, Lotte, b. Dresden. German dancer and mime. Studied with WIGMAN and Gret Palucca; debut Berlin. Left Germany and performed in Erika Mann's Kabarett Die Pfeffermühle, Zürich 1933. To USA 1937 with the same troupe and after a period in night clubs formed her own group in Hollywood 1943 and toured. Founded her Pantomime Circus 1954, a satirical entertainment of dance and mime, in which she clowned magnificently. GBLW

Goubé, Paul, b. Paris, 1912. French dancer and teacher. Studied Paris OBS. *Premier danseur* 1933. B. de Monte Carlo 1941. Founded B. de la Méditerranée, Nice, 1955; and his school, Centre de Danse de Paris, in the Salle Pleyel, 1969, where all forms of dance can be studied. M-FC

Gould, Diana, b. London, 1913. English dancer. Studied with RAMBERT and with KSHESSINSKA in Paris, and learned much from KARSAVINA when she danced with the BR. Danced in all the early Rambert productions; admired by both DIAGHILEV and A. PAVLOVA. Created Pavane in ASHTON's *Capriol Suite* (1930). Danced with BALANCHINE's Les Ballets 1933. Created Grille d'Égout in DE VALOIS's *Bar aux Folies-Bergère* (1934) with BR. Left Rambert 1935 to dance briefly with B. Russe de Monte Carlo then with MARKOVA–DOLIN B. 1935–7. Retired after m. to violinist Yehudi Menuhin. MC

Graduation Ball, ballet, 1 act, ch./lib. LICHINE; mus. Johann Strauss, arr. and orch. Antal Dorati; sc./c. BENOIS. Sydney, Australia, T. Royal, Original B. Russe, 28 Feb 1940; dan. RIABOUCHINSKA, Lichine, ORLOFF. Revived NY Met O., ABT, 8 Oct 1944; NY Met, B. Russe de Monte Carlo, 21 Sept 1949; Copenhagen, RDB, 22 Mar 1952; London, LFB, 9 July 1957. An immensely entertaining ballet about the visit of young cadets under their General to a girls' school for the graduation ball. After the production with the original cast, RDB's dancers have been most successful in maintaining the freshness of the work. MC

Graeme [Platts], Joyce, b. Leeds, 1918. English dancer. Studied with IDZIKOWSKI, CRASKE, VOLKOVA, RAMBERT, and at Vic-Wells S. Vic-Wells B. 1936–8; International B. 1941–3; BR 1945–8. Directed Australian B. 1948–51, LFB 1952. Assistant director, BR 1952–3. Danced and taught at Sc., Milan, 1955–62. A memorable Queen of the Wilis in GISELLE, she staged that ballet for Scottish TB 1971. Now teaches in London. DV

Martha Graham in her dance *Imperial Gesture*

Graham, Martha, b. Allegheny, PA, 1894. American dancer, teacher, choreographer, and co. director; one of the founders of modern dance in the USA. Both her American pioneer ancestry and a childhood spent in California probably exerted strong influence on her creative work. She studied and danced with DENISHAWN 1916–23, and many of her early choreographic efforts bore traces of the decorative exoticism associated with ST DENIS, whom Graham admired. After dancing in musical revues in NY and teaching at the Eastman S. of Music in Rochester, NY, for a year, she gave her first concert, consisting of solos and trios, at NY's 48th St T., 18 Apr 1926.

Almost immediately she moved away from pretty salon pieces and began exploring more personal and immediate ideas. *Lamentation* (1930) was one of several small essays that used the whole body to express an emotion or a mood, without relying on narrative incident or pantomime. She was already developing the classroom technique, based on centring the movement impulse in the solar plexus, that would enable her and her dancers to execute these ideas.

Graham's pivotal work of this early period was PRIMITIVE MYSTERIES. After this period she rarely dealt with her source material in such an abstract way. *Frontier* (1935) looked much more like the Graham that was to come. Instead of the strange, totemic figures she had created earlier, the dancer was unmistakably an American woman, on the threshold of a new life – but her dance gesture was far less literal, more earthbound and articulate through the whole body than ballet. Through the 1930s and 1940s Graham gave expression to the many lives of this woman, as participant in wars and migrations, as celebrant, mourner, and wife. Her most memorable depiction was the Bride in APPALACHIAN SPRING (1944). But the character began to have more specific identities: the poet Emily Dickinson (LETTER TO THE WORLD, 1940), the Brontë sisters (*Deaths and Entrances*, 1943), and Herodias, the first in a long series of victims and villains from antiquity (*Hérodiade*, 1944).

By the time she began tapping Greek mythology for her themes, Graham had already crystallized the main characteristics of her distinctive theatre: the movement style with its use of the centre of the body, its jagged and twisted shapes, its earthbound, slashing dynamics; the episodic way of presenting narrative by means of solos and small groups interspersed with larger unison choruses; the unheralded jumps back and forth in time and the use of more than one dancer to portray the same character at different times in the story; and the brilliantly conceived and coordinated use of props, sets, costumes, lighting, and music. She had begun her long-time collaboration with sculptor-designer NOGUCHI in *Frontier*, and under the guidance of HORST, her musical director, had adopted the policy of using scores written especially for the dance, usually by American composers.

The Greek dances usually seemed to emerge from the minds of their female protagonists, such as Medea (*Cave of the Heart*, 1946), and Jocasta (NIGHT JOURNEY, 1947), and they showed the heroine reliving the events of her life, seeking justification for her actions. The full-length CLYTEMNESTRA (1958) was a kind of culminating masterpiece in this genre, but Graham continued to explore the literature through the 1960s. She also made dances about other great women of history and myth. Her essays on Joan of Arc (*Seraphic Dialogue*, 1955) and Mary Queen of Scots (EPISODES, 1959) were the best known.

Graham's work was not always dramatic. In *Every Soul is a Circus* (1939) and *Acrobats of God* (1960) she poked fun at the performer's life and at herself as star. A succession of co. works, the most beautiful of which is DIVERSION OF ANGELS (1948), presented a more lyrical side of Graham and, without any plot or characters to draw the attention, they revealed her great compositional skill. Other key works included the patriotic tribute in the form of a minstrel show, *American Document* (1938); the Southwestern Indian folk drama, *El Penitente* (1940); and the strange transitional works, *Dark Meadow* (1946) and *Errand into the Maze* (1947).

Over the years, the often harsh, emphatic Graham technique gradually softened; the dancer's body line became rounder and the dynamics more fluid. Graham herself was declining as a performer, and since she had always thought of herself as the principal mover in her own work, the choreography became less personal, the themes more sweeping, the ideas more universal and diffuse. Criticism of her limitations on stage intensified, and at the same time she became increasingly reluctant to revive old works and assign her star roles to younger dancers.

After two years of anguish and desperate illness, Graham gave up dancing and returned to full command of her school and co. in 1973. Despite her proclaimed dislike for trying to hang on to the past, a surprising amount of the prodigious Graham

Mademoiselle N. TROUHANOWA
dans " LA PÉRI "

Aquarelle de Léon BAKST.

N. Gontcharowa.

ville's affection for her was not reciprocated and after early triumphs in Copenhagen she set out in 1838 on an international career, dancing in Paris, St Petersburg, and London, sealing her fame as a goddess of the Romantic ballet by appearing in the PAS DE QUATRE, London, 1845. She m. the Austrian tenor Friedrich Young in 1856 and retired from the stage although she worked as ballet mistress in Leipzig 1858–61, Munich 1869–75. She left her fortune to the poor of Munich, where Lucile-Grahn-Strasse is named after her. MC
See Ivor Guest, *The Romantic Ballet in Paris* (London and Middletown, CT, 1966)

Grand Ballet de Monte Carlo *see* GRAND BALLET DU MARQUIS DE CUEVAS

Grand Ballet du Marquis de Cuevas, a cosmopolitan co. that flourished under the patronage of DE CUEVAS. In 1944 he formed a co., B. International, which had a single season at the Park T. (renamed International T.), NY, 30 Oct–23 Dec 1944; it lost an estimated $800,000 but showed the first choreographic works of Edward Caton, DOLLAR, and Antonia Cobos. The co. incl. several celebrated American and Russian dancers, e.g. Viola Essen, MARIA-JEANNE, EGLEVSKY, Dollar. In 1947 de Cuevas bought the Nouveau B. de Monte Carlo, founded 1942 in Monte Carlo with dancers from the Paris O. and students from SEDOVA's S., and taken over by Paris impresario Eugène Grünberg 1945, which, with LIFAR as principal choreographer, had given seasons in France and London. The newly merged co. was called at first Grand B. de Monte Carlo and gave its first perf. 12 July 1947 in Vichy. In 1951 it became Grand B. du Marquis de Cuevas; although it danced under other names, often due to financial complexities, that is the title by which it is known. Dollar was the first ballet master, succeeded 1948 by TARAS, who was the co.'s most consistent choreographer, working, especially, in harmony with HIGHTOWER, its greatest star. De Cuevas was artistic director and employed the finest dancers (e.g. Marjorie TALLCHIEF, SKIBINE, GOLOVINE, SKOURATOFF, VYROUBOVA) and designers (e.g. Salvador Dali, André Levasseur, and the Marquis's nephew Raimundo de Larrain). The co. toured widely, admired for the very high standard of dancing and the opulence of its stagings. In 1960 de Larrain designed an extraordinarily elaborate production of SLEEPING BEAUTY. After de Cuevas's death, his widow and de Larrain kept the co. alive briefly but it disbanded in Athens, 30 June 1962. MC

Grands Ballets Canadiens, Les, Canadian B. co. founded in 1956 by Ludmilla Chiriaeff, from a group of dancers she had assembled to appear in ballets for Radio Canada TV, based on Montreal. DOLIN has been an artistic director since 1964 and the French-Canadian dancer Fernand Nault ballet master since 1966. The co. receives grants from the Canada Council and local authorities. The repertory ranges from GISELLE to *Tommy* (1971) a rock opera by the pop group The Who, ch. Nault. Brian Macdonald was appointed artistic director 1974; Nault is now resident choreographer. MC

Grant, Alexander, b. Wellington, 1925. New Zealand dancer. Dancing career entirely with the London RB. To London 1944 on RAD scholarship; joined SWB at CG 1946, soloist 1949. Created Barber in MASSINE's new version of MAM'ZELLE ANGOT, and became the RB's greatest *demi-caractère* dancer. Created Tirrenio in ONDINE, ALAIN, Bottom in DREAM, Meath Baker in ENIGMA VARIATIONS, and Yslaev (the husband) in MONTH IN THE COUNTRY. His unique gift was for dramatic timing in a solo; consequently he could, and often did, make indifferent choreography seem exciting. Director of Ballet For All 1971 but continued dancing until summer 1976 when he became Director of NB of Canada. His last perf. as Alain with the RB was in Washington when fans rained flowers onto the stage. Appeared as CARABOSSE with NB of Canada, NY, 1976 and still gives occasional perfs. in his great roles. CBE 1965. MC

Grantzow, Adèle, b. Brunswick, 1845; d. Berlin, 1877. German dancer, pupil of her father Gustav Grantzow of Brunswick (her mother was the teacher Mme Dominique in Paris). After dancing in Brunswick and Hanover she went to Moscow 1865 as a soloist. Paris debut 1866 in GISELLE. She created the title role in M. PETIPA's *Camargo* and would have done the same in SAINT-LÉON's *La Source* (1872) but had to return to Russia before the premiere. GBLW

Gray, Diane, b. Painesville, OH. American dancer. Studied at Juilliard S. and GRAHAM S., and with SCHWEZOFF, YOUSKEVITCH, Genia Melikova. Danced in the cos of MCGEHEE, J. DUNCAN, YURIKO, P. LANG, MASLOW, Kazuko Hirabayashi, and Graham. Has taken many leading roles in the Graham repertory, incl. the Bride in APPALACHIAN SPRING, Jocasta in NIGHT JOURNEY, the Woman in *Hérodiade*, Joan in *Seraphic Dialogue*, Helen of Troy in CLYTEMNESTRA. DV

Greco, José *see* SPAIN

Green Table, The, dance of death in 8 scenes, ch./lib. JOOSS; mus. Frederic (Fritz) Cohen; c./masks Hein Heckroth. Paris, T. des CE, Folkwang Tanzbühne (subsequently B. Jooss), 3 July 1932. Won first prize in a choreographic competition organized by the Archives Internationales de la

Colour Plate: Costume for the Chinese conjuror in PARADE by PICASSO (first produced 1917), as revived by MASSINE for LFB 1974, dan. Kerrison Cooke

Danse. A bitterly satiric ballet whose anti-war message is as powerful today as it was between the wars. Jooss's finest work, it has been revived by several cos incl. JOFFREY, CULLBERG, Northern Dance T., and NDT. Original German title *Der Grühne Tisch.* DV

Gregory, Cynthia, b. Los Angeles, CA, 1946. American dancer. Studied with MARACCI. Joined San Francisco B. 1961; ABT 1965. A classic ballerina of great purity of line and astonishing technical facility whose roles incl. ODETTE-ODILE, Nikia in BAYADÈRE, and the title roles in SYLPHIDE and NUREYEV's production of RAYMONDA. She also dances many ballets of the modern repertory incl. JARDIN AUX LILAS, DARK ELEGIES, UNDERTOW, and BALANCHINE's *Theme and Variations.* DV

Gregory, Jill, b. Bristol, 1918. English dancer and ballet mistress. Studied DE VALOIS, CRASKE, EGOROVA. Joined Vic-Wells B. 1933 and remained with the co. all her career. A soloist notable for the neatness and quickness of her style. Ballet mistress to the RB 1952, sharing with SOMES the credit for the quality of the RB *corps de ballet.* MC

Grey [Groom], Beryl, b. London, 1927. Trained with Madeline Sharp, then SWBS, from age 9 under SERGUEEFF, DE VALOIS and VOLKOVA, later with Audrey de Vos. Joined SWB 1941; by spring 1942 was dancing leading roles. On her 15th birthday danced full-length SWAN LAKE, adding GISELLE 1944 and SLEEPING BEAUTY (at CG) 1946. A famous LILAC FAIRY and Queen of the Wilis (*Giselle*), she had a triumph in the second ballerina role when the SWB revived BALLET IMPERIAL. Few major creations but a superb one was Winter Fairy in ASHTON's CINDERELLA. Left RB to freelance in 1957 but returned as guest until 1963. In 1957 danced as guest ballerina (the first English dancer to do so) with Kirov, Bolshoy, Kiev State and Tbilisi [Tiflis] State cos and wrote a book about her experiences, *Red Curtain Up* (London and New York 1958). Danced in S. Africa and New Zealand 1959–60, Peking 1964 and wrote another book, *Through the Bamboo Curtain* (London 1965; New York 1966). Toured worldwide. Artistic Director of LFB 1968. In 1950 m. Dr Sven Gustav Svenson and subsequently made many guest appearances in his native Sweden. As a dancer she used her exceptional height deliberately in magnificently expansive style. MC

Cynthia Gregory and MARKS of ABT in the Act III *pas de deux* of SLEEPING BEAUTY

Beryl Grey as Odile and David Paltenghi as von Rothbart in the stereoscopic film *The Black Swan*

Gridin, Anatoly, b. Novosibirsk, 1929. Soviet dancer. Graduated from Leningrad Choreographic S. 1952, class of Boris Shavrov. Began as both classical and character dancer, but gradually became leading dancer-actor of Kirov B., being noticed after GRIGOROVICH entrusted him with creation of Severyan in STONE FLOWER (1957). Since created many varied characters: Vizier (LEGEND OF LOVE), Mako (PATH OF THUNDER), Vanka (*The Twelve*, ch. YACOBSON), etc. A character dancer with an excellent classical style and dramatic expressiveness. Also studied at T. Directors' faculty of Leningrad T. Inst. NR
See M. Mikhailov, 'Anatoly Gridin' in *Leningrad Ballet Today*, No. 1 (Leningrad 1967)

Grigoriev, Serge, b. Tichvin, 1883; d. London, 1968. Russian dancer and *régisseur*. Trained St Petersburg Imperial S., graduating 1900. Sympathetic to the reforms of FOKINE from the beginning (he was in the original production of PAVILLON D'ARMIDE) he joined DIAGHILEV in planning and administering his first Paris season (1909) and remained his faithful *régisseur* for 20 years, resigning from the Imperial T. 1912. Grigoriev was not only responsible for keeping the ballets in good repair but played a vital part in the day-to-day running of the co. (he had the unenviable job of dismissing NIJINSKY). He appeared only in character roles but important ones, such as the Shah Shariar in SCHÉHÉRAZADE, and created the Russian merchant in BOUTIQUE FANTASQUE.

After Diaghilev's death he worked for DE BASIL, staging many revivals from the Diaghilev repertory, and published *The Diaghilev Ballet; 1909–1929* compiled from his diaries and translated by Vera Bowen (London 1953). It is a straightforward narration fascinating in detail (but some facts are challenged in BUCKLE's *Nijinsky*). To celebrate the 25th anniversary of Diaghilev's death he, with his wife, TCHERNICHEVA (m. 1909) revived OISEAU DE FEU as *The Firebird* for the SWB (Edinburgh Fest. 1954). Subsequently for the RB they staged PETRUSHKA, revised SYLPHIDES and finally, shortly before his death, PRINCE IGOR. Also worked on revivals with LFB and in Milan. MC

Grigorovich, Yuri, b. Leningrad, 1927. Soviet dancer, choreographer, and teacher. Graduated from Leningrad Choreographic S. 1946, pupil of PUSHKIN, PONOMARYOV, etc. Danced many character and *demi-caractère* roles at Kirov T. Showed early interest in choreography, creating *Baby Stork* (1948). With a group of young enthusiasts prepared first major work, STONE FLOWER (1957), returning to PROKOFIEV's autograph score and keeping close to the score's symphonic structure. This work marked a new stage in the development of Soviet ballet. Dance born from music became the new motto – but Grigorovich believes in ballet as total theatre. He is usually his own librettist. Appointed staff choreographer, Kirov B., 1961–9, creating LEGEND OF LOVE. From 1964 chief choreographer and artistic director, Bolshoy B., where he created his own versions of NUTCRACKER (1966), SWAN LAKE (1969), revived SLEEPING BEAUTY (1963, 1973) and choreographed a major work, SPARTACUS (1968), completely rethinking and rearranging the score with KHACHATURIAN's permission. Awarded Lenin prize in arts 1970 for this heroic epic work, together with his collaborators. In complete contrast is IVAN THE TERRIBLE, a series of psychological tableaux. Having developed his own theories on dance composition, Grigorovich now teaches them at the Leningrad Cons. Choreographers' Faculty, where he is Professor. President of the dance section at the Congress of International T. Inst., Moscow, from 1973. People's Artist, USSR. He m. N. BESSMERTNOVA. NR
See V. Vanslow, *Balety Grigorovicha i problemi choreografii (Grigorovich's Ballets and Problems of Choreography)*, 2nd ed. (Moscow 1971)

Grisi, Carlotta, b. Visinada, 1819; d. Saint-Jean, Geneva, 1899. Italian dancer. Studied under Guillet in Milan; debut Sc. 1829. In Naples 1833 she met PERROT who became first her teacher, then her lover, and helped shape her career. Paris debut, T. de la Renaissance, 1840; Paris O. 1841, dancing in Gaetano Donizetti's opera *La Favorite*, partnered by L. PETIPA. The same year she met GAUTIER, won his lifelong devotion, and, thanks to him and Perrot, became the first ballerina to dance GISELLE. Also created leading roles in PÉRI, ESMERALDA, PAQUITA, and in MAZILIER's *Le Diable à Quatre* (1845). Danced regularly in London 1842–51; debut 1850 at the Bolshoy T., St Petersburg, in *Giselle*, and spent three years in Russia (working again with Perrot). Danced in Warsaw 1854; then retired from the stage to settle in Saint-Jean. The close of her career came towards the end of the golden age of Romantic ballet of which she epitomized all the ideals. MC
See Serge Lifar, tr. Doris Langley Moore, *Carlotta Grisi* (Paris 1941, London 1947); Ivor Guest, *The Romantic Ballet in Paris* (London and Middletown, CT, 1966); *The Romantic Ballet in England* (London 1954)

Groke, Georg, b. Königsberg [Kaliningrad], 1904. German dancer. Pupil of WIGMAN. Danced in Essen 1926–7, Berlin Städtische O. 1927–33. Emigrated to Poland. To Germany 1939, danced in Strength Through Joy (Kraft durch Freude) B. in Berlin and was prisoner of the Russians. Resumed career 1948, dancing in E. Berlin and Leipzig; assistant ballet master Komische O., E. Berlin 1953–9. Later worked in E. German films. GBLW

Grosse Fuge, ballet, 1 act, ch. van MANEN; mus. Ludwig van Beethoven (Op. 133 and the cavatina from string quartet Op. 130); sc./c. Jean Paul Vroom. Scheveningen, Circus T., NDT, 8 Apr 1971. Revived for RB, 29 Apr 1972; Pennsylvania B., 1975. Male and female groups of four dancers each are set in marked opposition of styles in the opening section; the personalities of the various couples are next explored and then a vigorous ensemble, leading to an epilogue in contrasted mood, calm and gently erotic. JP

Gruber, Lilo, b. Berlin, 1915. German dancer and choreographer. Studied Berlin; a pupil of WIGMAN in Leipzig. In 1931 she joined the ballet in Berlin and became ballet mistress in Greifswald in 1945; in 1955 returned to the Berlin Staats O., E. Berlin, of which she was ballet director until 1970. Choreographed versions of GAYANÉ 1955, *Romeo and Juliet* (mus. PROKOFIEV) 1963, etc. GBLW

Gruca, Witold, b. Kraków [Cracow], 1927. Polish dancer and choreographer. Since 1952 principal, since 1961 also choreographer, Warsaw B. Toured with BITTNERÓWNA all over Europe 1956–60 with recitals of short dances; they won the 1st prize in Vercella, 1956. First Polish Romeo in ROMEO AND JULIET (ch. Jerzy Gogoł) and dances varied repertory of classical and character roles. As choreographer, he prefers short ballets with plots, often with the music of Polish contemporary composers. His ballets incl. *The Enchanted Inn* (mus. Antoni Szałowski); *Ad Hominem* (mus. Zbigniew Wiszniewski); *Mandragora* (mus. Karol Szymanowski); *The Loneliness* and *The Very Sleeping Beauty* (a parody of SLEEPING BEAUTY; mus. Augustyn Bloch). Has also prepared new versions of PAN TWARDOWSKI for film and for the Warsaw co. Choreographer for Warsaw TV. JPu

Gsovsky [Issatchenko], Tatiana, b. Moscow, 1901. Russian dancer, teacher, and choreographer. Daughter of actress Claudia Issatchenko. Studied St Petersburg with NOVIKOV, in the studio of I. DUNCAN, and at DALCROZE S. in Hellerau. She m. V. GSOVSKY and together they moved to Berlin where they opened their school 1928. She choreographed there for many organizations. In 1944 she choreographed *Princess Turandot* (mus. Gottfried von Einem) in Dresden. Ballet director, Staats O., E. Berlin, 1945–52; produced a great number of ballets, and used such dancers as DEEGE, Eleonore Vesco, REINHOLM and VAN DIJK. In 1952–3 she was at the T. Colón, Buenos Aires; 1954–66 director of ballet, Städtische (later Deutsche) O., W. Berlin. She founded the touring BERLINER B. in 1955; 1959–66 she jointly directed the ballet cos of W. Berlin and Frankfurt-am-Main. She continues to work at the ballet school of the Deutsche O. Greatly influenced by the WIGMAN style, her choreography and teaching epitomized German ballet 1930–55. She is the greatest single influence in ballet in Germany. GBLW

Gsovsky, Viktor, b. St Petersburg, 12 Jan 1902, d. Hamburg, 1974. Russian dancer, teacher, and choreographer. Pupil of E. SOKOLOVA in St Petersburg. In 1925 he went to the Berlin Staats O., with his wife T. GSOVSKY, as ballet master and in 1928 they opened a school there. After some film work he joined the MARKOVA–DOLIN B. in London in 1937, and in 1938 started teaching in Paris where his classes at the Studio Wacker were attended by SKORIK, MARCHAND, VERDY and others. In 1947 he choreographed *Dances of Galanta* and *Pygmalion* for the Metropolitan B. in London and was ballet master of PETIT'S B. des CE in 1948. Ballet master of the Munich B. 1950–2. Returned to Paris 1952 and staged *Cinderella* (mus. PROKOFIEV) for the Paris O., in 1954. His famous *Grand Pas Classique* (mus. AUBER) was created for a gala in 1949. Ballet master and teacher, Düsseldorf B. 1964–7, Hamburg 1967–70. GBLW

Guards at Amager, The *see* KING'S VOLUNTEERS OF AMAGER, THE

Guimard, Madeleine (Marie-Madeleine) b. Paris, 1743; d. Paris, 1816. French dancer, one of the most celebrated towards the end of the 18th c. Debut Paris O., May 1762 (replacing the injured ALLARD), *première danseuse* 1763. She danced in the ballets of NOVERRE and Maximilien Gardel and with all the great dancers of the time incl. DAUBERVAL. Essentially a *terre-à-terre* dancer, she disapproved of 'the modern mode of raising the foot to hip level'. She was nicknamed '*Le Squelette des Grâces*'. MC
See Parmenia Migel, *The Ballerinas, from the Court of Louis XIV to Pavlova* (New York 1972)

Guizerix, Jean, b. Paris, 1945. French dancer. *Corps de ballet,* Paris O. 1964; *premier danseur* 1971; *étoile* 1972. Notable creations incl. roles in *Un Jour ou Deux* (ch. CUNNINGHAM, 1973), *Tristan* (ch. TETLEY 1974). Other roles incl. AGON, PÉRI, FOUR TEMPERAMENTS, etc. He m. PIOLLET. M-FC

Gunn, Nicholas, b. Brooklyn, NY. Studied with LORING in Los Angeles, MCGEHEE in NY. Joined P. TAYLOR Dance Co., 1969, and has since danced leading roles in most of his works. DV

Gusev, Pyotr, b. St Petersburg, 1904. Soviet dancer, teacher, choreographer, and theoretician. Graduated from former Maryinsky S. 1922; danced JAMES in school perf. Danced various classical roles, but renowned for taking part in F. LOPUKHOV's experiments in 1920s, and the group BALANCHINE's Young B. Created Asak in ICE MAIDEN with Olga Mungalova in title role, introducing semi-acrobatic high lifts, also concert *pas de deux* exploiting this new style, being first performer of MOSZKOWSKI WALTZ. Partnered LEPESHINSKAYA in concerts. Considered one of the best performers of GIREY. Taught partnering in Leningrad and Moscow schools; headed latter 1937–40 and 1950. Headed Kirov B. 1946–51; Bolshoy B. 1956, Maly O. 1960–2, Novosibirsk B. 1963–6. Choreographed *Seven Beauties* (1952), new version of CORSAIRE (1956, 1963). Professor of choreographers' faculty, Leningrad Cons. Honoured Artist, RSFSR. NR

Hagar, the heroine of PILLAR OF FIRE

Häggbom, Nils Åke, b. Stockholm, 1942. Swedish dancer. Pupil of RSBS. Joined RSB 1959, became principal dancer 1966. AGS

Hallhuber, Heino, b. Munich, 1927. German dancer. Pupil of the Munich S. under Pino Mlakar and V. GSOVSKY. Joined Munich B. 1945, soloist 1949, and creating many principal roles, notably in H. ROSEN's *Josephslegende* (*see* LÉGENDE DE JOSEPH). Now works in film and TV, having retired from the co. in 1973. GBLW

Halprin, Anna [Ann], b. Winnetka, IL, 1920. American dancer and choreographer. Studied with Margaret H'Doubler, Univ. of Wisconsin, 1940–4. Debut in *Sing Out, Sweet Land*, choreographed by WEIDMAN. Joint studio with Welland Lathrop, San Francisco, 1948–55; opened her own studio and formed Dancers' Workshop, San Francisco, 1955. First public perfs 1959, with her own *Birds of America* and *Powerburger*. Toured Europe 1963 with *Five Legged Stool*, again in 1965 with *Parades and Changes* (also given in New York, 1967), both her own. Other works incl. *Ceremony of Us* (1969), *New Time Shuffle* (1970), *Kadosh* (1970), *Evocations of the Cement Spirit* (1971), *Initiations and Transformations* (New York 1971), many of them communally created by members of her inter-racial and inter-communal workshops. A seminal figure in American AVANT-GARDE DANCE; dancers who have worked with her incl. FORTI, RAINER, MONK. DV

Halte de Cavalerie, La (*Prival Kavaleriy*), *demi-caractère* ballet, 1 act, ch./lib. M. PETIPA; mus. Joseph Armsheimer; sc. G. Levogt; c. Ponomarev. St Petersburg, Maryinsky T., 2 Feb 1896, for the benefit perf. (20 years' service) of Marie Petipa; dan. Marie Petipa, P. GERDT, LEGNANI, Sergey Legat, Jozef Kschessinsky, Alfred Bekefi, Sergey Lukyanov. Each of the officers in a cavalry regiment flirts with Marie, a peasant girl, with senior officers sending the junior ones away on a mission as soon as rivalry occurs. A lively ballet calling for a gift for characterization especially among the male dancers, with plenty of good dancing. Marie Petipa danced her role until the beginning of the present century. Revived by GUSEV for Leningrad Chamber B. 1968, and for Maly OB 1975. NR
See COMPLETE BOOK

Hamel, Martine van, b. Brussels, 1945. Dutch dancer. Studied in Denmark, Netherlands, Venezuela, and Toronto, where she joined NB of Canada 1963. Gold Medal, Varna Competition, 1965. Also danced with RSB and CCJB before joining ABT 1970. Fully equal to the gruelling technical demands of such modern ballets as GEMINI, her authority, musicality, and majestic presence make her a superb interpreter of the classical repertory, incl. SWAN LAKE, BAYADÈRE, RAYMONDA, and as MYRTHA and AURORA. She revealed a subtle wit in her role in THARP's *Push Comes to Shove*. DV

Hamilton, Gordon, b. Sydney, 1918; d. Paris, 1959. Australian dancer. Studied to be a concert pianist but after seeing DE BASIL's B. Russe de Monte Carlo in Australia 1934 decided to become a dancer and went to Paris to study with PREOBRAZHENSKA and EGOROVA. To London 1939 to work with and dance for RAMBERT before joining the Anglo-Polish B. 1940 with which he appeared under the name of Alexander Walewski. With SWB 1941–6, dancing mostly character roles (DR COPPÉLIUS, CARABOSSE). Joined B. des CE 1946 after their first London season as principal character dancer (MADGE in V. GSOVSKY's SYLPHIDE), returned to SWB briefly in 1947 then rejoined PETIT and with B. de Paris created roles in CARMEN and CROQUEUSE DE DIAMANTS. In 1954 appointed ballet master at the reopened Vienna Staats O. to enlarge and improve the classical repertory; staged the full-length GISELLE there 1955, and did much to raise standards of teaching. MC

Hamlet, ballet, 1 scene, ch. HELPMANN; mus. TCHAIKOVSKY; sc./c. HURRY. London, New T., SWB, 19 May 1942; dan. Helpmann, FONTEYN, FRANCA, David Paltenghi. Revived CG, RB, 3 June 1946 and again 2 Apr 1964 as part of Shakespeare quatrocentennial program. The ballet is based on Hamlet's words: 'For in that sleep of death what dreams may come When we have shuffled off this mortal coil, Must give us pause.' The dying Hamlet recalls his life in hallucinatory fashion. The first ballet designed by Hurry; his brooding setting contributed greatly to the claustrophobic atmosphere. Helpmann's strong theatrical sense clinched its success. There have been many ballets on the Hamlet theme, incl. ones ch. NIJINSKA (1934), with herself as Hamlet, both T. and V. GSOVSKY (1950), SERGEYEV (1970), and NEUMEIER (1976), but none has captured so successfully the spirit of Shakespeare's play or understood the characters so well. MC

Hanka, Erika, b. Vincovci, Croatia, 1905; d. Vienna, 1958. Austrian dancer and choreographer. Early studies with BODENWIESER in Vienna, then JOOSS, with whose co. she toured Europe and USA. Soloist and acting ballet mistress, Düsseldorf O. 1936–9, then worked in Cologne, Essen, and Hamburg; invited 1941 to Vienna as guest choreographer. The success of her JOAN VON ZARISSA led to her appointment as ballet mistress, a position she held until her death. She choreographed some 50 ballets, the most successful probably being *Der Mohr von Venedig* (*The Moor of Venice*), mus. Boris Blacher, sc./c. Georges Wakhevitch, 29 Nov 1955 for the opening of the rebuilt Vienna Staats O. She worked mostly in the modern dance idiom herself but encouraged the teaching of the classic style and raised the importance of the ballet co., long regarded as a poor appendage to the opera. MC

Hanke, Susanne, b. Altdöbern, 1948. German dancer. Trained at the Stuttgart S. under WOOLLIAMS and at RBS. Joined Stuttgart B. 1966; soloist 1969. Created roles in CRANKO works (notably Bianca in TAMING OF THE SHREW 1969). To CAPAB B., S. Africa, 1973. Now teaching in Germany. GBLW

Harangozó, Gyula, b. Budapest, 1908; d. Budapest, 1974. Hungarian dancer, choreographer, and ballet master. Founder of Hungarian national ballet repertoire based on classical technique. Chief works (all in Budapest O.) incl.: *Scene in the Csárdas* (1936; mus. Jenő Hubay), ROMEO AND JULIET (1939; mus. TCHAIKOVSKY), WOODEN PRINCE (1939, revived 1958). In his post-war period he staged MIRACULOUS MANDARIN (1945, revived 1956), *Tricorne* (1947, revived 1959), *Platzmusik* (1948; mus. Jenő Kenessey after Johann Strauss), SCHÉHÉRAZADE (1959), and four full-length ballets: MISCHIEVOUS STUDENTS, KERCHIEF, COPPÉLIA (1953), and *Ludas Matyi* (*Matti the Gooseboy*, 1960; mus. Ferenc Szabó). They have frequently been revived in Budapest, Szeged, Pécs, and abroad. The first Hungarian to amalgamate authentic folk dance with classical ballet, to compose real ballet dramas, and sparkling ballet comedies. A brilliant character dancer and comedian. Eminent Artist, 1952; Kossuth Prize, 1956; Golden Order of Labour, 1958. GPD

Harkarvy, Benjamin, b. New York, 1930. American teacher and choreographer. Studied with George Chaffee, Edward Caton, and at SAB in New York, with PREOBRAZHENSKA in Paris. Opened his own school in New York 1955. Director of RWB 1957; ballet master of Nederlands B., 1958. In 1959 formed his own co. in Amsterdam, NDT, for which he choreographed many ballets. Left in 1969 to become joint director of HARKNESS B.; in 1970 became joint director (with van DANTZIG) of Dutch NB, but resigned after one year. Artistic director of Pennsylvania B., 1972, for which he has revived several of his earlier works and choreographed *Time Passed Summer* (1974; mus. TCHAIKOVSKY). DV

Harkness [Semple], Rebekah, b. St Louis, MO, 1915. American composer, ballet director, and president of the Harkness Foundation, established 1961, which sponsored ROBBINS's Ballets: USA in its European tour, 1961, and the JOFFREY B., 1962–4. After discontinuing her support of the latter, she formed her own co., the Harkness B., NY, 1964, with SKIBINE as director and his wife Marjorie TALLCHIEF as ballerina. The co. made its debut in Cannes, February 1965, and toured Europe with a repertory incl. AILEY's *Feast of Ashes*, a version of *Daphnis and Chloe* by Skibine, and ballets by BRUHN, Brian Macdonald, and Stuart Hodes. Later in the year the co. toured the USA; first NY perfs were in 1967, in which year Macdonald was appointed director. Changes in personnel and direction became increasingly frequent: RHODES, a principal dancer with the co., was appointed director 1968, joined by HARKARVY 1969. In 1969 Harkness formed a second co., the Harkness Youth B., and in 1970 combined the two cos under her own direction. In 1972 she bought a NY theatre and named it the Harkness T.; it opened with a brief season by her co. 1974. Shortly thereafter the co. went out of existence. The Harkness House for B. Arts, the school she had opened 1965, continues to operate under the direction of David Howard. DV

Harlem Dance Theatre *see* DANCE THEATRE OF HARLEM

Harlequinade, ballet, 2 acts, ch. BALANCHINE; mus. DRIGO; sc./c./ltg TER-ARUTUNIAN. NYST, NYCB, 4 Feb 1965; dan. MCBRIDE, VILLELLA. A modern reworking of MILLIONS D'ARLEQUIN, this ballet tells how Harlequin, helped by a Good Fairy, succeeds in releasing his beloved Columbine from her wealthy father's domination. FM

Harnasie *see* HIGHLANDERS, THE

Harper, Meg [Margaret Ann], b. Evanston, IL, 1944. American dancer. Studied dance at Univ. of Illinois, 1963–6 (BA), thereafter in NY with CUNNINGHAM, C. BROWN, CRASKE. Joined Cunningham's Co. 1967 and has danced in most of his pieces, creating roles in *Walkaround Time, Second Hand, Tread*, CANFIELD, *Landrover*, etc. Performed a solo of her own, *Earthrunner* (NY, Nov 1966). Teaches at Cunningham Studio, etc. DV

Hart, John, b. London, 1921. English dancer, ballet master, and director. Studied with Judith Espinosa, joined Vic-Wells B. 1938; won RAD GENÉE gold medal 1939. Before his own war service, RAF 1942–7, was mainstay of SWB young classical dancers, performing principal roles in SWAN LAKE, SLEEPING BEAUTY, GISELLE, COPPÉLIA all before the age of 20. In 1947 returned to the SWB as a principal dancer at CG, ballet master 1955, an assistant director of the RB 1963–70. Ballet director, International Univ. of Performing Arts, San Diego, from 1970; returned to RB as administrator 1975–7. Created Laertes in HELPMANN's HAMLET and Orion in ASHTON's SYLVIA. Published *Ballet and Camera*, photographs of RB (London 1956). CBE 1971. MC

Hartford Ballet *see* REGIONAL BALLET (USA)

Haskell, Arnold Lionel, b. London, 1903. English writer, critic, educator, and enthusiast for ballet. He was an early champion of the BR and later Vic-Wells B. and played a vital role in the growth of British ballet. Paradoxically, his book *Balletomania* (1934), an instant bestseller, was inspired largely by memories of the DIAGHILEV B. and delight in the young B. Russe de Monte Carlo. His books reached an enormous public and helped break down many prejudices against ballet, especially the myth that it is an elitist art. *The National Ballet* (London 1943) stated the case for the SWB to become Britain's national co. His *Ballet, A Complete Guide to Appreciation* (Harmondsworth 1938) sold more than a million copies throughout the world. He has travelled and lectured widely. He founded the SW (now RB) Benevolent Fund, is a vice-president of the RAD, and has constantly campaigned for closer links between dance and education. It was his insistence on proper academic education that led to the expansion of the SWS in 1947 with himself as director, a post he held until his retirement in 1964. From 1956 a governor of the RB; vice-chairman of the Varna Competitions 1964–73, and also a judge at international competitions in Moscow and Cuba. Author of the first detailed biography of Diaghilev (with Walter Nouvel, 1935) and two volumes of autobiography, *In His True Centre* (London 1951) and *Balletomane at Large* (London 1972). Also wrote the first book about Jacob Epstein, *The Sculptor Speaks* (London 1931) and in 1976 returned to sculpture to write a life of Émile Antoine Bourdelle. He m. Vera Saitzoff and after her death (1968) m. in 1970 Vivienne Marks (sister of MARKOVA). *Chevalier*, Légion d'Honneur, 1959; CBE 1954. MC

Havas, Ferenc, b. Budapest, 1935. Hungarian dancer. Pupil of NÁDASI; graduated from the State B. Inst. 1953; solo dancer since. Studied in Moscow under Aleksey Varlamov, L. LAVROVSKY, ULANOVA, and MESSERER. Typical *danseur noble* and excellent partner, danced almost all major classical roles in the Budapest repertoire, also the MILLER in HARANGOZÓ's *Tricorne* (1959), the title role in Harangozó's *Ludas Matyi* (1960), Lavrovsky's ROMEO (1962), and ASHTON's COLAS (1971). Apart from co. tours, he was guest of LFB five times 1960–4, incl. a Barcelona tour, and partnered STRUCHKOVA in Moscow (*Romeo and Juliet*, 1966). Permanent member of Grand B. Classique de France since 1974. Toured throughout Europe. Liszt Prize, 1962; Kossuth Prize, 1965; Merited Artist, 1973. GPD

Hawkins, Erick, b. Trinidad, CO. American modern dance choreographer, teacher, and dancer. Graduate of Harvard Univ., in Greek. Studied at SAB, becoming a member of American B. (1935–7) and B. Caravan (1936–9). Choreographed his first dance for the latter group 1937. Performed with GRAHAM 1938–51. The first male to dance with her co., creating the roles of the Husbandman in *Appalachian Spring*, the Ringmaster in *Every Soul is a Circus*, and He Who Beckons in *Dark Meadow*. He m. Graham 1948; they separated 1950, and were divorced 1954. Hawkins's first dances were dramatic in nature, but in 1955 he began to work in the abstract style for which he is now known. He has had a close collaboration with Lucia Dlugoszewski, a composer and musician who accompanies his dance on stage, using prepared instruments, and sculptor Ralph Dorazio. In his work, influenced by Greek and Oriental philosophy and art, and his teaching he stresses the importance of unforced, natural movement. Some of the best-known of his over 25 dances are HERE AND NOW WITH WATCHERS, *8 Clear Places* (1960), *Early Floating* (1962), *Geography of Noon* (1964), *Cantilever* (1966), all to music by Dlugozewski, and *Classic Kite Tails* (1972; mus. David Diamond). JD
See J. Baril, 'Rencontre avec Erick Hawkins', *Les Saisons de la Danse* (Paris, Dec 1973)

Erick Hawkins in his dance *Early Floating* (1962)

Top: Marcia Haydée with CLAUSS in the Stuttgart B's staging of ONEGIN

Left: Melissa Hayden in *The Combat* with NYCB

Haydée [Pereira da Silva], Marcia, b. Niteroi, State of Rio de Janeiro, 1939. Brazilian dancer. Studied with Yuco Lindenberg and Vaslav Veltchek. Joined T. Municipal Co. 1953. Entered RBS 1954; joined de Cuevas B. 1957 as a soloist. Left 1961 to become ballerina of Stuttgart B. Co. where she created many roles for CRANKO, incl. JULIET, Tatyana (ONEGIN), and Katharine (TAMING OF THE SHREW); also a great GISELLE. Artistic director, Stuttgart B., 1976. Created principal roles in HERMANAS and LIED VON DER ERDE. MLN
See H. Koegler, 'Marcia Haydée', *Les Saisons de la Danse* (Paris, Nov 1976), with list of roles

Hayden, Melissa [Mildred Herman], b. Toronto, 1922. Canadian dancer. Studied in NY with VILZAK and SCHOLLAR. Danced in Radio City Music Hall *corps de ballet*. Joined ABT 1945. After a season with B. Alicia ALONSO in S. America, joined NYCB 1950 and remained there until her retirement in 1973, except for a brief return to ABT, 1953–5, and some guest engagements with RB and NB of Canada, both 1963, etc. A ballerina with brilliant technique and strong dramatic gifts, she created roles in many ballets by BALANCHINE, incl. DIVERTIMENTO NO. 15, AGON, STARS AND STRIPES, LIEBESLIEDER WALZER, Titania in MIDSUMMER NIGHT'S DREAM, and ROBBINS's *Age of Anxiety* (1950) and *The Pied Piper*. As a farewell gift, Balanchine staged for her *Cortège Hongrois* (*see* RAYMONDA), 1973. On her retirement she took up an appointment at Skidmore College, Saratoga Springs, NY. In 1976 she was made artistic director, Pacific Northwest Dance, Seattle, WA. DV

Hayman-Chaffey, Susana, b. Tenterden, Kent, 1948. English dancer, choreographer, and teacher. Studied RBS 1957–60, and in Rome and Rio de Janeiro; modern dance in NY with GRAHAM and CUNNINGHAM, 1965–7. Danced with Cunningham and Dance Co. 1968–76; danced in nearly all his works during that time. Has also performed, choreographed, and taught at various US universities and in Brazil and Japan. Gave concert of her own choreography in NY, 1975. DV

Heart of the Hills (*Serdtse Gor*), ballet, 3 acts, ch. CHABUKIANI; mus. Andrey Balanchivadze (BALANCHINE's brother); lib. Georgy Leonidze and Nikolay Volkov; sc. VIRSALADZE; scenic advisor Nikolay Petrov. As *Mzechabuki* (or *Gargi*), 4 acts, Tbilisi T. of O. and B., 27 Dec 1936. As *Serdtse Gor*, 3 acts, Leningrad, Kirov T., 28 June 1938; dan. Chabukiani, VECHESLOVA, Elena Chikvaidze. Manizhe, a Caucasian prince's daughter, loves a peasant, Gargi, against the wishes of her father, who wants her to marry another prince. At the wedding feast she dies protecting Gargi with her own body from the knife of her bridegroom. A successful blending of classical and Georgian dancing, the latter used as a means of characterization rather than

divertissement. Typical of Soviet ballet of the time in having a legitimate-theatre director as scenic advisor. Other versions produced in the 1940s and early 1950s in different republics. NR
See V. Krasovskaya, *Vakhtang Chabukiani* (Leningrad 1960); L. Entelis, *Sto Baletnykh Libretto* (*One Hundred Ballet Librettos*) (Leningrad 1966)

Heaton, Anne [Patsy], b. Rawalpindi, India, 1930. English dancer and teacher. Studied with Janet Cranmore in Birmingham 1937–43, then SWBS. Debut 1945 with SW O. in Bedřich Smetana's opera *The Bartered Bride* at New T. (now Albery T.), London. Soloist with SWTB from its inception; created roles in HOWARD's *Assembly Ball* and *Mardi Gras* and FRANCA's *Khadra*, all 1946. To SWB at CG 1948, excelling in romantic roles e.g. in SYLPHIDES and title role in GISELLE 1954. Created the Woman in MACMILLAN's *The Burrow* (1958) and the Wife in INVITATION. Resigned from RB 1959 because of foot trouble; but was an occasional guest until 1962. Teaches at Arts Educational S., London. Has staged classical ballets, notably *Giselle* 1971, in Teheran for Iranian NB. She m. FIELD. MC

Heinel, Anna Friederike, b. Bayreuth, 1753; d. Paris, 1808. German dancer. Pupil of l'Épy; debut Stuttgart 1767 under NOVERRE. Debut at Paris O. 1768 and was called 'the Queen of the Dance'. First danced in London 1772; m. G. VESTRIS 1792. She is said to have invented the *pirouette à la seconde*. GBLW

Hellerau-Laxenburg S. *see* DALCROZE

Helpmann, Robert Murray, b. Mount Gambier, 1909. Australian dancer, actor, choreographer, producer, and director. Began dancing at age of five with Nora Stewart (Adelaide). J. C. Williamson Theatres Ltd, leading dancer, from 1927. Toured as student dancer with A. PAVLOVA's co., studying with NOVIKOV. Vic-Wells BS 1933. Joined Vic-Wells B. and within the year danced Satan (JOB) and partnered MARKOVA in full-length SWAN LAKE. *Stop Press* (revue), leading dancer, 1935, working with WEIDMAN. Remained as principal dancer with the Vic-Wells B. (later SWB) until 1950. His versatility in combining noble roles (ALBRECHT, SIEGFRIED) with dramatic ones (in e.g. RAKE'S PROGRESS) and comedy (Mr O'Reilly, *The Prospect Before Us*, ch. DE VALOIS; the Bridegroom, WEDDING BOUQUET; an Ugly Sister, CINDERELLA, all created) is unsurpassed. His celebrated partnership with FONTEYN had inestimable value in the development of the SWB (RB). His first ballet *Comus* (1942) was quickly followed by HAMLET and (1944) by MIRACLE IN THE GORBALS. His choreography stresses drama rather than dance invention but he unifies movement, music, and design into theatrically effective works.

Helpmann's exceptional range of talents launched him early on a double career in drama and ballet. In 1937 he played Oberon in William Shakespeare's *A Midsummer Night's Dream* at the Old Vic T., and later appeared in leading roles incl. Hamlet, at Stratford-upon-Avon and at the Old Vic. Has choreographed and danced and acted in films; directed opera, plays, musicals, and pantomime; and acted on TV and radio. His association with the Australian B. began in 1964 when his ballet *The Display* (mus. Malcolm Williamson, sc./c. Sidney Nolan) was staged in Adelaide. Appointed co-artistic director with VAN PRAAGH 1965. Promoted overseas tours of the co., choreographed ballets and appeared in mime roles. In 1973, with NUREYEV, directed film of the Australian B.'s DON QUIXOTE and appeared in title role. From Jan 1975 to June 1976 sole artistic director of Australian B., also staging MERRY WIDOW.

Robert Helpmann as Dr Coppélius, with SWB

Since leaving the RB, Helpmann has frequently returned as a guest in his created roles of the Red King (CHECKMATE) and Ugly Sister, and in 1977 appeared again as DR COPPÉLIUS with SWRB. He has narrated *A Wedding Bouquet* and compèred the co.'s gala tribute to ASHTON in 1970. CBE 1964, KBE 1968. KSW
See K. Sorley Walker, *Robert Helpmann* (London 1958)

Henze, Hans Werner, b. Gütersloh, 1926. German composer. Pupil of Wolfgang Fortner and René Leibowitz; originally a serialist, later an eclectic of marked individuality. A prolific writer for the theatre, he has written several ballets, incl. *Tancredi* (Munich 1954; ch. V. GSOVSKY; also Vienna 1966; ch. NUREYEV), *Maratona di Danza* (Berlin 1957; ch. Dirk Sanders), and ONDINE. His first opera, *Boulevard Solitude* (Hanover 1952) gave great prominence to dance. DH

Here and Now With Watchers, modern dance work, ch. HAWKINS; mus. Lucia Dlugoszewski;

c. Ralph Dorazio. NY, Hunter College Playhouse, 27 Nov 1957; dan. Hawkins, Nancy Lang. The relationships of a man and a woman expressed with tenderness at a calm, unhurried pace. DM

Hermanas, Las, ballet, 1 act, ch./lib. MACMILLAN (based on Federico García Lorca's play *La Casa de Bernarda Alba*, 1936); mus. Frank Martin (*Concerto for Harpsichord and Small Orchestra*); sc./c. GEORGIADIS. Stuttgart B., 13 July 1963; dan. HAYDÉE, BARRA. Revived Cardiff, New T., Western TB, 22 June 1966. NYST, ABT, 29 Nov 1967. London, SWT, RB, 2 June 1971. A claustrophobic Spanish household of five unmarried sisters dominated by their mother. The eldest is betrothed, but her fiancé seduces her youngest sister, the middle sister betrays him, he is banished, the eldest sister resigns herself to spinsterhood, and the youngest hangs herself in shame. MC

Heroic Poem *see* GEOLOGISTS

Hess, Günter, b. Berlin, 1903. German dancer and teacher. Pupil of Hans Storck, TERPIS, LABAN, and NOVIKOV. Taught in his own dance school in Berlin from 1920. Also taught in the Max Reinhardt S. and Berlin High S. for Music. Ballet master and choreographer in Osnabrück, Dessau, Hagen, Chemnitz, Wuppertal, Marburg etc., in 1920s to 1939. Choreographed a version of William Walton's FAÇADE in this period. After World War II worked in productions in Munich, Hamburg etc., and in films and TV. GBLW

Het Nationale Ballet *see* NETHERLANDS

Highlanders, The (*Harnasie*), ballet, 1 act, 3 scenes, ch. Jelizaveta Nikolska; mus. Karol Szymanowski; lib. Jarosław Iwaszkiewicz and Mieczysław Rytard. Prague, 11 May 1935; Paris, 27 Apr 1936; Poznań, 9 Apr 1938; Warsaw, 1 Oct 1938. A girl from the mountains has fallen in love with the leader of a band of highland robbers. During her wedding to a rich farmer's son, she allows herself to be kidnapped by her beloved robber. The ballet is closely connected with Polish folklore and dancing from the Tatra mountains in the central Carpathians. JPU

Hightower, Rosella, b. Ardmore, OK, 1920. American dancer and teacher. Studied with Dorothy Perkins in Kansas City, MO. Danced with B. Russe de Monte Carlo 1938–41, ABT 1941–5, becoming ballerina, MASSINE's B. Russe Highlights co. 1945–6, Original B. Russe 1945–6. Joined Nouveau B. de Monte Carlo in 1947 when it was being taken over by DE CUEVAS and, except for short guest seasons in the USA and Europe, remained first ballerina of that co. until its demise. She toured the world with the de Cuevas B., was the favourite dancer of the Marquis and one of the most popular dancers in continental Europe. She had an enormous repertory, incl. many creations for TARAS, also dancing SYLPHIDE (in H. LANDER's staging of the August BOURNONVILLE version) and SLEEPING BEAUTY. After the death of the Marquis she retired from the co. but continued to make guest appearances with various cos. In 1962 she gave three enormously successful perfs in Paris with Sonia Arova, BRUHN, and NUREYEV (she had danced with Nureyev when he made his London debut at a gala in 1961 in the BLACK SWAN *pas de deux*).

Since 1962 she has directed the Centre de Danse Classique in Cannes which attracts dancers from all over the world and where many of her famous colleagues give guest classes. Directed the B. de l'O. de Marseille 1969–71 and B. de Nancy 1972. Directed International Acad. of Dance at the Venice Fest. 1975. In 1976 organized her own co. in Cannes. She m. designer Jean Robier; their daughter Dominique dances, as Monet Robier, with BÉJART's co. *Chevalier*, Légion d'Honneur, 1975. MC
See I. Lidova, 'Rosella Hightower', *Les Saisons de la Danse* (Paris, Apr 1968) with list of roles

Rosella Hightower in PIÈGE DE LUMIÈRE with the de Cuevas B.

Horschelt, Friedrich, b. Cologne, 1793; d. Munich, 1876. German dancer and ballet master. Ballet master, T. an der Wien, Vienna, 1815–21, where he had a famous Children's B. (6–12-year-olds) of which Austrian dancer Thérèse Heberle was a member. He also choreographed in Munich for operas by AUBER, Giacomo Meyerbeer, etc.

His son August Horschelt was ballet master in Prague. GBLW

Horst, Louis, b. Kansas City, 1884; d. New York, 1964. American composer, teacher, and writer. Musical director for ST DENIS 1915–25, GRAHAM 1926–48. Composed scores for several Graham works incl. PRIMITIVE MYSTERIES (1931), *Frontier* (1935), *El Penitente* (1940). Taught dance composition at Bennington College, Connecticut College, Juilliard S. of Music, etc., and published *Pre-Classic Dance Forms* (New York 1937) and *Modern Dance Forms in Relation to the Other Modern Arts* (with Carroll Russell; San Francisco 1961). Editor of *Dance Observer* 1934–64. DV

Horton, Lester, b. Indianapolis, IN, 1906; d. Los Angeles, CA, 1953. American dancer. Studied with BOLM in Chicago. Strongly attracted by American Indian culture, he designed movement for a pageant *The Song of Hiawatha* in Chicago 1928 and accompanied the production to California which became the centre of his dance life. While continuing to collect handicrafts and instruments he formed his own dance co. 1932 and presented outdoor Indian pageants. In addition to creating the choreography, he also designed costumes and settings for his productions. A neck injury in 1944 forced him to retire from active performing but he continued to teach and design dances. Worked in film industry and nightclubs. Established his Dance T. in Los Angeles 1948 – the first hall devoted exclusively to dance all the year round. His most famous work is *The Beloved*, which has been perf. by many cos incl. the AILEY American Dance T. and DTH. His most noted pupils have been Ailey, LEWITZKY, Janet Collins, DE LAVALLADE, Joyce Trisler, and James Truitte. His style of dance movement emphasized a strong, quiet torso with asymmetrical arrangement of limbs building from the still centre. DM
See Larry Warren, *Lester Horton: Modern Dance Pioneer* (New York 1977)

House, modern dance work, ch. LAMHUT; mus. Steve Reich; c. Frank Garcia. NY, Barnard College, 19 Nov 1971; dan. Lamhut, Donald Blumenfeld, Rolando Pena. A woman cannot bear to leave the shelter of her small house. When she finally does she plunges through a paper hoop and collapses – her longed-for freedom is less important than it once seemed. DM

Houston Foundation for Ballet *see* REGIONAL BALLET (USA)

Hoving [Hovinga], Lucas, b. Groningen. Dutch dancer, choreographer, and teacher. Studied with GEORGI in Holland and JOOSS at Dartington, England. Danced with B. Jooss; moved to USA in mid-1940s; subsequently became US citizen. Danced with GRAHAM and BETTIS before beginning long association with LIMÓN in 1949, creating such roles as the Friend (Iago) in MOOR'S PAVANE, in which his malevolent intensity has never been equalled, as well as the Leader in *The Traitor*, the White Man in *Emperor Jones* (both ch. Limón), and roles in HUMPHREY'S *Night Spell* and *Ruins and Visions*. During the 1960s he choreographed several works for a co. of his own, notably *Icarus* (1964), which has been revived by AILEY and other cos. Appointed director, Rotterdam Dance Acad. in 1971, he now teaches, dividing his time between USA and Holland. DV

Howard, Andrée, b. 1910; d. London, 1968. English dancer and choreographer. Studied with RAMBERT and later in Paris with EGOROVA, KSHESSINSKA, PREOBRAZHENSKA, and TREFILOVA. A member of BR from its foundation, appearing in many of ASHTON'S earliest ballets and also in works by TUDOR, DE VALOIS, and FOKINE.

Her own first ballet, *Our Lady's Juggler* (1933), was a reworking of a 1930 work of that name by Susan Salaman. The choreography of *Mermaid* (1934) was also attributed to a collaboration between Howard and Salaman, although later it was accepted that the credit belonged mainly to Howard. An imaginative narration of a tale about a drowned man falling in love with the sea creature, it was admired for the way it achieved its effects by the simplest means. Further productions for Rambert incl. CINDERELLA (1935), *La Muse s'amuse* (1936), the slight but enduring *Death and the Maiden* (1937), and *Lady into Fox* (1939), which incl. a striking role for GILMOUR.

In 1939 Howard was invited to NY as one of the choreographers for ABT's inaugural season, staging and dancing in *Death and the Maiden* and *Lady into Fox*. Returning to England, she created her most successful ballet, FÊTE ÉTRANGE.

Henceforth Howard worked as a freelance choreographer. She did create further works for Rambert, notably the melodramatic *The Fugitive* (1944) and *The Sailor's Return* (first British 2-act ballet, based on David Garnett's novel; mus. Arthur Oldham; SWT, 2 June 1947; dan. Gilmour, GORE). For International B. she created *Twelfth Night* (1942). Her first connection with SWB was the production of *Le Festin de l'Araignée* (1944). When SWTB was formed in 1946 she made *Assembly Ball* for their opening program and later a popular parody of romantic ballet, *Selina* (1948); at CG she mounted *A Mirror for Witches* (1952) and *Veneziana* (1953). She designed many of her own ballets and also collaborated very successfuly with FEDOROVITCH. JP

Howes, Dulcie [Mrs Guy Cronwright], b. Little Brak River, Cape Province, 1908. S. African dancer, choreographer, and director. Educated at Herschel S., Cape Town. Early training from Helen Webb. At 17 she moved to London to study the CECCHETTI method with CRASKE, mime with KARSAVINA, national dancing with DERRA DE MORODA, and Spanish dancing with Elsa Brunelleschi. Toured with A. PAVLOVA's co.; returned to S. Africa and taught in Cape Town and Johannesburg. In 1934 she was invited to attach her ballet school to the Univ. of Cape Town. From the school grew the UCT BALLET CO., for which she choreographed many ballets.

Howes became director, Little T., Cape Town, 1936. In 1941 she began a three-year certificate course for teachers, later a diploma course for matriculated students. She kept her amateur co. going at a professional level against all odds, fostering such talent as Pamela Chrimes, POOLE, CRANKO, RODRIGUES, and Johaar Mosaval. From the co.'s profits she created (1950) a trust fund which finances new perfs and enables many dancers to further their studies. In 1963 her co. received a small state grant enabling her to appoint a ballet master and soloists. On 1 Apr 1965 the co. became fully professional and the name was changed to CAPAB BALLET. She became its first artistic director; retired 1969. Retired as principal of the UCT BS Dec 1972. Many awards, incl. Honorary Doctor of Music awarded by Univ. of Cape Town, 18 June 1976. Adjudicator for tri-annual National Education Choreographic Competition. MG

Hoyer, Dore, b. 1911; d. Berlin, 1967. German dancer. Pupil of DALCROZE S. at Hellerau, and Gret Palucca. Essentially a solo dancer; first recital in Dresden 1924. Danced in WIGMAN's group and was ballet mistress Hamburg 1949–51 and in 1950 choreographed her most famous solo, *Bolero* (mus. RAVEL). She gave recitals all over the world; a foremost exponent of the Central European style. GBLW

Hudova, Irina, b. Finland, 1930. Studied Helsinki NBS and also with Anna Northcote in London. Joined Finnish NB 1950, achieving ballerina status. Also danced and studied in Leningrad and Moscow and became internationally celebrated as a teacher. Taught for RAD, London, 1964; ballet mistress for a small RB group led by FONTEYN. Guest teacher RBS London 1967–8, subsequently taught in Ankara and Milan. In 1972 Director of Finnish NB. Returned to Milan Sc. as principal teacher 1973. MC

Humpbacked Horse, The (*Konyok-Gorbunok*) **or The Tsar Maiden**, ballet, 4 acts, 9 scenes with an apotheosis, ch./lib. SAINT-LÉON; mus. PUGNI. St Petersburg, Bolshoy T., 3 Dec 1864; transferred to Bolshoy T., Moscow, with same choreography, 1 Dec 1866. Though Saint-Léon failed to comprehend the nature of the popular Russian fairy tale by Pyotr Yershov, generations of Russian dancers made it into a true Russian ballet. Especially notable were Vasily Geltser as Ivan the Fool and his daughter GELTSER as the Tsar Maiden.

M. PETIPA choreographed a new prologue, apotheosis, and many dances for his revival at the Maryinsky T., 6 Dec 1895, for the benefit of LEGNANI, and it remained as a vehicle for many outstanding Russian ballerinas. GORSKY choreographed two new versions in 1901 and 1912, sc. Konstantin Korovin.

Entirely new score to same title in 4 acts with prologue and epilogue composed by Rodion Shchedrin; ch. RADUNSKY; Moscow, Bolshoy T., 4 Feb 1960. New version, ch. BELSKY; same lib./mus. Leningrad, Maly O., 21 Dec 1963. Productions to this score appeared elsewhere in the USSR. NR

Humphrey, Doris, b. Oak Park, IL, 1895; d. New York, 1958. Dancer, choreographer, and innovator of the American modern dance. After childhood studies in classical ballet, she attended the DENISHAWN S., Los Angeles and became a member of the Denishawn co., 1917–28. With her partner, WEIDMAN, she then founded a school and performing group in NY, giving concerts there and throughout the USA until the co. disbanded in 1940. During this period her artistic ideas were defined and developed.

She wrote of the basic principle of her approach then as 'moving from the inside out'. Unlike the contemporary ballet, which started with a set vocabulary, she began with a feeling and proceeded to devise whatever movements were necessary to communicate it. Spectacle and virtuosity were shunned, for this was serious art, not mere entertainment. The Humphrey dances were always strictly structured and meticulously crafted.

Some of her early works were inspired by nature: *Water Study* (1928) and *Life of the Bee* (1929). The experimental *Drama of Motion* (1931), devoid of music, costumes, and plot, was almost purely abstract; but *The Shakers* (1931), was a dramatic portrayal of an early American religious community. NEW DANCE (1935) envisioned an ideal society where each individual achieved personal fulfilment while contributing to the harmony of the group. *Passacaglia in C Minor* (1938), set to the music of Johann Sebastian Bach, proclaimed the grandeur of the human spirit in a dance of majestic architectural design. Characteristic of this period were intricate counterpointing of musical rhythms, often to serve expressive ends, and complex interweavings of movements for large groups, often symbolic of conflicting emotional forces.

In 1932, Doris Humphrey m. Charles Francis Woodford, an English merchant seaman. Their son, Charles Humphrey, was born 1933. The marriage made little change in the life of the artist.

In 1944 severe arthritis forced her to retire as a performer, but within two years she began to create some of her finest dances for the co. of her protégé LIMÓN: *Lament for Ignacio Sánchez Mejías* (1946) used the eloquent poetry of Federico García Lorca; *Day on Earth* (1947) traced the joys and sorrows of all human lives; *Theater Piece No. 2* (1956) was a venture

Doris Humphrey as the Matriarch in *With My Red Fires*

into what later became the popular style of mixed media. She continued to choreograph, for the Limón co. and also for her students at Connecticut College and the Juilliard S., until the time of her death.

Along with GRAHAM, Doris Humphrey created the form known as the American MODERN DANCE. Her greatest contribution came from her thought of dance as existing in an arc between two deaths: the body lying prone or standing firmly erect – both stable, both lacking in theatrical excitement. Kinetic interest was stirred when the body, venturing from its position of stability, encountered the pull of gravity, defied it, and triumphantly reclaimed its equilibrium. The theory of 'fall and recover', as it was called, was at once a pure movement idea and a dramatic concept. The threat motivated action that engendered designs in space and time; it also symbolized the eternal conflict between man's longing for security and his desire to risk the dangers of the unknown. In Humphrey choreography, he always dared the dangerous adventure and always emerged victorious. SJC
See Humphrey, *The Art of Making Dances* (New York 1959); her unfinished autobiography ed. and completed by Selma Jeanne Cohen in *Doris Humphrey: An Artist First* (Middletown, CT, 1972); 'New Dance', *Dance Perspectives* No. 25 (New York)

Hungary. Ballet was first seen in Hungary in the mid-18th c. at the court of Prince Esterházy, where Franz Josef Haydn regularly conducted the orchestra. NOVERRE's Vienna dancers performed at Fertőd 1772, VIGANÒ and his wife Maria Medina danced 1794 and 1797. After 1810 these gorgeous festivities were discontinued but pantomimes, harlequinades, etc., are recorded as having been shown in major Hungarian towns, incl. Pest, before that date. In the early decades of the 19th c. several Hungarian folk-dance 'societies' toured the European capitals with tremendous success. After the opening of the NT in Pest (1837) the first ballet produced was *La Fille Mal Gardée* (1839); ch. János Kolosánszky; mus. Ferenc Kaczér). CERRITO and SAINT-LÉON danced ONDINE 1846, GISELLE was staged 1847, and also danced by MAYWOOD (revived 1855 and 1879); GRAHN danced PÉRI 1851, M. and P. TAGLIONI were guests 1853. The first and greatest Hungarian prima ballerina of the c. was Emilia Aranyváry (active 1852–9). A very mediocre choreographer, Frigyes Campilli, headed the co. for 40 years (until 1886), mounting, e.g. ESMERALDA (1856), COPPÉLIA (1877), etc.

The co. of the Budapest OH (opened 1884 with one male dancer) danced Cézár Smeraldi's *Excelsior* (1887) and *Puppenfee* (1888); Lajos Mazzantini created ballets to music by Hungarian composers (Jenő Sztojanovits's *Csárdás* (1890), Károly Szabados's *Viora* (1891)). After the guest perfs of the Maryinsky Co. 1898 and 1901, Miklós Guerra (active 1902–14) was invited to produce ballets that incl. *The Dwarf Grenadier* (1903; mus. Adolf Szikla), *Pierrette's Veil* (1910; mus. Ernő Dohnányi), and *Prometheus* (1913; mus. Ludwig van Beethoven) with such solo dancers as Anna Pallai, Emilia Nirschy, and NÁDASI. Ede Brada staged WOODEN PRINCE 1917; MILLOSS did important work. HARANGOZÓ, Nádasi, and stage designer and director Gusztáv Oláh really built the national ballet. Harangozó's *Scene in the Csárdas* (1936; mus. Jenő Hubay) was seminal. Jan Cieplinski's best work then was *Bolero* (1943; mus. RAVEL). Nádasi began thorough classical training in the Budapest OS 1937. After World War II Harangozó staged MIRACULOUS MANDARIN, MISCHIEVOUS STUDENTS, etc. Cieplinski staged APRÈS-MIDI D'UN FAUNE (1948), and Ernő Vashegyi danced his own *Petrushka* (1949).

A new era started with the adoption of Soviet ballets incl. works by VAINONEN, MESSERER, ANISIMOVA, L. LAVROVSKY, KASATKINA, and VASILYOV. Harangozó continued his creative work by staging KERCHIEF (1951), *Coppélia* (1953), and *Ludas Matyi* (1960). Vashegyi staged *Bihari's Song* (1954;

mus. Jenő Kenessey), a blend of authentic Hungarian folk dance and classical ballet. ECK staged seven ballets 1959–69 incl. versions of SACRE DU PRINTEMPS and ONDINE. SEREGI created SPARTACUS, MIRACULOUS MANDARIN and WOODEN PRINCE, and staged other works. Sándor Barkóczy's works included *Classical Symphony* (1966; mus. PROKOFIEV). Antal Fodor's ballets incl. *Violin Concerto in E Major* (1971; mus. Johann Sebastian Bach) and *Metamorphoses* (1975; mus. Claudio Monteverdi). The principal dancers of the 1960s incl. LAKATOS, KUN, OROSZ, SZUMRÁK, FÜLÖP, RÓNA, DÓZSA, and HAVAS. ASHTON'S FILLE MAL GARDÉE was staged 1971, followed by Danish and French works.

The Budapest co. has toured abroad, visiting Bayreuth, Florence, various cities in Socialist countries, Turin, Helsinki, Edinburgh, Paris, Stockholm, many other European cities, and Cairo.

Another important ballet centre has been the NT at Pécs, where Eck in 1960 formed a young co. (known abroad as B. Sopianae) from a very talented class of the State B. Inst. and began creating works modern in form and message, devoted mainly to the problems of youth. Among his dancers Sándor Tóth was the first to make a ballet, *What is Under Your Hat?* (1964; mus. József Kinczes), revealing a penchant for comedy. In the late 1960s Eck created full-length ballets e.g. *Don Juan* (1966; mus. Christoph Willibald Gluck). Tóth took over the direction of the co. 1968 when Eck became artistic director. Pécs traditions of innovation have continued in such works as Tóth's miniature ballets and three symphonic ballets to Gustav Mahler's music (1974). With Eck he composed ballets to BARTÓK'S *Microcosmos* in a multigenre form for young audiences. He also choreographed *Verklärte Nacht* (mus. Arnold Schönberg) and a ballet-thriller *Keyholes* (both 1976). The co., about 35 strong, regularly tours the country with educational ballet programs performed in villages. Since 1961 its foreign tours have covered most of Europe, the USSR, some Arab countries, the USA, India, and Sri Lanka.

The Association of Hungarian Dance Artists has since 1954 united the profession, with about 200 members in sections for ballet, folk dance, teachers, and theoreticians. The State B. Inst. has trained about 15 dancers a year since its foundation in 1950, employing the VAGANOVA method combined with Nádasi's method. Directors have been Gyula Lőrinc, Hedvig Hidas, and (from 1972) Kun. GPD

See György Lőrinc (ed.), tr. G. P. Dienes, E. Rácz, and E. West, *The Budapest Ballet* (Budapest 1971)

Hurry, Leslie, b. London, 1909. English painter in the Surrealist-romantic style. HELPMANN, impressed by his paintings, invited him to design HAMLET, his first stage work, which launched him on a distinguished career as a designer for the legitimate theatre and opera. He designed SWAN LAKE for SWB in 1943, redesigned it 1952 and 1965; also *Scherzi delle Sorte* (ch. David Paltenghi) for BR (1951). MC

I

Icare (*Icarus*), ballet, ch. LIFAR; rhythms Lifar, orchestration Georges Szyfer; sc./c. Paul Larthe. Paris O., 9 July 1935; revived B. Russe de Monte Carlo, sc./c. BERMAN, 1938; revived Paris O., 5 Dec 1962, sc/c. PICASSO; dan. LABIS. The story of the Greek myth of Daedalus and Icarus, basically a long solo for Lifar as Icarus. M-FC

Icarus, modern dance work, ch. HOVING; mus. Chin-Ichi Matushita. New York, YM-YWHA 92nd St, 5 Apr 1964; dan. Hoving, Chase Robinson, Patricia Christopher. The classical myth is here seen both as a fall from a too-audacious flight and as an emotional disaster for a young man soaring beyond his capabilities. DM

Ice Dance. It is not recorded if Lydwina of Schiedam in Holland was performing a dance step on the ice when she sustained the fatal accident that led to her exalted position as Patron Saint of Skaters, but a report does exist of Samuel Pepys dancing on the ice with Nell Gwyn on the Thames during the Great Frost of 1683; some 300 years later.

Ice Dance now has the status of an Olympic event and since those early days it has developed in line with the social dances of the age. Steps and routines are closely related to the ballroom and this shielded them from other influences until ballroom dancing itself began to take in ideas from classical ballet. Even Russian skaters, who were to be the first to show this influence on the ice, relied heavily on ballroom and folk dance. One other influence has been the popular dance hall through commercial ice shows and films such as those of Sonja Henie, but in the early days it was slight, forming a framework for conventional skating rather than truly influencing it. Since 1950 the influence has been more imaginative and by the 1976 Olympic Games had reached a peak of invention.

Pair Skating as a competitive event has none of the restrictions of turns, lifts, and jumps that root Ice Dance firmly in the ballroom and this has led to greater freedom of expression and innovation. The arrival of the great Russian skaters, Oleg and Lyudmila Protopopov, in the World Championships in 1962, brought the first clear indication of a profound classical ballet influence. Their training in the Russian classical school helped produce for the first time a program conceived as an artistic entity. Relying on beautiful *adage* and big Russian lifts, they established firmly the importance of the interpretative element in skating. Their influence persuaded the public to expect more than technique and paved the way for the next creative thrust, which came in the individual free-skating event.

The culmination of this blending of technical brilliance and artistic expression came in 1976 when the British Champion, John Curry, won the European, World, and Olympic titles. From his earliest competitions he developed a concept of presentation derived almost totally from classical ballet. The choice of music became an integral part of the composition of the program, together with choreography of wit and intelligence. To sensitive interpretation he added quite recognizable ballet steps adapted to the limitations of the ice: speed, boots, and backward take-offs for the big jumps. Small attitude turns, simple *assemblés*, single *cabrioles*, and a variety of small beats were used in his programs, together with balletic placement and line. Perhaps the most important innovation was a wholly balletic approach to *port de bras*. This alone may prove to be the biggest contribution ballet has made to increasing the potential of skating as an interpretative medium. After his perf. at the Madison Square Garden, New York, Nov 1976, in THARP choreography, the world premiere of Curry's Theatre of Skating took place on 27 Dec 1976 at the Cambridge T., London, with special solo sequences for Curry choreographed by DARRELL and MACMILLAN. CD

Ice Maiden (*Ledyanaya Deva*), ballet, 3 acts, 5 scenes, ch./lib. F. LOPUKHOV; mus. Edvard Grieg arr. ASAFYEV; sc. Aleksandr Golovin. Leningrad, State T. of O. and B., 4 Apr 1927; dan. Olga Mungalova (title role); GUSEV (Asak); YERMOLAYEV (Winter Bird). Gusev choreographed a new version of this work, sc. V. Leventhal, Novosibirsk OH, 29 Dec 1964. Asak, a Norwegian village youth, sees a vision of the Ice Maiden in winter. In the spring, he meets Solveig in the woods, and falls in love with her. As the village wedding festivities are going on she disappears. He looks for her in the woods where they met, but finds that she is really the Ice Maiden. Winter has frozen everything in the woods and Asak dies surrounded by a circle of Ice Maidens. An earlier version was called *Solveig* (ch. P. Petrov, 1922). NR
See F. Lopukhov, *Sixty Years in Ballet* (Leningrad 1966); Yuri Slonimsky, *Sovietsky Balet* (Leningrad 1950); Yuri Slonimsky, 'About the Creation of *Ice Maiden*' in *Ice Maiden* (Leningrad 1936); booklet published by State Kirov Theatre

Idzikowski, Stanislas, b. Warsaw, 1894; d. London, 1977. Polish dancer and teacher. Studied with CECCHETTI, debut Empire T., London. Joined DIAGHILEV 1914, left 1926 but rejoined 1928. Created the Snob in BOUTIQUE FANTASQUE and the Dandy in TRICORNE. Also danced many of NIJINSKY's famous roles. Danced with Vic-Wells B. 1933, creating principal role in RENDEZVOUS. Taught for many years at his own studio in London (with Madame Evina his faithful pianist) and also worked for the RAD. After the death of Evina he retired from teaching. He was a very tiny dancer with prodigious elevation and technique, more suited to *demi-caractère* roles, like those created for him by MASSINE, than for romantic ones. He was co-author with BEAUMONT of *A Manual of the Theory and Practice of Classical Theatrical Dancing* (London 1922; new ed. 1940; New York 1975). MC

Illuminations, dramatic ballet, 1 act, ch. ASHTON; mus. Benjamin Britten (*Les Illuminations* song cycle); lib. Arthur Rimbaud's prose poems of the same name; sc./c. BEATON. NYCC, NYCB, 2 Mar 1950; dan. MAGALLANES, LECLERCQ, HAYDEN, Robert Barnett. The ballet depicts episodes from Rimbaud's life as performed by a troupe of pierrots. The songs are sung from the pit. FM

Imago, modern dance work, ch./mus./sc. NIKOLAIS. West Hartford, CT, 24 Feb 1963; dan. LOUIS, Gladys Bailin, Bill Frank, LAMHUT, Peggy Barclay, Albert Reid, Raymond Broussard, Roger Rowell. A full-length work in which strange quasi-human figures portray a society removed from our own but having recognizable correspondences. DM

Inbal Dance Theatre (Tel Aviv, Israel) was founded by Sara Levi-Tanai, choreographer and songwriter, in 1949. She combined the inherent talents of its Yemenite members, diverse Jewish traditional and poetic sources, and the life, art, and music of present-day Israel to create unusually perceptive choreographic visions, which are sung, spoken, and danced. In 1951, the still untrained Inbal members, headed by Margalit Oved, fascinated ROBBINS by their ability to express an age-old yearning for God, the land, and redemption, together with the earthy vitality of the pioneers. Trained by SOKOLOW and others, Inbal has toured widely since 1957. NM

Indes Galantes, Les (*The Gallant Indians*), *opéra-ballet*, prologue and 3 *entrées*, ch./mus. J.-P. RAMEAU; lib. Louis Fuzelier; sc. Giovanni-Niccolò Servandoni. Paris O., 23 Aug 1735. The theme is the universal appeal of love, expounded by the three *entrées*: *Le Turc Généreux*, *Les Incas de Peru*, and *Les Fleurs*. A fourth, *Les Sauvages*, was added 1736 (the first perf. had only the prologue and first 2 *entrées*). SALLÉ shone particularly in *Les Fleurs*. The work left the repertory 1773; revived with acclamation Paris O. (staged H. LANDER: prologue ch. AVELINE, sc. Jacques Dupont; 1st *entrée* ch. Aveline, sc. Georges Wakhevitch; 2nd *entrée* ch. LIFAR, sc. CARZOU; 3rd *entrée* ch. Lander, sc. Maurice Moulène and Raymond Fost; 4th *entrée* ch. Lifar, sc. Roger Chapelain-

Above: Interplay, ABT, CG, 1946

Below: The Invitation, with SEYMOUR as the Young Girl, DOYLE as the Husband, and HEATON as the Wife

Midy; epilogue ch. Lifar) 18 June 1952; dan. VYROUBOVA, DARSONVAL, Christiane Vaussard, DAYDÉ, Micheline Bardin, Lifar, KALIOUJNY, RENAULT. Some of the original splendour was recaptured. M-FC

India *see* ASIA

Inglesby [Kimberley], Mona, b. London, 1918. English dancer, choreographer, and co. director. Studied with CRASKE, RAMBERT, and EGOROVA and danced with BR, dancing Papillon in CARNAVAL (of which Rambert has a fragment of film). In 1940 founded own co. International B. and choreographed, notably *Endymion*, also a danced version of the morality play *Everyman*. She danced all the major classical roles with impeccable technique but little expression. Retired 1953 when the co. disbanded. MC

Initialen RBME, ballet, 1 act, ch. CRANKO; mus. Johannes Brahms (Concerto for Piano and Orchestra No. 2 in B Major, Op. 83); sc./c. ROSE. Stuttgart, Stuttgart B., 19 Jan 1973; dan. CRAGUN, KEIL, HAYDÉE, MADSEN. Cranko's acknowledgment of his love for the four principal dancers of his Stuttgart co. The initials are those of their Christian names. MC

Intermezzo, ballet, ch. FELD; mus. Johannes Brahms; c. Stanley Simmons. Spoleto, T. Nuovo, American B. Co., 29 June 1969. A plotless, romantic ballet to piano music by Brahms (the Opus 117 and 118 Intermezzos and some of the Opus 39 waltzes). Revived ABT and NB of Canada 1972; FELD B. 1974; Stuttgart B. 1975. FM

International Ballet *see* INGLESBY, Mona

International Council for Dance *see* CONSEIL INTERNATIONAL DE LA DANSE

Interplay, ballet, 4 movements, ch. ROBBINS; mus. Morton Gould; sc. Carl Kent. New York, Ziegfeld T., Billy Rose's *Concert Varieties*, 1 June 1945; dan. KRIZA, Janet Reed, Robbins. NY Met, ABT, 17 Oct 1945; sc. O. SMITH; c. Irene Sharaff; dan. Kriza, Reed, H. LANG. A plotless work to a lively contemporary score. Revived NYCB 1952. FM

In the Night, ballet, ch. ROBBINS; mus. Frédéric Chopin; c. Joe Eula; ltg Thomas Skelton. NYST, NYCB, 29 Jan 1970; dan. MAZZO, A. BLUM, VERDY, MARTINS, MCBRIDE, MONCION. A series of three dramatic *pas de deux* and a finale for all six dancers to four Chopin Nocturnes. Revived London, CG, RB, 10 Oct 1973; c. DOWELL. FM

Intime Briefe (*Intimate Letters*), ballet, ch. FURTWÄNGLER; mus. Leoš Janáček; c. Hans Anschütz. Cologne, 21 Apr 1968; dan. CARDÚS, BAUMANN, Hella Troester, Jonathan Watts. A psychological ballet inspired by the love letters of Janáček. GBLW

Invitation, The, ballet, 5 scenes, ch./lib. MacMillan; mus. Matyas Seiber; sc./c. Georgiadis. Oxford, New T., RB touring co., 10 Nov 1960; dan. Seymour, Gable, Heaton, Doyle. Revived CG, RB, 30 Dec 1960. Based on two novels, Beatriz Guido's *The House of the Angel* and Colette's *Le Blé en Herbe*. In a hothouse atmosphere of a family party two rapes are committed. A young girl and her cousin, just beginning to think of love, are seduced by an unhappy married couple. The boy matures from the experience; the girl, who suffers brutal handling from the husband, will obviously shrink into frigid spinsterhood. (The period is pre-World War I.) MC

Iran. In the early 1950s an American, Nila Cram-Cook, founded a small group to perform abroad using mostly Persian dance forms but to Western music. In 1958 the Minister for Culture requested Nejad and Aida Ahmadzadeh to open a ballet acad. and with help from Dollar and then with de Valois as dance adviser the Iranian NB quickly developed. In 1960–2 Miro Zolan and his wife Sandra Vane directed the co., followed by Richard Brown and Marion English, and 1965–71 Robert de Warren. In 1971, when de Warren devoted himself full-time (until 1976) to studying and developing the national dances of the country, Aida Ahmadzadeh took over the administration, succeeded in 1976 by Ali Pourfarrokh, an Iranian who had worked for some 15 years in the USA.

The co. performs in the Rudaki Hall OH, Teheran (built 1967) and in 1977 consisted of 45 dancers, backed by a symphony orchestra. The repertory consists of classical and contemporary works. Heaton staged Giselle 1970, Coppélia 1971; in 1970–1 Chabukiani mounted Swan Lake. In 1967 Empress Farah ordered the creation of a national organization to study, record, and produce for the stage the traditional dances of the country which, thanks largely to the work of de Warren, became the Mahalli Dancers of Iran; they are considered as the Court Ballet, have their own college, and have toured widely abroad as ambassadors of the folk art of their country. MC

Ireland. The Irish B. Co. was formed Sept 1973, as the national ballet of Ireland, with the aid of government money, and first performed at the Cork OH, 29 Jan 1974. This was the direct outcome of over 20 years' work by the teacher and choreographer Joan Denise Moriarty. Moriarty studied in London with Judith Espinosa and Rambert. In 1945 she set up a school of ballet in Cork, from which emerged the Cork B. Co. which gave its first perf. at the Cork OH June 1947 and held annual seasons thereafter, usually with guest artists. The Cork B. Co. is semi-professional, the Irish B. Co. fully professional, although small. Based on Cork, it tours widely and performs regularly in Dublin. Moriarty is artistic director; the first artistic adviser was the Israeli-born dancer and choreographer Domi Reiter-Soffer. MC

Irving, Robert, b. Winchester, 1913. English conductor. Musical director of RB 1949–58 and of NYCB from 1958 on. Also conducts for the Graham co. One of the finest contemporary ballet conductors. DH

Israel. In the Tel Aviv of the 1920s two main dance currents could be seen. First, a modern European stream, represented by Baruch Agadati's Chagall-like solo character dances and by Margalit Ornstein, who started the first dance studio and worked toward an aesthetic consciousness and natural truth of movement. Second, classical ballet as interpreted by Rina Nikova with the first Palestine O. Co. and at her studio.

With the large waves of Jewish immigration from Europe (1933–48) both these trends reached other cities as many of the teachers set up studios and formed short-lived dance groups. The classical current was opposed, quite groundlessly, on the score that this style was unsuited to the climate and the country's pioneering spirit. The creative 'moderns' won the day, mainly owing to Gertrud Kraus's exciting solo recitals and perfs with her group at the Folk O. and with the Palestine Symphony; inspired perfs acclaimed for their imaginative ideas and wide range of expression.

Alongside European dance themes of a general nature, a national style began to evolve, drawing on biblical subjects, and Near Eastern, and Eastern European Jewish traditions. Its first exponent was Nikova, surprisingly, who interpreted these themes with Yemenite dancers forming the Biblical B. in 1933. No less original was the Haifa-born Yardena Cohen's attempt to formulate Hebrew dance from Eastern music, nature, and archaeological remains.

The natural element in which to develop this current was obviously the Kibbutzim, out of whose vigorous spirit and new life style emerged the significant 'Masechet' form (recitations, song, and dances by groups and soloists) to celebrate ancient holidays and recent celebrations. The highly criticized but widespread and successful Folk Dance Movement also appeared on the scene at this time. In style, form, spirit, and content the third current achieved its foremost artistic fulfilment in the work of Sara Levi-Tanai with her Inbal Dance T.

In the 1950s, simultaneously with the work of Inbal, a fourth current could be felt in the marked infiltration of American Modern Dance. This became evident when the American-born and trained Rina Shaham and Rena Gluck settled in Israel (1951, 1954) and taught, danced, choreographed, and formed small groups with other dancers. Contributing greatly to this development were the frequent visits of Sokolow from 1953 onward. Her authoritative and serious teaching and the deeply moving work created for her Israeli group, The Lyric T. (1962–4) and other groups, left a firm imprint.

However, the country's reduced economic circumstances cut short the life of all such group efforts.

Fortunately, the former patron of GRAHAM, Bat Sheva [Bethsabe] de Rothschild, settled in Israel and established the BATSHEVA DANCE CO. (1964). Later she established the BAT DOR DANCE CO. (1968). Higher professional standards of choreography and performance were the outcome. Repertoires were mainly the work of Americans, which somewhat diminished the role of the Israeli choreographers. It was thus left to the music, the decor, and the dancers' interpretations to supply the Israeli character.

The American concern for disciplined technique was also to be the salvation of classical ballet in Israel. In 1967, Berta Yampolsky and Hillel Markman founded the ISRAEL CLASSICAL B. CO. Jeannette Ordman and Yvonne Narunsky introduced the English RAD syllabus. Lia Schubert opened her Russian-orientated Haifa Dance Centre in 1969 and in 1975 formed her Piccolo B.

In addition, there are the rarely seen but original chamber choreographies of Noa Eshkol. There are now some 10,000 students working in various techniques, some major and minor cos (including Judith Arnon's Kibbutz Co. and Dance Centre), the Israel Research Centre of Ethnic Dance (1972), and the Movement Notation Centre (1973). Financial support is given by various government and public funds. NM

Israel Classical Ballet, The. Founded by Berta Yampolsky and Hillel Markman 1967, the co. began to flourish when the Ministry of Absorption in 1973 enabled 15 American Jewish dancers to join the co. The results were a good ballet co. and a devoted public. The repertoire incl. established favourites like the BLUEBIRD and FLOWER FESTIVAL AT GENZANO *pas de deux*, also SERENADE (staged by NEARY), BALANCHINE'S MINKUS *pas de trois*, the *pas de deux* from AGON, and works by CHARRAT. Local choreographers incl. Berta Yampolsky, Gene Hill-Sagan, and Domi Reiter-Soffer. NM

Istomina, Avdotia, b. St Petersburg, 1799; d. St Petersburg, 1848. Russian dancer. Graduated St Petersburg TS 1815. Debut as Galatée in DIDELOT'S *Acis et Galatée* (mus. Catterino Cavos); occupied leading position in Bolshoy T., performing leading roles in most of Didelot's ballets, especially *Zéphire et Flore*. Inspired Aleksandr Pushkin's famous lines about her in *Eugene Onegin*. Excellent technique for her time with outstanding speed, musicality, and dramatic impact. She frequently appeared in dramas, comedies, and vaudevilles. Pushkin conceived the libretto for the ballet *Les Deux Danseuses* with her in mind, mentioning a famous duel fought over her (in 1817). About 1830 she retired from dancing, moving to mimed roles. She m. dramatic actor Pavel Ekunin. Died of cholera. NR

See N. Eliash, *Avdotia Istomina* (Leningrad 1971); Yuri Slonimsky, *Pushkin's Ballet Lines* (Leningrad 1974); A. A. Pleshcheyev, *Pod Seniu Kulis* (*In the Shadow of the Wings*), in Russian (Paris 1936)

Italy. Although the art of ballet traces its origins from Italy, it has had a chequered history in the country of its birth. The early spectacles (there are records of a *balletto conviviale* staged by Bergonzio di Botta at Tortona in 1489) were to inspire the BALLET DE COUR which flourished in France. The emergence of the 'rival' art of opera was totally to overshadow ballet in the Italian theatres but Italy made vital contributions, especially in the development of technique in the 19th c. (Significantly, the first dance treatises were published in Italy beginning with *De Arte Saltandi et Choreas Ducendi* by Domenico da Piacenza, or Ferrara, *c.* 1416). There was dance activity at all the courts and subsequently the theatres during the 17th and 18th centuries. During that period a 'European community' still existed *de facto* in the artistic world. While ANGIOLINI by no means confined his activities to Italy, GALEOTTI worked mostly in Copenhagen.

The Sc. T. can trace two centuries of ballet history from its opening in Milan 1778. The engagement of VIGANÒ as ballet master from 1812 until his death was largely responsible for its emergence as a prominent centre. In 1813 the 'Imperial Acad. of Dancing', attached to the Sc., was opened and in 1837 BLASIS became director. Viganò's works were produced all over Italy – Venice, Padua, Rome – and there are written testimonies to his greatness although none of his ballets survived. The publications of Blasis are still available and testify to the excellence of the training at the Sc. while his travels indicate how many theatres throughout Italy were still available to dancers and choreographers: CERRITO, for example, began her career in Naples which, like Milan, Turin, Venice, and other cities still has its famous theatre, the T. San Carlo, with school attached, but no record of creativity.

ZUCCHI and LEGNANI exerted their greatest influence in Russia. The creative impulse seemed to have deserted Italy. At the Sc., EXCELSIOR and other MANZOTTI works typified the subjugation of choreography to scenic effects and reflected the taste of the public. Not surprisingly, the great dancers of the era spent much time abroad. In the 1920s the offerings of the DIAGHILEV B. Russes were not appreciated. CECCHETTI returned to the Sc. in 1925 at age 75, too old to accomplish much-needed reforms although some of his pupils, notably RADICE, went on to do good work.

Since the late 1950s, individual dancers of talent have emerged to fame in Italy and abroad, incl. FRACCI, TERABUST, COSI, BORTOLUZZI, and many foreign cos have visited Italy but usually too briefly to have much influence. The opera houses with a sufficiently large ballet co. (Milan, Rome, Naples, and Palermo) use the dancers in the operas and incl. a couple of ballet programs in their subscription seasons. Some other opera houses (Venice, Turin, Florence) have a small co. of their own for use in the operas which they augment when necessary: in the case of Florence during the Maggio Musicale Fiorentino (Florence Musical May) fest. in particular.

Others such as those on the ATER circuit have no co. of their own but incl. one or two programs by visiting cos. Only Milan, Rome, Naples, and Palermo retain a school attached to the theatre and only the Sc. holds short independent ballet seasons (since 1965). A number of important perfs have also been given at the many summer fests such as the Nervi International B. Fest. (founded 1955 by Mario Porcile), the Fest. dei Due Mondi at Spoleto, in Florence, and at Verona, in both the Arena and the Roman T.

Italy's dance heritage sometimes seems more of a burden than an advantage: authorities seem reluctant to admit the necessity of a new start. In recent decades Italy has produced no choreographer of note, nor is there a first-class *corps de ballet* at any of the opera houses. Contemporary dance writings have seldom been translated into Italian and dance criticism too often reflects the insularity of the writers. However, if more and harder work is found for the dancers and a more demanding repertory established, Italy may soon regain a footing in the dance world. FP/MC

See Luigi Rossi, *Il Ballo alla Scala (1778–1970)* (Milan 1972); Alberto Testa, *Discorso sulla Danza e sul Balletto* (Rome 1970); Raffaele Carrieri, *La Danza in Italia 1500–1900* (Milan 1946) mainly pictorial; 'Italia – II. Balletto', *Enciclopedia dello Spettacolo* (Rome 1954–66 in 10 vols)

Ivanov, Lev, b. Moscow, 1834; d. St Petersburg, 1901. Russian dancer, choreographer, and teacher. Began training at Moscow TS, transferred to St Petersburg. Pupil of Emile Gredlu, Jean Petipa and others. While at school, attracted attention not only because of his dancing talents, but also his phenomenal musicality and musical memory. Debut in a *pas de deux*, 1850, aged 16. Graduated 1852 into the *corps de ballet*, in spite of obviously exceptional talents, and remained there for six years, never missing a single rehearsal and learning both the music and choreography of the entire current repertory. In 1858, his studious application paid off when he replaced M. PETIPA both as Hans the Postman in SAINT-LÉON's *La Vivandière* (partnering Anna Prikhunova) with one rehearsal on the day of the perf., and as Phoebus in ESMERALDA without any rehearsal at all. He was then awarded such roles as COLAS and others much less suitable for his lyric qualities. Also in 1858, he began teaching at the St Petersburg TS at a tiny remuneration despite repeated petitions to the Directors of the Imperial Theatres. In 1869, when Petipa replaced Saint-Léon as head of the St Petersburg B., Ivanov received the long overdue promotion to *premier danseur* but only a slight increase in salary.

He danced both classical and character roles. As a classical dancer, he was soon eclipsed by P. GERDT and passed on to mime roles, retiring in 1893.

His name survives in the history of dance as a brilliant choreographer, valued only by posterity. No more assertive in this field than as a dancer, he was first appointed *régisseur* of ballet 1882, and then second ballet master 1885 at Petipa's request. In this position, Ivanov revived FILLE MAL GARDÉE, and created TULIP OF HAARLEM and 1-act trifles such as *The Enchanted Forest* (1887). His first original choreography in 1890 was the Polovtsian Dances from PRINCE IGOR. So vivid was his realization of the music that years later FOKINE used some of Ivanov's work in his own version.

Ivanov choreographed NUTCRACKER (1892) to a detailed scenario prepared by Petipa who was prevented by illness from implementing his own concepts. His great contribution to choreography was in the lakeside scenes of SWAN LAKE. Neither the public nor the press appreciated his efforts. Still in Petipa's shadow, he died in penniless obscurity. NR

See Yuri Slonimsky, tr. Anatole Chujoy, 'Writings on Lev Ivanov' in *Dance Perspectives*, No. 2 (New York 1959); contains list of ballets staged by Ivanov in St Petersburg; Natalia Roslavleva, 'The Ballets of Ivanov', Ch. 6 in *Era of the Russian Ballet* (New York and London 1966)

Ivan the Terrible (*Ivan Grozny*), ballet, 2 acts, ch./lib. GRIGOROVICH; mus. PROKOFIEV (for film, *Ivan Grozny*, with some additions) arr. Mikhail Chulaki; sc. VIRSALADZE. Moscow, Bolshoy T., 20 Feb 1975; dan. VLADIMIROV (title role), N. BESSMERTNOVA (Tsarina Anastasia), Boris Akimov (Prince Kurbsky). VASILIEV later alternated in title role. Revived Paris OB, 14 Oct 1976. A powerful choreographic portrayal of the controversial personality of Ivan IV, a series of tableaux contrasting the gradual disintegration of the awe-inspiring Tsar with the gentle, loving Anastasia.

The same music has been used for the ballet *Tsar Boris*, after Aleksandr Pushkin's *Boris Godunov*; ch. Nikolay Boyarchikov. Perm, Tchaikovsky T. of O. and B., 27 Mar 1975. NR

Ivesiana, ballet, 6 episodes, ch. BALANCHINE; mus. Charles Ives; ltg ROSENTHAL. NYCC, NYCB, 14 Sept 1954; dan. Janet Reed, MONCION, WILDE, D'AMBOISE, KENT, BOLENDER. A set of short dramatic dances based on richly evocative scores – the well-known piece, 'The Unanswered Question,' among them. Revised version 1961, in 4 episodes. FM

Izmailova, Galiya, b. Tashkent, 1923. Soviet dancer and choreographer. Studied Tashkent Choreographic S. under the Leningrad teacher, Evgenia Obukhova, 1935–41. Tashkent Navoï T. of O. and B. 1941. In 1958 also graduated from the Producers' Faculty of Tashkent T. and Arts Inst. and started choreographing ballets: *Dream* (1960), *Bolero* and *Schéhérazade* (1964), *Legend of Cashmere* (1961), etc. Danced classical roles, but particularly known for parts in national ballets. Has vast repertoire of dances of all nations; has toured worldwide. People's Artist, USSR. NR

J

Jacobsen, Palle, b. Copenhagen, 1940. Danish dancer and choreographer. Entered RDBS 1952, but left 1957 to join various Danish and European cos. Soloist Johannesburg B. 1960–7. Soloist RDB 1967. Teacher at RDBS from 1972. Has danced all the great classic parts, SIEGFRIED to ALBRECHT, and Prince DÉSIRÉ in ÉTUDES. Choreographed *Albinoni* (1973), *The Blue Eyes* (RDB, 1975). SKJ

Jacobson, Leonid *see* YACOBSON

Jacob's Pillow, Becket, MA, is the home of the world-renowned Jacob's Pillow Dance Fest. and the SHAWN T. The name derives from a large boulder on a farm near a mountainous road called Jacob's Ladder. The 150-acre farm, purchased in 1930 by Shawn as a retreat, subsequently became a rehearsal place for the last of the DENISHAWN Dancers (1931) and then Shawn's Men Dancers. In 1940 Mary Washington Ball leased the property, started a school, and invited dancers to perform in varied styles, a policy continued to this day. In summer 1941 MARKOVA and DOLIN rented the farm, continuing the fest. and the school, primarily with members of the newly formed ABT. There, during the summer, TUDOR created PILLAR OF FIRE. In autumn 1941 a group of Massachusetts residents bought the farm from Shawn and the Jacob's Pillow Dance Fest. was incorporated as an educational, artistic, and non-profit organization, and Shawn became director. Under Shawn Jacob's Pillow became the first dance fest. in the USA, and it remains a unique institution. The Shawn T. was built 1942 by architect Joseph Franz. It has been enlarged over the years and at present the seating capacity is 618. This is the first theatre in the western hemisphere with a stage built exclusively for dance. Shawn conceived the dance perfs as a part of the necessary process for the students at the school, his 'University of the Dance'. For years the fest. was the only dance arena that welcomed equally ballet, modern, and ethnic dance. Over 300 choreographic works have been premiered at Jacob's Pillow and many US debuts have occurred there, notably Ten Leading Dancers from RDB 1955, BR 1959, the Western TB 1963, the NDT 1965, and the new JOFFREY Co., now CCJB, 1965. After Shawn's death the fest. was directed by John Christian (1972), TERRY (1973), Charles Reinhart (1974), and Norman Walker (from 1975). KC

James, the unhappy hero of SYLPHIDE

Jamison, Judith, b. Philadelphia, 1943. American dancer. Studied in Philadelphia with the Judimar S. and with J. JONES. New York debut as guest artist with ABT in DE MILLE's *The Four Marys* (1964). Has also danced with the HARKNESS B. and RSB. Soloist since 1965 with AILEY's co. Notable for her statuesque presence, faultless musicality, and the passionate intensity of her portrayals, which can transform even inferior choreography (e.g. Ailey's *Cry*). She m. the Puerto Rican dancer Miguel Godreau. DV

Japan. The Japanese zest and aptitude for acquiring 'things Western' are conspicuously exemplified by the growth of ballet in Japan. It had taken root by the 1930s; there were visits by foreign cos and soloists and ballet schools began to be established. Since 1945 the development has been prodigious, most of it in Tokyo, where, by 1975, there were eight reputable cos, the Tokyo, Komaki, Matsuyama, Tani, Maki Asami, Star Dancers, Tokyo City, and Tomoi, and where the ballet schools are legion. Only one of the cos, however, the Tokyo B., performs often and most of the others really amount to intermittent assemblies of dancers either for a very brief season or an isolated gala. The Tokyo B. (till recently the Tchaikovsky Memorial B.) has a permanent strength of 75 (some 20 men among them) and a record of many perfs, particularly of the classics, in Tokyo, the Japanese regions, and abroad. It was formed in 1964 by Tadatsugu Sasaki, a young, dynamic impresario widely interested in the performing arts. Its tours have included the USSR and W. Europe (chiefly France but also, in 1975, Britain). Exceptional in its professionalism, it has, however, like all the other Japanese cos, looked mainly to the USSR for its training, repertory, and general notions of ballet. More Soviet cos and 'concert pairs' come to Japan in a year than are seen in the USA or Britain in a decade. Most of the stars of the Bolshoy and Kirov cos have danced with the Tokyo B. MESSERER and other leading Soviet ballet masters have produced the classics for it. Non-Russian ballerinas, e.g., FONTEYN, and cos have also visited Japan, but much less abundantly. It is, again, characteristic that neither the Tokyo B. nor any other has so far developed any significant choreography of its own; the only notable, though still minor, supplement to the Soviet choreographic influence has been the French one. Leading dancers with Tokyo B. have incl. the ballerinas Chie Abe (largely trained in Paris), Kaoru Inoue, Yukiko Yasuda, Yumeko Wainai, and among the men, Hideteru Kitahara (the co.'s artistic director) and Chikahisa Natsuyama. But more remarkable than any of its stars is the co.'s generally high standard, in a style that blends the diminutive, stocky Japanese physique with Russian *bravura*. A fine, freelance ballerina is Yoko Morishita. The Matsuyama Co. is noteworthy for its association with Communist China, but it is like the rest in its Soviet Russian style, training, and approach to ballet. For the traditional dance theatre of Japan *see* ASIA. JM

Jaques-Dalcroze, Emil(e) *see* DALCROZE

Jardin aux Lilas (*Lilac Garden*), ballet, 1 act, ch./lib. TUDOR; mus. Ernest Chausson (*Poème*); sc./c. Hugh Stevenson. London, Mercury T., BR, 26 Jan 1936; dan. Maude LLOYD, VAN PRAAGH, LAING, Tudor. Revived NY, Center T., ABT, 15 Jan 1940; NYCC, NYCB, 30 Nov 1951; sc. Horace Armistead; c. (Barbara) Karinska; London, CG, RB, 12 Nov 1968; sc. Tom Lingwood. The costumes have always approximated the originals. Caroline, the Bride To Be, takes farewell of her Lover at a party in the lilac garden of her house on the eve of a marriage of convenience. At the same time the Man She Must Marry is ending his relationship with the Woman in His Past. In this work, Tudor (who much prefers the French title) for the first time explored human relationships with the greatest subtlety: quick glances, a suddenly outstretched arm, a gesture of sympathy. The first cast has never been surpassed but other famous Carolines have been GILMOUR and KAYE. Also revived by Tudor for NB of Canada (1954). MC

Jarre, La *see* GIARA

Jasiński, Roman [Czesław], b. Warsaw, 1912. Polish dancer. Studied at Warsaw OBS. Engaged by NIJINSKA for RUBINSTEIN Co., Paris, 1928, studied there with EGOROVA. Also danced with B. Russe de Monte Carlo (DE BASIL) 1932, BALANCHINE's Les Ballets 1933. Rejoined de Basil 1933–47. B. Russe de Monte Carlo 1948–50, ballet master 1951–2. Danced most leading classic roles. With his wife Moscelyne Larkin (Moussia Larkina), American ballerina, he now directs school and Civic Co. in Tulsa, OK. Their son Roman is also a dancer, currently with ABT. DV

Jazz dancing. A term frequently but inaccurately used to describe the kind of contemporary stage dancing usually to be found in musicals or TV shows. Jazz can be used to accompany any dancing in any technique. For instance, in the 1970s several classical ballet cos staged works on pointe to the music of Scott Joplin. MC

Jean de Brienne, the fiancé of RAYMONDA

Jeanmaire, Renée [known now as Zizi], b. Paris, 1924. French dancer and singer. Paris OS, studied with VOLININ, KNIASEFF. *Corps de ballet*, Paris O., 1939–44. Recitals with PETIT, Irène Lidova's Soirées de la Danse 1944. Nouveau B. de Monte Carlo 1946. Original B. Russe 1947, B. de Paris 1948. Created title role in Petit's CARMEN, then CROQUEUSE DE DIAMANTS 1950. In Samuel Goldwyn's film *Hans Christian Andersen* with Danny Kaye 1952 and was *The Girl in Pink Tights* in the Broadway musical (1953). She m. Petit 1954. Joined B. R. Petit. Created roles in many of his ballets, e.g. *Cyrano de Bergerac* (1959) and *Symphonie Fantastique* (1975) at the Paris O., and appeared in music-hall revues and various films. Director and star, Casino de Paris, from 1970. In spite of a brilliant classical technique she was not the right physique for the conventional repertory – gorgeous legs but a short neck – and the exuberance of her personality was not revealed until Petit began to create for her. By cropping her hair for *Carmen* the true 'Zizi' image was established and her success as a *chanteuse* in *La Croqueuse de Diamants* led her towards cabaret. M-FC
See I. Lidova, 'Zizi Jeanmaire', *Les Saisons de la Danse* (Paris, Jan 1975) with list of roles

Jenner, Ann, b. Ewell, Surrey, 1944. Studied with Marjorie Shrimpton, then RBS. Joined RB 1961, soloist 1964, principal 1970. Jenner's brightness and charm on stage made her an immediate favourite with the public. From classical solos she quickly progressed to principal roles, in none more delightful than as LISE. Her lightness, high soft jump, and the delicacy of her purely classical style are well suited to GISELLE. Danced her first AURORA 1972. MC

Jardin aux Lilas, danced by the RDB; left to right: KRONSTAM, LÆRKESEN, Flemming Ryberg, and Sorella Englund

Right: Jeux. Nijinsky in his ballet, one of the first to depict scenes of everyday life

Below: Le Jeune Homme et la Mort, dan. BABILÉE and PHILIPPART with B. des CE

Jensen, Lilian, b. Copenhagen, 1911. Danish dancer. Entered RDBS 1920; RDB debut, SYLPHIDE. Progressed to character parts where she gave new life to many of the obligatory roles with the originality of her mime. Danced roles from MADGE to all the great August BOURNONVILLE parts, especially the mothers in NAPOLI and GISELLE. She m. S. E. JENSEN. SKJ

Jensen, Svend Erik, b. Copenhagen, 1913. Danish dancer. Entered RDBS 1921. Debut 1936. Soloist RDB 1942. Throughout his career, which lasted till 1973, he danced character and classical parts from SPECTRE DE LA ROSE to Dandy in BEAU DANUBE and the General in GRADUATION BALL. Also celebrated as an August BOURNONVILLE stylist. He m. L. JENSEN. Now teaching. SKJ

Ruth Currier. In 1970 she struck out on a totally different path, with her partner, Fritz Ludin, in a repertory of works under the title 'Dances We Dance', by a variety of choreographers incl. Martha Wittman, LOUIS, WAGONER, THARP, with which they have toured widely in the USA and Europe. DV

Jones, John, b. Philadelphia, 1937. American dancer and choreographer. Studied with TUDOR and at SAB. Danced with DUNHAM Co., ROBBINS's Ballets: USA 1958–9 and 1961–2, as guest artist with NYCB in BALANCHINE's *Modern Jazz: Variants* (1961), JOFFREY B., HARKNESS B., DTH, and Pennsylvania B. Debut in a revival by Tudor of APRÈS-MIDI D'UN FAUNE (Philadelphia B. Guild, 1954); also an unforgettable interpreter of AFTERNOON OF A FAUN. Other roles incl. Death in GREEN TABLE. Choreographed *Eight Movements in Ragged Time* to music of Scott Joplin for Pennsylvania B. (14 Feb 1973). Now directs his own co. in Philadelphia. DV

Jones, Marilyn, b. Newcastle, NSW, 1940. Australian dancer and teacher. Studied with Lorraine Norton. Scholarship to SWBS 1956. RB 1957. BOROVANSKY B. 1959–61, junior ballerina, de Cuevas B. 1961, becoming ballerina. Australian B. 1962–71, principal ballerina, later guest artist. LFB, guest artist, 1963. Currently co-director, NTBS, Melbourne. Perhaps the finest classical ballerina produced by Australia, she has danced all the traditional leads incl. the full RAYMONDA. OBE 1972. KSW

Jong, Bettie de *see* DE JONG

Jooss, Kurt, b. Wasseralfingen, Württemberg, 1901. German dancer, choreographer, teacher, and director. Worked with LABAN in Mannheim and Hamburg 1922–3. In 1924 he formed the Neue Tanzbühne at the Münster T. with LEEDER, Aino Siimola (whom he m.), and the composer Frederic (Fritz) Cohen. Made dance director of the Folkwang S., Essen, on its foundation in 1927 and became ballet master of the ballet in Essen in 1930. His group performed his ballet GREEN TABLE at the first choreographic competition of the Archives Internationales de la Danse in Paris (1932), and won 1st prize. He then founded the B. Jooss and made a world tour, extending through the winter of 1933. Because of the Nazi persecution of the Jews, he did not return to Germany but moved the school and co. to Dartington Hall in Devon, England.

At the outset of World War II the co. left for the USA and toured both in N. and S. America, without Jooss himself, until 1942. On returning to Britain the co. was based in Cambridge and continued to tour in Britain during the rest of the war and afterwards. They returned to Essen 1951; the co. broke up after a London season in 1953. The school continued to function; 1963–4 Jooss organized a new co. on more eclectic lines.

In recent years several ballets by Jooss have successfully entered the repertories of other cos, notably *The Green Table* and BIG CITY (1975). GBLW/DV

See A. V. Coton, *The New Ballet. Kurt Jooss and His Work* (London 1946); J. Baril, 'Kurt Jooss', *Les Saisons de la Danse* (Paris, Nov 1975) with list of roles

Jordan, Olga, b. St. Petersburg, 1907; d. Leningrad, 1971. Soviet dancer. Brilliant VAGANOVA-trained ballerina, prominent in dramatic ballet of heroic style. Graduated into Kirov T. 1926, created Jeanne (FLAME OF PARIS), Diva (GOLDEN AGE), and ZAREMA. Strong, temperamental classical and dramatic dancer as ESMERALDA, ODETTE-ODILE, LAURENCIA, Pannochka (TARAS BULBA), etc. Headed ballet co., during siege of Leningrad, choreographed *Capriccio Espagnole* (Maly O., 1946). Taught in Vaganova and Moscow S., also Bolshoy T. Honoured Artist, RSFSR, Honoured Art Worker, Kirghiz SSR. NR

Josephslegende *see* LÉGENDE DE JOSEPH

Judgment of Paris, ballet, 1 scene, ch. TUDOR; mus. Kurt Weill; sc./c. LAING. London, Westminster T., London B., 15 June 1938; dan. Therese Langfield, DE MILLE, Charlotte Bidmead, Tudor, Laing. Revived London, BR, 1 Oct 1940. Revived NY, Center T., ABT, sc./c. Lucinda Ballard, 23 Jan 1940; dan. Viola Essen, de Mille, CHASE. In a sleazy Paris nightclub the 'goddesses', disillusioned and bored professionals, perform their weary dance routines for a drunken man about town. He chooses Venus but passes out, drunk. The goddesses quickly rob him of his possessions. Too often played for laughs, the ballet, like its music, the suite from the *Dreigroschen Oper*, is essentially sad. MC

Juice, 'theatre cantata in three instalments', ch. MONK; mus. Monk, Janet Zalamea, Don Preston, Carla Sydney Stone. New York, Solomon R. Guggenheim Museum, Minor Latham Playhouse, The House (lower Manhattan loft studio), 7 Nov–7 Dec 1969; dan. Dick Higgins, Madelyn Lloyd, Daniel Sverdlik, Monk, Monica Moseley (third section), augmented by six additional dancers in second section and by 74 in first section. An epic-scaled narrative of the relationships of six individuals in a loose social and artistic clustering on the journey of life. DM

Juliet, heroine of ROMEO AND JULIET

Junk Dances, modern dance work, ch. LOUIS; mus. collage of popular and operatic; sc. R. WILSON. New York, Henry St Settlement Playhouse, 11 Nov 1964; dan. Louis, LAMHUT. A proletarian couple caricatured in their humble and garish dwelling. He only wishes to sip his beer while she is driven to sartorial and romantic excesses approved by popular culture. Later redesigned by Murray Stern. DM

Karen Kain of NB of Canada as Odile with Sergiu Stefanschi as the Prince in SWAN LAKE

K

Kabuki *see* ASIA

Kain, Karen, b. Hamilton, Ontario, 1951. Canadian dancer. Studied at NBS, joining NB of Canada 1969; promoted to principal 1971. Won silver medal as soloist and, with Frank Augustyn, first place in *pas de deux* category at Moscow International B. Competition 1973. Guest artist with PETIT's B. de Marseille in created roles of Albertine (*Les Intermittences du Coeur* 1974) and NANA; with LFB as AURORA 1976. With NB of Canada, dances ODETTE-ODILE, SWANILDA, GISELLE, Aurora, and leading roles in van MANEN's *Four Schumann Pieces*, MONUMENT FOR A DEAD BOY, and KETTENTANZ, etc. PD

Kalioujny, Alexandre, b. Prague, 1923. Franco-Russian dancer. Pupil of PREOBRAZHENSKA. Danced with the B. de Cannes and with Nouveau B. de Monte Carlo 1946; created leading role in LIFAR's *Chota Roustaveli* (a full-length work based on a story by Roustaveli). *Étoile,* Paris O. 1947, dancing classical roles, as in PALAIS DE CRISTAL, and the works of Lifar. Celebrated for his superb vigour as the Chief Warrior in PRINCE IGOR and the GOLDEN SLAVE. Created leading role in BALANCE À TROIS 1955. Rejoined Paris OB 1956–61; retired to teach first in Nice then at the Paris O. MC

Kandyan *see* ASIA

Kapuste, Falco, b. Oels [Oleśnica], 1943. German dancer. Studied with GEORGI, KISS, and PERETTI. First danced in Wiesbaden B. 1963, Hamburg 1964, principal dancer Deutsche O., W. Berlin, 1965–70, and of Düsseldorf B. from 1970. He created the principal roles in several of MACMILLAN's works in Berlin and WALTER's in Düsseldorf. GBLW

Karalli, Vera, b. Moscow, 1889; d. Baden, near Vienna, 1972. Russian dancer. Daughter of provincial theatrical entrepreneur Aleksey Karalli-Tortsov. Graduated from Moscow TS 1906, class of GORSKY. A typical Gorsky ballerina, placing dramatic impact above technique and solid classical grounding. First soloist within two years, ballerina 1915. Her striking Oriental beauty, plastic expressiveness, and histrionic talent brought her widespread fame. Gorsky transposed classical ballets for her, turning GISELLE Act I into a suite of character dances, intensifying the pantomimic content of both acts according to his own artistic credo. Danced in all his major classical stagings, frequently with MORDKIN; also danced in DIAGHILEV's 1909 Paris season, title role in PAVILLON D'ARMIDE. Returned to Diaghilev's B. Russes 1919 (Polovtsian Girl in PRINCE IGOR) and 1920 (FOKINE's *Thamar*). Danced and taught in Kaunas, Lithuania, in 1920s, also Romanian O. as ballet mistress in 1930s. Had studio in Paris 1938–41, then taught in Vienna. NR
See S. L. Grigoriev, *The Diaghilev Ballet, 1909–1929* (London 1953); V. Krasovskaya, *Russian Ballet Theatre of the Beginning of the 20th Century*, Vol. 2, *Dancers* (Leningrad 1972)

Karelskaya, Rimma, b. Kaluga, 1927. Soviet dancer and teacher. Studied Moscow Bolshoy S. (a member of the experimental class for late starters) and with SEMYONOVA, graduating to the Bolshoy B. 1946. Created Tsar-Maiden in HUMPBACKED HORSE, RADUNSKY version. Other roles incl. ODETTE-ODILE, and MYRTHA, both of which she has danced in London. She m. YEVDOKIMOV. Retired from stage 1973; *répétiteur*, Bolshoy B. People's Artist, RSFSR. JS/NR

Karieva, Bernara, b. Tashkent, 1936. Soviet dancer. Prima ballerina, Navoï T. of O. and B., Tashkent, Uzbek SSR. Studied at Tashkent Choreographic S. and for four years at Bolshoy TS, graduating 1955. Solo parts from her first season. Exceptionally

musical ballerina with fine school and wide dramatic range. Dances classical as well as contemporary Soviet works and Uzbek roles, e.g. Nurkhon the dancer in *Tanovar* (ch. Nikolay Markarianz). Danced in London, Paris, Cairo, Cuba, Latin America. People's Artist, USSR. NR
See L. Avdeyeva, *The Dance of Bernara Karieva* (Tashkent 1973)

Karsavina, Tamara, b. St Petersburg, 1885. Russian dancer. Daughter of the dancer Platon Karsavin. She m. first Vasily Moukhin, then in 1917 a British diplomat, Henry James Bruce, with whom she escaped from Russia during the Revolution and eventually made her home in London. She studied at the St Petersburg Imperial S. and also with the Italian Caterina Beretta to strengthen her technique. Graduated 1902 as a soloist; by 1909 was dancing ballerina roles. She maintained her connection with the Maryinsky until the Revolution and her name is revered in the annals of Russian ballet. Her artistic education was furthered by FOKINE. She took part in all the early DIAGHILEV seasons and created immortal roles in SYLPHIDES, CARNAVAL, PETRUSHKA, SPECTRE DE LA ROSE, *Thamar*, and OISEAU DE FEU. Her intelligence and the deeply expressive nature of her dancing endeared her to Diaghilev; she was one of his favourite artists and returned to dance for him in 1919, creating the role of the Miller's Wife in TRICORNE and dancing NIJINSKA's *Roméo et Juliette* with LIFAR.

In England, through her friendship with RICHARDSON, she became a Vice-President of the RAD from its inception, and later devised important teaching syllabuses. She gave the infant BR her blessing by dancing with it in 1930. In later years she coached FONTEYN in some of her former roles, notably those of the Firebird (*Oiseau de Feu*) and GISELLE. She taught ASHTON the mime scene in Act II of FILLE MAL GARDÉE from her memories of the Maryinsky production. At her 90th birthday the toasts were proposed by Ashton and Sir John Gielgud. Perhaps the most universally loved dancer in the world. MC
See autobiography, *Theatre Street* (London 1930; New York 1931; paperback New York 1961), a classic of ballet history; H. J. Bruce, *Thirty Dozen Moons* (London 1949); *Silken Dalliance* (London 1946); Karsavina's technical manuals: *Ballet Technique* (London and New York 1956) and *Classical Ballet: The Flow of Movement* (London and New York 1962)

Karstens, Gerda, b. Copenhagen, 1903. Danish dancer. Entered RDBS 1911. *Coryphée* 1923. By 1935 she was renowned as a character dancer. Soloist 1942. The greatest mime of her period in Danish ballet; MADGE was her most famous creation but also well known as other August BOURNONVILLE characters. She m. the dancer Svend Karlog. Left the stage 1956 but continued for a period as mime teacher at RDB and later as mime actress outside RDB. SKJ

Kasatkina, Natalia, b. Moscow, 1934. Soviet dancer and choreographer. Graduated Bolshoy S. 1954, rapidly becoming a leading character dancer of the Bolshoy B. Developed an early interest in choreography, working invariably with husband VASILYOV. First joint ballet VANINA VANINI. Their next successful ballet was GEOLOGISTS. Their daring version of SACRE DU PRINTEMPS placed the action in the second millennium BC, making the Shepherd youth (VLADIMIROV) revolt against his elders in protest against the death of the Chosen Maiden (SOROKINA), with Kasatkina as the Possessed. STRAVINSKY personally encouraged the couple when this work was shown on tour in the USA. ROMEO AND JULIET was conceived entirely in terms of classical dance. Major works choreographed for Kirov T. incl. *The Creation of the World* (mus. Andrey

Tamara Karsavina as Columbine in FOKINE's CARNAVAL, one of her favourite roles

Niels Kehlet practising in the Royal Theatre, Copenhagen, in front of portraits of Antoine and August BOURNONVILLE. In addition to his prowess as a classical dancer, he is a great comedian.

Petrov; lib. after Jean Eiffel's cartoons), 23 Mar 1971. Other works incl. *Revelation* (mus. Yuri Butsko), Stanislavsky and Nemirovich-Danchenko B., 6 Apr 1974; *Preludes and Fugues* (1968; mus. Johann Sebastian Bach, arr. Mikhail Chulaki) with PLISETSKAYA; *Tristan and Isolde* (mus. Richard Wagner) with Kasatkina in the title role, Bolshoy T., 13 Apr 1963. Honoured Artist, RSFSR. NR
See Natalia Kasatkina and Vladimir Vasilyov, 'How We Invent a Ballet' in E. Bocharnikova, *The Magic Land of Ballet* (Moscow 1974)

Katalyse (*Catalysis*), ballet, ch. CRANKO; mus. Dmitri Shostakovich (1st Piano Concerto). Stuttgart, 8 Nov 1961; dan. Micheline Faure, Myrtha Morena, BARRA, Hugo Delavalle, Gary Burne. A ballet of transformation. Also in repertoire of Düsseldorf 1965, Munich 1968. GBLW

Katerina, ballet, 3 acts, 7 scenes, ch./lib. L. LAVROVSKY; mus. ADAM and Anton Rubinstein arr. Pavel Feldt and Evgeny Dubovskoy; sc. Boris Erbstein. Leningrad, Kirov T., Leningrad Choreographic S., 25 May 1935. Revived as part of the repertory of the Kirov T., 30 Jan 1936, with new musical arrangement by Feldt; dan. JORDAN, SHELEST, Boris Shavrov, Yuri Hofman. Ballet about the plight of serf dancers. Incl. a section in the style of DIDELOT based on Fedor Tolstoy's drawings, done with great taste. NR
See Yuri Slonimsky, *Soviet Ballet* (Leningrad 1950)

Kathak, Kathakali *see* ASIA

Kaye [Koreff], Nora, b. New York, 1920. American dancer of Russian extraction. Studied at NY Met BS with FOKINE, VILZAK, SCHOLLAR, and CRASKE, and at SAB. Danced in NY Met OB as a child, and at Radio City Music Hall. Joined ABT at its inception, 1939. Chosen by TUDOR for the role of HAGAR and was instantly recognized as the leading dramatic dancer of her time; also danced classic roles such as GISELLE. Danced with NYCB 1951–4, where ROBBINS created CAGE for her. Rejoined ABT 1954–60; MACMILLAN created *Winter's Eve* and *Journey* for her, 1957. She m. Herbert Ross, with whom she formed a co. that appeared at Spoleto, 1959 and 1960. Since her retirement from dancing in 1961 she has assisted Ross in his work as a choreographer and director of musical comedies and films. DV

Kchessinska *see* KSHESSINSKA

KDF-Ballett (*Kraft durch Freude, Strength Through Joy*), the official ballet of the 'Strength Through Joy' movement of the Nazi party (later its NB). It was led by its ballet mistress DERRA DE MORODA and gave its first perf. at the Kroll O., Berlin, 1941. It performed regularly in Berlin and toured. In 1943 a ballet school was added. The co. was evacuated to Hildburghausen in summer 1944 and eventually broke up. The principal dancers incl. LUIPART (then calling himself Frenchel); Derra de Moroda choreographed many of the ballets. GBLW

Keen, Elizabeth, b. Huntington, NY. American modern dance choreographer and dancer. She studied dance at SAB and at the TAMIRIS-NAGRIN S., NY, and composition with Robert Dunn. She has taught movement in the drama division of the Juilliard S. of Music. Performed with the Tamiris-Nagrin Dance Co. 1960–2, and the P. TAYLOR Dance Co. 1961–2. She started to choreograph 1962 under the aegis of the *avant-garde* Judson Dance T. with which she was associated for two years, although she was not a founding member. Since 1962 she has directed street theatre and off-Broadway musicals. Her choreography shows an interest in film, mime, court dance, and Americana. Many of her pieces are set to jazz. She uses both trained and untrained performers. Her work is usually short and often humorous. Of the more than 30 works she has choreographed, her best known are *Poison Variations* (1970; mus. Gwendolyn Watson and Joel Press), which takes off from the story of Hamlet, and *Quilt* (1971; mus. trad. Irish). JD

Kehlet, Niels, b. Copenhagen, 1938. Danish dancer. Entered RDBS 1948, soloist RDB 1961. From 1955 a leading Danish dancer with a great virtuosity in classic parts. Has danced with many European and American cos as guest artist. From his debut in ROBBINS's *Fanfare* he has covered a galaxy of roles, from Gennaro (NAPOLI) and JAMES to PIERROT LUNAIRE and COLAS. A favourite with the public of many countries, he has nevertheless remained a

permanent member of RDB. SKJ
See E. Aschengreen, 'Niels Kehlet', *Les Saisons de la Danse* (Paris, Mar 1970)

Keil, Birgit, b. Kovarov [Kowarschen, in former Sudetenland], 1944. German dancer. Studied at Stuttgart S. under CRANKO and RBS. Entered Stuttgart B. 1961. Soloist 1965, becoming a principal dancer and creating roles in many of Cranko's ballets (OPUS I, CARD GAME, *Brouillards* 1970, INITIALEN RBME etc.) and in HERMANAS; also dances the main ballerina roles in Stuttgart. GBLW

Kékesi, Mária, b. Budapest, 1941. Hungarian dancer. Studied State B. Inst. under Zsuzsa Merényi 1950–8, Leningrad with DUDINSKAYA 1966–7. Budapest O. 1958, soloist since 1968. Debut as MYRTHA 1960; has danced most major roles incl. MARIA, AURORA, and LILAC FAIRY, also the Princess in WOODEN PRINCE (1970) and the Muse in *The Cedar Tree* (1975), the last two ch. SEREGI, SWANILDA (1971), title role in SYLPHIDE and ÉTUDES (both 1973). Bronze Medal, Varna, 1960; Liszt Prize 1970; Merited Artist 1975. GPD

Kellaway, Leon [Jan Kowsky], b. London. English dancer, teacher, and ballet master. Studied with ASTAFYEVA and LEGAT. Anglo-Russian B. Partnered KYASHT. A. PAVLOVA B. 1929–31. Levitoff Russian B. 1934–5. Settled in Australia, becoming a distinguished teacher. Produced ballets for operettas etc. BOROVANSKY B., ballet master 1940–55, character dancer. NTB, Melbourne, ballet master 1948–51. Now Professor of Dance, Australian B. KSW

Kelly, Desmond, b. Penhalonga, Rhodesia, 1942. British dancer who moved to London for intensive work with FRENCH. Handsome, a good dancer although not a virtuoso, Kelly is a superb partner and fine actor. He joined LFB 1959, principal 1964. Guest artist with the New Zealand and Washington NB, he joined the RB as a principal 1970. A favoured partner of FONTEYN and indeed of many ballerinas, whom he 'presents' to the audience with nobility and grace, Kelly has a wide range and is one of the finest ALBRECHTS of our time. MC

Kent, Allegra, b. Santa Monica, CA, 1936. American dancer. Studied with NIJINSKA and MARACCI, then at SAB. Joined NYCB 1953. BALANCHINE has created many ballets for her, incl. SEVEN DEADLY SINS, IVESIANA ('The Unanswered Question'), and BUGAKU. One of the few Balanchine dancers to have made a successful transition into maturity, her perfs in such ballets as SERENADE, AGON, and DANCES AT A GATHERING, have gained tremendously in depth and authority. DV

Kerchief (*Keszkenő*), ballet, 3 acts, ch. HARANGOZÓ; lib. Viktor Lányi, Gusztáv Oláh, Harangozó; mus. Jenő Kenessey after Jenő Hubay; sc. Zoltán Fülöp; c. Tivadar Márk. Budapest O., 8 Mar 1951. Based on Harangozó's first choreography, a 1-act ballet *Scene in the Csárdas* (1936; mus. Hubay). Revived 24 Apr 1970 for the B. Sopianae, Pécs. Marika, a peasant girl, overcomes parental opposition and marries the boy she loves. Performed more than 100 times in Budapest. Same choreography abroad: Cluj 1954, Bratislava 1955, Saratov and Moscow 1956; ch. Stanislav Remar at Kosice 1955; ch. ULBRICH 1955. GPD

Kermis at Bruges, The (*Kermessen i Brügge*), ballet, 3 acts, ch. August BOURNONVILLE; mus. Holger Simon Paulli. Copenhagen, RDB, 4 Apr 1851. Still in the repertory as one of the most popular and amusing Bournonville ballets. A story about three magical gifts: a ring that makes everyone fall in love with the owner, a sword that gives its owner victory in all duels, and a violin that makes everyone dance. The setting is a fair in 17th-c. Flanders. SKJ

Kettentanz, ballet, ch. ARPINO; mus. Johann Strauss and Johann Simon Mayer; c. Joe Eula; ltg Thomas Skelton. NYCC, CCJB, 20 Oct 1972; dan. Rebecca WRIGHT, Dermot Burke, Susan Magno, Scott Barnard, Glenn White. A chain of dances (as the German title suggests) for six couples to polkas, galops, and waltzes. FM

Keuter, Cliff, b. Boise, ID, 1940. American modern dancer and choreographer. Early training with NAGRIN 1959. Joined TAMIRIS-Nagrin Dance Co. 1962. Won scholarships at the Juilliard S. of Music and GRAHAM S.; also studied SLAVENSKA, Jack Moore, SOKOLOW. Has performed with the Ruth Currier Co. and the P. TAYLOR Co. In 1969 formed the Cliff Keuter Dance Co., with a repertory of his own dances, which deal with fleeting dramatic situations, often surreal. Later works incl. *Station*, *Amazing Grace*, *Voice*, *The Murder of George Keuter*, and humorous dances *Museti di Taverni*, and *Plaisir d'Amour*. In 1972 he staged *Sunday Papers*, 'a serio-comic, somewhat surrealistic and hallucinatory dance' for NDT. EK

Khachaturian, Aram Ilyich, b. Tbilisi [Tiflis], 1903. Armenian composer. Studied Moscow Cons. Originally influenced by RAVEL, later by folk music, especially Armenian. His style is avowedly popular and in the Soviet Union he has achieved great official success. His ballets are *Happiness* (Erevan, Armenia, 1939; ch. Ilya Arbatov), which was recast as GAYANÉ, and the raucous and sentimental SPARTACUS. DH

Khlustin, Ivan, b. Moscow, 1862; d. Nice, France, 1941. Russian dancer, teacher, and choreographer. Graduated from Moscow TS, class of Gustav Legat. Bolshoy T. 1878–1903, *premier danseur* from 1886. First ballet, *Stars* (1898; mus. Antoine Simon), enabled him to display a constellation of Bolshoy

ballerinas incl. Adelina Giuri and ROSLAVLEVA, with himself as the hero Count de Castro. Another ballet, *Magic Dreams*, produced within one year to music by Yuri Pomerantsev, had less success. Retired with pension 1903; *maître de ballet*, Paris O., 1909–14, A. PAVLOVA's co. 1914–22, choreographing many ballets for her, incl. CHOPINIANA. NR
See Cyril W. Beaumont, *Ballets Past and Present, being a Third Supplement to the Complete Book of Ballets* (London 1955)

Khon *see* ASIA

Kidd, Michael, b. Brooklyn, NY, 1919. American dancer and choreographer. Studied with VILZAK and SCHOLLAR and at SAB. Danced with American B. 1937, B. Caravan 1937–40, Dance Players 1941–2, ABT 1942–7. Danced title role in BILLY THE KID, First Sailor in FANCY FREE, etc. Choreographed *On Stage!* for ABT 1945. Left to stage dances for musical, *Finian's Rainbow* (1947), and since then has choreographed many stage and film musicals, incl. *Guys and Dolls* (1951), *Can-Can* (1953), *Seven Brides for Seven Brothers* (film, 1954), *Hello Dolly!* (film, 1967). Also appeared with Gene Kelly in his film *It's Always Fair Weather* (1955). DV

Kinetic Molpai, modern dance work, ch. SHAWN; mus. Jess Meeker. Goshen, NY, Clark S., T. Shawn and his Men Dancers, 5 Oct 1935. A paean of praise to an athletic all-male society whose leader and followers are in happy rapport. Subsequently the piece became the third section, 'Future', of Shawn's full-length work *O Libertad!* Revived AILEY CCDT 1972. DM

King, Kenneth, b. Freeport, ME. American dancer. Formal training in dance began relatively late. Studied with Syvilla Fort and CUNNINGHAM. His undergraduate study concentrated on philosophy and he has in recent years constructed dance pieces that combine hypnotic and repetitive dance movement with speculative monologues. His use of words in these monologues is frequently idiosyncratic and highly personal. During the mid-1960s he performed with *avant-garde* choreographers MONK and Phoebe Neville among others and created his own works of which *Blow-Out* is the most accomplished. DM

King's Volunteers of Amager, The (*Livjægerne på Amager*), vaudeville ballet, 1 act, ch. August BOURNONVILLE; mus. Wilhelm Christian Holm, using compositions by Édouard Dupuy and popular tunes. Copenhagen, RDB, 19 Feb 1871. Still in the current repertory. The King's Volunteers, on guard against the British navy in 1808 (the ballet's subtitle is 'An Episode in 1808'), flirt with peasant girls in Dragør, a small village outside Copenhagen. The principal character is believed to have been based on the composer and tenor Édouard Dupuy, who worked in the Copenhagen and Stockholm opera houses and was a notorious Don Juan. The ballet has been performed with the English title *Lifeguards of Amager*, changed when it was taken on tour as the word 'lifeguard', besides being an inaccurate translation, has quite different meanings in Britain and the USA; also as *Guards at Amager*. SKJ

Kirkland, Gelsey, b. Bethlehem, PA, 1953. American dancer. Studied at SAB. Joined NYCB, 1968, where her repertory incl. BALANCHINE's *Theme and Variations* (in *Tchaikovsky Suite No. 3*), CONCERTO BAROCCO, SYMPHONY IN C, HARLEQUINADE, and *Divertimento* from BAISER DE LA FÉE; and ROBBINS's DANCES AT A GATHERING, GOLDBERG VARIATIONS, etc. She left the co. 1974 to join ABT as the chosen partner of BARYSHNIKOV, with whom she has danced SYLPHIDE, GISELLE, BAYADÈRE, *Theme and Variations*, and SHADOWPLAY. She also created the leading role in LEAVES ARE FADING . . . and dances Caroline in JARDIN AUX LILAS; with NAGY danced AURORA in 1976 revival of SLEEPING BEAUTY. DV

Kirnbauer, Susanne, b. Vienna, 1942. Austrian dancer. Trained at Vienna Staats OBS and joined Staats OB 1956. In 1965–6 worked with CHARRAT and MISKOVITCH in Paris. Returned to Staats O. 1967 to dance major classical roles, often in NUREYEV productions. MC

Kirov Ballet, Leningrad. Originally the Imperial B. Co., which danced at first at the Bolshoy T. of St Petersburg (*see* RUSSIA AND THE USSR). From 1860 the co. alternated between this theatre (rebuilt by 1896 to house the Conservatoire) and the Maryinsky T., built by Alberto Cavos (grandfather of BENOIS). From 1889 the Maryinsky became the sole stage for ballet *à grand spectacle* (smaller ballets were also shown at the Hermitage T. and elsewhere). In 1917–20 the theatre was named the State Maryinsky T., in 1920–35 the State Academic T. of O. and B. (abbreviated in Russian as GATOB), in 1935 it was named after Sergey Mironovich Kirov, the head of the Leningrad Communist Party who was assassinated in 1934, and became the S. M. Kirov State Academic Theatre of O. and B., Order of Lenin.

At the time of the 1917 October Revolution, ballet was in the hands of FOKINE, who had produced six new works since Nov 1915, the last of which, *Ruslan and Lyudmila* (dances in Mikhail Glinka's opera of that name) was mounted as part of the 70th Anniversary Celebrations of the first perf. of the Maryinsky B. Fokine was offered the post of chief ballet master and choreographer, but agreement could not be reached and he left the USSR in 1918, subsequent offers also proving unavailing. After his departure the dominant influence became that of VAGANOVA, after whom the Maryinsky/Kirov S. was renamed in 1957. Of post-Revolution prima ballerinas only E. GERDT and LYUKOM were not her students, other Kirov ballerinas SEMYONOVA, ULANOVA, DUDINSKAYA, SHELEST, OSIPENKO, and KOLPAKOVA all being

Vaganova pupils. The Vaganova system has been a major factor in the continuing acceptance of the Kirov style as the most refined and pure extant in the world.

The first post-Fokine choreographer was F. LOPUKHOV, chief choreographer in Leningrad 1922–60 with an interlude in Moscow in 1926; his works incl. ICE MAIDEN and *Dance Symphony* (1923) to the complete Fourth Symphony of Ludwig van Beethoven, which caused a scandal no less than did MASSINE's symphonic experiments a decade later; and *Le Renard* and OISEAU DE FEU (both mus. STRAVINSKY). The next choreographer of stature was VAINONEN, who created GOLDEN AGE, FLAME OF PARIS, a new version of NUTCRACKER (1934), and RAYMONDA, and by 1934 ZAKHAROV was producing FOUNTAIN OF BAKHCHISARAY, which provided Ulanova with her first important created role, MARIA. Other important choreographers were CHABUKIANI, who produced many ballets between 1938 and 1961, incl. LAURENCIA, and his contemporary L. LAVROVSKY, whose choreographic career began 1930 when he choreographed *Études Symphoniques* (mus. Robert Schumann) for the Leningrad BS, and incl. the masterpiece of Soviet ballet, ROMEO AND JULIET.

During World War II the Kirov B. was evacuated to Perm, returning 1944. SERGEYEV was in charge of the co. 1951–5 and 1960–70. GRIGOROVICH, who had graduated into the co. in 1946, emerged as choreographer with STONE FLOWER and LEGEND OF LOVE. Dancers to emerge in the 1950s and 1960s incl. Kolpakova and Osipenko, Vaganova's last pupils, also SIZOVA, KOMLEVA, MAKAROVA, and the outstanding male dancers SOLOVYOV and SOKOLOV. The latest choreographer to make an impact has been BELSKY, whose LENINGRAD SYMPHONY made a considerable impression in New York and London.

The Kirov S., now directed by Sergeyev and Dudinskaya, is still a magnet for the ballet world. Training is still based on the principles of Vaganova and pupils possess a unique lightness and aristocracy of movement. The dance archive in the Kirov S. in Theatre Street is one of the finest in the world. The Director and Curator, Marietta Francopoulo, is an ex-Kirov ballerina. JS

See Natalia Roslavleva, *Era of the Russian Ballet* (New York and London 1966); Mary Grace Swift, *The Art of the Dance in the USSR* (Notre Dame, IN, 1968; London 1969)

Kirsova, Helene [Ellen Wittrup], b. Denmark, *c.* 1911; d. London, 1962. Danish dancer, choreographer, and director. De Basil B. Russe 1932; R. Blum B. de Monte Carlo 1936; de Basil second co. 1936. Settled in Sydney 1937, founding a school (1940) and a co. (1941) and creating many ballets. Returned to Europe 1946. Created the Butterfly in ÉPREUVE D'AMOUR and was a celebrated dancer of the Valse in SYLPHIDES. Her ballets incl. *Faust, A Dream and a Fairytale, Revolution of the Umbrellas*. Pub. *Ballet in Moscow Today* (London 1956). KSW

Kirstein, Lincoln Edward, b. Rochester, NY, 1907. American writer, poet, and polemicist. Co-founder and director, NEW YORK CITY BALLET. It was due to Kirstein's drive and enthusiasm that BALANCHINE settled in the USA; for over 40 years Kirstein has dedicated himself to the creation of an American classic style through the training at the SAB and the ballets created by Balanchine. Kirstein's writings on the dance have provided some of the most important ballet literature of our time. He has also proved himself a distinguished art critic and patron of artists. American ballet's debt to him is incalculable. MC/CC

See his *Three Pamphlets Collected* ('Blast at Ballet', 1937; 'Ballet Alphabet', 1939; 'What Ballet is all About', 1959) with a new foreword, *Dance Horizons* (New York 1967); and General Bibliography

Kiss, Nora, b. Pyatigorsk, Russia, 1908. French teacher. Studied with BRIANZA, VOLININ. Boris Romanov and BALANCHINE cos 1929–35. Taught Rome, 1939–45, then Paris, Studio Wacker. Guest teacher, B. XXe S., Brussels Cons., RDB, many summer schools. Numbers most of today's international soloists among her pupils. M-FC

Kitri, the heroine in DON QUIXOTE

Kivitt, Ted, b. Miami, FL, 1942. American dancer. Studied with Thomas Armour and Alexander Gavrilov in Miami. Joined ABT 1961. Dances most leading roles in the classical repertory. DV

Klos, Vladimír, b. Prague, 1946. Czech dancer. Studied in Prague and joined Prague Studio B. 1968. Joined Stuttgart B. 1968, soloist 1973. Created CRANKO roles. GBLW

Kniaseff, Boris, b. St Petersburg, 1900; d. Paris, 1975. Russian dancer, choreographer, and teacher. Studied with GOLEIZOVSKY, MORDKIN, NELIDOVA. Debut Sofia 1917, then Paris 1921–32, partner of SPESSIVTSEVA to whom he was at one time m. *Maître de ballet*, OC, 1932–4. Opened a dance studio in Paris; among his pupils were CHAUVIRÉ, JEANMAIRE, SKOURATOFF, ALGAROFF, van DIJK. Also taught in Switzerland, then in Athens and Buenos Aires. Celebrated for his '*bar par terre*', making his classical dancers lie on the floor to perform exercises to improve turn-out. Ballets incl. *Berioska* (1931), *Piccoli* (1947). M-FC

Knust, Albrecht, b. Hamburg, 1896. German dancer and writer on dance notation. Pupil of LABAN and joined his group 1922. Directed the Laban S. in Hamburg 1924–5 and ballet master Dessau 1926. Began writing on and developing the Laban notation system and directed the dance section of the Folkwang S., Essen, 1934. Completed his monumental *Encyclopedia of Laban Kinetography* 1950 and from 1951 has taught at the Folkwang S. One of the great figures in dance notation. GBLW

Köchermann, Rainer, b. Chemnitz, 1930. German dancer. Pupil of T. and V. GSOVSKY and BLANK. Joined E. Berlin Staats O. 1949 and the Städtische O., W. Berlin, 1951. In Frankfurt B. 1955–9 and Hamburg from 1960 as principal dancer. Ballet master, Saarbrücken, 1976. GBLW

Kochno, Boris, b. Moscow, 1903. Russian librettist and poet. Secretary and assistant to DIAGHILEV from 1923. He was responsible for many librettos for the Diaghilev co., incl. FILS PRODIGUE and ODE. During the 1930s he collaborated with the R. BLUM–DE BASIL B. Russe de Monte Carlo and with BALANCHINE's Les Ballets 1933. In Mar 1945 he was associated with the renaissance of French ballet, devising the scenario of FORAINS; later that year he became artistic director, B. des CE. His two books on ballet, magnificently illustrated, are *Le Ballet* (Paris 1954) and *Diaghilev et les Ballets Russes*, tr. Adrienne Foulke as *Diaghilev and the Ballets Russes* (New York 1970; London 1971). MC/CC

Koegler, Horst, b. Neuruppin, 1927. German critic and author. Contributor to many German and international publications. Author of several books incl. *Friedrichs Ballett-Lexikon von A-Z* (Velber bei Hannover 1972) and *The Concise Oxford Dictionary of Ballet* (London, New York, and Toronto 1977); editor of the German annual *Ballett* since 1965. MC

Köhler-Richter, Emmy, b. Gera, 1918. German dancer and ballet mistress. Studied under WIGMAN and T. GSOVSKY and after dancing in Bonn, Strasbourg, Leipzig, appointed ballet mistress in Cologne 1947–51, in Basel 1953–5, in Weimar 1956–8. In 1958 became chief choreographer in Leipzig. Guest choreographer in Havana and Brno. GBLW

Irina Kolpakova of the Leningrad State Kirov B. as AURORA

Kölling, Rudolf, b. Hanover, 1904; d. Münster, 1970. German dancer, choreographer, and teacher. Pupil of the ballet school of Hanover and of LABAN and WIGMAN, he became a soloist in the Berlin Staats O. After World War II he was ballet master of the Städtische O., W. Berlin, Weimar, and, after a period in E. Berlin, of Munich 1948–50. He was ballet master at Münster 1955–64 and opened his own school there. He was the first to mount SACRE DU PRINTEMPS in Germany after the war (Munich 1949). He had a distinguished career as a teacher. He m. SPIES. GBLW

Kolosova, Evgenia, b. St Petersburg, 1780; d. St Petersburg, 1869. Russian dancer. Daughter of a dancer in the *corps de ballet*, Ivan Neyelov, she performed children's parts in numerous ballets, operas, and dramas. Pupil of VALBERG. Graduated from St Petersburg TS 1799; became soloist, St Petersburg B., creating title roles in *Medée et Jason* (NOVERRE's ballet revived by Charles Lepique), Adelaide in DIDELOT's *Raoul de Créquis*, and *Phèdre et Hyppolite*, with great dramatic impact; also appeared as dramatic actress in melodramas and comedies. Exerted considerable influence on M. DANILOVA and ISTOMINA among others. NR
See A. Glushkovsky, *Reminiscences of a Ballet Master* (Moscow and Leningrad 1940)

Kolpakova, Irina, b. Leningrad, 1933. Soviet dancer. Graduated from Leningrad Choreographic S. 1951, one of VAGANOVA's last pupils. Exquisite lyrical ballerina in perfect academic style of Kirov B., possessing ethereal lightness and nobility, enabling her to excel in classical repertoire. Also has a feeling for contemporary choreography: created roles of Katerina (STONE FLOWER), Shirien (LEGEND OF LOVE), Beloved (COAST OF HOPE – alternating with OSIPENKO), Desdemona (OTHELLO, CHABUKIANI's version), etc. She m. SEMYONOV, her permanent partner until his retirement. People's Artist, RSFSR and USSR. NR
See Irina Kolpakova, 'The Last Graduation', in *A. J. Vaganova* (Leningrad 1958); article by V. Chistiakova in *Leningrad Ballet Today*, No. 1 (Leningrad 1967)

Komar, Chris, b. Milwaukee, WI, 1947. American dancer. Bachelor of Fine Arts degree from Univ. of Wisconsin. Danced with Milwaukee B. Co. 1969–71. To NY to study with CUNNINGHAM; joined his co. 1972 and has created roles in all of his works since then, and also taken over Cunningham's own roles in *Winterbranch*, SUMMERSPACE, *Rune*, and *Signals*. DV

Komleva, Gabriella, b. Leningrad, 1938. Soviet dancer. Graduated from VAGANOVA Choreographic S. 1957, class of Vera Kostrovitskaya. Ballerina, Kirov B. Noted for perfect technique, great expressiveness and versatility. Roles incl. classical, e.g. RAYMONDA, GISELLE, ODETTE-ODILE, Nikia (BAYADÈRE), and contemporary, e.g. Asiat (GOR-

YANKA – created), Ophelia (HAMLET). She m. ballet critic Arkady Sokolov. People's Artist, RSFSR. NR *See* article by V. Krasovskaya in *Leningrad Ballet Today*, No. 2 (Leningrad 1968)

Kondratieva, Marina, b. Leningrad, 1934. Soviet dancer. Graduated from Bolshoy BS 1952, danced title role in CINDERELLA in second season. Elegant, lyrical, and technically impeccable, with exquisite feeling for romantic style in GISELLE. Numerous contemporary roles: JULIET, Muse (L. LAVROVSKY's *Paganini* – created), Katerina and the Mistress of the Copper Mountain (STONE FLOWER), PHRYGIA, Girl in SPECTRE DE LA ROSE, ANNA KARENINA (alternating with PLISETSKAYA), etc. People's Artist, RSFSR. NR

Kondratov, Yuri, b. Moscow, 1921; d. Moscow, 1967. Soviet dancer and teacher. Graduated from Bolshoy BS, class of GUSEV. Soloist Bolshoy T. 1940–60. Virile *premier danseur* as SIEGFRIED, BASILIO (at which he excelled), the Prince in CINDERELLA. Especially prominent in new Soviet ballets: created Ilko in SVETLANA and Fabricio in *Mirandolina* (ch. VAINONEN, after Carlo Goldoni's *La Locandiera*). Was Ma Lie-Chen (RED POPPY – L. LAVROVSKY version), Ali-Batyr (SHURALE), Lenny (PATH OF THUNDER). Partnered ULANOVA at her first appearance abroad, Maggio Musicale, Florence 1951. Taught at Moscow Choreographic S. from 1943, appointed its Artistic Director 1960, from 1964 headed Moscow Ice B. People's Artist, RSFSR. His son, Andrey, is a soloist with the Bolshoy B. NR

Koner [Mahler], Pauline, b. New York, 1912. American dancer and choreographer. Studied ballet with FOKINE, Spanish dance with Angel Cansino, Oriental dance with Michio Ito. Debut with Fokine B. 1926. Toured USA with Ito 1928–9. First solo recital, New York 1930. Toured USA giving solo concerts 1930–46, also Near East 1932, USSR 1935. Danced with LIMÓN Dance Co. 1946–60, creating many roles in works by HUMPHREY and Limón, incl. *La Malinche* (1949) and MOOR'S PAVANE (1949). Also directed her own co. 1949–63. Continued to choreograph solos incl. *Cassandra* (1953), *The Farewell* (1962), *Solitary Songs* (1963), and *Judith* (1965). Choreographed *Poème* for AILEY City Center Dance T. (1969). Has taught and/or choreographed in many American universities and also in Europe, S. America, and Japan. Since 1965 on faculty of North Carolina S. of the Arts, since 1975 on that of Brooklyn College. Formed new co., Pauline Koner Dance Consort, 1976. DV

Koren, Sergey Gavrilovich, b. St Petersburg, 1907; d. Moscow, 1969. Soviet dancer. Graduated 1927 from evening courses (for late starters) at Leningrad Choreographic S. From 1927 in the Maly OB; Kirov T. 1930–42, soloist 1942–60, from 1960 *répétiteur* Bolshoy T. Brilliant character dancer and actor, with feeling for national dances and gift for characterization. Created: Zaal (HEART OF THE HILLS), Ostap (TARAS BULBA), best performer of Kerim (*Partisans' Days*, ch. VAINONEN), etc. Danced Mercutio in the first Moscow production (1946) of L. LAVROVSKY's *Romeo and Juliet*. Honoured Artist, RSFSR; People's Artist, Kabardino-Balkarsky ASSR; Honoured Art Worker, North Osetian ASSR. NR

Kovich, Robert, b. San José, CA, 1950. American dancer. Studied at Univ. of California and then with Judith Dunn at Bennington College, VT, dancing in her co. 1971–2. Joined CUNNINGHAM and Dance Co. in 1973 and has created roles in most of Cunningham's new pieces since that time. DV

Krasovskaya, Vera, b. St Petersburg, 1915. Soviet critic and historian of ballet. Graduated from Leningrad Choreographic S. 1933, class of VAGANOVA. In *corps de ballet*, Kirov T. 1933–41. Graduated from theatre science faculty of Leningrad T. Inst. 1951, at present Professor of same. Doctor of Science (Arts). Principal works: *Vakhtang Chabukiani* (Moscow and Leningrad 1956); *Russian Ballet Theatre from Formation to the Middle of the 19th Century* (Leningrad 1958); *Russian Ballet Theatre of the Second Half of the 19th Century* (Leningrad 1963); *Russian Ballet Theatre of the Beginning of the 20th Century*, Vol. 1, *Choreographers* (Leningrad 1971), Vol. 2, *Dancers* (Leningrad 1972); *Anna Pavlova* (Leningrad 1964); *Nijinsky* (Leningrad 1974); 'Marius Petipa and *The Sleeping Beauty*', *Dance Perspectives*, No. 49 (New York). NR

Krassovska [Leslie], Nathalie, b. Petrograd, 1919. Russian dancer, whose mother and grandmother were also dancers. Studied with PREOBRAZHENSKA in Paris and LEGAT in London, also at SAB. Debut with NIJINSKA's co., Paris 1932. Danced with BALANCHINE's Les Ballets 1933, with LIFAR in S. America 1934, B. Russe de Monte Carlo 1936–50, LFB 1950–5. Danced most of the classic ballerina roles. Now teaches in Dallas, TX. DV

Kresnik, Hans, b. Bleiburg, 1939. Austrian dancer and choreographer. Pupil of Jean Deroc, WOIZIKOWSKI, APPEL in Cologne. Joined Graz B., then in Bremen. Cologne 1961–8 and returned to Bremen as ballet master. His choreography uses mixed media and handles controversial and political themes. GBLW

Kreutzberg, Harald, b. Reichenberg, 1902; d. Muri, Switzerland, 1968. German dancer. Studied in Leipzig and Dresden (with WIGMAN). Was engaged as soloist, Hanover 1922, and the Berlin Staats O. 1924 where he danced a Fool in TERPIS's *Don Morte* (1926) with a shaven head, which remained his 'trademark'. He became a principal exponent of the Central European Dance in the 1920s and '30s, in solos and as the partner of GEORGI with whom he

Mathilde Kshessinska in costume for a Russian dance. She appeared in a similar dance at CG as late as 1936

toured widely. In 1955 he opened a school in Bern where he taught for the rest of his life and ended his touring in 1959. He choreographed many solos for himself and for others, and epitomized the German contemporary style. GBLW

Kriger [Krieger], Viktorina, b. St Petersburg, 1893. Soviet dancer. Moscow TS 1903–10, graduating class of TIKHOMIROV. Accepted by Bolshoy T. as *coryphée* but within two months promoted to second soloist. Danced minor roles in SLEEPING BEAUTY 1911. Tsar-Maiden (HUMPBACKED HORSE) 1915, KITRI 1916, SWANILDA 1917, with NOVIKOV who was frequently her partner. Her virtuoso technique coupled with dramatic impact and temperament was noted by GORSKY who gave her many roles. Toured abroad, incl. Canada and USA, 1920–3. Invited into A. PAVLOVA Co. 1921, leaving it because of rivalry with Pavlova. Returned to Russia 1923, back to Bolshoy 1925, where she danced SWAN LAKE with MESSERER though it was not quite in her dynamic expressive style. Gave concerts with MORDKIN in the 1920s. Danced Tao-Hoa (RED POPPY) 1927. Created role of Stepmother in CINDERELLA (Bolshoy T., 1946; ch. ZAKHAROV) for which she received State Prize. Her role in the formation of the Moscow Art T. of B., which merged with Stanislavsky and Nemirovich-Danchenko Lyric T., was of paramount importance. Writes regularly on ballet. Honoured Art Worker, RSFSR. NR

See A. Abramov, *Viktorina Kriger* (Moscow 1928); V. Kriger, *Moi Zapiski* (*My Notes*) (Moscow 1930); M. Chudnovsky, *Viktorina Kriger* (Moscow 1964)

Kriza, John, b. Berwyn, IL, 1919; d. Naples, FL, 1975. American dancer of Czech parentage. Studied Stone-Camryn S., Chicago, also with DOLIN and TUDOR. Debut in WPA Federal Project and Chicago City OB (under PAGE) 1939. Joined ABT at its foundation; remained with the co. throughout his career, rising from *corps de ballet* to principal and once described as 'Mister Ballet Theatre in person'. He created the sentimental sailor in FANCY FREE and danced the role for over 20 years. Created roles in Robbins's *Interplay* 1945, in ABT's production of Herbert Ross's *Caprichos* 1950. Danced classical roles (SYLPHIDES) but will be remembered chiefly for *Fancy Free* and for his perfs as Billy in BILLY THE KID and as the Champion Roper in RODEO. Retired 1966 to work with ABT administration and stage revivals from its repertory. Died in a drowning accident. MC

Kröller, Heinrich, b. Munich, 1880; d. Würzburg, 1930. German dancer and choreographer. Pupil of the Munich S., joined the co. there, soloist from 1901. To Paris 1907 to study with ZAMBELLI and STAATS; returned to Dresden as principal dancer. To Munich as ballet master 1917; combined this responsibility with work at the Staats Os of Berlin (1919–22) and Vienna (1922–8). Among the many ballets he choreographed were Richard Strauss's *Josephslegende* (*see* LÉGENDE DE JOSEPH) and first productions of the same composer's *Couperin Suite* (1923) and *Schlagobers* (1924). GBLW

Kronstam, Henning, b. Copenhagen, 1934. Danish dancer and teacher. Entered RDBS 1943. Soloist RDB 1956. As a child he danced solo part in H. LANDER's *The Shepherdess and the Chimney Sweep* 1950; first adult role as the Drummer in GRADUATION BALL (1952). Poet in *Night Shadow* (*see* SONNAMBULA) 1955; created Romeo in ASHTON's ROMEO AND JULIET. For almost two decades he was the foremost Danish romantic dancer, then in mime parts such as the Dancing Master in LESSON and Iago in MOOR'S PAVANE (1973). Teacher at RDBS and from 1966 assistant ballet master. Guest appearances with RDB and SAND groups and as soloist in Europe and USA. Director, RDB, from 1978. SKJ
See E. Aschengreen, 'Henning Kronstam', *Les Saisons de le Danse* (Paris, Feb 1977) with list of roles

Kruuse, Marianne, b. Copenhagen, 1942. Danish dancer. Pupil of BARTHOLIN; Scandinavian B. 1959–61, T. d'Art du B. 1961–2, Mulhouse B. 1962–3, Stuttgart B. 1965–70. In 1970 she went with NEUMEIER to Frankfurt as soloist and with him to Hamburg 1973 as principal, creating chief roles in his version of ROMEO AND JULIET, NUTCRACKER, etc. GBLW

Krzesiński, Feliks, b. Warsaw, 1823; d. Krasnov, near St Petersburg, 1905. Polish dancer. First character dancer of Warsaw B. 1838–52. Excelled in Polish national dances, especially as the Best Man in CRACOW WEDDING. From 1853 principal character dancer in Maryinsky T., St Petersburg, also teacher of Polish dances. He taught the Tsar's family and Russian nobles. Father of KSHESSINSKA. JPU

Kshessinska [Kshesinskaya], Mathilde [Matilda-Maria] Feliksovna, b. Ligovo, near Peterhof [Petrodvorets], 1872; d. Paris, 1971. Russian dancer and teacher. A member of a Polish-born family of dancers (her father KRZESIŃSKI and brother Jozef were celebrated performers in St Petersburg), she studied at the Imperial S., St Petersburg, graduating into the ballet co. 1890. Eventually she was accorded the official rank of *prima ballerina assoluta*. A dancer of brilliant technique, strong dramatic gifts and great personal charm and beauty, Kshessinska owed some of her eminence in the Imperial B. to her association with members of the Imperial family (this story is delightfully told in her memoirs (tr. HASKELL) *Dancing in Petersburg*, London 1960, originally published in French as *Souvenirs de la Kschessinska*, 1960). She was the first Russian AURORA, and the first Russian dancer to perform the 32 *fouettés* in SWAN LAKE. Though the most glorious moments of her career lay in Russia, where she danced for 25 years, she also appeared with DIAGHILEV's B. Russes in London, Budapest, and Monte Carlo in 1911. She left Russia after the Revolution and settled in the S. of France where she became the morganatic wife of the Grand Duke Andrey, Tsar Nicholas II's nephew. She later moved to Paris where she opened a school and taught many of the best dancers of the 1930s and '40s, notably RIABOUCHINSKA. MC/CC

Kuchipudi *see* ASIA

Kun, Zsuzsa, b. Budapest, 1934. Hungarian dancer. Studied with NÁDASI, then at the Bolshoy and the Moscow Choreographic Inst. under E. GERDT, MESSERER, LEPESHINSKAYA, and Naima Baltacheyeva. Dancer at Budapest O. from 1949, solo dancer from 1953, excelling in lyric and dramatic, emotional and intellectual roles in all genres from classical to modern. Dances all principal roles in the Budapest repertoire, incl. L. LAVROVSKY's JULIET and ASHTON's LISE. With FÜLÖP choreographed *Mario and the Magician* (1964; mus. István Láng). In addition to touring with the co. she has performed abroad as a guest in her own right, first in the USSR (late 1950s), with LFB four times 1961–5; danced with NAGY, Sydney 1972. Director of the State B. Inst. since 1972. Liszt Prize, 1960; Kossuth Prize, 1966; Eminent Artist, 1971. GPD

Kunakova, Lyubov, b. Izhevsk, 1951. Soviet dancer. Studied Perm State S. of Choreography, graduating to the Perm OB, 1970. Gold medal, Varna, 1972. JS

Lydia Kyasht as she appeared at the Empire Theatre, London, 1913

Kurgapkina, Ninel, b. Leningrad, 1929. Soviet dancer and teacher. Studied with VAGANOVA, graduating to the Kirov B. in 1947. Roles with the Kirov incl. AURORA, ODETTE-ODILE, MYRTHA and appeared in many modern works incl. Parasha (BRONZE HORSEMAN). In 1972, appointed a Director of the Vaganova S., Leningrad. Honoured Artist, RSFSR. JS

Kyasht [Kyaksht], Lydia, b. St Petersburg, 1885; d. London, 1959. Russian dancer and teacher. Studied at Imperial S., St Petersburg; debut 1902; second dancer 1905; first dancer 1908. To London 1908 (one of the first Russian dancers to arrive) and succeeded GENÉE at the Empire T. Danced in USA and with DIAGHILEV but eventually settled in England and taught in London and Cirencester. In the 1940s, during the wartime ballet boom, had her own co., B. de la Jeunesse Anglaise, mostly drawn from her own pupils. MC
See her memoirs, *Romantic Recollections* (London and New York 1929); E. C. Mason, 'Lydia Kyasht', *Dance and Dancers* (London, Mar 1959)

Kylián, Jiří, b. Prague, 1947. Czech dancer and choreographer. Pupil of Prague Cons. and London RBS. Joined Stuttgart B. 1968, becoming a principal, and choreographed ballets for the NOVERRE SOCIETY there. In 1975 appointed joint director of NDT. GBLW

L

Laban, Rudolf von, b. Bratislava [Pozsony; Pressburg], 1879; d. Weybridge, Surrey, 1958. Hungarian dancer, teacher, and theorist. Studied Munich and Paris; appointed director of the Allied State Ts, Berlin, 1930 and staged large productions for 'movement choirs' throughout Germany. His best-known pupils were WIGMAN and JOOSS. Together they codified the laws of physical expression which they called Eukinetics, a system of controlling the dynamics and expressiveness of the human body. Laban's theories dominated dance in Germany during the prewar years. In 1938 to England where, during World War II, he devised a system of corrective exercises for factory workers. Author of several books – *Ein Leben für den Tanz* (*A Life for the Dance*; Dresden 1935) was reissued with valuable footnote material by Lisa Ullman in London 1975 – and inventor of a system of dance notation, *Kinetographie Laban* (1928) which was later codified as Labanotation. Laban's last years were spent in Surrey where with Lisa Ullman he conducted the Art of Movement Studio, now part of Goldsmiths' College, Univ. of London. His daughter Juana de Laban teaches dance in American universities. *See also* DANCE NOTATION. MC
See R. Laban and F. C. Lawrence, *Effort: Economy in Body Movement* (New York and London 1974)

Labis, Attilio, b. Vincennes, 1936. French dancer and choreographer. Paris OS 1947. *Corps de ballet* 1954, *premier danseur* 1959; *étoile* 1960. Prix Nijinsky 1961. Associate *maître de ballet* 1966. International guest artist. Created roles for DESCOMBEY and BESSY. Danced with RB at CG 1965, partnering FONTEYN with whom he has often appeared on tour with various cos. Dances in DOLLAR's *The Combat*, ICARE, FOUR TEMPERAMENTS, ÉTUDES, GISELLE, SWAN LAKE. Choreographed *Arcades* (1964; mus. Hector Berlioz), *Silk Rhapsody* (1968). He m. VLASSI. Virile, a brilliant technician, he spontaneously expresses the joy of dancing. M-FC
See I. Lidova, 'Attilio Labis', *Les Saisons de la Danse* (Paris, Apr 1971) with list of roles

Lac des Cygnes, Le *see* SWAN LAKE

Lacotte, Pierre, b. Châtou, 1932. French dancer, teacher, and choreographer. Entered Paris OS 1942, *corps de ballet* 1946. Created major role in *Septuor* for LIFAR 1950. *Premier danseur* 1952. Frustrated in his desire to choreograph, he left the O. 1955 to found with Josette Clavier the B. de la Tour Eiffel and staged many of his own modern works, incl. *La Nuit est une Sorcière*, *Solstice*, *Gosse de Paris*. Founded B. National des Jeunesses Musicales de France 1962 for which he choreographed *Hamlet*, *Penthésilée*, *La Voix*, *Combat de Tancrède*. He m. THESMAR for whom he produced SYLPHIDE for French TV (1972) with such success that the production was later mounted at the Paris O. Revived COPPÉLIA there 1973. Now a teacher at the Paris O. and concentrating on revivals of the 19th-c. ballets, researching meticulously to restore as much as possible of their original style. M-FC

Lady and the Fool, The, ballet, 1 act, 3 scenes, ch. CRANKO; mus: selected from Giuseppe Verdi's operas arr. Charles Mackerras; sc./c. Richard Beer. Oxford, New T., SWTB; 25 Feb 1954; dan. MILLER, MACMILLAN, Johaar Mosaval. Revived and revised CG, SWB, 9 June 1955; dan. GREY, Philip Chatfield, Ray POWELL. A rich beauty, La Capricciosa, on a whim takes two poor clowns, Moondog and Bootface, to an extravagant ball where they perform their 'routine' for the amusement of her friends. She is touched by the perf., falls in love with Moondog and rejects her aristocratic suitors. When first staged by a young co. in a small theatre the ballet had a sentimental charm which it lost when transferred to the CG stage. It persists in popularity, largely because of the score, the big *pas d'action* for La Capricciosa and her suitors, and the dance of the clowns. Revived London, SWRB, 1976. MC

Lærkesen, Anna, b. Copenhagen, 1942. Danish dancer. Studied with Edite Frandsen; accepted at RDB 1959. Soloist 1964, also studied with Bolshoy B. for a few months. Dances JULIET in ASHTON's ballet, MYRTHA, ODETTE-ODILE, Aili (CULLBERG's *The Moon Reindeer*), SYLPHIDE, and parts in more modern repertory, always with classic lines and clean style as her 'trademark'. Prima ballerina 1966 and the foremost soloist in Danish ballet, even if frequent periods of weakness have kept her from attaining the heights. Toured with RDB in Europe and USA and as guest soloist at Bolshoy T., Moscow. SKJ

Lafontaine, Mlle [Mlle de la Fontaine], b. Paris, 1655; d. *c.* 1738. The first 'ballerina'; debut 1681 in TRIOMPHE DE L'AMOUR, the first work at the Paris O. to feature female dancers. Critics hailed her as the 'Queen of the Dance'. Her style must have been stately and noble, in view of the costumes of the time. Retired 1693 and passed her last years in a convent. Succeeded by Marie-Thérèse Subligny. MC

Laing [Skinner], Hugh, b. Barbados, 1911. British dancer. Studied with CRASKE and RAMBERT in London, with PREOBRAZHENSKA in Paris. Joined BR 1932, created roles in TUDOR's *The Planets*, JARDIN AUX LILAS, DARK ELEGIES; also danced title role in APRÈS-MIDI D'UN FAUNE, etc. Left to join Tudor's

London B. 1938; with him to USA to join ABT 1939; created leading roles in further Tudor ballets (PILLAR OF FIRE, ROMEO AND JULIET, DIM LUSTRE, UNDERTOW), and in *Aleko* (1944; ch. MASSINE), *Tally-Ho* (1944; ch. DE MILLE). Danced with NYCB 1950–3 – in BALANCHINE's PRODIGAL SON and *Tyl Ulenspiegel*, and ILLUMINATIONS, etc. With ABT 1954–6. Though never a great technician, his personal magnetism and artistry made him an unequalled interpreter of dramatic roles, especially in Tudor's ballets. Successful in commercial photography since retiring from the stage; has also assisted Tudor in the restaging of his ballets for many cos. DV

Lakatos, Gabriella, b. Budapest, 1927. Hungarian ballerina. Pupil of NÁDASI. Solo dancer of Budapest O. since 1947. A powerful character dancer, excellent performer of classical parts. First outstanding role was the Miller's Wife in TRICORNE and has since danced all principal roles of the Budapest repertoire. A frequent guest performer abroad: danced with LFB several times in the early 1960s; danced in Barcelona etc. Kossuth Prize 1958, Merited Artist 1966, Eminent Artist 1971. GPD

Lake, Molly, b. Cornwall, 1900. English dancer and teacher. Pupil of CECCHETTI; one of the finest exponents of his method of teaching. Danced in A. PAVLOVA's co. and with MARKOVA–DOLIN B. In 1945 with her dancer husband Travis Kemp formed small Embassy B. and toured widely. In 1954 they went to Turkey to teach at the Cons. in Ankara. Returned to London 1974 and continued to teach master classes, notably at the LSCD where Kemp became administrator. MC

Lambert, Constant, b. London, 1905; d. London, 1951. English composer and conductor, student of Ralph Vaughan Williams. Introduced to DIAGHILEV, who commissioned ROMEO AND JULIET, the first English score for the B. Russes (Monte Carlo 1926; ch. NIJINSKA and BALANCHINE), but a source of great anguish to Lambert because of its surrealistic presentation. Lambert's other ballets are *Pomona* (Buenos Aires 1927; ch. Nijinska), *Horoscope* (London 1938; ch. ASHTON) and *Tiresias* (London 1951; ch. Ashton), which was badly received. Lambert arranged ballet scores from the music of AUBER (RENDEZVOUS), Franz Liszt (*Apparitions*, London 1936; ch. Ashton), Giacomo Meyerbeer (PATINEURS), François Couperin (*Harlequin in the Street*, London 1938; ch. Ashton), William Boyce (*The Prospect Before Us*, London 1940; ch. DE VALOIS), Henry Purcell (*Comus*, London 1942; ch. HELPMANN), and Emmanuel Chabrier (*Ballabile*, London 1950; ch. PETIT) – all for SWB, from whose inception Lambert was the sage musical director. As the co.'s chief conductor he was an important influence, his leadership guaranteeing remarkable musical standards. His conducting of SLEEPING BEAUTY was a great experience. DH

See Richard Shead, *Constant Lambert*, with a memoir by Anthony Powell (London 1973)

Lamhut, Phyllis, b. Brooklyn, NY, 1933. American modern dancer, choreographer, and teacher. Studied primarily with NIKOLAIS at the Henry St Playhouse, NY, also with CUNNINGHAM, ballet with Zena Romett, and circus arts with Hovey Burgess. Featured dancer with Nikolais Dance Co. 1948–69 where she created roles in over 25 works. Leading female dancer with the LOUIS Dance Co. 1963–9; roles incl. *Proximities*, *Go 6*, and JUNK DANCES. The Phyllis Lamhut Dance Co. was formed 1969. Since 1950 she has choreographed over 75 works, incl. solos and works for as many as 40 dancers. Her pieces have been performed in theatres, gymnasiums, and on streets. Known for her humour and unpredictable sense of drama, she has an innate sense of timing and is most often called a comedienne although not all her works are humorous. She is eclectic in her use of music, most frequently using collage sound scores or arranged sounds. Has taught in the USA and Canada, principally at the Henry St Playhouse and the Louis–Nikolais T. Lab, NY, and in many universities and colleges. Her recent works (1975) incl. *Conclave* (mus. Thomas Mark Edlun), *Solo with Company* (mus. Michael Czajkowski), and *Country Mozart* (mus. W. A. Mozart and Country Western). KC

Landé, Jean-Baptiste, b. ?; d. St Petersburg, 1748. French dancer and ballet master. Royal dancing master in Stockholm 1721–7; taught in Copenhagen 1726. To Russia 1734 as a dancer and teacher; in 1738 became the first director of the Imperial BS in St Petersburg. He laid the foundations of Russian ballet and served it until his death. *See* RUSSIA AND THE USSR. MC

See Natalia Roslavleva, *Era of the Russian Ballet* (London and New York 1966); Marian Hannah Winter, *The Pre-Romantic Ballet* (London 1974; New York and Toronto 1975)

Lander, Harald, b. Copenhagen, 1905; d. Copenhagen, 1971. Danish dancer, choreographer, teacher, and ballet master. Entered RDBS 1913, when BECK was still ballet master. Educated in the August BOURNONVILLE repertoire and entered the co. as *coryphée* 1923. Studied in USA, S. America, and Russia 1926–9 and also danced abroad. Returned 1929 to Copenhagen; successful as Bournonville's *The Toreador*. Choreographic debut with *Gaucho* 1931. Director RDB 1932–51. He developed a new repertoire, new dancers, and a *corps de ballet*, and under him the RDB flourished in a period of great creative activity (*see* DENMARK), even if it made very little impression outside Denmark. He created almost 30 ballets for the co., in all styles. He introduced the contemporary European repertory and choreographed many works incl. QARRTSILUNI. His masterpiece, ÉTUDES, became the most-danced Danish ballet of this c. Settled in Paris 1951; *Directeur de la* *danse*, Paris O., for two seasons and resident choreographer for almost 10 years. He re-created several of his works in Paris and some new ones – the final version of *Études* and, most important, part of INDES GALANTES. Became a French citizen 1956 but worked as guest choreographer with cos all over the world, producing *Études* more than a dozen times. Returned to Copenhagen several times to produce his works at the Royal T., and new ballets for Danish TV. SKJ

Lander [Florentz-Gerhardt], Margot, b. Oslo, 1910; d. Copenhagen, 1961. Danish dancer. Entered RDBS 1917, soloist RDB 1931; first dancer in Danish ballet to gain title of prima ballerina (1942). Debut as Eskimo girl in FAR FROM DENMARK (1926). Developed from *demi-caractère* to *sérieux* roles: SWANILDA, ODETTE, GISELLE. A rare combination of wit and poetry made her the most loved – and best – dancer in the RDB in the first half of this century. She m. H. LANDER 1932. In the 1930s with B. RALOV and BRENAA as her partners she brought Danish ballet to its third great flowering with the Lander repertoire (*see* DENMARK). World War II and the German occupation of Denmark made it impossible for her to gain the position in international ballet she was destined for. Retired 1950. SKJ

Lander [Pihl Petersen], Toni, b. Copenhagen, 1931. Danish dancer and teacher. Entered RDBS 1939. RDB debut 1947 in KING'S VOLUNTEERS OF AMAGER. Soloist 1950. She m. H. LANDER 1950. Left RDB 1951. Several guest appearances with RDB. With H. Lander in Paris and guest artist with Original B. Russe. Ballerina with LFB 1954–9. Created main role in TARAS's *Le Rendezvous Manqué* 1958, touring Europe. A principal with ABT 1961–71, where she danced the classic repertoire from ODETTE-ODILE to SYLPHIDE. The ballerina in ÉTUDES became her virtuoso part on stage and in a Danish TV version. RDB 1971–6 as dancer and teacher; farewell perf. (spring 1976) as Desdemona in MOOR'S PAVANE. Divorced from H. Lander, she m. MARKS 1966. SKJ

Lane, Maryon, b. Zululand, 1931. S. African dancer and teacher. RAD scholarship to London SWBS 1946 after early studies in Johannesburg. Joined SWTB 1947, soon becoming soloist. Created many roles for MACMILLAN, notably in *Laiderette* (1954), DANSES CONCERTANTES (1955), and at CG the hypnotist's assistant in *Noctambules* (1956). Soloist with RB at CG from 1955 with a repertoire ranging from COPPÉLIA to SWAN LAKE. Supremely musical, a tiny dancer of warmth and charm and a gifted actress. From 1971 teaching at RBS. She m. BLAIR. MC

Lang, Harold, b. San Francisco, CA. American dancer. Studied with Theodore Kosloff, Hollywood, and W. CHRISTENSEN, San Francisco. Danced with B. Russe de Monte Carlo 1941–2, ABT 1942–7, 1948–9, 1955–9. Danced some classic roles but chiefly known for such roles as First Sailor in FANCY FREE, which he created. In the intervals between engagements with ABT he danced with NYCB during its first London season, 1950, and made many appearances in Broadway musicals, especially ROBBINS's *Look Ma, I'm Dancin'*, *Kiss Me, Kate*, and in the title role of *Pal Joey*. Now teaches in California. DV

Lang, Maria, b. Stockholm, 1948. Swedish dancer. Studied RSBS, entered RSB 1965. Promoted to soloist and *première danseuse* 1974. Specializes in lyric and classical roles. She has danced as guest with RWB and on leave of absence in 1974 and 1975 with the Australian B. Joined Australian B. as soloist 1976. AGS

Lang, Pearl, b. Chicago, IL, 1922. American modern dancer and choreographer. Educated at Chicago City Jr College of the Univ. of Chicago 1938–41; studied dance at Frances Allis Studio and with GRAHAM, HORST, STUART, Nanette Charisse, and others. In Chicago she danced with the PAGE Dance T.; in NY she joined the Graham Co., debut in *Punch and the Judy* 1941. Graham created several roles on her; among them 'for Death' in *Canticle for Innocent Comedians*, the Girl in Red in DIVERSION OF ANGELS. Soloist with the Graham Co. 1942–52, dancing many important roles incl. NIGHT JOURNEY and LETTER TO THE WORLD. She was the first performer to take on Graham roles – the Three Marys in *El Penitente* (NY 1947), later the Bride in APPALACHIAN SPRING (NY 1953). Formed her own co. 1952 and choreographed works for them such as *Legend*, *Rites*, *And Joy is My Witness*, *Song of Deborah*, *Juvenescence*, *Night Flight*, *Falls the Shadow Between*, *Shirah*, *Apasionada*, *Encounter*, *Passover Moments*. Her solos for herself incl. *Windsung* and *Moonsung*. She has performed in several Broadway productions and in musicals, summer stock, TV. She has continued to appear as guest soloist with the Graham Co., as well as direct her own co. Received Guggenheim Fellowships 1960 and 1969. She has taught at schools in the USA and abroad, has served on the faculties of the Yale Univ. S. of Drama, the Juilliard S. of Music Dance Department, the Neighborhood Playhouse, and currently, the American Dance Center. She has a strong choreographic affinity with material from Jewish and biblical legend; in Jan 1975 she premiered a full-length work at the 92nd St YM–YWHA, *The Possessed*, based on the legend of the Dybbuk, in which she danced the leading role. EK

Lanner, Katti [Katherina], b. Vienna, 1829; d. London, 1908. Austrian dancer, choreographer, and teacher, daughter of the composer Joseph Lanner. Trained in the Vienna Court OS; debut Vienna 4 Aug 1845. Praised by ELSSLER and CERRITO, and chosen for a leading role by August BOURNONVILLE 1854.

Danced in several European capitals before travelling to NY to dance GISELLE at Fisk's T., 11 July 1870. London debut also in *Giselle*, 22 Apr 1871, Drury Lane T. To USA again in 1873 where she stayed two years. Eventually settled in London and took over direction of National Training S. of Dancing where she taught for 10 years, greatly improving training standards in London. Choreographer, Empire T., 1887–97, staging, among many other works, *Monte Cristo*, 26 Oct 1896, in which GENÉE made her London debut 1897. Her last ballet was *Sir Roger de Coverley* (1907). MC
See Ivor Guest, *The Empire Ballet* (London 1962); Phyllis Bedells, *My Dancing Days* (London 1954)

Lapauri, Aleksandr, b. Moscow, 1926; d. Moscow, 1975. Soviet dancer, mime, choreographer, and teacher. Graduated from Bolshoy TS 1944, in Bolshoy B. Co. for 23 years. Outstanding partner in semi-acrobatic *pas de deux* with his wife STRUCHKOVA, in MOSZKOWSKI WALTZ, GLIÈRE's *Étude* (own choreography) etc. First appearance with Bolshoy B. in London as GIREY. Superb HILARION. Other roles JEAN DE BRIENNE, ABDÉRÂME, Paris and Capulet in L. LAVROVSKY's ROMEO AND JULIET. Created André in *Fadetta* (ch. Lavrovsky). Choreographed (with Olga Tarasova) *Song of the Woods* (1961; mus. Germann Zhukovsky), and LIEUTENANT KIJË. Taught partnering at Moscow Choreographic S. From 1953 taught at Choreographers' Faculty of GITIS, of which he became Dean 1970. Honoured Artist, RSFSR. NR

Lapzeson, Noemi, b. Buenos Aires, 1940. Argentine dancer and choreographer. Studied jazz, ballet, and modern dance in New York. Joined GRAHAM Dance Co. 1959, and danced in almost every piece in the repertory. Left 1968 to help form LCDT, with which she remained as principal dancer, teacher, and choreographer until 1973. Her works there incl. *Cantabile* (1971), *One Was the Other* (1972), *Conundrum* (1972). Since leaving London she has been teaching and choreographing as a freelance in Europe, Israel, the USA, and Canada. DV

Larionov, Michel, b. Tiraspol, 1881; d. Fontenay-aux-Roses, 1964. Russian painter and designer. Lived in Paris from 1914 when invited there by DIAGHILEV for whom his first designs were for MASSINE's *Soleil de Nuit* (1915). Larionov's work was always based on Russian popular art but also conscious of contemporary trends. Creator with his friend Kazimir Malevich of *rayonnism*, near-abstract art 1909. Notable designs for Diaghilev were Massine's *Les Contes Russes* 1917 and NIJINSKA's *Renard* 1922. He also experimented in sketching choreographic ideas for *Chout* (with Tadeo Slavinski) 1921 and drew innumerable portraits and caricatures of Diaghilev and his entourage. Larionov was as influential in guiding Diaghilev's artistic taste in the postwar years as BENOIS had been earlier. MC

Larsen, Gerd, b. Oslo, 1921. Norwegian dancer, British subject. Trained with the great CECCHETTI teacher, CRASKE. Debut with TUDOR's London B. 1938. Created French ballerina in GALA PERFORMANCE. Joined International B. 1941 and SWB 1944; soloist 1954. Formerly a charming classical dancer, now one of the RB's great mime artists playing queenly roles and characters like the mother in GISELLE and the Nurse in MACMILLAN's ROMEO AND JULIET. Also teaches at the RBS. She m. TURNER. MC

Larsen, Niels Bjørn, b. Copenhagen, 1913. Danish dancer, choreographer, and ballet master. Entered RDBS 1920. Guest artist with SCHOOP 1936–7. Soloist RDB 1942. The foremost mime at the RDB in roles from DR COPPÉLIUS to MADGE and from Angekok (QARRTSILUNI) to WIDOW SIMONE. Produced several ballets for RDB, incl. *Capricious Lucinda* (1954) and *Peter and the Wolf* (1960). Teacher at RDB from 1946, producer at Royal T. from 1947. Acting ballet master RDB 1951, ballet master 1953–6 and 1960–6. From 1955 director of the Pantomime T., Tivoli. Started his own co., Niels Bjørn-Balletten, 1940, which for some years was popular at variety shows in Scandinavia. SKJ

Last, Brenda, b. London, 1938. English dancer. Pupil of Biddy Pinchard, VOLKOVA, and RBS. Won coveted GENÉE gold medal of RAD 1955. Joined Western TB 1957 and became a mainstay of that co. Joined RB 1963 (rejected originally as too small) and became a principal. A quick, precise, and ebullient dancer, she has also given sensitive perfs in SYLPHIDES. A 'trouper' in the best sense of the word, she is an indefatigable worker. Appointed ballet mistress to the touring RB 1974, she was at the same time dancing leading roles, notably SWANILDA. Director, Norwegian NB, 1977. MC

Laumer, Denise, b. Berlin, 1930. German dancer. Pupil of BLANK and T. GSOVSKY in Berlin. Entered the Staats O., E. Berlin, 1947. After dancing in Wiesbaden she joined the Wuppertal B. in 1953 when WALTER was the ballet master and she created the chief roles in nearly all his ballets for the next 10 years, incl. *Orpheus* (1954), *Pelleas und Melisande* (1955), *Romeo und Julia* (1959), *Undine* (1962), *Der Tod und das Mädchen* (1964), etc. Also danced in Düsseldorf, Essen and Gelsenkirchen as guest. GBLW

Laurencia, ballet, 3 acts, ch. CHABUKIANI; lib. Evgeny Mendelberg after Lope de Vega's *Fuenteovejuna*; mus. Aleksandr Krein; sc. VIRSALADZE; scenic advisor E. Kaplan. Leningrad, Kirov T., 22 Mar 1939; dan. Chabukiani (Frondozo), DUDINSKAYA (title role), VECHESLOVA (Paskuala), Elena Chikvaidze, Boris Shavrov. Revived 2 Feb 1956; sc. Vadim Ryndin; dan. PLISETSKAYA (title role).The plot concerns a peasant uprising in Castile. Many other versions in the USSR, also in Bulgaria and

Czechoslovakia. Chabukiani's production played an important role in the development of dance imagery in Soviet ballet and presented profound characterizations. NR
See V. Krasovskaya, *Vakhtang Chabukiani* (Moscow and Leningrad 1956)

Lavery, Sean (Owen), b. Harrisburg, PA, 1956. American dancer. Studied with Richard Thomas and FALLIS. At the age of 10 danced in the Pennsylvania B.'s NUTCRACKER and in *Ballet School* with the Bolshoy B. San Francisco B. 1972–4, Frankfurt OB 1974–6, US Terpsichore from 1976. Created Don José in Alfonso Cata's *Sweet Carmen*; also dances classic roles and BALANCHINE repertory. DV

Lavrovsky [Ivanov], Leonid, b. St Petersburg, 1905; d. Paris, 1967. Soviet dancer and choreographer. Graduated from Leningrad Choreographic Technicum (former TS) 1922, class of PONOMARYOV. Soloist, State T. of O. and B. (later the Kirov) 1922–35. Participant in 'Young Ballet' evenings organized by a group of enthusiasts headed by BALANCHINE, and in F. LOPUKHOV's *Dance Symphony* (1923). Danced in regular theatre repertoire: CHOPINIANA, JEAN DE BRIENNE, SIEGFRIED in the old Russian version and the Count in VAGANOVA's production of SWAN LAKE, Amoûn in *Nuits d'Égypte* (ch. FOKINE), etc. Was good classical dancer and partner. Started choreographing own recital items early in his stage career. First successful attempt was *Symphonic Études* (1930; mus. Robert Schumann) for pupils of the Leningrad Choreographic Technicum, where he created his first full-length ballets: *Fadetta* (1933; to music from DELIBES's *Sylvia*) and KATERINA, later transferred to Leningrad Maly O. (of which he was artistic director of ballet 1935–8), and to Kirov T. (1936).

From the start, with *Fadetta* and FOUNTAIN OF BAKHCHISARAY, Lavrovsky endeavoured to convey deep meaning through dance imagery and staging, bringing realistically live and poetically moving people on to the ballet stage. This remained his principle in all that he achieved. A new version of FILLE MAL GARDÉE (in 3 acts) and PRISONER IN THE CAUCASUS (1938) were but a foretaste of his greatest achievement, ROMEO AND JULIET (Kirov T., 1940), the apex of Soviet dramatic ballet of the 1930s.

He headed Kirov B. 1938–44 (from 1942 he simultaneously worked at Erevan O.). Chief choreographer and artistic director, Bolshoy B. 1944–64 (with some intervals), where he mounted the definitive version of *Romeo and Juliet* (1946), and revived GISELLE, preserving the choreography intact but giving the ballet a greater dramatic significance. Choreographed *Paganini* (1960), *Night City* (1961) to BARTÓK's *The Miraculous Mandarin* but with a different libretto. A founder member of GITIS Choreographers' Faculty, where he taught from 1950; Professor 1952. Artistic director, Moscow Choreographic S. 1964–7. People's Artist, USSR. NR
See L. Lavrovsky, 'From My Reminiscences about Sergei Prokofiev' in S. S. Prokofiev, *Materials, Documents, Reminiscences* (Moscow 1956); 'Paths and Destinies of Soviet Ballet' in *Soviet Culture* (Moscow, 3 and 8 Apr 1968)

Lavrovsky, Mikhail, b. Tbilisi [Tiflis], 1941. Soviet dancer. Son of L. LAVROVSKY and ballerina Elena Chikvaidze. Graduated from Moscow Choreographic S. 1961. In first season at Bolshoy T. danced Philippe in FLAME OF PARIS, showing the dynamic temperament that is his hallmark. Exquisite technique and great power of projection made his BASILIO outstanding. Danced ROMEO at memorial perf. for his father, but rehearsed role while he was still alive. His greatest perfs have been in GRIGOROVICH's ballets: as Ferhad in LEGEND OF LOVE, the Prince in NUTCRACKER, especially the tragic hero SPARTACUS, for which he was awarded the Lenin Prize. Studies at the Choreographers' Faculty of GITIS. He m. SEMENYAKA. People's Artist, RSFSR. Gold medal, Varna, 1965. Lenin Prize 1970. NR
See N. Avaliani and L. Zhdanov, tr. N. Ward, *Bolshoi's Young Dancers* (Moscow and London 1975)

Lazowski, Yurek, b. Warsaw, 1917. Polish dancer. M. dancer Galina Razoumova. Studied at Warsaw OBS. Debut with RUBINSTEIN co., Paris 1934. Danced with DE BASIL's B. Russe de Monte Carlo 1935–41, ABT 1941–3 and 1954–5, B. Russe de Monte Carlo 1944–6. One of the great character dancers of his time, a magnificent PETRUSHKA. Since retiring from the stage he has taught character dancing at SAB and other schools in NY. DV

Lazzini, Joseph, b. Marseille, 1927. French dancer and choreographer. Studied with F. Maylach. *Premier danseur*, B. de Nice 1945. *Étoile*, B. of Naples 1949–54. *Danseur étoile* and director, B. of the Liège O. 1954–7, of the Toulouse Capitole 1958, of the Marseille BO 1959–68. Invited to Sc. 1961, to the NY Met 1965, to BT Contemporain 1968, and Paris O. Founded T. Français de la Danse, 1969. Directed the Strasbourg B. du Rhin 1971–2. A prolific and ingenious producer who utilizes all the spectacular effects. Taken up with 'total theatre', he has had successes with e.g. $E = mc^2$ (1964), *Fils Prodigue* (1966), *Ecce Homo* (1968). M-FC
See L. Rossel, 'Joseph Lazzini', *Les Saisons de la Danse* (Paris, Apr 1969) with list of roles

Leaves are Fading . . . , The, ballet, ch. TUDOR; mus. Antonín Dvořák; sc. Ming Cho Lee; c. Patricia Zipprodt; ltg Jennifer Tipton. NYST, ABT, 17 July 1975; dan. KIRKLAND, Jonas Kage. A romantic, plotless ballet depicting young love remembered by a woman in the autumn of her life. FM

LeClercq, Tanaquil, b. Paris, 1929. American dancer. Studied at SAB. Danced with B. Society and NYCB 1946–56. Created many roles in BALANCHINE ballets, notably FOUR TEMPERAMENTS, SYMPHONY IN C, ORPHEUS, BOURRÉE FANTASQUE, VALSE, IVESIANA; also in *The Seasons* (CUNNINGHAM), ILLUMINATIONS, AFTERNOON OF A FAUN and CONCERT, etc. Her career was tragically cut short when she contracted poliomyelitis in Copenhagen during the NYCB's 1956 European tour. She m. Balanchine 1953, divorced 1969. Now teaches at DTH. DV

Lee, Mary Ann, b. Philadelphia, PA, 1823; d. 1899. American dancer. NY debut 1839 in *The Maid of Cashmere*, an English version of AUBER's *Le Dieu et la Bayadère*. When ELSSLER was in the USA 1840, Lee took lessons from her English partner James Sylvain and learned many of her celebrated solos. After successful US tours went to Paris to study with CORALLI and learn GISELLE, *La Fille du Danube*, and *Jolie Fille de Gand* which she took back to the USA. On 1 Jan 1846 was the first American to dance Giselle at the Howard Atheneum, Boston, partnered by G. W. SMITH. Failing health curtailed her perfs: she retired 1847 but on her husband's death occasionally returned to the stage until 1854. In 1860 opened her own school in Philadelphia. Considered the best American dancer after MAYWOOD but not in the class of her European contemporaries. MC
See Lillian Moore, 'First American Giselle', *Dance Index* (New York, May 1943)

Leeder, Sigurd, b. Hamburg, 1902. German dancer and teacher. Studied with LABAN in Hamburg; debut 1920 as a dancer and actor. In 1924 he joined JOOSS's Neue Tanzbühne; in 1928 moved with Jooss to Essen, where they founded the Folkwang Tanz T. and worked in the Folkwang S. Left Germany with Jooss 1934; co-director of Jooss–Leeder S. at Dartington Hall, Devon. In 1935 B. Jooss was formed, of which Leeder was co-director; they moved to Cambridge in 1940 and Leeder was ballet master until 1947, choreographing *Sailor's Fancy* (mus. Martin Penny). Taught in London 1947–58; taught in Santiago, Chile, 1959–65. Opened school in Herisau, Switzerland, 1966. GBLW

Legat, Nikolay [Nicolas], b. Moscow, 1869; d. London, 1937. Russian dancer, teacher, and choreographer. Son of Gustav Legat (1837–95), a dancer and teacher at the Moscow TS, and grandson of Ivan (Johann) Legat, a Swedish master of theatrical machinery who worked at the Imperial Ts (it is not known whether this is the same Ivan Legat who lost his life in an unsuccessful balloon flight over St Petersburg).

Nikolay graduated from St Petersburg TS 1888, pupil of JOHANSSON and P. GERDT, with whom he soon alternated in various roles. Of rather stocky build, he never became an ideal virtuoso dancer but strict adherence to perfect classical style, which he maintained throughout his life, grace and good carriage, and his flawless partnering, placed him in

Sergey Legat partnering LEGNANI in *La Camargo*, 1901

the first ranks of the Maryinsky B. In his youth, he was prominent in roles requiring *bravura* dancing, and he succeeded CECCHETTI as the BLUEBIRD after the premiere of SLEEPING BEAUTY. In his first season at the Maryinsky, he also danced Zephyr in M. PETIPA's *The Talisman*.

Danced his first principal role 1890–1 season, and in the following seasons appeared notably as FRANZ and COLAS, both roles requiring characterization. Never ideally suited to play romantic heroes, he nevertheless danced leading parts in the three TCHAIKOVSKY ballets, SWAN LAKE, *Sleeping Beauty*, and NUTCRACKER. He achieved acclaim as BASILIO and in other roles, e.g. Harlequin in MILLIONS D'ARLEQUIN, in which he half-danced and half-mimed, performing the role with extraordinary musical artistry.

In 1905 he was appointed second ballet master. Upon Petipa's dismissal, the post of first ballet master was left vacant and Legat thus became virtually the head of the Maryinsky B. He worked hard to maintain the high level of its classical school. Abandoning classes at St Petersburg TS, where he had taught from the early 1900s, he replaced Johansson as teacher of the *classe de perfectionnement*, and in 1909 founded a special new *pas de deux* class.

He tried his hand at choreography, but revealed little talent in this area. With his brother Sergey he created his best ballet in 1904, *The Fairy Doll* (mus. Joseph Bayer with interpolations by Tchaikovsky, DRIGO, Anatol Lyadov and Anton Rubinstein; dance for black dolls by Louis Moreau Gottschalk). The brothers devised this ballet in the same way they drew their book of caricatures; one would start the work, the other would add something, and so they continued until the dance or drawing was completed. Nikolay alone choreographed his next ballet, *Puss in Boots* (mus. Aleksandr Mikhailov, perf. only twice, Dec 1906). *The Crimson Flower* (a version of *Beauty and the Beast*, mus. Foma Gartman, Dec 1907) followed the set pattern of 19th-c. ballet and achieved some success because of the numerous *divertissements* in its five acts, performed by all the leading young dancers of the day, incl. A. PAVLOVA and FOKINE. In spite of Petipa's consternation, Legat also revived Petipa's *The Talisman* and *Les Saisons*.

Nikolay worked next with ASAFYEV, who composed music for small ballets produced privately, mostly at the Narodny Dom stage, where standards were far from academic. By 1917 he had not reached any agreement with the former Maryinsky T., where he was greatly appreciated as a teacher but where his dictatorial behaviour towards the co. was not tolerated. He then taught at several private ballet schools, notably Akim Volynsky's 'S. of Russian B.' where one of his first students was PUSHKIN. Late in 1920 he moved to Moscow, but could not find a teaching position either at the school, where TIKHOMIROV held the reins, or at the Bolshoy T., where he made himself unpopular by requesting that his second wife, Nadezhda (Nadine) Nikolayeva, his private student and nearly 30 years his junior, be awarded ballerina status – an impossible request at the formal and academic Bolshoy T. In Aug 1922 he was elected a member of the supreme choreographic council at the former Maryinsky T. but left Russia the same year.

He opened his first London studio in 1923; was ballet master to the DIAGHILEV B. 1925–6, but, according to GRIGORIEV, his teaching was too different from that of CECCHETTI to please the co. The last 15 years of his life were consequently spent teaching in London (among his pupils was EGLEVSKY). After his death his widow continued the school and at the outbreak of World War II transferred it to Sussex, the first fully educational, vocational ballet school in Britain.

Nikolay's brother Sergey (1875–1905) was also a dancer. He graduated from St Petersburg TS 1894 into the *corps de ballet*. Though six years his brother's junior, he soon outshone him as a dancer, and by 1903 had attained the rank of *premier danseur*. In 1896 he danced the title role in IVANOV's *Acis et Galatée*, and gradually danced all of P. Gerdt's best roles. His creation of JEAN DE BRIENNE was thought 'exemplary' by such critics as Valerian Svetlov. In 1901 he was asked to revive *La Camargo* for LEGNANI's farewell benefit perf., and, besides brilliantly dancing the role of G. VESTRIS and partnering the ballerina with great authority, he was responsible for a new adagio and two solos for the ballerina. The future looked bright. He taught mime at the school and worked as a *répétiteur* at the Maryinsky T. He was an incomparable partner, partly because of his constant involvement in all kinds of athletics (often with Nikolay); there was a standard joke at the theatre that he could lift even his common-law wife, Marie Petipa. Sadly, she brought more grief than joy to him: in 1905 she forced him to remove his name from a petition to the Maryinsky T. which many of the dancers had signed. In a fit of frustration and humiliation, he cut his throat on 19 Oct 1905.

Several other members of the Legat family were distinguished in Russian ballet. Gustav Legat, father of Nikolay and Sergey, m. Maria Granken, a pretty and versatile dancer, especially prominent in character roles. She bore nine children with practically no interruption to her career, several of whom were placed in the Moscow TS, incl., besides Nikolay and Sergey, Vera Legat (1865–?), who graduated from the TS 1884 as a *coryphée* and was a mediocre character dancer, m. her protector Count Shuvalov, and emigrated to Paris; Evgenia Legat (1870–?), who graduated from the TS 1889 into the *corps de ballet*, and was dismissed 1908 for lack of talent; and Ivan (1872–?), who graduated from the TS 1890, might have had a successful career, but, suffering from bouts of insanity, retired from dancing and became a monk. Their uncle, Ernest (1845–73), Gustav's brother, graduated from the TS 1864, and had an uneventful career as a *coryphée* until his death. Adelaide Legat (1844–1905), daughter of the Ivan Legat who lost his life in the balloon flight, may have been the sister of Gustav and Ernest. She graduated from the TS 1860; her career is not known.

The Legat dynasty continues today in both Russia and Britain. Tatiana Legat (b. Leningrad, 1934), Nikolay Legat's grand-daughter by his first wife, Antonina Chumakova, a Maryinsky dancer, is one of the Kirov T.'s leading *demi-caractère* dancers, particularly noted for the creation of the One Who Lost Her Beloved in COAST OF HOPE. Nikolay's daughter by his second wife, Anna Legat-Pinnes, is administrative principal of the Legat S. in Sussex, England, and her daughter Mimi in 1976 became a soloist with the RB de Wallonie at Charleroi in Belgium. NR/MC

See A. J. Alekseyev-Jakovlev (as told to Evgeny Kuznetzov), *Russian Folk Revels* (*Russkie Narodnye Gooliania*) (Leningrad and Moscow 1948); Nikolay and Sergey Legat, *Russky Balet v Karikaturakh* (St Petersburg 1903); Nikolay Legat, *The Story of the Russian School* (London 1932); Mikhail Borisoglebsky (ed.), *Materials for the History of Russian Ballet* (Vol. 1 Leningrad 1938; Vol. 2 1939)

Légende de Joseph, La (*Die Josephslegende*), ballet, 1 act, 2 scenes, ch. FOKINE; lib. Harry Kessler, Hugo von Hofmannsthal; mus. Richard Strauss; sc. José-Maria Sert; c. BAKST, BENOIS. Paris O., DIAGHILEV's B. Russes, 17 May 1914; dan. MASSINE, Maria Kusnetsova, Vera Fokina. The biblical story of Joseph and Potiphar's wife treated with Renaissance splendour, in 16th-c. Venetian costume, this was the ballet in which Diaghilev introduced Massine, his latest discovery, to the public; otherwise unmemorable, the score being one of Strauss's least distinguished compositions, though other choreographers have attempted it, incl. KRÖLLER (*Josephslegende*, Berlin 1921 and Vienna Staats O., 18 Mar 1922), BALANCHINE (RDB 18 Jan 1931, H. ROSEN (Munich Staats O. 1958); and TUDOR (Buenos Aires, T. Colón, 19 Aug 1958). DV

Legend of Love (*Legenda o Lyubvi*), ballet, 3 acts, ch. GRIGOROVICH; lib. Turkish writer and poet Nazym Khikmet after his play of the same title; mus. Arif Melikov; sc. VIRSALADZE. Leningrad, Kirov T., 23 Mar 1961; dan. Aleksandr Gribov (Ferhad), KOLPAKOVA (Shirien), MOISEYEVA (Mekhmene-Banu). Moscow, Bolshoy T., 15 Apr 1965; dan. LIEPA and M. LAVROVSKY (Ferhad, alternating), N. BESSMERTNOVA (Shirien), PLISETSKAYA (Mekhmene-Banu). Theme based on clash of love and duty. Queen Mekhmene-Banu sacrifices her beauty to save her sister Shirien from death, but regrets this when Shirien and Ferhad fall in love. The Queen contrives to keep the lovers apart and Ferhad sacrifices his love for Shirien because he must spend the rest of his days breaking through the Iron Mountain to bring water to his people. Mounted with same choreography all over the USSR, also in Prague. NR

Legnani, Pierina, b. 1863; d. 1923. Italian dancer. Studied Milan with Caterina Beretta; debut Sc.; joined the Maryinsky T., St Petersburg, 1893, where in CINDERELLA she performed 32 consecutive *fouettés* for the first time on any stage. At the Maryinsky until 1901, creating ODETTE-ODILE in the M. PETIPA/IVANOV revision of SWAN LAKE (1895). Other roles incl. SWANILDA and RAYMONDA, which she created. One of the only two dancers in the history of the Maryinsky T. to hold the title of *prima ballerina assoluta* (the other was KSHESSINSKA). She left Russia 1901; danced subsequently in Italy, France, and at the Alhambra T., London. JS/NR

Legong *see* ASIA

Lemaitre, Gérard, b. Paris, 1936. French dancer. Danced with several French cos before joining NDT (1960) where he soon became a leading soloist, creating roles in more than 80 ballets. Van MANEN has made notable use of his gifts and named *Opus Lemaitre* (1972) after him. Capable of strong drama, he is also a witty comedian. JP

Leningrad State Kirov Ballet *see* KIROV BALLET

Leningrad Symphony (*Leningradskaya Simfoniya*), ballet, 1 act, 2 scenes, ch./lib. BELSKY; mus. Dmitri Shostakovich, 1st movement of Seventh ('Leningrad') Symphony; sc. Mikhail Gordon. Leningrad, Kirov T., 14 Apr 1961; dan. SOLOVYOV, SIZOVA. Contemporary choreography grounded in classical ballet. Story of Soviet youth's heroic resistance to the German invasion in 1942. One of Belsky's most successful and highly moving works. NR

Lepeshinskaya, Olga, b. Kiev, 1916. Soviet dancer. Graduated Moscow Choreographic S. 1933, class of celebrated dancer and teacher Viktor Semyonov. Ballerina Bolshoy T. 1933–63, dancing LISE (GORSKY version) while at school, and debut as same. Brilliant technique, exceptional exhilaration of dancing, talent for vivid, optimistic portrayals. Created Suok (THREE FAT MEN), title role of SVETLANA, Jeanne (FLAME OF PARIS – Moscow version), Mirandolina in ballet of same title (ch. VAINONEN, after Carlo Goldoni's *La Locandiera*). Also brilliant classical virtuoso as KITRI, AURORA, Masha (NUTCRACKER), colouring these roles with her ebullient personality. Upon retirement a teacher in Berlin, Budapest, Rome, Paris, etc., bringing valuable experience of the Soviet method of teaching classical dance. People's Artist, USSR. Four State prizes. NR

Lepri, Giovanni, *fl. c.* 1850–60. Italian dancer and teacher. Pupil of BLASIS, he became a principal dancer at Milan Sc. 1857 but taught principally in Florence where CECCHETTI was among his pupils. He is a direct link between the teaching precepts of Blasis through Cecchetti to the teaching methods of classic ballet today. MC

Leskova, Tatiana, b. Paris, 1922. French dancer; Brazilian citizen since 1953. Artistic director of the T. Municipal, Rio de Janeiro. Studied with EGOROVA and joined Original B. Russe 1939. Was soon made *première danseuse* and performed the entire repertoire of the co. Left in 1945 to stay in Brazil. Was made ballet mistress, dancer, and choreographer of the T. Municipal 1950. Guest artist as ballet mistress with MASSINE's B. de Nervi. Choreographed many ballets for the Rio de Janeiro Co. and restaged all the classics. Has her own school in Rio de Janeiro and in late 1970s reorganized the T. Municipal *corps des ballet* as artistic director with Jorge García. MLN

Lesson, The (*Enetime*), ballet, ch. F. FLINDT, after Eugène Ionesco's 1-act *La Leçon*; mus. G. Delerue; sc. Bernard Daydé. Danish TV, 16 Sept 1963. Paris OC, 16 Apr 1964. In the repertory of RDB since 4 Dec 1964, this is Flindt's most original choreography, produced by him for many cos in Europe and USA. Flindt changed Ionesco's language teacher into a demented dance teacher. The scene is a dance studio, in which the teacher becomes absurdly and increasingly incensed by a girl pupil's work and eventually he kills her. The pianist folds her music away and closes the studio. The same pattern, with a different pupil, will be repeated the next day. SKJ

Lester, Keith, b. Guildford, Surrey, 1904. English dancer and choreographer. Studied with DOLIN, ASTAFYEVA and LEGAT. Toured with KARSAVINA on one of her European tours in the 1920s and also studied with her. Partnered SPESSIVTSEVA at the T. Colón, Buenos Aires, 1923, dancing SWAN LAKE and OISEAU DE FEU. Danced in Max Reinhardt's production of *The Miracle*, London 1932; then toured the USA in a ballet revue. Choreographed *David* for MARKOVA–DOLIN co. 1935 (mus. Maurice Jacobson, sc./c. Meninsky, curtain Jacob Epstein) and revived PAS DE QUATRE 1936. Formed a small co. to dance at the Arts T., London, during World War II and from 1945 until it closed was in charge of dancing at the Windmill T. From 1965 until 1975 principal teacher at the RAD and director of its teacher training. He devised the RAD's Dance in Education syllabus. A fine teacher of *pas de deux* work. MC

Letter to the World, modern dance work, ch./lib. GRAHAM; mus. Hunter Johnson; sc. Arch Lauterer; c. Edythe Gilfond. Bennington College, VT, Martha Graham Dance Co., 11 Aug 1940; dan. Graham, DUDLEY, HAWKINS, CUNNINGHAM. Based on the life of the American poet Emily Dickinson, excerpts from whose works are spoken in the piece (originally by an actress, in a later revision by the dancer Jean Erdman). DV

Levans [Levins], Daniel, b. Ticonderoga, NY, 1953. American dancer and choreographer. As a child studied tap and jazz in his home town, then ballet from the age of 13 in NY with Richard Thomas and FALLIS, and modern dance with Gertrude Shurr and O'DONNELL. Debut with FELD's American B. Co., 1969–71. Joined ABT 1971–4, NYCB 1974–5, then became principal dancer and resident choreographer of US Terpsichore, a co. directed by Thomas and Fallis. A talented character dancer, with ABT danced title roles in PETRUSHKA, BILLY THE KID, and APOLLO, the Transgressor in UNDERTOW, Third Sailor in FANCY FREE, the Champion Roper in RODEO, etc. With US Terpsichore he has not only danced but also choreographed: *Caprice* (1974; mus. STRAVINSKY), *Canciones Amatorias* (1975; mus. Enrique Granados), and *Italian Concerto* (1976; mus. Johann Sebastian Bach). In 1976 he retired from dancing to devote himself to choreography. DV

David Lichine and Tamara Grigorieva in a revival by the DE BASIL company of APRÈS-MIDI D'UN FAUNE

Levashov, Vladimir, b. Moscow, 1923. Soviet dancer. While still at Bolshoy TS created Rooster in LITTLE STORK. From 1941 one of the leading dancer-actors of Bolshoy B. Roles incl. VON ROTHBART, HILARION, etc. GRIGOROVICH productions enabled him to display an extraordinary blend of plastic and dramatic expressiveness – as DROSSELMEYER, CARABOSSE, Boyar (IVAN THE TERRIBLE). People's Artist, RSFSR. NR

Levinson, André, b. St Petersburg, 1887; d. Paris, 1933. Russian historian and writer on the dance. A strict upholder of the classical tradition, he did not succumb to the reforms of FOKINE or DIAGHILEV. In fact he criticized Diaghilev for being dominated by painters and musicians. (Concerning some of the productions of the Diaghilev B. in the 1920s he was right.) He settled in Paris after the Russian Revolution; wrote for the Paris papers and for many periodicals in France and England (on Spanish dance and music hall as well as classical ballet). His books incl. *La Danse au Théâtre* (Paris 1924), *La Vie de Noverre* (Paris 1925), *Anna Pavlova* (Paris 1928), *La Argentina* (1928), *Marie Taglioni, 1804–1884* (Paris 1929 in French, London 1930, tr. C. W. Beaumont in English), *La Danse d'Aujourd'hui* (Paris 1929) and *Les Visages de la Danse* (Paris 1933). MC

Lewitzky, Bella, b. San Bernardino, CA, 1915. American modern dancer and choreographer, of Russian parentage, with an exclusively West Coast career. Studied with HORTON; joined his co. In these early, innovative years he created his technique on her body. She danced the title roles in Horton's *Salome* and *The Beloved* (two character choreodramas), the role of The Chosen One in his *Sacre du Printemps* and Mexico in *¡Tierra y Libertad!* Performed with Paul Godkin in *Harvest Reel* (ch. DE MILLE) in the Hollywood Bowl, 1935. Later, with Horton, William Bowne, and her husband Newell Reynolds she formed the Dance T. Left Horton 1951 and founded Dance Associates, a group of 16 dancers. Since that time she has led three cos. The current one has been in existence for eight years; with them, Lewitzky has done performing and teaching residencies all over the USA and abroad, most recently at the American

Dance Fest., Connecticut College, and the T. de la Ville, Paris. She prefers to work with modern musical scores, often electronic, in a bright, quick movement style with stoptimes and isolations. Her dances incl. *Ceremony for Three*, *Spaces Between*, *Game Plan*, *Scintilla*, and others. She has done innovative work in dance for elementary schools, under the National Endowment for the Arts' Artists in the Schools program. In 1971 Lewitzky made a belated successful performing debut in concert with her own co. at the BAM, New York. EK

Lichine [Lichtenstein], David, b. Rostov-on-Don, 1910; d. Los Angeles, CA, 1972. Russian dancer and choreographer. He m. RIABOUCHINSKA. Studied with EGOROVA and NIJINSKA in Paris. Debut there with RUBINSTEIN's Co., 1928. Danced briefly with A. PAVLOVA's co., then with DE BASIL's B. Russe de Monte Carlo 1932–41. Created roles in MASSINE's *Jeux d'Enfants*, PRÉSAGES, BALANCHINE's *Cotillon*, and his own ballets, incl. *Protée*, FILS PRODIGUE, GRADUATION BALL. Other works incl. *Francesca da Rimini* for de Basil, 1937; *Helen of Troy* for ABT (revised from FOKINE's original), 1942; *La Création* (a ballet without music); and *La Rencontre* (mus. SAUGUET; sc./c. BÉRARD) for B. des CE, 8 Nov 1948. Danced with ABT 1944–5, 1952–3, 1954–5, mostly in his own works. Choreographed for films, at Milan Sc., and for LFB. Taught in Los Angeles 1955–72. DV

Lidström, Kerstin, b. Stockholm, 1946. Swedish dancer. Studied RSBS and London RBS. Joined RSB 1963, *première danseuse* 1974. Guest with NDT 1970. Among her roles the Bride in NOCES, LISE, and Titania in DREAM. AGS

Liebeslieder Walzer, ballet, 2 parts, ch. BALANCHINE; mus. Johannes Brahms; sc. David Hays; c. (Barbara) Karinska. NYCC, NYCB, 22 Nov 1960; dan. D. ADAMS, HAYDEN, Jillana, VERDY, W. CARTER, Conrad Ludlow, MAGALLANES, Jonathan Watts. A plotless ballet, part in Viennese style, part in dream sequence, to 33 waltzes by Brahms performed by a piano duet and a vocal quartet at the side of the stage. FM

Lieder eines Fahrenden Gesellen (*Songs of a Wayfarer*), ballet, ch. BÉJART, mus. Gustav Mahler. (As *Chant du Compagnon Errant*), Brussels, Forêt Nationale, B. XXe S., 11 Mar 1971; dan. NUREYEV (the young man), BORTOLUZZI (his double). A sustained piece of dramatic dancing for two men in which a young man and his double, his 'conscience', torment each other. Immensely popular; frequently given at galas with star dancers. DONN and LOMMEL have danced it with B. XXe S.; Lommel also with Nureyev in his 'Nureyev and Friends' seasons. M-FC

Lied von der Erde, Das (*Song of the Earth*), ballet, 1 act, ch. MACMILLAN; mus. Gustav Mahler; no decor; Stuttgart, Stuttgart B., 7 Nov 1965; dan. HAYDÉE, MADSEN, BARRA. Revived CG, RB, 19 May 1966; dan. Haydée, DOWELL, MACLEARY. The six Mahler songs are sung by two singers at each side of the stage. The music is Mahler's farewell to the joy and beauty of the world; MacMillan in his English version calls the main figure The Messenger of Death, who moves with calm inevitability throughout the work. The two other main characters are a man and a woman. Death takes the man; they return together for the woman. In the last song, *The Farewell*, there is, ultimately, acceptance and a hope of renewal. Considered by many to be MacMillan's masterpiece, the work is classically based but with much inventive movement, marvellously capturing the spirit of the songs.

The music has also been used by TUDOR for *Shadow of the Wind* (NY, ABT, 14 Apr 1948) and KONER (using the final song only, *Der Abschied*) for *The Farewell* (NY, 2 Feb 1962; solo dan. herself). MC

Liepa, Maris Rudolf, b. Riga, 1936. Soviet dancer. Studied Riga Choreographic S. 1947–50, Bolshoy TS 1950–4, graduating in class of Nikolay Tarasov. Soloist Riga Academic T. of O. and B. 1955. *Premier danseur*, Stanislavsky and Nemirovich-Danchenko Lyric T. 1956–60. From 1960 one of the leading dancers of the Bolshoy B. Excellent classical dancer noted for exceptionally clean and academically perfect technique. Dances all leading classical roles, especially famous for the depth of his characterizations, achieved through complete fusion of acting and dancing. He is beyond doubt one of the greatest dancer-actors of the 20th c. His CRASSUS (for which he was awarded the Lenin Prize, 1970) was hailed as one of the unique characterizations in the art of ballet. A versatile artist; has acted in films and TV; has taken part in many filmed ballets, and done incidental choreography. He teaches *pas de deux* at GITIS and at the Moscow Academic Choreographic S. He m. dramatic actress Margarita Zhigunova. People's Artist, RSFSR and Latvian SSR. NR
See Maris Liepa, 'Urge for Flight' in *Moskva*, No. 3 (Moscow 1976)

Lieutenant Kijë (*Podporuchik Kizhe*), ballet, 1 act, ch. LAPAURI and Olga Tarasova; mus. PROKOFIEV for film of same title; sc./c. Boris Messerer. Moscow, Bolshoy T., Bolshoy B., 10 Feb 1963; dan. STRUCHKOVA, BOGOMOLOVA, VASILIEV. Based on story by Yuri Tynianov; through a mistake of a negligent clerk, the name of a non-existent Lieutenant Kijë (which literally means 'blot') appears in a list of officers. A court lady exploits this opportunity to become Kijë's 'wife', and promotes him to a general's rank, etc., using these pranks as camouflage for her own affairs at court. Struchkova, piquant and saucy, was brilliant in the role, created with her flair for comedy in mind.

Staged 1964 with same choreography and decor at Kiev and Kazan. In Britain, as *Lieutenant Kijë*,

Serge Lifar in the title role of *Fils Prodigue*

choreographed Catherine Devillier, London, Cambridge T., 1963. The music also used by FOKINE for his *Russian Soldier* (NY Met, ABT, 6 Apr 1942). NR

Lifar, Serge, b. Kiev, 1905. Russian dancer, choreographer, and writer. Joined DIAGHILEV's co. 1923; studied with CECCHETTI and LEGAT. Created many leading roles, notably in *Apollon-Musagète* (*see* APOLLO) and FILS PRODIGUE. Endowed with exceptional beauty and magnetic stage presence he dominated the last four seasons of the Diaghilev co. Choreographic debut with the acrobatic version of *Le Renard* (1929).

After Diaghilev's death, he was invited by Jacques Rouché to stage at the Paris O. *Les Créatures de Prométhée* (*see* GESCHÖPFE DES PROMETHEUS) in which he created the principal role 1929. Named *danseur étoile* and *maître de ballet* of the Paris OB, he devoted to that co. nearly all the rest of his career. After daring creations like *Bacchus et Ariane* he turned, in 1932, towards classicism, dancing GISELLE (with SPESSIVTSEVA) and staging *Divertissement de Petipa* (a selection of dances from SLEEPING BEAUTY). He brought great nobility to the role of ALBRECHT in which he made his last appearance in 1956. His tragic second-act entrance, bearing lilies and trailing a long cloak, was as celebrated as his sensual interpretation of his own version of APRÈS-MIDI D'UN FAUNE (in which he dispensed with the nymphs). He inaugurated a class in *adage* which had an important influence on the French school for 20 years. The success of his ballet *Salade* (1935) prompted Rouché to give a complete evening of ballet at the O. once a week.

Lifar published his *Manifeste du Chorégraphe* (1935) which proclaimed the independence of dance from music, illustrating this by dictating to Arthur Honegger the rhythms for ICARE. Devised many ballets on heroic themes, e.g. *Alexandre le Grand* (1937). During World War II he created such varied works as CHEVALIER ET LA DAMOISELLE, *Joan de Zarisse* (*see* JOAN VON ZARISSA), and SUITE EN BLANC.

Forced for political reasons to leave the O. 1944, he joined Nouveau B. de Monte Carlo and staged DRAMMA PER MUSICA, *Chota Roustaveli*, and *Nautéos*. Re-engaged by the O. 1947, first as choreographer only, he staged *Les Mirages* and *Le Chevalier Errant*. He devised ballets as different in inspiration as PHÈDRE, the 3-act *Blanche-Neige* (*Snow White*), and the comic *Fourberies*, also *divertissements* in operas, part of INDES GALANTES, and *Le Martyre de Saint-Sébastien*. At the same time he worked with other cos. Left O. 1958, and pursued a peripatetic career.

He founded the Institut Chorégraphique 1947, which became the Université de la Danse 1957. He lectured; published historical works, *Carlotta Grisi* (1941), *Giselle* (1942), *Auguste Vestris* (1950), *L'Histoire du Ballet Russe* (1950; English translation by HASKELL); and aesthetic works such as *La Danse*, *Traité de Danse Académique*, *Traité de Chorégraphie* (1952); and memoirs, *Serge de Diaghilev* (1939) and his autobiography *Ma Vie* (1965); also *Le Manifeste du Chorégraphe* (Paris 1935); *À l'Aube de mon Destin: Sept Ans aux Ballets Russes* (Paris 1948); *La Musique par la Danse* (Paris 1955).

An original and controversial personality, Lifar exercised on French ballet a vitalizing influence and completely renovated the Paris OB. Closely weaving together dance and expression, he always knew how to show off his dancers – notably Spessivtseva and CHAUVIRÉ – while exploiting his personal gifts. He has devoted his life to ballet. M-FC
See 'Hommage à Serge Lifar', *Les Saisons de la Danse* (Paris, Feb 1970) with list of roles, etc.

Lifeguards of Amager *see* KING'S VOLUNTEERS OF AMAGER

Lighting *see* DESIGN

Lilac Fairy, the good fairy of SLEEPING BEAUTY

Limón, José, b. Culiacán, 1908; d. Flemington, NJ, 1972. Mexican dancer and choreographer. He m. costume designer Pauline Lawrence. After a year at the Univ. of California, he went to NY to study

Colour Plates. Facing page: A modern revival of EXCELSIOR, staged by Filippo Crivelli at the Scala, Milan, Sept 1974; dan. FRACCI and BORTOLUZZI

Overleaf: Oklahoma! by Richard Rodgers and Oscar Hammerstein II, ch. DE MILLE; sc./c. O. SMITH. The start of the nightmare ballet in which 'Laurey Makes Up Her Mind'. Judd, with his retinue of can-can girls, terrifies her and convinces her that she really loves Curley; an early example of the plot of a musical being carried forward through dancing (*see* MUSICALS).

PAX

painting, then in 1928 went to a perf. by KREUTZBERG, an experience that changed his life. He began to study dance with HUMPHREY and WEIDMAN, and danced in their co. 1930–40, as well as in Broadway musicals.

After serving in World War II he formed his own co. (1946), with Humphrey as artistic director. This co., José Limón and Dancers, made its New York debut 1947; its repertory incl. works by both Limón and Humphrey, and the principal dancers for many years were Limón, Ruth Currier, HOVING, B. JONES, and KONER. In 1949 he choreographed his most famous work, MOOR'S PAVANE.

In the 1950s the basic co. was considerably changed, making possible the presentation of works using a larger ensemble, such as Limón's *The Traitor* (mus. Gunter Schuller), dealing with the betrayal of Christ by Judas Iscariot, and *Missa Brevis* (mus. Zoltán Kodály), depicting the survival of religious faith in a war-torn society (now in the repertory of the AILEY Co.). The Limón Co. made many tours abroad under the auspices of the US Department of State, and also performed yearly at the American Dance Fest. at Connecticut College over a long period. Limón was on the dance faculty of the Juilliard S. of Music, NY, and choreographed works for its students as well as using them to augment his own co. for such works as *A Choreographic Offering* (1963; mus. Johann Sebastian Bach), a tribute to Humphrey.

Limón was a dancer of great dignity and magnificent, brooding intensity; he always remained keenly aware of his Mexican origin. Since his death the José Limón Dance Co. has continued, with the aim of preserving the works of both Humphrey and Limón, under the artistic direction first of Daniel Lewis and then of Ruth Currier (Humphrey's assistant 1951–8). The co. is now resident at New York's 92nd St YM-YWHA. DV

Lise, the heroine of FILLE MAL GARDÉE

Lisner, Charles, b. Paris. Australian dancer, choreographer, and director. Moved to Australia when nine years old. BOROVANSKY B.; opened studio in Brisbane 1953. Founder-director, Lisner B., 1960 (known as Queensland B. since 1962). Resigned directorship 1975. His ballets incl. *Images Classiques*. OBE 1976. KSW

Little Humpbacked Horse *see* HUMPBACKED HORSE

Little Mermaid, The (*Den Lille Havfrue*), fairy-ballet, 3 acts, ch. BECK; mus. Fini Henriques; lib. Julius Lehmann after Hans Christian Andersen's fairytale. Copenhagen, RDB, 26 Dec 1909. New version, ch. H. LANDER, 14 Mar 1936. Henriques's score is often heard in concert halls as a suite. SKJ

Little Stork, The (*Aistenok*), *or Friendly Hearts*, ballet, 3 acts, 4 scenes, ch. RADUNSKY, Nikolay

JOSÉ LIMÓN in *The Visitation*

Popko, Lev Pospekhin; mus. Dmitri Klebanov; sc. R. Makarov. Moscow, Affiliated Bolshoy T., 6 June 1937 (for graduation performance of Bolshoy BS). Revived 14 Feb 1955 in new version. The Little Stork, rescued by children, was first played by third-year pupil STRUCHKOVA. Other versions incl. one ch. GRIGOROVICH, Leningrad Palace of Culture 1948. Also known in English as *The Baby Stork*. NR

Litz, Katherine, b. Denver, CO, 1918. American dancer, choreographer, and actress. Studied modern dance with HUMPHREY and WEIDMAN, DE MILLE, H. HOLM, WIGMAN; ballet with FALLIS and Richard Thomas. With Humphrey–Weidman Co. 1936–42, also danced with de Mille's concert co. 1940–2 and in the Broadway musicals, *Oklahoma!* 1943–5 and *Carousel* 1945–7. Choreographed and danced title role in *Susanna and the Elders* for B. Ballads 1948. Gave first solo concert at YMHA, NY, April 1948, has since choreographed many solos for herself, as well as group works, incl. *Madame Bender's Dancing School* (1953), *The Enchanted* (1956; for ABT workshop), three versions of *Dracula* (1959, 1960, 1969), *Marathon* (1972), *They All Came Home Save One Because She Never Left* (1974). Formed her own co. 1967. Has taught and choreographed as artist-in-residence at many American universities. DV

Livry, Emma-Marie, b. Paris, 1842; d. Neuilly, 1863. French dancer. Pupil of Mme Dominique-Venettozza and M. TAGLIONI at Paris O. Debut Paris O. 1858 in SYLPHIDE. Taglioni recognized in the young dancer some of her own attributes and choreographed for her the ballet *Le Papillon* (1860). During a rehearsal for

Colour Plate: N. BESSMERTNOVA and M. LAVROVSKY in the *Black Swan pas de deux* from the Bolshoy B.'s staging of SWAN LAKE, Act III.

the mime role in AUBER's opera *La Muette de Portici* in 1862 her dress caught fire, she was badly burned but lingered for eight months. Her death ended the great days of romantic ballet; there was no ballerina of comparable gifts to succeed her. MC
See Ivor Guest, *The Ballet of the Second Empire, 1858–1870* (London 1953)

Lloyd, Gweneth, born Eccles, Lancashire, 1901. English, now Canadian, teacher and choreographer. To Winnipeg, Manitoba, with Betty Farrally in 1939 to found Winnipeg B. Club, later RWB and school. She has choreographed many works, incl. *Shadow on the Prairie*, first all-Canadian ballet. Director, Dance Division, Banff S. of Fine Arts, 1948–67; founded Canadian S. of B. in Kelowna, BC, in 1957. Officer, Order of Canada 1968. PD

Lloyd, Margaret, b. Braintree, MA, 1887; d. Brookline, MA, 1960. American dance writer, critic of the *Christian Science Monitor* 1936–60, and author of *The Borzoi Book of Modern Dance* (New York 1949). DV

Lloyd, Maude, b. Cape Town. S. African dancer and critic. Early studies with Helen Webb in Cape Town. To London 1927 to RAMBERT S.; appeared in early ballets of ASHTON. Returned to S. Africa 1928–30, but then to London to join BR. She inherited MARKOVA's ballerina roles. Especially sympathetic to the ideas of TUDOR, she created Caroline in JARDIN AUX LILAS and principal roles in DARK ELEGIES and GALA PERFORMANCE, also Châtelaine in FÊTE ÉTRANGE. Danced briefly with Markova–DOLIN B. where she worked with NIJINSKA and appeared as a 'grey girl' in BICHES. She m. art critic Nigel Gosling (who briefly studied at the Rambert S.) in 1939 and retired from the stage 1941. A dancer of exceptional beauty and aristocratic simplicity with an analytical mind. In 1951 BUCKLE persuaded her to collaborate with her husband as 'Alexander Bland' in contributing reviews to his magazine *Ballet*. Since 1952, Bland has been dance critic of *The Observer* newspaper and author of several books, among them *The Dancer's World* (London 1963), *The Nureyev Image* (London 1976), and *A History of Ballet and Dance* (London 1976). MC

Lommel, Daniel, b. Paris, 1943. French-Belgian dancer. Diploma in history of music. Studied with KISS. Debut 1960 in BÉJART's SACRE DU PRINTEMPS. With CHARRAT B. and B. of Hamburg O. B. XXe S. 1965. Created roles in Béjart's *Baudelaire* (1968), *Les Quatre Fils Aymon* (1969), *Erotica* (1971), NIJINSKY, CLOWN DE DIEU (1972), *Marteau sans Maître* (1973); *Stimmung, Tombeau, I Trionfi* (all 1974), etc. Dances Don José in PETIT's CARMEN and in Béjart's *Bhakti* and *Chant du Compagnon Errant* (*see* LIEDER EINES FAHRENDEN GESELLEN). He has elegant and virile technique, dramatic sense, and mischievous spontaneity. M-FC

London Ballet, The, co. formed by TUDOR and DE MILLE, which first performed at the Oxford Playhouse under the name of Dance T. Many BR dancers joined, incl. LAING, VAN PRAAGH, and Maude LLOYD. A base was established at Toynbee Hall for perfs in London. The repertory incl. Tudor's JARDIN AUX LILAS and DARK ELEGIES, to which he added the light-hearted *Soirée Musicale* and popular GALA PERFORMANCE. When Tudor and Laing left to join ABT the co. continued briefly under the direction of van Praagh and Lloyd and produced several works, notably FÊTE ÉTRANGE. In June 1940 it merged with BR as the Rambert–London B. until Sept 1941 when (since it was obvious that Tudor could not return) it was disbanded. Its dancers and repertory remained with BR. MC

London Ballet (GORE's), co. formed by Gore after leaving RAMBERT with HINTON as principal dancer and a repertory consisting mainly of Gore's choreography. First perf. at Hintlesham Hall, Suffolk, 28 July 1961, followed by Edinburgh Fest. that year and tours abroad. Disbanded 1963. RASSINE was principal classical dancer. The repertory incl. notably a production of GISELLE (in which SIBLEY, as a guest, danced the title role for the first time) and revivals of NIGHT AND SILENCE and DIE IM SCHATTEN LEBEN. MC

London Contemporary Dance Theatre. English dance co. founded 1969 by Robin Howard, with COHAN as director. Recruits its dancers principally from the LSCD, which Howard had earlier started to provide training in the modern-dance technique of GRAHAM. But only one of Graham's own creations, *El Penitente*, was in the initial repertory, danced by Cohan, LAPZESON, and LOUTHER, all of whom had been soloists in the Graham co.

Cohan soon suffered an injury and stopped dancing but has been the most prolific of the co.'s choreographers, responsible for many of its most successful productions. A few works by other established choreographers were mounted: AILEY, P. TAYLOR, SOKOLOW, CHARLIP, GOSLAR, and WAGONER; and in 1975 another Graham work, DIVERSION OF ANGELS. From the start, however, an important part of the co.'s activity was developing new creative talent within its ranks.

MORELAND showed promise in two early works but later turned his attention to classical ballet. Louther achieved an outstanding success with his second creation, *Vesalii Icones* (1969), in close collaboration with the composer Peter Maxwell Davies, but he too has pursued his career mainly outside LCDT. Two young men who produced apprentice works during that first season have since done more to shape the co.'s development: namely NORTH and ALSTON, who did not actually become a member of the co. but staged several works for LCDT.

When Lapzeson left the co. after its fourth year of working, the initial period of domination by dancers of Portugal, and the Pennsylvania B. He has also designed ballets and has had his own co. since 1968. JD

Ludmila, Anna [Jean Marie Kaley], b. Chicago, IL, 1903. American dancer. *Première danseuse* of Chicago OB 1918. Danced in Broadway musicals, and again at Chicago O. under BOLM 1924–5. Danced in PETRUSHKA with Bolm at T. Colón, Buenos Aires, 1925. Folies-Bergère, Paris, 1927. Soloist with RUBINSTEIN Co. 1928–9. With DOLIN at London Coliseum and elsewhere 1929. Created leading roles in NIJINSKA's *Aubade*, Paris 1924, and ASHTON's *Pomona* 1931. Injury forced her early retirement from the stage; turned to teaching. Founded National S. of Dance and its performing co., Panama 1948, and remained there for 20 years. Now lives in Texas. DV

Luipart [Fenchel], Marcel, b. Mulhouse [Mülhausen], 1912. German dancer and teacher. Pupil of LEGAT, EDOUARDOVA, and V. GSOVSKY. Joined Düsseldorf B. 1933. After dancing in Hamburg, Berlin, and Munich he joined the B. Russe de Monte Carlo 1936. During World War II (calling himself Frenchel) he was a principal dancer in KDF-Ballett. Ballet master, Munich 1946–8; choreographed *Abraxas* (1948, mus. Werner Egk). Danced in Frankfurt, Wiesbaden, and Düsseldorf; ballet master, Bonn 1957, Essen 1958–9, Cologne 1959–61 (with MILLOSS). Head of the Vienna Acad. of Dance in Schönbrunn 1971. GBLW

Luisillo [Luis Pérez Davila] *see* SPAIN

Lukom, Elena *see* LYUKOM

Lully, Jean-Baptiste [Giovanni Battista Lulli], b. Florence, 1632; d. Paris, 1687. French composer of Italian birth. Appointed Composer to the King (Louis XIV), 1661. A seminal figure in the history of dance music, which he invigorated with a new sprightliness. Lully composed over 30 ballets, incl. several *comédies-ballets* in collaboration with Molière, e.g. FÂCHEUX and *Le Bourgeois Gentilhomme* (Chambord 1670; ch. BEAUCHAMP). Upon taking over the Paris O. (1672) Lully composed a number of highly successful operas, in which dance played an important role, thus establishing an indispensable place for ballet in French opera. DH

Lumley, Benjamin, b. 1811; d. London, 1875. English lawyer in charge of finance at Her Majesty's T., London, 1836–41, and manager 1842–58 when the theatre closed and he returned to his law practice. A key figure in the presentation of Romantic ballet in England and famous for his diplomacy in dealing with artists – notably in settling the order of appearance of the four ballerinas in the PAS DE QUATRE. MC
See B. Lumley, *Reminiscences of the Opera* (London 1864; reprinted New York 1976); Ivor Guest, *The Romantic Ballet in England* (London 1954)

Lyman, Peggy [Margaret], b. Cincinnati, OH, 1950. American dancer. Studied in Chicago at Stone–Camryn S. An apprentice with the JOFFREY B. and also danced in NY City OB and Radio City Music Hall before joining GRAHAM Dance Co. 1973. Dances leading roles in most works of the Graham repertory. DV

Lynham, Deryck, b. Maisons Lafitte, France, 1913; d. Lausanne, 1951. English historian of the ballet. Educated in France. Subsequently to London where he gained practical knowledge of the theatre as a founder, with Judge Christmas Humphreys, of the Ballet Guild, a small co. lasting 1941–7. Its reference library was part of the nucleus of the London Archives of the Dance, now part of the Theatre Museum. Author of *Ballet Then and Now* (London 1947) and *The Chevalier Noverre, Father of Modern Ballet* (London and New York 1950). He died while working on *A Dictionary of Ballet* for Penguin Books; it was completed by G. B. L. Wilson and published London and Baltimore 1957 (rev. eds London 1961, 1974). MC

Lynne [Pyrke], Gillian, b. Bromley, 1926. English dancer, choreographer, and producer. Studied with Madeleine Sharp, at RAD and with Olive Ripman. Debut Arts TB 1940, danced with LAKE's co. and joined SWB 1943, becoming a principal. Her roles ranged from SYMPHONIC VARIATIONS to the BLACK QUEEN. Left 1951 to become principal dancer at the London Palladium. Subsequently appeared in many musicals and became the finest exponent of modern stage dancing of her generation. Wrote a series of articles on this technique for *The Dancing Times* (London) in the 1950s. Has worked as producer and choreographer of musicals, films and opera (Michael Tippett's *The Midsummer Marriage*, CG 1968). In 1976 she choreographed *The Prince Under the Hill* for the Australian B. for production on Australian TV. MC

Lyukom, Elena, b. St Petersburg, 1891; d. Leningrad, 1968. Soviet dancer. Graduated from St Petersburg TS 1909, class of FOKINE. While at Maryinsky T. participated in DIAGHILEV's B. Russes. Promoted to soloist 1912. Ballerina 1920 when she became one of the principal dancers of the Kirov B., creating new virtuoso *pas de deux* with her partner Boris Shavrov (1900–75) with whom she toured Germany, Denmark, and Sweden in the 1920s. She was an ethereal, fragile dancer possessing great charm and excellent technique. Created the Diva (GOLDEN AGE), Tao-Hoa in Leningrad version of RED POPPY, danced all the classical repertoire. *Répétiteur* Kirov B. 1953–65. Honoured Artist, RSFSR; Honoured Art Worker, RSFSR. NR
See E. Lyukom, *My Work in Ballet* (Leningrad 1940); V. Krasovskaya, *Russian Ballet Theatre of the Beginning of the 20th Century*, Vol. 2, *Dancers* (Leningrad 1972)

Patricia McBride of NYCB practising in one of the company's studios

M

McBride, Patricia, b. Teaneck, NJ, 1942. American dancer. Studied SAB. Joined EGLEVSKY Co. 1958; NYCB, 1959. A *demi-caractère* dancer of great piquancy and vivacity, she is capable of a greater depth when the occasion allows (e.g. in LIEBESLIEDER WALZER). Her solo to 'Fascinatin' Rhythm' in WHO CARES? is one of the greatest pieces of virtuoso dancing in contemporary ballet. Her partnership with VILLELLA was firmly established by such vehicles as HARLEQUINADE, *Tarantella*, and 'Rubies' in JEWELS. More recently she has danced with TOMASSON in BALANCHINE's *Divertimento* from BAISER DE LA FÉE, ROBBINS's *Dybbuk Variations*, and the A. DANILOVA-Balanchine COPPÉLIA. She m. BONNEFOUS. DV

McGehee (Umaña), Helen, b. Lynchburg, VA, 1921. American dancer, choreographer, and costume designer. BA, Randolph-Macon Woman's College, Lynchburg, VA. Studied dance there and with GRAHAM, with whose co. she made her debut in 1944; remained until 1971. Created many roles in the Graham repertory incl. Girl in Yellow in DIVERSION OF ANGELS, Electra in CLYTEMNESTRA: also danced for Graham in *Errand into the Maze*, *Cave of the Heart*, APPALACHIAN SPRING. On faculty of Graham S. and Juilliard S. Formed her own co. 1965 and has choreographed many works incl. *La Intrusa* (1953), *After Possession* (1965), *The Only Jealousy of Emer* (1967), *El Retratto de Maese Pedro* (1969). DV

McKayle, Donald, b. New York, 1930. American dancer and choreographer. Scholarship to New Dance Group Studio, 1947. Also studied with GRAHAM and CUNNINGHAM; danced with their cos, as well as those of SOKOLOW and ERDMAN. His first choreography was *Games* (1951) for his own co.; later in the repertories of the American B. Co., HARKNESS B., AILEY Repertory Workshop, and B. Hispanico, NY. Other works incl. RAINBOW 'ROUND MY SHOULDER (now in repertory of AILEY Co.) and *District Storyville* (1962). He has also choreographed and directed shows on and off Broadway and in London, films, and TV specials. Director, Inner City Repertory Dance Co. LA, 1970–3. DV

MacLeary, Donald, b. Glasgow, 1937. Scottish dancer. Pupil of Sheila Ross, then SWBS from 1951. Joined SWTB 1954, soloist 1955; principal, RB, 1959. Assumed princely roles at an early age; also created innumerable parts in the ballets of MACMILLAN. In the classical ballets, his partnership with BERIOSOVA was celebrated, their finest achievement being in SWAN LAKE. Became ballet master RB 1975 giving farewell perf. as the Prince in CINDERELLA, 27 Dec 1975. He subsequently danced several of his former roles with the RB, taking the place of injured dancers. MC

MacMillan, Kenneth, b. Dunfermline, 1929. Scottish choreographer and dancer. Trained at SWBS, graduating from there into SWTB at its inception in 1946. A fine classical dancer, he transferred to SWB 1948, returning to SWTB 1952. Created two apprentice ballets for the co.'s Choreographic Group 1953–4; his first professional work for SWTB was DANSES CONCERTANTES. Its bubbling wit and vivid response to music announced the arrival of an exceptional new talent. There followed a fairytale ballet, *House of Birds* (1955; a first attempt at narrative) and then, for the CG troupe, *Noctambules* (1956), in which a group of people play out their fantasies under the influence of a hypnotist.

In *The Burrow* (for SWTB, 1958) MacMillan was to discover the dance Muse who has enhanced so much of his later creativity: SEYMOUR. His style gradually became more relaxed and fluent. His first major achievement was BAISER DE LA FÉE (1960), an exquisite response to Stravinsky's score, with its unforced invention and admirable dramatic shape. He next produced a magnificent sequence of ballets, starting with INVITATION. Thereafter he showed that he could compose plotless works like the flowing *Diversions* (1961) and the darker, more introspective *Symphony* (1963); and the massive undertaking of RITE OF SPRING, in which he revealed how he could manipulate large forces and also guide and inspire a new talent – in this case MASON who was unforgettable as the Chosen Maiden. His taste for sharp dramatic effects was seen in HERMANAS. The culminating achievement of this period in his career was LIED VON DER ERDE. Two Shakespeare ballets 1964 and 1965 took some of their inspiration from words: in *Images of Love* (1964) a brief quotation could spark off a dance; in ROMEO AND JULIET both PROKOFIEV's score and the text's imagery fed the choreographer's imagination.

In 1966 MacMillan was invited to direct the Deutsche OB, W. Berlin, and for three years, with Seymour as his ballerina, he set himself the task of developing the range of dancers and repertory. He staged many ballets, the most important being the 1-act ANASTASIA, and made two fine classic productions: SLEEPING BEAUTY (1967) and SWAN LAKE (1969). In 1970 he returned to London to become Director of RB in succession to Ashton, and his major ballets since have celebrated the magnificent strength of the co. and sought to extend still further its powers. Very important have been the two full-length pieces: *Anastasia* (1971) and MANON (1974), the first being one of the most innovative and poetic of big ballets. Other 1-act ballets – ÉLITE SYNCOPATIONS, *The Four Seasons* (1975) – have proved most successful in displaying the virtuosity of RB. In 1967 he choreographed REQUIEM. CC

Madge, the witch in SYLPHIDE

Madsen, Egon, b. Ringe, 1942. Danish dancer. With the Stuttgart B. since 1961; now a principal dancer there, having created many roles in ballets by CRANKO and MACMILLAN in Stuttgart, incl. Lensky (ONEGIN), Gremio (TAMING OF THE SHREW), the Joker (CARD GAME), der Ewige (LIED VON DER ERDE), and a solo in REQUIEM. MC/CC

Magalhães, Renato, b. Rio de Janeiro, 1934. Brazilian choreographer. Studied ballet at the Municipal TS. Soon made first dancer and performed roles such as Koschey (OISEAU DE FEU), Harlequin (CARNAVAL). Guest artist in Chile, France, and Italy. Started doing choreographic works in 1971 for the Johann Strauss operetta *Le Baron Tzigane* in France where he also did *Le Malade Imaginaire* (1972). Noted for his strong work and extreme musicality which shows in his *Catulli Carmina* (1975) and *Nhamundá* (1976), both works created for the B. do Rio de Janeiro. MLN

Magallanes, Nicholas, b. Camargo, Chihuahua, Mexico, 1922; d. N. Merrick, Long Island, NY, 1977. American dancer. Studied at SAB. Danced with American B. Caravan, S. American tour, 1941; Littlefield B. 1942; B. Russe de Monte Carlo 1943–6. Created the Poet in BALANCHINE's *Night Shadow* (*see* SONNAMBULA) and danced leading classic roles. Joined B. Society, then NYCB 1946 and created roles in many ballets by Balanchine incl. SYMPHONY IN C, ORPHEUS (title role), VALSE, *Allegro Brillante*, DIVERTIMENTO NO. 15, LIEBESLIEDER WALZER, as well as the Poet in ILLUMINATIONS, 2nd Intruder in CAGE, etc. One of the best partners and teachers of adagio of his generation. DV

Magriel, Paul, b. Riga, Latvia, 1906. American writer. Compiled *A Bibliography of Dancing* (New York 1936) and supplements. First curator of Dance Archives at Museum of Modern Art, NY, 1939–42. One of the original editors of *Dance Index* (New York 1942). DV

Kenneth MacMillan rehearsing LAST for her role in his ballet *The Poltroon*

Makarov, Askold, b. Novo-Mosalskoye, Kalinin region, 1925. Soviet dancer and teacher. Candidate of Science/Arts. Graduated from Leningrad Choreographic S. 1943; GITIS 1957. Soloist Kirov B. 1943–70. Danced all classical roles but especially prominent in heroic roles of contemporary repertoire. Created Fisherman (COAST OF HOPE), Danila (STONE FLOWER), Poet (Mayakovsky) in YACOBSON's choreographic version of *Bed Bug*, Ali-Batyr (SHURALE), title role in CHABUKIANI's OTHELLO, etc. He had great feeling for heroic characterizations. Teaches at choreographers' faculty, Leningrad Cons. NR
See A. Makarov, 'In Search of My Hero', *Teatr*, No. 7 (Moscow 1968); A. Makarov, 'My Spartacus', *Soviet Music*, No. 11 (Moscow 1968); D. Zolotnitsky, article in *Leningrad Ballet Today*, No. 1 (Leningrad 1967)

Makarova, Natalia Romanovna, b. Leningrad, 1940. Russian dancer. Studied Kirov BS, Leningrad, joining Kirov B. Co. 1959. Her first GISELLE was danced in London during the Kirov B.'s visit to London CG, and was hailed as an exceptional debut; her repertoire incl. ODETTE-ODILE, AURORA, and various other roles in 19th-c. ballets as well as modern works. She was scheduled to dance Ophelia in a new HAMLET being prepared by SERGEYEV for the Kirov B. when that co. returned to Russia after a European tour in 1970, but remained in the West in order to dance a wider range of ballets, and travelled to NY where she joined ABT. Debut there as Giselle with NAGY. Also danced in ABT's productions of SWAN LAKE, SYLPHIDE, SLEEPING BEAUTY, and APOLLO, as well as TUDOR's JARDIN AUX LILAS, DARK ELEGIES, PILLAR OF FIRE, and ROMEO AND JULIET. For ABT staged and danced in Act IV (the Kingdom of Shades scene) of BAYADÈRE, 1974. Guest ballerina throughout the world, dancing the classic roles and some modern works. In London, with RB, from 1972, she danced notably in the MACMILLAN ballets MANON, *Romeo and Juliet Concerto,* and LIED VON DER ERDE; also *Cinderella,* CHECKMATE and BICHES. Her Giselle is generally regarded as the finest of our time, and her dancing is celebrated both for the aristocracy of her Kirov style and for its expressive intensity. Gold Medal, Varna Competition, 1965. CC

Mam'zelle Angot, ballet, 3 scenes with linking episode between first 2, ch./lib. MASSINE, based on operetta *La Fille de Madame Angot* by Charles Lecocq; sc./c. Mstislav Dobuzhinsky. (As *Mademoiselle Angot*) NY Met, ABT, 10 Oct 1943; dan. Massine, KAYE, EGLEVSKY, HIGHTOWER. Revised version; new music arr. Gordon Jacob; sc./c. DERAIN, London, CG, SWB, 26 Nov 1947, dan. GRANT, FONTEYN, SOMES, M. SHEARER. This version revived Melbourne, Princes T., Australian B., 9 Dec 1971. Mam'zelle Angot spurns the honest love of a little barber and is enamoured of an elegant artist who loves an aristocratic lady, the mistress of an elderly official. Eventually Mam'zelle Angot discovers the aristocrat is a childhood friend, the official is fooled, aristocrat and artist are united, and Mam'zelle Angot recognizes the true worth of her barber lover. Massine's casting of Grant in his original role of the barber established him as a great character actor dancer. MC

Natalia Makarova as CINDERELLA in ASHTON's version for the RB at CG; her Prince is DOWELL

Manen, Hans van, b. Nieuwer Amstel, 1932. Dutch dancer, choreographer, and ballet director. Danced with GASKELL's B. Recital, then (1952–8) with the Amsterdam OB. After a year with PETIT's co. was a founder member of NDT 1959. His first ballet was *Feestgerecht* (1957); with NDT he was a prolific creator, initially often in a jazzy manner but soon making a mark with *Symphony in Three Movements* (1963), *Essay in Silence*, and *Metaphors* (both 1965). His choreography puts an emphasis on form, often introducing an unusual element, such as the presence of a singer pursuing the dancers in *Solo for Voice 1* (1968, mus. CAGE), or a boxed-in set to heighten the relationships of the duets in *Situation* (1970). Joint director, NDT, 1961–71; left to become a freelance choreographer, creating works for the Düsseldorf B. and RB among others. Also began a close relationship with the Dutch NB as choreographer and rehearsal director. His recent ballets have incl. GROSSE FUGE, TWILIGHT, and ADAGIO HAMMERKLAVIER as well as humorous pieces such as *Septet Extra* (1973, mus. Camille Saint-Saëns), or his own interpretation of standard ballet scores. Influenced more by modern art and films than by other ballets, his cool manner and sense of structure sometimes disguise but do not prevent a sense of the drama inherent in the relationships of dancers on stage. In 1976 he was one of the first recipients of the Dutch H. J. Reinink Medal. JP

Manipuri *see* ASIA

Mank, Nora, b. Leipzig, 1935. German dancer. Studied with T. GSOVSKY and in Leningrad. Joined E. Berlin Staats O. 1950; ballerina 1961. GBLW

Manon, ballet, 3 acts, ch./lib. MACMILLAN; mus. Jules Massenet, chosen by Hilda Gaunt (but not incl. music from Massenet's opera of the same name), orch. Leighton Lucas; sc./c. GEORGIADIS. London, CG, RB, 7 Mar 1974; dan. SIBLEY (Manon), DOWELL (des Grieux), WALL (Lescaut). A spectacular adaptation of part of the novel *L'Histoire du Chevalier des Grieux et de Manon Lescaut* (1731), by the Abbé Antoine François Prévost, using the full resources of the RB. The role of Manon has also been interpreted by PENNEY, SEYMOUR, and MAKAROVA; Dowell and Wall have exchanged their roles as des Grieux and Lescaut; EAGLING has also shone as des Grieux.

An earlier treatment of the novel *Manon Lescaut*: ch. Jean Aumer; mus. Jacques-François-Fromental-Élie Halévy; Paris O., 3 May 1830. MC/CC

Manzotti, Luigi, b. Milan, 1838; d. 1905. Italian dancer and choreographer. Staged spectacular ballets at Milan Sc., notably *Sieba* (1886), EXCELSIOR, *Amor* (1886), and *Sport* (1897). MC

Maracci, Carmelita, b. Montevideo, Uruguay, 1911. American dancer, choreographer, and teacher. Of Italian and Spanish descent, brought to the USA as a child, studied ballet and Spanish dance in California and developed a personal style and technique combining elements of both. A legendary technician, she gave solo concerts and toured with her own co. for many years. Choreographed and danced in *Circo de España* for ABT, 1951, based on material from her repertory. Now teaches in Los Angeles. DV

Marceau, Marcel *see* MIME

Marchand, Colette, b. Paris, 1925. French dancer. Paris OBS, with V. GSOVSKY, VOLININ. *Corps de ballet*, Paris O.; Metropolitan B. 1947; B. de Paris 1948. Created roles in PETIT's *L'Oeuf à la Coque* (1949), *Ciné-Bijou* (1953), *Deuil en 24 Heures* (1953), and *Lady in the Ice* (1953). Danced in music hall with Maurice Chevalier in Paris; musical comedy in NY. Appeared in film *Moulin Rouge* (1953; director John Huston). Guest artist with the cos of Petit, MISKOVITCH, BT Contemporain. M. orchestra leader Jacques Bazire. Always a beauty, it was her long-legged elegance in *L'Oeuf à la Coque*, in which she appeared as a very sexy chicken, that made her name and earned her the nickname 'Les Legs'. M-FC

Marguerite and Armand, ballet, prologue and 4 scenes, ch. ASHTON; lib. after *La Dame aux Camélias* by Alexandre Dumas *fils*; mus. Franz Liszt (*La Lugubre Gondola* No. 1 and Sonata in B minor), orchestrated Humphrey Searle (later re-orchestrated Gordon Jacob); sc./c. BEATON. London, CG, RB, 12 Mar 1963; dan. FONTEYN, NUREYEV, SOMES, EDWARDS. A series of passionate duets that tell the story of the play in flashback as Marguerite lies dying, the ballet set the seal on the partnership of Fonteyn and Nureyev. DV

Maria, the heroine of FOUNTAIN OF BAKHCHISARAY

Marie-Jeanne [Marie-Jeanne Pelus], b. New York, 1920, of French parents. American dancer. Studied at SAB. B. Caravan 1937–40, created Mother and Sweetheart in BILLY THE KID. B. Russe de Monte Carlo 1940; American B. Caravan, S. American tour, 1941, created leading roles in CONCERTO BAROCCO and BALLET IMPERIAL. Original B. Russe 1942; de Cuevas B. 1944; B. Russe de Monte Carlo 1945–7; B. Society 1948; NYCB, European tour, 1943, retired 1954. A dancer of legendary technique and musicality who excelled in BALANCHINE ballets. Author of *Yankee Ballerina* (New York 1941) and *Opera Ballerina* (New York 1948). DV

Marin Civic Ballet *see* REGIONAL BALLET (USA)

Markó, Iván, b. Balassagyarmat, 1947. Hungarian dancer. Studied Budapest Inst. of B. 1958, with Heidi Hidas and LEPESHINSKAYA. *Corps de ballet*, Budapest O. 1967, soloist 1968; danced principal roles in classics, also LAURENCIA, and SYLVIA. B. XXe S. 1972; danced NIJINSKY, CLOWN DE DIEU; OISEAU

DE FEU; NINTH SYMPHONY (second movement). His natural elegance and purity of technique were ideal for classical roles; he has since discovered in BÉJART's work an opportunity to develop strength and authority. M-FC

Markova, Dame Alicia [Lilian Alicia Marks], b. London, 1910, English dancer. One of four devoted sisters. Studied with ASTAFYEVA in London, and taken into the DIAGHILEV co. at the age of 14. He called her 'my little English girl' and predicted a great future for her. She danced important roles with Diaghilev and created the title role in BALANCHINE's *Le Rossignol* (1926). After Diaghilev's death she danced for the young BR, London, and created roles in many early ASHTON ballets, incl. *Foyer de Danse* and *Les Masques*. For the Camargo Society she created the Polka in FAÇADE. Danced with the Vic-Wells B. 1931–3; ballerina 1933–5; created principal roles in RENDEZVOUS and RAKE'S PROGRESS. Above all, was first British dancer to appear as GISELLE and to dance ODETTE-ODILE. Her presence was vital in establishing the co. In 1935 she left to form with DOLIN the Markova-Dolin B., which toured widely in Britain. Joined the B. Russe de Monte Carlo as ballerina 1938–41; created roles in MASSINE's *Seventh Symphony* and *Rouge et Noir* and conquered NY, indeed the USA, with her Giselle. With ABT 1941–4 and 1945–6 creating roles as varied as the gypsy in MASSINE's *Aleko* and JULIET for TUDOR. The years in the USA were probably the greatest of her dancing career. With Dolin she also danced in Mexico and the Philippines and toured worldwide. They returned to Britain as guests of the RB in 1948 when Markova danced her first full-length SLEEPING BEAUTY. Co-founder with Dolin of LONDON FESTIVAL BALLET. Although Dolin has been her most frequent partner, she has danced with most of the great artists of her time such as the young BRUHN in *Giselle*. Retired as a dancer in 1963; director of the NY Met OB until 1969 when she became Professor of B. at the Univ. of Cincinnati, Cons. of Music, until 1974. Now gives master classes at the RBS and other centres. A dancer of exquisite purity and delicacy, the ideal SUGAR PLUM FAIRY, with a gentle humour best seen in her interpretation of M. TAGLIONI in PAS DE QUATRE. An entertaining talker on TV and radio both in the USA and Britain. CBE 1958. DBE 1963. MC

See Cyril W. Beaumont, *Alicia Markova* (London 1935); Anton Dolin, *Alicia Markova: her Life and Art* (London and New York 1953); Alicia Markova, *Giselle and I* (London 1960; New York 1961); I. Lidova, 'Alicia Markova', *Les Saisons de la Danse* (Paris, Apr 1975)

Alicia Markova as GISELLE

Marks, Bruce, b. New York, 1937. American dancer. Most of his early training and performing were in modern dance; debut at 14 in P. LANG's *Rites*, continued to dance in her co. as he grew older. Also studied at SAB and with CRASKE and TUDOR. Joined NY Met OB 1956, ABT 1961–71, becoming one of its leading *danseurs nobles* – danced lead in ÉTUDES, SIEGFRIED etc. Guest artist with RSB 1963–4, LFB 1965, RDB 1966. He m. T. LANDER 1966. Joined RDB as principal dancer 1971, leaving that co. in 1976 to take up position as director of B. West in Utah, USA DV

Marsicano [Petersen], Merle, b. Philadelphia, PA. American dancer and choreographer. Studied ballet with MORDKIN, modern dance with ST DENIS and GRAHAM. Began to give perfs in Philadelphia; moved to New York after her marriage to painter Nicholas Marsicano. Since 1952 has presented solo concerts in New York. Confined within the concentrated range of movement she permits herself, such solos as *Figure of Memory* (1954; mus. Morton Feldman) and *Fragment for a Greek Tragedy* (1956; mus. Jerry Petersen), are memorable for the spare intensity of their gesture. Formed her own co. 1976, for which she choreographed *Disquieting Muses* and *They Who Are Not Named*. DV

Martin, John, b. Louisville, KY, 1893. American dance writer, critic of *New York Times* 1927–62. A tireless advocate of the modern dance, it was only in later years that he became equally enthusiastic in support of ballet. Author of *The Modern Dance* (New York 1933), *Introduction to the Dance* (New York 1939), *The Dance* (New York 1946), *World Book of Modern Ballet* (Cleveland 1952). Took up appointment as lecturer in dance at Univ. of California, Los Angeles, 1965. DV

Martin, Keith, b. Doncaster, 1943. English dancer. Studied RAD and RBS, graduating into the co. 1962. As well as dancing such roles as the BLUEBIRD, and the BLUE SKATER, he created Puck in DREAM and Johnny Town Mouse in ASHTON's film of *Tales of Beatrix Potter* (US title: *Peter Rabbit and the Tales of Beatrix Potter,* 1970). With Pennsylvania B. 1971–4, Maryland B. 1974–5, San Francisco B. 1975–6, director, San Diego B. 1976. One of the most brilliant *demi-caractère* male dancers of his generation. He m. dancer Barbara Jean Martin. DV

Martins, Peter, b. Copenhagen, 1946. Danish dancer. Studied at RDBS, entered the co. at 18, dancing both the August BOURNONVILLE repertory and modern works, by BALANCHINE and others. After dancing APOLLO, at short notice, with NYCB, at the Edinburgh Fest. 1967, he was invited to join the co., first as a guest and then as a permanent member in 1970. In the 1972 STRAVINSKY Fest. Balanchine created roles for him in VIOLIN CONCERTO and DUO CONCERTANT. Also dances in DANCES AT A GATHERING and as FRANZ, etc.

A regular guest in Copenhagen, Martins is a magnificent example of the Danish tradition of great male dancing. DV

Martyn [Gill], Laurel, b. Brisbane, 1916. Australian dancer, choreographer, and director. Studied with BEDELLS. Choreographic scholarship to SWBS. SWB 1935–8. BOROVANSKY B. 1944, principal ballerina. Founded Victorian B. Guild 1946, now B. Victoria, of which she is artistic director. This co. has done much to encourage Australian choreographers, composers, and designers. Her ballets incl. *En Saga, Dithyramb, Voyageur, Cloth of Gold.* KSW

Maslow, Sophie, b. New York. American dancer. Studied with GRAHAM at Henry St Settlement Playhouse; joined her co. 1931. Featured in several major Graham productions such as *American Document* and PRIMITIVE MYSTERIES; remained with the Graham co. until starting her own independent concert career in the early 1940s. She was part of the DUDLEY-Maslow-BALES Dance Trio; created her noted *Folksay* (1942) for it. When the group disbanded, she continued to work with a variety of cos, incl. Batsheva Dance Co. for whom she restaged her nostalgic *The Village I Knew* (1950). Now teaches at the New Dance Group Studio (New York). DM

Mason, Monica, b. Johannesburg, 1941. S. African dancer. Early training in S. Africa (in the CECCHETTI method which she greatly admires) then London, RBS. Joined RB 1958; in 1962 created Chosen Virgin in RITE OF SPRING. Principal 1967. A dancer of exceptional strength and vitality, she is glorious in demanding variations, as in BAYADÈRE. Dances ODETTE-ODILE; has a range from the serene Lady Elgar (ENIGMA VARIATIONS) to the outrageous comedy of ÉLITE SYNCOPATIONS. She m. Austin Bennett, former RB dancer, now a successful sculptor. MC

Massine [Myasin], Leonid Fedorovich, b. Moscow, 1895. Russian dancer and choreographer. Trained in Imperial S., Moscow; graduated into the Moscow B. in 1912. In 1913 DIAGHILEV invited him to join his B. Russes to dance the leading role in LÉGENDE DE JOSEPH. At the outbreak of World War I he remained in Europe with Diaghilev; created his first choreographies incl. *Soleil de Nuit* (1915). For six years

Leonid Massine as the Peruvian in GAIETÉ PARISIENNE

Pamela May (left) as Mlle Théodore in DE VALOIS's comic ballet *The Prospect Before Us* (1940). On the right, ASHTON and MORETON as Noverre and his wife

thereafter he was Diaghilev's principal choreographer, creating FEMMES DE BONNE HUMEUR, PARADE, BOUTIQUE FANTASQUE, TRICORNE, SACRE DU PRINTEMPS. In 1921 he left Diaghilev but returned later to compose several more ballets, incl. *Le Pas d'Acier* (1927) and ODE. He visited the USA in the 1920s and also worked in revues in London during this period.

In 1932 he began his association with the B. Russe de Monte Carlo, creating a great variety of works ranging from comedies to the SYMPHONIC BALLETS. To USA in 1939 with B. Russe de Monte Carlo; worked with several cos during World War II. Returning to Europe 1946, he staged *La Boutique Fantasque* and *Tricorne* for the SWB at CG and danced his original roles. He has created and restaged many ballets for many cos throughout the world. In his B. Russe years he was one of the most important dancers and influential choreographers of his time. He m. dancers (1) Vera Savina (Clark), (2) Eugenia Delarova, (3) Tatiana Orlova. Published his autobiography, *My Life in Ballet* (London and New York 1968) and a book on his system of notation (London 1976). MC/CC

Maximova [Maksimova], Ekaterina, b. Moscow, 1939. Soviet dancer. Graduated Bolshoy TS, class of E. GERDT. Bolshoy B. since 1958. Versatile dancer with exquisite technique and stage presence in classical roles: AURORA, GISELLE, CINDERELLA, KITRI. Great impact and pliable body in modern roles: PHRYGIA, Muse (PAGANINI), Masha (NUTCRACKER, GRIGOROVICH version), and Katerina in Grigorovich's STONE FLOWER, her first created role in her first season at Bolshoy T. She m. VASILIEV. People's Artist, USSR. Gold medal, Varna, 1964. NR
See N. Avaliani and L. Zhdanov, tr. N. Ward, *Bolshoi's Young Dancers* (Moscow and London 1975); I. Lidova, 'Maximova', *Les Saisons de la Danse* (Paris, Nov 1972)

May, Pamela, b. Trinidad, 1917. English dancer. Studied with Freda Grant and with Russians in Paris, to SWBS 1933. Debut with SWB 1934 in soloist role in SWAN LAKE (the *pas de trois*). Created Red Queen in CHECKMATE, Moon in ASHTON's *Horoscope* (1938), and was in original cast of SYMPHONIC VARIATIONS. During World War II and immediately after shared ballerina roles in SWB repertory with FONTEYN. Knee injuries later hampered her dancing; since 1952 guest artist with the RB, bringing dignity and charm to queenly roles. As a classical dancer, she was noted for the beauty of her line, especially in arabesque. Taught at the RBS until 1977. MC

Maywood, Augusta, b. New York, 1825; d. Lemberg, Austria [now Lvov, USSR], 1876. American dancer. First American to have a career in Europe and to attain the rank of *prima ballerina assoluta*. Studied with M. and Mme Paul Hazard from 1836 in Philadelphia; became their star pupil; debut aged 12, rival of LEE. Lee won by default, as Augusta left for perfs at NY's Park T., 12 Feb–30 Apr 1838, and then for the Paris OBS to study with CORALLI and MAZILIER. Debut 16 Nov 1839 in *Le Diable Boiteux*, starring ELSSLER, at the Paris O. where Augusta continued for a year in all the repertoire, mainly in special *pas* and usually with Charles Mabille as partner, and was acclaimed as a phenomenon by GAUTIER and other critics. When Augusta and Mabille eloped, Nov 1840, their unauthorized absence automatically cancelled the O. contract. They m. a month later in Dublin. They then accepted a two-year engagement in Marseille. During those two summer seasons Augusta appeared with François Montessu in Lyon and then with her husband at Lisbon's T. São Carlo, autumn 1843 to spring 1845, after which she abandoned husband and child and eloped again. Mabille obtained a legal separation but fulfilled a one-year contract, 1846, as Augusta's partner at the Vienna Hof T., where she continued as solo dancer until Nov 1847.

Her first appearance in Italy was in 1848, at Sc., in PERROT's *Faust*, with Elssler in the leading role, but having immediately captivated the public of Milan, Augusta was awarded Elssler's role the following year together with the rank of *prima ballerina assoluta*. During her 10-year triumphant progress through Italy – Venice, Ravenna, Padua, Bologna, Florence, Rome, Ancona – she was hailed by the press and added to her laurels not only by staging such novelties as ballet versions of *La Dame aux Camélias* and *Uncle Tom's Cabin*, but also by being the first ballerina to found her own touring co., complete with managers, soloists, *corps de ballet*, decors and costumes. In 1848 and 1854, she reappeared briefly and successfully in Vienna and it was there that she settled when, after the death of Charles Mabille in 1858, she m. the Italian critic and impresario, Carlo Gardini. At this time, she retired from the stage and opened a ballet school which she directed until 1873. Her death from smallpox passed without notice, not only in Vienna but in all those cities where she had been the idol of the public. PME
See Parmenia Migel, *The Ballerinas from the Court of Louis XIV to Pavlova* (New York 1972)

Mazilier, Joseph, b. Marseille, 1801; d. Paris, 1868. French dancer and choreographer. Responsible for many of the ballets staged at the Paris O. in the mid-19th c., notably PAQUITA and *Marco Spada* (1857). As a dancer he is remembered as the first JAMES (for F. TAGLIONI). His ballets were admired for their skill in combining dramatic action and dance in grand settings. MC/CC
See Ivor Guest, *The Romantic Ballet in Paris* (London and Middletown, CT, 1966); *The Ballet of the Second Empire* (*1847–1858*, London 1955; *1858–1870*, London 1953)

Mazzo, Kay, b. Chicago, IL, 1946. American dancer. Studied at SAB. Joined ROBBINS's Ballets: USA 1961; NYCB 1962. She has a fragile beauty and a quality of vulnerability that make her interpretations of such ballets as AFTERNOON OF A FAUN and DUO CONCERTANT unusually touching. DV

Medea, ballet, ch. CULLBERG; mus. BARTÓK; sc. Alvar Granström. Sweden, Gävle, Riks T., 31 Oct 1950; dan. Anne Marie Lagerborg, BÉJART. New version: RSB, 1953; dan. E. VON ROSEN, Willy Sandberg. NYCB, 1958; dan. HAYDEN, D'AMBOISE. Has also been staged in other countries in Europe. A very intense and concentrated version of the Greek tragedy. AGS

Meditation, modern dance work, ch./c. CHARLIP; mus. Jules Massenet (from *Thaïs*). Penland S. of Crafts, NC, 1966; dan. Charlip. A timid man in civilian dress is torn between unruly desires and the repressive inhibitions induced by a sense of propriety. A second version was made for Maximiliano Zomosa in *Differences*, CCJB, 31 Mar 1968. DM

Medley, modern dance work, ch. THARP; c. street clothing, chosen by the dancers. Connecticut College Campus (outdoors), New London, CT, 19 July 1969; dan. RUDNER, Theresa Dickinson, Margery Tupling, Sheila Raj, Graciela Figueroa, Rose Marie WRIGHT, and 36 students of the American Dance Fest. The qualities of the six principal dancers celebrated and orchestrated through the use of student dancers in a work that begins and ends with imperceptibly slow movement suggesting the growth rate of foliage. DM

Meehan, John, b. Brisbane, 1950. Australian dancer and choreographer. Studied with Patricia MacDonald. Australian BS 1968. Australian B. 1970; soloist 1972; principal dancer 1974. An interesting and varied artist whose work ranges from ALBRECHT and Oberon (DREAM) to his created roles in GEMINI and Danilo (MERRY WIDOW). His ballet, *Night Episode,* which won the *Canberra Times* Award, 1974, is in the Australian B. repertoire. KSW

Mérante, Louis, b. Paris, 1828; d. Asnières, 1887. French dancer and choreographer. Principal dancer at the Paris O. 1848; created leading roles in many ballets, incl. SAINT-LÉON's *La Source* 1866. He choreographed several ballets during the last years of his life, notably SYLVIA and DEUX PIGEONS. He m. the dancer Zina Richard. MC/CC

Merry Widow, The, ballet, 3 acts, ch. Ronald Hynd; mus. Franz Lehár arr. John Lanchbery; sc./c. Desmond Heeley; staged HELPMANN. St Kilda, Melbourne, Palais T., Australian B., 13 Nov 1975. A balletic version of the famous operetta. The Lehár estate insisted on some vocal material which forced Lanchbery to incorporate 'heavenly choir' sections (instead of the original songs). A lavish spectacle, popular in Australia, and in Washington and on Broadway where FONTEYN was guest artist as the Widow, but failed at the London Palladium until Fonteyn was brought in to save the last two weeks of the season, which she did with a bewitching perf. MC

Messel, Oliver, b. Cuckfield, Sussex, 1905. English painter and designer whose work is notable for its charm and delicacy. Designed LICHINE's *Francesca da Rimini* for DE BASIL 1937, HELPMANN's *Comus* for SWB 1942 and, most celebrated of all, SLEEPING BEAUTY for the SWB 1946 (which he revived and revised for ABT 1976). Author of *Stage Designs and Costumes* (London 1933). CBE 1958. MC

Messe pour le Temps Présent (*Mass for Our Time*), *cérémonie*, 9 episodes, ch. BÉJART; mus. Pierre Henry; lib. extracts from Bible, Buddha, Friedrich Wilhelm Nietzsche; sc. Béjart, Roger Bernard, Joëlle Roustan. Avignon Fest., B. XXe S., 3 Aug 1967. This 'mass' evokes successively: the vital spirit, the body, the world prey to a frenzy of information, dance combining classical and Hindu vocabulary, the couple, war, night, silence, expectation. M-FC

Messerer, Asaf, b. Moscow, 1903. Soviet dancer, teacher, and choreographer. Entered Bolshoy TS aged 16, graduated from GORSKY's class 1921. Accepted at Bolshoy T. where he rapidly became leading *premier danseur noble*, remaining in the co. until 1954. Exceptional virtuosity and elevation: he performed triple *tours en l'air* and other feats. Was first to perform classical roles without conventional mime, making them more human. His versatility and talent enabled him to perform character and *demi-caractère* parts, e.g. Chinese Acrobat with ribbon in RED POPPY, also created Philippe in Moscow production of FLAME OF PARIS , Skater in PRISONER OF THE CAUCASUS, Nur-Ali in Moscow production of FOUNTAIN OF BAKHCHISARAY.

Choreographic debut 1924 with concert number, *Football Player*, performed by himself; choreographed first ballet *War of Toys*. Among later productions were SLEEPING BEAUTY, Act IV of SWAN LAKE (Bolshoy version), *On the Sea Coast* (at Vilnius), etc. Messerer's greatest achievement lies, however, as a teacher. He began teaching aged 20 at Bolshoy BS. At present he conducts the male *classe de perfectionnement*, Bolshoy T., visited by many ballerinas who prefer his system, which is famous for its gradual development of all the muscles, thus safeguarding the dancer from accidental injury. People's Artist, RSFSR. He m. TIKHOMIRNOVA.

His sister Sulamith Messerer, b. Moscow, 1908, was for many years his partner and ballerina at the Bolshoy T.; now teaches. Her son, Mikhail Messerer, is in the Bolshoy *corps de ballet*. Raisa Messerer, sister of Asaf and Sulamith (b. 1902), was a silent-screen actress. She is the mother of PLISETSKAYA and Aleksandr Plisetsky (b. 1931), Bolshoy T. 1948–70; at present ballet master in Peru; also of Azary Plisetsky (b. 1937), Bolshoy B. 1956–63, *premier danseur*, teacher, choreographer, and permanent partner of ALONSO at NB of Cuba, 1963–73. Azary m. ballerina Loipa Araujo (b. 1941); with the Bolshoy B. from 1975; toured Japan with Plisetskaya, partnering her as José in CARMEN. Their uncle, Azary Azarin, and aunt, Elizaveta Messerer, were prominent in legitimate theatre; their cousin Naum Azarin was *maître de ballet*, Stanislavsky and Nemirovich-Danchenko B. NR

See Asaf Messerer, *Lessons of Classical Dance* (Moscow 1967); contains his article 'Thoughts on Pedagogical Method' and lists roles and ballets choreographed by him; *Classes in Classical Ballet*, tr. Oleg Briansky (New York 1976)

Metropolitan Ballet. A co. founded in London 1947 by impresario Leon Heppner and patron Cecilia Blatch with an international cast incl. BRUHN, Sonia Arova, Poul Gnatt, MARCHAND, PERRAULT, and the very young BERIOSOVA. The ballet masters were V. GSOVSKY, BERIOZOFF, and FRANCA. Choreographers incl. TARAS, HIGHTOWER, and STAFF. Financial problems caused the co. to fold Dec 1949 but it launched several considerable talents. MC

Mexico. There is little evidence of theatrical dancing in Mexico before 1790, when the Marani Troupe visited the T. Coliseo, Mexico City. In the 1820s, André Pautret established the first dance school in Mexico, and presented *La Niña Mal Cuidada* (possibly FILLE MAL GARDÉE). Aimée Guenó gave a solo perf. in 1832. In 1902, a full dance co. performed a 'lyric pantomime' (the term 'ballet' was still unknown). But mild interest erupted into devotion with the arrival of A. PAVLOVA in 1919. During her first three-month visit, her co. danced both at the elegant T. Arbeu for the elite, and at the bullring, where 30,000 cheered. In 1925 her co. returned; during the 1930s and 1940s several famous cos appeared in the major cities.

Various foreign teachers, such as Nelsy d'Ambré (Paris O.), Sergio Unger (Kiev), and Lettie Carroll (USA) settled and taught in Mexico.

In 1947, Guillermina Bravo, SOKOLOW and Waldeen (von Falkenstein) founded the official government school of dance, the Academia de la Danza Mexicana, which concentrated on modern dance. Two years later, ballet instruction in private schools was organized by Ana Castillo around the London RAD syllabus. Thirty-six member schools of the RAD, training about 5,000 students, developed quickly from her initial efforts. With Sylvia Ramírez, Castillo introduced the Cuban grading system in 1973–4. In 1975–6 Cuban teachers formally established this grading system at the Government Academia.

The first established co., B. de la Ciudad de México, founded 1944 by the Campobello sisters, survived only three seasons. Unger's B. Concierto (founded 1952), directed by Felipe Segura, maintained a repertory of 18 ballets but also lasted a short time. A third co., the B. Clásico de México (founded 1963), was financed by the government but has achieved only sporadic success in 12 years. Mexican dance officials have asked the Cuban government for help. The new Compañía Nacional de Danza, thanks to assistance from Cuba (and ALONSO) now has a *corps de ballet* of a good standard but there is a need for male dancers and soloists of both sexes.

In spite of the international reputations of such dancers as SERRANO, CARDÚS, Marcos Paredes (ABT), and Elena Carter (DTH) and the national stature within their own country of others (Laura Urdapilleta, Susana Benavides), Mexico still lacks its own personality in the world of ballet. AC

Meyer, Yvonne, b. Rio de Janeiro. Brazilian dancer and teacher. Studied with Yuco Lindenberg, Marylla Gremo, and Vaslav Veltchek. Joined the T. Municipal 1953 as a soloist; left Rio 1954 to join de Cuevas B. Created several roles in the co. and left to join the B. MISKOVITCH. Was soloist of MASSINE's B. de Nervi, guest artist with PAGE's Chicago Co. and CHARRAT's B. Later joined GORE's London B. She m. dancer Ivan Dragradze. Now principal teacher at Yvonne Goubé's school in Paris. MLN

Michaut, Pierre, b. Paris, 1895; d. Paris, 1956. French critic and writer. Author of *Histoire du Ballet* (Paris 1945) and *Le Ballet Contemporain, 1929–1950* (Paris 1950). Was president of the Association des Écrivains et Critiques de la Danse. M-FC

Midsummer Night's Dream, A, ballet, 2 acts, 6 scenes, ch. BALANCHINE; mus. Felix Mendelssohn; sc./ltg David Hays; c. (Barbara) Karinska. NYCC, NYCB, 17 Jan 1962; dan. MITCHELL (Puck), VILLELLA (Oberon), HAYDEN (Titania), Roland Vasquez (Bottom). A full-length dance version of William Shakespeare's play set to Mendelssohn's incidental music and other works. Act I recapitulates the action of the play, Act II celebrates the resolution of the plot with a series of *divertissements*. FM

Milan. The T. alla Scala, Italy's most famous opera house, opened 1778, capacity about 2,000. In 1975 *corps de ballet* of 34, plus 19 soloists, 12 principals and four *primi ballerini assoluti*: COSI, SAVIGNANO, FASCILLA, and PISTONI. Ballet director 1962–4 NOVARO, 1971–4 FIELD, Pierre Dobrievich appointed 1975. Joint *maîtres de ballet* Giulio Perugini and Gilda Maiocchi. Head of school attached to theatre (founded 1813), Anna Maria Prina. Two ballet programs usually incl. in subscription opera season (Dec–June); the co. also dances in operas. Sc. is the only Italian opera house to hold two short independent ballet seasons annually, one in the courtyard of the Castello Sforzesco, Milan, in July (not held 1975) and one in Sept at Sc. Guest artists are frequently invited for principal roles. FP

Milhaud, Darius, b. Aix-en-Provence, 1892; d. Geneva, Switzerland, 1974. French composer. Member of Les Six (with POULENC, AURIC, Arthur Honegger, Germaine Tailleferre, and Louis Durey), all of whom, save the last, collaborated on *Les Mariés de la Tour Eiffel* (Paris 1921; ch. BÖRLIN) for B. Suédois. Contributed a polka to *L'Éventail de Jeanne* (Paris 1929; ch. Yvonne Franck and Alice Bourgat), music by, among others, Poulenc, RAVEL, Jacques Ibert, Albert Roussel, and Florent Schmitt. A prolific composer, Milhaud wrote several ballet scores, incl., for B. Suédois, ch. Börlin, *L'Homme et son Désir* (Paris 1921) and *La Création du Monde* (Paris 1923). For DIAGHILEV he wrote TRAIN BLEU and orch. SATIE's three piano pieces *Jack in the Box* (Paris 1926; ch. BALANCHINE). For DE BEAUMONT's Soirées de Paris, 1924, *Salade* (ch. MASSINE). For RUBINSTEIN *La Bien-Aimée*, after Franz Schubert and Franz Liszt (Paris 1928; ch. NIJINSKA). For Les Ballets 1933 *Les Songes* (Paris 1933; ch. Balanchine). For Chicago Univ. *The Bells* (1946; ch. PAGE). For B. de Paris *'Adame Miroir* (Paris 1948; ch. CHARRAT). DH

Miller, The, hero of TRICORNE

Miller, Patricia, b. Pretoria, 1927. S. African dancer and teacher. Trained by HOWES, Cecily Robinson, and Yvonne Blake. In 1947 joined London SWBS and then SWTB. She m. D. DAVIES 1954. She created important roles for SWTB in CRANKO's ballets, incl. Beauty (*Beauty and the Beast*), Columbine (*Harlequin in April*), and La Capricciosa (LADY AND THE FOOL); also danced SWANILDA. Returned to S. Africa with her husband 1956 to teach at the UCT BS, dancing as guest artist with UCTB until 1963 when she appeared as guest artist for B. Transvaal in Johannesburg. Ballerina with PACOFS B., Bloemfontein, 1965–7; guest artist with NAPAC B. Durban, 1963; ballerina there 1968–73 and assistant director from 1973. MG

Millions d'Arlequin, Les (*Arlekinada*), ballet, 2 acts, ch. M. PETIPA; mus. DRIGO; sc. Orest Allegri; c. Evgeniy Ponomarev. St Petersburg, Hermitage T., 10 Feb 1900; St Petersburg, Maryinsky T., 13 Feb 1900; dan. KSHESSINSKA, PREOBRAZHENSKA. Ballet in *commedia dell'arte* style: Harlequin and Columbine outwit her father's attempts to marry her off to a rich suitor. A. PAVLOVA danced in this ballet with FOKINE; later she incl. a *pas de trois* derived from it in her own repertory, under the title *Les Coquetteries de Colombine*, ch. LEGAT. London, Palace T., 15 Apr 1912. Recent presentations of a *pas de deux* said to be from the original ballet seem to be of dubious authenticity. Sometimes called HARLEQUINADE, under which title BALANCHINE produced a new version in 1965. DV

Milloss, Aurelio [Aurel (von) Milloss (de Miholy)], b. Ujozora, Hungary [now Uzdin, Yugoslavia], 1906. Hungarian dancer, choreographer, and director (Italian nationality from 1960). Studied Budapest and Berlin. Resident choreographer T. dell'O., Rome, 1938–45. Ballet master Cologne 1960–3. Ballet director Vienna Staats O. 1953–66, and again 1971–4, when he left Rome after a further period there as director (1966–9). Prolific choreographer for a number of cos, incl. most Italian opera houses as well as T. Colón, Stockholm, Vienna, B. des CE (*Portrait de Don Quichotte*, 1947; mus. Goffredo Petrassi), Baalbeck Fest., etc. Has frequently collaborated with composers (Luigi Dallapiccola, Petrassi, etc.) and famous artists such as Corrado Cagli. FP
See A. Testa, 'Les 70 Ans de Aurelio Milloss', *Les Saisons de la Danse* (Paris, Dec 1976) with list of activities

Mime. The art of conveying meaning without speech (*see* Glossary under MIME) has evolved in W. Europe and the USA largely from the innovative activities of Étienne Decroux. A speaking actor trained by Jacques Copeau, Charles Dullin, and Louis Jouvet, Decroux performed on the Paris stage, in films, and radio from the late 1920s through the 1940s. During this period he developed corporal mime, a term he coined to distinguish his work from the white-face pantomime of the Romantic era, personified by Jean Gaspard Deburau. Decroux's interest in corporal mime was sparked by Copeau's masked improvisation exercises at the Vieux Colombier TS. In corporal mime the face is masked or inexpressive, while the body is expressively articulated, as opposed to pantomime of the Romantic era in which the face and hands draw the focus of attention.

Decroux's first pupil was Jean-Louis Barrault, an actor and director who has used mime throughout his long career in the theatre. Barrault starred as Baptiste in Marcel Carné's film *Les Enfants du Paradis* (1945), in which Decroux played the role of Baptiste's father. A re-creation of the life and times of Deburau, the film is rich in pantomime of the Romantic era.

Marcel Marceau, another Decroux pupil, combines the charm of romantic pantomime with some of the elements of corporal mime. He has become one of the most popular solo artists of our time, performing as many as 300 times a year in various parts of the globe. Marceau cites as influences Decroux, Charlie Chaplin, and Buster Keaton.

In E. Europe, contemporary mime has two outstanding exponents, Ladislav Fialka of Czechoslovakia and Henryk Tomaszewski of Poland. Both began their career as ballet dancers, both were influenced by AUSDRUCKSTANZ, or modern dance, and both created forms of mime in response to a need for greater expressivity than either felt dance would allow. Being exponents of mime as a group expression rather than a solo form, both created theatres rich in costume, scenic elements, lighting, and music. Whereas Fialka has continued as the leading performer as well as the director of his co., Tomaszewski soon gave directing his full attention. The Czech ensemble of eight prefers small theatres; the Polish co. numbers 30 and favours large-scale productions.

Mime training in Poland and Czechoslovakia is carried on by the two major figures and their disciples; in France Decroux and Jacques Lecoq are the leading teachers. Decroux perfects corporal mime; Lecoq works with masks, *commedia dell'arte*, improvisation, text, clowning, and acrobatics in a creative approach to actor and mime training.

Mime in America is taught and practised by disciples of Decroux, Lecoq, Marceau, and to a lesser

Mime. Jean-Louis Barrault impersonating the great mime Deburau in Marcel Carné's film *Les Enfants du Paradis*

European Dance (or AUSDRUCKSTANZ) were DALCROZE and LABAN. The Central European School, whose leading exponents were WIGMAN, KREUTZBERG, and JOOSS, had some influence on the American Modern Dance through their visits to the USA, and more particularly through the teaching and choreography of H. HOLM.

Although the modern dancers of the first generation all produced some works that consisted of pure movement, for the most part they were concerned with the communication of 'important' subject matter, in contrast to what was considered the 'trivial' content of ballet: especially in the 1930s, many pieces were laden with social significance and several dancers were involved in the government-sponsored Works Progress Administration (WPA) which gave employment to artists during the Depression. Others, especially Graham, were profoundly influenced by Freudian psychology, especially in works reinterpreting Greek myths.

Although each of the leading figures of this generation had followers who were content to accept the principles they laid down – for Graham, P. LANG and others, for Humphrey, LIMÓN and KONER – there were others who repeated the pattern of their original rebellion, notably CUNNINGHAM. Cunningham generally eliminated literary content of any kind from his works, as did NIKOLAIS (originally associated with Holm): they in their turn have been followed by young choreographers whose experiments are even more extreme (see AVANT-GARDE DANCE).

Throughout its brief history, however, Modern Dance has continued to produce solitary figures whose work resists categorization but may be said to carry on the tradition of Duncan – dancers like S. SHEARER, LITZ, and MARSICANO, whose solos could be described in the words used by the silent-movie star Louise Brooks (who began her career as a Denishawn dancer) to define the art of film acting: 'the movements of thought and soul transmitted in a kind of intense isolation.' DV

See Margaret Lloyd, *The Borzoi Book of Modern Dance* (New York 1949); John Martin, *The Modern Dance* (New York 1933); *Introduction to the Dance* (New York 1939); Selma Jeanne Cohen (ed.), *The Modern Dance: Seven Statements of Belief* (Middletown, CT, 1966)

Moiseyev, Igor, b. Kiev, 1906. Soviet dancer and choreographer. At age 12 entered private ballet class of Vera Mosolova who within one year recommended him for Bolshoy BS. Graduated 1924, class of GORSKY. Character soloist and choreographer, Bolshoy B., 1924–39. Choreographed several works in the 1930s. Returned to choreograph first Bolshoy version of SPARTACUS. Always interested in folk dancing, in his early youth walked and hitchhiked from Ukraine to Pamir region, studying and recording dances, songs, and customs of various nationalities. An invitation to head the dance department of

The Moiseyev Folk Dance Company in *The Partisans* (dan. Boris Kretyaninov)

the T. of Folk Art (founded Moscow 1936) came from these interests and encouraged him to decide that the time had come to found a professional folk-dance co. (born 10 Feb 1937). At first there were no permanent premises and about 30 dancers, mostly from amateur folk groups who had attracted attention at the 1936 Folk Dance Fest. When one of the men fell ill, Moiseyev had to dance in his stead. The repertoire consisted of about 10 numbers such as the Georgian *Khorumi*, the Byelorussian *Liavonikha*, the Moldavian *Moldavenskaya*, etc. From the start Moiseyev was against presenting folk dances just as they were performed by the people, with only a few steps and a primitive pattern. His idea was to develop the dances and give them a highly professional theatrical form. Moreover, in many cases, he literally created folk dances for the people. For example, the Byelorussian nation had been so poor and downtrodden before the Revolution that it had lost or forgotten most of its dances. Moiseyev took a Byelorussian song, *Bulba* (*Potato*), and created a merry dance about girls planting, weeding, and collecting potatoes into one huge bag (formed by their own bodies), which was accepted by the Byelorussian people as one of their own and firmly believed to be so. There are many such examples. Moiseyev created many choreographic scenes that should rightly be called 1-act ballets: e.g. *A Day on a Battleship*, *Old Moscow Scenes*, *Holiday on a Collective Farm*, *Football*, and the unforgettable *Partisans*. The Moiseyev Folk Dance Co. also has a vast repertoire of dances of other nations from the 50 countries visited by them. There are now 116 dancers and a total repertory of over 300 dances. The accompaniment for such a serious and varied folk-dance theatre is provided by a good symphony orchestra, supplemented by groups playing Russian and Oriental instruments. The co. performs for roughly three months on tour abroad, spending the rest of the year dancing in all the 15 republics of the USSR.

In 1967 Moiseyev founded a sister professional co., the State Ensemble of Classical Ballet. He invited the pick of young graduates and soloists from various ballet schools and theatres, and created a repertoire of purely classical dances and miniatures. However, finding it impossible to divide himself between two cos, he handed over the direction of the classical co. to ZHDANOV in 1971. Hero of Socialist Labour (awarded 1976 on his 70th birthday), People's Artist, USSR (1953), Lenin and three State Prizes. NR

Moiseyeva, Olga, b. Leningrad, 1928. Soviet dancer. Graduated Leningrad Choreographic S. 1947, class of VAGANOVA. Created Queen Mekhmene-Banu (LEGEND OF LOVE), Queen Gertrude (HAMLET; SERGEYEV version), Bianca (OTHELLO; CHABUKIANI version). Other roles incl. ZAREMA, Suimbike (SHURALE), title role in LAURENCIA, Aegina in YACOBSON's SPARTACUS, GISELLE, ODETTE-ODILE, Nikia (BAYADÈRE), KITRI. TV film *Olga Moiseyeva Dances*, also in *Choreographic Miniatures*. Her roles incl. lyrical-romantic, heroic, and even comic impersonations, e.g. an Ugly Sister in Sergeyev's CINDERELLA. People's Artist, RSFSR. NR
See V. Mironova, 'Olga Moiseyeva' in *Leningrad Ballet Today*, No. 2 (Leningrad 1968)

Moncion, Francisco, b. La Vega, Dominican Republic, 1922. American dancer and choreographer. Joined DE CUEVAS's B. International 1944, created title role in *Sebastian* (ch. Edward Caton). Also danced in Broadway musicals for BALANCHINE and with B. Russe de Monte Carlo before joining B. Society 1946. A member of NYCB since its inception, a superb partner and dramatic dancer. Created roles in many Balanchine ballets incl. ORPHEUS (Dark Angel), and also in AFTERNOON OF A FAUN. His choreography incl. *Pastorale* (1957) for NYCB, also given by Boston and Pennsylvania Bs. DV

Monk, Meredith, b. New York, 1942. American modern dancer, musician, and choreographer. Associated with *avant-garde* dance. Early training in DALCROZE Eurhythmics, later at Sarah Lawrence College with Judith Dunn and Beverly Schmidt. Monk began presenting her work at the Judson Church in the middle 1960s. In her first important solo, *Break* (1964), she explored a proscenium space, wearing a clear plastic raincoat over tights and leotard, accompanied by automobile noises. After *Blackboard*, *Beach*, and *Cartoon* she made *16 Millimeter Earrings* 1966, a dance in which she interwove film and live images. Monk developed her own theatrical iconography further in *Duet with Cat's Scream and Locomotive* (1966) with KING. She used props, film, sounds, and a slow repetitive pace. Since *Overload* for the Expo '67 Youth Pavilion and *Blueprint* for two buildings in Woodstock, New York, Monk's work has been designed for specific sites. Audiences received maps; their journey was part of the perfs, which had spread beyond the conventional

Monotones (mus. *Trois Gymnopédies* by SATIE) with (left to right) DOWELL, LORRAYNE, ASHMOLE

dance framework, as in JUICE, performed in three instalments at different places. *Needlebrain Lloyd and the Systems Kid* (1970) she called 'a live movie' and *Vessel* (1971) 'an opera epic'. *Vessel* was seen by audiences through windows and across parking lots, angles which approximated movie viewing. The material of Monk's work often refers to myth. Repeated combinations of strange gestures and strange characters become the event, enhanced by costumes, colours, voice sounds. In *Education of a Girlchild* (1973) Monk's group of dancers, called 'The House' acted out a communal evolution from childhood to old age or from morning to night. In *Paris/Chacon* (1974) the group performed a work dance, with chanting. Music – Monk's own haunting voice, and her piano or organ themes – plays an important part in her work and she has made musical scores for other dancers as well. Her own most recent pieces are *Small Scrolls* (1975) for 'three mortals and two gods' and a solo, *Anthology* (1975). EK

Monkshood's Farewell, modern dance work, ch./sc. PILOBOLUS DANCE T.; mus. collage, arr. Pilobolus Dance T. New London, CT, Palmer Auditorium, Connecticut College, 28 July 1974. A humorous and slightly macabre series of vignettes that celebrate a medieval sense of grotesque drama, ending with a shadowy parade into fading light. DM

Monotones, *pas de trois*, ch./c. ASHTON; mus. SATIE (*Trois Gymnopédies*), orchestrated DEBUSSY and Roland-Manuel. London, CG, RB, 24 Mar 1965; dan. LORRAYNE, DOWELL, Robert Mead. Intended as a *pièce d'occasion* for a gala, this dance, a further distillation of Ashton's classicism in the same vein as SYMPHONIC VARIATIONS, proved so successful that it was retained in the repertory, with the addition of a second *pas de trois* with the same title, also to music of Satie (*Prélude d'Éginhard* and *Trois Gnossiennes*), orchestrated John Lanchbery. CG, RB, 25 Apr 1966; dan. SIBLEY, PARKINSON, SHAW. The dances are performed in reverse order of their composition. Revived W. Berlin, Deutsche OB, 20 June 1971; Chicago B., 9 Feb 1974; New York, CCJB, 11 Oct 1974; Brisbane, Australian B., 18 July 1975, etc. DV

Monteux, Pierre, b. Paris, 1874; d. Hancock, ME, 1964. French conductor. With DIAGHILEV 1911–14 and on tour of USA, 1916–17. Conducted premieres of PETRUSHKA, SACRE DU PRINTEMPS, DAPHNIS ET CHLOÉ, and JEUX. DH

Month in the Country, A, ballet, 1 act, ch. ASHTON; mus. Frédéric Chopin, arr. John Lanchbery; lib. freely adapted from Ivan Turgenev's play; sc. Julia Trevelyan Oman. London, CG, RB, 12 Feb 1976; dan. SEYMOUR, DOWELL, GRANT, SLEEP, RENCHER, Marguerite Porter, Denise Nunn. The ballet concentrates on the central situation of Turgenev's play, revolving around the young tutor and his effect on the various members of the Yslaev household – husband, wife, their son, their ward, the wife's 'admirer' – all translated into some of Ashton's most beautiful and brilliant choreography. DV

A Month in the Country. SEYMOUR as Natalia Petrovna

Monument for a Dead Boy (*Monument voor een Gestorven Jongen*), ballet, 1 act, ch. van DANTZIG; mus. Jan Boerman; sc. SCHAYK. Amsterdam, Stadsschouwburg, Dutch NB, 19 June 1965; dan. Schayk. At the moment of death, a boy sees the main events of his life which separated him from his vulgar quarrelling parents, led him in pursuit of an inner artistic vision, and caused him to recognize his homosexual leanings. Inspired by the suicide of a young poet, the ballet was admired for its frankness and vivid dramatic situations; revived for many cos in the USA, Denmark, Germany, etc. JP

Monumentum pro Gesualdo, ballet, 1 act, ch. BALANCHINE; mus. STRAVINSKY (an arrangement for orchestra of 3 madrigals by Carlo Gesualdo); sc. David Hays. NYCC, NYCB, 16 Nov 1960; dan. D. ADAMS, Conrad Ludlow. Plotless ballet usually paired in repertory with MOVEMENTS. FM

Moore, Lillian, b. Chase City, VA, 1917; d. New York, 1967. American dancer, teacher, and historian. Remembered for her extensive and very scholarly writings about dance, in many journals and publications. As a dancer she was principal of NY Met OB; later was director of the apprentice program of the JOFFREY B. MC/CC

Moor's Pavane, The, modern dance work, ch. LIMÓN; mus. Henry Purcell, arr. Simon Sadoff; c. Pauline Lawrence. New London, CT, Palmer Auditorium, Connecticut College, 17 Aug 1949; dan. Limón, HOVING, B. JONES, KONER. Within the fabric of a formal pavane, interrupted by private 'asides', the four principal characters of William Shakespeare's *Othello* portray their conflicts and passions. In the repertory of many ballet cos. DM

Mordkin, Mikhail, b. Moscow, 1880; d. Millbrook, NJ, 1944. Russian dancer, teacher, and choreographer. Trained Moscow TS; debut as student 1898 in a part arranged by his teacher TIKHOMIROV. In 1899, a year before graduation, danced COLAS and became immediately a popular favourite. Handsome, virile, and an excellent actor, he soon rivalled Tikhomirov and claimed artistic recognition for the male dancer as the equal of the ballerina. His dramatic gifts made him an ideal GORSKY dancer, achieving great success as ALBRECHT in Gorsky's 1907 production of GISELLE. With equal veracity he played the repulsive Nubian king in FILLE DU PHARAON. Seeking to widen his activities, he began to teach at the Moscow TS; assistant ballet master to Gorsky 1905 although he was allowed to choreograph only opera ballets. From 1906 he taught at the Moscow actor Aleksandr Adashev's Art T., pursuing his goal of expanding the expressiveness of the human body. Konstantin Stanislavsky admired his work and invited him to collaborate on productions.

Mikhail Mordkin in his 'Bow and Arrow' dance which he choreographed himself; it was one of the most popular dances in his repertory

In 1909 Mordkin appeared in the first DIAGHILEV Paris season but his style was at variance with the mostly St Petersburg-trained co., and GRIGORIEV described him as 'rather angular'. He was of an independent and uncompromising nature and soon parted with the Diaghilev co. to tour with A. PAVLOVA. In Feb 1910 they had a triumph at the NY Met O., dancing a version of COPPÉLIA and *divertissements* incl. their famous *Bacchanale* (mus. GLAZUNOV) and Mordkin's 'Bow and Arrow' dance which he choreographed himself (mus. Andrey Arends from the ballet *Salammbô*). In 1910 with Pavlova made a second coast-to-coast tour of the USA; 1911 danced with her in London at the Palace T. He had been obliged to resign from the Imperial Ts for taking such long leave of absence and after quarrelling with Pavlova (who was jealous of his success) he formed his own co. 1911 called, without any authority, 'The Imperial Russian B. of Stars', which incl. GELTSER, SEDOVA, ZAMBELLI, and had Hilda Munnings (later L. SOKOLOVA) in the *corps de ballet*. Its life ended in New Orleans.

In 1912 Mordkin successfully petitioned for reinstatement at the Imperial Ts and thanks to the support of the director Vladimir Teliakovsky rejoined his favourite Moscow co. where he was received jubilantly. He built up a concert repertory (with BALASHOVA, his regular partner), his most famous solo being 'The Italian Beggar' (mus. Camille Saint-Saëns's *Gipsy*). In 1918 his ballet *Aziade*, on Oriental themes, was filmed with himself and Margarita Froman. In the early 1920s he worked in both Tiflis and Moscow but his Jan 1923 concert in Moscow was badly received (he was 43 and heavily built) and after touring the country with KRIGER he left for W. Europe and the USA. He appeared in the Greenwich Village Follies 1924 and toured for two years under Morris Guest with Xenia Makletsova (formerly of the Bolshoy) and NEMCHINOVA. He subsequently taught in NY and Philadelphia and in 1937 formed the Mordkin B. Co. to show his pupils' talents. By 1938 it had become professional with Sergei Soudeikine as designer, Eugene Fuerst as musical director, and CHASE a principal dancer. From this co. grew ABT. Mordkin, typically, could not work in the new organization, resigned and returned to teaching, embittered, until his death. He m. former character dancer Bronislava Porzychka (Pozhitskaya). Their son Mikhail Mordkin, Jr, became a businessman. NR
See V. Krasovskaya, *Russian Ballet Theatre of the Beginning of the 20th Century* (Leningrad 1972); George Amberg, *Ballet in America* (New York 1949); Doris Hering, 'Wild Grass, The Memories of Rudolf Orthwine' in *Dance Magazine* (New York 1967)

Moreau, Jacqueline, b. Bandol, 1926. French dancer and teacher. Studied Paris OBS, *première danseuse* 1948. Joined B. des CE as soloist 1951; *étoile*, de Cuevas B. 1952–9. A dancer of great beauty, she shone in the neoclassical repertory. Now teaches at the Paris O. M-FC

Moreland, Barry, b. Melbourne, 1943. Australian dancer and choreographer. Joined Australian B. 1962 from its S. Coming to Europe he danced in musicals and studied at the LSCD, joining its co., where he made his first choreographies: *Summer Games*, *Kontakion*, *Hosannas*. In 1971 he was invited to join LFB, for whom he choreographed *Summer Solstice* (1972), *In Nomine* (1973) and the 2-act *Prodigal Son in Ragtime* (1974) which has proved immensely popular with LFB's audiences. In 1975 he resigned from LFB. Now a freelance choreographer. MC/CC

Moreton, Ursula, b. Southsea, 1903; d. London, 1973. English dancer and teacher. Pupil of CECCHETTI and member of the DIAGHILEV B. Russes 1920–2. In 1926 she joined DE VALOIS's school as a teacher; thereafter her career was devoted as dancer and teacher to de Valois's enterprise in building an English national ballet. Greatly admired, she directed the RBS 1952–68. OBE 1968. MC/CC

Moroda, Derra de *see* DERRA DE MORODA

Morrice, Norman, b. Agua Dulce, Veracruz, Mexico, 1931. English dancer, choreographer, and director. Entered Rambert BS 1952 and BR 1953, becoming a principal dancer but mainly in character roles such as the Man She Must Marry in JARDIN AUX LILAS. Created his first ballet, *Two Brothers*, 1958 and gave a sensitive and moving perf. as the younger, 'mixed-up' brother whose behaviour results in a tragic killing. Visited the USA 1961–2 for five months on a Ford Foundation Fellowship. In 1965 he choreographed *The Tribute* for RB but it did not live long in the repertory. Greatly impressed by contemporary dance in the USA, he was ready when the BR image was changed in 1966 not only to accept the post of associate director but also to stage many ballets in the contemporary dance idiom, among them *Blind-Sight* and THAT IS THE SHOW. In 1970 he was appointed joint artistic director of the co. but resigned in 1974. As a choreographer Morrice is deeply concerned with the world today (he was much influenced by dancing in the TUDOR repertory of the 'old' BR) but his choreographic language can be obscure. MC

Morris, Margaret, b. London, 1891. English dancer and movement theorist. She founded her own school 1910 in London and was a pioneer in the teaching of free dance. In 1925 founded the Margaret Morris Movement (still extant) and devised a system of notation. In 1947 founded her short-lived Celtic B. in Glasgow. An influential figure, she published several books incl. her autobiography, *My Life in Movement* (London 1969). MC/CC

Mosolova, Vera, b. Moscow, 1875; d. Moscow, 1949. Russian dancer and teacher. Graduated from Moscow TS 1893 into Bolshoy B. Transferred for *classe de perfectionnement* under JOHANSSON to Maryinsky T. 1896–1903, where she performed solo parts. Bolshoy 1903–18; danced AURORA, LILAC FAIRY, Tsar-Maiden (HUMPBACKED HORSE), but not promoted to ballerina position until 1917. In extravaganza *Dance Dream*, London, 1911; taught in A. PAVLOVA's co. 1913. At period when GORSKY's choreography neglected technique, she was invariably praised by critics for clean lines and virtuosity. Taught at Moscow S. from 1918, teaching Sulamith Messerer among others; had own school; also taught at Meyerhold, Stanislavsky and Nemirovich-Danchenko and many other theatres. Her unpublished memoirs preserved at Bakhrushin T. Museum, Moscow. Honoured Art Worker, RSFSR. NR

The Moszkowski Waltz as danced by STRUCHKOVA and LAPAURI of the Bolshoy B.

Moszkowski Waltz, *pas de deux*, ch. VAINONEN; mus. Moritz Moszkowski. Leningrad, 1930; dan. GUSEV, Olga Mungalova. The prototype of spectacular Soviet *pas de deux*, it is still in the repertory. When Gusev moved to Moscow in the mid-1930s and became LEPESHINSKAYA's concert partner during World War II, he taught it to her; she was the only partner who performed three revolutions mid-air (instead of two) before throwing herself into Gusev's arms for the 'fish dive'. In 1947, when preparing young dancers for the World Youth Fest. in Prague, Gusev passed on the *Moszkowski Waltz* to STRUCHKOVA and LAPAURI; it has since become identified with them. NR
See Klaudia Armashevskaya and Nikita Vainonen, *Baletmeister Vainonen* (Moscow 1971)

Motte, Claire, b. Belfort, 1937. French dancer. Paris OBS 1948; *corps de ballet* 1951; *première danseuse* 1957, *étoile* 1961. Dances the classical repertory, especially ÉTUDES, but her strong personality and powerful technique are really more suited to the contemporary repertory: SYMPHONIE FANTASTIQUE, LIFAR's *Chemin de Lumière* (1957), DESCOMBEY's *But* (1963), PETIT's NOTRE-DAME DE PARIS and *Turangalila. Chevalier*, Légion d'Honneur 1972. M-FC
See I. Lidova, 'Claire Motte', *Les Saisons de la Danse* (Paris, Feb 1972)

Movements, ballet, 1 act, ch. BALANCHINE; mus. STRAVINSKY; sc./ltg David Hays and Peter Harvey. (As *Movements for Piano and Orchestra*) NYCC, NYCB, 9 Apr 1963; dan. FARRELL, D'AMBOISE. Plotless ballet usually paired in repertory with MONUMENTUM PRO GESUALDO. FM

Moves, ballet, ch. ROBBINS; without music or decor. Spoleto, T. Nuovo, Ballets USA, 3 July 1959; dan. Erin Martin, Michael Maule. Subtitled 'A ballet in silence about relationships'. Revived CCJB 1968. FM

Moylan, Mary Ellen, b. Cincinnati, OH, 1926. American dancer. Studied at SAB. Debut in ballets staged by BALANCHINE for New O. Co., NY, 1942, incl. *Rosalinda* (*Die Fledermaus*), opposite LIMÓN, and a revival of BALLET IMPERIAL, B. Russe de Monte Carlo, 1943–4 and 1947–9; B. Society 1946, creating Sanguinic in FOUR TEMPERAMENTS; ABT 1949–55; NY Met OB 1955–7. Retired on her marriage, 1957. One of the first contemporary US dancers to achieve ballerina status. DV

Muller, Jennifer, b. Yonkers, NY, 1944. American modern dancer and choreographer. Studied Juilliard S. of Music, ABTS, and with LIMÓN, GRAHAM, TUDOR, P. LANG, Alfredo Corvino, CRASKE, HORST, and SOKOLOW. She has performed with Lang, MASLOW, Frances Alenikoff, and the NY City OB. Joined the Limón Dance Co. 1963 and performed with FALCO and Featured Dancers (1967–74). She formed her own co., Jennifer Muller and The Works, 1974. Among her works are *Nostalgia* and *Rust* (both 1971; mus. Burt Alcantara). JD

Mulys, Gérard, b. Strasbourg, 1915. French dancer and teacher. Studied with RICAUX and AVELINE. *Maître de ballet*, Monte Carlo, 1941, then Nice 1948–56, Paris OC 1957. Taught at Paris O. 1958, then *régisseur général* and *répétiteur général* 1971; appointed administrator of ballet 1972. In 1946 he danced ALBRECHT at very short notice, to replace an injured dancer, with BR in London. A stylish dancer, now a revered teacher. Author (with Georges Detaille) of *Les Ballets de Monte-Carlo, 1911–1944* (Paris 1954). M-FC

Museums of Dance *see* ARCHIVES AND MUSEUMS

Musicals. Musical comedy, almost by definition, has always involved dance in one form or another. In fact, the musical entertainment often cited as the great-grandparent of musical comedy, BLACK CROOK (1866), was primarily distinguished not by its music, nor by its comedy, but by its interpolation of dance into the traditional structure of the musical revue.

The Black Crook established the conventions according to which dance would be utilized (or exploited) by musical comedies for many years to come. Dance was employed in these revues and extravaganzas either as a sinuous allurement or as a small, 'tolerable' dose of 'high culture'. The most interesting aspect of these primitive musical entertainments which followed in the wake of *The Black Crook* is the occasional guest stint by a legendary dancer. For example, FULLER is said to have performed her famous butterfly dance in a musical play called *A Trip to Chinatown* in 1891. A. PAVLOVA danced excerpts from SLEEPING BEAUTY in the Hippodrome extravaganza *The Big Show* in 1916. The 'Ziegfeld Follies of 1922' featured two dances choreographed by FOKINE. And even a performer as certifiably 'non-commercial' as GRAHAM appeared in the 'Greenwich Village Follies' 1923–5.

The first major choreographer to work in a bona-fide musical comedy (that is, an entire evening of song, dance, and dialogue organized around a single storyline) was BALANCHINE. Significantly, his first Broadway musical, *On Your Toes* (1936), was also the first musical comedy to take dance as its central theme. This Richard Rodgers and Lorenz Hart musical concerns a down-and-out Russian ballet co. touring the USA with a stuffy and unpopular ballet called *La Princesse Zénobia*. The desperate co. is persuaded to perform instead a jazz ballet called *Slaughter on Tenth Avenue* which is infinitely more acceptable to its American audience.

Balanchine's choreography for *On Your Toes* was instrumental in exposing a new mass audience to the conventions of ballet for the very first time; but he engineered no major structural innovations in the musical comedy form itself. Despite the fact that he was the first choreographer elevated to the status of overall director (for *Cabin In The Sky*, 1940), he did not achieve a fluid intermingling of song, dance, and dialogue. Even a magnificent stretch of choreography like *Slaughter on Tenth Avenue* exists within *On Your Toes* as a self-contained unit: i.e. a 'production number'. It was shown separately, excerpted from its original context, by NYCB in 1968.

In much the same way, other distinguished choreographers contributed dances to Broadway musicals in the 1930s and '40s without attempting to integrate dance into the narrative more organically. WEIDMAN contributed the choreography to Rodgers and Hart's *I'd Rather Be Right* (1937), TUDOR created the dances for one of Alan Jay Lerner and Frederick Loewe's first musicals *The Day Before Spring* (1945), and SOKOLOW did the same for Kurt Weill's *Street Scene* (1947).

But it was DE MILLE whose choreography revolutionized the musical comedy form beginning with Rodgers and Hammerstein's *Oklahoma!* in 1943. Before *Oklahoma!*, song, dance, and dialogue remained strictly compartmentalized. Here de Mille created the dream ballet 'Laurey Makes Up Her Mind' which sought to reveal, choreographically, the subconscious fears and longings of a seemingly uncomplicated *ingénue*. In addition to its psychological seriousness, de Mille's choreography for *Oklahoma!* emerged fluidly from the body of the work, capturing in movement what could not be captured in music or dialogue alone.

Unlike Balanchine, de Mille continued to work on Broadway throughout her career; and one can observe a continuing interaction between her choreography for musical comedies and her work for the concert stage. The seeds which blossomed into *Oklahoma!* for example, can be glimpsed in RODEO. She also created the choreography for a number of successful musicals incl. *One Touch Of Venus* (1943), *Carousel* (1945), *Brigadoon* (1947), and *Gentlemen Prefer Blondes* (1949). In 1954 she choreographed Sigmund Romberg's last musical, *The Girl In Pink Tights*, a nostalgic recounting of the events surrounding the original production of *The Black Crook*.

Like Balanchine before her, de Mille was given the opportunity to direct as well as choreograph for the Broadway stage (she did both for *Allegro* in 1947). But it was not until ROBBINS began to focus his creative energies on the musical comedy form that anyone realized how completely a choreographer's vision might dominate the entire conception of musical comedy. Under Robbins's guidance, the Broadway musical was transformed into something more closely resembling Wagnerian 'music drama', but a drama pulsating to the beat of contemporary urban America.

Robbins's Broadway career can be viewed as an odyssey in which he evolves from 'mere' choreographer (for *On The Town* 1944, which grew out of FANCY FREE) to co-director (with George Abbott on *Pajama Game*, 1954) to director-choreographer with his magnificent *West Side Story* in 1957. It was Robbins – even more than his composer Leonard Bernstein – who conceived of *West Side Story* as one living, breathing organism, expanding and contracting into an endless variety of shapes and patterns. The clearest example of this poetic principle was a recurring image in Robbins's *Fiddler On The Roof* (1964), that of the fiddler playing and dancing the 'Tradition' motif.

Although Robbins retired from the musical stage after *Fiddler On The Roof* in order to devote his time more exclusively to NYCB, his accomplishments continue to exert an enormous influence over other directors and choreographers.

KIDD, who danced for Robbins in *Fancy Free* while a member of ABT, went on to create some of the most ingenious choreography ever seen on Broadway. His choreographed prologue for *Guys and Dolls* (1950) was a model of economical storytelling

Musicals. *Above: West Side Story*, the Dance at the Gym as staged in London, 1959; *below: Show Boat* with Miguel Godreau in the wedding celebrations scene, as revived in London, 1971

and complex characterization achieved entirely through movement. Onna White, who assisted Kidd on *Guys and Dolls*, established herself as a leading Broadway choreographer with her dances for *The Music Man* (1957). H. HOLM, a WIGMAN disciple, forsook her German expressionist heritage and created the dances for musicals such as *Kiss Me Kate* (1948), *My Fair Lady* (1956), and *Camelot* (1960). Bob Fosse, who worked with Robbins on *Bells Are Ringing* (1956) as well as on *The Pajama Game* (1954), is probably most responsible for the sleek, sexy, razzle-dazzle look of ultra-professionalism which so often compensates for the sentimentality and simple-mindedness of the Broadway musical plot. Fosse's choreography for musicals such as *Sweet Charity* (1966), *Pippin* (1973), and *Chicago* (1975) made it perfectly clear that the Broadway musical had broken away completely from the lilting waltz time of European operetta. Gower Champion, director-choreographer of musicals such as *Bye, Bye, Birdie* (1960), *Hello Dolly* (1964), and *I Do, I Do* (1966) also reflected the Robbins influence in achieving a style of swirling, seamless, utterly fluid scene-to-scene transitions for each of his musicals.

Today, the director-choreographer most likely to carry on where Robbins left off is Michael Bennett. Like Robbins, Bennett is interested in creating serious works of musical theatre rather than stylish after-dinner diversions. As choreographer of *Company* (1970) and *Follies* (1971) he demonstrated a capacity for mocking the mindless conventions of most Broadway musicals in a very dry, bitter, brittle way. As director-choreographer for *A Chorus Line* (1975), he created the most disciplined and fully danced musical comedy to appear on Broadway since *West Side Story*. RC

Music for Ballet. Ballet music (i.e., music especially designed to accompany the theatrical presentation of dancing) has its origins in the BALLET DE COUR, with such works as BALLET COMIQUE DE LA REINE. But it was not until the advent of LULLY that a really unified approach became manifest, particularly in those *comédies-ballets* (a form that combined spoken drama and dance) on which he collaborated with Molière (e.g. *Le Bourgeois Gentilhomme*, 1670). Though ballet was not to become an independent activity for some time, it flourished as an integral part of French opera because of the powerful influence of Lully, who was appointed head of the recently founded Paris O. in 1672. Lully, in his young days a dancer as well as musician, replaced the stately, slow airs that dominated the *ballet de cour* of his youth with short, fast pieces especially designed to exhibit the dancers' speed and liveliness.

After Lully's death the opera-ballet which had developed in his last years continued to flourish in the work of J.-P. RAMEAU, to whom dancing was also a necessary feature of musical theatre. Of Rameau's 25 stage works ballet has an important place in no fewer than 19. But though his dance music is certainly practical – it includes elegant gavottes, minuets, and gigues, as well as rhythmically vigorous rigaudons, bourrées, tambourins and *contre-danses* – his use of ballet was diversionary rather than organic.

However, in 1761, three years before Rameau's death, Christoph Willibald Gluck initiated a new expressive approach to dance. With his *Don Juan* (ch. ANGIOLINI), the first self-sufficient *ballet d'action* to have music by an important composer, Gluck claimed to have returned to the principles of pantomime that guided the Ancients. As with the reform opera, *Orfeo ed Euridice* (1762), *Don Juan* gave ballet a decisively humanistic direction by stressing drama over virtuosity. Though Gluck's score consists of several, mainly short, symphonic pieces, with relatively few formal dances, it is propulsive, melodic and emotionally powerful, and therefore eminently danceable.

After *Don Juan* Gluck wrote only one more ballet score, the unremarkable *Semiramide* (1765; ch. Angiolini). In the following decades other distinguished figures composed ballets, among them Luigi Boccherini (*Ballet Espagnol*, 1775), Wolfgang Amadeus Mozart (*Les Petits Riens*, 1778) and Ludwig van Beethoven (GESCHÖPFE DES PROMETHEUS, ch. VIGANÒ, 1803). Yet the first half of the 19th c. brought a marked decline in the musical prestige of ballet. Because ballet had become an indispensable ingredient of French grand opera many first-rate composers did, in fact, write dance music throughout the 19th c. Giacomo Meyerbeer's *Robert le Diable* (1831), Gaetano Donizetti's *La Favorite* (1840), Hector Berlioz's *Les Troyens à Carthage* (1863), and Giuseppe Verdi's *Les Vêpres Siciliennes* (1855) all contain significant dance episodes. So does Bedřich Smetana's *Bartered Bride* (1866), produced in Prague, and Richard Wagner's *Die Meistersinger* (1868), produced in Munich, and so do a whole series of Russian operas, from Mikhail Glinka's *Ivan Susanin* (1836) to TCHAIKOVSKY's *Eugene Onegin* (1879) and Aleksandr Borodin's *Prince Igor* (1890).

But until the arrival of DIAGHILEV in the first decade of the present century, the provision of independently conceived ballet music remained – with a handful of remarkable exceptions – a specialized but unprestigious job, one often left to a theatre's staff composer, music director, or conductor. Thus DRIGO, who composed MILLIONS D'ARLEQUIN for Marius PETIPA, was the principal conductor for ballet at the Maryinsky in St Petersburg and led the first perfs there of SLEEPING BEAUTY (1890), NUTCRACKER (1892), and the revised SWAN LAKE (1895). MINKUS, staff composer of the Bolshoy in Moscow 1864–71 and at the Maryinsky 1871–86, when the position was abolished, supplied Petipa with more than a dozen works, including DON QUIXOTE and BAYADÈRE.

Today figures like these are largely alluded to, if at all, in contemptuous terms. PUGNI, staff composer at London CG until 1851 and in St Petersburg from then until his death in 1870, does not find a place in the fifth edition of *Grove's Dictionary of Music and*

Musicians, yet his reputed 312 ballets incl. some of the most influential works of the 19th c., among them PAS DE QUATRE, ESMERALDA, and HUMPBACKED HORSE. Every student of dance history knows that among the great reforms initiated by, first, I. DUNCAN and then, Diaghilev, was the restoration to dance of high musical standards. Yet, as the persistent survival of *Les Millions d'Arlequin* (in BALANCHINE's HARLEQUINADE, 1965), *Don Quixote*, and *Bayadère* suggests, we should not be overhasty in dismissing such music from serious consideration, any more than in our admiration for FOKINE's reforms we should undervalue the genius of Petipa.

Neither Minkus nor Drigo was a genius. They were simply craftsmen who attempted little more than to supply a necessary service – what Balanchine once referred to as the floor the dancer walks on. Their music is melodious, rhythmically clear and varied, both in mood and form. Above all, it is kinetic. It implies its realization in movement. To write such music is a rarer accomplishment than has generally been acknowledged. An examination of an often-heard contemporary ballet score like Nicolas Nabokov's *Don Quixote* (NYCB, 1965) can only increase admiration for these 19th-c. composers.

ADAM's music for GISELLE (1841) has also been scoffed at as merely serviceable; it remains, nevertheless, one of the most admirable works of its kind, possessing not only the virtues of Minkus and Drigo but, too, a perfect understanding of stage time (which is to say, drama), the ability to characterize without wasting a note, and a gift for atmosphere and locale. It also has some specifically French merits: clarity of texture, directness, and charm. *Giselle*, indeed, springs from a tradition of French music-making that exemplifies elegance, vivacity, tenderness, and wit. These inform the surviving ballet scores of composers like Ferdinand Hérold (FILLE MAL GARDÉE), Jean-Madeleine Schneitzhoeffer (SYLPHIDE), AUBER (*Marco Spada*, 1857), Édouard Lalo (*Namouna*, 1882; ch. Charles Nuitter and L. PETIPA), and André Messager (DEUX PIGEONS). The same characteristics can be found in the work of composers who though not born in France adopted the country and absorbed its attitudes, e.g. Friedrich Burgmüller (PÉRI) and Jacques Offenbach (*Le Papillon*, 1860; ch. Marie TAGLIONI). They are to be discerned even in the music of such German-influenced musicians as the Danes Niels Vilhelm Gade, Edvard Helsted, and Holger Simon Paulli, all of whom contributed to the score of August BOURNONVILLE's NAPOLI. But the most talented exponent of this tradition in ballet, the composer who carried it to its consummation, is DELIBES, whose COPPÉLIA and SYLVIA, at once brilliant and heartfelt, are among the masterpieces of dance music.

Tchaikovsky's admiration for *Sylvia* caused him to regret that he had not heard the score before embarking on his own SWAN LAKE. Nevertheless, this work and his other two ballets, *Sleeping Beauty* and *Nutcracker*, may be said to epitomize for most people the sound of ballet music, largely because of their incomparable theatrical vividness. Especially in his masterpiece, *Sleeping Beauty*, Tchaikovsky shows an awesome gift for apposite and memorable melody, for variety of imagination, and for richness of orchestral sound – though the latter initially stood in the way of the work's wholehearted acceptance by those, incl. Tsar Nicholas II, who found his music too symphonic. In both *Sleeping Beauty* and *Nutcracker* Tchaikovsky worked from a highly detailed scenario by M. Petipa that prescribed the length and form of virtually every number, but his genius was in no way hobbled by the necessary practical considerations the choreographer was wise enough to take account of. GLAZUNOV, who also collaborated with Petipa (e.g. RAYMONDA), continued with distinction, if with less inspiration, along the same lines.

Changes, however, were at hand. One of I. Duncan's most consequential reforms was her replacement of music written for dancing by absolute music, usually of the highest quality. She opened her first Russian concert (1905) by dancing to Frédéric Chopin. Not long afterwards, FOKINE used the same composer, though in orchestral transcriptions (by Glazunov), for what in due course came to be known as SYLPHIDES. Whether the conversion of self-sufficient compositions to balletic purposes represents an improvement in artistic standards is questionable, especially when the music is subject to the hazards of arrangement. Though under Diaghilev's guidance the change in attitude led to such pleasant confections as the Gioacchino Rossini–Ottorino Respighi BOUTIQUE FANTASQUE, it also led to the hodge-podge of Anton Arensky, Sergey Taneyev, Glinka, Glazunov, Modest Musorgsky, Nikolay Rimsky-Korsakov, and Aleksandr Cherepnin that was pressed into service for Fokine's *Cléopâtre* (1909). Similarly, since Diaghilev it has resulted in, on the one hand, a delightful assemblage of diverse material like John Lanchbery's *Fille Mal Gardée* and, on the other, in an unnatural union like NEUMEIER's *Don Juan* (Hamburg B., 1972), where Gluck's 18th-c. score is combined with a mass by the Spanish composer, Tomás Luis de Victoria (1548–1611).

But with a ballet like NIJINSKY's APRÈS-MIDI D'UN FAUNE (1912) Diaghilev demonstrated that a tone poem could serve admirably as a basis for dance and since his death all kinds of absolute music have been annexed for dance purposes. Though MASSINE's first symphonic ballets, PRÉSAGES, to Tchaikovsky's Fifth Symphony and CHOREARTIUM, to Brahms's Fourth Symphony (both 1933) were greeted by charges of musical presumptuousness, the controversy no longer exists. Today a choreographer is free to choose whatever accompaniment he deems suitable for his needs, whether Gustav Mahler's *Lied von der Erde* (TUDOR, 1948 and MACMILLAN, 1965), the Brahms-Schönberg *Quartet* (ch. Balanchine, 1966) or Johann Sebastian Bach's *Goldberg Variations* (ch. ROBBINS, 1971). Whatever the reaction to his ballet, the choreographer is unlikely any longer to face censure on the grounds of musical impiety. (Or, conversely, triviality, if like THARP in DEUCE COUPE, 1973, he uses music by a pop group.)

To a large extent this change results from the serious recognition which ballet has been accorded in the last generation, and which must ultimately be ascribed to Diaghilev. By his discovery of STRAVINSKY's genius for the theatre and the steady use he made of it over a period of 18 years, Diaghilev gave ballet music a prestige it had not enjoyed since the age of Lully, and because of it he was able to obtain works from composers like RAVEL, SATIE, FALLA, PROKOFIEV, POULENC, DEBUSSY, and Richard Strauss (LÉGENDE DE JOSEPH).

There are few distinguished 20th-c. composers who have not written at least one ballet score. The greatest of them remains Stravinsky, whose appeal to Balanchine from *Le Chant du Rossignol* (1925) to DUO CONCERTANT has produced an *œuvre* of astonishing quality and range. Not only has Balanchine collaborated directly with the composer on important commissions like ORPHEUS and AGON, he has in works like MONUMENTUM PRO GESUALDO and MOVEMENTS *(for Piano and Orchestra)* demonstrated the ability of dance to use with great effectiveness abstruse and rarefied scores such as would never have been considered theatrical before he showed them to be so. He has also thereby demonstrated the validity of his observation: 'I think the greatest music is never far from dancing.'

Equally valid, however, is the view that music and dance, though equals, are not inevitable partners. There have been some attempts at eliminating musical accompaniment altogether (e.g. LICHINE's *La Création*, 1948 and Robbins's MOVES), but the most successful readjustment of the time-honoured relationship between music and dance has been made by CUNNINGHAM. Cunningham has insisted that the components of theatrical dance – choreography, music, and decor – be given individual autonomy. His 30-year collaboration with CAGE has given dance music a decisive new direction. DH

Musil, Karl, b. Vienna, 1939. Austrian dancer. Studied at the Vienna Staats OBS; entered the co. in 1953 becoming a principal dancer. Guest artist with many cos, incl. LFB. He m. BOROWSKA. MC/CC

Musitz, Suzanne, b. Hungary, 1937. Hungarian dancer, choreographer, and director. Sydney B. Group (Australia). De Cuevas B. Western TB, founder member, 1957–61. Australian B., soloist, ballet mistress. Founded B. in a Nutshell 1965, now The Dance T. (NSW). Resigned from the directorship 1974. An emotionally expressive dancer (the Wife in PRISONERS, which she created, or the Woman in SONATE À TROIS) identified mainly with modern psychological ballets. Her ballets incl. *Family of Man*, *Romeo and Juliet*. KSW

Myrtha, the Queen of the Wilis in GISELLE

Napoli, as danced by the RDB in the early 1950s, the last act *divertissement*, with children from the RDBS appearing as extras on the bridge

N

Nádasi, Ferenc, b. Budapest, 1893; d. Budapest, 1966. Hungarian ballet dancer, teacher, and choreographer. Trained the first generations of Hungarian dancers to a European classical standard. He also studied with CECCHETTI in St Petersburg. Solo dancer, Budapest O. 1913 where his first principal role was Miklós Guerra's *Dwarf Grenadier*. Partnered ASTAFYEVA 1914 during her Budapest guest perf. and danced most major roles. In 1921 m. Aranka Lieszkovszky and undertook long tours abroad (Berlin, Prague, Munich, etc.). Studied in Paris with EGOROVA and PREOBRAZHENSKA. He m. Swiss dancer Marcelle Vuillet-Baum 1930 and together returned to Budapest 1937 to start the OBS producing such dancers as KUN, LAKATOS, RÓNA, FÜLÖP etc. He choreographed SYLVIA 1942, SPECTRE DE LA ROSE 1948. Merited Artist 1955, Kossuth Prize 1958. GPD

Nagrin, Daniel, b. New York, 1917. American dancer and choreographer. Studied modern dance with TAMIRIS, GRAHAM, H. HOLM, SOKOLOW, ballet with Elizabeth Anderson-Ivantzova and Edward Caton. Began to perform 1940, danced with Tamiris, MASLOW, WEIDMAN, Sokolow, and in many Broadway musicals incl. *Annie Get Your Gun* (1946) and *Plain and Fancy* (1955). Best known as a soloist: *Spanish Dance*, *Strange Hero*, and *Man of Action*, all created 1948, later formed part of a program called *Dance Portraits* with which he toured the USA from 1957. He m. Tamiris and formed a co. with her, 1960–3; divorced 1964. Continues to choreograph and perform solos, incl. two full-length works, *The Peloponnesian War* (1968) and the autobiographical *Ruminations* (1976). DV

Nagy, Ivan, b. Debrecen, 1943. Hungarian dancer. Studied first with his mother, Viola Sarkozy, then at Budapest NBS, joining the co. there on his graduation. Joined NB, Washington DC, 1965; NYCB 1968; ABT 1968. A true *premier danseur noble* who

performs such roles as ALBRECHT and JAMES with moving conviction and notable *ballon*, he has been the chosen partner of many ballerinas, incl. FONTEYN and MAKAROVA. He m. Australian ballerina Marilyn Burr, formerly with LFB and NB, Washington. Silver Medal, Varna Competition, 1965. DV

Nana, ballet, 9 scenes, ch. PETIT; mus. Marius Constant; lib. Edmonde Charles-Roux based on the novel by Émile Zola; sc. Ezio Frigerio. Paris O., 6 May 1976; dan. KAIN (title role), ATANASOFF (Muffat). The splendours and final degradation of a courtesan during the Second Empire in Paris, symbolizing the downfall of the regime as well. M-FC

NAPAC (Natal Performing Arts Council) **Ballet Company,** founded 1963 in Durban, Natal, S. Africa, when government grants for the arts were given to all four provinces. The Alhambra T. was acquired for perfs in 1970. The co. served country towns, schools, and the cities of Durban and Pietermaritzburg. D. DAVIES became artistic director 1968. In 1973 MILLER, the co.'s ballerina, was appointed assistant director. Producers such as STAFF, Mischa Slavensky, and Davies, as well as guest artists SCHULTZE, PARK, MACLEARY, SAMSOVA, and PROKOVSKY worked there. The co. was disbanded 1976. MG

Napoli (*or The Fisherman and his Bride*) (*Napoli, eller Fiskeren og hans Brud*), romantic ballet, 3 acts, ch./lib. August BOURNONVILLE; mus. Holger Simon Paulli, Edvard Helsted, Niels Vilhelm Gade and Hans Christian Lumbye. Copenhagen, RDB, 29 Mar 1842. Bournonville's most popular ballet, of which Act III has been given on its own at hundreds of special perfs; the whole ballet has been performed by the RDB more than 700 times. The story takes place in Naples, with Vesuvius glowing in the background across the bay. The first scene is full of dance and bustle in the marketplace with many comic characters. A young fisherman, Gennaro, takes his bride Teresina for a boat trip but is shipwrecked in a storm and loses her. She is taken to the Blue Grotto by naiads and transformed into a naiad herself by the King of the Sea. Gennaro arrives in his boat and with the help of a Madonna picture breaks the spell. The last act is a cascade of dance and wedding celebrations. Traditionally, children from the RDBS make their stage debuts standing on the bridge to watch the festivities. As Gennaro and Teresina leave in their wedding chariot, flowers are thrown, hats flung in the air, and muskets fired. The Tarantella and Finale are among the most exhilarating moments in ballet. SKJ

Naranda, Ludmilla, b. Zagreb, 1936. Yugoslav dancer. Pupil at the Zagreb State S.; joined Zagreb B. 1954. To Frankfurt, Heidelberg, Lübeck, then *prima ballerina* in Wuppertal. In 1974 to T. am Gärtnerplatz, Munich, as ballerina. She m. SERTIĆ. GBLW

National Ballet of . . . *see* the appropriate country

Nativo, Marga, b. Sfax, Tunisia, 1943. Italian dancer. At T. Comunale, Florence, since 1967. Resident *prima ballerina*, Maggio Musicale Fiorentino. At her best in modern roles, but opportunities limited by Italian preference for guest artists. FP

Nearhoof, Pamela, b. Indiana, PA, 1955. American dancer. Studied Jacksonville, FL, and at American B. Center, NY. Danced with Joffrey II Co., then joined CCJB 1972; was cast by THARP in both her ballets for that co., DEUCE COUPE and AS TIME GOES BY. Her magnificent extensions caused a sensation in the second version of MONOTONES. DV

Neary, Patricia, b. Miami, FL, 1942. American dancer. Studied NB of Canada S. and danced with co. 1956; then to SAB, New York; joined NYCB 1960.

Nederlands Dans Theater in *Arena* (ch. TETLEY)

Danced leading roles in many BALANCHINE ballets and in DIM LUSTRE and SUMMERSPACE. Ballet mistress, Deutsche O., W. Berlin, 1971–3; director, Geneva B. from 1973. Has staged Balanchine ballets for many cos. Her sister, Colleen Neary, b. 1952, is a soloist with NYCB. DV

Nederlands Dans Theater. Dutch dance co. founded 1959 by a breakaway group from Het Nederlands B. (*see* NETHERLANDS). The first leader was HARKARVY, an American teacher and ballet master. In 1960 he was joined in the artistic direction by van MANEN. Since 1961 the co. has been supported by the city of The Hague and has made its home there although appearing regularly all over the Netherlands.

The original policy was a mixture of new works based on the classical ballet technique and others in modern-dance style. Harkarvy supplied most of the former; guest choreographers such as BUTLER, in addition to van Manen, provided the latter. From the first, NDT was open to American influences and employed several American dancers, among them TETLEY who soon also became one of the resident choreographers. In 1970, Tetley succeeded Harkarvy as joint director but he and van Manen both resigned the following year. FLIER then took charge for two seasons, after which Carel Birnie, who had been the administrative and financial director throughout the co.'s existence, took charge of artistic policy until 1975 when KYLIÁN was appointed director jointly with Hans Knill.

Under Flier's direction, the influence of American modern dance became stronger, as did the tendency towards the use of more *avant-garde* musicians and artists. The classical side of the work was almost entirely relinquished, and after his departure this development continued with the arrival of the American choreographers FALCO and MULLER, who staged a series of mixed-media works with pop scores by Burt Alcantara.

Throughout its history, NDT has produced about 10 new works every year, most of them created specially for the co. and the great majority to 20th-c. music. In its early days, this creative policy and the attempt to combine the classical and modern-dance styles was widely influential, being copied by BR 1966 and also having a considerable effect on the RB when MACMILLAN first became director. However, one or two of the productions have played a crucial part in NDT's success. BUTLER's CARMINA BURANA could for years be guaranteed to sell out the house, and thus helped to draw audiences for more experimental works. Later, this function of guaranteeing audiences fell to *Mutations* (1970), which combined experimental dance films by van Manen and Jean-Paul Vroom with choreography on stage by Tetley. Two short film sequences and a few brief passages on stage were performed nude, as part of the work's general theme of contrasts and changes, but these episodes were exaggerated out of all proportion in public comment on the work.

NDT attracted many of the best Dutch dancers (incl. BIJE, SARSTÄDT, and Flier) and gave their first opportunities to RADIUS and EBBELAAR, who later achieved success elsewhere. Charles Czarny, LEMAITRE, and Arlette van Boven have been notable among the dancers from other countries. JP

Neglia, José, b. Buenos Aires, 1929; d. 1971. Argentine dancer. Studied Colón TS with Michel Borowski, Esmée Bulnes, and RUANOVA, joining the Colón co. 1948. A very versatile dancer, his repertory ranged from ALBRECHT to the title role in WITCH BOY. Awarded gold medal as best male dancer, International Dance Fest., Paris, 1968. His tragic death in a plane crash ended a brilliant career. JUL

Negro Spirituals, modern dance work, ch./c. TAMIRIS; mus. traditional, arr. Genevieve Pitot. New York, Little T., 29 Jan 1928 ('Nobody Knows the Trouble I See' and 'Joshua Fit de Battle ob Jerico'); New York, Martin Beck T., 7 April 1929 ('Swing Low, Sweet Chariot'); New York, Craig T., 7 Feb 1931 ('Crucifixion'); New York, New S. for Social Research, 18 Dec 1932 ('Git on Board, Lil' Chillun' and 'Go Down, Moses'); New York, Tamiris Studio, 2 Feb 1941 ('When the Saints Go Marchin' In'); New York, Rainbow Room, 1 Apr 1942 ('Little David, Play Your Harp' and 'No Hidin' Place'); dan. Tamiris. Solos reflecting the pious and playful moods of the individual hymns. In the repertory of the 5 × 2 Dance Co.; dan. Tamiris's nephew, Bruce Becker. DM

Nelidova [Lupandina; orig. Bartho], Lydia, b. Moscow, 1863; d. Moscow, 1929. Russian dancer. Daughter of a British manufacturer, Richard Bartho, who settled in Russia. Graduated from Moscow TS into Bolshoy B. 1884–97. Performed secondary solo parts with mediocre success. Danced Empire T., London, 1895; praised for lightness and beautiful *port de bras*. Repeated petitions to be granted ballerina status refused. After 13 years at Bolshoy Nelidova retired to found private school with her sister, Katarina Bartho (*c.* 1870–*c.* 1943). Lydia was the first Russian dancer to tour Australia. She also wrote on ideals of ballet and called for government support of private schools.

Her daughter Lydia Nelidova [Redega, married name Podobed], b. Moscow, 1888; d. Moscow, 1946, studied at her school. She was a character dancer invited by DIAGHILEV (1912) to dance the Goddess in *Dieu Bleu* (ch. FOKINE) and Principal Nymph in APRÈS-MIDI D'UN FAUNE. NR
See Ivor Guest, *The Empire Ballet* (London 1962); Serge Grigoriev, *The Diaghilev Ballet, 1909–1929* (London 1953; paperback Harmondsworth 1960); Lydia Nelidova, *Letters on Ballet* (Moscow 1894)

Nemchinova, Vera, b. Moscow, 1899. Russian dancer and teacher. Studied privately in Moscow and joined DIAGHILEV's B. Russes in 1915, becoming principal dancer 1924. Created many principal roles, notably in BICHES. In 1927–8 organized the Nemchinova–DOLIN B. in London in which her husband A. OBUKHOV later appeared. Prima ballerina, Lithuanian State B. 1931–5, and with R. BLUM and DE BASIL cos. Guest with ABT 1943. Now teaches in NY. MC/CC

Nerina, Nadia, b. Cape Town, 1927. S. African dancer. Early studies in Durban with Eileen Keegan and Dorothea McNair. To England 1945 to RAMBERT S., then SWBS, joining SWTB 1946 and making an immediate impression as the Circus Dancer in HOWARD's *Mardi Gras*, which she created Nov 1946. To SWB at CG 1947 as soloist, principal 1952. An enchanting soubrette, likened by many to L. LOPUKHOVA, by determination and hard work, especially with her teacher Cleo Nordi, earned her right to the whole classical repertory, AURORA, ODETTE-ODILE, GISELLE. She danced for a wider public than any of her generation, appearing in six major roles in complete TV screenings from the classic repertory, dancing in commercial TV variety programs, even with a circus. She toured S. Africa and S. Rhodesia in 1952 with RASSINE and also in 1954. Guest artist at the Bolshoy T., Moscow, 1960. ASHTON created the Spring solo for her in CINDERELLA and a solo in *Birthday Offering*, both using her quick, light and very high jump. The peak of her career was the creation of Ashton's LISE. Retired 1966. Patron of the CECCHETTI Society. MC
See Clement Crisp (ed.), *Ballerina: Portraits and Impressions of Nadia Nerina*, designed by Barney Wan (London 1975)

Netherlands, Ballet in. Although the cos of DIAGHILEV, A. PAVLOVA, and others visited Holland, there was virtually no dance tradition there until the 1930s, when modern dance began to establish itself, largely through the efforts of GEORGI, who formed a small co. (1936) which in 1941 was engaged at the newly constituted Amsterdam Municipal O. Its activities were suspended after the liberation in 1945, in which year Hans (actually Johanna) Snoek organized the Scapino B. to perform for children. This co. still has a small group that appears in schools while the main troupe plays to young or family audiences in theatres, with a high standard and a

Nadia Nerina as ASHTON's LISE, with BLAIR as COLAS

widely based repertory. The Amsterdam O. was reopened 1946 and a new ballet co. formed for it, directed first by Darja Collin (a Dutch dancer and choreographer who had worked mainly abroad) and later by ADRET. In 1947, Mascha ter Weeme, a former soloist of Georgi's co., formed the B. der Lage Landen (B. of the Low Countries), which produced many works specially created by Dutch or British choreographers; among these WITCH BOY. GASKELL formed a small group called B. Recital and in 1958 a larger co., Het Nederlands B., based in The Hague. HARKARVY, an American teacher engaged as ballet master, left the following year and with like-minded Dutch colleagues formed NEDERLANDS DANS THEATER which, after some initial difficulties, became one of Holland's two leading cos. In 1959, the Amsterdam OB and the B. der Lage Landen combined to form the Amsterdams B. under ter Weeme's direction; this in turn amalgamated in 1961 with Het Nederlands B. to form Het Nationale B. (*see below*). Holland also receives many visiting cos at the Holland Fest. every June; for some years the Fest. ignored the indigenous cos but nowadays they customarily take part and additionally hold their own B. Fest. in Amsterdam each July. Every city in Holland has a theatre and the cos regularly perform all over the country. Several small modern-dance groups also exist; that of Pauline de Groot did particularly interesting work but has now disbanded, leaving Koert Stuyf as the leading independent choreographer, with his wife Ellen Edinoff as leading dancer.

Nationale Ballet, Het (Dutch NB). Dutch co. founded in Amsterdam 1961 by amalgamation of Amsterdams B. and Het Nederlands B., initially under joint direction of Gaskell and Mascha ter Weeme. The former soon took sole charge and over the next seven years built up a large co. with an exceptionally eclectic repertory. From the first, however, she encouraged young Dutch choreographers to develop their abilities, notably van DANTZIG, who with Robert Kaesen succeeded to the direction of the co. on Gaskell's retirement in 1968. Van Dantzig soon became sole director and has concentrated on the best aspects of the existing policy, with a smaller, more selective repertory of standard works (by BALANCHINE, TUDOR, and others as well as the 19th-c. classics) and a strong creative wing.

With the success of MONUMENT FOR A DEAD BOY, the Dutch NB began to acquire an international reputation. The same work marked the recognition, as dancer, designer, and choreographer, of SCHAYK. Since 1973 van MANEN has also been associated with the co. as choreographer and rehearsal director. With three resident choreographers of such standing, the NB has toured widely and been greatly admired for the originality of its modern repertory. All three men have been influenced by modern art (painting and sculpture) and by developments in the cinema and literature; van Manen has pursued a path much concerned with formal qualities while the other two have shown an interest (unusual in ballet) in the problems of society and mankind. The creations show a recognizable 'house style' but with individual qualities that became especially apparent when the three resident choreographers collaborated on the production of *Collective Symphony* (to STRAVINSKY's Symphony in C) for the 700th anniversary celebrations of the city of Amsterdam in 1975; their contributions were recognizable though not credited.

The large-scale classics are intended for home consumption only; an essential part of the co.'s work, they do not match its modern works either in quality of production or in standard of perf. Nevertheless, some of them (notably a revival of the Kingdom of Shades scene from BAYADÈRE) show promise in the younger dancers. The lack of a national ballet school in the Netherlands has been a restricting factor in this respect, and the co. has traditionally drawn a high proportion of its dancers from abroad, with Sonja Marchiolli (from Zagreb) and Francis Sinceretti (from France) prominent among the principals in 1975 together with RADIUS, EBBELAAR, and Henry Jurriëns from Holland.

In 1968 NUREYEV first danced with the co., at his own suggestion, and he has returned on a number of occasions, incl. the creation of the central role in van Dantzig's *Blown in a Gentle Wind* (1975). Guest stars from the Bolshoy and Kirov cos have also appeared. The co.'s home is the Stadsschouwburg (Municipal T.), Amsterdam. JP

Neumeier, John, b. Milwaukee, WI, 1942. American dancer, choreographer, and director. Studied locally, then at Stone-Camryn S. in Chicago, London RBS, and with VOLKOVA. As a student appeared with S. SHEARER's co. Danced 1963–9 with Stuttgart B. and created his first professional ballet, *Separate Journeys* (1968; mus. Samuel Barber). There followed commissions from the Harkness B. (*Stages and Reflections*, 1968; mus. Benjamin Britten), and Scottish B. (*Frontier*, 1969; mus. BLISS). Directed Frankfurt B. 1969–73, for which his most important productions were ROMEO AND JULIET (mus. PROKOFIEV) and NUTCRACKER (both 1971), *Dämmern* (mus. Aleksandr Skriabin piano music), *Don Juan* (mus. Christoph Willibald Gluck and Tomás Luis de Victoria), and *Le Sacre* (mus. STRAVINSKY) all 1972. Since 1973 he has been director of the Hamburg State OB for which his creations have included *Meyerbeer/Schumann* (1974), *Die Stille* (mus. George Crumb), *Mahler's Third Symphony* (both 1975), *Illusions – like Swan Lake* (mus. TCHAIKOVSKY) and *Petrushka Variations* (mus. Stravinsky), both 1976. For ABT he created *Epilogue* (1975; mus. Gustav Mahler; dan. MAKAROVA and BARYSHNIKOV) and *Hamlet: Connotations* (1976; mus. COPLAND; dan. HAYDÉE, KIRKLAND, Baryshnikov, and BRUHN). Many of his ballets have been revived for other cos in Canada and Germany. Highly regarded in continental Europe for the originality of his treatment of music and plots and for the flair with which he develops his dancers. Choreographed *Josephslegende* for Vienna

New York City Ballet in BALANCHINE's *Chaconne*, 1976

Staats OB and *The Fourth Symphony* (or *Humoresque*, mus. Gustav Mahler) for RB, both 1977. JP
See Horst Koegler, *John Neumeier Unterwegs* (Frankfurt 1972)

New Dance, modern dance work, ch. HUMPHREY and WEIDMAN; mus. Wallingford Riegger; c. Pauline Lawrence. Part I, *Theater Piece*, NY, Guild T., 19 Jan 1936; dan. Humphrey, Weidman, LIMÓN, Edith Orcutt, George Bockman, with ensemble. Part II, *With My Red Fires*, Bennington, VT, Bennington College Summer S. of the Dance Fest., 13 Aug 1936; dan. Weidman, LITZ, Humphrey, Lillian Burgess, Maxine Cushing, with ensemble, and student dancers. Part III, *New Dance* (7-part version), NY, Guild T., 27 Oct 1935: dan. Humphrey, Weidman, Beatrice Seckler, S. SHEARER, Litz, and ensemble. The trilogy is designed on a heroic scale. It opens with the competitiveness and wastefulness of contemporary society, then details the destructiveness of possessive matriarchal love, and concludes with a harmonious society where individuals work in a spirit of cooperation without abrasive rivalry. DM

New York City Ballet, formed 1948, the culmination of a 14-year effort by BALANCHINE and KIRSTEIN to create an American ballet co. In 1933 Balanchine, at Kirstein's invitation, arrived in the USA from Paris to set up and direct a ballet school, with the idea of training his own dancers for a future co. Within six months, he staged a student perf., presenting, notably, the lyrical ensemble ballet SERENADE. In Mar 1935 a professional group, the American B., made its first NY appearance and soon became associated with the Met (autumn 1935–spring 1938). Here Balanchine produced the famous but critically maligned opera *Orpheus and Eurydice* (1936; mus. Christoph Willibald Gluck; sc./c. TCHELITCHEV) and his first STRAVINSKY Fest. (1937): BAISER DE LA FÉE, *The Card Party* (*see* CARD GAME), and his seminal DIAGHILEV work *Apollon-Musagète* (*see* APOLLO). At the same time (1936–9) Kirstein, with L. and H. CHRISTENSEN, organized a small touring group, B. Caravan, to create works on American subjects, with commissioned music and decors by Americans. Its most significant production was BILLY THE KID. In 1941, sponsored by the US State Department, Kirstein organized an eight-month tour of S. America with dancers from both cos under the name American B. Caravan, for which Balanchine created two of his lasting masterpieces, CONCERTO BAROCCO and BALLET IMPERIAL.

After World War II (1946) Balanchine and Kirstein undertook a subscription venture named B. Society, again concentrating on new works (mostly by Balanchine), with commissioned scores and decors, although no longer on American themes. The resulting works were more often 'theatre' than 'dance', with the important exceptions FOUR TEMPERAMENTS, SYMPHONY IN C, and ORPHEUS. B. Society was not financially sound, and through the assistance of financier Morton Baum, the troupe was taken on as a constituent co. of NYCC, ensuring it a home base and regular performing seasons.

As NYCB, the co. opened Oct 1948 with a program of *Concerto Barocco*, *Orpheus*, and *Symphony in C*. Its first box-office success was *Firebird* (*see* OISEAU DE FEU), which marked the emergence of Maria TALLCHIEF as a home-grown ballerina of international standing. ROBBINS joined as dancer and choreographer in 1949, creating *Age of Anxiety* (1950; mus. Leonard Bernstein; c. Irene Sharaff; sc. O. SMITH) and CAGE, and dancing the lead in Balanchine's Expressionist PRODIGAL SON. In 1950 the co. danced in London and in later years appeared throughout Europe, the USSR (1962, 1972), and the Far East, to critical acclaim. In 1954 Balanchine staged a full-evening NUTCRACKER, his most ambitious project to date, in the manner of the Russian classical spectacles. In 1957 came the premiere of AGON, a reductive 'modern' work to a partially serial score, the apex in Balanchine's extraordinary 50-year collaboration with Stravinsky, which began in 1928 (with *Apollo*) and which he continued even after the composer's death, with his brilliant Stravinsky Fest. of 21 new ballets in 1972. EPISODES, a joint effort with GRAHAM, followed, in which Balanchine showed himself to be more 'modern' than the high priestess of modern dance herself. The period was marked by the rise of two of the earliest distinguished American male dancers, D'AMBOISE and VILLELLA, as well as the prominence of the dramatic ballerina HAYDEN. MIDSUMMER NIGHT'S DREAM was the first original full-length ballet created in America.

In 1963 the Ford Foundation granted $7 million to the NYCB and its affiliate acad., SAB, to be spread over 10 years, tacit recognition that Balanchine was the most vital force in US ballet. A year later, the co. took up residence in the NYST, a component of the new arts complex of Lincoln Center and the first house built expressly to accommodate a dance troupe. With his new resources Balanchine began to mount more costly, larger works (never neglecting his *avant-garde* wing), some in a traditionalist vein, e.g. HARLEQUINADE and COPPÉLIA, others original, notably his controversial DON QUIXOTE, in which Dulcinea was assigned to his favoured interpreter of the period, FARRELL. The co. grew to almost 100 dancers and regularly played as many as 30 weeks a year in NY. In 1969, after several years' absence, Robbins returned in triumph with his hour-long celebration of pure dance, DANCES AT A GATHERING. Among his foremost interpreters (and outstanding in Balanchine works of the period) was MCBRIDE.

Night Journey, with GRAHAM as Jocasta, ROSS as Oedipus, and COHAN as Tiresias

The presence of Balanchine, both as creative artist and inspiring leader, has always given the co. its distinctive profile and forward momentum. In his classes (he teaches frequently) and in his ballets he requires a mastery of classical technique, which he then heightens, quickens, streamlines, and gives new accents. He is known for his supreme musicality. His characteristic 'look' is spare, non-allusive, unmannered, and supercharged kinetically, although he has also created in a lush, romantic vein (VALSE, *Brahms–Schönberg Quartet*, 'Emeralds' in JEWELS, LIEBESLIEDER WALZER). In fact, his range is enormous (he has choreographed over 100 ballets), from the experimental works to once-unknown music (*Opus 34, Metastaseis and Pithoprakta*, IVESIANA); to full-co. Americana (*Stars and Stripes, Western Symphony*, WHO CARES?); to any number of classical display pieces, large and small. In his costumed, full-length story ballets, with their many *divertissements*, his debt to M. PETIPA is most evident; beyond that, it is difficult to find precedents for his seemingly inexhaustible supply of inventive movements.

Other artists associated with the NYCB have incl. Leon Barzin and IRVING (music directors); D'Amboise, ASHTON, BOLENDER, Ruthanna Boris, BUTLER, John Clifford, CULLBERG, CUNNINGHAM, CRANKO, DOLLAR, Lorca Massine, Richard Tanner, TARAS, TUDOR (choreographers); D. ADAMS, Herbert Bliss, BONNEFOUS, Bolender, BRUHN, Gisella Caccialanza, Dollar, EGLEVSKY, Farrell, Jillana, KAYE, KENT, KIRKLAND, LECLERQ, Sara Leland, MAGALLANES, MARIE-JEANNE, MARTINS, MAZZO, MITCHELL, MONCION, Janet Reed, P. SCHAUFUSS, Suki Schorer, VERDY, WILDE (dancers). NRe

See Anatole Chujoy, *The New York City Ballet* (New York 1953); Lincoln Kirstein, *The New York City Ballet*, with photographs by Martha Swope and George Platt Lynes (New York 1973; London 1974); Nancy Reynolds, *Repertory in Review: 40 Years of the New York City Ballet* (New York 1977)

N.Y. Export, Opus Jazz, ballet, ch. ROBBINS; mus. Robert Prince; sc. Ben Shahn; c. Florence Klotz.

Spoleto, T. Nuovo, Ballets: USA, 8 June 1958; dan. Wilma Curley, Pat Dunn, Barbara Milberg, J. JONES. A plotless ballet that responds to the moods and rhythms of the 1950s among young people in NY. Revived Harkness B., 1969, CCJB, 1974. FM

Night and Silence, The, ballet, 1 act, ch. GORE; mus. Johann Sebastian Bach; arr. Charles Mackerras; sc./c. Ronald Wilson. Edinburgh, Empire T. (as part of the Edinburgh International B. during the Fest.), 25 Aug 1958; dan. HINTON, POOLE. One of Gore's most effective ballets, on the theme of jealousy. MC

Night City *see* MIRACULOUS MANDARIN

Night Journey, modern dance work, ch. GRAHAM; mus. William Schuman; sc/c. NOGUCHI. Cambridge, MA, Graham Dance Co., 3 May 1947; dan. Graham, HAWKINS, Mark Ryder. The classical myth of Oedipus, seen in flashback from the point of view of Jocasta, his mother and later his wife. DV

Night Shadow *see* SONNAMBULA

Nijinska, Bronislava, b. Minsk, 1891; d. Los Angeles, CA 1972. Russian dancer and choreographer; sister of NIJINSKY. She m. (1) Alexander Kochetovsky (2) Nicholas Singaevsky, both dancers. Studied at Imperial S., St Petersburg, graduated into Maryinsky TB 1908, danced in first seasons of DIAGHILEV's B. Russes 1909–13. Created Papillon in CARNAVAL. Danced in her brother's short-lived co., London, 1914, then returned to Russia, heading her own school in Kiev. Left in 1921 and rejoined Diaghilev, dancing in and helping with staging of SLEEPING BEAUTY (London 1921); became his only woman choreographer, creating eight ballets incl. NOCES (1923), BICHES, FÂCHEUX, and TRAIN BLEU (all 1924), ROMÉO ET JULIETTE. Choreographed several ballets for RUBINSTEIN's Co., 1928–9, incl. *Bolero*, BAISER DE LA FÉE, and VALSE. Ballet mistress of O. Russe à Paris 1930–4; formed her own co. 1932, for which she choreographed and danced the title role in *Hamlet* (mus. Franz Liszt). Also in 1932 was choreographer at T. Colón, Buenos Aires. For DE BASIL's B. Russe de Monte Carlo she choreographed *Les Cent Baisers* (1935), *Danses Slaves et Tziganes*, and a revival of *Les Noces* (1936). Ballet mistress of MARKOVA–DOLIN B., 1937, reviving *Les Biches*, etc. Also in 1937 choreographed several ballets for Polish NB. Settled in California 1938 and established school there, but continued to choreograph for various cos, incl. B. Russe de Monte Carlo, ABT, B. International (New York) and de Cuevas B. Invited by ASHTON to revive *Les Biches* and *Les Noces* for RB in 1964 and 1966, respectively; the latter finally achieved recognition as one of the great ballets of the 20th c. DV

Nijinsky, Vaslav Fomich, b. Kiev, 1888; d. London, 1950. Russian dancer and choreographer, brother of NIJINSKA. From 1898 to 1907 a student at the Imperial S. of B., St Petersburg. His powerful musculature and extraordinary elevation soon attracted notice. Danced at the Maryinsky T., St Petersburg, both in works of the old repertory and in the early ballets of the reformer FOKINE. In 1908 he met DIAGHILEV who became his mentor. From 19 May 1909, when Diaghilev presented his first Paris season, Nijinsky became a legend. In 1911, in a much-publicized scandal over an inadequacy of his costume in GISELLE, Nijinsky was dismissed from the Maryinsky, left Russia for good and became *premier danseur* of Diaghilev's now independent B. Russes, as well as Diaghilev's constant companion. Most of Nijinsky's famous roles (almost all of which were created for him) were in the new Fokine works: PAVILLON D'ARMIDE, *Cléopâtre*, and SYLPHIDES (1909); SCHÉHÉRAZADE (1910); SPECTRE DE LA ROSE, CARNAVAL, PETRUSHKA, and *Narcisse* (1911); *Le Dieu Bleu* and DAPHNIS ET CHLOÉ (1912). His

Bronislava Nijinska (left) as the Street Dancer in the DIAGHILEV B. Russes production of PETRUSHKA, with K. Kobelev as the Organ Player and SCHOLLAR as the Gypsy

partner was nearly always KARSAVINA. His remarkable hovering leap as the Spectre of the Rose, his flickering comic Harlequin (*Carnaval*), the animal savagery of his GOLDEN SLAVE and the pathos of his puppet Petrushka were the most admired of his achievements. He had prodigious technique, but his greatest quality was interpretative genius, the ability to transform himself completely in each of his roles.

Disenchanted at last with Fokine's ideas and methods, and encouraged by Diaghilev, Nijinsky devised an entirely new style of choreography, flat and frieze-like, inspired by Greek art, for his first ballet, APRÈS-MIDI D'UN FAUNE, at first a *succès de scandale* because of Nijinsky's erotic gestures as the Faune. His second work, JEUX, in which he danced with Karsavina and SCHOLLAR, was the first ballet on a modern sporting theme, and dismissed by critics as obscure. But his greatest achievement, the choreography for SACRE DU PRINTEMPS, with its primitive contortions to match the elemental score, antagonized the fashionable audience who battled with approving intellectuals on its notorious first night. The work had only seven perfs.

Vaslav Nijinsky as the Golden Slave in SCHÉHÉRAZADE, *c.* 1911

Diaghilev had faith in Nijinsky's new choreography: he planned with him a Bach ballet and Richard Strauss's *Légende de Joseph*, and had in mind also STRAVINSKY's NOCES (which was eventually produced by Nijinska). On the B. Russes' American tour in 1913, Nijinsky married in Buenos Aires a Hungarian, Romola de Pulszky. The jealous Diaghilev dismissed him abruptly. There followed an abortive season at the Palace T., London, 1914, for which Nijinsky had formed his own co.; then he was interned in Hungary as an alien. Diaghilev pulled influential strings and secured Nijinsky's release to rejoin the co. in NY, Apr 1916. For the B.'s second US tour (winter 1916–17) Nijinsky took over as artistic director, Diaghilev returning to Europe. Nijinsky's last ballet, *Till Eulenspiegel* (mus. R. Strauss, sc./c. Robert Edmond Jones: Manhattan OH, 23 Oct 1916), which he had conceived while a prisoner, suffered from his illness and increasingly unpredictable behaviour and from dissension within the co., but was a popular success and had 22 perfs. After the dispiriting tour Nijinsky rejoined Diaghilev in Spain, and was obliged to dance in the second S. American season. There his persecution mania gained ground, and he gave his last perf. with the Diaghilev B. on 26 Sept 1917 in Buenos Aires.

The Nijinskys retired to Switzerland, where after a frightening dance recital at St Moritz early in 1919 he was pronounced insane. His famous Diary and drawings date from this period. Nijinsky spent most of the next 20 years in sanatoria, but was again interned in Budapest in World War II. The Nijinskys escaped to Austria in 1945 and moved to England in 1947. Nijinsky died in London in 1950, survived by his widow and two daughters. In 1953 he was reburied in Paris, near the grave of A. VESTRIS.

It is now clear that Nijinsky's illness cut short not only a memorable dancing career, but also an important choreographic talent. He was undeniably a pioneer of modern dance. *Le Sacre du Printemps* was a seminal work. *L'Après-midi d'un Faune*, the only one of his ballets still performed, has long been recognized as a masterpiece. DD

See Richard Buckle, *Nijinsky* (London 1971; New York 1972); Lincoln Kirstein, *Nijinsky Dancing* (New York and London 1975)

Nijinsky, Clown de Dieu (*Nijinsky, Clown of God*), ballet, 2 parts, ch. BÉJART; mus. TCHAIKOVSKY and Pierre Henry; sc./c. Joëlle Roustan and Roger Bernard. Brussels, Forêt Nationale, B. XXe S., 8 Oct 1971; dan. DONN, FARRELL, BORTOLUZZI, Victor Ullate. Huge lyric fresco evoking the drama of the dancer divided between his love for his art, his subservience to DIAGHILEV, the woman who is the incarnation of his ideal, and his vision of God. M-FC

Nikolais, Alwin, b. Southington, CT, 1912. American dancer, choreographer, composer, teacher,

Les Noces, as revived by the RB at CG, 1966, with BERIOSOVA (centre) as the Bride

and theatrical innovator. Of Russian and German parentage. First an accompanist for silent movies, he was later director of a marionette theatre in Hartford, CT, 1935–7. In 1933 after seeing a perf. of WIGMAN, he began to study dance. Formed his own dance co. 1937–9, taught and choreographed. His first commissioned work, *Eight Column Line*, was performed at the Avery Memorial T., Hartford, May 1939. During the summers of these years Nikolais studied at the Bennington (VT) S. of Dance where he worked with H. HOLM. After a transcontinental tour with 'Dancers on Route' he was in the US Army 1942–6. Assistant to H. Holm at Colorado College 1947–8, as well as being the director of the dance department of Hartford Univ. Went to the Henry St Playhouse, NY City, 1948; appointed co-director (with Betty Young) 1950. He stopped dancing and turned to teaching and choreography for the Playhouse Dance Co., which later became the Alwin Nikolais Dance Co. While at the Playhouse he began to evolve his concept of total theatre in which dancers, props, lights, sounds, and colour are united as equally important parts of a production. The first work in this multi-media abstract form was *Masks, Props and Mobiles* (1953). During the following years Nikolais began to experiment with sounds and to compose tape-music scores for his works. In 1963 he made compositions on a specially constructed Moog synthesizer and he was the first to use this instrument in a concert. His use of props as extensions of the dancer's bones and muscles, the designs of light and colour which illumine the stage, and the sophisticated slides which project changing features on dancers and stage properties are hallmarks of the Nikolais Dance T., as the co. is now called. It is the abstract interaction of motion, time, space, shape, colour, light, and sound that forms the dramatic meaning. Among Nikolais's works are *Kaleidoscope* (1956), *Totem* (1960), IMAGO (1963), *Sanctum* (1964), *Vaudeville of the Elements* (1965), *Somniloquy* (1967), *Tent* (1968), *Scenario* (1971), *Cross-Fade* (1974), and *Tribe* (1975). The co. tours extensively: e.g. the Fest. dei Due Mondi, Spoleto, 1962; major European tour 1968; SW, June 1969.

Nikolais has been the subject of films and TV programs. Awarded two Guggenheim Fellowships, a Fellowship from the Rockefeller Foundation, and numerous other awards and commissions. Choreographed and designed *Help! Help! the Globolinks* by Gian-Carlo Menotti, 1968; produced a multi-media spectacle, *Kyldex I*, 1973, both for the Hamburg O. Left the Henry St Playhouse 1970 and moved into 'The Space for Innovative Development' in NY City. In 1974 the co. moved to 33 East 18th St, Manhattan, where the Nikolais Dance T. together with the LOUIS Dance Co., the Louis–Nikolais Dance T. Lab, and Chimerafilm comprise the Chimera Foundation for Dance Inc. KC

See Marcia B. Siegel, 'Nik: A Documentary Study of Alwin Nikolais', *Dance Perspectives*, No. 48 (New York 1971)

Ninth Symphony, ballet, ch. BÉJART; mus. Ludwig van Beethoven. Brussels, Cirque Royale, B. XXe S., 27 Oct 1964. After a text by Friedrich Wilhelm Nietzsche, this choreographic symphony, awarded the Prix de la Fraternité 1966, celebrates the reconciliation of peoples in joy and universal love. Revised 1976; still in the co.'s repertoire. M-FC

Noces, Les (1) ballet, 4 consecutive scenes, ch. NIJINSKA; mus. and words STRAVINSKY (composed 1917); sc./c. GONCHAROVA. Paris, T. Gaîeté-Lyrique, DIAGHILEV's B. Russes, 13 July 1923; dan. DUBROVSKA (the Bride). Revived for DE BASIL's US tour 1936; London, CG, RB, 23 Mar 1966; dan. BERIOSOVA. The celebration of a Russian peasant wedding, Diaghilev's last production, to look back at the Holy Russia of his youth. The four scenes are: The Blessing of the Bride, The Blessing of the Groom,

The Bride's Departure from her Parents' Home, The Wedding Feast. Nijinska rejected the first highly coloured, primitive peasant art designs of Goncharova and asked instead for earthy browns and blacks and a very sparse setting. The work is a deeply religious portrayal, the innocence of the bride and her gentle femininity strongly contrasted with the virile dancing of the men. Nijinska throughout used sculptural blocks of dancers in icon-like effect. When she revived the work for RB more than 40 years after its creation, it was still remarkable for its 'modernity'. There are four solo pianists (originally on stage), percussion, and a chorus. Nijinska's masterpiece. MC *See* 'The Creation of *Les Noces*' in Mary Clarke and Clement Crisp, *Making a Ballet* (London and New York 1975)

(2) dance cantata, ch. ROBBINS; mus. STRAVINSKY; sc. O. SMITH; c. Patricia Zipprodt; ltg ROSENTHAL. NYST, ABT, 30 Mar 1965; dan. Erin Martin, William Glassman. Following the composer's intentions for the first presentation of this work, Robbins observes that his purpose was 'not to reproduce the wedding or show a stage dramatization with descriptive music, but rather to present a ritualized abstraction of its essences, customs, and tempers'. FM

Noguchi, Isamu, b. Los Angeles, CA, 1904. Japanese-American sculptor and designer. Son of the poet Yone Noguchi. Educated Yokohama until age 13 when returned to USA although he spends much time in Japan. In sculpture he works in metal abstractions and natural substances, wood, bones, stone, etc. Collaborated with GRAHAM from 1934, designing the properties which she incorporates into her choreography. An extraordinary range, from the purely American settings for her solo *Frontier* (1935) and APPALACHIAN SPRING, to the heavier, symbolic constructions for her Greek dramas such as CLYTEMNESTRA. Designed *The Bells* for PAGE 1946, *The Seasons* for CUNNINGHAM 1947, and ORPHEUS for BALANCHINE 1948. His golden metallic setting for Graham's *Seraphic Dialogue* (1955) is a masterpiece of design for contemporary dance. MC

Noir et Blanc *see* SUITE EN BLANC

Norman, Gary, b. Adelaide, 1951. Australian dancer. Australian BS 1967. Ballet in a Nutshell (small touring co.) 1969; Australian B. 1970, soloist 1971, principal dancer 1972. Studied with PETIT in Marseille. NB of Canada 1974, principal dancer. A young *danseur noble* with a strong technique and effective personality (ALBRECHT, COLAS) and a natural ability in widely divergent modern roles (he created one of principal roles in GEMINI; Don José in CARMEN). KSW

North [Dodson], Robert, b. Charleston, SC, 1945. American dancer and choreographer. Studied London RBS and LSCD. Debut with LCDT 1967, then danced with GRAHAM's co.; rejoined LCDT as leading male dancer 1969, later becoming associate choreographer. His productions often involve close collaboration with other choreographers: LAPZESON in *One was the Other* (1972), SLEEP in *David and Goliath*, and SEYMOUR in *Gladly Sadly Badly Madly* (both 1975); or with film makers in *Still Life* (1975). His most successful dance creation has been *Troy Game* (1974), a comic piece for the men of the co. JP

Northern Dance Theatre. The first dance co. in England set up to serve a specific region, the North West, with Arts Council support and also helped by local institutions. The first perf. was 28 Nov 1969 in Manchester where the co. now performs regularly in the theatre of the Royal Northern College of Music. The first director was Laverne Meyer who resigned in 1974. The co. was run by its own teaching and administrative staff until 1976 when Robert de Warren was appointed director. MC

Norway. A co. called the Ny Norsk B. was founded in 1948 by Gerd Kjölaas and Louise Browne in Oslo. It did valuable pioneer work – FONTEYN and HELPMANN appeared as guests – and in 1958 became the nucleus of a newly formed state-subsidized co., the Norwegian NB, based on the Oslo (Ny Norsk) opera house. The first director was ALGERANOFF and the first production COPPÉLIA, 25 Feb 1959. In 1960 ORLOFF was director but was succeeded the following year by the English dancer and teacher Joan Harris. She introduced several English ballets to the repertory but in 1965 resigned from the co. to give all her time to its school. Following the example of Louise Browne she introduced the RAD syllabus with excellent results. As director of the co. she was succeeded by, in turn, Brian Macdonald and Henny Mürer, Sonia Arova, Anne Borg and, in 1977, LAST. The co. is essentially classical. MC

Notre-Dame de Paris, ballet, 2 acts, ch. PETIT; mus. Maurice Jarre; sc./c. René Allio; based on Victor Hugo's novel of the same title. Paris O., 11 Dec 1965; dan. Petit (as Quasimodo); MOTTE (as Esmeralda). Petit's first choreography for the O., 20 years after he had left. *See also* ESMERALDA. M-FC

Notre Faust (*Our Faust*), spectacle, 2 parts, ch./lib. BÉJART; mus. Johann Sebastian Bach (sections of the B minor Mass) and Argentine tangos; sc./c. Thierry Bosquet. Brussels, T. Royal de la Monnaie, B. XXe S., 12 Dec 1975. A typically Béjart personal interpretation of the Faust story with quotations from Goethe in German and French; a kind of black mass with Lucifer, Satan, and Beelzebub in attendance, and the characters of Faust and Mephistopheles interchanged and finding redemption at last in humility. M-FC

Nouveau Ballet de Monte Carlo *see* GRAND BALLET DU MARQUIS DE CUEVAS

Novaro, Luciana, b. Genoa, 1923. Italian dancer and choreographer. Joined Milan Sc. S. 1933 (teachers incl. Esmée Bulnes and VOLKOVA); then Sc. co.; prima ballerina 1946. Her own ballets show a preference for Spanish themes; she has also choreographed GIARA and *Chout* (mus. PROKOFIEV). Produced operas abroad. Director Sc. B. co. 1962–4. FP

Noverre, Jean-Georges, b. Paris, 1727; d. Saint-Germain-en-Laye 1810. French dancer, choreographer, writer, and reformer of Swiss extraction. He studied with Louis Dupré of the Paris O. but did not enter the co. His fame as a dancer was slight; he was, for instance, listed in the *corps de ballet* in Berlin 1747 in a co. formed by Jean-Barthélemy Lany, headed by the Italian dancer Barbara Campanini ('La Barbarina') but seems to have abandoned dancing early to concentrate on choreography. His first production in Paris was at the OC 1754 when he staged *Les Fêtes Chinoises* (previously given in Lyon in the season 1751–2). This greatly impressed the English actor David Garrick who is said to have called Noverre 'the Shakespeare of the dance' and became a great friend. He invited Noverre to London to stage *The Chinese Festival* at Drury Lane T. in 1755 but perfs were disrupted by anti-French riots. In 1757 Noverre returned to Lyon. In 1760 he became ballet master in Stuttgart where he staged his most famous ballet *Medée et Jason* (mus. Jean Joseph Rodolphe) in 1763. He left Stuttgart in 1767 (his productions had become too expensive even for the pleasure-loving Grand Duke Charles II of Württemberg) and went to Vienna where he worked until 1774. He then went to Milan and in 1776, thanks to Queen Marie-Antoinette, whom he had taught in Vienna, became ballet master at the Paris O. One of his most important productions there was *Les Horaces* (21 Dec 1776). There was much jealousy from DAUBERVAL and Maximilien Gardel and in 1779 Noverre submitted his resignation. He left for London during the Revolution and staged his last ballets there at the King's T. He returned to France *c.* 1795 to work on a new edition of his famous book *Lettres sur la Danse et sur les Ballets* (first edition, Lyon and Stuttgart 1760) and lived in retirement until his death.

Noverre's great influence on ballet was his campaign for greater dramatic truth in his productions, for the abandonment of masks, the use of freer costume, and even, in his last writings, for safety curtains and proper fire drill. His writings are still valid and he is recognized as the father of the *ballet d'action* and the kind of ballet we know today. Some of his ideas had already been implemented by WEAVER, HILVERDING, and ANGIOLINI, but he remains a giant figure. Of his 150 ballets only librettos and music have survived but contemporary accounts testify to their quality. MC

See Jean Georges Noverre, *Letters on Dancing and Ballets*, tr. from the revised and enlarged edition (St Petersburg 1803) by Cyril W. Beaumont (London 1930); Deryck Lynham, *The Chevalier Noverre, Father of Modern Ballet* (London and New York 1950); Marian Hannah Winter, *The Pre-Romantic Ballet* (London 1974; New York and Toronto 1975); Lincoln Kirstein, *The Book of the Dance* (New York 1942; first published as *Dance*, New York 1935)

Noverre Society (Noverre Gesellschaft), ballet club founded in Stuttgart 1958 during the regime of BERIOZOFF. It was intended to form a link between Stuttgart B. and the general public and greatly succeeded in this. Lectures, film evenings, and student perfs are given, with new ballets choreographed by members of the co. In 1970 CRANKO founded a Noverre B., which was a 'second co.' and gave perfs in the small theatre of the Württemberg Staats T., Stuttgart. It disbanded 1973. GBLW

Novikov, Laurent, b. Moscow, 1888; d. New Buffalo, MI, 1956. Russian dancer and teacher. Graduated from Imperial S., Moscow, 1906. Debut in HUMPBACKED HORSE at the Bolshoy T. 1908, joined DIAGHILEV for first Paris season 1909. Principal dancer Moscow Imperial B. 1910; same year danced DON QUIXOTE with GELTSER in St Petersburg. With A. PAVLOVA 1911–14. Returned to Russia to stage dances for Moscow O. but left in 1918, rejoining Diaghilev in London 1919. Partnered KARSAVINA on her tours for two seasons but rejoined Pavlova 1921–8. Taught briefly in London 1928. In 1929 became ballet master to Chicago Civic OB co., remaining four years and staging SWAN LAKE, his *El Amor Brujo* (mus. FALLA) and many other ballets. Ballet master NY Met OB, 1941–5. Later taught in Chicago until his death. A powerful dancer and strong partner. MC

Nureyev, Rudolf, b. nr Irkutsk, USSR, 1938. Tartar dancer. Brought up in Ufa. First studied folk dancing and appeared with children's troupes, then had his first ballet lessons from local teachers. Appeared as an extra with the Ufa ballet and opera cos while still at school, and went with the Ufa B. (as an apprentice member) to Moscow 1955. Auditioned there for entry to Bolshoy BS, then went to Leningrad and auditioned at Kirov S.; accepted by both and preferred the Kirov. His late start and his 'nonconformist' attitude caused difficulties, but with the aid of an exceptionally able and sympathetic teacher, PUSHKIN, he graduated with distinction and was acclaimed at a competition in Moscow. Offered contracts as a principal dancer by three cos and again chose the Kirov (1958).

During three years with that co. he danced the leading parts in most of the 19th-c. classics and several modern works. Had an outstanding personal success during the co.'s first visit to Paris (1961) and was then ordered back to Russia before they went on to London; fearing that official disapproval would mean the end of his career, he sought and was given permission to stay in France. Has subsequently appeared as guest star with many cos in the West.

His London CG debut in Feb 1962 began a historic partnership with FONTEYN in which each gained much from the other. Her maturity and his quick mind, together with a mutual grasp of style, resulted in memorable perfs together all over the world. But from the beginning he was interested in dancing with other ballerinas also and has appeared with literally dozens of partners, both famous and unknown. Among nearly 100 different roles, he has been particularly admired for his interpretation of the classic heroes; for his perf. of roles by FOKINE (SYLPHIDES, PETRUSHKA), BALANCHINE (APOLLO and PRODIGAL SON) and ASHTON (especially MARGUERITE AND ARMAND, created for him and Fonteyn, but also notably in FILLE MAL GARDÉE). He danced the first perf. of MACMILLAN's ROMEO AND JULIET and has also appeared with particular success in ballets by ROBBINS, BÉJART, and NEUMEIER.

Rudolf Nureyev in CORSAIRE

In addition, he has widened this already impressive range by seeking out opportunities to perform modern-dance works, first in MONUMENT FOR A DEAD BOY, then in works by P. TAYLOR, TETLEY, LIMÓN, GRAHAM, and LOUIS.

The diversity of his characterizations partly accounts for his success, but his gripping stage presence and ability to use an unusually strong virtuoso technique for purposes of expression are even more important. Since his earliest days in the West he has staged many productions, the most successful being his own interpretations of NUTCRACKER, DON QUIXOTE, RAYMONDA, and 'The Kingdom of the Shades' from BAYADÈRE. JP

See Nureyev (ed. Alexander Bland), *Nureyev, An Autobiography With Pictures* (London 1962; New York 1963); John Percival, *Nureyev* (New York 1975; London 1976); Alexander Bland, *The Nureyev Image* (London and New York 1976)

Nutcracker, The (*Casse Noisette*), ballet, 2 acts, 3 scenes; ch. IVANOV; mus. TCHAIKOVSKY; lib. after Ernst Theodor Hoffmann; sc. M. I. Bocharov, Ivanov, and VSEVOLOZHSKY. (As *Casse Noisette*), St Petersburg, Maryinsky T., 18 Dec 1892; dan. Antonietta Dell'Era, P. GERDT, LEGAT, PREOBRAZHENSKA, KYASHT. At a Christmas party, Clara is given a nutcracker which comes to life to lead an army of toy soldiers in a victorious battle against invading mice, then turns into a handsome prince and leads her to the Kingdom of Sweets. (In Russia the little girl is called Masha.) The production was planned in detail by M. PETIPA, who fell ill and handed the realization over to his assistant, Ivanov.

Probably the most frequently performed ballet in the world, though all that now survives of the original choreography is the final *pas de deux* of the Sugar Plum Fairy and her cavalier. Among many new versions are those by ASHTON (London, SWTB, 1952), BALANCHINE (NYCB 1954), GRIGOROVICH (Moscow, Bolshoy B., 1966), CRANKO (Stuttgart 1966), NUREYEV (RSB 1967, RB 1968), BARYSHNIKOV (Washington DC, Kennedy Center for the Performing Arts, ABT, 1976). Because of the Christmas party in Act I, the ballet has become a staple Christmas attraction. DV

See Mary Clarke and Clement Crisp, *Making a Ballet* (London and New York 1975)

The Nutcracker, the Act I party scene, RB, 1968

L'Oiseau de Feu. KARSAVINA as the Firebird and BOLM as the Tsarevich in the original production

O

Obukhov, Anatoly, b. St Petersburg, 1896; d. New York, 1962. Russian dancer and teacher. Member of a family of dancers, nephew of M. OBUKHOV. Graduated from Imperial S., St Petersburg, 1913, dancing the CHOPINIANA Waltz with SPESSIVTSEVA at their graduation perf. Partnered A. PAVLOVA in her last perfs in Russia, 1914. Principal dancer 1917. Left Russia 1920, joined Boris Romanoff's Russian Romantic B. in Berlin, dancing leading classic roles. With NEMCHINOVA (whom he m.) to Lithuanian State B., Kaunas, in early 1930s; danced with that co. in London, 1935. R. BLUM's B. Russe de Monte Carlo, 1936–7. Created role of Ambassador in ÉPREUVE D'AMOUR, also danced PETRUSHKA, SIEGFRIED, ALBRECHT. Briefly with DE BASIL co. as instructor, Australia, 1939, then in USA from 1940 until his death, a member of faculty of SAB. Responsible for revival of DON QUIXOTE *pas de deux* for ABT, 1944, which introduced that showpiece to contemporary Western repertories. As a teacher, he was a strict disciplinarian who inspired his pupils with his own love of classic dance in its purest form. DV

Obukhov, Mikhail, b. St Petersburg, 1879; d. St Petersburg, 1914. Russian dancer and teacher. Graduated from Imperial S. (class of CECCHETTI); from 1898 *coryphée*; soloist 1901. Partnered A. PAVLOVA in the Waltz from CHOPINIANA at its first perf., 1907. His main roles were SIEGFRIED, the Gypsy in PAQUITA. From 1900 he taught at the St Petersburg Imperial S. One of the first to recognize NIJINSKY's great gifts. Uncle of A. OBUKHOV and brother of E. OBUKHOVA. MC

Obukhova, Evgenia, b. St Petersburg, 1874; d. 1946. Russian dancer and teacher. Graduated from St Petersburg TS; danced at the Maryinsky T. 1892–1910; taught at the A. Volyinsky S. of Russian B. 1917–24; senior teacher, T. Hanoum S. of B., Tashkent, 1934–42. She was one of the founders of choreographic education in the Uzbekistan NB. Many leading dancers of that co. (incl. IZMAILOVA) were her pupils. Sister of M. OBUKHOV. MC

Ode, spectacle, 2 acts, ch. MASSINE; mus. Nicolas Nabokov; lib. KOCHNO; sc./c. TCHELITCHEV and Pierre Charbonneau. Paris, T. Sarah Bernhardt, DIAGHILEV's B. Russes, 6 June 1928; dan. DUBROVSKA, Alice Nikitina, Massine, LIFAR, Irina Beline. Based on a text by the 18th-c. Russian poet Mikhail Lomonosov, a meditation on the marvels of Nature and their relation to Man. This subject was treated in abstract form; the ballet introduced many innovations in staging e.g. light projections, film, now commonplace in 'mixed media' events and commercial theatre. DV

Odette-Odile. Odette is the enchanted Swan Queen heroine of SWAN LAKE; Odile the magician's daughter who impersonates her; usually the same ballerina dances both roles

Odissi *see* ASIA

O'Donnell, May, b. Sacramento, CA, 1909. American dancer, teacher, and choreographer. Studied with GRAHAM, danced with her co. 1932–8 and 1944–52, creating many roles. In 1939 organized San Francisco Dance T. with her husband, the composer Ray Green, and former Graham dancer Gertrude Shurr. Danced with LIMÓN Co. 1941–3. Gave concert of her own works NY, 1945; formed her own co. 1949. Now teaches in NY. Works incl. SUSPENSION, *Dance Sonata No. 1* (1952), *Dance Concerto* (1954), *Dance Sonata No. 2* (1956). DV

Oiseau de Feu, L' (*Firebird*), ballet, 1 act, 3 scenes, ch./lib. FOKINE, based on Russian fairytales; mus. STRAVINSKY; sc. Aleksandr Golovin; c. Golovin and BAKST. Paris O., DIAGHILEV's B. Russes,

Ondine, ASHTON's production, RB at CG, with FONTEYN as Ondine and GRANT as Tirrenio, King of the Sea, in the last act of the ballet

Right: Opera, Ballet in. The Ballet of the Nuns in *Robert le Diable* by Giacomo Meyerbeer, Pierre-Luc-Charles Ciceri's design for Act II of the first performance, 1831. The nuns were led by M. TAGLIONI.

25 June 1910; dan. KARSAVINA, Vera Fokina, Fokine, CECCHETTI. London, Lyceum T., 25 Nov 1926; sc./c. GONCHAROVA. With the aid of the Firebird, Prince Ivan rescues a beautiful Princess and her companions from the spell of the evil magician Koschey. Stravinsky's first ballet score. Revived DE BASIL's B. Russe de Monte Carlo, 1934; RB 1954. Versions by many choreographers, none an improvement on the original, incl. those by F. LOPUKHOV, Petrograd, Maryinsky T., 1921, sc./c. Golovin; BOLM, Ballet T., 1945, sc./c. Marc Chagall; BALANCHINE (*Firebird*), NYCB, 1949, sc./c. Chagall (revised in collaboration with ROBBINS 1970 and 1972); LIFAR, Paris O., 1954, sc./c. Georges Wakhevitch; BÉJART, Paris O., 1970, revived B. XXe S. 1970. Also revived Moscow B. 1964, staged Stanislas Vlasov and Anatoly Simachev after Fokine, sc./c. Golovin; dan. PLISETSKAYA. DV

Oliphant, Betty, b. London, 1918. English, now Canadian, dancer and teacher. Studied classical ballet with KARSAVINA and NOVIKOV, stage dancing with Zelia Raye and Joan Davis. Choreographed and performed in London musicals. To Canada in 1948, first ballet mistress of NB of Canada. Principal of NBS 1959 to the present. Associate artistic director of NB 1969–75. At BRUHN's invitation, reorganized BS of Royal Swedish O. 1967. Fellow and Examiner of Imperial Society of Teachers of Dancing. Officer, Order of Canada 1972. PD

Ondine (1), **Ondine, ou la Naïade,** ballet, 6 scenes, ch./lib. PERROT and CERRITO; mus. PUGNI; sc. William Grieve. London, Her Majesty's T., 22 June 1843; dan. Cerrito, Perrot, Marie Guy-Stephan. In spite of its title, this ballet had little in common with Friedrich de la Motte Fouqué's novel *Undine*, though it retained the basic theme of a mortal torn between his love for his fiancée and for a supernatural being. Famous for Cerrito's *pas de l'ombre*, in which the Naiad sees her shadow for the first time.

(2) ballet, 3 acts, ch. ASHTON; mus. HENZE; lib. Ashton, freely adapted from la Motte Fouqué; sc./c. Lila de'Nobili. London, CG, RB, 27 Oct 1958; dan. FONTEYN, SOMES, FARRON, GRANT. Ashton returned to la Motte Fouqué for his lib. but incorporated Perrot's idea of the *pas de l'ombre*. Described as a 'concerto for Fonteyn'; considered by many to be her greatest created role. DV

Onegin, ballet, 3 acts, 6 scenes, ch./lib. CRANKO (based on Aleksandr Pushkin's poem); mus. TCHAIKOVSKY (but not from his opera *Eugene Onegin*) arr. Kurt-Heinze Stolze; sc./c. ROSE. Stuttgart B., 13 Apr 1965; dan. BARRA (Onegin), MADSEN (Lensky), HAYDÉE (Tatyana), CARDÚS (Olga). Slightly revised 1967 with CLAUSS as Onegin. One of Cranko's biggest successes, a most effective translation of the story into dance terms with characteristic sympathy for the individuals caught in tragedy. The 'letter scene' is a *pas de deux* in which Tatyana dances with a dream image of Onegin. The farewell *pas de deux* in the last act is one of Cranko's most beautiful inventions. Since his death the ballet has been staged for RSB and the Australian B. (both 1976). MC

Opera, Ballet in. Opera came into existence in Italy at the end of the 16th c. and immediately sought the aid of ballet, especially for scenes of general rejoicing. The happy endings of Jacopo Peri's *L'Euridice* (Florence 1600), the first opera whose music survives, of Claudio Monteverdi's *La Favola d'Orfeo* (Mantua 1607), and of Marco da Gagliano's *Dafne* (Mantua 1608) are all enlivened by festive dancing. Throughout the 17th and 18th centuries Italian opera (which flourished in N. Europe as well as in Italy) continued to make use of ballet, usually as an adjunct to lavish spectacle.

But ballet was also employed by composers as an organic element of music drama. In the Act II finale

of George Frideric Handel's *Ariodante* (London 1735) the heroine's plight is clarified after she falls asleep by a danced encounter between the forces of good and evil that contend within her. In Act II of Gluck's *Orfeo ed Euridice* (Vienna 1762) the Dance of the Furies and the subsequent Dance of the Blessed Spirits create with incomparable vividness the dramatic and psychological situation of the hero. During the 19th c., when Italian opera ceased to be international in origin, ballet virtually disappeared from it, Italian composers by and large preferring to give undisputed primacy to the human voice. The celebrated Dance of the Hours from Act III of Amilcare Ponchielli's *La Gioconda* (Milan 1876) is an exception to this tendency.

In France, on the contrary, the relationship continued to prosper. LULLY's achievement in developing a native form of opera from court spectacle, of which ballet was an essential ingredient, helped to earn dance a prominent place in the new genre. The operatic success of J.-P. RAMEAU, equally sympathetic to dance, ensured it a permanent one. By the 19th c. a formal ballet midway in the action was an obligatory feature of every French grand opera even when written by non-French composers. Gioacchino Rossini's *Guillaume Tell* (Paris 1829) no less than AUBER's *La Muette de Portici* (Paris 1828) contains a substantial ballet sequence, as do the many imitations of French grand opera throughout the rest of Europe – e.g. Richard Wagner's *Rienzi* (Dresden 1842) or Ferenc Erkel's *Hunyady László* (Pest 1844).

Paris, the world's music capital during most of the 19th c., saw the premieres of many grand operas with notable ballet scores, among them: Giacomo Meyerbeer's *Robert le Diable* (1831), *Les Huguenots* (1836) and *Le Prophète* (1849); Gaetano Donizetti's *La Favorite* (1840) and *Dom Sébastien* (1843); Jacques François Fromental Halévy's *La Juive* (1835); Giuseppe Verdi's *Les Vêpres Siciliennes* (1855) and *Don Carlos* (1867). Before his *Tannhäuser* (Dresden 1845) could be presented in Paris (1861) Wagner had to augment the score with a full-scale ballet. Verdi similarly wrote special ballet music for the French productions – 1857 and 1894 respectively – of his *Il Trovatore* (Rome 1853) and *Otello* (Milan 1887). It should be emphasized that in Paris during this period the finest dancers and choreographers were engaged in the presentation of opera ballets, which often achieved memorable distinction. It was M. TAGLIONI at the head of a rout of ghostly nuns in the ballet devised by her father Filippo in Act II of *Robert le Diable* that began the cult of balletic supernaturalism and led directly to SYLPHIDE and GISELLE.

The situation in 19th-c. France suggests that ballet flourishes as an adjunct to opera when the public has a taste for spectacle and where a steady supply of first-rate dancers is available – a notion supported by the prominence of ballet in Russian opera from the latter's origins in Mikhail Glinka's *A Life for the Tsar* (*Ivan Susanin*) (St Petersburg 1836) to PROKOFIEV's *War and Peace* (staged complete Leningrad 1955). Dance is prominent in Russian works as aesthetically different as Aleksandr Serov's *Judith* (St Petersburg 1863), Modest Musorgsky's *Boris Godunov* (St Petersburg 1874), TCHAIKOVSKY's *Eugene Onegin* (Moscow 1879), and Nikolay Rimsky-Korsakov's *Sadko* (Moscow 1898).

In Central Europe during the 19th c. dance was often used to increase the jollity of comic operas – e.g. Albert Lortzing's *Zar und Zimmermann* (Leipzig 1837), Bedřich Smetana's *The Bartered Bride* (Prague 1866), Wagner's *Die Meistersinger* (Munich 1868) – though it was also frequently called upon for supernatural and fantastic ends, as in Wagner's *Parsifal* (Bayreuth 1882) and Antonín Dvořák's *Rusalka* (Prague 1901). In our own time opera has shown no disinclination to avail itself of dance's unique attributes, despite the expense in which it involves opera houses – e.g. HENZE's *Boulevard Solitude*

(Hanover 1952), Michael Tippett's *Midsummer Marriage* (London 1955), Arnold Schönberg's *Moses und Aron* (staged Zürich 1957) and Benjamin Britten's *Death in Venice* (Aldeburgh Fest. 1973). DH

Opéra-ballet, a form of lyric theatre, more spectacular than dramatic, though usually with a tenuous connecting theme between one act and another, in which singing and dancing are of equal importance. *Opéra-ballet* came into existence at the end of the 17th c., its first outstanding composer being André Campra (1660–1744), who wrote several, incl. *L'Europe Galante* (Paris 1697), *Les Fêtes d'Hébé* (Paris 1739), and *Les Fêtes Vénitiennes* (Paris 1710). J.-P. RAMEAU brought *opéra-ballet* to its culmination, especially with INDES GALANTES and *La Guirlande* (Paris 1751), though the form lasted well into the 19th c., e.g. ADAM's *L'Écumeur de Mer* (2 acts; St Petersburg 1840; ch. F. TAGLIONI) for M. TAGLIONI; AUBER's *Le Dieu et la Bayadère* (Paris 1830; ch. F. Taglioni) for M. Taglioni; and the same composer's *Le Cheval de Bronze* (Paris 1857). DH

Opus 1, ballet, ch. CRANKO; mus. Anton (von) Webern (Passacaglia); no decor. Stuttgart B., 7 Nov 1965; dan. KEIL, CRAGUN. An impression of Man's life cycle. Revived Deutsche O. am Rhein (1968), CCJB, 2 Oct 1975. GBLW

Orange Free State Ballet Group *see* PACOFS BALLET COMPANY

Orbs, modern dance work, ch. P. TAYLOR; mus. Ludwig van Beethoven: Quartets Op. 127 (no. 12),

Orpheus. Dancers of the NYCB in BALANCHINE's ballet with HAYDEN as Eurydice, BONNEFOUS as Orpheus and MONCION as the Dark Angel, 1972 revival

Op. 133 (Grosse Fuge), Op. 130 (no. 13); sc./c. Alex Katz. The Hague, Royal T., Paul Taylor Dance Co., 4 July 1966; dan. DE JONG, Taylor, WAGONER, C. ADAMS, CROPLEY. Taylor's first full-length work, based on the theme of the planets revolving around the sun, used also as a metaphor for human society. DV

Oriental Dance *see* ASIA

Original Ballet Russe *see* BALLET RUSSE DE MONTE CARLO

Orlando, Mariane, b. Stockholm, 1934. Swedish ballerina. Studied RSBS, with Lilian Karina, and at London SWS. Entered RSB 1948; principal dancer 1953. Leading ballerina since her debut as ODETTE-ODILE. Studied Leningrad Kirov S. 1960. Guest artist with ABT 1961–2. Dances the great classical roles as well as roles in modern dance e.g. CULLBERG's *The Moon Reindeer*, MEDEA, and PILLAR OF FIRE. Critics' prize, Paris, 1959; Order of Vasa 1967; awarded Hon. Doctor of Arts and Letters, 1977. AGS

Orlikovsky, Vaslav, b. Kharkov, 1921. Russian dancer, choreographer, and ballet master. Studied with PREOBRAZHENSKY. Danced in Russia; arrived in W. Europe just after World War II. First settled in Munich; in 1950 founded a small touring group; 1952 became ballet master in Oberhausen, where he staged the first of his many ambitious productions of CINDERELLA (1952) and SWAN LAKE (1955). These led to his being invited to direct the ballet in Basel, 1955, where, with financial assistance from rich backers, he built up the co. As guest choreographer he staged his Basel *Peer Gynt* for LFB 1963; for Raimundo de Larrain's co. in Paris he produced his *Cinderella* the same year. For Vienna, as director of ballet, he produced his own versions of SLEEPING BEAUTY (1963), PRINCE OF THE PAGODAS (1967), SACRE DU PRINTEMPS (1968) etc. In 1971 he produced ice shows for the Vienna Ice Revue. To Graz 1974. GBLW

Orloff, Nicholas, b. Moscow, 1914. Russian dancer. He m. dancer Nina Popova. Studied Paris with PREOBRAZHENSKA and V. GSOVSKY. Joined DE BASIL's Original B. Russe 1939; created role of Drummer in GRADUATION BALL; ABT 1941–50, 1954–5, 1958–9; de Basil B. 1947; de Cuevas B. 1950. Director, Norwegian OB 1960–1. Now teaches in NY. DV

Orosz, Adél, b. Budapest, 1938. Hungarian dancer. Pupil of NÁDASI, graduated from State B. Inst. 1954, studied in Leningrad under DUDINSKAYA and PUSHKIN 1959. Solo dancer since 1957, Budapest O., good classical technique, danced almost all classical roles in the Budapest repertoire, and Flavia in SPARTACUS, the Princess in WOODEN PRINCE, LISE (ch. ASHTON). Besides taking part in the co.'s tours, has also toured China, Vietnam, Korea (1959); the European countries in the mid-1960s; visited Cuba 1966 and 1967. Danced title role in the TV film *The Girl Danced into Life*, and *The Wooden Prince*. Liszt Prize, 1961; Kossuth Prize, 1965; the Finnish White Rose Order, 1968; Merited Artist, 1972; Eminent Artist, 1976. GPD

Orpheus, ballet, 3 scenes, ch. BALANCHINE; mus. STRAVINSKY; sc./c. NOGUCHI; ltg ROSENTHAL. NYCC, B. Society, 28 Apr 1948; dan. MAGALLANES, Maria TALLCHIEF, MONCION. A contemporary retelling of the legend of Orpheus, the poet and musician who journeyed to the underworld to bring back from the dead his wife Eurydice. FM

Osato, Sono, b. Omaha, NE, 1919. American dancer, of Japanese–Irish parentage. Studied with BOLM in Chicago and with EGOROVA in Paris. Joined de Basil's B. Russe de Monte Carlo 1934; created Siren in LICHINE's version of PRODIGAL SON, etc. ABT 1941–3, 1954–6. A dancer of striking beauty, used to great effect in the Broadway musicals *One Touch of Venus* (1943; ch. DE MILLE) and *On the Town* (1944; ch. ROBBINS). DV

Osipenko, Alla, b. Leningrad, 1932. Soviet dancer; Graduated from Leningrad Choreographic S. 1950, class of VAGANOVA. Kirov T. 1950–71. Excellent classical ballerina with perfect line in classical works; also renowned for roles created in contemporary ballets with great understanding of style: Mistress of the Copper Mountain (STONE FLOWER), Beloved (COAST OF HOPE), Cleopatra (*Antony and Cleopatra*, Leningrad, Maly T.); soloist in YACOBSON's *Choreographic Miniatures* 1971–3. Has taught at Vaganova S. since 1966. She m. John Markovsky, soloist Kirov B. and in *Choreographic Miniatures*. People's Artist, RSFSR, 1960; Prix Anna Pavlova. NR
See article by G. Dobrovolskaya in *Leningrad Ballet Today* (Leningrad 1967)

Østergaard, Solveig, b. Skjern, 1939. Danish dancer. Entered RDBS 1947; soloist 1962. Debut as Cupid (WHIMS OF CUPID) when a child; dances *demi-caractère* roles with vivacity and has a special brilliant August BOURNONVILLE style in allegro dancing. Among her best parts are the junior student in GRADUATION BALL, pupil in LESSON, SWANILDA, and the great Bournonville solos. SKJ

Othello, ballet, 4 acts, 13 scenes; ch./lib. CHABUKIANI; mus. Aleksey Machavariani; sc. VIRSALADZE. Tbilisi T. of O. and B., 27 Nov 1957; dan. Chabukiani (title role), Vera Zignadze (Desdemona). Kirov T., same choreography, 1960. Has also been filmed. Follows William Shakespeare's tragedy closely, but has prologue showing Desdemona's elopement with Othello from her father's home, and a pantomime illustrating his speech in the Senate. NR

P

PACOFS (Performing Arts Council of the Orange Free State) **Ballet Company,** founded 1963 (as the Orange Free State B. Group), Bloemfontein, Orange Free State, S. Africa, when government grants for the arts were given to all four provinces. The first professional ballet was presented in association with CAPAB B. in 1964; D. DAVIES was appointed director the same year. In 1965 the name was changed to PACOFS B.; professional dancers with MILLER as ballerina replaced the original group of scholars and teachers. They presented lecture demonstrations and performances. In 1968 Davies and Miller joined NAPAC and were succeeded by George Golovine. Golovine was succeeded by STAFF in 1969; at his death in 1971 the co. was disbanded. *See also* BALLET INTERNATIONAL. MG

PACT Ballet Company, founded 1963 in Johannesburg, S. Africa; subsidized by the S. African Government, provincial, and municipal funds. In Apr 1963 the Johannesburg City B. merged with PACT to present ballet seasons. Artistic Directors have been Hermien Dommisse (1963), Faith de Villiers (1964–7), Paul Grinwiss (1969), John Hart (1972), SCHULTZE, and GODFREY from 1973; the post was vacant in 1968, 1970, and 1971. The co. has over 50 dancers and a large and varied repertoire of the classics as well as works by contemporary choreographers. PACT B. tours the Transvaal and has appeared in all the main S. African cities as well as Rhodesia, Zambia, and Maputo (Lourenço Marques) in Mozambique. MG

Pagava, Ethéry, b. Paris, 1932. French dancer and choreographer. Studied with EGOROVA. B. des CE 1945. Created roles in FORAINS, AMOURS DE JUPITER. De Cuevas B. 1947. Danced LIFAR's *Roméo et Juliette,* MASSINE's *Tristan Fou,* SONNAMBULA. From 1952 guest artist Netherlands, France. Massine's B. Europeo 1960. Staged *Facettes* (mus. Pierre Schaeffer) 1969, *La Parole* (mus. Krystof Penderecki) 1972 for Dutch NB. Has headed her own co. since 1973, L'Animation-Danse du Centre Culturel de Malakoff. Early noticed for poetic radiance and dramatic freshness. M-FC

Page, Ruth, b. Indianapolis, IN, 1905. American dancer and choreographer. Studied with BOLM, KHLUSTIN, and CECCHETTI. Danced with A. PAVLOVA's Co. in S. America 1918–19; title role in Bolm's *Birthday of the Infanta,* Chicago O. 1919; Bolm's B. Intime 1920–2; Irving Berlin's Music Box Revue, NY 1922–4; Chicago Allied Arts (Bolm) 1924–6; briefly with DIAGHILEV 1925, when BALANCHINE arranged dances for her; T. Colón, Buenos Aires, 1925. First choreography, *The Flapper and the Quarterback* (1925). Danced at Met and with Adolph Bolm B., both 1927–8 (danced Terpsichore in Bolm's original version of APOLLO 1928). Toured Europe and Asia with small group 1928. Gave solo recitals in Moscow 1930. Toured USA in solo concerts 1930–5, USA and Orient with KREUTZBERG 1932–4. *Première danseuse* and director of Chicago OB 1934–7 and 1942–5, of Ruth Page B. 1934–8, Federal T. Project 1938–9, (with Bentley Stone) of Page–Stone B. 1940–6, Les B. Américains, Paris 1950. Choreographer and director of ballet of Chicago Lyric O. 1954–70, Chicago OB 1955–6, Ruth Page's International B. 1966–9, Chicago B. 1972–.

Her ballets incl. *Iberian Monotone* (1931; mus. RAVEL), *La Guiablesse,* with a black cast led by DUNHAM (1933; mus. William Grant Still); *Hear Ye! Hear Ye!* (1934; mus. COPLAND); *Frankie and Johnny* (with Bentley Stone, 1938; mus. Jerome Moross); *The Bells* (1946; mus. MILHAUD); *Billy Sunday* (1946; mus. Remi Gassmann) – the last three were all taken into the repertory of the B. Russe de Monte Carlo; *Revanche* (1951; mus. Giuseppe Verdi; revived B. des CE 1951); and three versions of *Carmen,* to music from Georges Bizet's opera; *Guns and Castanets* (with Bentley Stone; 1939), *Carmen* (1961), and *Carmen and José* (for DTH, 1976). In many of her ballets she has had the collaboration of distinguished designers such as CLAVÉ, NOGUCHI, TCHELITCHEV, and Georges Wakhevitch. One of the first choreographers to attempt ballets on contemporary American themes. DV

Palais de Cristal, ballet, 4 movements, ch. BALANCHINE; mus. Georges Bizet; sc./c. Léonor Fini. Paris OB, 28 July 1947; dan. DARSONVAL, TOUMANOVA, Micheline Bardin, Madeleine Lafon. Renamed *Symphony in C*; NYCC, B. Society, 22 Mar 1948; dan. Maria TALLCHIEF, LECLERCQ, Beatrice Tompkins, Elise Reiman. A plotless ballet, typically designed to display the gifts of four distinguished ballerinas. The score, written when Bizet was 17, was suggested to Balanchine by STRAVINSKY. FM

Panov, Valery, b. Vitebsk, 1938. Russian dancer. Graduated from Leningrad S. into Maly T. Co. 1957, danced PETRUSHKA in 1961 revival; Kirov B. 1963. A brilliant character dancer who won many awards in USSR, he was not permitted to dance in the West except for one perf. in New York in 1958. Created

Colour Plates. Facing page: SIBLEY as Titania, DOWELL as Oberon, and GRANT as Bottom in DREAM, as staged by the RB at CG

Overleaf: MACMILLAN's production of ROMEO AND JULIET for the RB at CG, the ballroom scene with FONTEYN as Juliet (left) and NUREYEV as Romeo; sc./c. GEORGIADIS

title role in SERGEYEV's *Hamlet*, 1970. He m. Galina Ragozina (b. Archangel 1949), who had graduated from Perm BS into the co. there 1967, then joined Kirov 1970. In 1972 the Panovs were dismissed from the co. after they had been refused visas to emigrate to Israel. Theirs became a *cause célèbre* when dancers, writers, artists, and theatre people all over the world appealed on their behalf. They were finally allowed to leave in 1974, on the eve of the opening of the Bolshoy B. season in London. Since then they have appeared as guest artists in many countries. Valery Panov has also fulfilled his long-held ambition to choreograph: *Adagio Albinoni*, a *pas de deux* for his wife and himself (Bridgeport, CT, 1975) and *Heart of the Mountain* (San Francisco B., 1976). Lenin prize 1969. DV

Pan Twardowski (*Mr Twardowski*), ballet: (1) 5 acts, ch./lib. Virgilius Calori; mus. Adolf Sonnenfeld. Warsaw, 6 July 1874, in the repertory until 1917. (2) 3 acts, 8 scenes, ch. ZAJLICH; mus. Ludomir Różycki; lib. Stefania Różycka; sc. Wincenty Drabik. Warsaw, 9 May 1921. Most popular of Polish ballets. The plot is based on the legend of the Polish Dr Faustus, who sells his soul to the Devil on condition that the Devil will take his soul only in Rome. As Twardowski never visits Rome, the Devil entices him to a village inn called Roma. Twardowski's prayers save him from the Devil but he is taken to the moon. JPu

Paquita (*Pakhita*), pantomime-ballet, 2 acts, 3 scenes, ch. MAZILIER; mus. Édouard Marie Ernest Deldevez; lib. Paul Foucher and Mazilier. Paris, T. de l'Académie Royale de Musique, 1 Apr 1846; dan. GRISI (title role), L. PETIPA (Comte d'Hervilly). A story of a noble girl stolen by gypsies and restored to her family. Another version: 3 acts, ch. M. PETIPA, St Petersburg, 26 Sept 1847; dan. ANDREYANOVA (title role), M. Petipa (debut as d'Hervilly). Revived 27 Dec 1881; ch. M. Petipa; dan. VAZEM (title role). Act III expanded by Mazurka performed by pupils of St Petersburg TS (now in the repertory of the Moscow Choreographic S. in a version by Vladimir Varkovitsky) and a *grand pas* (mus. MINKUS) for ballerina, *premier danseur*, six first and eight second soloists. In the USSR only this *grand pas*, a Spanish-flavoured classical ensemble calling for virtuosity and a grand manner, has survived and is performed by many Soviet cos and some cos abroad. NR
See COMPLETE BOOK; Mikhail Borisoglebsky (ed.), *Materials for the History of Russian Ballet*, Volume II (Leningrad 1939)

Parade, *ballet réaliste*, 1 act, ch. MASSINE; lib. COCTEAU; mus. SATIE; sc./c. PICASSO. Paris, T. du Châtelet, DIAGHILEV's B. Russes, 18 May 1917; dan. L. LOPUKHOVA, Maria Chabelska, Massine, Nicholas Zverev, WOIZIKOWSKI. Circus performers try without success to attract the public to their perf. An attempt to translate the principles of Cubism into a theatrical spectacle; naturalistic mime and vernacular movement were incorporated into the choreography, and Satie used sirens, typewriters, and pistol shots in the score. Revived Brussels, T. de la Monnaie, B. XXe S., 1964; NYCC, CCJB, 22 Mar 1973; London Coliseum, LFB, 22 May 1974. DV

Colour Plate: Julia Blaikie and BRUCE of B. Rambert in PIERROT LUNAIRE

Paris Opéra Ballet. The Paris O. boasts a longer tradition of ballet than any other theatre in the world. From the foundation of the O. by Louis XIV's *privilège* of 1669 it has always had a strong co. of dancers, and it has remained the main centre of French ballet.

During the O.'s early years, under the direction of LULLY who had himself been a dancer, BEAUCHAMP laid the foundations of the ballet co. which was formed to take part in the danced passages in the lyric tragedies of Lully. At first the co. consisted only of men, and it was not until 1681 that women first danced at the O. in TRIOMPHE DE L'AMOUR. In 1687 Beauchamp was succeeded as composer of ballets by PÉCOUR, who held the post until 1729.

As the 18th c. dawned the technique of theatrical dancing was becoming increasingly intricate and brilliant, and the dance occupied an important position in the opera-ballets of André Campra and J.-P. RAMEAU. Ballerinas such as CAMARGO, La Barbarina (Barbarina Campanina) and Louise-Madeleine Lany extended the range of technical virtuosity, while the noble style of male dancing was for many years in the hands of Louis Dupré, who danced with great panache and a style that he hardly varied from one perf. to another. Simultaneously with this development, awareness was spreading of the importance of emotional expression in the dance, a development associated particularly with the ballerina, SALLÉ, Camargo's rival.

The growing desire for expressive content produced a trend towards separating ballet from opera and making it an independent form. This trend made its appearance in Paris at the Comédie Italienne and the OC, and it was not until NOVERRE was appointed ballet master in 1776 that the new form of the *ballet d'action* was accepted at the O. The time was then ripe for it, and after Noverre the *ballet d'action* was firmly established by the GARDEL brothers, Maximilien and Pierre, the latter of whom dominated French ballet throughout the Revolution and the First Empire, holding the post of chief ballet master 1787–1820. Pierre Gardel raised the popularity of ballet to new heights in the early 1800s. His most successful ballets were based on classical themes and were the mainstay of the repertory for many years.

After Gardel's retirement the O. ballet enjoyed a period of great splendour under the influence of the Romantic movement. Becoming a private, though subsidized, enterprise after the Revolution of 1830, the O. shed some of its antiquated traditions, incl. the division of the dancers into the three genres (serious, *demi-caractère* and comic). M. TAGLIONI was

Right: Paris Opera Ballet. LIFAR with six *étoiles* of the Paris O., for whom he created his *Variations:* (left to right) Madeleine Lafon, DAYDÉ, VYROUBOVA, DARSONVAL, Christiane Vaussard, Micheline Bardin; *opposite left:* 'La Danse' as depicted by the sculptor Jean-Baptiste Carpeaux on the front of the Paris O.; *far right;* 'Le Pas de Quatre', lithograph by A. E. Chalon, with M. TAGLIONI (centre), GRISI, GRAHN and CERRITO

elevated to the supreme position of star ballerina, being followed shortly afterwards by ELSSLER and GRISI. The choreographers active in this period were F. TAGLIONI, CORALLI, and MAZILIER; the ballets produced incl. SYLPHIDE and GISELLE.

After 1850 ballet began to lose its vitality, and a decline set in that was to last until the 20th c. SAINT-LÉON's COPPÉLIA is the only ballet to survive from these years with its original choreography. Later, under the ballet masters MÉRANTE and Joseph Hansen, the old repertory was neglected and the male dancer almost totally eclipsed, attention being concentrated on star ballerinas such as Rita Sangalli, Rosita Mauri, and ZAMBELLI, who were sometimes cast opposite a *travesti* dancer playing the hero's role.

The regeneration began almost simultaneously with the arrival in W. Europe of DIAGHILEV's B. Russes. During his long regime as director of the O. (1914–45), Jacques Rouché did much for the ballet, which benefited greatly from his advanced ideas on stage design and his understanding of the new ideas stimulated by Diaghilev. His first ballet master was STAATS, but very soon he began to inject a direct Russian influence. In the 1920s both FOKINE and NIJINSKA were invited to produce ballets, and SPESSIVTSEVA was engaged as star ballerina. The engagement of LIFAR in 1929 was a logical consequence of this policy, his arrival coinciding with the retirement of Zambelli as ballerina. Lifar dominated French ballet as completely as Gardel had done. He created a wide following for ballet among the public, encouraged French dancers – his pupil, CHAUVIRÉ, became the first French dancer within living memory to win international renown – and generally restored dignity to French ballet.

After Lifar the ballet of the O. relied largely on guest choreographers, and has been directed by non-choreographers.

The organization of the co. evolved in its present form in the mid-19th c., with a hierarchy headed by the *étoiles*. Under them, in descending order, come the *premiers danseurs* and *premières danseuses*, the *sujets* (formerly divided into two classes, *grands* and *petits sujets*), the *coryphées* and the *quadrilles* of the *corps de ballet*. Promotion depends on the results of examinations, except that *étoiles* must be nominated by the administrator.

The school of dance attached to the O. has supplied a continuous stream of dancers for the co. since it was established in 1713. Among the great teachers there have been Jean-François Coulon, M. Taglioni, Mme Dominique, Mauri, Zambelli, and Chauviré. The school has given continuity and strength to the ballet, supporting it in good times and bad, and justifying the addition, albeit unofficial, of the word dance to the O.'s official title – the Académie Nationale de Musique et de la Danse. In 1977 VERDY was appointed artistic director. IG

See Ivor Guest, *Le Ballet de l'Opéra* (Paris 1976)

Park, Merle, b. Salisbury, 1937. Rhodesian dancer. Studied with Betty Lamb, then to Elmhurst BS, England. Joined RB 1954, soloist 1958, principal 1959. Small, light, exceptionally musical and with a faultless technique, Park shone first in soubrette roles but understudied NERINA and was the second RB dancer to appear as LISE. Dazzling in short, swift solos, she also dances a sunny AURORA and effective GISELLE. She did not attempt SWAN LAKE until 1973 when she had a notable success. Created ballerina role in NUREYEV's staging of NUTCRACKER for RB at CG. Many guest perfs overseas, often dancing with Nureyev. CBE 1974. MC

Parkinson, Georgina, b. Brighton, 1938. English dancer. Studied RBS. Joined RB 1957, soloist 1959, now a principal. Although she dances many classical roles, mostly soloist, she is happiest in the modern repertory, especially in the ballets of MACMILLAN. Danced JULIET in MacMillan's revival for RSB of ROMEO AND JULIET, Stockholm 1969, and created Winifred Norbury in ENIGMA VARIATIONS, a role in which she is unrivalled. She m. photographer Roy Round. MC

Parlić, Dimitri, b. Salonika, Greece, 1919. Yugoslav dancer and choreographer. Studied with Natalia Bosković, Yelena Poliakova, T. GSOVSKY, PREOBRAZHENSKA. Joined Belgrade NB 1938, principal dancer 1941. Choreographer from 1949. His works incl. a version of COPPÉLIA, *Orpheus* (mus. STRAVINSKY), and *Macedonian Tale* (mus. Gligor Smok-

varski) based on a Macedonian theme and staged by the Skoplje B. Also versions of *El Amor Brujo* (mus. FALLA), and MIRACULOUS MANDARIN. Parlić has also staged ballets for the Vienna Staats OB, where he was ballet master and choreographer 1958–61. Also worked in Germany, Greece, and Rome (1963–6). Returned to Yugoslavia after short stay with NB of Finland 1970–1; now freelancing. MC

Pas de Quatre, Le, *divertissement* for four dancers, ch. PERROT; mus. PUGNI. London, Her Majesty's T., 12 July 1845; dan. M. TAGLIONI, GRISI, CERRITO, GRAHN. It was LUMLEY's idea to bring four of the greatest stars together in one work. Performed four times in 1845 and in 1847 revived for two more perfs with ROSATI replacing Grahn. In 1936 LESTER reconstructed the ballet in the style of 1845 for the MARKOVA–DOLIN B., using the original music orch. Leighton Lucas. A charming suite of solos and group dances. Another version staged by Dolin for ABT, 16 Feb 1941, has been reproduced by him all over the world. He introduced much more difficult *pointe* work than could have been in the original and a note of comedy. MC
See Ivor Guest, *The Romantic Ballet in England* (London 1954) and *The Pas de Quatre* (London 1970, Tokyo 1976)

Path of Thunder (*Tropoyu Groma*), ballet, 3 acts, ch. SERGEYEV; mus. Kara Karayev; lib. SLONIMSKY, after the novel of same title by S. African author Peter Abrahams. Leningrad, Kirov T., 31 Dec 1957; dan. DUDINSKAYA (Sari), Sergeyev (Lenny). First performed Bolshoy T. same ch.; sc. Valery Dorer, 27 June 1959. A white girl and a black teacher are caught in the Veldt and killed by her father, a landowner, and his companions, for daring to oppose their way of life. Many other versions to the same music. NR
See V. Prokhorova, *Konstantin Sergeyev* (Leningrad 1974)

Patineurs, Les (*The Skaters*), *ballet-divertissement*, 1 act, ch. ASHTON; mus. Giacomo Meyerbeer, arr. LAMBERT; sc./c. William Chappell. London, SWT, Vic-Wells B., 16 Feb 1937; dan. Mary Honer, Elizabeth Miller, TURNER, FONTEYN, HELPMANN, June Brae, MAY. The convention that the dancers are supposed to be ice skaters provided the pretext for a display of virtuosity more brilliant than had been seen before in British ballet. Revived by many cos incl. ABT, sc./c. BEATON, 1946; Australian B. 1970; Noverre B. (Stuttgart second co.) 1973. DV

Paul [Wiedersheim-Paul], Annette av, b. Stockholm, 1944. Swedish dancer. Studied RSBS; debut 1962 in GRIGOROVICH's STONE FLOWER. Principal dancer 1966; guest artist, RWB, same year; created title role in *Rose Latulippe* (ch. her husband Brian Macdonald). Danced with HARKNESS B. 1967–8, RSB 1968–72. Grands B. Canadiens 1970; soloist 1974. GISELLE and JULIET are among her roles. Freelanced since 1972. AGS

Paul, Mimi, b. Nashville, TN, 1943. American dancer. Studied with Lisa Gardiner, Mary Day, FRANKLIN, Washington, and at SAB. Danced with Washington DC B. 1955–60, NYCB 1961–8, ABT 1969–72, NUREYEV and Friends 1974. DV

Pavillon d'Armide, Le, choreographic drama, 1 act, 3 scenes, ch. FOKINE; lib. BENOIS, from GAUTIER's *Omphale*; mus. Nikolay Cherepnin; sc./c. Benois. St Petersburg, Maryinsky T., 25 Nov 1907; dan. A. PAVLOVA, P. GERDT, NIJINSKY. A single scene, *The Animated Gobelins*, had been presented at the Annual Pupils' Perf. of the Imperial S., 28 Apr 1907, as a result of which Fokine was invited to stage the complete ballet. Though not one of Fokine's 'reform' ballets – it was essentially a ballet *à grand spectacle* in the M. PETIPA manner, though shorter in length – this was the first completely original production by

Anna Pavlova with NOVIKOV in *Christmas*

artists who were to be among DIAGHILEV's collaborators in his first Paris seasons of B. Russes, and was incl. in the opening program at the T. du Châtelet, *répétition générale* 18 May 1909; dan. KARALLI, MORDKIN, Nijinsky, KARSAVINA. DV

Pavlova, Anna, b. St Petersburg, 1881; d. The Hague, 1931. Russian dancer. A document in the Leningrad Archives of the Imperial Ts says she was the daughter of a reserve soldier Matvey Pavlov and a laundress Lyubov Pavlova. She was rumoured to be of more exalted origin and possibly of Jewish blood. She certainly changed her patronymic Matveyevna to Pavlovna either because she disliked it or because the other sounded better. After seeing a perf. of SLEEPING BEAUTY at the Maryinsky T. 1890, she resolved to become a dancer and appear as AURORA. E. SOKOLOVA helped her gain a place in the St Petersburg TS in 1891, where P. GERDT, JOHANSSON, and later CECCHETTI were her mentors. Two years before graduating she danced on the Maryinsky stage in the *Pas des Almées* in FILLE DU PHARAON for Johansson's benefit. She graduated 11 Apr 1899 in a small ballet arranged by Gerdt, *False Dryads* (mus. PUGNI) and immediately attracted the attention of critics.

She first danced her incomparable GISELLE in 1903 and appeared in the fairy variations in the Prologue of *The Sleeping Beauty* before achieving her goal of Aurora in 1908. She received ballerina status in 1906. M. PETIPA gave her the title role in his ballet *The Awakening of Flora* (mus. DRIGO) 1900 and for her ten-year jubilee on the stage she danced Nikia in his BAYADÈRE. An assiduous worker, she studied during the summer vacations with Caterina Beretta in Milan and admired I. DUNCAN's fluent and expressive style. The Annals of the Imperial Ts mention her talent, agility, and mime. She was no less outstanding in parts requiring playful grace and coquetry such as LISE and KITRI, and was delightful in many smaller, supporting roles. She danced no fewer than 18 leading parts on the Maryinsky stage, was FOKINE's first Armida in PAVILLON D'ARMIDE 1907, and in the same year he created for her CYGNE (*The Dying Swan*) which became her most famous solo.

In 1906 she went to Moscow to dance in GORSKY's version of *Fille du Pharaon*, attracted by the bold strength of the Moscow B. It was then she first danced with MORDKIN, who was to partner her on tours abroad. She later chose as partners such Moscow dancers as NOVIKOV and VOLININ. She also danced with more lyric St Petersburg dancers such as M. OBUKHOV (with whom she created the C-sharp-minor Waltz in CHOPINIANA) and NIJINSKY, with whom she performed the same *pas de deux* in SYLPHIDES. She last appeared in Russia in a full-length work 25 Feb 1913 in *La Bayadère*; her final Russian appearance was 7 June 1914 in a series of *divertissements*.

Pavlova began her tours abroad in 1908, visiting Stockholm, Copenhagen, and Berlin. She made her debut in both NY and London in 1910; in 1912 bought Ivy House, North End Road, Golders Green, in London, which was her home for the rest of her life. Although sympathetic to the ideas of Fokine she danced only in the early DIAGHILEV seasons, preferring to star in her own co. and tour worldwide. More than any other dancer she epitomizes the public image of a ballerina. As well as pretty trifles, she staged many of the classical ballets (notably *The Sleeping Beauty* in NY) and transformed everything with her artistry. She inspired a love of dance in all who saw her – among them ASHTON.

Many of her dancers were English girls and her former costumier, Manya Charchevnikova, settled in London and organized each year a memorial service at the Russian Church on 23 Jan, the date of her death in the Netherlands (from pneumonia). On 3 Feb 1974 the enthusiasm of two balletlovers, John and Roberta Lazzarini, led to the setting up of a small museum devoted to Pavlova in a room at Ivy House. Fragments of her dancing were filmed by Douglas Fairbanks in Hollywood 1924–5, dubbed with music and edited by BRINSON 1956. Her husband Victor Dandré incl. them in a film he made about her in 1936, *The Immortal Swan*, and there also exists some newsreel footage. The Lazzarinis formed a Pavlova Society in 1975, and since Manya's death in 1974 have continued to hold the memorial service. NR/MC

See V. Krasovskaya, *Anna Pavlova* (Leningrad 1964); *Russian Ballet Theatre of the Beginning of the 20th Century*, Vol. 2, *Dancers* (Leningrad 1972); Natalia Trouhanova, '*Vstrechi s Proshlym*' (*Meeting the Past*); in volume of materials from the Central State Archives of Literature and Art of the USSR, issue I, '*Sovietskaya Rossiya*' (Moscow 1970); Valerian Svetlov, *Anna Pavlova* (London 1930); Victor Dandré, *Anna Pavlova* (London 1932; Berlin 1933); Cyril W. Beaumont, *Anna Pavlova* (London 1932)

Peter and the Wolf, ballet or dance-mime work, ch. BOLM; lib. (text)/mus. PROKOFIEV; sc./c. Lucinda Ballard. NY, Center T., ABT, 13 Jan 1940; dan. LORING. Another version ch. STAFF; sc./c. Guy Sheppard. Cambridge, Arts T., BR, 1 May 1940; dan. Helen Ashley (Lulu Dukes, younger daughter of RAMBERT). The Staff version has been revived for PACT B. Johannesburg, and Northern Dance T. The little boy Peter with the help of his friends, the Cat and the Bird, captures the wicked Wolf despite his grandfather's warnings. The cheerfulness and clarity of the Prokofiev music and narration have made *Peter and the Wolf* a firm favourite with choreographers and also with schoolchildren who delight in making their own versions. MC

Petipa, Lucien, b. Marseille, 1815; d. Versailles, 1898. French dancer and choreographer, brother of M. PETIPA. Studied with his father Jean Antoine Petipa (b. Paris, 1796; d. St Petersburg, 1855) and danced in his productions in Brussels and Bordeaux before debut at Paris O. 1840, partnering ELSSLER in SYLPHIDE. The following year created role of ALBRECHT, partnering GRISI as he did in many ballets. A fine dancer and handsome man, his choreography was mostly for ballets in opera incl. that in Richard Wagner's *Tannhäuser* (Paris O., 13 Mar 1861). *Namouna* (1882) was to music by Édouard Lalo. *Maître de ballet*, Paris O., 1860–8; a hunting accident forced him to retire. MC
See Ivor Guest, *The Romantic Ballet in Paris* (London and Middletown, CT, 1966); *The Ballet of the Second Empire 1847–1858* (London 1955); *1858–1870* (London 1953)

Petipa, Marius, b. Marseille, 1818; d. Gurzuf, Russia, 1910. French dancer and choreographer and architect of the Imperial Russian B. Son of Jean Antoine Petipa (and totally eclipsed as a dancer in the West by his brother L. PETIPA) he made his first appearances with his father's co. in Brussels and staged his first ballets in Nantes, 1838. With the family to the USA, disastrously, 1839, followed by successful appearances at the Comédie Française, dancing with GRISI. In 1843–6 toured Spain with Marie Guy-Stephan, learning the national dances later featured in his ballets. In 1847 to Russia as principal dancer in Imperial T., St Petersburg. In 1862, following the success of FILLE DU PHARAON, he was appointed *maître de ballet* but worked in the shadow of SAINT-LÉON until 1869 when he finally became chief ballet master. From then until his retirement in 1903 he ruled the St Petersburg B. He not only choreographed more than 60 full-length ballets but, by combining his French schooling with the virtuosity of the Italians and the temperament of the Russians, created the classic dance we know today. ASHTON and BALANCHINE are his heirs. Petipa was a master of the giant spectacles demanded by the Imperial court but he was also a master choreographer of solos and *pas de deux*. To dance a Petipa variation in SLEEPING BEAUTY, RAYMONDA or BAYADÈRE is still the test of a ballerina. In addition to the many new works created in Russia, Petipa restaged there GISELLE and a version of COPPÉLIA. With his assistant IVANOV he staged the first successful production of SWAN LAKE in St Petersburg and in Moscow 1869 produced DON QUIXOTE, restaging it in St Petersburg 1871. Petipa's first wife was Maria Surovshchikova (1836–82), a dancer celebrated in character parts. They separated in 1867 and he married Lyubov Savitskaya, a dancer in the Moscow B. His daughter by his first wife, Maria Mariusovna Petipa (1857–1930), created the LILAC FAIRY. MC
See Lillian Moore, 'The Petipa Family in Europe and America', *Dance Index* (New York, May 1942); Yuri Slonimsky, 'Marius Petipa', tr. Anatole Chujoy, *Dance Index* (New York, May–June 1947); Marius Petipa, *Russian Ballet Master: The Memoirs of Marius Petipa*, tr. Helen Wittaker, ed. Lillian Moore (London and New York 1958); Y. Slonimsky, *Marius Petipa, Materiali Vospominaniya Stati* (*Materials, Reminiscences, Letters*) (Leningrad 1971), tr. Eberhard Rebling as *Marius Petipa: Meister des klassischen Balletts* (E. Berlin 1975); Vera Krasovskaya, 'Marius Petipa and *The Sleeping Beauty*', *Dance Perspectives*, No. 49 (New York)

Petit, Roland, b. Villemomble, 1924. French dancer and choreographer. His French father was the proprietor of a Paris bistro (and helped to finance his first ballets) and his Italian mother opened the Repetto shop, which specializes in tights and ballet shoes. Entered Paris OBS 1934, studying with RICAUX and LIFAR; *corps de ballet* 1940. *Premier sujet* Jan 1943, when he created principal role in Lifar's *L'Amour Sorcier*. Recitals with CHARRAT 1941–3. In 1944 left the O. to work with the group of young artists that was to become the BALLETS DES CHAMPS-ÉLYSÉES. His friendship with COCTEAU, BÉRARD, KOCHNO, and SAUGUET formed his taste. His first ballet was FORAINS. He staged many works for the B. des CE incl. AMOURS DE JUPITER, JEUNE HOMME ET LA MORT, *Bal des Blanchisseuses*, and *Treize Danses*. Left the co. 1948 and founded BALLETS DE PARIS, staging for it many works incl. DEMOISELLES DE LA NUIT, *L'Oeuf à la Coque* (1949), CARMEN, CROQUEUSE DE DIAMANTS, and LOUP.

In the USA, he staged the choreography for many films such as *Hans Christian Andersen* (dir. Charles Vidor, 1952), *Daddy Long Legs* (dir. Jean Negulesco, 1955), *The Glass Slipper* (dir. Charles Walters, 1954), *Anything Goes* (dir. Robert Lewis, 1955).

He m. JEANMAIRE 1954, and staged a revue for her at the T. de Paris (1956), then the revue *Zizi Jeanmaire* (1957) at the T. de l'Alhambra. In the 1950s and 1960s he staged many ballets in Paris, London, Milan, Toronto, and Hamburg. In 1970 took over with Jeanmaire the direction of the Paris Casino, where he staged revues, and, at the same time from 1972, that of the B. de Marseille, for which he staged *Allumez les Étoiles* (1973), *La Rose Malade* (1973),

Petrushka, revived by GRIGORIEV, RB at CG, 1957

L'Arlésienne (1974), *Jeux d'Enfants* (1974), *Les Intermittences du Cœur* (1975), and his own versions of COPPÉLIA (1975) and NUTCRACKER (1976). Choreographed for the Paris OH (1976) several ballets, NOTRE-DAME DE PARIS, *Turangalila* (1968), and NANA.

Influenced by Lifar's neoclassicism, Petit has a brilliant sense of theatre. He has always surrounded himself with fashionable collaborators, such as the designers CARZOU, Max Ernst, Bernard Buffet, Christian Dior, Yves Saint-Laurent, and composers who could provide not necessarily great music but music ideal for his ballets. He served his dancers well: Jeanmaire, MARCHAND, VERDY, BLASKA, DENARD. He was himself an elegant dancer and a superb dramatic actor. M-FC
See C. W. Beaumont, *Ballets of Today, being a Second Supplement to the Complete Book of Ballets* (London 1954); Irène Lidova, *Roland Petit* (Paris 1956); article in *Les Saisons de la Danse* (Paris, summer 1968) with list of roles

Petroff [Petersen], Paul, b. Helsingør [Elsinore], 1908. Danish dancer. Studied Copenhagen. *Premier danseur* of de Basil's B. Russe de Monte Carlo 1932–43, ABT 1943–6, International B. 1947. He m. GOLLNER. Now teaching in California. DV

Petrushka, burlesque scenes in 4 tableaux, ch. FOKINE; lib. STRAVINSKY and BENOIS; mus. Stravinsky; sc./c. Benois. Paris, T. du Châtelet, DIAGHILEV'S B. Russes (as *Petrouchka*), 13 June 1911; dan. NIJINSKY, KARSAVINA, Aleksandr Orlov, CECCHETTI. At the Shrovetide fair in St Petersburg in the 1830s, a magician displays three puppets, Petrushka, a Ballerina, and a Moor. Behind the scenes, they continue to act out the triangle indicated in their pantomime; Petrushka seems to have human feelings within his misshapen doll's body. In a frenzy of jealousy, the Moor finally chases him out into the square and kills him before the horrified crowd. The Magician picks up the body and shows them it is just sawdust and wood. The crowd disperses; suddenly Petrushka's ghost appears above the little theatre and curses his master. Possibly Nijinsky's greatest role.

Revived by most major cos, for whom Benois, before he died in 1960, made several new versions of his designs: Petrograd, Maryinsky T., 1920, ch. Leonid Leontiev (presumably after Fokine); RDB, 1925; de Basil's B. Russes de Monte Carlo, 1934; R. BLUM'S B. de Monte Carlo, 1936; ABT, 1942 (new production using original designs, 1970); Paris O., 1948; de Cuevas B., 1950; LFB, 1950; RB, 1957; CCJB, 1970. First revival for many years in USSR was at Maly T., Leningrad, 1961, ch. Konstantin Boyarsky after Fokine; dan. PANOV. DV

Phèdre, ballet, ch. LIFAR; mus. AURIC; lib./sc./c. COCTEAU. Paris O., 14 June 1950; dan. TOUMANOVA, LIFAR. A powerful translation of Jean Baptiste Racine's tragedy to the ballet stage, it blended mime and dance and even included a representation of a chariot race. Brilliantly simple setting and strong perfs by the creators of the main roles. M-FC

Philippart, Nathalie, b. Bordeaux, French dancer. Studied with EGOROVA and V. GSOVSKY. She m. BABILÉE. Soloist, B. des CE; B. de Paris 1947; ABT. Created principal role in JEUNE HOMME ET LA MORT with Babilée, also AMOUR ET SON AMOUR. Unmistakably French, her chic and sophistication were also used by PETIT in the role of Danae in AMOURS DE JUPITER. M-FC

Photography and Ballet. There has been remarkably little change since the early days of photography in the approach to the subject in the studio. The photographer's ambition has always been to capture the beauty of the dancer and as much as possible of the characterization in any particular role. This is as true of the early photographs of artists of the Imperial Russian B., such as A. PAVLOVA and KARSAVINA, and of the exotic pictures of NIJINSKY taken by Baron de Meyer just before World War I, as it is of studio pictures taken today. In every case the lighting is unobtrusive and allows all attention to be on the dancer; clever photographic technique is at the dancer's service and does not intrude.

What is surprising is to discover how very early photographers could succeed in 'freezing' movement, at a time when it might be thought to have been impossible for the technical resources of camera and film to stop dancing in action. This is shown, for example, in the series of photographs of LEGNANI, taken in Italy in the 1890s, which show her in process of executing a step. Legnani possessed an exceptionally strong technique and probably could hold positions longer than her Russian contemporaries, who are nearly always depicted stationary or supported in a more difficult position. None of the Legnani photographs would be accepted by a dance publication today, for no attempt has been made to improve on the balletic position or to prettify the feet. This suggests that the photographer was no specialist in ballet and was more concerned with capturing the charm and personality of the ballerina than with illustrating a perfect attitude or arabesque. Dance photographers today have to know a great deal about dance technique and there is danger in becoming obsessed with this knowledge; the photographer, like the dancer, must use technique always as the servant, not the master.

A new approach in studio work occurred in the 1930s and 1940s when Hollywood's insistence upon unnatural glamour forced photography in all theatrical areas to follow suit. Extremely gifted people in this area were the American Maurice Seymour and the Englishman Houston Rogers. The luscious skin tones and the aura of glamour were achieved by using small spotlights, backlighting the hair, shoulders and legs, and a soft fill-in light from high in front. From this period, retouching becomes an integral part of the work. A great deal of this retouching was done straight on to the large format negatives with brush and knife, with a smaller amount of final touching-up on the positive print itself, done by brush and knife again. (Perfectionists would fill in the knife marks on the emulsion of the print with wax, to conceal from cruel eyes the 'plastic surgery' that had been done.)

A photographer who combined the best of the glamorized approach with a strong involvement with the world of ballet and dance was Gordon Anthony. His published collections, notably *Ballet* (London 1937), *The Vic-Wells Ballet* (London 1938), *Russian Ballet* (London 1939), and *Massine* (London 1939), capture the essence of what people thought of as B. Russe in the 1930s, with its starry personalities, and also the springtime years of RB. Gordon Anthony's sister is DE VALOIS, so he was always in close contact with working dancers and he had a unique understanding of ballet.

By the 1930s cameras had already found their way into the theatre. A pioneer of 'action' photography during perf. was Merlyn Severn whose book, *Ballet in Action*, was published in London in 1938. The technical data which she gives, in detail, are amazingly similar to the technique of the best action photographers working today. The small format negative, the high-speed shutter, and the open diaphragm are all techniques still used when taking pictures in the theatre. Her immediate successors were Peggy Delius (most of whose work was destroyed in World War II), Fred Fehl, still active in NY, Baron (Nahum), and Roger Wood, whose photographs are now in the Dance Collection of the NY Public Library. Contemporary dance photography and photographers can be judged – and admired – from the illustrations in this book.

There are no hard-and-fast rules about photographic technique when working in a theatre at a dress rehearsal or a perf. Equipment, exposure and processing must all be selected to suit the requirements of the dance that is to be photographed. For example, in taking pictures of SLEEPING BEAUTY it is important to show the opulence of the setting in the full stage picture whereas in a contemporary dance piece like CELL all that is important is that the claustrophobic intensity of the work is faithfully captured in the pictures. This can often be achieved by the use of blur and grainy film.

A problem all photographers have to cope with when working at rehearsal or in perf. is the habit of lighting directors to use low (dim) lighting for theatrical effect and to put 'follow spots' on the principal dancers. In these conditions, the ballerina may be caught centre stage in an impeccable pose but the stage picture in which she really shines is lost in murky darkness. For special photo-calls, rare now because of the enormous expense, most photographers ask for the light to be built up at the sides of the stage instead of being concentrated on the centre so that the exposure is kept level. But a careful balance must be maintained. The photographer's task is to show the full stage, but to show it in the appropriate atmosphere of light.

Colour presents further problems. In the theatre most lamps have coloured gelatine over them and the colour temperature of the lamps is not right for colour film. The best ploy is to look at the lamps and then balance the colour film by the use of filters. For example, to balance an over-all green lighting of a set a magenta filter is used. The more filters used, the slower the speed of the film and the more you have to compensate with longer exposures. Nearly all colour film is already very slow so in photographing a perf. in action there are times when it is technically impossible to get a good picture.

Superimposing, if done deliberately in the studio for a purpose, can say something about dance; too often it is used as a 'clever' photographic device which may be pictorially effective but tells nothing about the dancer or the dance.

The real technical revolution in the studio has been the advent of strobe lighting. A development of the flashgun from a trough of magnesium which could be ignited to a blinding flash has become a sophisticated powerpack, capable of intensity regulation to the smallest degree, and with a recharging cycle-time of a quarter of a second. In the present writer's experience, the danger of using strobe is that it is now all too easy to 'freeze' movement. The photograph of a dancer caught in mid-air in a spectacular jump is popular with editors and will earn its keep as it will always find a publisher. More rewarding to the photographer, however, in personal fulfilment if not in monetary rewards, are those sessions when editors can be forgotten and photographer and dancer work together to produce *truthful* pictures, in which no commercial considerations are allowed to get between the aspiration of the dancer and the aspiration of the photographer to catch the actual communication of emotion through dancing. ACY

Phrygia, the wife of SPARTACUS

Picasso, Pablo Ruiz, b. Malaga, 1881; d. Mougins, Cannes, 1973. Spanish painter, resident in France. Leader of the École de Paris and the dominating influence on 20th-c. art. COCTEAU drew him into the DIAGHILEV entourage and together they planned PARADE, the first Cubist ballet. Subsequently for Diaghilev he designed TRICORNE, PULCINELLA, *Cuadro Flamenco* (1921), a backcloth for APRÈS-MIDI D'UN FAUNE (1922), and the celebrated curtain for TRAIN BLEU. Designed MASSINE'S *Mercure* for DE BEAUMONT (1924), curtain for PETIT'S *Le Rendezvous* (B. des CE, 1945), curtain and decor for ICARE (1962). Picasso's first wife was a dancer in the Diaghilev B., Olga Khokhlova (d. 1955), a sister of NEMCHINOVA. He made many sketches of dancers in rehearsal. MC
See Douglas Cooper, *Picasso: Theatre* (London and New York 1968)

Piège de Lumière (*Trap of Light*), ballet, ch. TARAS; mus. Jean-Michel Damase; lib. Philippe

Photo by Baron de Meyer, Paris, *c.* 1909, of NIJINSKY in PAVILLON D'ARMIDE

Photo by Gordon Anthony of June Brae as the BLACK QUEEN in CHECKMATE, 1937

Hériat; sc. Félix Labisse; c. André Levasseur. Paris, T. de l'Empire, de Cuevas B., 23 Dec 1952; dan. HIGHTOWER, SKOURATOFF, GOLOVINE. NYST, NYCB, 1 Oct 1964; ltg David Hays; dan. Maria TALLCHIEF, PROKOVSKY, MITCHELL. A fantasy in which escaped convicts in a forest become enchanted with butterflies, which they catch in a trap of light, only to become ensnared and vulnerable like them. Also in repertory of LFB (1969). FM

Pierrot Lunaire, modern dance work, ch. TETLEY; mus. Arnold Schönberg; sc. TER-ARUTUNIAN. NY, Fashion Inst. of Technology, 5 May 1962; dan. Tetley, Linda Hodes, Robert POWELL. The eternal triangle as seen through the *commedia dell'arte* figures of the dark and white clowns and the fickle woman between. Also in repertories of RDB and BR. DM

Piletta, Georges, b. Paris, 1945. French dancer. Paris OBS; *corps de ballet*; *étoile* 1970. Prix R. BLUM 1962. PETIT quickly realized his talents; Piletta created roles in Petit's *Adage et Variations* (1965), *Turangalila* (1968), *Kranerg* (1969), *Formes* (1971), and in *Ecce Homo* (ch. LAZZINI, Paris OC 1971). Dances PRODIGAL SON, AGON, FOUR TEMPERAMENTS, and the classical repertory. M-FC

Pillar of Fire, ballet, 1 act, ch./lib. TUDOR; mus. Arnold Schönberg; sc./c. Jo Mielziner, NY Met, ABT, 8 Apr 1942; dan. KAYE, LAING, CHASE, Annabelle Lyon, Tudor. A ballet about passion and forgiveness; the story of Hagar, a repressed spinster, who fears that her beloved prefers her younger sister. In desperation, she throws herself at a stranger. Her fears were unfounded and she is finally reunited with the man she loves. Revived RSB, 1962; Vienna Staats OB, 1969. FM

Pilobolus Dance Theater, co. formed 1971 at Hanover, NH, by Robb (Moses) Pendleton, Jonathan Wolken, Robby Barnett, and Lee Harris, all undergraduates at Dartmouth College. The unique style of the co. derives from its skilful use of gymnastic body configurations in successive tableaux that link in a narrative flow. A prime example of the co.'s early work is *Anaendrom*. With the acquisition of two women, Martha Clarke and Alison Chase, the co.'s work began to display a male–female dramatic tension that has led to its further artistic development, as in MONKSHOOD'S FAREWELL. The co. is a cooperative; all choreographic design is worked out by the members jointly, as are costume and decor. Occasionally an individual musical credit is listed in their programs. DM

Pineapple Poll, ballet, 1 act, 3 scenes, ch./lib. CRANKO, adapted from William S. Gilbert's Bab Ballad, *The Bumboat Woman's Story*; mus. from Arthur Sullivan's operas, selected and arr. Charles Mackerras; sc./c. Osbert Lancaster. London, SW, SWTB, 13 Mar 1951; dan. FIFIELD, BLAIR, POOLE. Cranko transformed the bumboat woman, Poll, into a pretty young seller of trinkets who, like all the sailors' sweethearts and wives of Portsmouth, is infatuated with the handsome Captain Belaye. She is loved by the potboy Jasper but mocks his devotion. Poll disguises herself as a sailor and, like all the other girls, boards Belaye's ship. To the horror of his 'crew' Belaye returns from shore with his bride Blanche and her chattering Aunt Dimple, but eventually all are placated, Belaye appears resplendent in Admiral's attire, Jasper assumes the glamour of a Captain's uniform, and Poll accepts his suit.

Cranko's first big success with a comedy ballet, brimful of brilliant *demi-caractère* dancing. Also in the repertories of Australian B., NB of Canada, and Joffrey B. Never out of the repertory of the RB. MC

Piollet, Wilfride, b. Drôme, 1943. French dancer. Paris OBS, studied with EGOROVA, R. FRANCHETTI. *Corps de ballet* 1960; *première danseuse* 1966; *étoile* 1969. Created roles in *Zyklus* (ch. DESCOMBEY) 1968; *Constellations* (LIFAR) 1969; *Un Jour ou Deux* (CUNNINGHAM) 1973; *Tristan* (TETLEY) 1974. Dances ballerina roles in the classics, also APOLLO, AGON, FOUR TEMPERAMENTS, ÉTUDES. Guest artist, LFB, 1969; Avignon Fest. 1970. Has a remarkably sure technique and excels in contemporary repertory. She m. GUIZERIX. M-FC

Piper, John, b. Epsom, 1903. English painter and designer. Surrealist in style until 1930 when he reverted to Romantic Naturalism, painting architectural fantasies. Designed ASHTON's *The Quest* (SWB, 1943) and then JOB (CG, 1948). This led to many commissions from Glyndebourne O. and elsewhere. For CRANKO designed *Harlequin in April* (SWTB, 1951) and PRINCE OF THE PAGODAS (RB, 1957). MC

Pistoni, Mario, b. Rome, 1932. Italian dancer and choreographer. Since 1951 at Sc. where partnered FRACCI in SYLPHIDE 1962, also in many works which he created for her, incl. *Francesca da Rimini* (1965) and *La Strada* (1966), based on Federico Fellini's film of the same name. The Sept 1975 Sc. ballet season incl. three Pistoni works: *Francesca* (SAVIGNANO replacing Fracci), *Specchio a Tre Luci*, and *Concerto dell'Albatro*. He m. Fiorella Cova, principal dancer at Sc. FP

Place, The *see* LONDON CONTEMPORARY DANCE THEATRE

Platt, Marc [Marcel LePlat], b. Seattle, WA, 1915. American dancer and choreographer. Studied with Mary Ann Wells and at Cornish S., Seattle. Joined DE BASIL's B. Russe de Monte Carlo as Marc Platoff and became one of the leading character dancers, creating such roles as Malatesta in LICHINE's *Francesca da Rimini* and King Dodon in COQ D'OR. B. Russe de Monte Carlo 1938, danced Devil in ASHTON's *Devil's*

Maya Plisetskaya of the Bolshoy B. in CYGNE

Holiday, etc., and choreographed *Ghost Town* (1939; mus. Richard Rodgers), an American genre ballet. Changed his name to Marc Platt as featured dancer in the Broadway musical *Oklahoma!* (1943). Appeared in many film musicals incl. *Tonight and Every Night* (1945), *Seven Brides for Seven Brothers* (1954). Director of ballet, Radio City Music Hall 1962. DV

Plisetskaya, Maya, b. Moscow, 1925. Soviet dancer. Entered Bolshoy S. 1934, studying with E. GERDT, later with VAGANOVA and MESSERER, her uncle. Danced solo roles with the Bolshoy B. before her graduation 1943, therefore never appeared as a member of the *corps de ballet*. Before graduation created the Cat in LITTLE STORK; roles immediately after graduation incl. the Mazurka in CHOPINIANA, the LILAC FAIRY, and Masha (NUTCRACKER), to which in 1945 she added the title role of L. LAVROVSKY's new version of RAYMONDA. In 1947 danced ODETTE-ODILE, AURORA, MYRTHA and the TSAR-MAIDEN in HUMPBACKED HORSE. Danced Suimbike in SHURALE (1950) and PHRYGIA (1962).Other roles incl. ZAREMA, the title role in LAURENCIA, KITRI, the Mistress of the Copper Mountain in STONE FLOWER, and Lavrovsky's JULIET, which she studied for five years before attempting. Created Carmen in *Carmen Suite* (ch. Alberto Alonso, mus. Georges Bizet, arr. Rodion Shchedrin (her husband), sc./c. Boris Messerer; Moscow, Bolshoy T., 20 Apr 1967); in 1972 choreographed and danced the leading role in ANNA KARENINA. Has danced widely outside Russia, and as guest artist at Paris O. 1961 and 1964. She has also performed with B. XXe S. since 1975. Since ULANOVA's retirement in 1962, Plisetskaya is considered to be the leading dancer in the USSR. She is *prima ballerina assoluta*; People's Artist, USSR, 1959; Lenin Prize, 1964. JS
See Natalia Roslavleva, *Maya Plisetskaya* (Moscow 1968); J. Baril, 'Maya Plisetskaya', *Les Saisons de la Danse* (Paris, Oct 1968) with list of roles and activities

Plucis, Harijs, b. Riga, 1900; d. Vienna, 1970. Latvian dancer and teacher. Trained Latvian NBS, graduating into the co. 1920 and quickly assuming leading roles in all the great classics, also in national ballets. To Paris 1927 to study with LEGAT; joined RUBINSTEIN B. 1928. Returned to Latvia 1931 to set up its State BS which he directed 1932–44. Ballet master of the SWB 1947–56, doing much to broaden its style of dancing. Later taught in Switzerland; 1961–8 was head of the Vienna Staats OBS. His son Andris trained at the London RBS and is now a professional dancer. MC

Poland. Ballet was known in Poland from the 16th c. as a court entertainment. The first Polish co. was founded 1785 during the reign of the last Polish king, Stanislas II Augustus, and lasted until the end of Polish independence (1794), when the country was divided among Russia, Prussia, and Austria. Warsaw belonged to Russia and in 1818 became the cradle of a permanent Polish co., directed by French choreographers Louis Thierry (1818–23) and Maurice Pion (1825–43). The first (1838) of three visits of M. TAGLIONI brought the beginning of Romanticism to Warsaw ballet. The co. already had a high level of dancing, was rich in gifted dancers and had its own good school. Pion and F. TAGLIONI, who succeeded him as director (1843–53), built the repertory mostly of Taglioni's widely known works, such as SYLPHIDE, *Le Pirate* (1841), *La Gitana* (1843) and some created specially for the co. R. TURCZYNOWICZ became assistant director and choreographer 1845, introducing the first Polish versions of many works, e.g. GISELLE (1848), CATARINA (1850), ESMERALDA (1851), CORSAIRE (1857). He took over the directorship of the co. and ballet school 1853. Until his retirement (1866) the co. was at the height of its development and an important centre of European ballet. The Taglioni family, GRISI, and BLASIS were the most prominent of its guest collaborators. It had over 100 dancers, led by K. TURCZYNOWICZ, Aleksander and Antoni TARNOWSKI, and KRZESIŃSKI.

After 1866 the co., under various Italian directors, lost its high level of artistry, although the dancing, in the Italian style, was still good. The best dancer of the period was CHOLEWICKA. At the end of the 19th and beginning of the 20th c., the repertory was strongly influenced by Russian ballet (the first perf. of SWAN LAKE in Poland was 1900). Many Russian ballerinas, e.g. KSHESSINSKA, A. PAVLOVA, and KARSAVINA, visited Warsaw. CECCHETTI, as director of the co. 1902–5, taught a generation of dancers who, after 1910, joined DIAGHILEV, among others IDZIKOWSKI and WOIZIKOWSKI.

The Warsaw co. hardly existed 1910–17, but under the directorship of ZAJLICH was revived and modernized. Under Russian government, the co. was not allowed to create ballets on national plots, so during this period only a few such ballets were staged, the most important being CRACOW WEDDING and the first version of PAN TWARDOWSKI. When the country was freed again in 1918, the most important trend was to fill this gap, the best works being the second version of *Pan Twardowski* and HIGHLANDERS. Another trend was to incl. among the classics some of Diaghilev's ballets. The most prominent dancer was SZMOLC. In 1920 a new centre of ballet was founded in Poznań. The newly founded B. Polonais toured all over Europe 1937–9 with a repertory of Polish ballets. Its director was NIJINSKA, succeeded by Woizikowski.

After World War II Polish ballet had to start again almost from the beginning due to great losses in artists and theatre buildings. Today there are eight state cos, connected with opera houses, the most important in Warsaw. DRZEWIECKI's very important Polish Dance T. was founded 1973 in Poznań. Among the best dancers are BITTNERÓWNA, BONIUSZKO, Maria Krzyszkowska, SAWICKA, GRUCA, STRZAŁKOWSKI, and SZYMAŃSKI. A new generation is studying in five state ballet schools under Polish and Russian teachers. JPU

Ponomaryov, Vladimir, b. St Petersburg, 1892; d. Budapest, 1951. Soviet dancer and teacher. Graduated from St Petersburg TS 1910; soloist Kirov T. 1917–51. An excellent partner, he danced all the great classical roles. Renowned for his teaching: he formed most of the leading dancers of the Kirov B., conducted a *classe de perfectionnement* from 1931. Assistant artistic director, Kirov B. 1935–8; acting artistic director 1941–4. Choreographed version of RED POPPY with F. LOPUKHOV and Leonid Leontiev; revived SYLPHIDE, BAYADÈRE (with CHABUKIANI). Senior *répétiteur*, Kirov B. Honoured Artist, RSFSR. NR

Pontois, Noëlla, b. Vendôme, 1943. French dancer. Paris OBS 1953. *Corps de ballet* 1961. Prix R. Blum 1964. *Première danseuse* 1966; *étoile* 1968. Guest artist, LFB, 1967, partner of NUREYEV. She m. dancer Daini Kudo 1967. Dances in ballets by PETIT, BALANCHINE, and ROBBINS; excels particularly in the classical repertory. Possesses lightness, exceptional balance, romantic grace, and delicate style. M-FC
See J. C. Diénis, 'Noëlla Pontois', *Les Saisons de la Danse* (Paris, Jan 1973) with list of roles and other activities

Poole, David, b. Cape Town, 1925. S. African dancer, choreographer, and producer. Trained by Cecily Robinson and HOWES at UCT BS. Danced with SWTB 1947–55, SW and BR 1955–6. At SWTB he created many roles in CRANKO's ballets, incl. Jasper in PINEAPPLE POLL; also danced leading roles in other ballets in SWTB's repertoire, most notably Pierrot in CARNAVAL. In 1957 he taught at JOOSS's Folkwang S., Essen, and danced at the Edinburgh Fest. Produced ballets and appeared as guest artist and producer with UCT 1952, 1957, and 1958. Joined staff of UCT BS and co. 1959, producing ballets for the co. and the Eoan Group, Cape Town. When UCT B. became CAPAB B. in 1963, Poole continued as ballet master; artistic director from 1969. In 1973 he succeeded Howes as principal of the UCT BS. He produced all the classics for CAPAB; has also choreographed original works, e.g. *The Snow Queen* (1961), *Le Cirque* (1973), *Rain Queen* (1973), based on a local African theme as conceived by STAFF, *Kami* (1976). MG

Portugal. As in other European countries, the Portuguese national dance style grew from court perfs and the combined effects of large casts and sumptuous productions. In the 16th c., the playwright Gil Vicente added dramatic structure to the dance of courtly feasts, and thus achieved a kind of BALLET DE COUR. But the Portuguese renaissance was brief, and the decline of court life prevented further development of Vicente's theatre. The 60 years of Spanish occupation (1580–1640) and the austere restoration that lasted until nearly 1700 smothered most dance activity. Only with the reign of João V, who imported gold and diamonds from Brazil in the first half of the 18th c., did the arts flourish again in a flamboyant mockery of Louis XIV's court. Italian artists built public and royal theatres.

In 1755, Lisbon's earthquake put an end to Portuguese baroque extravaganzas, and the new Royal OH that opened in 1793 was a public theatre built by a new capitalist aristocracy. The opening perf. in this theatre incl. an allegorical ballet, *La Felicità Lusitana* ch. Gaetano Gioja, a former pupil of VIGANÒ. These allegorical ballets dominated dance in Lisbon for the first half of the 19th c. Their librettos were based on current events; real troops joined the dancers on stage, e.g. Wellington's soldiers who came to fight Napoleon celebrated their victory in dance.

For years, their popularity prevented any acceptance of the Romantic ballet. In 1838 Mlle Clara danced SYLPHIDE and other roles of M. TAGLIONI, and MAYWOOD danced GISELLE 1843 (staged Gustave Carey), to a lukewarm reception. Even the seasons of Romantic ballet produced by SAINT-LÉON (1854–6) created only brief interest, and when BLASIS arrived in 1858, he was all but ignored. The decline of the Portuguese OH followed hard on the decline of Italian dance, and until the 20th c., only LANNER's Austrian co., which presented *Giselle* 1870, provoked any interest.

Sociology and politics in the 20th c. have worked against the development of a lasting dance tradition in Portugal. DIAGHILEV's B. Russes were poorly received in 1917, and the National OH has produced only brief seasons.

Even the creation of three dance groups, Verde Gaio (founded 1940), a folk co., Margarida de Abreu's Circulo de Iniciação Coreográfica (founded 1944), and the sponsored Grupo Gulbenkian de Bailado (founded 1966) have not produced a national policy for dance. However, professionalism has grown through the Gulbenkian Group, with GORE and Milko Sparemblek as artistic directors. It has staged the works of such choreographers as BUTLER, CULLBERG, SANASARDO, LUBOVITCH, and Sparemblek as well as the classics. Young Portuguese choreographers have begun to show their own work. But the future of dance in Portugal depends on the chances afforded the art by the newborn democratic government of the country. JSAS

See José Sasportes, 'Feast and Folias: The Dance in Portugal', *Dance Perspectives*, No. 42 (New York 1970); José Sasportes, *História da Dança em Portugal* (Lisbon 1970)

Poulenc, Francis, b. Paris, 1899; d. Paris, 1963. French composer. Member of Les Six (with AURIC, MILHAUD, Arthur Honegger, Germaine Tailleferre, and Louis Durey), all of whom, save the last, collaborated on *Les Mariés de la Tour Eiffel* (Paris 1921; ch. BÖRLIN) for B. Suédois. Poulenc also collaborated on *L'Éventail de Jeanne* (Paris 1929; ch. Yvonne Franck and Alice Bourgat) with, among others, RAVEL, Auric, Milhaud, Jacques Ibert, Albert Roussel and Florent Schmitt. Poulenc's other ballet scores incl. BICHES; *Aubade* (Paris 1929; ch. NIJINSKA) for a *soirée* of Vicomte de Noailles (Paris 1930; ch. BALANCHINE, for Nemchinova Co. 1930), and *Les Animaux Modèles* (Paris 1942; ch. LIFAR). All of them exemplify Poulenc's gaiety and sophistication, qualities equally apparent in his *Trio for Oboe, Bassoon and Piano* (1926), which ASHTON used for *Les Masques* (London 1933). DH

Powell [Needham], Ray, b. Hitchin, 1925. English dancer, ballet master, choreographer, and director. SWBS 1941. SW (Royal) B 1942–62 (Army Service 1944–7), soloist, assistant ballet master. Australian B. 1962, ballet master, character principal; assistant artistic director; associate director 1975. An outstanding character dancer with a gift for pathos (he danced Bootface in LADY AND THE FOOL) and a relish for comedy (SANCHO PANZA, filmed 1973). His own ballets incl. *One in Five* (1960; mus. Josef and Johann Strauss), *Just for Fun* (1963; mus. Dmitri Shostakovich), *Symphony in Gold* (1969; mus. Felix Mendelssohn). MBE 1976. KSW

Powell, Robert, b. Hawaii, 1941. American dancer. Graduated from High S. of Performing Arts, NY, 1958, and joined GRAHAM Dance Co., dancing leading roles in most of the repertory. Has also danced with the cos of O'DONNELL, LIMÓN, Norman Walker, MCKAYLE, and TETLEY, and with LCDT. As well as dancing in Graham's co., he is now its rehearsal director. DV

Preobrazhenska [-ya], Olga, b. St Petersburg, 1870; d. Paris, 1962. Russian dancer and teacher. Graduated from St Petersburg Imperial S. 1889, pupil of IVANOV, M. PETIPA, and Anna Johansson. Entered Maryinsky T. 1889, remaining for 25 years. Studied privately with CECCHETTI and Caterina Beretta (in Milan). Starting in the *corps de ballet*, she was a ballerina by 1893 and became one of the greatest dancers of her time. She had 35 ballets in her repertoire including RAYMONDA, PAQUITA, GISELLE, CORSAIRE, HALTE DE CAVALERIE, DON QUIXOTE. She was impeccable in technique and especially charming in vivacious roles such as LISE. Intensely musical, she gave her own rendering to each role and her range extended from the old ballets to the first creations of FOKINE: *Les Nuits d'Égypte*, PAVILLON D'ARMIDE, CHOPINIANA. Guest appearances at Milan Sc. 1904, the Paris O. 1909, London Hippodrome 1910, and danced in South America 1912. Taught in Petrograd S. and at Akim Volynsky's private 'S. of Russian B.' 1917–21. Exerted considerable influence on VAGANOVA. In 1922 she went to Paris (after spending a short time in Berlin) and in 1923 opened her famous studio in the Salle Wacker. She taught there until 1960, and formed countless great dancers. NR/MC

See Valerian Svetlov, *Preobrazhenskaya* (St Petersburg 1902), containing many illustrations and the ballerina's own statements

Preobrazhensky, Vladimir, b. St Petersburg, 1912. Soviet dancer, choreographer, and teacher. Graduated from Leningrad Choreographic S., class of PONOMARYOV; in State T. of O. and B., Leningrad, 1931–5; from 1935 Kirov B.; a leading soloist at Sverdlovsk O. 1935–9, and Kiev 1939–41; at Moscow, Bolshoy T., 1942–58, partnering ULANOVA, LEPESHINSKAYA, and other prominent ballerinas. Roles incl. SIEGFRIED, Evgeny (BRONZE HORSEMAN), Frondozo (LAURENCIA), ALBRECHT, Vaslav (FOUNTAIN OF BAKHCHISARAY). Had vast concert repertoire. Manager Bolshoy B. Co. 1960–3. From 1965 headed ballet co. of Mosconcert. Taught at

Moscow S. 1945–50. A tall, excellently built *premier danseur noble*. Honoured Artist, RSFSR, and Ukrainian SSR. NR

Présages, Les, ballet, 4 parts, ch./lib. MASSINE; mus. TCHAIKOVSKY (Fifth Symphony); sc./c. André Masson. Monte Carlo, B. Russe de Monte Carlo, 13 Apr 1933; dan. VERCHININA, BARONOVA, RIABOUCHINSKA, LICHINE, WOIZIKOWSKI. The first of Massine's 'symphonic' ballets. The underlying theme was man's triumph over adversity. MC

Price family. A dynasty of dancers started by James Price (1761–1805), an English circus rider and member of a pantomime troupe who settled in Copenhagen, Denmark. His granddaughter Juliette Price (1831–1906) was the most famous; she created principal roles in August BOURNONVILLE's FOLK LEGEND and FLOWER FESTIVAL AT GENZANO, and was his favourite SYLPHIDE, after GRAHN, who created the role in Copenhagen. Her brother Valdemar (1836–1908) was also a leading dancer at the Royal T., Copenhagen. Their grandniece Ellen created the title role in BECK's LITTLE MERMAID and was the model for the famous little statue at Langelinie. Several cousins of Juliette also became dancers and one of them, Julius, danced and then taught at the Vienna Staats O. SKJ

Primitive Mysteries, modern dance work, ch./c. GRAHAM; mus. HORST; dan. Graham, and ensemble. NY, Craig T., 2 Feb 1931. With a group of 12 women and herself as the central figure who could be both Virgin and Crucified, Graham sketched an entire religious ritual based on the faith of the Christian Indians of the American Southwest, but her bold, severe stage canvas looks nothing like any known church rite. DM/MBS

Primus, Pearl, b. Trinidad, 1919. American dancer and choreographer. Ph.D. in anthropology, Columbia Univ. Dance debut 1943. Visited Africa 1948. Her interest in the dances of Africa and the Caribbean has shown its influence in many works, notably *Fanga* (1949) and *The Wedding* (1961). She has also demonstrated an interest in racial questions in *Strange Fruit* (1943), a dance examining a lynching. Choreographed many Broadway musical shows and also the dances in Eugene O'Neill's play *The Emperor Jones* (1947). Her works have been performed by the AILEY American Dance T. as well as her own co. She has also been active as a teacher. She m. dancer Percival Borde. DM

Prince Igor (strictly, Polovtsian Dances from *Prince Igor*), ballet, 1 scene, ch. FOKINE; mus. Aleksandr Borodin (from his opera); sc./c. Nicholas Roerich. Paris, T. du Châtelet, DIAGHILEV's B. Russes, 19 May 1909; dan. BOLM, S. FEDOROVA, Elena Smirnova. A plotless work but with a hint of 'story' in the relationships of the warriors to their captive maidens. The choreography is rooted in Tartar folk dance with authentic variety between the powerful dancing of the men and the delicate steps of the women. Roerich's brooding set of a Tartar camp and above all the dancing of the men electrified Paris. The work has been revived for countless cos. Ironically, when GRIGORIEV revived it for the RB at CG 24 Mar 1965 for a real Tartar (NUREYEV) it was a failure. MC

Prince of the Pagodas, The, ballet, 3 acts, ch./lib. CRANKO; mus. (commissioned) Benjamin Britten; sc. PIPER; c. Desmond Heeley. London, CG, RB, 1 Jan 1957; dan. BERIOSOVA, FARRON, BLAIR, Anya Linden, LANE, SHAW, EDWARDS. A wicked princess, Belle Épine, tricks her father and his favourite daughter, Belle Rose, out of his kingdom. The Prince of the Pagodas is bewitched as a salamander until (as in the *Beauty and the Beast* fairy story) Belle Rose truly loves him. He then returns to his proper shape, restores the King and marries Belle Rose. Act II consists of a journey through the elements to the land of the pagodas and the last act is one of general rejoicing. Despite the beauty of the score, its length in relation to the dramatic events has always robbed the ballet of success – Britten refused to make any changes. Cranko revived the original at Milan, Sc., 1957 and for his Stuttgart co., 1960. Other choreographers (A. CARTER in Munich, ORLIKOVSKY in Basel) have used the score but encountered similar problems. In Russia, VINOGRADOV staged it at Leningrad, Kirov T., 30 Dec 1972, under the title *Enchanted Prince* (*Zacharovanniy Prints*) but, again, its life was short. The first British full-length ballet and the only one to have a score specifically written by Britten, who conducted the first perf. MC

Prisoner of the Caucasus, The (*Kavkazsky Plennik*), ballet, 3 acts with prologue, ch. L. LAVROVSKY; mus. ASAFYEV; lib. Nikolay Volkov in collaboration with L. Lavrovsky and I. Zilberstein after Aleksandr Pushkin's poem of same title. Leningrad, Maly T., 14 Apr 1938; dan. Elena Chikvaidze. New version, ch. ZAKHAROV. Moscow, Bolshoy T., 26 Apr 1938; dan. Marianna Bogolubskaya, GABOVICH, LEPESHINSKAYA. Circassian national dances, picturesque scenes of old St Petersburg, and the touching image of the Circassian Maid throwing herself into the river having liberated the Prisoner from her mountain village proved a formula for success. The Prisoner's part was mimed rather than danced since he spent most of the time in chains. NR

See Yuri Slonimsky, *Soviet Ballet* (Leningrad and Moscow 1952)

Prisoners, The, ballet, 1 act, 2 scenes, ch. DARRELL; mus. BARTÓK; sc./c. Barry Kay. Dartington Hall, Devon, Western TB, 24 June 1957; dan. MUSITZ. Two prisoners escape and make their way to the house of the older prisoner. His wife falls in love with the younger one and incites him to murder her husband. Terrified to leave the house, he has exchanged one prison for another. MC

Prix de Lausanne *see* SWITZERLAND

Prodigal Son, ballet, 3 scenes, ch. BALANCHINE; mus. PROKOFIEV; lib. KOCHNO; sc./c. Georges Rouault. (As *Le Fils Prodigue*) Paris, T. Sarah Bernhardt, DIAGHILEV's B. Russes, 21 May 1929; dan. LIFAR, DUBROVSKA. The Biblical parable (St Luke 15: 11–32) of the son who wastes his inheritance in riotous living but is yet welcomed home again. This version revived NYCB 1950, RB 1973. LICHINE used same music and decor for his version, Sydney, de Basil co., 1938. FM

Prodigal Son, The, ballet, ch. CRAMÉR; mus. Hugo Alfvén; sc. Rune Lindström. Stockholm, RSB, 27 Apr 1957; dan. E. VON ROSEN, HOLMGREN. Based on early wall paintings of Biblical themes in farmhouses in Dalarna, Sweden. Folklore, folk music, and folk dances given character to the ballet, but classical movements are also used. AGS

Prokhorova, Violetta *see* ELVIN

Prokofiev, Sergey Sergeyevich, b. Sontsovka, Ukraine, 1891; d. Moscow, 1953. Russian composer. For DIAGHILEV he wrote *Chout* (Paris 1921; ch. LARIONOV and Taddeo Slavinsky), *Le Pas d'Acier* (Paris 1927; ch. MASSINE), PRODIGAL SON; for the Paris O. *Sur le Borysthène* (1932; ch. LIFAR). In 1933 Prokofiev returned to Russia and henceforth faced increasing criticism for his lack of musical accessibility, and lack of 'socialist realism'. His ROMEO AND JULIET, rejected by the Bolshoy B., Moscow, was first produced Brno. CINDERELLA fared better, but his last ballet, STONE FLOWER, ran into difficulties and was much revised before its posthumous premiere. Today his later ballet scores, especially *Cinderella* and *Romeo and Juliet*, are popular throughout the world. DH

Prokovsky [Pokrovsky], André, b. Paris, 1939, of Russian parents. French dancer, choreographer, and director. Studied with Nicholas Zverev, PERETTI, KISS. Early appearances in Paris with cos of CHARRAT and PETIT. Silver medal, Moscow Youth Fest., 1957. Principal dancer with LFB 1957–60 (sharing limelight with GILPIN) and with DE CUEVAS B. 1960–2. With NYCB 1963–6. Principal dancer with LFB 1966–72, where his partnership with SAMSOVA (his wife) became celebrated. They formed their own co., New London B., 1972 to present new ballets as well as their own virtuoso numbers such as the CORSAIRE *pas de deux*. By 1977 it was in dire financial straits, having failed to win any regular subsidy. As a dancer, Prokovsky is powerful and exciting with an engaging stage personality. A good actor (PIÈGE DE LUMIÈRE) and brilliant in works like ÉTUDES. For his own co. choreographed several ballets well tailored to the talents of the group, since they were all of soloist standard. MC

Pugni, Cesare, b. Genoa, 1802; d. St Petersburg, 1870. Italian composer and conductor. Educated Milan Cons. Wrote ballets for Sc., and Paris O. Resident ballet composer Her Majesty's T., London, where his many scores incl. the following, all ch. PERROT: ONDINE, ESMERALDA, PAS DE QUATRE, CATARINA. In 1851 he went to St Petersburg, where he composed HUMPBACKED HORSE, and many works for M. PETIPA, among them: FILLE DU PHARAON, *Roi Candaule* (1868). A quick worker, Pugni is said to have written the music for more than 300 ballets and is usually derogated for his prolific output. His surviving scores, however, are melodic and have a good deal of charm. DH

Pulcinella, ballet with songs, 1 act, ch. MASSINE; mus. STRAVINSKY after Giovanni Battista Pergolesi; lib. from the *commedia dell'arte*; sc./c. PICASSO. Paris O., DIAGHILEV's B. Russes, 15 May 1920; dan. KARSAVINA, TCHERNICHEVA, NEMCHINOVA, Massine, IDZIKOWSKI, CECCHETTI. Diaghilev's choice of Pergolesi as the musical source of this *commedia dell'arte* ballet set Stravinsky on the path of neoclassicism: the score and Picasso's Cubist evocation of a moonlit Naples street were the most distinguished features of the piece. Revived Milan, Sc., 10 Dec 1971; Wolftrap Farm Park, VA, CCJB, 15 Aug 1974. Many versions by other choreographers, incl. F. LOPUKHOV, Leningrad, 1925; JOOSS, Essen, 1932; WOIZIKOWSKI for his own co., 1935; BALANCHINE and ROBBINS, NYCB, 1972. DV

Puppenfee, Die (*The Fairy Doll*), pantomime-*divertissement*, 1 act, ch. Josef Hassreiter; mus. Josef Bayer; lib. Franz Gaul; sc./c. Anton Brioschi. Vienna, Hof O., 4 Oct 1888. The story concerns dolls who come to life at night in a toyshop (as in BOUTIQUE FANTASQUE). In 1905 LANNER choreographed a version for GENÉE at the Empire T., London. In 1906 SERGUEEFF and LEGAT staged another version in St Petersburg which was revived by A. PAVLOVA (ch. KHLUSTIN, sc./c. Mstislav Dobuzhinsky) in NY in the early 1920s and became one of the most famous *divertissements* in her repertory. Still in the repertory of the Vienna Staats O. MC

Pushkin, Aleksandr, b. St Petersburg, 1907; d. Leningrad, 1970. Soviet dancer and teacher. Graduated from Leningrad Choreographic S. 1925, class of PONOMARYOV. Debut with SEMYONOVA in SAINT-LÉON's *La Source*. Danced in all classical ballets and partnered many celebrated ballerinas. Taught male class and *pas de deux* from 1932, developed into outstanding teacher. His pupils are distinguished by nobility of manner, excellent classical form, and devotion to their art. From 1951 he conducted the *classe de perfectionnement* at Kirov B. Honoured Art Worker, RSFSR. NR

Q R

Qarrtsiluni, ballet, 1 act, ch./lib. H. LANDER and Knudåge Riisager; mus. Riisager; sc. Svend Johansen. Copenhagen, RDB, 21 Feb 1942; dan. N. B. LARSEN. A ritual dance of celebration as the Eskimos watch the sun begin to rise again after the long, dark Greenland winter. Performed in Germany and Italy with new choreographies, and at the Paris O. 1960 with Lander's choreography, staged by himself. SKJ

Quadri, Alicia, b. 1954. Argentine dancer. Studied with Gloria Kazda and RUANOVA; joined the co. of the T. Colón 1970. Auditioned for and danced with the NB of Canada, NY 1974. A romantic ballerina, charming in SPECTRE DE LA ROSE and as Effie in SYLPHIDE, a bright hope of Argentine ballet. JUL

Radice, Attilia, b. Taranto, 1913. Italian dancer and teacher. Entered Milan Sc. BS 1923. Principal dancer Sc. and later T. dell'O., Rome, where she took over the direction of the BS 1958. FP

Radius, Alexandra, b. Amsterdam, 1942. Dutch dancer. Studied with Nel Rooss and at age 15 joined Netherlands B. as a soloist. In 1959 became a founder member of NDT; created many roles in ballets by van DANTZIG and van MANEN. Went with her husband and usual partner EBBELAAR to ABT 1968 as soloist; from 1969 principal; 1970 returned to the Netherlands as a principal dancer with Dutch NB, with which she danced the great classics as well as the BALANCHINE repertory, and modern works by van Dantzig and van Manen, notably in the latter's TWILIGHT and ADAGIO HAMMERKLAVIER. Danced with NUREYEV autumn 1975 on European tour (BAYADÈRE, CORSAIRE) and in summer 1976 with Nureyev and Friends at London Coliseum. Joined B. International 1976; also stayed with Dutch NB. MC

Radunsky, Aleksandr, b. Moscow, 1912. Soviet dancer, choreographer, and teacher. From a family of famous circus clowns. Graduated from Moscow Bolshoy BS 1930 into *corps de ballet*, Bolshoy T. Prominent character soloist and dance actor 1935–62. Created Peter I in BRONZE HORSEMAN, Capulet in L. LAVROVSKY's Moscow version of ROMEO AND JULIET. Unsurpassed in mime roles of the classical repertory, especially the Duke of Courland (GISELLE). Choreographed, with Nikolay Popko and Lev Pospekhin, LITTLE STORK, *Svetlana*, CRIMSON SAILS, HUMPBACKED HORSE. Now ballet master of Soviet Army Song and Dance Ensemble. Honoured Art Worker, RSFSR. NR

Rainbow 'Round My Shoulder, modern dance work, ch. McKAYLE; mus. prison songs of the American South; c. Domingo A. Rodriguez. NY, YM-YWHA 92nd St, 10 May 1959; dan. HINKSON, McKayle. The harsh reality of life on a prison chain gang and the momentary escape into dreams of a happier past. DM

Rainer, Yvonne, b. San Francisco, CA, 1934. American *avant-garde* choreographer and dancer. Studied acting and, later, dance with GRAHAM, CUNNINGHAM, HALPRIN, and Edith Stephen, and composition with Robert Dunn. Began to choreograph 1961. Associated with the *avant-garde* Judson Dance T. at its inception in 1962. Performed with WARING, Aileen Passloff, Beverly Schmidt, and Judith Dunn, and has had her own co. intermittently. She m. and was divorced from painter Al Held. Has worked with artists such as Robert Morris and Robert Rauschenberg. She is concerned with the physical quality of simple tasks and natural, non-dance movement. The form of her dances is often open-ended with parts that can be interchanged or inserted into other dances. She has worked with film and has written about her dances, most notably in *Work 1961–1973* (New York 1974). Works incl.: *At My Body's House* (1964; mus. Dietrich Buxtehude and radio transmission by Billy Klüver), *Parts of Some Sextets* (1965; taped excerpts of the diary of William Bentley), *The Mind Is a Muscle* (1966–8; mus. Dimitri Tiomkin, Henry Mancini, Greenbriar Boys, Frank Sinatra, John Giorno, and Jefferson Airplane), *Rose Fractions* (1969; mus. Chambers Brothers), and *Continuous Project – Altered Daily* (1970; popular music). JD

RainForest, modern dance work, ch. CUNNINGHAM; mus. David Tudor; sc. Andy Warhol. Buffalo, NY, Upton Auditorium, 9 Mar 1968; dan. Cunningham, C. BROWN, DILLEY, Albert Reid, Sandra Neels, SOLOMONS. The dancers' simple, direct reactions to one another are unclouded by complex social demands. DM

Rainò, Alfredo, b. Rome, 1938. Italian dancer. Rome OHS 1947–57. Debut as principal dancer Rome 1961. TERABUST's partner Rome O. in COPPÉLIA, NUTCRACKER, CINDERELLA, SYMPHONY IN C, SYLPHIDE, ROMEO AND JULIET, GISELLE, etc. FP

Rake's Progress, The, ballet, 6 scenes, ch. DE VALOIS; mus./lib. Gavin Gordon after William Hogarth (1697–1764); sc./c. Rex Whistler after Hogarth. London, SWT, SWB, 20 May 1935; dan. GORE, MARKOVA, TURNER. Revived CG, RB, 18 Mar 1946. Closely based on the series of Hogarth's paintings depicting the ruin of a young man who

Dame Marie Rambert, with a statuette of herself and ASHTON in TRAGEDY OF FASHION, made by Astride Zydower to celebrate the 50th anniversary of the B. Rambert

dissipates his fortune and dies in a madhouse, despite the efforts of a young girl (whom he has betrayed) to save him. An early example of the dramatic power of English dancers, every character being sharply realized. The structure of the scenario and the music are theatrically stunning. Still in the RB repertory; a great success in the USSR when the RB toured there. Staged by de Valois in Turkey 1969 and Zürich 1976. Also danced Munich, 1956; Ghent 1972. MC

Ralov [Petersen], Børge, b. Copenhagen, 1908. Danish dancer and choreographer. Entered RDBS 1918; soloist 1933; first solo dancer 1942–57, the first to receive this title in Denmark. The foremost Danish dancer of his time in both August BOURNONVILLE and international style, dancing over a long period with M. LANDER. Among his best roles were those in PETRUSHKA, SPECTRE DE LA ROSE, and NAPOLI (Gennaro). Became instructor at the RDB 1934 and teacher RDBS. His ballets incl. *Widow in the Mirror* (1934) and *Four Temperaments* (mus. Carl Nielsen, Symphony No. 2). Left the Royal T., became ballet instructor and choreographer, Danish Radio and TV. He m. but later divorced K. RALOV. SKJ

Ralov [Gnatt], Kirsten, b. Bạden bei Wien, Austria, 1922, of Danish parents. Danish dancer and choreographer. Grew up in Copenhagen; entered RDBS with her brother Poul Gnatt 1929; soloist 1942–62, then left the stage but stayed in the ballet as instructor. Danced international repertory from *L'Apprenti Sorcier* to AURORA'S WEDDING as well as the chief August BOURNONVILLE parts in FAR FROM DENMARK to NAPOLI. As a teacher and producer she has worked with success both in Denmark and from Australia to the USA, specializing in the Bournonville repertory and technique. After divorcing B. RALOV, she m. BJØRNSSON. SKJ

Rambert, Dame Marie [Cyvia Rambam], b. Warsaw, 1888. Polish dancer and teacher. Daughter of a Warsaw bookseller and his equally cultivated wife (of Russian origin), she soon acquired a passion for Russian literature, later to spread to poetry and drama of other lands. Sent by her parents to Paris after the 1905 Warsaw uprising, ostensibly to study medicine but really to keep her out of trouble, she entered the city's artistic life. Began to arrange her own dances for fashionable parties, in the style of I. DUNCAN. In 1910 she went to study at DALCROZE's summer school at Geneva and remained with him for three years, becoming an assistant teacher at his Dresden school. When DIAGHILEV and NIJINSKY visited Dresden Dalcroze recommended her to help NIJINSKY with the difficult rhythms of SACRE DU PRINTEMPS. She became his friend and joined the co. Inspired by KARSAVINA, her interest in classical ballet caught fire on the co.'s 1913 S. American tour. At the outbreak of World War I she left Paris for London, where she created a ballet *La Pomme d'Or* (1917) in which she danced and in which she first attracted attention. On 3 Mar 1918 she married the playwright Ashley Dukes and became a British subject. She opened a studio in 1920 while continuing her own studies in ballet with ASTAFYEVA and CECCHETTI; among her first pupils was ASHTON.

In 1930 the first perf. was given by The Marie Rambert Dancers, soon to become the BALLET RAMBERT and the BALLET CLUB was formed. It was her indomitable spirit that kept her co. alive through many vicissitudes. She not only had a shrewd eye for possible choreographic talent but also a remarkable gift for finding and encouraging designers and an ability to draw from dancers gifts of expression they did not know they possessed. Her ever-inquiring mind and the breadth of her knowledge and interest in the arts fuelled her co. The liveliness of her personality, her wit, perception and gaiety were undimmed in old age. CBE 1954; *Chevalier*, Légion d'Honneur 1957; DBE 1962. D.Litt., Univ. of Sussex 1964. Wrote her autobiography *Quicksilver* (London and New York 1972) and helped KIRSTEIN with his book *Nijinsky Dancing* (London and New York 1975) – a task that gave her intense happiness.

Her two daughters became dancers. Angela (Mrs David Ellis) now directs the Rambert S., Lulu retired from the stage after marriage. MC

See Mary Clarke, *Dancers of Mercury* (London 1962); Clement Crisp, Anya Sainsbury, and Peter Williams, eds, *Fifty Years of Ballet Rambert* (souvenir program) (London 1976); list of her activities in *Les Saisons de la Danse* (Paris, Nov 1971)

Rameau, Jean-Philippe, b. Dijon, 1683; d. Paris, 1764. French composer, important for the brilliance and variety of his dance music, by means of which he also attempted to depict character and situation. Rameau continued the work of LULLY in giving ballet a predominant place in the lyric theatre. He wrote several ballets (e.g. *Pigmalion*, Paris 1748) and *opéra-*

ballets (e.g. INDES GALANTES), and his operas (e.g. *Dardanus*, Paris 1739) feature much dancing. DH

Rameau, Pierre, French dancing master and author. His book *Le Maître à Danser* (Paris 1725) is principally a guide to social dancing but had considerable effect on theatrical dance as he used great stage dancers as models of perfection of form. The book was translated as *The Dancing Master* by the English teacher John Essex in 1728, and by C. BEAUMONT (London 1931, New York 1975). MC

Rao, Shanta, b. Mangalore, 1930. Indian dancer. The first woman to master the male *Kathakali* style of SW India. Also a fine dancer of *Mohini Attam* and *Dasi Attam*. RM

Rassine [Rays], Alexis, b. Kaunas, Lithuania, 1919, of Russian parentage. Russian dancer and teacher. Grew up in S. Africa, where he had first lessons. Studied Paris with PREOBRAZHENSKA and VOLININ, London with VOLKOVA and IDZIKOWSKI. Professional debut in French revue *Bal Tabarin*. To England 1939 to dance with various cos before joining SWB 1942; quickly assumed principal roles. Partnered FONTEYN and CHAUVIRÉ with SWB and RB; toured S. Africa with NERINA 1952, 1955. Made a vital contribution to British ballet during World War II and immediate postwar years as a *danseur noble*, when most British male dancers were on war service. His endearing personality made him an ideal FRANZ; he had a unique gift for illuminating minor but important roles e.g. the Rake's friend in RAKE'S PROGRESS and Elihu in JOB. Resident in England; opened a school in London 1976. MC

Ravel, Maurice, b. Ciboure, Basse-Pyrenées, 1875; d. Paris, 1937. French composer, whose ballet scores are marked by brilliant orchestration and vivid theatricalism. For DIAGHILEV he wrote DAPHNIS ET CHLOÉ, for RUBINSTEIN *Boléro* (Paris 1929, ch. NIJINSKA), and, again for Diaghilev, though rejected by him and then accepted by Rubinstein, VALSE. He also orchestrated two of his piano works for the stage: *Ma Mère l'Oye* and, as *Adelaïde, ou le Langage des Fleurs* (Paris 1912; ch. Natalia Trouhanova), his *Valses Nobles et Sentimentales*. Ravel's music has often been appropriated by later choreographers, notably ASHTON (*Daphnis and Chloe*, London 1951). Balanchine used *La Valse* and *Valses Nobles et Sentimentales* for his *La Valse* (NY 1951) and also staged Ravel's '*fantaisie lyrique*', *L'Enfant et les Sortilèges* three times: Monte Carlo 1925, and New York 1946 and 1975, the last as part of a Ravel centennial festival given by NYCB, when 16 new productions were staged, incl. Balanchine's *Sonatine* and TOMBEAU DE COUPERIN and ROBBINS's CONCERTO IN G. DH

Rayet, Jacqueline, b. Paris, 1932. French dancer. Paris OBS 1942; studied with ZAMBELLI, EGOROVA, KISS. *Corps de ballet* 1946, *première danseuse* 1956, *étoile* 1961. Guest artist Hamburg and Geneva. Created important roles in ballets by contemporary choreographers. Dances in GISELLE, SWAN LAKE, FOUR TEMPERAMENTS, *Apollon-Musagète* (*see* APOLLO), PETRUSHKA. Organized Brantôme Fest. 1958–75. Exceptionally musical, versatile, with strong dramatic gifts. *Chevalier*, Légion d'Honneur, 1973. M-FC
See J.-P. Hersin, 'Jacqueline Rayet', *Les Saisons de la Danse* (Paris, Nov 1969)

Raymonda, ballet, 3 acts, 4 scenes with an apotheosis, ch. M. PETIPA; mus. GLAZUNOV; lib. Lydia Pashkova and Petipa; sc. Orest Allegri, Konstantin Ivanov, Piotr Lambin; c. Ekaterina Ofizerova and Ivan Kaffi. St Petersburg, Maryinsky T., 19 Jan 1898; dan. LEGNANI. The ballet was written in close collaboration: Petipa prepared the detailed plan, Glazunov composed superb symphonic music for it in three movements, but they were handicapped by the idiotic and virtually incomprehensible libretto, set in medieval Provence and involving the beautiful Raymonda, her Crusader lover Jean de Brienne, the wicked Saracen Abdérâme, who tries to abduct her, the ghost of a White Lady, and even King Andrew II of Hungary. However, Petipa's ch., especially the *Grand Pas Hongrois*, Raymonda's many variations, and the famous male *pas de quatre*, brought long life to this work, which served as a vehicle for generations of Russian ballerinas incl. GELTSER, PREOBRAZHENSKA, KARSAVINA, SPESSIVTSEVA, E. GERDT, SEMYONOVA, PLISETSKAYA. Remained in original version in Leningrad repertoire until late 1930s; revived with new lib. by SLONIMSKY and VAINONEN, with ULANOVA in title role, 18 Mar 1938. Revived in version closer to original, ch. SERGEYEV; sc. VIRSALADZE; Leningrad, Kirov T., 30 Apr 1948. First Moscow production Bolshoy T., 23 Jan 1900, ch. KHLUSTIN and GORSKY, who made his own new version, sc. Konstantin Korovin and Aleksandr Golovin, 30 Nov 1908, and another 1918. L. LAVROVSKY revived the ballet with most of Petipa's ch., Moscow, Bolshoy T., 7 Apr 1945; dan. Semyonova (title role). Innumerable other productions exist in the USSR, invariably with best of Petipa's ch. retained.

The *Grand Pas Hongrois* from Act III formed part of the *divertissement Le Festin* included in the opening program of DIAGHILEV's first Paris season, 1909, with NIJINSKY in the men's *pas de quatre*. A. PAVLOVA presented a 2-act version of the whole ballet by Khlustin, *c.* 1914, and later the *Grand Pas* as a separate *divertissement*. The complete ballet was revived 1933 or 1934 by Nicholas Zverev for the Lithuanian NOB in Kaunas; sc. Mstislav Dobuzhinsky; London, 1935; dan. NEMCHINOVA and A. OBUKHOV. A slightly abbreviated version was made 1946 by A. DANILOVA and BALANCHINE for B. Russe de Monte Carlo; sc./c. BENOIS; dan. Danilova and MAGALLANES. The *Grand Pas* from this production was revived by FRANKLIN for ABT 1961; Balanchine made his own version of it under the title *Pas de Dix* for NYCB, 1955, later expanded into *Cortège Hongrois*, 1973. His *Raymonda Variations* (1961) uses a selection of music from the complete score (revived Pennsylvania B., 1971).

There have also been several versions of the complete ballet by NUREYEV: Spoleto, RB touring section, 1964, sc./c. Beni Montresor; Act III alone given by main RB, London, CG, 1966, sc./c. Barry Kay; Australian B., 1965, sc. Ralph Koltai, c. N. BAYLIS; Zürich OB, 1972, sc./c. GEORGIADIS, revived ABT 1975. NR/DV

See A. K. Glazunov, *Musical Legacy*, Vol. 1 (Leningrad 1959); Marius Petipa, *Materials, Reminiscences, Letters* (Leningrad 1971); David Vaughan, 'Nureyev's *Raymonda*' and Marius Petipa, 'Scenario of *Raymonda*', *Ballet Review*, Vol. 5, No. 2 (New York 1975–6)

Redlich, Don, b. Winona, MD, 1933. American dancer, choreographer, and teacher. Studied dance at the Univ. of Wisconsin; in NY studied with H. HOLM and danced in several Broadway and off-Broadway shows in addition to TV work. Concert debut 1958. Choreographed *Passin' Through* (1959), a portrait of a travelling man. He has designed dances for conventional stage as well as unconventional outdoor spaces with a keen sense of theatrical excitement. Teaches at Sarah Lawrence College, NY. DM

Red Poppy (*Krasniy Mak*), ballet, 4 acts, 8 scenes, ch. Lev Lashchilin and TIKHOMIROV; mus. GLIÈRE; sc./lib. Mikhail Kurilko; theatrical director Aleksey Dikiy. Moscow, Bolshoy T., 14 June 1927; dan. GELTSER (Tao-Hoa); Tikhomirov, then Aleksey Bulgakov (Soviet Captain). Tao-Hoa, a Chinese dancer, saves the life of a Soviet captain whose merchant ship has brought grain to her people during a coolie uprising. Tikhomirov created all the dances for Geltser and Tao-Hoa's Dream in Act II.

Second version Leningrad, State T. of OB, 20 Jan 1929, ch. F. LOPUKHOV (Act I), PONOMARYOV (Act II) and Leonid Leontiev (Act III); sc. Boris Erbstein.

Revived Moscow, Bolshoy T., 12 Dec 1949, ch. L. LAVROVSKY; sc. Mikhail Kurilko. In 1957 the title was changed to *Red Flower*. Since then produced by most Soviet opera and ballet theatres; also staged round the world, notably by SCHWEZOFF for B. Russe de Monte Carlo in Cleveland, OH (1943) and in Rio de Janeiro (1945), and by various choreographers in Eastern Europe. NR

See N. Roslavleva (ed.), *V. D. Tikhomirov, Artist, Balletmaster, Teacher* (Moscow 1971)

Red Sails *see* CRIMSON SAILS

Regional ballet (USA). Halfway through the 19th c. the American publisher Horace Greeley uttered his galvanic slogan, 'Go West, young man.' Greeley's injunction bore fruit. The sturdiest voyagers crossed the Rocky Mountains to California and Washington. Others were lured by the fertile and more accessible Midwestern plains. Texas and its bordering states offered the challenge of limitless grazing land. For their entertainment these American pioneers were contented with an occasional itinerant troupe, often from abroad. Their rugged existence did not leave them time to make perfs of their own. This was still true by the 20th c. Although Oakland, CA, Fullersburg, OH, and Sommerville, NJ, had by then produced I. DUNCAN, FULLER, and ST DENIS, these innovators were to find initial acceptance in Europe. Their own country was slow to recognize them.

The most widespread catalytic effect on American dance came from the extensive touring of A. PAVLOVA between 1910 and 1930. She performed in small communities as well as large, also selected American girls along the way, making them part of her *corps*.

After Pavlova's death (1931), the next major influence was exercised by the B. RUSSE DE MONTE CARLO, which toured 1933–62, sometimes triumphantly, sometimes in decline. Either way, its impact was intense. To this day residents of Houston, TX, think of the last week of December as 'Ballet Russe Week'! The first two directors of the Houston B., Tatiana Semyonova and Nina Popova, were former B. Russe dancers. Other former B. Russe dancers who settled in Texas and Oklahoma to teach and/or direct their own regional cos are YOUSKEVITCH, KRASSOVSKA, Miguel Terekhov and Yvonne Chouteau, Fernando and Nancy Schaffenburg, Eugene Slavin and Alexandra Nadal, JASIŃSKI and Moscelyne Larkin, SKIBINE and Marjorie TALLCHIEF.

Before 1940 most young Americans who were brave enough to seek a dance career flocked to NY to study with Russian émigré teachers. Jobs were desperately scarce for the serious dancer. The small cos formed by Russian luminaries like FOKINE and MORDKIN in NY and BOLM in Chicago were short-lived.

With the founding of ABT (1940) and the activities of the various groups which laid the grounding for the NYCB (1948), NY became even more strongly the country's dance Mecca. Yet simple common sense indicates that an art cannot thrive and develop, especially in a nation as large as the USA, unless it takes root at the community level.

A generation of fine American teachers began to shed light far from NY. Among them were Edith James of Dallas, TX, Mary Ann Wells of Seattle, WA, Lillian Cushing of Denver, CO, and Edna McRae of Chicago, IL. Others went beyond their studios and formed cos.

The great visionary of these American regional pioneers is Dorothy Alexander (née Dorothea Sydney Moses, b. Atlanta, GA, 1904). Teaching was to be her living, as well as a basic dedication. She received a degree from the Atlanta Normal Training S. (1925) and a BA from Oglethorpe College (1930). She made many concert appearances as soloist and subsequently

Branch YMCA; c. Lawrence Maldonado. NY, YM-YWHA 92nd St, Ailey Dance T., 31 Jan 1960. The stages of man's religious sentiment; sorrow and joy in a series of telling episodes. Ailey's most successful work; an infallible 'closing' ballet because of its exultant finale. DM

Reyn, Judith, b. Wankie, Rhodesia, 1944. British dancer. Studied with Dorothy Ainscough in Rhodesia and London RBS. Joined RB 1962; Stuttgart B. 1966 as soloist, creating roles in several CRANKO ballets. Guest artist Munich and Frankfurt from 1967. GBLW

Rhodes, Lawrence, b. Mount Hope, WV, 1939. American dancer. Studied B. Russe S., American B. Center (JOFFREY) and with S. WILLIAMS. *Corps de ballet*, B. Russe de Monte Carlo, 1958; Joffrey B. 1960–4, HARKNESS B. 1964, of which he became director 1968, Dutch NB 1970, Pennsylvania B. 1972–6, FELD B. 1974–5. Combines strong classic technique with powerful dramatic presence. In Italy, danced ALBRECHT to FRACCI's GISELLE, Nov 1974, and Mercutio in FASCILLA's ROMEO AND JULIET, also with Fracci, 1975–6. Now freelance. He m. dancer Lone Isaksen, who retired on the birth of their child. DV

Riabouchinska, Tatiana, b. Moscow, 1917. Russian dancer. She m. LICHINE. Studied with KSHESSINSKA in Paris. Debut with Nikita Balieff's *Chauve-Souris* revue, Paris, at 15. One of the three 'baby ballerinas' in DE BASIL's B. Russes de Monte Carlo 1932–41, creating many roles incl. Frivolity in PRÉSAGES, Child in *Jeux d'Enfants*, both by MASSINE, title role in COQ D'OR, Florentine Beauty in *Paganini*, both by FOKINE, Junior Girl in GRADUATION BALL; also famous for her Prelude in SYLPHIDES, Columbine in CARNAVAL, etc. With her husband danced in many cos incl. ABT, 1944–5, 1952–3; returned to de Basil 1947; B. des CE 1948; DE CUEVAS B. 1949, when she danced GISELLE for the first time; LFB, 1951. Now teaches in California. DV

Riabynkina [Ryabinkina], Elena, b. Sverdlovsk, 1941. Soviet dancer. Studied Moscow, Bolshoy S. from 1950 with Vera Vasilyeva, joined the Bolshoy B. 1959; debut as ODETTE-ODILE while still a student. Later studied with E. GERDT. Roles incl. the Tsar-Maiden (HUMPBACKED HORSE, RADUNSKY version), KITRI, and PHRYGIA. Created the leading female role in VANINA VANINI. Honoured Artist, RSFSR. Her sister Xenia Riabynkina (b. Moscow, 1945), also dances leading roles with the Bolshoy B. and has attracted attention in film roles. JS/NR

Ricaux, Gustav, b. Paris, 1884; d. Aubagne, 1961. French dancer and teacher. Paris OBS; *premier danseur*, partner of SPESSIVTSEVA. Famous teacher; his pupils incl. PERETTI, PETIT, BABILÉE, and RENAULT. M-FC

Ricercare, ballet, 1 act, for 2 dancers, ch. TETLEY; mus. Mordecai Seter (*Ricercar*, 1956); sc./c. TER-ARUTUNIAN. NY, State T., ABT, 25 Jan 1966; dan. HINKSON, DOUGLAS. Revived Nottingham Playhouse, BR, 24 Feb 1967; dan. Sandra Craig, Jonathan Taylor. The setting is a concave structure on which and from which lovers play. MC

Richardson, Philip J. S., b. Newark, Nottinghamshire, 1875; d. London, 1963. English editor, author, and propagandist for dance. His interest in dancing stemmed from his appointment as editor of *The Dancing Times* when the magazine first appeared in Oct 1910. His involvement became complete. He was instrumental in getting the RAD established, the CAMARGO SOCIETY functioning, and also worked in the field of ballroom dancing, establishing the Official Board of Ballroom Dancing and the International Council of Ballroom Dancing. Through the pages of his magazine he campaigned from the early 1920s for the establishment of a British national ballet; his was the organizing spirit that brought other talents together. His remarkable collection of rare dance books is now in the RAD library and available on microfilm. OBE 1951. MC
See Ifan Kyrle Fletcher (ed.), *Bibliographical Descriptions of Forty Dance Books in the collection of P. J. S. Richardson OBE* (London 1954, 1977)

Rinker, Kenneth, b. Washington, DC, 1945. American dancer and choreographer. BA, Univ. of Maryland; studied dance there and in Washington and Berlin; in NY with WEIDMAN, CUNNINGHAM, GRAHAM, HAWKINS, and YOUSKEVITCH. Danced with Ethel Butler Co. in Washington. With the composer Sergio Cervetti, founded Berlin Dance Ensemble 1969. Joined THARP's co. 1971; has danced in most of her works for her own co. since, also the original version of DEUCE COUPE. His own works incl. *Prisons* (Berlin 1969), *Zinctum* (Honourable Mention, Cologne Choreographic Competition, 1969), *Raga II* (NY 1971), *Melodies* (WNET-TV 1972), *Alberti Bass – Alberti Bounce* (NY 1975). DV

Rite of Spring, The, ballet, ch. MACMILLAN; mus. STRAVINSKY; sc./c. Sydney Nolan. London, CG, RB, 3 May 1962; dan. MASON. The first tableau is danced against a rocky setting, the second backcloth features an enormous gold phallus shape. Using a huge ensemble, MacMillan devised particularly inventive floor patterns. This version is ideally seen from the upper part of a theatre. For other ballets to the same music, *see* SACRE DU PRINTEMPS. MC

Rites de Passage, modern dance work, ch. DUNHAM; mus. Pasquita Anderson (percussion Gaucho); c. John Pratt. Los Angeles, Biltmore T., 30 Oct 1941; dan. Lavinia Williams, BEATTY, Dunham. One of the earliest explorations of African folk material shaped for conventional stage presentation, depicting the initiation of a young boy into the life of a tribe. DM

Road of the Phoebe Snow, The, modern dance work, ch. BEATTY; mus. Duke Ellington, Billy Strayhorn; sc. Lew Smith. NY, YM-YWHA 92nd St, 28 Nov 1959. Life in the raw hostility engendered by poverty under the railroad tracks of a big city of the American Midwest; disillusionment, rape, and indifference, with flurries of violence. The *Phoebe Snow* was a luxury train of the Erie–Lakawanna Railroad, whose right of way brushed past poor districts. DM

Robbins [Rabinowitz], Jerome, b. New York City, NY, 1918. American choreographer. The man whom many consider to be the foremost American-born choreographer working in classical ballet did not embark upon a career in dance until 1936, after completing one year at NY Univ. He danced in the chorus of several musical comedies 1938–40, incl. *Keep Off The Grass* (1940; ch. BALANCHINE). Joined ABT, then in its second season, 1940; during the next four years played a number of important roles, such as PETRUSHKA; Mercutio in TUDOR's ROMEO AND JULIET; Alias in BILLY THE KID. On 18 Apr 1944, his own remarkably successful first ballet, FANCY FREE, was presented during ABT's season at the NY Met. This adroitly made work demonstrated what came to be considered important ingredients of his style: theatrical clarity and a skill at blending vernacular styles and natural gestures with the vocabulary of classical ballet.

On 28 Dec 1944, *On The Town*, a musical by Betty Comden and Adolph Green, based on *Fancy Free*, received its premiere. Robbins collaborated on the book and provided the choreography. From then on, he divided his time between Broadway and the ballet world. His appearances as a dancer became sporadic, although he performed in the ABT premieres of his *Facsimile* (1946) and *Summer Day* (1947) and also danced in his INTERPLAY and *Fancy Free*. In the ballets that he created during the 1940s, as well as in such musicals as *Billion Dollar Baby* (1946), *High Button Shoes* (1947), and *Look Ma I'm Dancing* (1948), he continued to develop his gift for capturing the essence of a particular era or social stratum through the way dancers moved or treated each other.

He joined NYCB 1949, and as associate artistic director (1950–9) created nine ballets, particularly CAGE, AFTERNOON OF A FAUN, and CONCERT, which further demonstrated the range of his interests and choreographic abilities. During his first three years with NYCB, he also danced – giving particularly vivid perfs in the title roles in BALANCHINE's PRODIGAL SON and *Tyl Eulenspiegel*. It was also during the 1950s that Robbins adapted, directed, and choreographed the musical *Peter Pan* (and several TV versions of it); created the *Small House of Uncle Thomas* ballet in *The King and I* (both play and film); and, most importantly, conceived, directed, and choreographed *West Side Story*.

West Side Story (1957) is generally acknowledged to be a landmark in the history of American musical theatre: its ending is a tragic one, its characters are violent, its setting unglamorous. Like an early Robbins ballet, *The Guests* (1949), it is a variation on the Romeo–Juliet tale. What made *West Side Story* so remarkable, aside from Leonard Bernstein's brilliant score, was Robbins's pacing of the entire action like a tense, restless, volatile dance. This production seems to have awakened in Robbins an interest in the tough and alienated youth of the 1950s, and several of the ballets that he choreographed for his own co., Ballets: USA, such as MOVES and N.Y. EXPORT, OPUS JAZZ, reflect this interest. Ballets: USA, which made its debut at the Spoleto Fest. in summer 1958, toured the USA, and was sent abroad by the US State Department.

After directing two non-musical plays, *Oh Dad, Poor Dad, Mama's Hung You In The Closet And I'm Feelin' So Sad* (1962) and *Mother Courage And Her Children* (1963), Robbins returned to musical comedy with the very successful *Fiddler on the Roof* (1964) and to ballet with the controversial NOCES, staged for ABT 1965. In 1966, he received a government grant for two years to explore theatre forms involving dance, song, and speech, and worked in seclusion with a group of performers, American T. Laboratory, on a number of experimental projects, none of which was ever shown to the public.

When this project ended, Robbins returned to NYCB as a choreographer. He is now one of its three ballet masters. Beginning with his extraordinarily inventive DANCES AT A GATHERING, Robbins has made many ballets for the co. (including two in collaboration with Balanchine); among the most prominent are GOLDBERG VARIATIONS, *Watermill* (1972), *Dybbuk Variations* (1974), and *Ma Mère l'Oye* and *Piano Concerto in G* (both made in 1975 for the co.'s RAVEL FEST.). Except for the sparse, meditative, barely moving *Watermill,* his recent ballets demonstrate a new willingness to rely more on the idiom of classical ballet. He has seemed less concerned than formerly with delineating specific characters and situations and more tolerant of ambiguity. Robbins has dances in the repertories of many major ballet cos and has won many awards for his achievements. Although critics have, on occasion, found his work contrived or over-facile, they praise his clarity, musicality, eloquent movement, and his unusual ability to make dancers on stage look human. DJ
See I. Lidova, 'Jerome Robbins', *Les Saisons de la Danse* (Paris, Dec 1969)

Rodeo, ballet, 2 scenes, ch. DE MILLE; mus. COPLAND; lib. de Mille; sc. O. SMITH; c. Kermit Love. NY Met, B. Russe de Monte Carlo, 16 Oct 1942; dan. de Mille, FRANKLIN, Casimir Kokitch. Subtitled *The Courting at Burnt Ranch*; the story of a cowgirl who gets her man. Revived ABT 1949. FM

Rodrigues, Alfred, b. Cape Town, 1921. S. African dancer and choreographer. Early training Cape Town Univ. B. Club with Cecily Robinson. To London

Jerome Robbins's comedy-ballet CONCERT, as staged by the RB at CG, 1975; SEYMOUR in the strange and poetic Umbrella Dance

1946, studied with VOLKOVA and joined SWB 1947. Choreographed *Île des Sirènes* (1950) for a FONTEYN-HELPMANN tour, *Blood Wedding* (1953) and *Café des Sports* (1954) for SWTB, and for SWB *The Miraculous Mandarin* (Edinburgh Fest., 1956). Staged many musicals and choreographed many large-scale ballets in Italy; has also worked in Turkey, Denmark, and Poland. He m. FARRON. MC

Roleff, Peter, b. Quadrath, Cologne, 1906. German dancer, ballet master, and teacher. Pupil of V. GSOVSKY in Berlin. Danced in Berlin, Augsburg, Essen, etc. From 1935 taught and choreographed in Berlin; ballet master and soloist Wiesbaden, 1946–7; directed a co. in Cologne 1948–51; ballet master, Bonn 1951–3, and Bielefeld 1953–6. In 1956 opened a ballet school in Munich with the German dancer Karl-Heinz King, the Roleff-King S. GBLW

Romantic era, the period in ballet which reflected the ideals of the Romantic movement in the other arts. The first flowering was with SYLPHIDE and the heyday the 1830s and 1840s. MC

Rome. Teatro dell'Opera (T. Costanzi, built by Domenico Costanzi 1880; rebuilt and modernized 1926–7, renamed T. Reale dell'Opera 1928; now known as T. dell'O.); school attached. After a long succession of ballet masters from various countries, in 1974 pressing financial difficulties made it impossible to invite choreographers or dancers, or to stage new productions. In 1975 the ballet master was Guido Lauri (termed Assistant Choreographer 1976). Notable productions incl. SYLPHIDE, staged BRUHN for FRACCI and NUREYEV, 1966; in the same program Bruhn appeared with Fracci in his choreography of the Balcony Scene from ROMEO AND JULIET. Moscow Bolshoy B. visited 1970. Many classics staged by Zarko Prebil. Director of the school from 1975 Walter Zappolini. The ballet is almost totally subservient to opera. FP

Romeo and Juliet. William Shakespeare's tragedy has fascinated choreographers from the late 18th c. Although there are references to earlier versions, the first precise date is that of the premiere of GALEOTTI's ballet for the RDB, mus. Claus Schall, 4 Feb 1811. TCHAIKOVSKY's fantasy-overture *Romeo and Juliet* has been used for innumerable 1-act versions but by far the most important stagings have been to PROKOFIEV's score for a 3-act work to a libretto by Adrian Pyotrovsky and Sergey Radlov (a theatrical director and authority on Shakespeare). The music was first used by Vania Psota, Brno, 30 Dec 1938. On 11 Jan 1940 a new production was staged by L. LAVROVSKY for the Kirov B. in association with Radlov, sc./c. Pyotr Williams, dan. ULANOVA and SERGEYEV. It was a milestone in Soviet ballet, not only portraying the literary theme but penetrating human emotions. Staged Moscow, Bolshoy T., same choreography; dan. Ulanova and GABOVICH, 28 Dec 1946. (With this production the Bolshoy B. first conquered the West in London, CG, 1956.) There have been other productions all over the USSR, of which the most notable are those by VINOGRADOV (Novosibirsk 1965); A. Shekero (Kiev 1971); KASATKINA and VASILYOV (Novosibirsk 1972); and Nicolay Boyarchikov (Perm 1971).

Outside the USSR, ASHTON choreographed a 3-act ballet to Prokofiev's music, sc./c. Peter Rice, for

Romeo and Juliet, L. LAVROVSKY version, as staged at the Bolshoy T., Moscow; Act II, scene 3, the death of Tybalt; sc./c. Pyotr Williams

the RDB, 19 May 1955, dan. VANGSAAE and KRONSTAM – before the Lavrovsky version had been seen in the West. It was remarkably successful in both Copenhagen and NY but has been lost from the repertory.

CRANKO staged his fine version for the Stuttgart B., sc./c. ROSE, 2 Dec 1962; dan. HAYDÉE and BARRA; he mounted it for NB of Canada 1964 and in Munich 1968.

MACMILLAN made his version for the London RB at CG, sc./c. GEORGIADIS, 9 Feb 1965; dan. FONTEYN and NUREYEV but choreographed for SEYMOUR and GABLE. He stressed the role of Juliet as the motive force of the action, seeing her as a 'positive' girl with a passionate will to react against the conventions of her society and it was one of his finest collaborations with Seymour. This version was revived RSB 1969.

An entirely different treatment of the story – but no less successful than the Prokofiev versions – is TUDOR's narrative ballet, 1 act, mus. Frederick Delius, arr. Antal Dorati; sc./c. BERMAN. NY Met O., ABT, 6 Apr 1943 (incomplete; first complete perf. 10 Apr); dan. MARKOVA, LAING, ORLOFF, Tudor, ROBBINS, OSATO, CHASE. Though described as a 'narrative' the ballet is rather a meditation on Shakespeare's tragedy; Delius's music (*Over the Hills and Far Away*, *A Walk to the Paradise Garden* from *A Village Romeo and Juliet*, Prelude to *Irmelin*, *Eventyr*, and *Brigg Fair*) induces a trancelike suspension of real time. This version was revived by RSB 1962. NR/DV/MC

See G. Ulanova 'Author of Favourite Ballets' and L. Lavrovsky, 'From the Deposit of Talent' in *S. S. Prokofiev, Materials, Documents, Reminiscences* (Moscow 1956)

Roméo et Juliette (*Romeo and Juliet*), 'rehearsal without scenery, in two parts', ch. NIJINSKA (*entr'acte* by BALANCHINE); mus. LAMBERT; curtains and scenic adjuncts Max Ernst and Joan Miró. Monte Carlo, DIAGHILEV's B. Russes, 4 May 1926; dan. KARSAVINA, LIFAR. Not about William Shakespeare's lovers but two dancers who elope while rehearsing a ballet on the theme of his play. Short-lived but typical of Diaghilev's search for novelty. MC

Róna, Viktor, b. Budapest, 1936. Hungarian dancer. Pupil of NÁDASI; graduated from the State B. Inst. 1954; studied with PUSHKIN in Leningrad 1959. Dancer, Budapest O. 1950; solo dancer 1957, performing all major classical and character roles of the Budapest repertoire. Besides the tours of the co. he toured China, Vietnam, and Korea (1959), partnered FONTEYN in London and the USA (1962), and SAMSOVA in Paris in CINDERELLA, toured the USA with DAYDÉ (1965), and danced with OROSZ in Cuba (1966, 1967), and elsewhere. Principal roles in TV films of SEREGI's WOODEN PRINCE, and MISCHIEVOUS STUDENTS. Also principal dancer and ballet master of the Norwegian NB. Merited Artist, 1972; Eminent Artist, 1976; Liszt Prize, 1961; Kossuth Prize, 1965; Finnish White Rose Order, 1968. GPD

Rooms, modern dance work, ch. SOKOLOW; mus. Kenyon Hopkins. NY, YM-YWHA 92nd St, 24 Feb 1955; dan. J. DUNCAN, Beatrice Seckler, Jack Moore, MCKAYLE, Eve Beck, Sandra Pine, Judith Coy, SANASARDO. A series of solos depicting the fantasies and frustrations of a group of city dwellers, each enclosed in his or her private world. Revived NDT, AILEY Dance T., CCJB. DV

Rosanova, Bertha, b. Rio de Janeiro, 1930. Brazilian dancer. Studied with Maria Olenewa and at 13 entered the T. Municipal Co. At 15 made first dancer. Performed all the classical roles but specially renowned for her GISELLE. Many Brazilian ballets written for her; has danced throughout the country and all over S. America. The most famous and popular dancer in Brazil; in 1959 awarded title of *prima ballerina assoluta* by the direction of the T. Municipal, Rio de Janeiro. MLN

Rosario (Florencia Pérez Padilla) *see* SPAIN

Rosati [Galletti], Carolina, b. Bologna, 1826; d. Cannes, 1905. Italian dancer. Pupil of BLASIS, Antonia Torelli, and Giovanni Briol. Engaged by Nestor Roqueplan for the Paris OB 1853–9; reputedly received the highest salary ever paid up to that time to a dancer. She appeared in London between 1847 and 1858 and in St Petersburg 1859–61, retiring 1862. A very strong dramatic dancer, she created roles in many of MAZILIER's ballets, incl. his CORSAIRE. She m. dancer Francesco Rosati. MC
See I. Guest, *The Ballet of the Second Empire, 1847–1858* (London 1955); *1858–1870* (London 1953)

Rose, Jürgen, b. Bernburg, 1937. German artist and designer. Worked in close collaboration with CRANKO as well as designing for other German cos, and for the NB of Canada. A versatile and exceptionally practical designer, sympathetic both to the choreographer's demands and the dancers' needs. Also possesses a gift for re-creating in the style of other artists, notably Gustav Klimt in CRANKO's *Poème de l'Extase*. MC

Rosen, Elsa-Marianne von, b. Stockholm, 1927. Swedish dancer, choreographer, and ballet director. Studied with Vera Aleksandrova, Albert Kozlovsky, and Jenny Hasselquist. RDBS 1945–7. Debut in recitals. Joined B. Russe de Monte Carlo 1947. Created the title roles in MISS JULIE and MEDEA for the Riks T. on tour in 1950. Ballerina, RSB, 1951–9. Formed, with her husband Allan Fridericia, Scandinavian B. 1960 and toured Scandinavia. Director, Gothenburg B., 1970–6. She was an outstanding personality as a dancer, with dramatic talent. Became a specialist on August BOURNONVILLE, staging his SYLPHIDE for BR, London; B. Municipale, Santiago; Monte Carlo B. with NUREYEV; National B., Washington; and the Maly OB, Leningrad. She has also staged NAPOLI. AGS

Rosen, Heinz, b. Hanover, 1908; d. Lake Constance, 1972. German dancer and choreographer. Pupil of LABAN, JOOSS, and V. GSOVSKY. Toured with Jooss B.; in Basel as ballet master 1945–51. He was the first to choreograph *Dame à la Licorne* (1953). Director, Munich B., 1959–69; choreographed LÉGENDE DE JOSEPH (as *Josephslegende*, 1958), CARMINA BURANA, and CATULLI CARMINA etc. Also staged operas and operettas. GBLW

Rosenthal, Jean, b. New York, 1912; d. New York, 1965. American lighting designer. Lit all productions of B. Society and NYCB 1946–57, GRAHAM's works 1958–65, ROBBINS's Ballets: USA 1959–60, as well as many musical comedies, operas, and plays. She also designed the set for AFTERNOON OF A FAUN. Robbins dedicated DANCES AT A GATHERING to her memory. DV

Roslavleva, Lyubov, b. Moscow, 1874; d. Zürich, 1904. Russian dancer. Daughter of an army officer who went bankrupt; her mother placed her, a 'nobleman's child' in the Moscow TS, then a rare event. Studied there 1885–92 (as a ward of the State), class of Aleksey Bogdanov, graduating under José Mendez. In Bolshoy B. from 1892, by early 1893 danced SWANILDA, replacing the then reigning ballerina Lydia Geiten. To St Petersburg 1895, 1897, and 1899, to replace LEGNANI, KSHESSINSKA, and PREOBRAZHENSKA, etc. when they were indisposed. At first criticised for rigidity in her *ports de bras*, through hard work under CECCHETTI, IVANOV, and M. PETIPA, and the good influence of her Moscow partner TIKHOMIROV, she overcame her defects and, though not endowed with elevation, succeeded in hiding this through grace and breadth of dancing. She was also a strong dramatic actress. Her roles incl. Tsar-Maiden (HUMPBACKED HORSE), CINDERELLA, KITRI, Medora (CORSAIRE). She was the first Moscow AURORA and only illness prevented her from becoming the first RAYMONDA. Her last role was Nikia (BAYADÈRE). She m. Prov Sadovsky, of the famous Maly T. family of dramatic actors. NR
See V. Svetlov, *Terpsichore* (articles, essays, notes) (St Petersburg 1906)

Ross, Bertram, b. Brooklyn, NY, 1925. American dancer, teacher, and choreographer. First attracted attention in title role of FONAROFF's *Lazarus*, 1952. Joined GRAHAM Dance Co. 1953, danced nearly all principal male roles, creating that of St Michael in *Seraphic Dialogue* (1955), Agamemnon and Orestes in CLYTEMNESTRA (1958), etc. Taught at Graham S. for many years. Presented first concert of his own choreography in NY, 1965. Left Graham in 1974, now teaches at NY Univ. S. of the Arts. DV

Rouché, Jacques *see* PARIS OPÉRA BALLET

Rousanne, [Rousanne Sarkissian; Madame Rousanne], b. Baku, 1894; d. Paris, 1958. French-Armenian teacher. Studied with KHLUSTIN, TREFILOVA, VOLININ. Taught privately in Paris from 1928 at the Studio Wacker. Her class quickly became one of the most celebrated, notably through her pupils DARSONVAL, Yves Brieux, SCHWARZ, ALGAROFF, KALIOUJNY, BABILÉE, PETIT, VAN DIJK, BÉJART, and VERDY. M-FC

Rowe, Marilyn, b. Sydney, 1946. Australian dancer. Studied with Frances Lett. Australian BS 1963; Australian B. 1964, becoming soloist; principal ballerina 1969. A brilliant classicist, aerial and vivacious (Queen of the Dryads in DON QUIXOTE, title role in MERRY WIDOW) but capable of adapting sensitively to modern work (created role in GEMINI). Silver Medal, Second International B. Competition, Moscow, 1973. KSW

Royal Academy of Dancing (RAD). Founded 31 Dec 1920 by RICHARDSON and ESPINOSA as the Association of Teachers of Operatic Dancing of Great Britain to watch over standards of teaching of operatic (ballet) dancing. Royal Charter 1936, henceforth known as RAD. It conducts examinations throughout the world, ranging from children's work to its highest performing award, the Solo Seal. Since 1947 it has conducted a teacher training course and graduates may use the letters L (Licentiate) RAD after their names. The first president was GENÉE until 1954, when she was succeeded by FONTEYN. Kathleen Gordon was director 1924–68; in 1969 Ivor Guest became chairman and in 1976 FIELD became director. The headquarters are in Battersea, London. MC

Royal Ballet, The, Britain's national ballet. It grew out of an association, from 1926, between two redoubtable women, L. BAYLIS and DE VALOIS. De Valois was producing the dances in operas and drama at London's Old Vic T. and when Sadler's Wells T. reopened 1931 she moved her existing and prosperous school into that theatre and established a nucleus of six dancers and herself. The Vic-Wells B., as it was known, gave its first perf. 5 May 1931 at the Old Vic, supplemented by guests (notably DOLIN). Perfs soon became regular, every two weeks at first, and from 1935 the co. was solely based on Sadler's Wells T. Consequently when that theatre was bombed in 1940 and the co. began to tour widely it changed its name to Sadler's Wells B. until, in 1956, having achieved world fame, it was granted a 'charter of incorporation' from Queen Elizabeth II and became 'Royal'.

MARKOVA was the co.'s ballerina 1932–5, ASHTON joined permanently in 1935; LAMBERT was from the start musical director, and FONTEYN, having entered the school aged 14, in 1934, became, in effect, ballerina when Markova left. Ashton, Lambert, and Fonteyn, under the dynamic leadership of de Valois, gave the infant co. its distinctive quality and eventually its worldwide fame. De Valois built on a triple foundation: a school, a home theatre, and the classical

Royal Ballet, the *corps de ballet* of swans in the last act of SWAN LAKE

ballet and inspiring Russian dancers, among whom ANDREYANOVA ranks as the most exciting. On her last visit (1842) Taglioni brought JOHANSSON as her partner. At this time in St Petersburg ballet perfs were given on Mondays, Wednesdays, and Fridays during the season which began at the end of Easter and ended on the second day of Lent the following year (though later summer perfs were suspended and the season usually began in Oct). Despite the prowess of the Russian dancers, the director of the Imperial Ts (a court appointment entailing responsibility for overseeing all the theatrical perfs in the royal theatres) continued to invite foreign stars and choreographers to St Petersburg. GRAHN made her debut there in 1843, ELSSLER in 1848. In the same month PERROT arrived to start his decade of work there.

In 1847 M. PETIPA had arrived to take up an appointment as principal dancer in the city where his father, Jean Petipa, was teaching in the Imperial S. The subsequent development of the Imperial B. results from the work of Perrot, then of SAINT-LÉON, and supremely of Petipa in the creation of a repertory and in the evolution of a Russian style of dancing. From 1860 (when the Maryinsky was built by Alberto Cavos, grandfather of BENOIS) ballet perfs alternated between the Bolshoy and the Maryinsky Ts. In 1881 the appointment of VSEVOLOZHSKY brought to a magnificent climax the 19th-c. development of the Imperial B. In 1889 the Maryinsky became the sole stage for ballet *à grand spectacle*. Notable at this time were the technical developments among Russian dancers such as KSHESSINSKA and PREOBRAZHENSKA, inspired by the virtuosity of visiting Italian stars – LEGNANI, CECCHETTI – and the inspiration offered by the dramatic power of ZUCCHI. On Petipa's enforced retirement in 1903 the St Petersburg B. fell on dark times. The prodigious generation of dancers now emerging from the school – TREFILOVA, A. PAVLOVA, KARSAVINA, NIJINSKY, EGOROVA, etc. – could look to no fresh challenges beyond those of the existing repertory. The inhibiting conservatism of both audiences and directorate was to restrict the further development of ballet in Russia. FOKINE was faced with every obstacle in the staging of his early ballets in St Petersburg (PAVILLON D'ARMIDE was given its first perf. *after* an evening perf. of SWAN LAKE) and it was the DIAGHILEV enterprise that was to show the wealth of creative and interpretative talent existing in the St Petersburg B. in the first decade of this century.

In Moscow, ballet traditions had also been established in the latter years of the 18th c. In 1773 Filippo Beccari, an Italian ballet master who had been dancing in St Petersburg, undertook to start dancing classes for the children of the Moscow Orphanage. Of the 62 pupils with whom he worked, no fewer than 24 were judged suitable to take the stage three years later (Beccari's contract stipulated payment by results: 250 roubles per dancer) and in 1776 the perf. by these children marks the real beginning of the Moscow B. Housed first in the Znamensky T., it moved to the Petrovsky T., then under the management of an Englishman, Michael Maddox. When that theatre burned down, the new Bolshoy Petrovsky T. was built on the same site; when this in turn was destroyed by fire, a splendid building went up to replace it. Called simply the Bolshoy ('big') T., like the Maryinsky T. designed by Cavos, it opened its doors in 1856. The Imperial B. in Moscow suffered from the prime importance of St Petersburg and its development throughout the 19th c. must always be considered secondary. In 1869 Petipa staged his DON QUIXOTE there (the contrast in staging between the vivid dramatic Moscow presentation and the cooler and far more 'classical' St Petersburg staging epitomizes the aesthetic difference between the two cos) and in 1877 the first perf. of *Swan Lake* was given.

The crucial figure in Moscow's balletic history was GORSKY, whose revisions of the Petipa repertory and his own creations sharpened the image of Moscow ballet as something more emotionally vivid and dramatic than St Petersburg's. This difference reflected both in stagings and in dance style can be noted even today. With the 1917 Revolution and the transfer of government to Moscow the pre-eminence of the Bolshoy B. became official policy. Supremely important among Moscow dancers of the early 20th c. were GELTSER and her partner TIKHOMIROV.

At the time of the 1917 Revolution ballet was still essentially a court entertainment, financed by the Tsar. Although it might have been expected that such an élitist art form would have been swept away, it was not only saved (primarily by Anatoly Lunasharsky, first Soviet Commissar of Education) but has spread throughout the country until by 1976 there were no fewer than 34 cos in the major cities of the USSR. It has been recognized that in its technical achievements, thanks to teachers like VAGANOVA and MESSERER, and the dramatically expressive power of its dancers – SEMYONOVA, ULANOVA, PLISETSKAYA – it can communicate to the people and also bring great prestige on tours abroad. This prestige is reflected in the encouragement of children to enter the profession of classical ballet and the high standard of training. *See* USSR, BALLET EDUCATION IN.

The major choreographers to emerge after Fokine's departure have been VAINONEN, ZAKHAROV, L. LAVROVSKY, CHABUKIANI and GRIGOROVICH. The schools of the KIROV and BOLSHOY ballets continue to produce galaxies of dancers, some of whom – NUREYEV, MAKAROVA and BARYSHNIKOV – have elected to dance in the West and have brought with them the incomparable inheritance of their training. MC/CC/JS

See C. W. Beaumont, *A History of Ballet in Russia (1613–1881)* (London 1930); Natalia Roslavleva, *Era of the Russian Ballet* (London 1966); Mary Grace Swift, *The Art of the Dance in the USSR* (Notre Dame, IN, 1968); Yuri Slonimsky, *The Bolshoy Theatre Ballet* (Moscow 1956 and later editions, in English)

S

Sabirova, Malika, b. Dyushambe [Stalinabad], 1942. Soviet dancer. Prima ballerina, Aini T. of O. and B., Dyushambe, Tadzhik SSR. Studied Vaganova S., Leningrad, 1953–61. Small, a brilliant technician and a fine actress. On frequent visits to Moscow rehearses with ULANOVA and attends MESSERER's class. Her roles incl. KITRI, GISELLE, Nikia (BAYADÈRE), and JULIET. Permanent partner Musafar Burkhanov (*premier danseur*, Aini O.), whom she m. She has danced in Britain, Italy, Canada, Cuba, Japan, and Burma. People's Artist, USSR. Silver medal, Varna. Gold medal and 1st prize, First International B. Competition, Moscow, 1969. NR

Sacramento Ballet *see* REGIONAL BALLET (USA)

Sacre du Printemps, Le (*The Rite of Spring*), pictures of Pagan Russia in 2 acts, ch. NIJINSKY; lib. STRAVINSKY and Nicholas Roerich; mus. Stravinsky; sc./c. Roerich. Paris, T. des CE, DIAGHILEV's B. Russes, 29 May 1913; dan. Marie Piltz. New version ch. MASSINE; T. des CE, 15 Dec 1920; dan. L. SOKOLOVA. A primitive ritual in which a virgin is chosen as a sacrificial victim. The first perf. was one of the key events in the history of 20th-c. art: there was an uproar in the theatre that almost drowned out the music. Nijinsky's choreography treated the theme in an essentially abstract fashion with the classic technique completely inverted; performed very few times, its importance in the development of contemporary choreography is belatedly coming to be recognized. Massine revived his version in Philadelphia, 11 Apr 1959, with GRAHAM, for the RSB, 30 May 1956, and in Milan, Sc., 18 Jan 1962. There have been many versions by other choreographers, notably WIGMAN (sc. Wilhelm Reinking; Städtische O., W. Berlin, 1957); BÉJART (sc. Pierre Caille; dan. BARI, T. de la Monnaie, Brussels, 9 Dec 1959); MACMILLAN (*see* RITE OF SPRING); VASILYOV and KASATKINA (dan. Kasatkina, VLADIMIROV, Moscow, Bolshoy T., 28 June 1965). DV

Le Sacre du Printemps, costume design by Nicholas Roerich

Sadler's Wells Royal Ballet, Sadler's Wells Theatre Ballet *see* ROYAL BALLET

St Denis [Dennis], Ruth, b. NJ, 1877; d. Hollywood, CA, 1968. American dancer, choreographer, teacher, and actress. With very little formal training, she created for herself a Hindu ballet, *Radha* (1906), a measure of whose authenticity is that it was originally danced to music of DELIBES. Later the same year she added *Cobras* (mus. Delibes) and *Incense* to her repertory, and in 1908 *Nautch* and *Yogi*. Toured Europe and the USA, where she played in vaudeville theatres, with these and other exotic numbers. In 1914 SHAWN became her partner and her husband, and together they founded the DENISHAWN S. and Co. Except during his army service in World War I, they danced together until their separation in 1932; GRAHAM, HUMPHREY, and WEIDMAN all began their careers in Denishawn. St Denis was finally obliged to give up the school but continued to perform as a soloist well into her 80s, incl. in her repertory the dances that had launched her career. Author of an autobiography, *Ruth St Denis: An Unfinished Life* (London and New York 1939). DV

Saint-Léon, Arthur (Charles Victor), b. Paris, 1821; d. Paris, 1870. French dancer, violinist, and choreographer. Son of the ballet master at the Württemberg Ducal T., Stuttgart, he studied with his father and made his debut in Munich at age 14, dancing and playing the violin. He subsequently danced and mounted ballets all over Europe. He met CERRITO in Milan, m. her in 1845, and in 1847 staged his ballet *La Fille de Marbre* for her debut at the Paris O. It was so successful that he staged some 16 ballets and *divertissements* there, among them *Le Violon du Diable* (1849) in which he played a violin solo. He worked at the Paris O. 1847–52 but also danced in London with Cerrito and was her constant partner until they separated 1851. In 1859 he went to Russia where he staged many of his earlier works (sometimes under different titles) and created new ones incl. HUMP-BACKED HORSE, the first ballet based on Russian themes. In 1869 Saint-Léon, who had maintained his contacts with the Paris O. and staged *La Source* (mus. MINKUS and DELIBES) there in 1866, left Russia. His last ballet and the only surviving one was COPPÉLIA, at the Paris O. His book *La Sténochorégraphie* (1852) recorded his pin-figure system of notation; decipherable by experts today, it indicates how greatly technique had developed by that time. MC
See Ivor Guest, *Fanny Cerrito* (London 1956, rev. ed. 1974); *The Ballet of the Second Empire, 1847–1858* (London 1955); *1858–1870* (London 1953); Natalia Roslavleva, *Era of the Russian Ballet* (London and New York 1966)

Sakharoff [Zuckerman], Alexander, b. Mariupol [Zhdanov], 1886; d. Siena, 1963. Russian dancer and choreographer. Studied law and painting in Paris; decided to become a dancer after seeing Sarah Bernhardt dance a minuet in a play there. Studied in Munich and gave his first perfs there in 1910. In 1911 he went into partnership with Clothilde von der Planitz (b. Berlin, 1895; d. Rome, 1974; danced as Clothilde von Derp; he m. her in 1919) and they developed an individual style of plastic dancing and mime. MASSINE was influenced by them. Retired 1953 and opened a school in the Palazzo Doria, Rome. GBLW

Sallé, Marie, b. 1707; d. Paris, 1756. French dancer. Member of a French family troupe of itinerant actors. Studied with BALON, Blondy, Michel and Françoise Prévost at Paris OS; first appeared aged nine with her brother Francis at John Rich's T., Lincoln's Inn Fields, London, for 100 perfs, Oct 1716–June 1717; appeared with him at Paris Foires Saint-Laurent and Saint-Germain 1718–24; at Lincoln's Inn Fields again, Oct 1725–Apr 1727; Paris O. 1727–30 and 1731–2, where her delicate grace and eloquent miming pitted against the ostentatious brilliance of CAMARGO became a *cause célèbre*. Was a favourite dancer at the French Court. Under Rich at London CG, she created a furore with her ballets *Pygmalion* (14 Feb 1734) and *Bacchus and Ariane* (26 Mar 1734), forerunners of NOVERRE's *ballets d'action*. To be consistent with such classical subjects she abandoned the paniered, bejewelled, elaborate costumes, headdresses and heeled shoes required at the Paris O. and danced in Grecian tunic and sandals with her hair unbound. During 1734 and 1735 at London CG, she created and danced in *divertissements* for the operas of George Frideric Handel, who also composed his only ballet, *Terpsicore* (a 'Dramatick Entertainment') for her. Returned to Paris O. in a *pas seul* in the flower scene of INDES GALANTES (23 Aug 1735), which she later choreographed with great success. For five years she held the important roles in the repertoire but she chafed under the conventions and restrictions of the O. and, after several attempts to resign, finally retired with a pension in June 1740. Following five years of seclusion, she reappeared in 20 ballets at court in Versailles, 1745–7, after which her pension was doubled. Another five years passed and she emerged in four ballets at court in Fontainebleau, with her last appearance 7 Nov 1752. Her partners incl. many great dancers, e.g. Louis ('le Grand') Dupré and G. VESTRIS. Portraits of her were painted by Nicolas Lancret, and Maurice-Quentin de La Tour, among others, and Voltaire and Noverre praised her in the highest terms. Louis de Cahusac wrote that she '. . . stepped out of the rank of mere performer and rose to the rare category of creative artist'. PME
See Parmenia Migel, *The Ballerinas, from the Court of Louis XIV to Pavlova* (New York 1972)

Samsova [formerly Samtsova], Galina, b. Stalingrad, 1937. Byelorussian dancer. Studied Kiev BS, joined Kiev B. 1956, becoming soloist. She m. Alexander Ursuliak, a Canadian engineer of Russian extraction, and became a British subject. Joined NB of Canada 1961 (dancing GISELLE); in 1963 created title role in Raimundo de Larrain's staging of *Cendrillon* in Paris (ch. ORLIKOVSKY). She made an immediate impact with her strong, fluent dancing and unmistakably Russian training. Principal dancer with LFB 1964–73, she also toured with her present husband, PROKOVSKY, and their own group. From 1973 devoted herself entirely to this group and toured worldwide. After its demise in 1977, guest artist with many cos incl. RB. Essentially a romantic dancer, Samsova also commands the virtuoso repertory and dazzles in such numbers as the CORSAIRE *pas de deux* and MESSERER's *Spring Waters*. MC

Sanasardo, Paul, b. Chicago, IL, 1928. American modern dance choreographer, teacher, and dancer. A graduate of the Art Institute of Chicago, he studied dance with TUDOR, Erika Thimey, GRAHAM, and SLAVENSKA. Joined the Erika Thimey Dance T.

1952, and appeared with SOKOLOW 1955 (creating a role in ROOMS). He appeared in a Broadway production of Sean O'Casey's *Red Roses For Me* (1955) and was a member of the NY City O. ballet (1956); appeared frequently on TV. He joined P. LANG as a guest artist, 1957 and 1964. Established the Paul Sanasardo–Donya Feuer Dance Co. 1957, and in 1958 opened a school which is still in operation in NY. In the early 1960s he formed his own co., which has toured the W. Indies and Canada. Most of the over 20 dances he has choreographed deal with gloomy themes. Among his best-known works are *Metallics* (1969; mus. Henry Cowell and Henk Badings), *Cut Flowers* (1966; mus. Kazimierz Serocki), and *Pain* (1969; mus. Witold Lutowski). JD

Sancho Panza, servant of DON QUIXOTE

Sand, Inge, b. Copenhagen, 1928; d. Copenhagen, 1974. Danish dancer. Entered RDBS 1936; soloist 1950. Debut in H. LANDER's *Spring* 1945; from 1951 SWANILDA, the role that best showed her rare combination of wit and airy dance. Danced most of the big *demi-caractère* parts from FAR FROM DENMARK to ROBBINS's *Fanfare*. She was the indefatigable organizer of tours with smaller groups of the RDB, taking them first to Jacob's Pillow and other places in the USA in the 1950s and 1960s. In Copenhagen she organized a summer season at the New T. 1965 which brought new choreography to Copenhagen. From 1969 until her untimely death she was in charge of the Royal T.'s official tours. SKJ

San Francisco Ballet *see* REGIONAL BALLET (USA)

Sankovskaya, Ekaterina, b. Moscow, 1816; d. Moscow, 1878. Russian dancer. Studied Moscow TS 1825–36 under Felicité Hullin, who did much for her development and took her to Paris (1836) to see M. TAGLIONI dance SYLPHIDE. Upon return made her debut in this role 6 Sept 1837, while Taglioni made her debut as Sylphide in St Petersburg on the same date. Sankovskaya's talent was noticed at school; she performed children's parts in plays, having been taught by the great dramatic actor Mikhail Shchepkin. From 1829, while still a pupil, she danced ballets, and from 1836 occupied a leading position, becoming the idol of Moscow Univ. students and serious writers. Her technique might have been weaker than Taglioni's but she won hearts by great depth of characterization. Roles incl. GISELLE, CATARINA, ESMERALDA. She performed mime roles in operas and dramas and revived PERROT's ballets. Upon retirement in 1854 she lived in straitened circumstances, teaching ballroom dancing, especially in merchants' houses, incl. that of the Alekseyevs (parents of theatre director Konstantin Stanislavsky). NR
See Yuri Bakhrushin, *History of Russian Ballet*, 2nd ed. (Moscow 1973)

Mrinalini Sarabhai with Chatunni Panicker

Sarabhai, Mrinalini, b. Madras, 1923. Celebrated Indian dancer who has trained in *Dasi Attam*, *Kathakali*, Greek and Javanese dance, and Russian ballet. Toured worldwide and in 1948 founded the Darpana acad. of dance in Ahmedabad. RM

Sardanapal, ballet, 4 acts, ch. P. TAGLIONI; mus. Peter Ludwig Hertel. Berlin, Royal OH, 24 Apr 1865. Extremely popular ballet about Assyria; chosen as the first ballet presented in the new Vienna Hof O. 1869. Also given in Milan. GBLW

Sarry, Christine, b. Long Beach, CA, 1946. American dancer. Studied with MARACCI in California, Richard Thomas and FALLIS, New York. Danced with CCJB 1963–4, ABT 1964–8 and 1971–4, American B. Co. (FELD), 1969–71, Eliot Feld B. 1974 to date.

A dancer of great piquancy and infallible musicality, she has danced a wide range of roles in classic and contemporary ballets. DV

Sarstädt, Marian, b. Amsterdam, 1942. Dutch dancer. Danced with Scapino B. 1957–60, de Cuevas B. 1960–1, then NDT, where she became a leading soloist. Created many leading parts, especially in ballets by HARKARVY and van MANEN. Since her retirement in 1972 has been ballet mistress of Scapino B. of which her husband Armando Navarro is artistic director. JP

Satie, Erik (Alfred Leslie), b. Honfleur, Calvados, 1866; d. Paris 1925. French composer, who, despite his small output, became one of the seminal influences in 20th-c. music – especially on POULENC, MILHAUD, AURIC, SAUGUET – for his iconoclastic wit and his clarity, objectivity, and openness to popular influences like the music hall. For DIAGHILEV he wrote PARADE, for DE BEAUMONT's Soirées de Paris *Mercure* (Paris 1924; ch. MASSINE), for Les Ballets

Sergueeff [Sergeyev], Nicholas [Nikolay], b. St Petersburg, 1876; d. Nice, 1951. Russian dancer and *régisseur*. Trained in Imperial S., St Petersburg; graduated 1894, danced with the Maryinsky B.; *régisseur* 1904; *régisseur-général* 1914. He recorded the classic repertory in the Stepanov system of notation and after leaving Russia in 1918 brought his precious notebooks to the West. In 1921 he mounted *The Sleeping Princess* (*see* SLEEPING BEAUTY) for DIAGHILEV. When DE VALOIS began to build the RB she sought him out in Paris to stage the classics for her co. He also worked for INGLESBY's International B. It is thanks to him that such ballets as SWAN LAKE and *Sleeping Beauty* could be staged in the West more or less in their original choreography; when the RB took its *Sleeping Beauty* to Leningrad 1961 older ballet-goers recognized the version at once. The Sergueeff notebooks are now in the Harvard T. Collection. MC

Serrano, Lupe [Guadalupe], b. Santiago, 1930. Chilean dancer. Studied in Mexico, then in NY with SCHWEZOFF and TUDOR. Joined B. of Mexico City at 13, B. ALONSO 1949, B. Russe de Monte Carlo 1949–51, ABT 1953–72. Ballerina with strong technique and presence, especially in classic roles. Now teaches for Pennsylvania B. DV

Sertić, Ivan, b. Zagreb, 1922. Yugoslav dancer and ballet director. Studied London, Paris, and Moscow. Joined Belgrade B. 1947; principal dancer 1953. Soloist, Frankfurt, 1956–61; ballet master, Heidelberg, 1961–3; Lübeck 1963–5. To Wuppertal 1965 as assistant; ballet master 1968. In 1973 became ballet master, T. am Gärtnerplatz, Munich. Has choreographed many ballets. He m. NARANDA. GBLW

Setterfield, Valda, b. Margate, Kent, 1939. English dancer. Studied with RAMBERT and Audrey de Vos, London. Danced with BR. Toured Italy in a revue 1956. To USA 1958. Danced with the cos of WARING 1958–60 and 1965; LITZ (*Dracula*, 1959); CUNNINGHAM 1960–1 and 1965–74; and RAINER 1971–2. She m. GORDON, danced in his works. Appeared in the films *The Wedding Party* (1966; dir. Bryan de Palma) and Rainer's *Lives of Performers* (1972). Performed with Grand Union 1976. Teaches at Cunningham Studio. *See* AVANT-GARDE DANCE. DV

Seven Deadly Sins, ballet, ch. BALANCHINE; mus. Kurt Weill; lib. Berthold Brecht; sc./c. Casper Neher. Paris, T. des CE, Les Ballets 1933, 7 June 1933; sung Lotte Lenya; dan. Tilly Losch. NYCC, NYCB, 4 Dec 1958; tr. W. H. Auden and Chester Kallman; sc./c. TER-ARUTUNIAN; sung Lenya; dan. KENT. The heroine, doubly cast as dancer and singer, in search of enough money to build a home for her family back in Louisiana, travels to seven US cities in each of which she encounters one of the seven deadly sins: sloth, pride, anger, gluttony, lust, avarice, and envy. There have been many versions by other choreographers incl. MACMILLAN. FM/MC

Seymour [Springbett], Lynn, b. Wainwright, Alberta, 1939. Canadian dancer and choreographer. Studied in Vancouver and London SWS. Danced with CG OB 1956, RB 1957, first with touring co., soloist of main co. 1958–66, from 1970; with MACMILLAN to Deutsche OB, W. Berlin, 1966–9. MacMillan picked her out of the Royal *corps de ballet* to dance leading roles in *The Burrow* 1958, BAISER DE LA FÉE, and INVITATION 1960. Later he made his ROMEO AND JULIET for her 1965 (though FONTEYN danced in the premiere), and ANASTASIA. ASHTON created DEUX PIGEONS for her, MONTH IN THE COUNTRY, and *Five Brahms Waltzes in the Style of Isadora Duncan* (solo) 1975–6. The leading dramatic ballerina of her generation. Guest artist with many cos incl. LFB 1969 and 1970; NB of Canada 1965; AILEY Dance T. 1971; LCDT 1975 (when she choreographed and danced a duet with NORTH, *Gladly Badly Sadly Madly*); ABT 1976, when she danced TUDOR's PILLAR OF FIRE and ROMEO AND JULIET, as well as SWAN LAKE. First commissioned

Lynn Seymour as Anna Anderson in ANASTASIA

ballet *Rashomon,* London, SWT, SWRB, Nov 1976. CBE 1976. DV
See C. Crisp, 'Lynn Seymour', *Les Saisons de la Danse* (Paris, May 1976) with list of roles

Shabelevsky, Yurek, b. Warsaw, 1911. Polish dancer. Studied at Wielki (Grand) O., Warsaw, later with NIJINSKA. Danced with RUBINSTEIN co. in Paris and on tour 1928; 1932–9 was with DE BASIL's co., creating roles in several MASSINE ballets and dancing such roles as PETRUSHKA and the Chief Warrior in PRINCE IGOR. Handsome and virile, Shabelevsky epitomized the high standard of male dancing in the B. Russe cos of the 1930s. In 1940 appeared briefly with ABT as a guest. Toured the USA with his own group, then to S. America and Italy. From 1967 ballet master, New Zealand B. MC

Shadow of the Wind *see* LIED VON DER ERDE

Shadowplay, ballet, 1 act, ch./lib. TUDOR; mus. Charles Koechlin (*Les Bandar-Log* and *La Course de Printemps*); sc./c. Michael Annals. London, CG, RB, 25 Jan 1967; dan. DOWELL (the Boy with Matted Hair), RENCHER (the Terrestrial), PARK (the Celestial). Inspired partly by Rudyard Kipling's *Jungle Book* stories, the ballet suggests the forces that mould individuals and shows the individual (the Boy) struggling for self-assertion. Tudor gives no clue or program note; the ballet could be about 'growing up'. Revived NY State T., ABT, 23 July 1975; dan. BARYSHNIKOV, Jonas Kage, KIRKLAND. MC

Shankar, Uday, b. Udaipur, 1900. Indian dancer and choreographer. After studying many types of dance, he evolved his own distinctive style. In his youth he studied art and partnered A. PAVLOVA in London, and was the first to make Indian dancing understood in the West. He is the pioneer of choreography and creative dance in India, where he founded his own school in 1938. RM

Shaw, Brian, b. Golcar, Yorkshire, 1928. English dancer and teacher. Studied with Ruth French and made first appearances (as Brian Earnshaw) with RAD Production Club and with SW OB. Joined SWB 1944, becoming the finest classical male dancer of his generation. Created virtuoso role in SYMPHONIC VARIATIONS; a famous BLUEBIRD and BLUE SKATER, impeccable in technique in classical variations. A brilliant teacher, he still appears in mime roles, notably as the WIDOW SIMONE. MC

Shawn, Ted [Edwin Meyers], b. Kansas City, MO, 1891; d. Orlando, FL, 1972. American dancer, choreographer, and teacher. Studied at Univ. of Denver, CO, began to study ballet to strengthen his legs after an illness. He m. ST DENIS and became her partner 1914; together they founded the DENISHAWN S. and Co. Separated from St Denis 1932. Formed his Co. of Male Dancers 1933, with the express purpose of destroying public prejudice against dancing by men. His choreography, especially for this co., made use of American native material, aboriginal, folk, and popular. Disbanded the co. 1940; became director of the Jacob's Pillow Dance Fest. and Summer S. 1941, both of which followed the Denishawn principle of embracing dance in all its aspects. Continued to perform there until he was over 70. His works incl. many solos and duets for St Denis and himself, and group works such as *Prometheus Bound* (1929; mus. Aleksandr Skriabin), and, for his male co. KINETIC MOLPAI (1935). Author of several books incl. *Ruth St Denis: Pioneer and Prophet*, *Gods Who Dance*, *Every Little Movement* (2nd ed. Pittsfield, MA, 1963), and an autobiography (with Gray Poole), *One Thousand and One Night Stands* (New York 1960). DV

Shearer[-King], Moira, b. Dunfermline, 1926. Scottish dancer and actress. Early studies in Rhodesia and from 1936 with English teacher Flora Fairbairn and at Legat S. working mostly with Nadezhda (Nadine) Nikolayeva Legat. In 1940 joined SWBS, professional debut International B. 1941, returned to SWS for further study and joined co. 1942. ASHTON cast her in the role of Pride in *The Quest* (1943) in which she made her name. In 1944 she was named a ballerina of the SWB, a title she retained until in 1952 she withdrew from the co. to pursue a new career as an actress. Her red hair and porcelain beauty gave her a 'fairy princess' image, fully exploited in the film *The Red Shoes* (dir. Michael Powell and Emeric Pressburger, 1948) which has probably introduced more people to ballet than any other event. With SWB created one of ballerina roles in SYMPHONIC VARIATIONS, and title role in Ashton's CINDERELLA. Danced all the major ballerina roles. She m. writer and TV personality Ludovic Kennedy. Occasional TV, stage, and lecture appearances. MC

Shearer, Sybil, b. Toronto. Canadian dancer and choreographer. Studied at Skidmore and Bennington Colleges. Soloist in HUMPHREY–WEIDMAN Co., assisted DE MILLE in 1941 on two ballets, *Three Virgins and a Devil,* for ABT, and *Drums Sound in Hackensack*, for B. JOOSS. First solo concert 1942. Settled in Chicago 1943, though she continued to give regular concerts in NY, usually devoted to cycles of dances, some untitled and abstract (1949 and 1955), others with titles suggesting a theme, such as *Once Upon a Time* (1951), *Shades Before Mars* (1955), *Seven Images of the Answer* (1957). Formed the Sybil Shearer Co. 1959, for which she choreographed *Within This Thicket* (1959), her first major group work; *Fables and Proverbs* (1961); *Wherever the Web and the Tendril* (1964); *In Place of Opinions* (1965); *Ticket to Where?* (1972). After this she disbanded the co. and devoted herself to making films with Helen Morrison, her associate and lighting designer since 1943. The first of these, *A Sheaf of Dreams* (1975), uses material from some of her dances. Mysterious, lyric, or witty, her dances are unlike any others, though she shares with other great modern dance soloists from I. DUNCAN onward the quality of being a force of nature. DV

Shelest, Alla, b. Smolensk, 1919. Soviet dancer. Graduated from Leningrad Choreographic S. 1937, pupil of E. GERDT, VAGANOVA. Kirov T. 1937–63. A fine, expressive dancer in romantic, heroic, and tragic vein, colouring each role with her own personality. Her extraordinary versatility was shown in different creations such as Aegina (YACOBSON's SPARTACUS), Nikia (BAYADÈRE), ZAREMA, LAURENCIA, Suimbike (SHURAVE), etc. Taught at Ballet Masters' Faculty, Leningrad Cons., 1965–70. Now choreographs in various opera houses; staged exquisite GISELLE in Tartu, Estonia, for Vanemuine TB. People's Artist, RSFSR. NR
See A. Shelest, 'Shakespeare in My Life', *Teatr* magazine no. 4 (Moscow 1964); B. Lvov-Anokhin, *Alla Shelest* (Moscow 1964)

Shurale, ballet, 3 acts, 4 scenes, ch. YACOBSON after Tartar folk tales; mus. Farid Yarullin. Leningrad, Kirov T., 28 June 1950; dan. BELSKY (Shurale), SHELEST (Suimbike, the Bird-girl), Askold Makarov (Ali-Batyr). Originally intended for production at the Tartar Fest. of Art, Moscow, 1941, but because of World War II not produced until 1945 in Kazan. Staged Moscow, same choreography, 1955. Shurale, a Tartar wood spirit, steals Suimbike's wings to separate her from Ali-Batyr, but Suimbike learns how to love humans and stays with the people and her beloved of her own free will. Yacobson artfully blends classical dance with Tartar national idiom. Other versions staged in Kazan, Sofia, etc. NR

Sibley, Antoinette, b. Bromley, Kent, 1939. English dancer. Studied first at Arts Educational S., then RBS at age 10 where she received her full training. Joined RB 1956 and in 1959 danced SWANILDA in the first RBS matinée at CG. A principal by 1960. She had an

Alla Shelest in BAYADÈRE, 1950

Antoinette Sibley as JULIET

overnight triumph that year dancing ODETTE-ODILE at very short notice for an indisposed NERINA. Since then has danced all great ballerina roles, the undisputed successor to FONTEYN in SLEEPING BEAUTY. Created Titania in DREAM to the Oberon of DOWELL, with whom she established an internationally celebrated partnership. Created Dorabella in ENIGMA VARIATIONS and title role in MANON. Her dancing combines the lyric qualities of the English school with the grandeur of the Russians, especially in BAYADÈRE. CBE 1973. MC
See N. Dromgoole (text) and L. Spatt (photos), *Sibley and Dowell* (London and New York 1976)

Siedova, Julie *see* SEDOVA, Julia

Siegfried, Prince, the hero of SWAN LAKE

Simone, Kirsten, b. Copenhagen, 1934. Danish dancer. Entered RDBS 1945; soloist 1956; first solo dancer 1966. Debut 1952 as Hilde in August BOURNONVILLE's FOLK LEGEND, and has danced many of his parts from SYLPHIDE to Teresina in NAPOLI. With VOLKOVA as teacher, however, she grew into the neo-Russian style and found her place in the M. PETIPA repertory from SLEEPING BEAUTY to ODETTE-ODILE and NUTCRACKER. With PETIT's CARMEN she entered the *caractère* genre, and as Carmen and MISS JULIE found new ways to express her personality, combined with a technique in which she has excelled from ASHTON's JULIET to NEUMEIER's Lady Capulet (ROMEO AND JULIET). SKJ
See E. Aschengreen, 'Kirsten Simone', *Les Saisons de la Danse* (Paris, Mar 1971)

Simonov, Yuri, b. 1941. Russian conductor, graduate Leningrad Cons. 1965. After winning first prize at the International Conducting Competition, Rome, 1967, Simonov was invited to the Bolshoy, Moscow, where in 1969 he was appointed chief conductor. In the West he has led the Bolshoy O., the Bolshoy B. (London, summer 1974) and Stars of the Bolshoy B. (NY, autumn 1974), on each occasion with great success, his conducting being marked by enormous theatrical skill and irresistible ardour. DH

Sisyphus, ballet, ch. ÅKESSON assisted by Kåre Gundersen; mus. Karl-Birger Blomdahl; lib. Erik Lindegren; sc. Tor Hörlin; ltg Göran Gentele. Stockholm, RSB, 18 Apr 1957; dan. Åkesson (alternating with ORLANDO), HOLMGREN, Mario Mengarelli, Teddy Rhodin, Viveka Ljung. The Greek myth treated in a modern dance idiom, very stylized and beautiful. AGS

Sizova, Alla, b. Moscow, 1939. Soviet dancer. One of leading ballerinas, Kirov B. Graduated from VAGANOVA S. 1958; danced Masha (NUTCRACKER; VAINONEN version). Ethereal, lyrical dancer, lovely line, faultless technique. She first danced GISELLE 1963, JULIET 1965. Created Girl in LENINGRAD SYMPHONY, Ophelia (SERGEYEV's HAMLET), Princess Belle Rose in VINOGRADOV's *Enchanted Prince* (*see* PRINCE OF THE PAGODAS). Danced Snow Maiden and Firebird in YACOBSON's *Choreographic Miniatures*. People's Artist, RSFSR. Gold medal, Varna, 1964. Prix A. PAVLOVA for AURORA in Sergeyev's film of SLEEPING BEAUTY. NR
See article by V. Kiselev in *Leningrad Ballet Today*, No. 2 (Leningrad 1968)

Skeaping, Mary, b. Woodford, Essex, 1902. English dancer, teacher, scholar, and authority on the ballet style of the 17th and 18th centuries. Studied with Francesca Zanfretta, NOVIKOV, EGOROVA, TREFILOVA, CRASKE, and LABAN. Danced with A. PAVLOVA's co. Ballet mistress, SWB, 1948–51; director, RSB, 1953–62. Choreographed *Cupid out of his Humour* (mus. Henry Purcell) at Drottningholm T., for state visit of Queen Elizabeth II, Sweden, 1956; subsequently re-created many of the old court ballets there, since 1967 in collaboration with CRAMÉR. Directed the film *The Little Ballerina* (London 1947) and the first live full-length classic ballet for BBC TV, SLEEPING BEAUTY, 1951, then SWAN LAKE 1952 (prod. Christian Simpson). Has staged classic ballets all over the world, notably in Finland, Cuba, Sweden, Canada, and USA. Adviser on historical works to the RB's Ballet For All. MBE 1958; Dame, Vasa Order, Sweden 1961. MC

Skibine, George, b. Yasnaya Polyana, Russia, 1920. Russian-American dancer and choreographer. Studied with PREOBRAZHENSKA, SEDOVA, VOLININ, LIFAR, EGOROVA. Debut Bal Tabarin nightclub 1936. B. de la Jeunesse 1937. B. Russe de Monte Carlo 1938–41. To the USA, ABT, 1941–2. Danced in MASSINE's *Seventh Symphony*, *Nobilissima Visione*, and *Aleko*, and FOKINE's *Bluebeard*. Original B. Russe 1946; MARKOVA-DOLIN Co. 1947; DE CUEVAS B. 1947–56, where he danced notably Edward Caton's *Sebastian*, SONNAMBULA, CONCERTO BAROCCO, *Inès de Castro* (ch. Ana Ricarda). Choreographed and danced *Tragédie à Vérone* (1950), *Annabel Lee* (1951), *Le Prisonnier du Caucase* (1951), *Idylle* (1954), etc. After a brief stay with PAGE co. 1956–7, engaged at the Paris O. as *danseur étoile* and choreographer, then *maître de ballet* 1958–62. Artistic director, HARKNESS B. 1964–6; Dallas Civic B. 1969. Reims B. 1974. He m. Marjorie TALLCHIEF. An elegant dancer and good partner, the best part of his choreographic work has been his feeling for *pas de deux*. M-FC
See I. Lidova, 'George Skibine', *Les Saisons de la Danse* (Paris, May 1970)

Skorik [Beaudemont], Irène, b. Paris, 1928. French dancer. Studied with ZAMBELLI, PREOBRAZHENSKA, and V. GSOVSKY. Debut 'Vendredis de la Danse', T. Sarah-Bernhardt 1944. B. des CE 1945–50. Created roles in CHARRAT's *Jeu de Cartes* (*see* CARD GAME),

PETIT's *Déjeuner sur l'Herbe* (1945) and AMOURS DE JUPITER. Prima ballerina, Munich 1950–2, W. Berlin 1956–7. MISKOVITCH Co. 1957–60; Basel B. 1960–5. Guest artist LFB 1963. Her youthful promise was not wholly fulfilled as a ballerina as, after leaving Petit, she did not find another choreographer who understood so well her classical style and poetic sweetness. Now teaches in Paris. M-FC

Skouratoff, Wladimir, b. Paris, 1925. French dancer. Studied with PREOBRAZHENSKA and KNIASEFF. Galas with JEANMAIRE. Soloist, Nouveau B. de Monte Carlo 1946. Created roles in LIFAR's *Chota Roustaveli* and *Aubade* 1946. Original B. Russe 1947. B. de Paris 1948; created roles in CHARRAT's *'Adame Miroir* and *La Femme et son Ombre* (1948; also ch. Charrat). B. des CE 1951; DE CUEVAS B. 1952–8. Created roles in PIÈGE DE LUMIÈRE 1952, SKIBINE's *Idylle* (1954), *Le Rendez-vous Manqué* (ch. TARAS and Don Lurio; mus. Michel Magne; sc. Bernard Buffet; lib. Françoise Sagan, Monte Carlo, 3 Jan 1958). Guest artist Scandinavian B., LFB 1960. *Maître de ballet*, Strasbourg O. 1967–9, Bordeaux 1970–6. He had the looks of a French film star, dark and romantic, and shone in the modern repertory where his great dramatic gifts could also be used. M-FC

Slavenska [Čorak], Mia, b. Slavonski-Brod, 1914. Yugoslav dancer. Studied Zagreb, Vienna, with NIJINSKA in Paris, and Vincenzo Celli in NY. Debut with Zagreb NO, of which she became ballerina 1933. Danced in Nijinska's Co., Paris, 1933, under her real name. First prize at Dance Olympiad, Berlin, 1936. Appeared in film *La Mort du Cygne* (1937). B. Russe de Monte Carlo 1938–42; Slavenska B. Variante 1947–52; guest artist, LFB 1952; Slavenska-FRANKLIN B. 1952–5; NY Met OB 1955–6. Classic ballerina of great virtuosity, she also danced contemporary dramatic roles such as Blanche in BETTIS's *A Streetcar Named Desire*, created for her in 1952. Now teaches in CA. DV

Slayton, Jeff [Jeffrey Clarke], b. Richmond, VA, 1945. American dancer and choreographer. Studied tap, ballet, and modern dance; debut with CUNNINGHAM and Dance Co. 1968. Left to join FARBER Dance Co. 1970, having earlier danced in Farber's *Duet for Mirjam and Jeff* (1969). He m. Farber, with whom he shared Gold Medal at 9th International Dance Fest., Paris, 1971. DV

Sleep, Wayne, b. Plymouth, 1948. English dancer, pupil of Muriel Carr and then RBS. Succeeded in appearing in no fewer than three RBS annual matinées and had won a public before he entered the RB in 1966; soloist 1970; principal 1973. His lack of inches is compensated for by abundance of personality and a stunning technique. An intelligent actor (he has appeared in plays, films, and operas), he is at his best in *demi-caractère* roles such as Puck (DREAM) and the Jester (CINDERELLA). Created

The Sleeping Beauty, SWB at CG, 1946; ELVIN and RASSINE in the BLUEBIRD *pas de deux*

small but brilliant role in ENIGMA VARIATIONS and was also the son in MONTH IN THE COUNTRY. His passion for dancing is insatiable; he willingly gives up free time to appear with school or amateur groups. LCDT with NORTH, choreographed and danced in *David and Goliath* (1975). MC

Sleeping Beauty, The (*La Belle au Bois Dormant*; Russian title: *Spyashchaya Krasavitsa*), ballet, prologue and 3 acts, ch. M. PETIPA; lib. Petipa and VSEVOLOZHSKY, after the fairytale by Charles Perrault; mus. TCHAIKOVSKY; sc. Heinrich Levogt, Ivan Andreyev, Mikhail Bocharov, Konstantin Ivanov, Matvey Shishkov; c. Vsevolozhsky. St Petersburg, Maryinsky T., 16 Jan 1890; dan. BRIANZA, P. GERDT, CECCHETTI, Varvara Nikitina, Marie Petipa. After Brianza's departure, the title role of Aurora was danced by KSHESSINSKA. Although it represents the summation of late 19th-c. classicism, the ballet was not an immediate success – the music was considered 'too symphonic'. However, it gradually established itself as a favourite and has had a fairly continuous performance history in Russia.

Moscow, Bolshoy T., 17 Jan 1899, ch. reproduced by GORSKY from Vladimir Stepanov notation; sc. Anatoli Geltser and Karl Valts; this version revived at St Petersburg, Maryinsky T., 16 Feb 1914; sc. Konstantin Korovin. New versions were staged at the Kirov by F. LOPUKHOV, 8 Oct 1922, and SERGEYEV, 25 Mar 1952; at the Bolshoy by TIKHOMIROV, 25 May 1924, and by MESSERER, 20 Dec 1936, and again 9 Apr 1952. On 27 Dec 1963 the Bolshoy presented a production by GRIGOROVICH that attempted to restore a more authentic choreographic text (some revisions, June 1973).

The first production outside Russia seems to have been that given at Milan, Sc., 11 Mar 1896, ch. Giorgio Saracco, in which Brianza again danced the title role – it is a safe assumption, therefore, that some of the choreography followed that of the original.

This too was unsuccessful and the ballet was not revived again there until 24 Jan 1940, ch. Nives Poli. On 31 Aug 1916 A. PAVLOVA presented an abridged version, arr. KHLUSTIN, as part of an extravaganza called *The Big Show* at the Hippodrome, NY, chiefly significant because decor was designed by BAKST, who was to design the first important Western production, that presented at the Alhambra T., London, 2 Nov 1921, by DIAGHILEV; many of the designs were in fact identical or nearly so. Diaghilev's was the most lavish production of a full-length classic ballet ever produced; again, it was a financial failure and left him bankrupt. The choreography had been reproduced by SERGUEEFF, again from Stepanov, with additions by NIJINSKA, and STRAVINSKY edited the score. The title role was danced at alternate perfs by SPESSIVTSEVA, EGOROVA, L. LOPUKHOVA, and TREFILOVA, with VLADIMIROFF or VILZAK as the Prince. Brianza appeared as the Wicked Fairy, Carabosse. Diaghilev salvaged a 1-act *divertissement*, (AURORA'S WEDDING) from the production.

When DE VALOIS formed the Vic-Wells B. an important part of her policy was the systematic revival of the great classic ballets; *The Sleeping Beauty* (called *The Sleeping Princess* as it had been by Diaghilev) was revived at SW, 2 Feb 1939, reproduced by Sergueeff; sc./c. Nadia Benois; dan. FONTEYN, HELPMANN. It was the ballet with which the co. reopened CG after World War II, 20 Feb 1946 – again with Fonteyn and Helpmann; additional choreography by de Valois and ASHTON; sc./c. MESSEL – and with which it opened its first NY season at the Met, 9 Oct 1949. The production was finally supplanted on 17 Dec 1968 by a new one staged by P. WRIGHT and Ashton (sc. Henry Bardon; c. Lila de'Nobili and Rostislav Dobuzhinsky), in turn replaced by MACMILLAN's version 15 Mar 1973 (sc./c. Peter Farmer).

In the USA, there were attempts to present more or less complete versions by MORDKIN, 1936, Catherine Littlefield (Philadelphia B.), 1937, and A. OBUKHOV, San Francisco, *c.* 1947. ABT presented a 1-act *divertissement* called *Princess Aurora*, reproduced by DOLIN, Mexico, 23 Oct 1941 (revised by TUDOR, 1947, and by BALANCHINE, 1949). A new production of Act III of the complete ballet, ch. BLAIR, was given 19 Feb 1974, as the first instalment of a projected complete production. This did not materialize, at least not as planned. When *The Sleeping Beauty* in its entirety finally entered the repertory of ABT, at the Met, 15 June 1976, ch. was reproduced by SKEAPING; sc./c. Messel, based on his 1946 designs for the London SWB; dan. MAKAROVA, BARYSHNIKOV.

Other notable productions incl.: Lithuanian National OB, Kaunas, 1934 (ch. reproduced by Nicholas Zverev; sc./c. Mstislav Dobuzhinsky); International B., London, 24 May 1948 (ch. reproduced by Sergueeff; sc. Prince Aleksandr Schervachidze; c. Hein Heckroth); RSB, Stockholm, 13 Jan 1955 (ch. reproduced by Skeaping; sc./c. Yngve Gamlin); RDB, Copenhagen, 8 May 1957 (ch. reproduced by de Valois and VAN PRAAGH; sc./c. André Delfau); DE CUEVAS Co., Paris, 25 Oct 1960 (ch. reproduced by Helpmann; sc./c. Raimundo de Larrain); Sc., Milan, 22 Sept 1966 (ch. reproduced and considerably revised by NUREYEV; sc./c. GEORGIADIS), revived NB of Canada, 1 Sept 1972, LFB, 16 Apr 1975; Deutsche OB, W. Berlin, 8 Oct 1967 (ch. reproduced by MacMillan; sc./c. Barry Kay); NB of Cuba, Havana, 3 Nov 1974 (ch. ALONSO; sc./c. Salvador Fernandez), revived Paris O., 31 Dec 1974 (sc./c. José Varona). DV

See D. Vaughan, 'Further Annals of *The Sleeping Beauty*', *Ballet Review*, Vol. 3, No. 2 (New York 1969); F. Lopukhov and B. Asafyev, 'Annals of *The Sleeping Beauty*' in *Ballet Review*, Vol. 5, No. 4 (New York 1975–6); Mary Clarke and Clement Crisp, *Making a Ballet* (London and New York 1975)

Sleeping Princess, The *see* SLEEPING BEAUTY

Slonimsky, Yuri, b. St Petersburg, 1902. Soviet ballet historian, critic, and author of ballet librettos. Candidate of Science/Arts. Educated at Law School, Univ. of Petrograd and the Inst. for History of Arts (Theatre division). Developed interest in ballet in his youth; took part in activities of the Young B. founded by BALANCHINE and others. Started writing on ballet 1919. First important monographs *Giselle* (1926), *La Sylphide* (1927). His next important work, *Masters of the Ballet of the XIXth Century* (1937), brought him wide recognition, partly translated by CHUJOY for *Dance Index* (New York). Taught at Moscow and Leningrad S. in 1930s, also Choreographers' Faculty, GITIS, and at Leningrad Cons. He was the first Soviet scholar to bring a sound academic approach to the study of ballet. His libs incl. COAST OF HOPE. NR

See Yuri Slonimsky, *The Bolshoy Ballet* (Moscow 1956, 1963), which incl. lists of his scenarios and works; '*Raymonda*: An Analysis' in *A. Glazunov, Musical Legacy*, Vol. 1 (Leningrad 1959); (ed.) *M. Fokine* (Leningrad 1962); *Seven Ballet Stories* (Moscow 1968), a personal account of his own libs; *In Honour of Dance* (Moscow 1968), a collection of articles, some previously unpublished; (ed.) *Petipa* (Leningrad 1971); *Pushkin's Ballet Lines* (Leningrad 1974); *Dramaturgy of Ballet* (Leningrad 1976), containing libs of famous ballets with analyses; 'Balanchine: The Early Years', tr. John Andrews, in *Ballet Review*, Vol. 5, No. 3 (New York 1976)

Smith, George Washington, b. *c.* 1820; d. Philadelphia, PA, 1899. American dancer and teacher. One of the many young Americans to be enslaved by ELSSLER on her US tour 1840–2, he joined her co. and studied with her then partner James Sylvain. He became LEE's partner and danced ALBRECHT with her, Boston, 1 Jan 1846. In 1859 was principal dancer with the Ronzani B., the first Italian co. to tour the USA (it incl. the young CECCHETTI and his parents). In the early 1880s opened a successful school in Philadelphia. MC

See Lillian Moore, 'George Washington Smith', *Dance Index*, Vol. 4, No. 6 (New York, June–Aug 1945)

Smith, Oliver, b. Waupun, WI, 1918. American designer and producer. His special gift is for evoking American settings. RODEO captured the spirit of the prairies and FANCY FREE a NY bar and street on a hot summer night. His set for FALL RIVER LEGEND could be manipulated effortlessly to change from an indoor to an outdoor setting. Also successfully designed ABT's production of NOCES. Has worked extensively for musicals, for plays and opera, and received many awards for his designs. Co-director of ABT since 1945. MC

Snow Maiden (*Snegurochka*), ballet (1) 2 acts, ch. Vladimir Varkovitsky; mus. TCHAIKOVSKY; sc. Pyotr Williams. Moscow Choreographic S., graduation perf., 5 July 1946; dan. Tamara Tuchnina. Revived 1948, also for graduation perf. (2) 3 acts, ch./lib. BURMEISTER; same mus. arr. with other Tchaikovsky music, some from the *Children's Album*; sc. Yuri Pimenov and Gennadi Epishin. London, Royal Festival Hall, LFB, 17 July 1961. Moscow, Stanislavsky and Nemirovich-Danchenko Lyric T., 2 Nov 1963; sc. Boris Volkov; dan. VINOGRADOVA (title role), VLASOVA (Kupava).

All versions of this ballet are based on the play of the same title by Aleksandr Ostrovsky, for which Tchaikovsky composed the music. The Snow Maiden lives in a forest with her father, the Frost. Wishing to know humans and hearing sounds of revels coming from a nearby village, she goes there, sees a village youth, and experiences the feeling of love for the first time. With the first rays of the hot spring sun, however, she melts away. NR

Söffing, Tilly, b. Apolda, 1932. German dancer. Studied at Bornhacke-Urlichs S., Jena, and with BESOBRAZOVA. Danced in Gera, Weimar, Aachen, and Augsburg Bs; a principal in Cologne 1960–5, and Düsseldorf from 1965. An outstanding dancer in the German late modern style. GBLW

Sokolova, Evgenia, b. St Petersburg, 1850; d. Leningrad, 1925. Russian ballerina and teacher. Graduated from St Petersburg TS 1869, but as early as 1861 danced successfully in *The Pearl of Seville* (ch. SAINT-LÉON; mus. PUGNI). Danced principal part in *L'Amour Bienfaiteur*, created for her by M. PETIPA (mus. Pugni) at school perf., 6 Mar 1868. In 1869 accepted into St Petersburg Bolshoy T. as *première danseuse*. A soft, lyrical dancer, inferior to her contemporary VAZEM in technique, but graceful and expressive. Abandoned stage 1886; taught and rehearsed in St Petersburg, replacing JOHANSSON on his recommendation. Her pupils incl. A. PAVLOVA, KARSAVINA, EGOROVA. After the October Revolution returned to the Maryinsky T., revived old ballets, taught and rehearsed until 1923; was awarded an honorary pension. Her roles incl. those in FILLE DU PHARAON, DON QUIXOTE, CORSAIRE, ESMERALDA, and *Les Offrandes à l'Amour ou le Bonheur est d'Aimer*, created for her by Petipa (mus. MINKUS) July 1886, in which she danced Chloe. She appeared in this role for her farewell perf. 25 Nov 1886. NR

Sokolova, Lydia [Hilda Munnings], b. Wanstead, Essex, 1896; d. Sevenoaks, 1974. English dancer. Studied with A. PAVLOVA and MORDKIN; joined DIAGHILEV co. 1913, his first English dancer. Remained with his co. until the end, dancing principal roles, mostly *demi-caractère* but incl. the Chosen Maiden in MASSINE's version of SACRE DU PRINTEMPS. After 1929, worked in musicals in London and taught for the RAD. In 1962 appeared as a guest with the RB as the Marquise Silvestra in a revival of FEMMES DE BONNE HUMEUR. In the course of his Diaghilev Exhibition in 1954 BUCKLE discovered her gifts as a *raconteuse* and she gave several talks. A warm personality of great loyalty, she suffered much hardship with Diaghilev during World War I. MC
See L. Sokolova, ed. R. Buckle, *Dancing for Diaghilev: The Memoirs of Lydia Sokolova* (London 1960; New York 1961)

Sokolow, Anna, b. Hartford, CT, 1915. American modern dance choreographer, teacher, and dancer. Studied with GRAHAM, HORST, at the NY Met OBS, and at the Bennington (VT) S. of Dance; left home at 15 to join the Graham co., with which she danced until 1938. In 1934 she formed the first of several cos which appeared intermittently until the late 1960s. She has a close attachment to Mexico and Israel, where she taught, founding the first Mexican modern dance co. 1939. She has also taught movement and choreography in Sweden, Switzerland, Germany, the Netherlands, Japan, and at the Juilliard S. of Music, NY. Her works have been performed by NDT, Inbal, and the Lyric T. of Tel-Aviv (founded by her but no longer in existence), the BR, London, the NY CCJB, the Boston B. and the AILEY Dance T. She began to choreograph 1933 and has worked in theatre, opera, and musicals as well as modern dance. She uses music as diverse as that of Jelly Roll Morton and Edgard Varèse, but much of her work has been set to jazz, often that of Teo Macero. Her earliest works dealt with social conditions. Her dances are dramatic, with sombre themes of loneliness, alienation, and the ills of contemporary civilization. Of a repertory of over 50 works, among her best known are *Lyric Suite* (1953; mus. Alban Berg), ROOMS, *Dreams* (1961; mus. Anton (von) Webern), and *Steps of Silence* (1968; mus. Anatol Vieru). JD

Solomons, Gus Jr [Gustave Martinez], b. Boston, MA, 1938. American dancer and choreographer. Studied architecture at Massachusetts Inst. of Technology, and dance with Jan Veen in Boston, in NY with CUNNINGHAM, COHAN, GRAHAM, American B. Center, and NYSB. Danced with the cos of McKAYLE 1961–4, P. LANG 1961–8, Graham 1964–5, and Cunningham 1965–8. Formed his own co., The Solomons Co./Dance, 1972. Has choreographed many works for his own co. and for various college dance groups in the USA, the AILEY Repertory Workshop, and Maryland Dance T. The formal meticulousness of his work reflects his early training as an architect, though he has also experimented with various indeterminate structures. Appointed Dean of Dance, CA Inst. of the Arts, 1976. DV

Solovyov, Yuri, b. Leningrad, 1940; d. Sosnova, nr Leningrad, 1977. Soviet dancer. Graduated from VAGANOVA S. 1958, class of Boris Shavrov. Debut as BLUEBIRD. Had extraordinary elevation, noted for very soft landing, and virtuosity of technique, especially in turns. Danced all classical repertory, and created many roles in contemporary ballets incl. Youth (LENINGRAD SYMPHONY), God (*Creation of the World*, ch. KASATKINA and VASILYOV). He m. Tatiana Legat, a soloist with Kirov B. People's Artist, USSR. Prix Nijinsky 1963. NR
See article by L. Linkova in *Leningrad Ballet Today*, No. 1 (Leningrad 1967)

Michael Somes dancing with FONTEYN in ASHTON's *Horoscope*, 1938

Sombert, Claire, b. Courbevoie, 1935. French dancer. Studied with Yves Brieux, ROUSANNE, PREOBRAZHENSKA. B. CHARRAT 1951, B. de Paris 1953, Milan Sc. 1955. Has danced with BABILÉE, MISKOVITCH, LIFAR, CHAUVIRÉ; and on TV. *Étoile* and director, B. du Rhin 1972. Created gypsy girl in LOUP and roles in BÉJART's *Créatures de Prométhée* 1956, and LAZZINI's *Pour Orchestre à Cordes* (1965). Dances JEUNE HOMME ET LA MORT, BALANCE À TROIS, GISELLE. Much admired in Russia for her classical style but has proved her ability to break free from traditional conventions and excel in the contemporary repertory. M-FC
See I. Lidova, 'Claire Sombert', *Les Saisons de la Danse* (Paris, Apr 1973) with list of roles

Somes, Michael, b. Horsley, Gloucestershire, 1917. English dancer and *répétiteur*. After early training in the W. of England and then with ESPINOSA, Somes won the first male scholarship to the SWS, 1934. Joined the co. in 1936 and was noticed for his exceptional elevation, while still in the *corps de ballet*, in PATINEURS. First created role was the Young Man in ASHTON's *Horoscope* (1938; mus. LAMBERT, sc./c. FEDOROVITCH) in which he danced with FONTEYN. Many creations in Ashton ballets, notably in SYMPHONIC VARIATIONS, *Daphnis and Chloe* (*see* DAPHNIS ET CHLOÉ) and ONDINE. After HELPMANN left the SWB in 1950, Somes became Fonteyn's regular partner, dancing all the major classics and also creating the role of Ivan Tsarevich in the RB's revival of OISEAU DE FEU – in which he has never been equalled. Retired from dancing roles in 1961 but continues to appear in mime roles; created the father in MARGUERITE AND ARMAND and Capulet in MACMILLAN's ROMEO AND JULIET. An assistant director of the RB 1963–70. Since 1970 a principal teacher and *répétiteur*, with special responsibility for the Ashton ballets. He has a quietly commanding stage presence, and great nobility of bearing. From KARSAVINA he learned much about the ballets in her repertoire. He choreographed one ballet, *Summer Interlude* (1950; mus. Ottorino Respighi, sc./c. Fedorovitch) for SWTB but showed no more interest in choreography. His entire career has been devoted to the RB; the quality of the *corps de ballet* owes much to his vigilance. CBE 1959. MC

Sonate à Trois, ballet, 1 scene, ch. BÉJART; mus. BARTÓK; c. contemporary dress. Essen, BT de Maurice Béjart, 27 Apr 1957; dan. SEIGNEURET, BARI, Béjart. Paris, T. Marigny, 19 June 1957. A danced version of Jean-Paul Sartre's play *Huis Clos*. Revived London, SW, Western TB, 22 Apr 1960. In repertory of Scottish B. Béjart gave the ballet to Western TB in admiration for its work with his dancers at the T. Royal de la Monnaie. MC

Song of the Earth *see* LIED VON DER ERDE

Songs of a Wayfarer *see* LIEDER EINES FAHRENDEN GESELLEN

Sonnambula, La (*The Sleepwalker*), ballet, 1 act, ch. BALANCHINE; mus. Vittorio Rieti, partly after Vincenzo Bellini's opera *La Sonnambula*; lib. Rieti; sc./c. Dorothea Tanning. NYCC, B. Russe de Monte Carlo, 27 Feb 1946 (as *Night Shadow*); dan. A. DANILOVA, MAGALLANES, Maria TALLCHIEF, Michel Katcharoff. At a masked ball, a Poet encounters a Sleepwalker, the Host's wife. The Host's mistress, attracted by the Poet, observes them together and betrays them to the Host, who kills the Poet. The Sleepwalker carries his body away. Revived by many cos, usually staged TARAS, incl. London CG, de Cuevas B., 24 Aug 1948; sc./c. Jean Robier (later André Delfau); dan. PAGAVA, SKIBINE, Marjorie TALLCHIEF; Copenhagen, RDB, 9 Jan 1955 (as *La Sonnambula*, a title the choreographer now prefers); sc./c. Delfau; dan. SCHANNE, KRONSTAM, VANGSAAE; NYCC, NYCB, 6 Jan 1960; sc./c. André Levasseur; dan. KENT, BRUHN, Jillana; London, SW, BR, 18 July 1961; sc./c. Alix Stone; dan. June Sandbrook, MORRICE, ALDOUS; Venice, Fenice T., LFB, 20 Mar 1967; sc./c. Peter Farmer; dan. Dianne Richards, GILPIN, Carmen Mathé. DV

Sorkin, Naomi, b. Chicago, IL, 1949. American dancer. Studied with Bentley Stone and Walter Camryn, Chicago; MARACCI, Los Angeles; Vincenzo Celli, Margaret Black, and David Howard, New York. Debut with Chicago Lyric O. 1962. Danced with ABT 1967–73, San Francisco B. 1973, FELD B. from 1974. As well as her roles in the Feld repertory, she has danced ODETTE, the DON QUIXOTE *pas de deux*, and SYLPHIDES. DV

Sorokina, Nina, b. near Moscow, 1942. Soviet dancer. Upon graduation from Moscow Choreographic S. accepted as soloist, Bolshoy T.; in first season danced Jeanne in FLAME OF PARIS. Created Girl in GEOLOGISTS, Beloved in VASILIEV's *Icarus* (1971) and other roles; dances PHRYGIA. Has feeling for contemporary roles. Excellent classical technique as AURORA, in the Peasant *pas de deux* in GISELLE, and as KITRI. She m. classmate and frequent partner VLADIMIROV. People's Artist, RSFSR. Gold Medal, Varna (1966) and First International B. Competition, Moscow (1969). NR
See N. Avaliani and L. Zhdanov, tr. N.Ward, *Bolshoi's Young Dancers* (Moscow and London 1975)

South Africa. Although the early European settlers brought with them no tradition of dancing, S. Africans show a considerable talent for ballet. Until 1963 there were no professional cos to support them at home and there was a steady exodus of choreographers, e.g. STAFF, CRANKO, and RODRIGUES, and dancers, e.g. Maude LLOYD, HOWES, NERINA, RASSINE, POOLE, MILLER, LANE, Johaar Mosaval, DOYLE, to cos in Britain, the European continent, and the USA. Some returned, but it was not until 1963 that government subsidies were made available to the performing arts, enabling the country to retain its talent in CAPAB BALLET, PACT BALLET and NAPAC BALLET.

The cradle of ballet in S. Africa is Cape Town, where amateur and professional cos have performed since the 19th c. As early as 1802 perfs were given by pupils of local dance masters and 1805–15 many original ballets were produced. In 1834 a ballet with a local theme, *Jack at the Cape, or All Alive among the Hottentots*, was performed against a backdrop of Table Mountain and the Bay. Productions followed the fashion in Europe, but the perfs remained amateur and no professional co. was established.

In the first half of the 20th c. the earliest pioneers were Helen Webb and her assistant Helen White, who taught Maude Lloyd, Rassine, Howes, and Staff. By 1926 the Cape Town Dance Teachers' Association was formed; ESPINOSA visited S. Africa as the first examiner.

Howes returned from touring Europe with A. PAVLOVA's co. and started the Univ. of Cape Town BS 1934, and later the UCT Ballet Co. Other valuable training grounds for both dancers and choreographers were the B. Club, founded 1938 by Cecily Robinson on her return from the DE BASIL B. Russe de Monte Carlo, and her co., S. African NB, 1946–8. The Eoan Group, which draws its dancers mainly from the Coloured community, also presents annual perfs in Cape Town.

The Dancing Teachers' Association was established in Johannesburg 1923 by Madame Ravodna (Ray Espinosa), Violet Kirby, Ivy Conmee, Poppy Frames, Madge Mann, STURMAN, and Poppins Salomon. These teachers were to stage the early ballet perfs in Johannesburg. In the early 1940s the Johannesburg Fest. B. and the Pretoria B. Club were formed; in 1947 Faith de Villiers and Joyce van Geems started a professional co., BT, collaborating with UCT B. for their first program. Staff founded the S. African B. Co., producing 15 original ballets for them 1955–8, but all the Transvaal cos were short-lived, mainly because they had no financial backing. Johannesburg City B., founded 1960 by de Villiers, was used as a nucleus for PACT B. in 1963. Before then many young dancers, e.g. SPIRA, MASON, BERGSMA, DERMAN, and LORRAYNE, left to work in Britain.

Although the same high standard of teaching is to be found throughout S. Africa, no professional cos were founded in other centres before 1963, and the Orange Free State co., PACOFS, was disbanded after Staff's death in 1971, in spite of being subsidized. *See also* BALLET INTERNATIONAL. MG

Spain. Spanish dance cos have typically evolved around single individuals, who have been able to bring the broad spectrum of Spanish dance to a worldwide audience. Large-scale cos have therefore regularly formed and disbanded because, without State support or patronage, the ability to maintain a co. has depended very largely on the artist's own financial resources.

The first person to make a worldwide impact this c. was Antonia Mercé (b. Buenos Aires, 1888; d. Bayonne, 1936) who took her artistic name of 'La Argentina' from the country of her birth. Having studied under her father she made her debut, aged nine, in the Royal O., T. Real, Madrid, becoming prima ballerina when 11. As a concert artist she toured the world before forming a partnership 1925 with Vincente Escudero (b. Valladolid, *c.* 1889), and a co. 1928. Her technique of castanet playing and her use of the music of Albeniz, Granados, FALLA, and Turina were revolutionary. After the success of her ballet *El Amor Brujo*, she determined to present a series of 1-act Spanish ballets using the music of Ernesto Halffter, Oscar Espla, Joaquin Nin among others. Her ballets incl. *Juerga*, *El Contrabandista*, *Sonatina*, *Triana*, and *El Fandango de Candil*. She is considered by many to be the greatest Spanish dancer of all time.

Another Argentine, Encarnación López Julvez (b. Buenos Aires, 1895; d. New York, 1945) took her stage name of 'La Argentinita' in homage to Antonia Mercé. Taken to Spain as a child, her early dance background was with the regional dances of Spain. She founded her B. de Madrid with Federico García Lorca in 1927. The first appearance abroad of her group (NY 1928) was highly successful. In 1933 she attempted the first large-scale theatrical presentation of authentic flamenco in *Las Calles de Cadiz* (*The Streets of Cadiz*), bringing out of retirement such dancers as La Macarrona, La Malena, La Sordita, Fernanda Antúnez, and singers and guitarists of equal calibre. In 1939 she collaborated with MASSINE on *Capriccio Espagnole,* and appeared as guest artist with ABT in 1945 in *Goyescas* and *Bolero*.

Pilar López Julvez (b. San Sebastian, 1912), sister of the legendary Encarnación López, began her career in her sister's co. After her sister's untimely death, Pilar López felt it her duty to carry on the work of her sister and so created her own co., B. Español, in 1946 with José Greco (b. Montorico-Nei-Frentani, 1919), a discovery of her sister's, Nila Amparo, Elvira Real, and Manolo Vargas. She has become as legendary as her sister, training in her co. nearly all the famous male Spanish dancers of today. José Greco, Vargas, Roberto Ximenez, Alejandro Vega, Roberto Iglesias, and Antonio Gades (b. Elda, Alicante, 1936) all left to form their own cos.

Although now retired, Pilar López occasionally appears as guest artist at galas. Her last appearance in Madrid (partnered by Gades) was at a homage to Escudero in 1974.

Another woman who made an important contribution to the popularity of Spanish dance through her worldwide appearances in the 1930s and 1940s was Mariemma.

Spanish dance on the American scene has largely, in recent years, been influenced by Greco. With his wife Nila Amparo, he formed his own co. 1951, and has toured widely. Many young artists have had their initial start from Greco's talent scouting. His co. has diminished in size in recent years, necessitated by financial reasons. Having established a Foundation of Spanish Dance in America he retired 1975.

Probably the finest of all dancers to come out of the Pilar López Co. is Gades. Before forming his own co. he collaborated with DOLIN in choreographing *Bolero* for the Rome O. He followed this by becoming choreographer and teacher at Sc. 1962. Representing Spain, he took a co. of 14 to the NY World's Fair 1964. In the succeeding years his co. has come to be recognized as a major co. contributing new ideas to the theatrical vision of Spanish dance.

A dancer who appeared with Gades in NY in 1964 was Manuela Vargas (b. Seville), after making her London debut with her own co. 1963. In latter years she has featured as the only woman in her otherwise all-male co.

The most extraordinary personality of all time in flamenco dance was Carmen Amaya (b. Somorrostro, Barcelona, *c.* 1913; d. 1963), who earned and spent legendary fortunes in her lifetime. Born into a gypsy family she began dancing at the age of four in the waterfront bars of Barcelona, accompanied on the guitar by her father. Her international career began in the co. of Raquel Meller, Paris 1923. After appearing at the Barcelona International Exposition 1929 she went to Buenos Aires, not returning to Spain until 1940. NY debut 1941, London debut 1948. Her co. was very much a family affair with sisters, brothers, aunts, uncles, and cousins performing, but it was Amaya's own electrifying flamenco that ensured its success. Shortly before her death she filmed *La Historia de los Tarantos*, a gypsy version of *Romeo and Juliet*, which also starred Gades. Her records *Queen of the Gypsies* and *Flamenco* are still the most sought-after records of flamenco dance.

Two dancers who emerged from her co. were Luisillo (Luis Pérez Davila, b. Mexico, 1928) and Lucero Tena (b. Mexico, *c.* 1936). Luisillo formed his first co. in partnership with his wife, Teresa, 1949, but after its break-up he formed another co., Luisillo and his T. of Spanish Dance, 1954. Lucero Tena, although she has never formed a co., is famous for her castanet playing, giving recitals with orchestras all over the world.

The two dancers who have done more than anyone else to show the artistic heights to which Spanish dance can attain are the cousins Antonio (Ruiz Soler, b. Seville, 1921) and Rosario (Florencia Pérez Padilla,

Colour Plates. Facing page: Linda Gibbs and NORTH in LCDT's *Duet* (ch. P. TAYLOR)

Overleaf: The NIKOLAIS Dance T. in *Cross-Fade*, 1974

b. Seville, 1918). They studied under Realito (Manuel Real) in Seville and later with various maestros including Otero, Pericet, 'el Estampio' (Juan Sanchez) and 'Frasquillo' (Francisco Leon). They formed a childhood partnership known as 'Los Chavalillos Sevillanos', debut Liège 1928. The pair danced as partners all over the world for over 20 years: US debut 1940, Edinburgh Fest. 1950, London 1951. In 1953 Antonio formed his own Spanish ballet co., Antonio and the Ballets de Madrid, without Rosario. Shortly after Rosario formed her own co. and was partnered by Iglesias. She rejoined Antonio and his co. 1964 as guest artist, with appearances in London and NY.

The first co. in Spain to be government-sponsored on a permanent basis is The National Dance Co. of Spain (previously known as the B. Antología Española). This co. grew out of the dance interludes in an anthology of Spanish *zarzuelas* produced *c.* 1970. From small beginnings the co. numbers over 30 artists. Both the principals, Marisol and her husband, Mario de la Vega, have been with the co. since its inception. For the first appearance of the co. in London in 1975, Antonio appeared as guest artist, and many of the ballets from Antonio's own co. have been taken into the repertoire. PH
See La Meri, *Spanish Dancing* (New York 1948; Pittsfield, MA, 1967); Anna Ivanova, *The Dancing Spaniards* (London 1970); Don Pohren, *The Art of Flamenco* (Jerez de la Frontera, Spain, 1962); *Lives and Legends of Flamenco* (Madrid 1964)

Spartacus (*Spartak*), ballet, 4 acts, ch. YACOBSON; mus. KHACHATURIAN; lib. Nikolay Volkov; sc./c. Valentina Khodasevich. Leningrad, Kirov T., 27 Dec 1956; reproduced with some changes Moscow, Bolshoy T., 4 Apr 1962; new sc. Vadim Ryndin, but the off-*pointe* dancing (main principle) remained undisturbed.

New version ch. MOISEYEV, sc. Aleksandr Konstantinovsky. Moscow, Bolshoy T., 11 Mar 1958. Danced on points, had some interesting group dances, but did not last.

New version ch./lib. GRIGOROVICH; sc. VIRSALADZE. Moscow, Bolshoy T., 9 Apr 1968; dan. VASILIEV, M. LAVROVSKY (Spartacus), and LIEPA (Crassus). Remains in permanent repertoire. Awarded Lenin Prize in Arts, 1970. Khachaturian received Lenin Prize for the score, 1959.

About 30 productions of this work have been shown in different opera houses of the USSR. Other productions abroad by choreographers in Hungary (e.g. SEREGI, 1968), Romania, Czechoslovakia, and Poland. NR
See N. Roslavleva, 'Spartacus at the Bolshoy', in *The Dancing Times* (London, June 1969)

Colour Plate: SUMMERSPACE, ch. CUNNINGHAM, sc./c. Robert Rauschenberg, danced by (left to right) KOMAR, KOVICH, Cathy Kerry, and HARPER

Spartacus, Bolshoy B., 1968; dan. VASILIEV and MAXIMOVA

Spectre de la Rose, Le, choreographic tableau, ch. FOKINE; lib. Jean-Louis Vaudoyer, from a poem by GAUTIER; mus. Carl-Maria von Weber, orch. Hector Berlioz; sc./c. BAKST. T. de Monte Carlo, DIAGHILEV's B. Russes, 19 Apr 1911; dan. KARSAVINA, NIJINSKY. A young girl returning from a ball falls asleep and dreams that the spirit of the rose she holds is dancing with her. A *pas de deux* made to display Nijinsky's spectacular elevation and the poetry of Karsavina's presence, it has rarely worked when danced by others. Revived BR 1930, Paris O. 1931, Vic-Wells B. 1932 (new prod. 1944 with sc. Rex Whistler), DE BASIL 1935, R. BLUM's B. de Monte Carlo 1936, ABT 1941, LFB 1962. First danced in Russia by NB of Cuba 1964. Revived for Bolshoy B., Havana, Cuba, 12 Nov 1966; dan. N. BESSMERTNOVA, LIEPA.

Perhaps the most convincing perf. of the male role has been by BARYSHNIKOV, with SEYMOUR, Hamburg, 22 June 1975, and with TCHERKASSKY, ABT, 4 Jan 1976. DV

Spessivtseva [Spesivtseva], Olga, b. Rostov, 1895. Russian dancer. Daughter of a provincial opera singer who died prematurely in 1902 leaving five children who were sent to an orphanage founded by the great actress Maria Savina in St Petersburg. Olga, her sister Zinaida (1903–71), and brother Aleksandr (b. 1892) were later placed in the Imperial TS and all danced in the Maryinsky B. Olga graduated 1913, class of Klaudia Kulichevskaya, a pupil of E. SOKOLOVA, FOKINE, and VAGANOVA. First danced AURORA 4 Oct 1915. Ballerina 1918. She had perfect technique, an exquisite romantic dancer with a tragic mien ideally suited for GISELLE and ODETTE-ODILE. Toured USA with DIAGHILEV's co. 1916, replacing KARSAVINA and dancing with NIJINSKY in BLUEBIRD, SYLPHIDES, and SPECTRE DE LA ROSE. Returned to Russia at the beginning of 1917 dancing such roles as SUGAR PLUM FAIRY, *grand pas* from

Olga Spessivtseva as GISELLE, in Act II

PAQUITA and others. Started working with Vaganova on the recommendation of her friend Akim Volynsky and added Medora in CORSAIRE and Nikia in BAYADÈRE (1920) to her repertory. In 1921 danced Aurora in Diaghilev's *The Sleeping Princess* (*see* SLEEPING BEAUTY) in London, returned to Russia 1922, danced FILLE DU PHARAON, DON QUIXOTE and SWAN LAKE but departed in the spring of 1924. From 1924 until 1932 danced, with short intervals, at the Paris O. In 1927 she created the title role in BALANCHINE's *La Chatte* (mus. SAUGUET) with the Diaghilev B. In 1932 danced *Giselle* with DOLIN for the CAMARGO SOCIETY in London. Later that year danced again at T. Colón, Buenos Aires (her first visit had been briefly in 1923) working with Fokine for six months. In 1934 became ballerina of Victor Dandré–Alexander Levitov B. (formerly A. PAVLOVA's co.) to tour Australia, partnered by VILZAK. Signs of depression were already evident. She moved to the USA in 1939 and in 1943 suffered a complete nervous breakdown and was placed in a hospital for mental diseases. In Feb 1963 with the help of friends, among them DUBROVSKA, Dolin and Dale Edward Fern, she was discharged and settled in the Tolstoy Farm, Rockland County, NY, a Russian settlement maintained by the Tolstoy Foundation and headed by Alexandra Tolstoy, daughter of Leo Tolstoy. NR/MC

See Valerian Bogdanov-Berezovsky, 'Spessivtseva' in *Encounters* (Moscow 1967); Léandre Vaillat, *Olga Spessivtzeva, Ballerine* (Paris 1944); André Schaiké-vitch, *Olga Spessivtzeva, Magicienne Enroutée* (Paris 1954); Anton Dolin, *The Sleeping Ballerina* (London 1966); Olga Spessivtseva, with an introduction by Anton Dolin, *Technique for the Ballet Artiste* (London 1967)

Spies, Daisy, b. Moscow, 1905. German dancer and ballet mistress. Pupil of, among others, V. GSOVSKY and TERPIS. Soloist, Staats O., Berlin, 1924–31; Weimar 1946; director, Staats O., W. Berlin, 1951–5; then ballet mistress, Hamburg Operettenhaus to 1959, Linz B. 1959–61. Taught classical ballet, WIGMAN S., Berlin, 1962–5. Guest choreographer Leipzig 1950. With KÖLLING and her brother the composer Leo Spies, she gave the first ballet evening in Berlin after World War II, in 1945. She m. Kölling. GBLW

Spira, Phyllis, b. Johannesburg, 1943. S. African dancer. Studied in Johannesburg with Renée Solomon and Reina Berman, London RBS 1959. After a few months joined RB touring co.; soloist 1961, remaining with the co. for five years. Joined PACT B. in Johannesburg as its principal dancer, 1963–4, dancing classical roles. Danced as CAPAB B.'s ballerina in Cape Town 1965–6, leaving for one year, 1967–8, to dance with NB of Canada in productions by FRANCA, CRANKO, BRUHN, BALANCHINE, and MACMILLAN, with that co. touring Canada, the USA, and Mexico. Returned as guest artist to CAPAB B. 1968; remained there as ballerina. MG

Staats, Léo, b. Paris, 1877; d. Paris, 1952. French dancer, choreographer, and teacher. Pupil of MÉRANTE. Debut Paris O. at 10, choreographed his first ballet at 16. His most famous role was that of Jean in Mariquita's *Javotte*, revived at O. 1909. Artistic director, T. des Arts, 1910–14, where he choreographed *Le Festin de l'Araignée* (1913; mus. Albert Roussel). Returned to O. 1915, choreographed many ballets incl. *Cydalise et le Chèvre-pied* (1923; mus. Gabriel Pierné) for ZAMBELLI and AVELINE, and *Soir de Fête* (1925; mus. DELIBES, from *La Source*), considered by many a precursor of BALANCHINE's plotless ballets, and also revived many works by other choreographers. Choreographed dances in Hector Berlioz's *La Damnation de Faust* at CG, 1933, and many numbers for music hall and revue. Taught in his own studio until his death. DV

Staff, Frank, b. Kimberley, 1918; d. Bloemfontein, 1971. S. African dancer and choreographer. Studied with Helen Webb and Maude LLOYD in Cape Town; encouraged by Lloyd to return with her to London to study with RAMBERT and dance with BR. He also appeared with the Vic-Wells B. 1935 and 1938–9. For BR choreographed his first short ballet *The Tartans* (1938; mus. William Boyce); followed by *Peter and the Wolf* (1940); a plotless work to Edward Elgar's *Enigma Variations* (1940); and two charming suites of dances that made fun of ballet conventions of the time, *Czernyana* (1939) and *Czerny 2* (1941). Handsome and with a facile technique, he inherited many of LAING's roles in the BR repertory and for the London B. created Julian in FÊTE ÉTRANGE. For Metropolitan B. he choreographed *Fanciulla delle Rose* (mus. Anton Arensky) which starred the young BERIOSOVA. He worked with the B. des CE and the San Francisco B. and choreographed for London and

Broadway musicals before returning to S. Africa 1953. He started his own S. African B. (1955–8), choreographing 15 ballets before becoming resident choreographer for the UCT/CAPAB B. For that co. he revived earlier works and staged a full-length *Romeo and Juliet*. He was with PACT B. 1966–8 and director of PACOFS B. from 1969 until his death, creating for that co. six new ballets incl. *Mantis Moon* (mus. Hans Maske) and was working on his first full-length indigenous ballet, *The Rain Queen* (mus. commissioned from Graham Newcater) when he died. He m. four times, the dancers Elisabeth Schooling and Jacqueline St Clere, the actress Heather Lloyd-Jones, and the dancer Veronica Paeper. MG

Stages, ballet, 2 acts, ch. COHAN; mus. Arne Nordheim (Act 1), Bob Downes (Act 2); sc. Peter Farmer. London, The Place, LCDT, 22 Apr 1971; dan. LOUTHER, LAPZESON. Freely based on several different myths, it shows an anti-hero of the space age involved with various frightening creatures before deciding to destroy the world about him. It became LCDT's first widely popular work, playing to enthusiastic audiences on tour. The production incorporated acrobatics and film sequences. JP

Stars and Stripes, ballet, ch. BALANCHINE; mus. John Philip Sousa, adapted and orch. Hershy Kay; sc./ltg David Hays; c. (Barbara) Karinska. NYCC, NYCB, 17 Jan 1959; dan. KENT, Robert Barnett, D. ADAMS, HAYDEN, D'AMBOISE. A celebration of the American parade and the marches of Sousa. FM

State Ensemble of Classical Ballet (USSR) *see* MOISEYEV

Still Point, The, ballet, ch. BOLENDER; mus. DEBUSSY. USA (on tour), Dance Drama Co., 1954; NY, YMHA, 10 Apr 1955 (as *At the Still Point*); dan. Emily Frankel, Mark Ryder. Danced to the first three movements of Debussy's String Quartet, Op. 10; a young girl endures rejection to find love. FM

Stock, Gailene, b. Ballarat, 1946. Australian dancer. Studied with Paul Hammond. Australian B. 1962. RAD scholarship to RBS 1963. Grand B. Classique de France. T. del B. di Roma. Studied with HIGHTOWER. Australian B. 1965–74, becoming soloist and principal ballerina. NB of Canada 1974, principal dancer. A remarkably versatile dancer, in both modern dramatic and classical roles. KSW

Stone Flower, The (*Kamenniy Tsvetok*), ballet, 3 acts; (orig. *Tale of the Stone Flower*) ch. L. LAVROVSKY; mus. PROKOFIEV; lib. Mira Prokofieva and L. Lavrovsky after folktales from the Ural mountains collected and edited by author Pavel Bazhov; sc. Tatiana Starzhenetskaya. Moscow, Bolshoy T., 12 Feb 1954; dan. ULANOVA (Katerina), PREOBRAZHENSKY (Danila), PLISETSKAYA (Mistress of the Copper Mountain). This version did not survive, being overburdened with mimed scenes.

New version ch. GRIGOROVICH, the Sixth World Fest. of Youth and Students, Moscow, summer 1957. Leningrad, Kirov T., 22 Apr 1957; dan. KOLPAKOVA (Katerina), Aleksandr Gribov (Danila), OSIPENKO (Mistress of the Copper Mountain), GRIDIN (Severyan). The choreography and decor were hailed as milestones in contemporary Soviet ballet. Same version: Moscow, Bolshoy T., 7 Mar 1959; dan. MAXIMOVA (Katerina), VASILIEV (Danila) – their first created roles – Plisetskaya (Mistress of the Copper Mountain), LEVASHOV (Severyan). Grigorovich version mounted in many O. and B. theatres of USSR, also Stockholm (RSB, 1962).

An earlier independent version ch. Yuri Kovalyov; mus. Aleksandr Friedlender, Perm OH, 1954. Also ch. Vitaly Timofeyev; mus. Friedlender, Sverdlovsk OH, 1975. NR
See V. Vanslov, *Balety Grigorovicha i Problemi Choreografii (Grigorovich's ballets and problems of choreography)* (Moscow 1971)

Strange Hero, modern dance work, ch./c. NAGRIN; mus. Stan Kenton, Pete Rugolo. NY, Hotel Ballroom 8th Ave & 51st St, spring 1948; dan. Nagrin. A jazz solo depicting the brutal life and death of a gangster with overtones of knightly honour as he acknowledges the superior skill of his killer. DM

Stravinsky, Igor Fyodorovich, b. Oranienbaum [Lomonosov], 1882; d. New York, 1971. Russian composer (US citizen from 1943). Pupil of Nikolay Rimsky-Korsakov. Discovered by DIAGHILEV, who commissioned OISEAU DE FEU and presented PETRUSHKA, SACRE DU PRINTEMPS, PULCINELLA, *Le Chant du Rossignol* (Paris 1920; ch. MASSINE), *Le Renard* (Paris 1922; ch. NIJINSKA), NOCES, and APOLLO. For RUBINSTEIN's co. Stravinsky wrote BAISER DE LA FÉE and *Persephone* (Paris 1934; ch. JOOSS). Stravinsky's remarkable collaboration with BALANCHINE produced *Card Party* (*see* CARD GAME), ORPHEUS, and AGON. Balanchine has also choreographed many works to already-existing Stravinsky music. Stravinsky's capacity for self-renewal and his awareness of the importance of form, line, rhythmic clarity, and dynamic energy have kept his influence in ballet a strong one. In 1972 (18–25 June) NYCB performed 31 of his works, incl. 21 creations, though few of great consequence. ASHTON's SCÈNES DE BALLET is notable. DH
See Nancy Goldner, *The Stravinsky Festival of the New York City Ballet* (New York 1974)

Street Games, ballet, 1 scene, ch. GORE; mus. Jacques Ibert; sc./c. Ronald Wilson. London, Wimbledon T., Gore's New London B., 11 Nov 1952. Children's games such as hopscotch, skipping ropes, hoop rolling, translated into dance. Revived by many cos, it is a light-hearted work too often distorted by exaggerated comedy. MC

Struchkova, Raisa, b. Moscow, 1925. Soviet dancer. Graduated from Moscow Bolshoy TS 1944, class of E. GERDT. Debut as LISE (GORSKY version), 1945. Fine technique coupled with deep penetration into character enabled her to perform a great variety of classical and contemporary roles, incl. GISELLE, JULIET, MARIA, and Kijë's Wife (LIEUTENANT KIJË). She m. her classmate LAPAURI, who partnered her in semi-acrobatic showpiece *pas de deux*, e.g. MOSZKOWSKI WALTZ, in which she was unsurpassed. Teaches classical repertoire, Choreographers' Faculty, GITIS. People's Artist, USSR. NR

Strzałkowski, Zbigniew, b. Radom, 1929. Polish dancer. Principal, Bytom B. Co. 1952–4; Warsaw from 1952. A *danseur noble* with unique stage personality, powers of acting and master of partnering. One of the best Polish interpreters of SIEGFRIED, ALBRECHT, ROMEO, PAN TWARDOWSKI; also danced the Chief of Mountain Robbers (HIGHLANDERS), GOLDEN SLAVE, the Prince in CINDERELLA, etc. Created many principal roles in Polish ballets. Danced all over Europe, and in N. America. JPu

Stuart [Popper], Muriel (Mary), b. London, 1903. British dancer and teacher. Studied with A. PAVLOVA at Ivy House, London, from the age of eight, and danced in her co. 1916–26. Also studied with KHLUSTIN, CECCHETTI, SHANKAR, KREUTZBERG, GRAHAM, MARACCI. Ballet mistress and soloist, Chicago Civic OB 1930. Taught in San Francisco 1927 and 1931–4, Los Angeles 1931; at SAB since 1934. Author of *The Classic Ballet: Basic Technique and Terminology* (New York 1952; London 1953). DV

Stukolkin, Timofey, b. St Petersburg, 1829; d. St Petersburg, 1894. Russian character dancer, son of a theatre usher. Performed circus acts while a student at St Petersburg TS and nearly graduated as a circus equestrian, but finished his ballet studies instead 1848, spent an extra year after graduation polishing his style, and became the public's favourite for 50 years as a comic dancer and mime in such roles as DON QUIXOTE, Pierre Gringoire in ESMERALDA, John Bull in FILLE DU PHARAON. Also performed in comedy and vaudeville, and taught dance at various institutes for the aristocracy. He m. the daughter of the mime Nikolay Golts. Died 18 Sept 1894 in costume as DR COPPÉLIUS after Act II of COPPÉLIA at the Mikhailovsky T. (now the Maly OT).

His namesake, Lev Stukolkin (1837–1895), mime and character dancer, taught ballroom dancing and published a textbook about it. Also wrote an interesting reminiscence of his dance contemporaries, *Historical Essay on St Petersburg Ballet*, preserved in MS. at the Leningrad Archive of Art. NR
See Mikhail Borisoglebsky (ed.), *Materials for the History of Russian Ballet*, Vol. 1 (Leningrad 1938)

Sturman, Marjorie, b. London, 1902. English teacher who has worked mostly in Johannesburg. Studied there with Madame Ravodna (Ray Espinosa), also worked with Judith and Édouard ESPINOSA in London and with VOLKOVA. An early member of the RAD, she introduced the system to S. Africa when she opened her own school in Johannesburg 1934. One of the foremost teachers in S. Africa, she was also instrumental in laying the foundations of what is now the PACT B. From its inception in 1953, principal teacher, Art B. and Music S., Johannesburg, established by the Transvaal Education Authority. MC

Stuttgart Ballet. The earliest record of a *ballet de cour* of the state of Württemberg is of 1609 and there has been a continuous history of ballet in Stuttgart since that time. NOVERRE was ballet master at the court 1759–67, mounting his *Rinaldo und Armida*, *Medea und Jason*, etc. and G. VESTRIS, Maximilien Gardel, DAUBERVAL, and HEINEL danced there. In 1824 F. TAGLIONI came as ballet master and his daughter M. TAGLIONI was ballerina. His popular DANINA *oder Joko der brasilianische Affe* was premiered there 1826.

In 1922 Oskar Schlemmer's *Triadisches Ballett* (*Triadic Ballet*) had its first complete perf. at the Landes T. Osvald Lemanis, appointed 1949, was the third ballet master of the postwar period and was succeeded by Robert Mayer 1950–7. In 1957 BERIOZOFF mounted the full-length SLEEPING BEAUTY in Stuttgart, at the time when Germany was turning away from modern dance, and was appointed ballet master. It was the turning point in Stuttgart's fortunes. He mounted GISELLE (1958), NUTCRACKER (1959), SWAN LAKE (1960), and many of the FOKINE masterpieces. In this way an audience was formed that was eager for the classical ballet. A ballet club (NOVERRE SOCIETY) was established, 1958, and preparations made for a school.

In 1960 Beriozoff invited CRANKO to mount his PRINCE OF THE PAGODAS. Beriozoff then moved to Zürich and the *Intendant* of Stuttgart, Dr Walter Schäfer, appointed Cranko in his place, 1961. Thenceforth, until his tragic death in 1973, Cranko, with HAYDÉE as his ballerina, built up the Stuttgart B. to a preeminent position on the Continent and made it one of the leading cos of the world. Besides mounting some of the works he had already created for the London SWB, Cranko brought in MACMILLAN and P. WRIGHT from England to make ballets (the former's HERMANAS was premiered there 1963). The repertoire received Cranko's ROMEO AND JULIET (1962), *Swan Lake* (1963), CARD GAME (1965), ONEGIN (1965, his masterpiece), TAMING OF THE SHREW (1969), and MacMillan's LIED VON DER ERDE (1965). Among his colleagues in building up the Stuttgart B., Cranko had WOOLLIAMS to head the school (made residential from 1971; now called the John-Cranko S.), BEALE to teach the co., CRAGUN and MADSEN as dancers; and, drawn from the school, KEIL and HANKE have been principals. Other outstanding dancers with the co. are or have been REYN, CUOCO, Jane Landon, BERG,

CLAUSS, Reid Anderson, Jan Stripling, Ruth Papendick.

German critics were slow to recognize the importance of the Stuttgart B. but not only did it become immensely popular in its mother city but had a success at the Edinburgh Fest. 1953 and first visited NY 1969, the USSR 1971. In 1974 the co. made its first visit to London (CG). On Cranko's death TETLEY was appointed ballet master (1974) but his work was not liked in Stuttgart and he resigned in 1976, when Haydée was made director. The outstanding features of the Stuttgart B. are the fine repertoire and outstanding dancers who work with immense devotion and enthusiasm – qualities which they derive from Cranko himself and his memory. GBLW

See Walter Erich Schäfer, *Bühne eines Lebens* (Stuttgart 1975); the section of his memoirs relating to Cranko tr. into English by Jean Wallis, published in six instalments, *The Dancing Times* (London, May–Oct 1976); Madeline Winkler-Betzendahl and Zoe Dominic, *John Cranko und das Stuttgarter Ballett* (Pfullingen 1969; revised with photographs 1975)

Sugar Plum Fairy, the ballerina role in NUTCRACKER

Suite en Blanc, ballet, 1 scene, ch. LIFAR; mus. Édouard Lalo (*Namouna*). Zürich, Paris OB, 19 June 1943; Paris O., 23 July 1943. One of the rare ballets by Lifar consisting of pure dance; designed to show off the *étoiles* and the full strength of his co. Remained in the repertory a long time. Revived as *Noir et Blanc*, Nouveau B. de Monte Carlo, 1946, and as such entered repertory of de Cuevas B. Revived London RFH, LFB, 15 Sept 1966. The costumes are plain white tutus for the girls; the men wear tights (either white, originally, or black; hence the change of title) and white shirts. When performed by a strong co. it is a thrilling display of classicism. MC

Summerspace, a lyric dance, ch. CUNNINGHAM; mus. Morton Feldman; sc./c. Robert Rauschenberg. New London, CT, Connecticut College, 17 Aug 1958; dan. Cunningham, C. BROWN, FARBER, Cynthia Stone, Marilyn Wood, CHARLIP. Revived NYST, NYCB, 14 Apr 1966; Stockholm, Stads T., CULLBERG B., 22 Oct 1967; Boston Music Hall, Boston B., 7 Nov 1974. The dancers are like winged insects in a summer landscape; at rest, they are camouflaged against Rauschenberg's decor, whose pointillist effect is repeated in the costumes. DV

Suspension, modern dance work, ch. O'DONNELL; mus. Ray Green; sc. Claire Falkenstein. San Francisco, O'Donnell Dance Studio, 3 Feb 1943. A floating, calm dance beneath a suspended mobile. One woman at the centre is the focal point around which the others weave a tangential web of movement bespeaking a quiet and peaceful order. Also in the repertory of AILEY Dance T. DM

Sutherland, Paul, b. Louisville, KY, 1935. American dancer. Studied with DOLLAR in NY. Danced with RWB and ABT before joining the JOFFREY B. 1959. Rejoined ABT 1964, returned to CCJB 1967. Virile and athletic, he is an excellent interpreter of ballets by ROBBINS and ARPINO. He m. dancer Brunilda Ruiz. DV

Svetlana, ballet, 3 acts, with prologue, ch. RADUNSKY, Nikolay Popko, Lev Pospekhin; mus. Dmitri Klebanov; lib. Ivan Zhiga; sc. Rodion Makarov. Moscow, Affiliated Bolshoy T., 20 Dec 1939; dan. LEPESHINSKAYA (Svetlana), KONDRATOV (Ilko). A girl sets her own house on fire so as to signal the presence of a saboteur. Kondratov created the principal male role while still at school. Other versions have been produced, incl. one ch. Vitaustas Grivickas (Vilnius 1951). NR

See Yuri Slonimsky, *Soviet Ballet* (Leningrad 1950)

Svetlov [Ivchenko], Valerian, b. 1860; d. Paris, 1934. Russian ballet critic, writer, and editor. Wrote innumerable articles on ballet in Russian and French. His book *Le Ballet Contemporain* was published simultaneously in Russian and French (St Petersburg 1911), and contains glorious reproductions of designs by BAKST together with many other illustrations. In 1917 settled in Paris. He m. TREFILOVA and was mentor to the young HASKELL. MC

Swaine, Alexander von, b. Munich, 1905. German dancer and teacher. Studied with EDOUARDOVA in Berlin 1924–8 and danced in Max Reinhardt's *A Midsummer Night's Dream*, working with him in Berlin and Salzburg. He gave solo recitals of modern dance. To London 1932 to study with CRASKE. Soloist Berlin 1935; guest artist Milan and Rome 1936. Toured with Darja Collin and Rosalia Chladek. During World War II he was interned in Sumatra. After a period working in India he returned to Germany 1947 and began his famous partnership with CZOBEL which took them all over the world with their modern dances until 1965. Since 1960 he has taught modern dance, notably in Mexico City and at Jacob's Pillow, MA. He was one of the greatest and most active exponents of AUSDRUCKSTANZ or modern dance style. GBLW

Swanilda, heroine of COPPÉLIA

Swan Lake (*Lac des Cygnes, Le*; Russian title: *Lebedinoe Ozero*), ballet, 4 acts, lib. V. P. Begichev and Vasily Geltser; mus. TCHAIKOVSKY. Prince Siegfried, hunting wild swans by a lake near his castle, sees their Queen, Odette, transformed into a beautiful maiden. She tells him that she is under the spell of von Rothbart, an evil magician, which can be broken only when a man falls in love with her and swears eternal fidelity. Siegfried does so, but at a ball in the castle the following evening von Rothbart appears with his daughter, Odile, whose resemblance to Odette is such that Siegfried is tricked into swearing to make her his bride. Von Rothbart and Odile disappear, and Siegfried rushes back to the lake, where he and Odette defy von Rothbart and throw themselves into the waters. The spell is finally broken, and the lovers are united in eternity.

Moscow, Bolshoy T., 4 Mar 1877 (OS 20 Feb 1877); ch. REISINGER; sc. H. Shangin, Karl Valts, H. Gropius; dan. Pelageia Karpakova, Gillert II. This first production is generally described as a failure, owing to Reisinger's poor choreography; the score was misunderstood and considerably rearranged. However, the ballet remained in the repertory, with choreography revised by Joseph Hansen in 1880 and again 1882. (Hansen soon afterwards became ballet master at the Alhambra T., London, and in 1884 produced there a ballet called *The Swans*, with music by George Jacobi, whose story was clearly derived from that of *Swan Lake*.) In 1893, following the success of SLEEPING BEAUTY, it was decided that M. PETIPA should mount a new version of *Swan Lake* at the Maryinsky T., St Petersburg. He entrusted the 'white' Acts (II and IV) to his assistant IVANOV, and the score was edited by DRIGO. Act II was given at a memorial concert of Tchaikovsky's works at the Maryinsky, 1 Mar 1894, and the complete ballet on 27 Jan 1895 (OS 15 Jan 1895); sc. Mikhail Bocharov and Heinrich Levogt; dan. LEGNANI, P. GERDT. Revived Moscow, Bolshoy T., 1901 with ch. revised by GORSKY, which version long remained in the Soviet repertory, with further revisions by MESSERER.

Swan Lake was one of the first classic ballets to be shown widely outside Russia: A. PAVLOVA presented it on her tour of Germany and Austria in the spring of 1909, before she joined DIAGHILEV in Paris, PREOBRAZHENSKA in London, Mar 1910, GELTSER at the NY Met, Dec 1911. Diaghilev gave it in an abridged version (2 acts and 3 scenes), CG, 30 Nov 1911; ch. revised FOKINE; sc./c. Konstantin Korovin and Aleksandr Golovin (brought by Diaghilev from the Imperial T. in Moscow); dan. KSHESSINSKA, NIJINSKY.

It became the custom with many cos, e.g. the various B. Russes de Monte Carlo, to give Act II only, but the Vic-Wells B. revived the complete ballet, reproduced by SERGUEEFF from Vladimir Stepanov notation, SW, 20 Nov 1934; sc./c. Hugh Stevenson; dan. MARKOVA, HELPMANN. Revived London, New T., SWB, 7 Sept 1943; sc./c. HURRY; dan. FONTEYN, Helpmann. Another production with new sc./c. Hurry, CG, 18 Dec 1952; dan. GREY, FIELD. Yet another: CG, RB, 12 Dec 1963, with some new ch. ASHTON; sc./c. Carl Toms; dan. Fonteyn, BLAIR. The RB touring co. gave a new version, CG, 18 May 1965; sc./c. Hurry; dan. NERINA, LABIS. This last production, with some changes, is now in the repertory of the main co.

New, or partly new, versions by many choreographers incl.: BALANCHINE (1 act), NYCC, NYCB, 20 Nov 1951; sc./c. BEATON; dan. Maria TALLCHIEF, EGLEVSKY, BURMEISTER, Moscow, Stanislavsky and Nemirovich-Danchenko T., 24 Apr 1953; sc. Anatole Lushin; c. Archangelskaya; dan. BOVT, Oleg Chichinadze; and Paris O., 21 Dec 1960; dan. AMIEL, VAN DIJK. CRANKO, Stuttgart B., 14 Nov 1963; sc./c. ROSE; dan. HAYDÉE, BARRA. NUREYEV, Vienna, Staats OB, 15 Oct 1964; sc./c. GEORGIADIS; dan. Ully Wülmer, Nureyev. GRIGOROVICH, Moscow, Bolshoy T., 25 Dec 1969; sc. VIRSALADZE; dan. N. BESSMERTNOVA, FADEYECHEV. A complete version based on the traditional choreography, revived by Blair, Chicago, ABT, 6 Feb 1967; sc. O. SMITH; c. Freddy Wittop; dan. Nerina, FERNANDEZ. DV

See C. W. Beaumont, *The Ballet Called 'Swan Lake'* (London 1952)

Sweden. Ballet came to Sweden in the 17th c. when the country became an important political power. Ballet master Antoine de Beaulieu introduced court ballet in the French style 1638. Court entertainments were especially brilliant during Queen Christina's reign. The first professional troupe was organized 1773 when King Gustav III founded the Royal O. Louis Gallodier, formerly of the Paris O., was the first ballet master. The ballet school started the same year. Under Gallodier, Stockholm saw the pre-NOVERRE style. New ideas of *ballet d'action* were brought by Antoine BOURNONVILLE 1781. The young co. kept in touch with France and Italy, as many artists and ballets visited from these countries. F. TAGLIONI was *premier danseur* 1803–4 and ballet master 1818. He married a Swede; their daughter Marie, born in Stockholm, returned once in 1841 to give perfs. Her Swedish partner was JOHANSSON, a very promising artist. At this time RSB had turned to Copenhagen for inspiration. August BOURNONVILLE often visited Stockholm. Twelve of his ballets were staged at the Royal O. by him or by his pupils. Soon after the Taglioni season, Johansson left for St Petersburg and began a career as dancer and teacher. Johansson had his final studies with August Bournonville and was much influenced by him.

In 1833 Anders Selinder became RSB's first native ballet master. He had a vivid interest in Swedish folklore and inserted folk dances into *divertissements* and lyric plays. These dances, adapted for the stage, have been preserved and are still performed, but at folk festivals rather than in the theatre.

Ballet suffered a decline towards the end of the 19th c. Interest in dance as an art grew again after I. DUNCAN (1906) and A. PAVLOVA (1908) danced in Stockholm. Of lasting effect was the engagement of FOKINE 1913 and 1914. He staged his *Cléopâtre*, CARNAVAL, SCHÉHÉRAZADE, and SYLPHIDES and danced leading roles with Vera Fokina. He discovered and used young talents like Jenny Hasselquist, ARI, and BÖRLIN. There were advanced plans to sign Fokine as ballet director, but World War I prevented the theatre from realizing them. In 1920 Rolf de Maré founded B. SUÉDOIS in Paris with some of the best dancers in RBS. Remaining with the parent co. was Lisa Steier, the first ballet mistress and a gifted choreographer. She staged PULCINELLA and OISEAU DE FEU with her own choreography. She died early, a loss to the co. Several decades passed without anything of real interest happening. The ballet lived in the shadow of the opera. Some talented dancers appeared, but they were given little to dance.

In 1949 the Royal T. engaged TUDOR to reform the ballet. He started with the school and entrusted the teaching to Nina and Albert Kozlovsky. Tudor staged GISELLE as first classic for the repertory and added JARDIN AUX LILAS and GALA PERFORMANCE. SKEAPING succeeded him in 1953 as ballet director. She stayed eight years. The ballet acquired a repertory of classics like SWAN LAKE, SLEEPING BEAUTY, and COPPÉLIA. The three important Swedish choreographers at the time, CULLBERG, ÅKESSON and CRAMÉR, were invited to create new works for the co. The standard improved and RSB was invited to visit theatres and festivals abroad. Leading dancers were Ellen Rasch, ORLANDO, E. M. von ROSEN, ANDERSSON, Björn Molmgren, Teddy Rhodin, Julius Mengarelli, SELLING, BORG. Skeaping retired 1962 after a tour through China. Now ballet directors began to change too often. Tudor returned for a brief period, dividing his time between Stockholm and NY, 1961–3. He choreographed ECHOING OF TRUMPETS 1963. Brian Macdonald arranged a ballet festival that has now become a tradition. New principal dancers were PAUL and HÄGGBOM. BRUHN arrived in 1967, reformed the school with Gösta Svalberg as new director, and invited major choreographers like ROBBINS, TETLEY, LIMÓN, and MACMILLAN. James Moore succeeded Bruhn for a couple of seasons in 1972. New leading dancers were LIDSTRÖM, Astrid Strüwer, M. LANG, SEGERSTRÖM, and ALHANKO. Cramér became ballet director 1975, the first Swede in that capacity for 50 years.

Sweden also has ballet cos with classical and modern repertories in Gothenburg [Göteborg] and Malmö, and two touring cos under the management of the Riks T. organization, the Cullberg and Cramér Ballets. Small groups of dancers are organized in the Dance Centre, Stockholm, also for touring. AGS

Switzerland. There is no national ballet in Switzerland but ballet cos are attached to the opera houses in Zürich, Bern, Basel, St Gallen, Lucerne, and Geneva. These cos work in the same way as those in GERMANY. The major co. is that in Zürich. BERIOZOFF was ballet master there 1964–71, staging many of the great classical ballets and those of FOKINE, with FULTON as ballerina. His successors Geoffrey Cauley and Hans Meister widened the repertory with ASHTON'S FILLE MAL GARDÉE (1974) and DE VALOIS'S RAKE'S PROGRESS (1976). In the French-speaking region, BALANCHINE was invited to direct the ballet at the Geneva OH, after CHARRAT and GOLOVINE had been ballet masters. He installed NEARY 1973, who mounted APOLLO, NUTCRACKER, *Symphony in C* (*see* PALAIS DE CRISTAL), etc., and engaged many dancers from the USA.

The annual Prix de Lausanne, competed for in that city, was founded and endowed 1973 by Philippe and Elvire Braunschweig for students aged 16–19; an international jury awards prizes and scholarships enabling the winners to continue their studies at the London RBS; the Centre de Danse International, Cannes; the Mudra S., Brussels; the Paris OBS; and the ABTS, NY. GBLW

Sylphide, La (1) ballet, 2 acts, ch. F. TAGLIONI; mus. Jean Schneitzhoeffer; lib. Adolphe Nourrit based on Charles Nodier's story *Trilby ou le Lutin d'Argail*; sc. Pierre-Luc-Charles Ciceri; c. Eugène Lami. Paris O., 12 Mar 1832; dan. M. TAGLIONI, MAZILIER. James, a young Scotsman engaged to a local girl, Effie, is haunted by a beautiful Sylph whom only he can see, and lured away to the forest on the eve of his wedding. James fears she will fly away from him and seeks the help of a witch, Madge, whose anger he has earlier incurred. She gives him a magic scarf that will destroy the Sylph's power of flight. After a happy dance in which James teases her with the scarf he wraps it round her: her wings drop off but with them she loses her life. As Madge exults over the hapless James, he sees in the distance the wedding procession of Effie who has accepted the hand of a neighbour farmer.

The ballet enjoyed an immediate success and remained Taglioni's greatest role. It skilfully combined subjects dear to the Romantic movement then sweeping Europe – an exotic setting (Scotland) and the artist's dream of the unattainable ideal. *La Sylphide* launched the whole Romantic period of ballet; it also for the first time used dancing on *pointe* imaginatively to suggest the flight of the Sylphide, and the use of stage machinery heightened the effect of the supernatural as she appeared among the treetops. The costume (attributed to Lami) for the Sylphide, a close-fitting bodice with shoulders bare and a bell-shaped skirt falling below mid-calf, became the accepted attire of the ballerinas of the period and is still worn – the Romantic tutu as compared with the short, classical tutu evolved at the end of the 19th c. Taglioni danced the ballet in London, CG, 28 July 1832; St Petersburg, Bolshoy T., 18 Sept 1837; Milan, Sc., 29 May 1841. The F. Taglioni choreography has been lost but V. GSOVSKY revived the ballet using the same music for B. des CE, sc. Serebriakov, c. BÉRARD, at the T. des CE, Paris, 15 June 1946 (dan. VYROUBOVA and PETIT) and succeeded in capturing the style of the original by using many of the poses recorded of Taglioni. The Taglioni version was reconstructed by LACOTTE for French TV, 1 Jan 1972; dan. THESMAR, DENARD; this entered Paris O. repertory, 7 June 1972; dan. PONTOIS, ATANASOFF.

(2) *Sylfiden*, romantic ballet, 2 acts, ch. August BOURNONVILLE, based on his memories of the Taglioni version; mus. Hermann Løvenskjøld. Copenhagen, Royal T., RDB, 28 Nov 1836; dan. GRAHN, Bournonville. This version has been in the

Les Sylphides, as revived by MARKOVA for the Australian B., 1976

Danish repertory ever since and is now danced all over the world. H. LANDER was the first to take it out of Denmark, staging it for the DE CUEVAS B., sc./c. Bernard Daydé, Paris, Empire T., 9 Dec 1953; dan. HIGHTOWER, GOLOVINE. His production was staged in Milan (1962), Holland (1963), and by ABT in San Antonio, TX, 11 Nov 1964. Another notable staging was by E. M. von ROSEN for BR, sc./c. Robin and Christopher Ironside, London, SWT, 20 July 1960; dan. von Rosen, F. FLINDT. This contained additions made in Denmark by Ellen Price de Plane, an authority on Bournonville's ballets. Acquired by Scottish B. 1973, staged BRENAA. BRUHN, the greatest James of all time, has also produced versions in Italy and Canada. The role of James was undoubtedly strengthened by Bournonville to give himself a better part, especially in Act II (Mazilier was noted for his good looks rather than his dancing). MC
See Ivor Guest, *The Romantic Ballet in Paris* (London and Middletown, CT, 1966)

Sylphides, Les, 'romantic reverie', ballet, 1 act, ch. FOKINE; mus. Frédéric Chopin; sc./c. BENOIS. Paris, T. du Châtelet, DIAGHILEV's B. Russes, 2 June 1909; dan. A. PAVLOVA, KARSAVINA, Alexandra Baldina, NIJINSKY. Fokine had earlier presented a ballet called CHOPINIANA at a charity perf., St Petersburg, 23 Feb 1907; most of the dances were in national costume but Pavlova danced a Waltz *pas de deux* with M. OBUKHOV, wearing a costume similar to the Romantic tutu of SYLPHIDE. Still called *Chopiniana* it was danced at a charity perf. at the Maryinsky T., St Petersburg, 8 Mar 1908; dan. PREOBRAZHENSKA, Pavlova, Karsavina, Nijinsky. It was this version, in which all the female dancers wore Romantic dress, that Diaghilev rechristened *Les Sylphides*. The ballet has no plot; a poet dances with ghostly sylphs against the setting of a ruined monastery. Everything depends on musicality and delicacy of style; the solo dances are as demanding in expressive nuance as in smooth technique. The *corps de ballet* is on stage almost throughout, used in decorative groups when not actually dancing.

Although the title pays homage to M. TAGLIONI, the ballet bears no resemblance to *La Sylphide* except in its Romantic mood. In the repertory of nearly every co. in the world today, the music having been constantly reorchestrated. The Vic-Wells B. acquired the Benois setting in 1937 and the London RB has used it ever since. Most cos use a sylvan setting, sometimes attributed 'after Corot'. MC
See Richard Buckle, *Nijinsky* (London and New York 1971)

Sylvia, *ou la Nymphe de Diane,* ballet, 3 acts; ch. MÉRANTE; lib. Jules Barbier and Baron de Reinach; mus. DELIBES; sc. Jules Chéret, Auguste Alfred Rubé, Philippe Marie Chaperon; c. Eugène Lacoste. Paris O., 14 June 1876; dan. Rita Sangalli, Mérante, Louise Marquet, Marie Sanlaville. The theme is drawn from Torquato Tasso's pastoral *Aminta*: Sylvia, a votary of Diana, rejects the love of Aminta, a shepherd. She is captured by Orion, the hunter, and rescued by Eros. Her union with Aminta is finally blessed by Diana. Delibes's score is one of the greatest composed for ballet in the 19th c. It was the cancellation of a revival planned by DIAGHILEV for the St Petersburg Maryinsky T. (sc. BENOIS, BAKST, Konstantin Korovin, *et al.*) that prompted his resignation from the Imperial Theatres in 1900. The ballet was staged for the Maryinsky 15 Dec 1901: ch. IVANOV (who died before he could complete it) and P. GERDT; dan. PREOBRAZHENSKA. Other versions incl. ones ch. STAATS, Milan, Sc., 1895; ch. Fred Farren, lib. revised (1 act) C. Wilhelm, dan. KYASHT, London, Empire T., 18 May 1911; Staats's version given at Paris O., 1919 (where it was revived with ch. LIFAR, 1941, AVELINE, 1946). *Pas de deux* only, ch. BALANCHINE, NYCC, NYCB, 1 Dec 1950; dan. Maria TALLCHIEF, and MAGALLANES. Complete ballet presented by SWB, CG, 3 Sept 1952; lib. revised and ch. ASHTON; sc./c. Robin and Christopher Ironside; dan. FONTEYN, SOMES. DV

Symphonic Ballet. Term used to describe the ballets made by MASSINE in the 1930s which were danced to complete symphonies and often aroused the ire of musicians. The first, PRÉSAGES, was a huge popular success but the second, CHOREARTIUM, staged later the same year, provoked a storm from those who sought to keep classical music sacrosanct, although the distinguished musicologist Ernest Newman defended Massine. SYMPHONIE FANTASTIQUE was accepted because Hector Berlioz had given his symphony a definite story line. Some said impresario DE BASIL favoured them because the music was out of copyright. Today, although these three revolutionary works have disappeared, choreographers frequently use complete symphonies with success. BÉJART has taken extreme liberties with Ludwig van Beethoven's Ninth Symphony. MC

Symphonic Variations, ballet, 1 act, ch. ASHTON; mus. César Franck; sc./c. FEDOROVITCH. London, CG, SWB, 24 Apr 1946; dan. FONTEYN, MAY, M. SHEARER, SOMES, Henry Danton, SHAW. Ashton's first postwar ballet. Originally conceived with a mystical theme, it finally emerged as a plotless work, Ashton's credo of classicism. DV

Symphonie Fantastique, choreographic symphony, 5 scenes, ch. MASSINE; mus./lib. Hector Berlioz; sc./c. BÉRARD. London, CG, DE BASIL's B. Russe de Monte Carlo, 24 July 1936; dan. Massine, TOUMANOVA. A musician, in a series of opium-induced dreams, sees his Beloved (Berlioz's *idée fixe*) at a ball, in an idyllic countryside, in a prison, and, hideously transformed, at a witches' sabbath. Revived Paris O., 17 Apr 1957. A new version of the work was ch. PETIT 1975. DV

Symphony in C *see* PALAIS DE CRISTAL

Symphony in Three Movements, ballet, ch. BALANCHINE; mus. STRAVINSKY; ltg Ronald Bates. NYST, NYCB, 18 June 1972; dan. TOMASSON, Sara Leland, VILLELLA. Plotless ballet illuminating the score; presented at the opening of the NYCB's Stravinsky Fest. FM

Szmolc, Halina, b. Warsaw, 1892; d. Warsaw, 1939. Polish dancer. Soloist of A. PAVLOVA's, MORDKIN's, VOLININ's and other cos 1911–19; prima ballerina, Warsaw B., 1919–34. Danced GISELLE, ODETTE, CATARINA, SWANILDA, ZOBEIDE, Ballerina in PETRUSHKA, and created roles in Polish ballets, e.g. in PAN TWARDOWSKI. Gave recitals of small solo dances. Killed by a bomb during the siege of Warsaw. JPu

Szumrák, Vera, b. Budapest, 1938. Hungarian dancer. Studied under NÁDASI, graduating from State B. Inst. 1954. Acquired teacher's diploma 1964. Dancer, Budapest O. since 1954, soloist since 1966, mainly *demi-caractère* and modern style. Debut 1959 as MYRTHA. Major roles incl.: ZAREMA, the Girl in MIRACULOUS MANDARIN (ch. SEREGI), the Chosen Virgin (SACRE DU PRINTEMPS, 1973; ch. BÉJART), the Black Woman in *The Cedar Tree* (1975; ch. Seregi). Liszt Prize 1969, Merited Artist 1976. She m. DÓZSA. GPD

Szymański, Stanisław, b. Kraków, 1930. Polish dancer. Principal dancer, Warsaw B. since 1956. Danced Mercutio in Jerzy Gogoł's ROMEO AND JULIET and Romeo in the second version of Aleksey Chichinadze's ballet, the Prince in CINDERELLA, the title role in ORPHEUS, the Mandarin (MIRACULOUS MANDARIN), the Devil in PAN TWARDOWSKI. Created many roles in Polish ballets, incl. the title role in *Mazepa* (ch. Stanisław Miszczyk after Juliusz Słowacki's play). Master of episodic solo dances in great ballets. JPu

T

Tacoma Performing Dance Company *see* REGIONAL BALLET (USA)

Taglioni, Filippo, b. Milan, 1777; d. Como, 1871. Italian dancer and choreographer. Debut Pisa 1794, subsequently principal dancer in Florence, Venice, Paris (where he studied with Jean François Coulon) and in 1803 to Stockholm where he was also choreographer and where his daughter Marie TAGLIONI was born. He staged ballets throughout Europe but his place in history is secured by his creation of SYLPHIDE which launched the Romantic movement in ballet. It was his intensive training that made Marie a great dancer; he knew how to exploit her gifts. MC
See Ivor Guest, *The Romantic Ballet in Paris* (London and Middletown, CT, 1966)

Taglioni, Marie, b. Stockholm, 1804; d. Marseille, 1884. Italian dancer, daughter of F. TAGLIONI and Sophie Hedwige Karsten (daughter of the Swedish singer Cristoffer Karsten). While her father toured Europe producing his ballets she lived in Paris with her mother and studied with Jean François Coulon. Although she was a skinny and unprepossessing child he recognized her talent and his enthusiasm led her father, somewhat prematurely, to obtain an engagement for her in Vienna. When she arrived he realized his mistake and years of unremitting toil began during which he made her the foremost dancer of her time (rivalled only by ELSSLER). Her debut was at the Hof T. 10 June 1822 in a *divertissement* by her father appropriately called *La Réception d'une Jeune Nymphe à la Cour de Terpsichore*. Debut Paris O. 1827 where she was immediately admired for her exceptional lightness and grace and the aerial quality of her dancing. On 21 Nov 1831 she appeared as the abbess Hélène, leading the 'Ballet of the Nuns', staged by her father in Giacomo Meyerbeer's opera *Robert le Diable*. Her spiritual perf. contributed greatly to the success of the work and delighted Meyerbeer but she withdrew after a few perfs to work on a new ballet her father was planning for her. The ballet in *Robert le Diable* was the first flowering of the Romantic style, to be established firmly in F. Taglioni's next work, SYLPHIDE. It made Marie's name internationally famous. Thereafter she danced in London regularly, in Russia between 1837 and 1842 – where she was idolized – and danced in Vienna (where 40 young aristocrats unhitched the horses and pulled her carriage through the streets), and toured Poland. At the height of her career she amassed great riches and returned from Russia loaded with jewels and sables. She retired to a villa at Lake Como in 1847 but returned to Paris in 1858, lured by reports of the young LIVRY who was said to be a reincarnation of the original '*Sylphide*' (as Taglioni was always known). She became *Inspectrice de la Danse* at the Paris O. 1859, retaining the post until 1870, teaching the most advanced class. She choreographed her only ballet *Le Papillon* (1861) for Livry (mus. Jacques Offenbach). During her absence from Como her fortune mysteriously diminished (some say her old and eccentric father made foolish speculations). She then taught dancing and deportment, first in London (Queen Mary was a pupil), then Paris. In 1880 she went to live with her son Georges Gilbert de Voisins and his family in Marseille. She had married Comte Gilbert de Voisins in 1832 but they separated 1835. She also had a daughter Nini (b. 1835) and absented herself from the Paris O. during her pregnancy with a pretended knee injury. *Mal au genou* thenceforth became a euphemism in ballet circles for the pregnancy of ballerinas. MC
See André Levinson, *Marie Taglioni* (Paris 1929; English tr. Cyril W. Beaumont, London 1930); Léandre Vaillat, *La Taglioni ou La Vie d'une Danseuse* (Paris 1942); Ivor Guest, *The Romantic Ballet in Paris* (London and Middletown, CT, 1966); *The Romantic Ballet in England* (London 1954); Parmenia Migel, *The Ballerinas, from the court of Louis XIV to Pavlova* (New York and Toronto 1972)

Taglioni, Paul, b. Vienna, 1808; d. Berlin, 1888. Italian dancer and choreographer, son of F. and brother of M. TAGLIONI. Studied with his father and with Jean François Coulon in Paris. Debut Stuttgart 1825; danced in most European capitals, notably in Berlin where he partnered Amalia Galster, whom he m. Some of his most important and successful ballets (mostly mus. PUGNI) were staged in London at Her Majesty's T. between 1847 and 1851. *Electra* (17 Apr 1849) was the first ballet in which electric light was used; *Les Plaisirs de l'Hiver* (5 July 1849) was one of the first to represent skating on stage. He also produced many ballets in Berlin.

His daughter Marie Paul Taglioni (b. Berlin, 1833; d. Neu-Aigen, 1891), not to be confused with her aunt M. Taglioni, danced mostly in her father's ballets but at Her Majesty's T., London, appeared in PERROT's *divertissement Les Quatre Saisons* 1848, as MYRTHA 1849 and in SYLPHIDE 1851. Principal dancer, Berlin Staats O. 1848–65; guest appearances throughout Europe. In 1866 she m. Prince Joseph Windisch-Grätz and retired from the stage. MC
See Ivor Guest, *The Romantic Ballet in England* (London 1954)

Taglioni, Salvatore, b. Palermo, 1790; d. Naples, 1868. Italian dancer and choreographer, brother of F. TAGLIONI. His career was almost entirely in Naples where he worked for 50 years. He founded the school at the San Carlo T. there 1812, at the invitation of King Joachim I Napoleon (Murat) and staged over 200 ballets incl. his own version of SYLPHIDE in the 1830s. He turned mostly to historical and literary subjects for his ballets, e.g. *Les Fiancés* based on Alessandro Manzoni's novel *I Promessi Sposi*. He m.

the dancer Adélaide Perraud; their daughter Louise Taglioni (1823–93) danced at the Paris O. 1848–57, debut there 21 Aug 1848 in Auguste Mabille's ballet *Nisida, ou les Amazones des Açores* (mus. François Benoist). She also appeared in the USA in 1855. MC

Tait, Marion, b. London, 1950. English dancer. Joined RBS at age of 15; joined RB touring co. 1968, becoming RB principal 1974. First major role was the Girl in a revival of INVITATION (1974) in which her dramatic and lyric gifts were both evident. Danced GISELLE the same year and created her first role in a contemporary dance work, BRUCE's *Unfamiliar Playground.* In 1975 created leading role in J. CARTER's *Shukumei* and danced SWANILDA and Titania (to NUREYEV's Oberon) in DREAM. She m. RB soloist David Morse. MC

Takei, Kei, b. Tokyo, 1946. Japanese dancer. Brought to the USA with the encouragement of SOKOLOW. Her dance training has incl. study at the Juilliard S. of Music, the GRAHAM S. of Contemporary Dance, CUNNINGHAM Studio, and the Henry St Settlement Playhouse. She has evolved her own personal style of movement, strongly dramatic and full of sustained poses and interludes of struggle. Since 1969 she has been choreographing a long sequence of loosely related dances called *Light* which suggest a personal odyssey. DM

Tallchief, Maria, b. Fairfax, OK, 1925. American dancer, sister of Marjorie TALLCHIEF. Studied with NIJINSKA and at SAB. B. Russe de Monte Carlo 1942–7 and 1954–5, where she became particularly identified with the ballets of BALANCHINE, whom she later m. Created Coquette in *Night Shadow* (*see* SONNAMBULA), *pas de trois* in DANSES CONCERTANTES. Danced with B. Society and NYCB 1947–60 and 1963–5, where Balanchine continued to create many roles for her, incl. *Symphony in C* (*see* PALAIS DE CRISTAL, First Movement), ORPHEUS (Eurydice), *Firebird*, revival of PRODIGAL SON (Siren), *Scotch Symphony*, *Allegro Brillante*. Guest artist in Balanchine ballets, Paris O., 1947. Also danced with ABT 1948–9, and as guest artist with PAGE's Chicago OB 1961, RDB 1961, Chicago Lyric O. 1962. Now teaches in Chicago. DV

Tallchief, Marjorie, b. Denver, CO, 1927. American dancer, sister of Maria TALLCHIEF. She m. SKIBINE. Studied with NIJINSKA and LICHINE, California. ABT 1944–7, DE CUEVAS Co. 1947–56, dancing her sister's role of the Coquette in *Night Shadow* (*see* SONNAMBULA), and later the Sleepwalker, CONCERTO BAROCCO, BICHES, etc. Toured USA with PAGE's Chicago OB 1956 and 1958. *Étoile* of Paris O. 1957–62, the first American to be so designated. HARKNESS B. 1964–6. Now teaches in Dallas, TX. DV

Talvo, Tyyne, b. Helsinki, 1919. Finnish dancer and choreographer, Swedish by m. with CRAMÉR. After a dancing career in Cramér productions, she studied at the Choreographic Inst., Stockholm, 1964–7. Has created and staged ballets for Cramér B., other Scandinavian cos and TV, incl. *The Hill of the Winds* (from the *Kalevala*, the Finnish national epic), and *Sauna*. Director, Cramér B., since 1975. AGS

Taming of the Shrew, The, ballet, 2 acts, ch./lib. (after William Shakespeare's play) CRANKO; mus. Kurt-Heinz Stolze after Domenico Scarlatti; sc./c. Elisabeth Dalton. Stuttgart, Stuttgart B., 16 Mar 1969; dan. HAYDÉE, CRAGUN, MADSEN. A brilliantly comic retelling of the story with superb roles for the two principals and a delightful cameo for the unlucky suitor, Gremio. The roles of Katharine and Petruchio are virtuoso ones but also credible characters whose love for each other, despite stormy passages, gives the ballet humanity. Revived RB at CG, 1977. MC

Tamiris [Becker], Helen, b. New York, 1905; d. New York, 1966. American dancer and choreographer. Studied with FOKINE, danced at NY Met for three seasons during the 1920s, *Music Box Revue*, 1924. Concert debut 1927; appeared as soloist at Salzburg, Berlin, Paris. Appeared annually in NY with her own co. from 1930, was director of S. of American Dance 1930–45, choreographer of Federal Dance Project, NY, 1936–9. With her husband, NAGRIN, formed Tamiris–Nagrin Dance Co. 1960–3. Choreographed many solos incl. NEGRO SPIRITUALS

Maria Tallchief as BALANCHINE's Firebird

Tap. ASTAIRE in
Three Little Words (1950)

(1928–42); group works incl. *Walt Whitman Suite*, 1934 (returning to the same source of inspiration for *Dance for Walt Whitman*, 1958), *Salut au Monde* (1936), *How Long Brethren?* (1937), *Adelante* (1939); many musicals incl. a revival of *Showboat* (1946), *Annie Get Your Gun* (1946), *Inside USA* (1948), *Touch and Go* (1949), *Plain and Fancy* (1955). DV

Tap dancing, a style of dance in which the percussive sound of the footwork is the distinguishing characteristic. The basic tap steps produce distinct sounds described by step names such as *flap*, *hop*, *brush*, *stamp*, *shuffle*, *heel drop*, *ball-change*, and *cramp roll*. These steps are performed in intricate rhythmical combinations which may be applied to any style of music or form of dance movement. In the tradition of American tap dancing, small metal plates are attached to the toe and heel of the dancing shoes to articulate the dancer's rhythm and movement.

The roots of tap dancing lie in Europe and Africa, but the separate elements of the form were first brought together in the USA. The earliest Irish jigs and reels made lively 'shoe music'. Irish step dancers and English clog dancers kept the upper body and arms nearly motionless in order to concentrate on footwork. In Africa, the various tribal dances involved the whole body in head, shoulder, hip, and loin movements to syncopated ritual rhythms. With the beginning of the slave trade in America, the two dance forms came together in a blend of European footwork and African timing that took on a uniquely American character. By the 1820s, Irish immigrants had begun performing clog dances on American stages. In 1828 one white dancer, Thomas Dartmouth 'Daddy' Rice, parodied an old slave's contorted dance and sang 'Jump Jim Crow' in the first blackface performance of the American minstrel genre. In the 1840s, the most famous black minstrel, William Henry Lane, billed throughout the USA and Europe as 'Juba: King of All Dancers', took on white competitors in refereed challenge tap matches. American minstrels continued to blend cultural influences and create new dances, such as the Essence of Old Virginia, a slow-tempoed shuffle, which evolved into the gentle Soft Shoe popularized by the renowned George Primrose.

In 1881 the first vaudeville show opened in NY, offering family entertainment and an expanded showcase for tap dancing. Major figures of white vaudeville were Tom Patricola, who gave tap dancing a classic step that bears his name; Eddie Horan, who introduced clog and cane dancing; and Pat Rooney, who contributed the colourful steps 'Falling Off a Log' and 'Off to Buffalo'. The black vaudeville circuit presented celebrated 'hoofers' such as King Rastus Brown, the master of flat-footed tap dancing; Eddie Rector, who gave black tapping a new elegance and grace; John Bubbles, originator of the subtle Rhythm Tap style; and Bill 'Bojangles' Robinson (1878–1949), America's most famous black tap dancer, remembered for his superb footwork and his 'Stair Dance'.

In the 1920s, black choreographers adapted emerging jazz rhythms to the Broadway stage to give tapping a new dimension and complexity. In Hollywood in the 1930s, the incomparable ASTAIRE brought years of ballet, ballroom, and acrobatic training to his love for tap dancing and perfected a cinematic dance form that reached new heights of sophistication in films such as *The Gay Divorcee* (1934) and *Top Hat* (1935). Astaire integrated his naturally easy-going tap style with ballet carriage and a firm sense of motivation to shape each screen dance into its own story. Great women tappers of the era include Ruby Keeler, Vera-Ellen, Ginger Rogers, Ann Miller, and Eleanor Powell. Other male tap stars were James Cagney, Ray Bolger, Donald O'Connor, and Gene Kelly. An exceptional actor in his own right, Kelly used his powerful physique and strong cinematic personality to raise screen tap dancing to new aesthetic heights in *Cover Girl* (1944) and *Singin' in the Rain* (1951). In the concert field, Paul Draper applied tap technique to classical music in an attempt to give tap more artistic validity.

By the late 1940s, tap dancing's audience appeal started to wane as popular taste swung from tap to ballet. Musical comedies such as *Oklahoma!* offered audiences fresh and imaginative ballet numbers. With the introduction of bold jazz dances on Broadway in the 1950s in e.g. *West Side Story*, tap dancing was virtually banished from American entertainment.

A series of nostalgic tap revivals on stage and film in the early 1970s once again placed before the public the artistry and heritage of America's only indigenous dance form. Alongside aspiring professionals, a new breed of amateur 'hoofer' enrolled in tap-dancing classes, in search of exercise, enjoyment, and a lost era of elegance. JHS

Taras, John, b. New York City, 1919. American dancer, choreographer, and ballet master. Studied with FOKINE, VILZAK, SCHOLLAR, at SAB and with others. Early appearances in musicals. Joined American B. Caravan 1940, Littlefield B. 1940–1, American B. for S. American tour 1941, ABT 1942–6. With ABT progressed from *corps de ballet* to soloist and ballet master and choreographed his first ballet *Graziana* 1945. Choreographed DESIGNS WITH STRINGS. Joined DE CUEVAS B. as ballet master 1948 and from then until 1959, with short breaks, was principal choreographer to the co., staging among other works PIÈGE DE LUMIÈRE and working closely with HIGHTOWER. Returned to NY in 1959 to revive and dance the role of the Baron in SONNAMBULA for NYCB and joined the co. as assistant to BALANCHINE. He has since staged Balanchine's ballets all over the world. Ballet master, Paris O., 1969–70; 1971–2 in W. Berlin. Returned to NYCB 1972 as one of the three ballet masters (with Balanchine and ROBBINS). He has created ballets for fests throughout Europe, notably in France and at Monte Carlo, and has worked in S. America. MC

Taras Bulba, ballet, 4 acts, 11 scenes, ch. Boris Fenster; mus. Vasily Solovyov-Sedov; lib. after Nikolay Gogol's classic novel of same title; sc. Aleksandr Konstantinovsky. Leningrad, Kirov T., 28–30 June 1955; dan. Mikhail Mikhailov (title role), MAKAROV (Ostap), SERGEYEV (Andriy), DUDINSKAYA (Pannochka). Andriy, the second son of Taras, a 16th-c. Ukrainian chief, is in love with a Polish girl, Pannochka, and goes over to the enemy's side. Taras kills him with his own hand. His other son, Ostap, is executed before his eyes.

Original version: ch. F. LOPUKHOV; sc. Vadim Ryndin; Kirov T., 12 Dec 1940. The same music was used for ZAKHAROV's version, Bolshoy T., 26 Mar 1941; dan. GABOVICH and Sergeyev (as guest artist) as the two sons, and SEMYONOVA as Pannochka. Revived Novosibirsk 1960. The Gopak from this production is a popular number in the Bolshoy B.'s highlights recitals on tour. NR

Tarnowski, Aleksander, b. Warsaw, 1822; d. Warsaw, 1882. Polish dancer. Principal classical dancer, Warsaw B., 1845–58. The first Polish ALBRECHT, Salvator Rosa (CATARINA), Phoebus (ESMERALDA), etc. Twin brother of Antoni TARNOWSKI. JPu

Tarnowski, Antoni, b. Warsaw, 1822; d. Warsaw, 1887. Polish dancer. Principal classical dancer, Warsaw B., 1850–66. Danced ALBRECHT, JAMES, Conrad (CORSAIRE), Gringoire (ESMERALDA), etc. Twin brother of Aleksander TARNOWSKI. JPu

Taylor, Burton, b. White Plains, NY, 1943. American dancer. Studied ABTS. Debut with EGLEVSKY B. 1959. Later danced with ABT; with CCJB 1969–75. Now freelance. One of America's

Paul Taylor and members of his dance company in his *Book of Beasts*

finest *danseurs nobles*, his roles incl. Oberon in DREAM, Othello in MOOR'S PAVANE, and MONOTONES I. DV

Taylor, Paul (Bellville), Jr, b. Pittsburgh, PA, 1930. American choreographer and modern dancer. Studied painting at Syracuse Univ. and dance with TUDOR and CRASKE at Juilliard S. of Music, NY, and at Connecticut College, GRAHAM S. and NY Met OBS. Performed with P. LANG and CUNNINGHAM 1953; formed his own co. 1954. He performed with Graham as a soloist 1955–61, creating such roles as Aegisthus (CLYTEMNESTRA), the dancing Tiresias (NIGHT JOURNEY), and the Stranger (*Embattled Garden*). In 1959 BALANCHINE created a solo for him in EPISODES. He has also appeared on TV and Broadway. With his co., Taylor has toured S. America, Europe, N. Africa, and Asia, and has appeared in Mexico (1963), Fest. dei Due Mondi, Spoleto, in Paris, in London (1964), and at the Holland Fest. (1966). He received many prestigious awards. His works are in the repertories of the Dutch NB and the RDB. Taylor's works to 1961 were *avant-garde* to the point that *Epic* (1957), an almost motionless dance performed to telephone time signals, was reviewed by HORST with a blank page in *Dance Observer*. Of the major figures of US modern dance, he is one of the most classically orientated, although he does not use formal ballet technique. AUREOLE, a pure dance piece which might be said to be his most classical work, has been performed by NUREYEV. Taylor has consistently used dancers with strong stage personalities and often atypical dancers' bodies. Much of his work has decor or costumes by US artists like Robert Rauschenberg and Alex Katz. His choreography is characterized by humour and a sense of the macabre. Of the over 50 works he has choreographed since 1955, some of his best-known pieces are THREE EPITAPHS, *Insects and Heroes* (1961; mus. John Herbert McDowell), *Aureole*, the full-length ORBS, and *Esplanade* (1975; mus. Johann Sebastian Bach). JD

See Selma Jeanne Cohen, *The Modern Dance, Seven Statements of Belief* (Middletown, CT, 1966); J. Baril, 'Paul Taylor', *Les Saisons de la Danse* (Paris, July 1973) with list of roles and other activities

Tchaikovsky, Piotr Ilyich, b. Kamsko-Votinsk, Viatka, 1840; d. St Petersburg, 1893. Russian composer. Though Tchaikovsky wrote only three ballets, SWAN LAKE, SLEEPING BEAUTY, and NUTCRACKER, almost all his music is imbued with theatricality and the qualities of dance, especially in its rhythmic energy, vivid melody, and emotional clarity. His symphonies, concertos, tone poems, orchestral suites, chamber music, and even songs, have all made fine ballet scores. DH

Tchaikovsky Concerto No. 2 *see* BALLET IMPERIAL

Tchelitchev, Pavel, b. Moscow, 1898; d. Rome, 1957. Russian-born painter and designer who lived and worked in the USA 1934–51, becoming a US citizen. Neo-Romantic in style, influenced by PICASSO and his 'Blue Period' and by the Surrealists. Designed ODE for DIAGHILEV, but his close friendship with KIRSTEIN and BALANCHINE led to many extraordinarily beautiful collaborations, notably Balanchine's *Errante* (Paris 1933), Christoph Willibald Gluck's opera *Orfeo ed Euridice* (NY Met, 1936), *Balustrade* (Original B. Russe, 1941). Designed MASSINE's *Nobilissima Visione* (also known as *Saint Francis*; B. Russe de Monte Carlo, 1938). Made many designs and projects for ballets that were never produced, e.g. *The Cave of Sleep* (1941, a Balanchine–Kirstein project).

The Museum of Modern Art in NY owns some of his best work. MC

Tcherina [Tchemerzina], Ludmilla (Monique) b. Paris, 1924. French dancer and actress. Studied with KHLUSTIN and PREOBRAZHENSKA. Created JULIET for LIFAR. O. Marseille, Nouveau B. de Monte Carlo 1946; created principal roles in *À la Mémoire d'un Héros* (in which she was Napoleon), and *Mephisto Valse*, both by Lifar. She m. dancer Edmond Audran (d. 1951). International guest artist. Appeared in the film *Tales of Hoffmann* (1951; directed Michael Powell). Created leading role in Lifar's *Le Martyre de Saint-Sébastien* (Paris O., 1957). Founded her own co. 1959 and with it created leading role in *Les Amants de Téruel* (ch. Milko Sparemblek) which she brought to London 1959. Also danced in Venice, and at Milan Sc. in *Excelsior* (ch. DELL'ARA) 1967. An elegant, sophisticated woman, she has a strong stage personality and shows a preference for dramatic roles. M-FC

Tcherkassky, Marianna, b. Glen Cove, NY. American dancer. Early training with her mother, Lillian Tcherkassky, later at Washington S. of B. and SAB. Danced with EGLEVSKY B., joined ABT 1970. One of the most promising younger American ballerinas, she has danced opposite BARYSHNIKOV in SPECTRE DE LA ROSE, GISELLE, and in THARP's *Push Comes to Shove*. DV

Tchernicheva, Lyubov, b. St Petersburg, 1890; d. London, 1976. Russian dancer and ballet mistress. Studied Imperial S., St Petersburg, graduating 1908. She m. GRIGORIEV 1909 and in 1911 joined DIAGHILEV co., resigning from Imperial Ts in 1912; a leading dancer with Diaghilev until 1929, ballet mistress to the co. from 1926. In 1932 joined B. Russe de Monte Carlo and stayed with DE BASIL until the end. Subsequently, with her husband, restaged much of the Diaghilev repertory. A great beauty, her most famous roles were ZOBEIDE, the Miller's wife in TRICORNE, and the title roles in FOKINE's *Thamar* and LICHINE's *Francesca da Rimini* (1937, which she created). MC

Television. Television was in the early years a development of sound broadcasting, rather than film, and like radio, it provided 'entertainment' between informative programs.

The British Broadcasting Corporation began transmitting public TV programs on 2 Nov 1936, and on 5 Nov 1936 presented its first dance program, a *divertissement* of nine items by RAMBERT's dancers. 'Entertainment' on BBC radio was primarily music, so for TV instead of just showing musicians it seemed sensible to put dancers in front of them, dancing to 'good' music. The music was played in the same studio by the TV Orchestra, and the program given twice, at 15.15 and 21.37, 'live' on both occasions, and transmitted over an area of 30 miles. On 11 Nov 1936 JOB was televised. The outbreak of World War II temporarily put an end to all TV.

Since the war, most of the countries of the world have developed nationwide TV coverage. The TV organizations fall into three categories: those owned and controlled by the Government or State as in E. Europe and the USSR; those financed by advertising and operating commercially as in the USA; those financed by licence fees and operating as a public service as in Britain, some other European countries, and Japan. All have legal obligations to provide information, entertainment, and education. The way in which they do this, and the order of priority, shifts under social, economic, and political pressures.

The economic existence of any broadcasting organization depends upon satisfying a mass audience. The cost of TV to the viewer is relatively low; the cost of maintaining the service is high. The economy of TV, therefore, works only if there is 'investment' by the viewer on a very large scale.

The relationship between dance and TV so far has been that TV hires and controls, dance provides.

Unlike the relationship between drama and TV where there is a large pool of professional performers on which TV can draw, with dance there is no pool of professional dancers free of co. commitments, and virtually no choreographers working specifically for TV. Theatre dance cannot command a regular audience and has never succeeded in any country in becoming regular TV fare. Admirable as many programs have been, they are nearly always 'once offs'. Dance usually requires both dancers and musicians, two sets of artists (also paid for repeats); it is therefore more costly than drama, a bigger risk, and thus not loved by TV controllers.

Nevertheless, by the early 1950s the BBC was televising educational programs about ballet (directed by Felicity Gray and Philip Bate) and in 1952 a full-length SLEEPING BEAUTY directed by SKEAPING with an international cast assembled for the occasion (the SWB was too fully committed to live perfs to spare time for TV). In 1957 DALE began a series of condensed versions of the classical ballets, adapting them to take place in the small space of the studio (faithfully reproducing stage perfs means that the cameras have to be so far from the stage that the dancers appear minute), and making subtle use of TV techniques so that the ballets really came alive on the screen. She found a willing collaborator in NERINA, who danced in COPPÉLIA (27 Oct 1957), GISELLE (23 Nov 1958), and, with the RB, FILLE MAL GARDÉE (27 Dec 1962).

The arrival of colour in 1967 both helped and hindered dance on TV. The magnificence of national dance troupes, especially the *Kathakali* dancers from India, dazzled with their gorgeous costumes and exotic make-up. But the carefully planned black-and-white productions of the classic ballets were replaced by colour relays of actual stage perfs, ill-suited to the small screen. Typically, the Bolshoy B.'s ROMEO AND JULIET, filmed for international TV in live perf. to celebrate the Bolshoy T.'s 200th anniversary in 1976, lost nearly all its dramatic impact.

In France, Juan Corelli and LACOTTE have done valuable work in mounting ballets specially for TV. In Sweden, CULLBERG has had many successes incl. a brilliant condensation of GREEN TABLE (1976). In 1974 several of BALANCHINE's ballets were filmed for TV in Munich, using his dancers from the NYCB, produced by Reiner Moritz and directed by Klaus Lindermann and Hugo Niebeling. From Canada, Norman McLaren's *Pas de Deux*, filmed in high speed, became so celebrated that an entire documentary on his work, *The Eye Hears, The Ear Sees*, was made by Dale in 1969 (shown on BBC Jan 1970). The work of NIKOLAIS lends itself well to TV; *Nik The Relay*, directed by Bill Fitzwater, made in 1971, was about the man and his choreography. From Germany an excellent version of CRANKO's ONEGIN was produced by ZDF in 1976, directed by David Sutherland.

Little dance has been shown on US television. Grants from the National Endowment for the Arts and other bodies made possible the production of a series, 'Dance in America', for the Public Broadcasting Service by WNET/13, NY, in 1976. The programs devoted to GRAHAM and to THARP were shown on BBC under the title 'Bicentennial Summer'.

Televising RB's production of CINDERELLA with FONTEYN for NBC TV, 1957

However, the public's fascination with physical movement demonstrated by the viewing figures for Olympic ice skaters and gymnasts (mostly ballet trained) has not yet spilled over into dance. On TV, as in the theatre, dance still goes cap in hand, dependent on grants and subventions. The BBC has a relatively good record (it has transmitted documentaries on major dance personalities – notably John Drummond's two programs on DIAGHILEV (1968) – as well as dance works). But even for Britain the 1976 *World Radio and TV Handbook* gives the following figures: out of 8,000 hours' transmission on two channels 1,101 were devoted to sport, 482 to drama, 137 to music. Dance, as dance, is not listed. MC

Tena, Lucero *see* SPAIN

Tennant, Veronica, b. London, England, 1947. Canadian dancer. Studied at NBS of Canada, joining co. as principal 1965; debut as JULIET in CRANKO's ROMEO AND JULIET. Appeared in award-winning TV films of *Romeo and Juliet*, FRANCA's CINDERELLA, NUREYEV's SLEEPING BEAUTY. Guest appearances with NAGY and BUJONES in USA. Dances all leading ballerina roles, incl. GISELLE, SWANILDA, SYLPHIDE. Officer, Order of Canada, 1975. PD

Terabust, Elisabetta, b. Varese, 1946. Italian dancer. Rome OHS 1955–63; appointed prima ballerina 1966, and appeared in wide range of roles from modern to classical and romantic. Frequent guest artist, LFB and PETIT's Marseille Co. Debut Milan, Sc., Sept 1975. Dances classical roles and in many MILLOSS ballets. FP

Ter-Arutunian, Rouben, b. Tiflis [Tbilisi], 1920. American designer of Armenian parentage. Studied in Berlin, Vienna, and Paris. Emigrated to USA 1951, US citizen 1957. A prolific designer of remarkable range, his work in ballet has been mostly for NYCB and for TETLEY. He designs with equal facility the sugary confections of BALANCHINE's NUTCRACKER and the simple shell-shaped set for RICERCARE. MC

Terpis [Pfister], Max, b. Zürich, 1889; d. Zürich, 1958. Swiss dancer and teacher. Studied architecture; then danced under Suzanne Perrotet, a pupil of LABAN and WIGMAN. Ballet master, Hanover, 1923; followed KRÖLLER as ballet master, Berlin Staats O. 1924–30, choreographing many ballets there. Opened a school in Berlin with Rolf Arco. He returned to Switzerland 1939; and worked as an opera *régisseur* in Basel 1941–3 and in Milan. Wrote *Tanz und Tänzer* (Zürich 1946). GBLW

Terrain, modern dance work, ch. RAINER. NY, Judson Memorial Church, 28 Apr 1963; dan. T. BROWN, William Davis, Judith Dunn, Alex Hay, PAXTON, Rainer, Albert Reid. An exercise in controlling space while leaving some leeway to the performer to determine his own movements within the overall structure. It emphasized great physicality with no attempt to glamorize the process of the dance. DM

Terry, Walter, b. Brooklyn, NY, 1913. American writer and lecturer. BA, Univ. of NC; studied dance there. Dance critic, *Boston Herald* 1936–9, *NY Herald Tribune* 1939–42, 1945–66, *Saturday Review* from 1967. Served in US Army Air Force during World War II. Author of many books incl. *Ballet* (New York 1958), *The Ballet Companion* (New York 1968), *Frontiers of Dance: The Life of Martha Graham* (New York 1975). DV

Tetley, Glen, b. Cleveland, OH, 1926. American dancer and choreographer. Studied with HOLM, CRASKE, TUDOR, and danced with a variety of ballet and contemporary dance cos, incl. those of BUTLER, JOFFREY, GRAHAM, ROBBINS, and with ABT. This catholicity of experience, plus the fact that Tetley came late (in his 20th year) to dance and was concerned to accept training in both classic and contemporary styles, is a key to much of his later creativity. He made his first ballets for his own group in NY in 1962, most notably PIERROT LUNAIRE.

In 1964 Tetley was asked to join NDT and his first ballet for that co., *The Anatomy Lesson* (mus. Marcel Landowsky; sc./c. Nicolas Wijnberg; The Hague, 28 Jan 1964), was inspired by Rembrandt's painting on this theme. Since then he has staged some 16 ballets for NDT and for a year, 1969–70, was joint artistic director with van MANEN. He has also staged ballets elsewhere, for ABT, Batsheva Dance Co. of Israel, but perhaps his most influential work was with BR for whom he restaged and created several ballets. These were important in helping to fix an identity for the new BALLET RAMBERT. Tetley's ballets were an example of how a new image and power could be given to dance. After Tetley had become a freelance choreographer and had been recognized in Europe (though not in the USA) as an important innovator, he was invited to make two ballets for RB: *Field Figures* (sc./c. N. BAYLIS; mus. Karlheinz Stockhausen) was created for RB's touring group (Nottingham, 9 Nov 1970), and *Laborintus* (mus. Luciano Berio; sc./c. TER-ARUTUNIAN) was mounted for the CG troupe.

In autumn 1974, succeeding CRANKO, Tetley was invited to direct the Stuttgart B. and just before taking up his appointment he created VOLUNTARIES to POULENC's Organ Concerto as a tribute to Cranko and his two stars, HAYDÉE and CRAGUN. As director, Tetley has introduced some of his existing ballets into the Stuttgart repertory and has staged a *Daphnis and Chloe*. In 1976, he resigned and was succeeded as director of the Stuttgart B. by Haydée. CC

Tharp, Twyla, b. Portland, IN, 1942. American modern dancer and choreographer. Graduate of Barnard College, NYC, art history. Studied dance with, among others, CUNNINGHAM, CRASKE, Richard Thomas, and NIKOLAIS. Debut with P. TAYLOR Dance Co. In 1965 formed her own co. and began choreographing. First work, *Tank Dive* (Hunter College, NYC, spring 1965).

Before 1972 Tharp worked almost exclusively without musical accompaniment and usually in non-theatre spaces – art galleries, gymnasiums, outdoors, often choreographing for a combination of her own co. and large groups, e.g., MEDLEY. In Feb 1969, she was the youngest of eight major US choreographers to take part in the NY Dance Marathon on Broadway at the Billy Rose T. *Dancing in the Streets of Paris and London, Continued in Stockholm and Sometimes Madrid*, Wadsworth Atheneum, Hartford, CT, later at Metropolitan Museum of Art, NYC (autumn 1969), involved simultaneous performing in multiple spaces viewed on closed-circuit TV. The audience was free to move from one perf. area to another.

Eight Jelly Rolls (Oberlin College, OH, Jan 1971; revised NYC autumn 1971), marks a turning point in Tharp's career and the beginning of her rapidly growing popularity. Set to eight pieces by jazz pianist Jelly Roll Morton, this is the first in a group of dances using American jazz and popular music; among them BIX PIECES, *Sue's Leg* (mus. Fats Waller; St Paul, MN, Feb 1975), *Ocean's Motion* (Spoleto, Italy, mus. Chuck Berry, Festival dei Due Mondi, June 1975), *Give and Take* (NY, BAM, Mar 1976, mus. John Philip Sousa *et al.*), as well as her first work for a ballet co. DEUCE COUPE. Tharp also wrote AS TIME GOES BY for the JOFFREY B. In Jan 1976 she choreographed *Push Comes to Shove* (mus. Franz Joseph Haydn's 82nd Symphony and Joseph Lamb's *Bohemia Rag 1919*) for ABT, becoming the first US choreographer to create a work for BARYSHNIKOV.

Twyla Tharp in *Sue's Leg*

Tharp's iconoclastic style blends the vitality and offhanded freedom of pop forms (jazz, tap, social dance) with the virtuosity and discipline of formal ballet technique. The speed and flexibility of her multi-focused, non-narrative work cloaks her complex, tightly organized musical structures in a spontaneous, often seemingly improvised, surface *déshabillé*.

She was awarded the Brandeis Univ. Creative Arts Citation 1972. Tharp's was one of 10 American modern dance cos to share a $1,400,000 grant awarded by the Andrew W. Mellon Foundation, Dec 1975. AR
See T. Tharp, 'Group Activities', *Ballet Review*, Vol. 2, No. 5 (New York 1969); 'Questions and Answers', *Ballet Review*, Vol. 4, No. 1 (New York 1971); Arlene Croce, 'Twyla Tharp's Red Hot Peppers', *Ballet Review* Vol. 4, No. 1 (New York 1971)

That is the Show, ballet, 1 act, ch. MORRICE; mus. Luciano Berio (*Sinfonia for Eight Voices and Orchestra*, 1968–9); c. N. BAYLIS; ltg John B. Read. London, Jeannetta Cochrane T., BR, 6 May 1971; dan. BRUCE. Inspired by Berio's music, Morrice was stimulated both by the juxtaposition of musical quotations and by the sung text performed by the Swingle Singers. A study of the hero as victim. MC

Theilade, Nini, b. Java, 1915. Danish dancer, choreographer, and teacher. Studied in Copenhagen with Asta Mollerup and later in Paris with ARI and EGOROVA. As a child prodigy, she was engaged in Max Reinhardt's production of Giacomo Puccini's opera *Turandot* in Germany, then returned to Copenhagen for her debut as choreographer 1936 with *Psyche* for RDB. She choreographed the first Danish symphonic ballet, *Cirklen* (*The Circle,* 1938; mus. TCHAIKOVSKY's 6th Symphony), *Metaphor* (1950), *Concerto* (1950), and *Kalkbillede* (*Chalk Picture*, 1968). She never stayed long in Denmark during her dancing years but was attached to B. Russe de Monte Carlo 1938–40, when she created important parts in MASSINE's *Nobilissima Visione* and *Seventh Symphony*. She m. in Brazil in 1940s, lived in S. America for 20 years and occasionally produced ballets there but returned to Europe in the 1960s. She formed her own school in Denmark in 1970 on the island of Thurø, near Svendborg; her group dances all over Scandinavia and occasionally at the NT, working with the theatre in Odense. SKJ

Thesmar, Ghislaine, b. Peking, 1943. French dancer. Studied with Yves Brieux, SCHWARZ, Tatiana Grantseva. DE CUEVAS B. 1960–2. With LACOTTE's B. National des Jeunesses Musicales de France; m. Lacotte 1968. Guest artist with BR, Grands B. Canadiens; *étoile*, Paris O. 1972. Created roles in her husband's ballets and danced in his revivals of SYLPHIDE (1971), COPPÉLIA (1973). Dances roles in SLEEPING BEAUTY, AFTERNOON OF A FAUN, etc. An elegant and confident dancer, has stage presence and style. Guest artist, NYCB, 1976. M-FC

Thibon, Nanon, b. Paris, 1944. French dancer. Paris OBS, *corps de ballet* 1958. Prix René Blum 1960; *première danseuse* 1963; *étoile* 1965. Dances *Scotch Symphony* (1963; ch. BALANCHINE), NOCES (1965), *Turangalila* (1968; ch. PETIT), *Grand Cirque* (1969; ch. LIFAR). Also leading roles in GISELLE, SWAN LAKE, FOUR TEMPERAMENTS. Her interesting and vivid personality has not yet been fully used by choreographers. M-FC
See A.-P. Hersin, 'Nanon Thibon', *Les Saisons de la Danse* (Paris, Dec 1971) with list of roles

Thompson, Clive, b. Kingston, 1936. Jamaican dancer, US resident since 1960. Studied ballet with May Soohih in Kingston; modern dance in NY with DUNHAM, GRAHAM, and FONAROFF, also ballet with

Margaret Black. Danced in Broadway and off-Broadway musicals, with Graham Co. 1960–70, AILEY Co. since 1968. Also in concerts with BEATTY, P. LANG, PRIMUS, YURIKO. Created several roles in works by Graham (incl. Helmsman in *Circe*, Paris in *Cortège of Eagles*) and Ailey (incl. Preacher in *Mary Lou's Mass*, duet in *Hidden Rites*). Other roles in Ailey repertory incl. all principal male roles in REVELATIONS, LIMÓN's own role in his *Missa Brevis*, Daedalus in ICARUS. In 1967 collaborated with Walter Nicks in choreographing a dance version of *Othello* for Norwegian TV, also staged movement in TV play *The Pueblo Incident*. DV

Thorogood, Alfreda, b. Lambeth, London, 1942. English dancer. Studied with VOLKOVA as a child, then RBS. Joined RB 1960, principal by 1968. A classical dancer of typically English accuracy and restraint, she won a great following during her years with the touring RB. Blessed with big, dark and expressive eyes, she has a gamine charm best revealed in DEUX PIGEONS. She m. WALL. MC

Three-Cornered Hat, The *see* TRICORNE

Three Epitaphs, modern dance work, ch. P. TAYLOR; mus. 'folk proto-jazz'; c. Robert Rauschenberg. NY, Master Inst. T., Dance Associates, 27 Mar 1956. The dancers are entirely covered in black body tights incl. their faces, with metallic 'eyes'. They carry on casual romantic attachments or momentary alliances that are at the same time hilarious and profoundly sad. First given under the title *Four Epitaphs* with a section subsequently dropped. In the repertory of LCDT from 1970. DM

Three Fat Men (*Tri Tolstyaka*), ballet, 4 acts, 8 scenes, ch./lib. MOISEYEV, after a fairytale of the same title by Yuri Olesha; mus. Viktor Oransky; sc. Boris Matrunin. Moscow, Bolshoy T., 1 Mar 1935; dan. LEPESHINSKAYA (Suok), A. Rudenko (Tibul), RADUNSKY (Doctor Gaspard), MESSERER (Balloon Vendor). Suok, a circus child performer, pretends to be a doll in order to save Tibul, fighter for his people, from enslavement by the Three Fat Men, tyrant rulers of the country. She is helped by kind Doctor Gaspard. There were many interesting interpolated danced roles, e.g. the Balloon Vendor, but although the music was illustrative, the colourful and inventive action lacked depth. Production lasted two seasons; revived 1941 for several perfs. NR
See Yuri Slonimsky, *Soviet Ballet* (Leningrad 1950)

Tikhomirnova, Irina, b. Moscow, 1917. Soviet dancer. Bolshoy TS 1926–36. Soloist and ballerina, Bolshoy B. 1936–59. Debut as Princess Florine in the BLUEBIRD *pas de deux* with MESSERER (whom she later m.) in first season. Created Assol in CRIMSON SAILS. Danced the great classical roles. She had a crisp, clean technique. Acted frequently as husband's assistant. Now teaches and takes rehearsals for Mosconcert, an organization that arranges concerts on the vaudeville stage. Toured and has taught abroad. Honoured Artist, RSFSR. Her son Mikhail (by first marriage) is in Bolshoy B. NR

Tikhomirov, Vasily, b. Moscow, 1876; d. Moscow, 1956. Russian dancer, teacher, and choreographer. Placed in Moscow TS 1886 by Bolshoy T. dancer Maria Svetinskaya, who had noticed the boy, son of a poor seamstress, dancing in a courtyard to hurdy-gurdy music. Graduated 1891, when the Bolshoy T. (as did all Imperial Ts) accepted dancers of 16. Sent to St Petersburg as exceptionally promising pupil, for *classe de perfectionnement* under P. GERDT, so that he could be prepared as a much-needed *premier danseur* for Moscow. Stayed two years instead of one, using every chance to study as well in JOHANSSON's classes. Offered a place at Maryinsky T. but returned to Moscow, where in his first season he gained a reputation as a brilliant dancer and influenced his first permanent partner, ROSLAVLEVA. From 1894 began teaching at Bolshoy BS, where he introduced more progressive methods of ballet education and the virile style that is still the hallmark of the Bolshoy male dancers. By 1896 officially appointed teacher of Moscow S.; senior teacher 1898; from Mar 1917 headed the S. until early 1930s, when he retired because of serious illness.

Danced at London Alhambra T. 1911 with partner and first wife GELTSER, also partnered A. PAVLOVA, 1913. ESPINOSA in his *Technical Vademecum* (London 1948) named Tikhomirov among the greatest Russian dancers. He shone in the whole repertoire but especially in manly roles such as JEAN DE BRIENNE in GORSKY's version of RAYMONDA.

Tikhomirov directed the Bolshoy B. 1927–30. He created a new production of ESMERALDA, dancing Phoebus and providing Geltser with one of her greatest dramatic roles. He also revived SLEEPING BEAUTY and SYLPHIDE (Act II only), which he had seen in his youth in St Petersburg, revived by M. PETIPA, and participated in the creation of the first Soviet contemporary ballet, RED POPPY.

MORDKIN and NOVIKOV were his pupils; all the male dancers of the Bolshoy B. today are heirs to his style and teaching. He was one of the greatest teachers of classical ballet. People's Artist, RSFSR. NR
See N. Roslavleva (ed.), *V. D. Tikhomirov, Artist, Balletmaster, Teacher* (Moscow 1971), a volume of his own writings, letters, etc. with list of roles and ballets; N. Roslavleva, 'Isadora Duncan and the Bolshoy Ballet School, *Dance Perspectives*, No. 64 (New York 1975).

Tikhonov, Vladimir, b. Kishinev [Chisinău], 1935. Soviet dancer. Studied Leningrad, danced in Kishinev, thence to the Bolshoy B., becoming soloist 1960, dancing BASILIO, etc. Created the leading male role in VANINA VANINI. Shared 1st prize and gold medal with M. LAVROVSKY, Second Varna Competition, 1965. People's Artist, RSFSR and the Moldavian SSR. JS/NR

Timofeyeva, Nina, b. Leningrad, 1935. Soviet dancer. Graduated from VAGANOVA Choreographic S. 1953; debut in SWAN LAKE. Invited to join Bolshoy B. 1956. Her brilliant and impeccable technique, good training, and great talent for deep and varied characterizations enabled her to take leads in all the classical ballets and create many roles in the contemporary repertory incl. Girl in *Night City* (L. LAVROVSKY's version of MIRACULOUS MANDARIN), Aegina in SPARTACUS (GRIGOROVICH version), and JULIET (VINOGRADOV's version of ROMEO AND JULIET). People's Artist, USSR. NR

Tivoli. The Pantomime T., in the Tivoli Gardens, Copenhagen, is the only stage in the world where the old Italian *commedia dell'arte* is kept alive with a tradition going back to troupes of Italian and English strolling players. They first arrived in Denmark at the end of the 18th c. when two families, the Casortis and the PRICES, gave perfs of these 'pantomimes' at their own theatre. A theatre for them was opened in Tivoli 1843. In 1874, the present Pantomime T., in Chinese style, was built by Vilhelm Dahlerup and Ove Petersen, who also designed the Royal T. Here the traditional pantomime repertory is given each night 1 May–mid-September. It became the custom to stage a short ballet later in the evening. SKJ

Tomasson, Helgi, b. Reykjavik, 1942. Icelandic dancer. Studied with VOLKOVA and BRUHN in Copenhagen, and at SAB. Danced at Tivoli T., Copenhagen; joined JOFFREY B. 1961, HARKNESS B. 1964, NYCB 1970. One of the finest male dancers of his generation. BALANCHINE created an extraordinary solo for him in *Divertimento* from BAISER DE LA FÉE during the 1972 STRAVINSKY Fest. Dances opposite MCBRIDE in this and also ROBBINS's *Dybbuk Variations*, COPPÉLIA, etc. DV

Tomaszewski, Henryk *see* MIME

Tombeau de Couperin, Le (*Couperin's Tomb*), ballet, ch. BALANCHINE; mus. RAVEL; ltg Ronald Bates. NYST, NYCB, 29 May 1975. A six-part plotless ballet to Ravel's tribute to the composer François Couperin. Revived Paris O., 1975. FM

Tomsky, Aleksandr, b. Moscow, 1905; d. Rome, 1970. Soviet dancer, ballet master, and choreographer. Graduated 1923 from evening classes, Bolshoy TS. Until 1954 soloist musical theatres, Moscow, Sverdlovsk, Kharkov, and Tashkent Os. Artistic director, Bolshoy B., 1957–8; Leningrad Maly OB 1959–60, deputy artistic director, Stanislavsky B., 1962–4. Widely known and respected for activity in his last position, co. manager, Bolshoy B. Choreographed versions of RED POPPY, CORSAIRE, SVETLANA, *Capriccio Espagnole*, and *Shahida* in the USSR; FOUNTAIN OF BAKHCHISARAY, SWAN LAKE, and STONE FLOWER in Czechoslovakia and Poland. Honoured Artist, Uzbek SSR. NR

Toumanova, Tamara, b. near Shanghai (in a railway train as her parents were leaving Russia), 1919. Russian dancer. Studied in Paris with PREOBRAZHENSKA. Debut at Paris O. in *L'Éventail de Jeanne* (*see* POULENC), at the age of nine. Engaged for DE BASIL's B. Russe de Monte Carlo 1932 by BALANCHINE, who choreographed *Cotillon* and *La Concurrence* for her. Left to dance in his Les Ballets 1933, then returned to de Basil as one of three 'baby ballerinas'. Went with MASSINE when he took over the R. BLUM B. Russe de Monte Carlo in 1938. Danced in the Broadway musical *Stars in Your Eyes* (1939), and appeared as dancer and actress in several films. Rejoined de Basil, Australia 1939; Balanchine created *Balustrade* for her 1941; returned to B. Russe de Monte Carlo 1941. Guest artist with many cos incl. ABT 1944–5, Paris O. 1947 and 1950 (when she created the title role in PHÈDRE), DE CUEVAS Co. 1949, Milan Sc. 1951 and 1952, LFB 1952 and 1954. Her repertory incl. all the great classic roles, the Miller's Wife in TRICORNE, the Beloved in SYMPHONIE FANTASTIQUE, etc. DV

Tamara Toumanova, a studio portrait

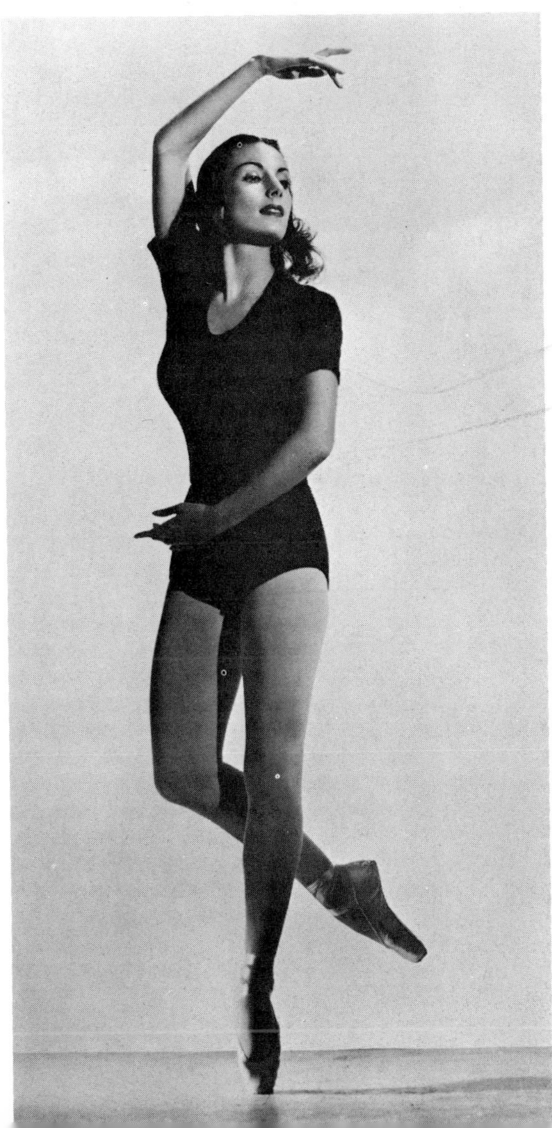

Tragedy of Fashion, A, *or the Scarlet Scissors*, ballet, 1 act, ch. ASHTON; lib. Ashley Dukes; mus. Eugene Goossens, arr. Ernest Irving; sc./c. 'F.E.D'. (FEDOROVITCH). London, Hammersmith, Lyric T., 15 June 1926; dan. RAMBERT, Ashton. A couturier stabs himself with his shears when his creations fail to please his clients. Ashton's first ballet and his first collaboration with Fedorovitch. Although given as part of a revue, *Riverside Nights*, it was produced by Rambert and her co. is therefore considered to have originated with this ballet. DV

Trailine, Boris, b. Lemnos, Greece, 1921. French dancer and teacher. Brother of H. TRAILINE. Studied with SEDOVA, KHLUSTIN, VOLININ. B. de Cannes 1941, Nouveau B. de Monte Carlo 1943. Created a leading role in *Chota Roustaveli* (ch. LIFAR) 1946. Has partnered such stars as CHAUVIRÉ and TOUMANOVA. Took part in Salzburg and Florence festivals. Created Chevalier in H. ROSEN's version of *La Dame à la Licorne* (Munich 1953). Now teaching in Paris and also acting as an impresario. M-FC

Trailine, Hélène, b. Bombas, 1928. French dancer and teacher. Sister of B. TRAILINE. Studied with SEDOVA, EGOROVA. Nouveau B. de Monte Carlo 1946, B. des CE 1949–50, also danced with the cos of DE CUEVAS, CHARRAT, MISKOVITCH, BÉJART, and RAMBERT. Created roles in Béjart's *Haut Voltage* (1956) and *Équilibre* (1959), also in Charrat's *Electre* (1960). Teaches in Paris. M-FC

Train Bleu, Le (*The Blue Train*), ballet, 1 act, ch. NIJINSKA; mus. MILHAUD; lib. COCTEAU; sc. Henri Laurens; c. Coco Chanel; curtain PICASSO. Paris, T. des CE, DIAGHILEV's B. Russes, 20 June 1924; dan. DOLIN, Nijinska, L. SOKOLOVA, WOIZIKOWSKI. Set on a Riviera beach (the Blue Train was then the fashionable mode of travel to the S. of France) the ballet was based on beach games, swimming, tennis, and golf movements, and exploited Dolin's acrobatic skills. It was never given after he left the co. MC

Trecu [Aldabaldetrecu], Pirmin, b. Zaraus (Basque Province), 1930. Spanish dancer and director. Sent to England as refugee from Spanish Civil War. Entered SWS 1946, joined SWTB 1947 and SWB at CG 1955. A leg injury curtailed his dancing career in 1961 when he gave his last perf. at CG on 27 Jan as the Boy in FÊTE ÉTRANGE, one of his finest roles for which his strange and compelling personality was ideal. He was also an authoritative Miller in TRICORNE. He now directs his own school in Oporto, Portugal, and enters pupils for the examinations of the English Imperial Society of Teachers of Dancing. MC

Trefilova, Vera, b. Vladikavkaz, 1875; d. Paris, 1943. Russian dancer. Daughter of a dramatic actress. VAZEM recommended her to St Petersburg TS; graduated into *corps de ballet* 1894. Through hard work and constant studying for perfection under CECCHETTI, Catarina Beretta, E. SOKOLOVA, and LEGAT, she reached the position of prima ballerina 1906 but danced her first AURORA 1904. Other ballets incl. *La Source* (ch. SAINT-LÉON), HALTE DE CAVALERIE, DON QUIXOTE. She was a perfect classical ballerina and virtuoso, and her domain was in the ideal harmony of classical forms. SVETLOV often criticized her for her lack of dramatic expressiveness, yet in 1916 she m. him (her third marriage). Farewell benefit in SWAN LAKE, 24 Jan 1910, but in 1921 DIAGHILEV persuaded her to return in *The Sleeping Princess* (*see* SLEEPING BEAUTY). She knew how to convey each musical nuance; HASKELL justly called her 'the Ingres of ballet'. Taught in Paris until the end of her life. NR
See V. Krasovskaya, *Russian Ballet Theatre of the Beginning of the 20th Century* (Leningrad 1972); C. W. Beaumont, *The Diaghilev Ballet in London* (London 1940; 3rd ed. 1951)

Left: Le Train Bleu as danced by DIAGHILEV's B. Russes; sc. Henri Laurens; c. Coco Chanel, 1924

Right: Trend, as performed by HOLM and Concert Group at Bennington, 1937

Trend, modern dance work, ch. H. HOLM; mus. Wallingford Riegger and Edgard Varèse; c. Betty Joiner. Bennington Fest., Bennington, VT, 13 Aug 1937; dan. Holm and Concert Group. Cast also included students from summer school. The dance was divided into several sections – some solos, some danced by the group – and depicted a society being destroyed by its own false values, which were finally wiped out in a cataclysm leading to an affirmative conclusion. DV

Tricorne, Le (*The Three-Cornered Hat*), ballet, 1 act, ch. MASSINE; mus. FALLA; lib. Martínez Sierra, after Pedro Antonio de Alarcón; sc./c. PICASSO. London, Alhambra T., DIAGHILEV's B. Russes, 22 July 1919; dan. KARSAVINA, Massine, WOIZIKOWSKI, IDZIKOWSKI. A miller and his beautiful wife outwit an elderly official bent on her seduction. Choreography in part derived from dances Massine had seen in Spain when the co. toured there during World War I. Revived by many cos incl. DE BASIL 1934, B. Russe de Monte Carlo 1938, ABT 1943, SWB 1947, CCJB 1969, LFB 1973. DV

Trinity, ballet, ch. ARPINO; mus. Alan Raph and Lee Holdridge; ltg Jennifer Tipton. NYCC, CCJB, 9 Oct 1969; dan. C. HOLDER, CHRYST, Rebecca WRIGHT, Dermot Burke, Donna Cowen, Starr Danias, James Dunne. An open tribute to the rebellious and thoughtful youth of the 1960s, *Trinity* is named for its three separate sections, Sunday, Summerland, and Saturday. FM

Triomphe de l'Amour, Le (*Love's Triumph*), ballet, 25 *entrées*, dances arranged by BEAUCHAMP and PÉCOUR; mus. LULLY; sc./c. Jean Bérain. Saint Germain-en-Laye, by the French court, 21 Jan 1681. On 16 May 1681 it was staged at the Paris O. with LAFONTAINE, the first ballet in which a professional female dancer appeared. MC

Triumph of Death, The (*Dødens Triumf*), dance drama, 12 scenes, ch. F. FLINDT after Eugène Ionesco's drama, *Le Jeux de Massacre*; mus. Thomas Koppel; sc./c. Poul Arnt Thomsen; ltg Jørgen Mydtskov. Danish TV, 23 May 1971; first staged Copenhagen, RDB, 19 Feb 1972. Flindt's third Ionesco ballet and biggest success; illustrates how death comes to people of all ages and in all situations. Danced by RDB in Copenhagen, also on tour in London and New York. SKJ

Trümpy, Berthe, b. Glarus, 1895. Swiss dancer and teacher. Pupil of DALCROZE, CECCHETTI, LABAN, and WIGMAN, whose group she joined in Dresden 1920. In 1924 she founded, with Vera Skoronel, a school in Berlin for modern dance and gymnastics. Now lives in Switzerland. GBLW

Tudor, Antony, b. London, 1909. English dancer, teacher, and choreographer; resident NY City since 1939. His output has been small, his influence enormous. He was a 'late starter', going to RAMBERT for his first lessons at the age of 19 and consequently never a strong dancer but a strong stage presence. Impressed by his desire to learn, she employed him in various capacities in her theatre and gave him his first opportunities as a choreographer; he made for her JARDIN AUX LILAS, DARK ELEGIES, and JUDGMENT OF PARIS. In 1938 he left, with some of Rambert's best dancers, to form his own London B., and created GALA PERFORMANCE. World War II put an end to London B.; some of the dancers were absorbed back in BR but Tudor, with LAING and HOWARD, accepted an invitation to participate in the founding of ABT and in 1939 moved to the USA. Howard soon returned to England but Tudor and Laing remained. The best of Tudor's existing ballets went into the ABT repertory and his reputation was assured after the production of PILLAR OF FIRE, followed by ROMEO AND JULIET, UNDERTOW, and DIM LUSTRE.

Antony Tudor and Elizabeth Schooling in his *The Descent of Hebe*, B. Rambert, 1935

In 1950 he left ABT to take over the NY Met OB, working with his own former teacher CRASKE, and although he continued to make occasional ballets for professional cos and for the Met students, his muse seemed to have deserted him. In 1963 his ECHOING OF TRUMPETS was a success with the RSB but his great 'comeback' was in 1967 when, at ASHTON's invitation, he made his first ballet for the RB: SHADOWPLAY. Tudor is now an associate director, ABT. His great contribution to ballet is his extraordinary ability to convey human relationships of the subtlest kind through movement. MC
See John Percival, *Dance Perspectives* (New York 1963) Antony Tudor No. 17: Part One: 'The Years in England' by John Percival; No. 18: Part Two: 'The Years in America and After' by Selma Jeanne Cohen

Tulip of Haarlem, The (*Garlemsky Tyulpan*), ballet, 3 acts, 4 scenes; ch. IVANOV and M. PETIPA; mus. Baron Boris Shel; lib. Ivanov. St Petersburg, Maryinsky T., 4 Oct 1887; dan. Emma Bessone, P. GERDT. Emma, a Dutch peasant girl, is turned into a tulip and is returned to human shape by a kiss from her sweetheart Peter. Ivanov's first multi-act ballet, it was said to contain enough dances for two, but suffered from pedestrian music and an uninteresting lib. Petipa's contribution was probably slight. The *scène de séduction* was especially praised, and Act II, of which it was part, was frequently revived, under the title of *Field of Tulips*, for graduation perfs of St Petersburg TS. NR

Tulsa Ballet *see* REGIONAL BALLET (USA)

Turczynowicz [Damse], Konstancja, b. Warsaw, 1818; d. Warsaw, 1880. Polish dancer and teacher. Principal, Warsaw B. 1842–53; teacher, Warsaw BS 1853–63. First Polish GISELLE, ESMERALDA, CATARINA, etc. Excellent executor of character dances, especially Polish, e.g. the Bridesmaid in CRACOW WEDDING. Danced the Polish dances Mazur and Krakowiak, Paris Grand O. 1842. She m. R. TURCZYNOWICZ. JPu

Turczynowicz, Roman, b. Radom, 1813; d. Warsaw, 1882. Polish dancer, choreographer, and teacher. Principal and teacher, Warsaw B., 1835–44, assistant director 1845–53, director, Warsaw B. and BS, 1853–66. Partnered M. TAGLIONI in SYLPHIDE 1842, later that year danced the Polish dances Mazur and Krakowiak at Paris Grand O. Choreographer of first Polish versions of GISELLE, CATARINA, ESMERALDA, CORSAIRE, and other romantic ballets. Wrote the first stage version of Polish national dances for Stanisław Moniuszko's operas (from 1858). He m. K. TURCZYNOWICZ. JPu

Turin. The original T. Regio was opened 1740 and the ballet school attached to it 1752. One of the most important Italian theatres in the 18th and 19th c. for opera and ballet, but it had begun to decline before it was (accidentally) burned down 1936. From then until 1973 seasons, incl. one or two ballet programs a year, were given at various Turin theatres, particularly T. Nuovo. On 10 Apr 1973 the new Regio (seating 1,800) was opened with Giuseppe Verdi's *I Vespri Siciliani*, incl. ballet *Four Seasons* (ch. LIFAR; dan. MAKAROVA). There is no school yet, and only a small *corps de ballet* (prima ballerina Loredana Furno). Choreography by ballet master Giuseppe Carbone (from 1976 Giuliana Barabaschi), by the teacher and choreographer Susanna Egri, etc. Many school perfs, also in small theatre in basement (Piccolo Regio). FP

Turkey. Although Turkey has a long and honourable tradition of dancing, and ballet perfs were given there by visiting cos over a long time (there is even a record of a court entertainment with dancing in 1524), national ballet is a recent achievement. In 1947 the Turkish government invited DE VALOIS to study the possibility of setting up a school of ballet within the State Cons. of Music; a school was established by the Government in a suburb of Istanbul, 11 boys and 18 girls, aged 7–10 years, selected as the first pupils. Training was modelled on English principles with some modifications to adapt to local traditions. Officially opened in Jan 1948, the school was moved in 1950 to the capital, to the Ankara State Cons. and soon grew to a capacity of 100 students. Joy Newton was in charge of the school for four years; she was succeeded by Beatrice Appleyard (another early member of the SWB). The school was directed 1954–74 by two other English dancer/teachers, Travis Kemp and his wife LAKE. After nine years of training the dancers were ready to give occasional perfs and had the good fortune (thanks to de Valois's continuing interest) to appear with visiting guest stars of the calibre of FONTEYN, NERINA, SOMES, BLAIR, and RASSINE, all from England. In 1960 the English choreographer Robert Harrold staged *El Amor Brujo* (mus. FALLA) with Turkish dancers; the program was completed with *Salome* (mus. Richard Strauss) in which the English dancer Valerie Taylor was guest artist. In the 1961–2 season Ailne Phillips staged the full-length COPPÉLIA and BOLENDER staged two of his ballets, *Création du Monde* and STILL POINT for the students. Ballets from the English repertory were gradually added, PATINEURS and RAKE'S PROGRESS. In 1962–3 HOWARD staged some of her ballets and created the first Turkish ballet for the co., *Les Baricades Mystérieuses*. In the 1963–4 season de Valois staged the full-length SLEEPING BEAUTY and in 1966 SWAN LAKE. Gradually, however, ballets with Turkish themes were introduced to the repertory. Among the ballet masters who ran the co. (as distinct from the school) in its early years were Claude Newman, Joy Newton, who returned in 1964 with Dudley Tomlinson (a former RB dancer), and the S. African Richard Glasstone (now teaching at the RBS). Glasstone staged 3-act works such as new versions of SYLVIA and PRINCE OF THE PAGODAS. The first ballet by a native choreographer, Sait Sökmen, was *The Wheel* (Ankara, 6 Nov 1968), an abstract work to RAVEL's String Quartet in F. Other choreographers who have emerged from the co. are Oytún Turfanda and Duygu Aykal. The standard of dancing can be judged from the fact that when *Sleeping Beauty* was revived in the 1971–2 season there were no fewer than three AURORAS: Meriç Sümen (who has danced GISELLE as a guest in the USSR in Odessa, Kiev, at the Kirov and at the Bolshoy), Gülcan Tunççekiç, and Jale Kazbek. The principal male dancer is Oytun Turfanda. In 1975–6 a major production was DON QUIXOTE, staged by two *répétiteurs* from the Bolshoy, Revaz Sulukidze and Nina Tchkalova in scenery and costumes by the Turkish designer Osman Sengezer.

In 1976 the Turkish B. had 74 dancers, 47 female and 27 male, and a full staff of native teachers, designers, and notators. It is able to work independently of foreign help. The guidance and vision of de Valois has always been recognized by the Turks as the inspiration for their ballet and she has been much honoured by the Turkish government. MC
See Metin And, *A Pictorial History of Turkish Dancing* (in English) (Ankara 1976)

Turner, Harold, b. Manchester, 1909; d. London, 1962. English dancer. Debut 1927 with the Alfred Haines English B. Then studied with RAMBERT and in 1930 partnered KARSAVINA in SPECTRE DE LA ROSE. Danced with both BR and Vic-Wells B. in early 1930s, joining Vic-Wells as principal dancer in 1935 and remaining with the co. (except for a brief spell with International B. and war service in the 1940s) until his death. Turner was the first virtuoso male dancer produced by British training. He created the taxing roles of the BLUE SKATER and the Red Knight in CHECKMATE, also a brilliant 'double' as the Dancing Master and the Man with a Rope in RAKE'S PROGRESS; a fine BLUEBIRD. He retired from the stage in 1955 to teach at the RBS but made occasional guest appearances. He was to dance the old Marquis in the RB's revival of FEMMES DE BONNE HUMEUR but died on his way to his dressing room after a rehearsal. He m. (1) May Honer, (2) G. LARSEN. MC

Turney, Matt, b. Americus, GA. American dancer. Studied Univ. of Wisconsin. Danced with GRAHAM Dance Co. 1951–72, during which time she created roles in many dances incl. Graham's *Canticle for Innocent Comedians*, *Seraphic Dialogue*, CLYTEMNESTRA, etc. Has also danced with the cos of MCKAYLE, AILEY, P. TAYLOR, P. LANG, and in joint concerts with COHAN. Now teaches in NY. DV

Twilight, *pas de deux*, ch. van MANEN; mus. CAGE (*The Perilous Night*); sc./c. Jean Paul Vroom. Amsterdam, Dutch NB, 20 June 1972; dan. RADIUS, EBBELAAR. London, CG, Dutch NB (Fanfare for Europe), 13 Jan 1973. Revived Stratford-upon-Avon, RB, 2 Mar 1973; dan. RUANNE, Paul Clarke. The pianist sits on stage; the setting shows an apparently romantic scene gradually revealed as an industrial landscape. The two dancers appear to be mutually attracted but distrustful and wary; the woman wears high-heeled shoes which she later removes to dance barefoot. By breaking most of the conventions of *pas de deux* form, this piece has a strong emotional impact. JP

Two Pigeons *see* DEUX PIGEONS

Harold Turner in NUTCRACKER

Galina Ulanova as Juliet with LAPAURI as Paris in the bedroom scene of L. LAVROVSKY'S ROMEO AND JULIET, as staged by the Bolshoy, Moscow

U

UCT (University of Cape Town) **Ballet Co.,** S. Africa. In 1934 HOWES joined the Faculty of Music of the Univ. of Cape Town to establish a ballet school. Yearly perfs were given at the Univ.'s Little T., and gradually from a teachers' training course, established 1941 (B. Certificate or B. Diploma), a co. grew. The Little T. proved too small and the co. appeared at the City Hall, Alhambra, and the open-air T. at Maynardville. It visited surrounding towns; in 1941 toured to Port Elizabeth and Johannesburg. Annual tours around the Republic of S. Africa, Rhodesia, Zambia, Mozambique, and SW Africa (Namibia) brought ballet of a professional standard to several hundred thousand people. It was not professional, however: students danced in the *corps de ballet* while members of the staff danced the leading roles. Until 1965 the co. was financed by the Howes B. Trust. In 1963 it became professional when it received a grant from the government to appoint paid soloists and a ballet master, a post filled by POOLE. In 1965 it received a subsidy from the Cape Performing Arts Board and appeared under the title CAPAB BALLET CO. for all perfs other than those within the Cape Town municipal boundaries, where it still performed as the UCT B. Co. In 1967 the UCT B. Co. ceased to exist; it continued, as it started, as a school only. It performed in Lausanne, Switzerland, at the 1972 Youth Music Fest. Past and present teachers incl. most of S. Africa's important artists. MG

Ulanova, Galina, b. St Petersburg, 1910. Russian dancer. Daughter of Sergey Ulanov, dancer and *régisseur* of the Maryinsky B. and his wife Maria Romanovna, dancer of the Maryinsky and teacher at its BS. Studied for five years with her mother at the Maryinsky S. and for her four remaining student years with VAGANOVA. On graduation in 1928, danced the Waltz and the Mazurka in CHOPINIANA and the SUGAR PLUM FAIRY. In her first and second seasons, danced both Princess Florine and AURORA in SLEEPING BEAUTY, and 1932 the name role in GISELLE. Created MARIA and JULIET for L. LAVROVSKY, in both ballets dancing with her regular partner, SERGEYEV. She repeated Juliet when the ballet was staged by the Bolshoy B. in 1946, two years after her transfer to that co. Also created for L. Lavrovsky leading roles in his RED POPPY (Tao-Hoa) and STONE FLOWER (Katerina). Other roles incl. Masha (NUTCRACKER), RAYMONDA, Nikia (BAYADÈRE), the Tsar-Maiden (HUMPBACKED HORSE), Mireille in FLAME OF PARIS, and CYGNE.

After 1959 limited her stage appearances to SYLPHIDES and FOUNTAIN OF BAKHCHISARAY. Became ballet mistress, Bolshoy T. 1959, passing on her stage experience to such young dancers as MAXIMOVA, whom she coached for *Giselle.* Has frequently travelled abroad as ballet mistress and Artistic Director Bolshoy B., and has contributed many articles to Soviet periodicals. Chairman of the Jury at the Varna Competition 1964–72. People's Artist, USSR. Lenin Prize, 1957. *Prima ballerina assoluta*, Bolshoy B. Her m. to Yuri Zavadsky, a stage director, ended in divorce; she later m. the principal designer of the Bolshoy B., Vadim Ryndin, who died 1974.

Ulanova has in her lifetime become a legend quite as potent as that of A. PAVLOVA, and on the strength of an immeasurably smaller number of perfs. Never in any sense a virtuoso, her essential qualities of musicality, sincerity and delicacy made her a dancer once seen, never forgotten. Some echo of her quality has been preserved in films of ROMEO AND JULIET, made in the USSR, and *Giselle* and *Le Cygne*, made during her first perfs in Britain, 1956. JS

See Galina Ulanova, *'Shkola Baleriny'* (Ballerina's School), *Novy Mir*, No. 3 (Moscow 1954); *The Making of a Ballerina* (Moscow 1955); V. Bogdanov-Berezovsky, Ulanova (Moscow 1961); M. Sizova, tr. M. Rambert, *Ulanova, Her Childhood and Schooldays* (London 1962); A. E. Kahn, *Days With Ulanova,* introduction by Arnold L. Haskell (London and New York 1962); B. Lvov-Anokhin, *Galina Ulanova* (in English, Moscow 1970) with list of roles

Ulbrich, Werner, b. Dresden, 1928. German dancer and choreographer. Pupil of HOYER and BLANK, he danced at the Komische O., E. Berlin, 1951–6, excelling in character parts. Ballet master, Chemnitz [Karl-Marx-Stadt], 1954–6, and of Leipzig B., 1954–8, also freelancing in Hamburg. Director, Düsseldorf B., 1960–4. Now works as choreographer. Choreographed ROMEO AND JULIET (Stuttgart 1959), COPPÉLIA, and *Undine* (both Düsseldorf 1961) etc. GBLW

Undertow, ballet, 1 act with prologue and epilogue; ch./lib. TUDOR after a suggestion by John Van Druten; mus. William Schuman; sc./c. Raymond Breinin. NY Met, ABT, 10 Apr 1945; dan. LAING, ALONSO, D. ADAMS, GOLLNER, Shirley Eckl, Patricia Barker, CHASE. Reveals the psychological background to a murder. FM

United States of America. Considering that in W. Europe and the Americas, classic ballet was popularly known as 'Russian' ballet during at least the first half of the 20th c., we may note some curious facts: in 1735, a year before the first professional ballet dancing was seen in Russia, Henry Holt, an Englishman, gave the first ballet perf. in Charleston, SC, in what were then the American Colonies; M. PETIPA's appearance in the USA, in 1839, preceded by eight years his arrival in St Petersburg; and Americans saw CECCHETTI as a child prodigy in 1857, 30 years before he went to dance in Russia.

By the end of the 18th c., in all the States but especially in NY, Philadelphia, Baltimore, Charleston, and New Orleans, there was an enthusiastic public for the influx of lesser or more accomplished foreign dancers, conditioned only by some rather prudish social attitudes. Philadelphia, which later became one of the most important ballet centres, was especially strict in this respect; all theatrical perfs were banned there 1786–9 and, in spite of the subsequent visits of such talented dancers as Pierre Landrin Duport (1790), M. du Moulin (1791), and Alexandre Placide's co. (1792), the prejudices persisted.

The first major ballet season in the USA was presented by the co. of Alexandre Placide (1750–1812) at the John St T., NY, Jan–May 1792. Although the programs consisted mainly of numbers popular in the London theatres, Placide was trained in Paris in classic ballet and was besides a dazzling tight-rope performer and acrobat, actor, and theatre manager. Following a successful stay in NY, the co. went on to Philadelphia and Boston and, 1794, arrived in Charleston. After a duel between Placide and the singer Louis Douvillier, a member of the troupe, 'Mme' Placide (Suzanne Vaillande, 1778–1825) married the latter 1796 and finally settled with him in New Orleans, where for 19 years she reigned alternately as *première danseuse* and as America's first woman choreographer while Placide chose to stay in Charleston, dancing and staging ballets and plays until the end of his life.

Before 1800, if many of the ballet programs derived from NOVERRE, DAUBERVAL, Maximilien Gardel and other choreographers of the Paris O., CG and Drury Lane, nevertheless there was a solid beginning of American productions. First and notable was *La Forêt Noire*, at the New T., Philadelphia, 1794, staged for Mme Anna Gardie (*c.* 1773–98), as well as Placide's original work in Charleston and a long series of revised or new productions by Jean-Baptiste Francisquy and the British James Byrne.

During the early 19th c., a steady succession of visiting celebrities monopolized most of the theatres. The Ravel family, in a kaleidoscopic repertoire of original ballets, pantomimes, high-wire acts and tumbling, were on the road in the USA for over 30 years, beginning with the 1830s, supported by the 'immortal Gabriel' and, 1853–8, by Yrca Matthias (1829–58), a ballerina who had created a sensation in Moscow in 1847 and who married François Ravel. Charles and Mme Ronzi Vestris were in NY, 1828, under the auspices of the Bowery T.'s ballet master, Claude Labasse, and then toured for a year. The Parisian Mlle Céleste (Céline Céleste Keppler, 1811–82) arrived 1827 on the first of several visits, presented the first American showing of F. TAGLIONI's SYLPHIDE (1835), married an American, Henry Elliot, and then continued her dancing and acting career in England until the age of 64. The Munich-born Mlle Augusta (Caroline Augusta Fuchs, 1806–1901) came 1836 and staged NY's first GISELLE (1846 – the American LEE had staged it and danced the title role a month earlier in Boston). Mme Lecomte, at her Philadelphia debut, 1837, was described by theatre manager Francis Wemyss as being a skilful dancer but as having a figure too ample to attract any public. Optimistically she assembled a co. in 1839 with her husband as manager, her brother Jules Martin as *premier danseur*, Jean Petipa as ballet master and young M. Petipa among the dancers, a first-rate troupe, but from the start in NY they were dogged by misfortune. Their first theatre burned to the ground, at the second, poor receipts obliged the owner to cancel their engagement, and when they reopened at the Bowery a fortnight later, they were again financially unsuccessful. Perhaps their season followed too closely on the exciting visit at the Park T. of P. TAGLIONI, with his wife Amalia Galster. At any rate, the Petipas sailed home in disgust while the undaunted Mme Lecomte and her brother stayed on permanently, becoming teachers in Philadelphia.

Philadelphia by now had become a leader in ballet activities and novelties, due no doubt to the influence of two enlightened English theatre managers, Wemyss and Robert Maywood, who jointly or alternately directed the programs of the Arch St, Chestnut St, and Walnut St Theatres. Local interest was also stimulated by the establishment of the BS of

M. and Mme Paul Hazard. The Hazards, veterans from the opera houses of Europe, trained many accomplished dancers and especially MAYWOOD who shared her debut with a fellow pupil Mary Ann Lee, but whereas Augusta departed for Europe the following spring and never returned, Mary Ann remained in the USA and thus is considered the first native ballerina.

As for the American male dancers, John Durang (1768–1822) began with the Placide Co., was active in the theatres until 1819, and sired a family of dancers, but the emphasis was on entertainment and ballroom dancing rather than classic ballet. The one great *premier danseur noble* of the period was G. W. SMITH.

By the time ELSSLER arrived, in 1840, the American public had observed enough top-ranking dancers in a whole range of successful European ballets to appreciate what they were seeing. But Elssler was something apart. With her brilliant technique, beauty and charm, novel repertoire, and generosity in donating her receipts to local charities, her conquest was absolute.

United States. *Above, left*: Mary Ann Lee, aged 15, as Fatima in *The Maid of Cashmere*; *below, left*: Augusta Maywood; *above*: George Washington Smith

Hippolyte Monplaisir (Hippolyte Georges Sornet, 1821–77) and his wife Adèle, fresh from their fruitful association at Sc., with M. Taglioni, ROSATI, and PERROT (Augusta Maywood was also there, 1847–8, in Perrot's *Faust*) embarked in 1847 on a coast-to-coast tour with their co. ably managed by Adèle's father, the well-known director Victor Bartholomin. Monplaisir returned to Europe for 20 years of further triumphs, staging hit ballets in Lisbon and at Sc.; but Domenico Ronzani (1800–68), who brought his troupe in 1857, remained in the USA for the rest of his life. Briefly with Ronzani were the Cecchetti family, little Enrico and his parents, and in 1859 G. W. Smith joined as *premier danseur*.

In 1866, at Niblo's Garden, NY, SANGALLI and Maria Bonfanti (1847–1921) were the ballet stars of a theatrical extravaganza, BLACK CROOK. Also at Niblo's, and again with Bonfanti, a similar show, *The White Fawn*, was presented in 1868. Bonfanti, who toured, taught, married, and settled in the USA, and Sangalli, who became leading ballerina of the Paris O. 1872, arrived in America on the heels of an Italian invasion. Besides those already mentioned, the most distinguished were Giuseppina Morlacchi in 1868, followed by BRIANZA and Malvina Cavallazzi, 1883, Maria Giuri, 1886, FORNAROLI in 1910, continuing right up to the present day.

From Vienna came LANNER to shine in *Giselle*. This present-day favourite ballet was dropped by the Paris O. from the time of GRANTZOW, 1868, until after World War I and suffered the same fate in the USA where it disappeared after Lanner's 1870 perf. until A. PAVLOVA brought it in 1910 to the NY Met.

First ballerina to appear at the Met OH, for its inauguration in 1883, was Malvina Cavallazzi (?–1924) and she returned there 26 years later to establish the ballet school. However, ballet in opera in the USA, in spite of superb guest artists, never acquired the stature that it has in Europe. After Cavallazzi, Bonfanti did her stint, 1885–6; Pavlova with MORDKIN created a furore in 1910; the five visits to the USA of GENÉE incl. a transcontinental tour and culminated in her appearance at the NY Met in 1912 with VOLININ; Arturo Toscanini's daughter-in-law, Cia Fornaroli, stayed 1910–13; and the following year Rosina Galli was *première danseuse*, and then ballet mistress, 1919–35. Even though Galli's husband, Giulio Gatti-Casazza, was director of the OH for 27 years, nothing much ever came of all this, the Met always having preferred singers to dancers.

With Pavlova's many and prodigious tours to all corners of the 48 States and with the advent of DIAGHILEV's dancers, a new era began and Americans were inspired to form important cos of their own. A further incentive was the decision of many great dance personalities to settle permanently in the USA, among them such performers and teachers as Theodore Koslov, in 1911, BOLM, 1916, FOKINE and Mordkin in 1923, and eventually BALANCHINE, VILZAK, and others, many of them propelled to the New World by political changes in Russia.

America's immense debt to Europe was not to be repaid for a long time. Though Maywood decided to pursue her career in Europe, it was only in 1937 that Catherine Littlefield (1908–51) took the first all-American co. to London, Paris, and Brussels. The Littlefield B., with native dancers and a program built around native themes, was the precursor of the indigenous American cos of today, which, in turn, have influenced the European scene. PME

For later development of American ballet *see* AMERICAN BALLET THEATRE, BOSTON BALLET, DANCE THEATRE OF HARLEM, JOFFREY BALLET, NEW YORK CITY BALLET, PENNSYLVANIA BALLET, REGIONAL BALLET (USA), UNIVERSITIES, DANCE IN (USA).
See also AVANT-GARDE DANCE, DENISHAWN, MODERN DANCE.

Universities, Dance in (USA). Since the mid-1950s the establishment of dance departments in American universities has become increasingly important in dance in America. The movement began modestly but, as events proved, most significantly when the famous dance educator Margaret H'Doubler began in 1917 to teach dance as part of the physical-education program at the Univ. of Wisconsin. She initiated and developed the idea of college dance clubs, which she named Orchesis, in 1918. Her pioneer work began to be taken up in more and more universities. In the early years this form of modern dance was at a fairly elementary level. There was no idea of training students to a high degree of technical excellence, but with the passing years came programs concentrating on dance itself for students who wanted to develop in that single area. A big step forward came in 1934 when Bennington College for Women, VT, established its S. of the Dance, offering the first college degree in dance. An intensive training course was held each summer 1934–41 at which such great dance figures as GRAHAM, HUMPHREY, H. HOLM, WEIDMAN had the opportunity of working. Such seminal modern dance works as Graham's *El Penitente*, Humphrey's *With My Red Fires*, and Holm's TREND had their premieres at Bennington. The summer programs were discontinued after 1941 but Bennington still has one of the finest modern dance departments in the country, from which have come some of the leading dancers of this generation.

Its original concept has been carried on each summer since 1948 at Connecticut College for Women, New London, CT. The plans for bringing together student and teacher, artist, and audience, were initiated by Dr Martha Hill who had been director of the original Bennington program. Each year students from all over the USA and from abroad have the opportunity of working with the foremost dance teachers and performers of the day. Here too important dance works have been premiered at the public fests that are always a feature of these summer schools. Graham, Humphrey, KONER, LIMÓN, P. TAYLOR, CUNNINGHAM, NIKOLAIS, AILEY represent only a handful of the dance 'greats' who have taught and staged works at Connecticut.

Modern dance continues to function modestly as a part of all physical-education programs. But today many universities have departments offering advanced training in technique, composition, teaching, etc. leading to degrees up to MA, and most of today's modern dancers have graduated from such schools. It is impossible to mention them all, but Ohio State Univ., Columbus, OH, may stand as one of the best representatives. In NY the Juilliard S. of Music set up a dance department in 1952 under Martha Hill, still its director. Here Humphrey and Limón worked and taught until their deaths, developing the Juilliard Dance Ensemble from the student ranks. P. Taylor is a Juilliard graduate.

Because of its special nature and the general recognition that training must begin at an early age, ballet came much later to American universities. In 1951, David Preston at Texas Christian Univ., Fort Worth, and W. CHRISTENSEN at Univ. of Utah, Salt Lake City, established schools of ballet at their respective universities. These pioneering projects were soon taken up by the Jordan S. of Music, Butler Univ., Indianapolis, IN, and at Indiana Univ., Bloomington. The acceptance of ballet as part of a university curriculum came more slowly than the acceptance of modern dance, but again today it is growing rapidly and majors and minors in ballet are offered at many universities. In some cases the programs are basically geared to students not seriously considering ballet as a career since they have probably entered the university with too little early training. However, in addition to those already mentioned there are a number of universities where a high technical level is expected of the student at the outset, and a rigorous schedule of classes quickly separates the serious student from the dilettante.

W. Christensen himself, in the 1950s, developed a performing co. from the best of his students. Called Utah B., it attracted considerable local patronage. Because of its excellence, the co. received a Ford Foundation grant of $175,000 in 1963 enabling it to be established as a professional co. Now known as B. West and touring widely, it is the first professional co. to grow out of a university program.

The second is Cincinnati B., under the artistic direction of David McLain, who is also chairman of the Dance Division at Univ. of Cincinnati College-Cons. of Music. Realizing in the early 1970s that a nucleus of talented dancers would be lost to Cincinnati when they all graduated in the same year, he asked the co.'s board of directors (made up of interested local citizens) if it would be prepared to undertake the financial responsibility of transforming a university performing group into a professional co.

Special problems are involved where ballet is concerned. Ideally, students should begin a regime of regular daily training at around age 10 so that by 17 the dancers are prepared to perform at a professional level. This rarely happens, with the result that at college age only a handful of the thousands of dance students in the USA are sufficiently prepared. This is why intensive training in colleges, with its attendant studies in music, dance history, and related courses, has its validity, and why professional cos growing out of such programs are likely to play an even greater part in the future of Dance in America. PWM

Ursuliak, Alexander, b. Edmonton, 1937. Canadian dancer and teacher. Early studies with Fred Seychuk in Canada; also studied Kiev, where he m. SAMSOVA and brought her to Canada. Danced with NB of Canada 1961–3; taught in London 1963–5; taught at Vienna Staats O. 1965–73 (where he m. the dancer Christl Himmelbauer); from 1973 teacher, ballet master, and character dancer, Stuttgart B. GBLW

USSR *see* RUSSIA AND THE USSR

USSR, Ballet Education In. Professional dancers in Soviet ballet are trained in state choreographic schools, of which there were 19 in 1976. (It should be understood that in Russia the word 'choreography' has two meanings: the art of dancing as a whole, and the art of ballet-making. However, a choreographer is very often called 'ballet master' which means a 'maker of ballets', not a *répétiteur* or company teacher.) Pupils enter at the age of 10, having already completed the first three years of elementary education in an ordinary school, and spend eight years in the Choreographic S.

Thus, their remaining six years of general education are spread over the next eight years. Music, history of art, and ballet are added to a detailed program of academic subjects. In the ballet school, a 'teacher-choreographer' takes charge of classical ballet, character dancing, and mime; a 'teacher' teaches mathematics or any other academic subject.

The teaching of classical ballet and character dancing is based on a unified pedagogical system, practised by all Soviet teachers, whether in Moscow, Leningrad, Tashkent, or Ulan-Ude. This system has evolved through many slow stages of advancement in the Soviet professional performing arts.

It would be wrong to identify the Russian method as taught by LEGAT and other teachers of his generation as the present Soviet method of ballet education, though the second is, of course, a progressive development of the first. JOHANSSON, P. GERDT, TIKHOMIROV, and many other excellent teachers, whose names have not lived in history, contributed nevertheless to the present system. Thanks to the experience of its best teachers, the principles of the Russian School have been scientifically analysed and codified over many years.

This process started in the early 1920s when VAGANOVA began defining her method on a group of talented pupils. By teaching them, she taught herself, and grew to be the leading figure in the great constructive work conducted by the entire staff of the school that now bears her name. The publication of her *Basic Principles of Classical Ballet* (1934) marked a new period in Soviet pedagogy. She distilled the experience of generations and offered a clear and concise system for teaching the performance of the complete classical dance vocabulary. However, she never denied the close relation between teaching and contemporary practice. The soaring leaps, proud stance, and many other details taught in her class developed in direct response to the needs of the heroic ballets created in the 1930s. Were she alive today, she would undoubtedly introduce many changes into her teaching. From the seed of the great 'Vaganova method' has grown the present system of dance education, which has been developed and nurtured by special 'Method departments' (Russian: *metodichesky kabinet*) of the leading Soviet schools.

On the basis of the joint experience of the Leningrad and Moscow Schools, new syllabuses were created by 1961, exactly ten years after Vaganova's death. These covered the eight-year program of study and included all the material taught formerly in nine years. By 1967 this program had finally been perfected, officially adopted, and printed for the use of State Ballet Schools.

In 1969 a six-year syllabus was created at the Leningrad S. in order to accelerate study for those talented boys and girls who had missed entrance at the required age. Pupils may enter these classes (still known as 'experimental', although the experiment has long ago proved successful) at the age of 12, having completed five years of intermediary education. The entire eight-year course is then compressed into six years. The first three years of the eight-year syllabus take the first two years of the six-year program, and the sixth, seventh, and eighth years are all fitted into the last year. Many leading dancers in Soviet opera houses have been in these 'experimental' classes, but the public cannot see any difference in their performance, for indeed there is none. As in the eight-year course, the necessary prerequisites for the student are talent and a body particularly suited to the needs of the profession. Without these, even an eight-year course will not save the pupil from the last lines of the *corps de ballet*.

Aside from the syllabuses constructed to indicate not only what to teach, but how to teach it, there are many other ways of keeping ballet teachers all over the country in touch with the latest educational developments.

Methodological instructions are issued in written form by the Method department of the Moscow S., which is preeminent in this field. Once every four years, teachers' seminars are held in Moscow for representatives of all the 19 schools, and the entire process of education is discussed and evaluated.

Besides these large-scale seminars on the general principles of the Method, the Moscow S. organizes, at some time during the academic year, a seminar on one individual topic, using its own classes for demonstration. The Moscow S. has also begun filming the entire course of study, grade by grade, and in the future these films will be sent to other schools for practical application.

At each school, teachers are regularly assembled for methodological analyses after the students' yearly examination, during which meetings both faults and merits in teaching are openly judged by the teachers' colleagues.

It goes without saying that teachers in the Soviet Choreographic Schools are highly professional. But much has changed since the time when any retired dancer could claim the right to teach. Preference in the schools is now given to teachers with special pedogogical training in ballet. This is provided by the two-year teachers' course, at the Moscow and Leningrad Schools, which has existed for more than ten years. Teachers from other schools are sent here for refinement of their methodological skills. Many, of course, are former professional dancers with stage experience (usually of 20 years) and a complete ballet education behind them. Their experience, however, is not equal to a diploma of Higher Education, provided by two institutions: the pedagogical departments of the Ballet Masters' Faculty of GITIS (State T. Inst.) in Moscow, and of the Leningrad Conservatory. These institutions each offer a four-year course, during which the Choreographic Schools' study programs and the methods of teaching are themselves taught in great detail, along with many academic subjects. For a diploma, the pupil must finally prove he knows how to teach a given class.

Publication of many new textbooks on classical ballet in the last few years has also added much to the dissemination of precise knowledge. Especially valuable are Vera Kostrovitskaya's and Aleksey Pisarev's *School of Classical Dance* (1968) and Professor Nikolay Tarasov's *Classical Dance* (1971) for which he received (posthumously) the State Prize in Arts for 1975. This book concentrates on teaching male dancing and emphasizes expressive acting as the ultimate goal of all teaching.

There are also valuable books on character dancing, the latest by Nina Stukolkina and Aleksey Andreyev, former leading Kirov character dancers. Character dancing is also taught in the schools, according to a defined syllabus and method, complete with character barre.

Methodological work in arts education, in theatre as well as dance, is continuing at the present time, and can benefit foreign teachers along with those in the USSR. Information on methodology can be obtained by the foreign teacher through official channels between the USSR and the teacher's country. Preference is usually given to younger students. NR

Utah Ballet *see* UNIVERSITIES, DANCE IN (USA)

Uthoff, Ernst, b. Duisburg, 1904. German dancer and ballet master. Pupil of JOOSS and LEEDER, he danced from 1927 at the Folkwang S., Essen, and became assistant ballet master. When the B. Jooss was in Santiago, Uthoff and his wife Lola Botka left, founded the Chilean NB, and started a school there. In GREEN TABLE he created the Flag Bearer.

His son, Michael, b. Santiago, 1943, is a dancer. Studied Juilliard S., NY, and with GRAHAM; joined the LIMÓN Co. 1964, JOFFREY B. 1965; in 1970 founded, with his wife Lisa Bradley, the First Chamber Dance Co.; director, Hartford B., since 1973. GBLW

USSR, Ballet Education in. *Below*: Boys' class in the school of the Bolshoy Ballet; *right*: DUDINSKAYA teaching senior students in the famous Leningrad school in 'Theatre Street'

Vaganova, Agrippina, b. St Petersburg, 1879; d. Leningrad, 1951. Russian dancer and teacher. Graduated from St Petersburg TS 1897; pupil of Ivanov, Vazem, P. Gerdt and Legat. Also attended *classe de perfectionnement* of Preobrazhenska. In Maryinsky B. 1897–1916; first soloist from 1906, ballerina only from 1915, shortly before her retirement. Known as the 'queen of variations', very strong on *pointe* and with outstanding elevation, but lacked personal charm. Started teaching 1920, at private S. of Russian B. founded by Akim Volynsky, a great admirer of her art. She also had a small private school where she gave classes to selected pupils. Taught regularly at main (Petrograd) Leningrad Choreographic S. 1921–51, working out her own teaching method on first graduates Natalia Kamkova, Semyonova (the ideal embodiment of the Vaganova method), Elena Tangieva-Birzniece, and Dudinskaya. Later she taught classes only in the last two or three grades and in the last years only the graduation pupils. The last Kirov ballerina trained by her was Kolpakova.

Agrippina Vaganova as Odile in Swan Lake

Vaganova not only created a galaxy of ballerinas, teaching them to dance with their entire bodies, but also exerted great influence on the style of male dancing in Soviet ballet and on the work of Soviet choreographers who were able to achieve more with dancers with such complete command of their bodies. She never stopped working to perfect her system, collating all that was best in the experience of teachers of the Russian school and of Soviet choreographers of her period, who sought dancers capable of creating powerful heroic characters through effortless technique which enabled them to concentrate on living the parts. She also unswervingly defended classical ballet against the frequent attacks of the 1920s. She perfected the expressiveness of the dancers' bodies and taught them to dance, not merely to perform movements, and in this way proved the great expressive power of classical ballet. To sum up the Vaganova method briefly, everything was subordinated to the main goal of bringing the human body into a state of harmony, with complete coordination of all its members. The 'Vaganova back' was the first thing that struck the eye in Vaganova-trained dancers. Her method was based on perfect mastery of the torso, assisted by coordinated movements of the head and arms.

Choreography did not occupy as important a place in Vaganova's artistic life as teaching, but she created new versions of classical ballets (Esmeralda, Swan Lake). Her 'Diana and Actaeon' *pas de deux* from the *divertissement* in *Esmeralda* has entered the permanent recital repertoire of many Soviet ballerinas and *premiers danseurs*.

Vaganova taught the *classes de perfectionnement* for Kirov B. up to 1951 and headed the co. 1931–7. She headed the pedagogical department of the Leningrad Choreographic S. 1934–41, and of the Leningrad Cons., 1946–51, when she was awarded the rank of Professor. In 1957 the Leningrad Choreographic S. was named after her. People's Artist, RSFSR. State Prize, USSR, in Arts, 1946. NR
See V. Bogdanov-Berezovsky, *A. J. Vaganova* (Moscow and Leningrad 1950); A. J. Vaganova, volume of materials and reminiscences with list of her own articles (Leningrad 1958); *Osnovy Klassicheskogo Tanza* (*Fundamentals of the Classic Dance*) with introduction by I. I. Sollertinsky (Leningrad 1934); tr. into English by A. Chujoy as *Basic Principles of Classical Ballet, Russian Ballet Technique*, with introduction by Ninette de Valois, ed. Peggy van

Praagh (New York 1946; London 1948; with all the material from the fourth Russian edition, incl. Vaganova's sample lesson with musical accompaniment tr. John Barker, New York 1969); also published in Spanish, German, Czech, Hungarian, Polish and Georgian

Vainonen, Vasily, b. St Petersburg, 1901; d. Moscow, 1964. Soviet dancer and choreographer. Graduated Petrograd TS 1919. Character dancer, State T. of O. and B. 1919–38. Participated in experiments of the Young B. group headed by BALANCHINE. Started his own experiments in choreography in the early 1920s; his first choreographed ballet was GOLDEN AGE. Outstanding success with FLAME OF PARIS. His version of NUTCRACKER (1934) lives in the repertory of the Kirov and many other theatres. *Partisan Days* (1936) was another successful attempt at choreography grounded in character dance. Worked for many other theatres, staged own version of GAYANÉ, Bolshoy T., 1957. NR
See Klaudia Armashevskaya and Nikita Vainonen (Vainonen's wife and son), *Balletmaster Vainonen* (Moscow 1971)

Valberg [Lesogorov], Ivan, b. Moscow, 1766; d. St Petersburg, 1819. Russian dancer, teacher, and choreographer of distant Swedish origin. Son of a theatrical tailor. Studied St Petersburg TS under Giuseppe Canziani, graduated 1786 into the court ballet co. as *premier danseur*. Wide reading and studying French and Italian provoked an early interest in choreography. His first ballet, *Happy Repentance* (1795), was based on the usual mythological subject matter but seen from a sentimentalist, rather than classicist, viewpoint. Valberg called his works 'moral ballets' and emphasized in them logical and realistic development of both action and character. Examples are *New Werther* (1799) based on a contemporary incident, and *New Heroine* (or *Woman-Kozak*; 1810) about a Russian woman successfully disguised as a soldier at the battle of Friedland. His *Romeo and Juliet* (1809), 'a tragic ballet with choruses', was probably based on Daniel Steibelt's opera *Roméo et Juliette* (after William Shakespeare) altered by a happy ending. Valberg danced the title role.

With Canziani's departure in 1790, Valberg took charge of the St Petersburg BS, introducing progressive methods with excellent results. DIDELOT succeeded him 1801; a year later, Valberg was sent to Paris to study French ballet.

In the next nine years, he created 24 ballets, 15 danced scenes for opera, and many *divertissements*. He also translated Le Sieur Charles Compan's *Dictionnaire de Danse* (Paris 1787) and many French plays into Russian, and wrote a delightful diary of his experiences at the Paris O.

Valberg returned to Moscow 1807 to teach; in 1811, upon Didelot's departure, took sole charge of the St Petersburg co., concentrating on creating patriotic ballets such as *Love of Motherland* (1812), performed four days after the battle of Borodino. These displays of dance, song and even dialogue, though perhaps naïve, were rousing enough to make spectators enlist.

Didelot expressed his respect for Valberg in the preface to the libretto of *Amour et Psyché*, and Valberg's contributions to the formation of Russian national ballet cannot be overlooked. NR
See I. I. Valberg, ed. Yuri Slonimsky, *From the Balletmaster's Archive* (*Iz Arkhiva Baletmeistera*) (Moscow and Leningrad 1948)

Valse, La (1) choreographic poem, mus. RAVEL, originally commissioned by DIAGHILEV, whose failure to produce the ballet caused a permanent breach between the two men; ch. NIJINSKA; sc./c. BENOIS. Monte Carlo, RUBINSTEIN Co., 12 Jan 1929; dan. Rubinstein, VILZAK. New version ch. FOKINE, Paris O., 25 June 1931. (2) ballet, 2 parts, ch. BALANCHINE; mus. Ravel; c. (Barbara) Karinska; ltg ROSENTHAL. NYCC, NYCB, 20 Feb 1951; dan. LECLERCQ, MAGALLANES, MONCION. A dramatic interpretation of two Ravel scores, the *Valses Nobles et Sentimentales* and *La Valse*, creating a fantasy around Ravel's 'fantastic and fateful carousel'.

Both the scores used by Balanchine have been ch. separately by ASHTON. *Valses Nobles et Sentimentales*, first version as *Valentine's Eve*, lib. Ashton; sc./c. FEDOROVITCH; London, Duke of York's T., BR, 4 Feb 1935; dan. Pearl Argyle, Ashton, Maude LLOYD; second, plotless version as *Valses Nobles et Sentimentales* with revised sc./c. Fedorovitch; London, SW, SWTB, 1 Oct 1947; dan. HEATON, FIFIELD, Donald Britton. *La Valse*; sc. André Levasseur. Milan, Sc., 31 Jan 1958; dan. COLOMBO, PISTONI. Revived London, CG, RB, 10 Mar 1959; dan. Deirdre Dixon, Gary Burne. DV/FM

van Dijk (Dyk) *see* DIJK

Vangsaae, Mona, b. Copenhagen, 1920. Danish dancer, choreographer, and teacher. Studied RDBS and Paris. Soloist 1942; until her retirement in 1962 danced the main parts in national and international repertory. Created JULIET in ASHTON'S ROMEO AND JULIET (Copenhagen 1955), one of her greatest successes, combining dance and mime with enormous effect. After she left RDB, she staged NAPOLI, Act III, for LFB 1971, and CONSERVATORY 1973, and danced with NB of Canada 1968. For many years m. to F. SCHAUFUSS whom she divorced; mother of P. SCHAUFUSS, with whom she danced in Canada. SKJ

Vanina Vanini, ballet, 1 act, ch. KASATKINA and VASILYOV; mus. Nikolay Karetnikov. Moscow, Bolshoy T., Bolshoy B., 25 May 1962; dan. RIABYNKINA, TIKHONOV. Based on a story of the same title by Stendhal (Henri Beyle) about Italians fighting for their freedom in the first half of the 19th c., and created by dancers of the Bolshoy B. in their spare time; the first of a series of successful collaborations between Kasatkina and Vasilyov. JS/NR

Peggy van Praagh in DARK ELEGIES with B. Rambert, 1937

van Praagh, Dame Peggy, b. London, 1910. English dancer, teacher, and director. Began dancing at age of four. Studied with Aimée Phipps and later with CRASKE, L. SOKOLOVA, VOLKOVA; BODENWIESER and DE MILLE (modern dance); KARSAVINA (mime). First appeared with DOLIN in *Revolution* (London Coliseum, 1929). Camargo Society 1932. BR 1933–8. De Mille's 'Modern Group'. CGOB, under TUDOR's direction, 1936. Founder member and principal dancer, Tudor's London B., 1938. On the directing committee, London-Rambert B. 1940–1, initiating 'lunchtime ballet' programs. Leading dancer, Players' T., 1941. SWB, 1941, dancer and teacher. SWO (later T.) B., 1946, ballet mistress and producer; assistant director 1951–6. Van Praagh was largely responsible for the flowering of talent within this co., which incl. BERIOSOVA, NERINA, BLAIR, CRANKO, MACMILLAN. Freelance producer from 1956, staging works by Tudor, DE VALOIS, ASHTON, for many cos. Ballet producer, BBC TV, 1949–58. Director, Edinburgh Fest. B. 1958. Taught at Jacob's Pillow, MA, and conducted seminars for the CECCHETTI Society in the USA.

In December 1959 van Praagh was invited to direct the final season of the BOROVANSKY B., Australia. She did this with great success, staging the 3-act COPPÉLIA and RENDEZVOUS. After the season ended, the Australian B. Foundation asked her to become the first artistic director of a new co. to be called the Australian B. Before this co. was launched (Nov 1962) she was resident teacher with the DE CUEVAS B.

She was artistic director of Australian B. 1962–74, when ill-health forced her resignation, joined in 1965 by HELPMANN. As founding director, she aimed at creating a balanced repertoire, encouraging Australian creative artists, establishing a school, and providing educational programs on ballet. Her influence on dancers in their formative years again resulted in some outstanding young talent. Van Praagh has been an examiner and member of the London Committee of the Cecchetti Society since 1935, has given worldwide lecture demonstrations and seminars. She was awarded a D.Litt. from the Univ. of New England, Armidale (NSW), 1974. Roles as a dancer incl. notable creations in Tudor ballets such as The Woman in his Past in JARDIN AUX LILAS; the Moscow Ballerina in GALA PERFORMANCE; and a delightful virtuoso perf. as SWANILDA. She has published *How I Became a Ballet Dancer* (London and New York 1954); *The Choreographic Art* (with BRINSON) (London and New York 1963); *Ballet in Australia* (Melbourne 1965). OBE 1966; DBE, 1970. KSW

Vargas, Manuela *see* SPAIN

Varna, International Competition. Initiated 1964, then held 1965, 1966, thereafter biennially. The competition was chaired by ULANOVA to 1972 then GRIGOROVICH. Jury members have incl. ALONSO (every competition to 1976), HASKELL, DOLIN, BRUHN, F. FLINDT, FRANCA, LIFAR, CRANKO, CULLBERG and many from E. Europe. Dancers may compete up to age 29; in 1968 a junior section to age 19 was introduced. Notable prizewinners have been VASILIEV, SIZOVA, MAKAROVA, MAXIMOVA, M. LAVROVSKY, BARYSHNIKOV, N. BESSMERTNOVA, and Galina Ragosina (PANOV) from the USSR; FUKAGAWA and Yoko Morishita from Japan; many Cubans; and the US citizens EVDOKIMOVA and BUJONES (the last though of junior age, entered as a senior in 1974 and won a gold medal).

The competition is in three stages, only the first consisting of 'set pieces'; accompaniment may be taped or played live by a pianist and non-competing partners are permitted; entrants may also perform solos. Competitors receive a minimum per round of two 15-minute stage rehearsals which for lighting calls necessitates working at any time to 5 a.m. An interpreter is provided for all competitors. Dancers from Communist countries are at an obvious advantage as they are sponsored and arrive accompanied by teachers, coaches, pianists and masseurs, whereas the independent entrants from W. Europe and America must not only do all preparatory work unsponsored but also pay their fares to Bulgaria. Once in Varna, all expenses are paid. Prizes are generous but only part of the sums won may be exported.

To dancers, Varna offers a unique opportunity to mix quite freely with performers from the entire world, while spectators have the equally unique chance to watch all extant styles of ballet performed in succession without the 'padding' of full-scale productions. The greatest endurance test for the audience is how many times they can sit through the favourite showpiece, the DON QUIXOTE *pas de deux*. Similar international competitions are now held in Moscow, Havana, and Tokyo. JS

Vasiliev, Vladimir, b. Moscow, 1940. Soviet dancer. Graduated from Moscow Choreographic S. 1958, soon partnering ULANOVA in one of her last appearances, in CHOPINIANA. Created roles of Danila (STONE FLOWER) and Ivanushka (HUMPBACKED HORSE; 1960 version) in first two seasons at Bolshoy, where choreographers exploited his physical prowess and Russian type to advantage. Gradually developed from strength to strength, becoming Bolshoy *premier danseur* and dancer of international reputation. Prodigious virtuosity in DON QUIXOTE, BLUEBIRD, GISELLE, etc., coupled with outstanding projection and dramatic impact. Created title role in GRIGOROVICH's SPARTACUS, expressing idea of self-sacrificing heroism through incredible technique, totally submerged in complete identification with the concept. He also created IVAN THE TERRIBLE, alternating with VLADIMIROV. Danced *Icare* in his first ballet, of the same title, choreographed for Bolshoy B., mus. Sergey Slonimsky; Kremlin Palace of Congresses, 1971. People's Artist, USSR. Prix Nijinsky, 1964. Grand Prix, Varna Summer Competition, 1964 (the only recipient of this award to 1976). Lenin Prize 1970. M. former classmate MAXIMOVA. NR
See A. Iloupina, 'Vasiliev', *Les Saisons de la Danse* (Paris, June 1970) with list of roles; N. Avaliani and L. Zhdanov, tr. N. Ward, *Bolshoi's Young Dancers* (Moscow and London 1975)

Vasilyov, Vladimir, b. Moscow, 1931. Soviet dancer and choreographer. A character dancer with the Bolshoy B. 1949–71. He m. KASATKINA, with whom he has choreographed many ballets, incl. VANINA VANINI, GEOLOGISTS, and versions of SACRE DU PRINTEMPS and ROMEO AND JULIET. NR
See Natalia Kasatkina and Vladimir Vasilyov, 'How We Invent A Ballet' in Ella Bocharnikova, *The Magic Land of Ballet* (Moscow 1974)

Vazem, Ekaterina, b. St Petersburg, 1848; d. Leningrad, 1937. Russian dancer and teacher. St Petersburg, Bolshoy T. 1867–84, rapidly becoming ballerina. Created many roles, in particular Nikia (BAYADÈRE), choreographed by M. PETIPA for her pure style and virtuosity. Other roles incl. PAQUITA, Medora (CORSAIRE), GISELLE, and Fenella in AUBER's opera *La Muette de Portici*, though mime was not her special talent. Taught at TS 1886–96; pupils incl. A. PAVLOVA and VAGANOVA. After 1917 taught privately until an advanced age. Wrote valuable memoirs, *Notes by a Ballerina of the St Petersburg Bolshoy Theatre, 1867–1884* (Leningrad 1937). NR

Vecheslova, Tatiana, b. St Petersburg, 1910. Soviet dancer. Graduated from Leningrad Choreographic S. 1928, classes of Marie Romanova and VAGANOVA. ULANOVA's classmate. Strong dramatic dancer. Roles she created incl. Manizhe (HEART OF THE HILLS), Paskuala (LAURENCIA), Nuné (GAYANÉ), Florine (LOST ILLUSIONS), one of the Ugly Sisters (CINDERELLA; SERGEYEV's version), and ESMERALDA (Vaganova version). Toured USA with CHABUKIANI 1934. Retired from stage 1953; worked as teacher and ballet mistress, Kirov T. and abroad. Writes on ballet. Honoured Artist, RSFSR. Honoured Art Worker, RSFSR. NR
See T. Vecheslova, *I am a Ballerina* (Leningrad 1964); G. Kremshveskaya, *Honoured Artist of the RSFSR: Tatiana Mikhailovna Vecheslova* (Leningrad 1951)

Ventana, La, *divertissement,* 1 act, ch. August BOURNONVILLE; mus. Spanish melodies and Hans Christian Lumbye. Copenhagen, 19 June 1854; dan. Casino, PRICE family; RDB, 6 Oct 1856. Originally only a mirror dance, where a young Señorita dances before her mirror to the tunes of a serenade outside her window (using the old *commedia dell'arte* trick of one dancer in front of and another behind the frame of the mirror); developed to a dance showing the young girl meeting her lover and their friends, with a special *pas de trois.* Still in the Danish repertory; the work has also been performed by other cos, staged BRENAA. SKJ

Verchinina, Nina, b. Moscow. Russian-American dancer, teacher, and choreographer. Studied in France with PREOBRAZHENSKA and NIJINSKA. Developed her own style of dancing and teaching after having studied the LABAN method. Danced with DE BASIL's B. Russe, creating roles in MASSINE's PRÉSAGES, CHOREARTIUM, and SYMPHONIE FANTASTIQUE, in which he used her Laban style. Guest choreographer 1937–45 in several ballet cos and in 1946 rejoined the B. Russe, leaving it to be ballet mistress and choreographer for the T. Municipal, Rio de Janeiro. Toured S. America dancing and choreographing and returned to Rio de Janeiro to form her own group and school 1957. Her choreographic work incl. *Narcisse* (mus. RAVEL), *Zuimaaluti* (1960; mus. Claudio Santoro), and *Metathasis* (1967). MLN

Auguste Vestris, 1781

Verdy, Violette [Nelly Guillerm], b. Pont-l'Abbé-Lambour, 1933. French dancer. Studied with ROUSANNE and V. GSOVSKY, Paris. Debut with B. des CE, Paris, 1945. Joined B. de Paris 1953, created leading role in LOUP. LFB 1954; ABT 1957; NYCB 1958. Guest artist with many cos incl. London RB (in SLEEPING BEAUTY), Paris OB, Milan Sc. A ballerina of great piquancy, noted for the subtlety of her musical phrasing, used to advantage by BALANCHINE in *La Source*, etc, and in DANCES AT A GATHERING. Appointed director, Paris OB, Jan 1977. DV

Veredon, Gray, b. Tauranga, New Zealand, 1943. New Zealand dancer and choreographer. Studied London RBS and with IDZIKOWSKI and HIGHTOWER. In 1960 he danced in New Zealand and with the London CGOB 1963. Joined Stuttgart B. 1964 and from 1968 has been in Cologne where he founded (with Hermuth Baumann and Jochen Ulbrich) the Cologne Tanz-Forum Co., becoming sole director. M. dancer Sveinbjorg Alexanders. Choreographed many ballets. GBLW

Vernon [Herzfeld], Konstanze, b. Berlin, 1939. German dancer. Pupil of T. GSOVSKY, KISS, and PERETTI. Städtische OB, W. Berlin, 1954; soloist 1956. Munich B. 1962, where she is principal dancer. Danced with T. Gsovsky's Berliner B. 1959. Co-director, ballet dept, Munich Music Acad. from 1975. GBLW

Vestris, Auguste, b. Paris, 1760; d. Paris, 1842. Italian dancer and teacher whose career was spent in Paris. The son of G. VESTRIS and ALLARD. Debut Paris O. 1772 and reigned there for 36 years. He is a key figure in the development of classical ballet technique. His father had been a pupil of Louis Dupré (1697–1774) and he himself taught August BOURNONVILLE, DIDELOT, and PERROT who continued his work in Copenhagen and Russia. His father had been called '*Le Dieu de la Danse*' and he inherited the title which had been given, by public acclaim, to very few men in the history of ballet. At the age of 75 he partnered M. TAGLIONI at the Paris O. His skill in footwork, strong *pirouettes*, and soaring elevation are reflected in the Bournonville-style trained RDB male dancers. MC
See Serge Lifar, *Auguste Vestris, le Dieu de la Danse* (Paris 1950); Gaston Capon, *Les Vestris* (Paris 1908); Marian Hannah Winter, *The Pre-Romantic Ballet* (London 1974; New York and Toronto 1975)

Vestris, Gaetano (Apolline Baldassare), b. Florence, 1729; d. Paris, 1808. Italian dancer. From a theatrical family; the most celebrated of his generation at the Paris O. Studied there with Louis Dupré, entered the co. 1749, and became soloist, but was dismissed in 1754 after a quarrel with the ballet master, Jean-Barthélémy Lany. Returned 1756 when his reputation earned him the nick-name '*le Diou* [*Dieu*] *de la Danse*', previously applied to Dupré and later to Gaetano's son, A. VESTRIS. In 1761 appointed assistant to Lany; ballet master 1770–5, Paris O. Worked in Stuttgart in mid-1760s on leave from Paris O. where he met NOVERRE, danced in his ballet *Medée et Jason* and arranged for him to work at the Paris O. His noble style and technique, especially in jumps and the newly developed *pirouette*, made him not only the foremost dancer in Paris but also throughout Europe. He had a succession of liaisons with female dancers; ALLARD bore his son Auguste and the German HEINEL (credited with perfecting the *pirouette*) another son, Apollon. After being rivals for years, Heinel and Vestris retired in 1782 and married in 1792. Proud, quarrelsome, and vain, Gaetano said his century had produced only three great men: Frederick the Great of Prussia, Voltaire, and himself. In 1772 in the ballet *Castor et Pollux*, he discarded all use of the mask and astonished the audience with the clarity of his mime. MC

Vic-Wells Ballet *see* ROYAL BALLET

Vienna. The munificence of the Austrian court brought to Vienna the greatest ballet masters of the 18th c. – HILVERDING, ANGIOLINI, NOVERRE, VIGANÒ – and in the 19th c. the most celebrated dancers of the Romantic era appeared there, the Viennese-born ELSSLER becoming the greatest of all Austrian dancers although much of her career was elsewhere. As in Italy, however, ballet soon became subservient to opera. When the Staats O. was built (destroyed 1945, rebuilt 1955) a major ballet production was staged in 1869 shortly after its opening, a revival of SARDANAPAL. Karl Telle, the German dancer and ballet master (1826–95), was in charge of the ballet co. until 1890, staging productions of COPPÉLIA 1876 and SYLVIA 1877. He was succeeded in 1891 by Josef Hassreiter whose PUPPENFEE had achieved great success in 1888. Hassreiter reigned until 1920, staging nearly 50 ballets and employing

Austrian dancers. His favoured composer was Josef Bayer. KRÖLLER was ballet master 1922–8, staging ballets to music by Richard Strauss who was then director of the Staats O. Margarethe Wallman, an Austrian dancer who had studied with WIGMAN and was a principal choreographer for Salzburg Fests in the 1930s, was director of the Staats OB and its school 1934–9.

During World War II FRÄNZL helped conserve the old repertory. (The co. danced in the Volks O. and T. an der Wien after the bombing of its own theatre.) HANKA was in charge of the co. from 1942, choreographing many ballets characterized by their strong dramatic impact but using a style of dance that owed much to the European modern dance techniques. She was instrumental, however, after the reopening of the Staats O. in 1955, in introducing classic ballets to the repertory. HAMILTON's staging of GISELLE shared the bill with Hanka's *Der Mohr von Venedig* (mus. Boris Blacher) on the first evening of ballet in the new house, 29 Nov 1955. Teaching standards were improved (the Staats OBS, housed in the theatre, has some of the finest studio facilities in the world) but after Hanka's death in 1958 a period of unrest and constant change began. Succeeding ballet masters were PARLIĆ (1958–61), MILLOSS (1961–6 and again 1971–4), and ORLIKOVSKY (1966–71). NUREYEV's 1964 staging of SWAN LAKE won a new and fervent audience for classical ballet, as did the production of NUTCRACKER by GRIGOROVICH in 1973, and the visits of star dancers from the USSR and the West.

In 1975–6 the ballet master Richard Novotny took charge of the co. and from 1 Sept 1976 the former music and dance critic Gerhard Brunner became director. The head ballet mistress then was Maria Fay, with Oprea Petrescu as ballet master and former dancers Gerlinde Dill and Richard Novotny as *répétiteurs*. The principal dancers were Gisela Cech, KIRNBAUER, Lilly Scheuermann, Michael Birkmeyer, K. MUSIL, Ludwig Musil, Paul Vondrak, and Franz Wilhelm. The school is also directed by Brunner with former ballerina Edeltraud Brexner as assistant director. The repertory incl. PALAIS DE CRISTAL (revived 1972) and LIEBESLIEDER WALZER (revived 1977), CRANKO's ROMEO AND JULIET (revived 1975) and works by MASSINE, NEUMEIER, and van MANEN. The more classical and varied repertory, presenting a greater challenge to the dancers, together with improved teaching initiated by Hamilton and the American Georgia Hiden, may well make the Vienna Staats OB more prominent internationally.

There are also ballet cos attached to the T. an der Wien and the Volks O. and the Raimund-T.; these appear mostly in operettas. MC
See J. Gregor, *Kulturgeschichte des Ballets* (Vienna 1944)

Viganò, Salvatore, b. Naples, 1769; d. Milan, 1821. Italian dancer and choreographer. While visiting Madrid he m. the Austrian dancer Maria Medina and met DAUBERVAL who influenced his thinking about the new realism and drama to be found in choreography. He worked mostly in Vienna and Italy and Milan Sc. knew its greatest ballet triumphs during his regime. It was for Viganò that the young Ludwig van Beethoven wrote his only ballet, GESCHÖPFE DES PROMETHEUS. MC
See Marian Hannah Winter, *The Pre-Romantic Ballet* (London 1974; New York and Toronto 1975)

Vikulov, Sergey, b. Leningrad, 1937. Soviet dancer. Graduated from VAGANOVA S.; from 1956 one of the leading soloists, Kirov B. A lyrical, classical dancer, performing with artistic and technical brilliance as Solor (BAYADÈRE), DÉSIRÉ, BLUEBIRD, SIEGFRIED, ALBRECHT. Created Roderigo in CHABUKIANI's OTHELLO. Studied Choreographers' Faculty of Leningrad Cons. Choreographed *Koriolanus* (*Coriolanus*, 1966) for Chamber B. and concert numbers. He m. dancer Tatiana Udalenkova. People's Artist, RSFSR and USSR; Gold Medal, Varna, 1964. NR
See article by Y. Golovashenko in *Leningrad Ballet Today*, No. 2 (Leningrad 1968)

Villella, Edward, b. Bayside, NY, 1936. American dancer. Studied SAB. Joined NYCB 1957, and

Edward Villella in ROBBINS's *Watermill* with NYCB

immediately assumed leading roles, e.g. in AFTERNOON OF A FAUN. A dancer of great virility and athletic prowess, he has become a star through his TV appearances. BALANCHINE created HARLEQUINADE, 'Rubies' in JEWELS, and PULCINELLA for him; he was in the original cast of DANCES AT A GATHERING, and the protagonist of ROBBINS's controversial *Watermill*. DV

Vilzak, Anatole, b. St Petersburg, 1896. Russian dancer. He m. SCHOLLAR. Graduated from Imperial S. into Maryinsky, 1915, partnered KSHESSINSKA, TREFILOVA, KARSAVINA, SPESSIVTSEVA. Left Russia 1921 and joined DIAGHILEV, danced in *The Sleeping Princess* (*see* SLEEPING BEAUTY) at Alhambra T., London. RUBINSTEIN's Co. 1928–9, *premier danseur* and ballet master at State O., Riga, Latvia, in early 1930s, joined R. BLUM's B. de Monte Carlo 1936, creating title role in FOKINE's *Don Juan*. *Premier danseur*, NY Met 1936–7, when BALANCHINE was choreographer. Taught at B. Russe S. in NY, Washington 1963–5, since 1965 at San Francisco BS. DV

Vinogradov, Oleg, b. Leningrad, 1937. Soviet dancer and choreographer. Graduated from Vaganova Choreographic S. 1958; until 1963 in Novosibirsk B., dancing character roles. From 1963 assistant ballet master, Novosibirsk B., and began choreographing and designing, with versions of CINDERELLA (1964), ROMEO AND JULIET (1965) and *Asel* (Bolshoy T., 1967). Choreographer, Kirov T. 1967–72 (from 1971 member of artistic collegium). Choreographed GORYANKA; also own version of *Enchanted Prince* (1972; *see* PRINCE OF THE PAGODAS). Has choreographed his own *Lise and Colin or La Fille Mal Gardée* to original score by Louis Joseph Hérold (discovered in Leningrad archives), Maly OB, 1971. Has headed Maly OB since 1973, choreographing his own version of COPPÉLIA and an original ballet, YAROSLAVNA. Uses modern idiom boldly and has individual and original choreographic conceptions. Designs his own ballets, or provides ideas for designers. Under his guidance Maly OB regained a reputation as an experimental, advanced co. Graduated GITIS and teaches at Ballet Masters' Faculty, Leningrad Cons. Honoured Artist, Daghestan ASSR. NR

Violin Concerto, ballet, ch. BALANCHINE; mus. STRAVINSKY; ltg Ronald Bates. NYST, NYCB, 18 June 1972; dan. Karin von Aroldingen, MAZZO, MARTINS, BONNEFOUS. A plotless ballet in four movements to Stravinsky's Violin Concerto. One of the most inventive and masterly works of NYCB's 1972 Stravinsky Fest. Balanchine first used this music for *Balustrade*, sc./c. TCHELITCHEV; New York, 51st Street T., Original B. Russe, 22 Jan 1941. The title was taken from the white balustrade of the decor. Now called *Stravinsky Violin Concerto*. FM/DV

Virsaladze, Simon, b. Tbilisi [Tiflis], 1909. Georgian painter and designer. Studied Tbilisi Acad. of Arts, Moscow Arts Inst. and Leningrad Acad. of Arts under Professor Mikhail Bobyshov. Started theatre designing 1927 in Tbilisi, chief designer Tbilisi O. and BT 1932–6; Kirov T. from 1937, chief designer there 1940 and 1945–62. Leading Soviet ballet designer, with great feeling for colour scheme and costumes suitable for dancing. Ballets he designed incl. CHABUKIANI's HEART OF THE HILLS, LAURENCIA, OTHELLO, etc. and (from 1957) GRIGOROVICH's STONE FLOWER, LEGEND OF LOVE, SPARTACUS, IVAN THE TERRIBLE, etc. People's Painter, RSFSR and Georgian SSR. Lenin Prize 1970 for *Spartacus*. Corresponding Member of the Acad. of Arts, USSR. NR
See V. Vanslov, *Simon Virsaladze* (Moscow 1969), containing full list of ballets designed by Virsaladze

Vision of Salome, modern dance work, ch. ALLAN; mus./sc. Marcel Remy. Munich, Apr 1907; dan. Allan. A solo meditation on the seductive dancer who caused the beheading of St John the Baptist. DM

Vladimiroff, Pierre [Pyotr], b. St Petersburg, 1893; d. New York, 1970. Russian dancer. He m. DUBROVSKA. Graduated from Imperial S. into Maryinsky 1911. On leave, danced with DIAGHILEV's B. Russes 1912 and 1914, taking over several of NIJINSKY's roles. Left Russia 1918, rejoined Diaghilev 1921–2 and 1925–8, dancing DÉSIRÉ etc. Partnered A. PAVLOVA from 1928 until her death in 1931. Invited by BALANCHINE to join faculty of SAB 1934, taught there until he retired in 1966. DV

Vladimirov, Yuri, b. near Moscow, 1942. Soviet dancer. Athletic virtuoso, at his best in contemporary roles, e.g. Leader (GEOLOGISTS, created 1964), Shepherd (*Sacre du Printemps*, version by KASATKINA and VASILYOV, created 1965), VASILIEV's *Icare* (created 1971) and title role of SPARTACUS. His creation of the title role in IVAN THE TERRIBLE (1975) revealed him as an outstanding dance actor. Also dances various classical parts. He m. classmate SOROKINA. People's Artist, RSFSR. Gold Medal, Varna, 1966, and First International B. Competition, 1969. NR
See N. Avaliani and L. Zhdanov, tr. N. Ward, *Bolshoi's Young Dancers* (Moscow and London 1975)

Vlasova, Eleonora, b. Moscow, 1931. Soviet dancer. Graduated from Moscow Choreographic S., class of Maria Leontyeva; from 1949 accepted as soloist Stanislavsky and Nemirovich-Danchenko B. Technically strong; a dramatically expressive ballerina. Roles incl. ODETTE-ODILE and ESMERALDA (BURMEISTER versions). People's Artist, RSFSR. NR

Vlassi [Bassi], Christiane, b. Paris, 1938. French dancer. Paris OS 1948, *corps de ballet* 1952, *étoile* 1963. Leading roles in modern works as well as classics, e.g. COPPÉLIA, DAMNATION DE FAUST,

Apollon-Musagète (*see* APOLLO). She m. LABIS. She possesses femininity, elegance, a flowing technique, and a sense of humour too rarely exploited. M-FC

Volinin, Aleksandr, b. Moscow, 1882; d. Paris, 1955. Russian dancer and teacher. Graduated from Moscow TS, class of TIKHOMIROV, also studied with GORSKY, joining (1901–10) in the constellation of *premiers danseurs* typical of the Gorsky period, though he was more lyrical and soft than his rival MORDKIN. By 1909–10 had danced all leading classical roles, also the Prince in Gorsky's version of *Magic Mirror*. Danced with DIAGHILEV B. summer 1910 with GELTSER; also toured with GENÉE as her partner, and 1914–25 permanent partner of A. PAVLOVA. He did not return to Russia but taught in Paris in his own school until his death. Greatly influenced DAYDÉ, CHAUVIRÉ, BABILÉE, LICHINE, RIABOUCHINSKA, JEANMAIRE, etc. Praised by GRIGORIEV for classical technique and extraordinary lightness, which he owed to Tikhomirov. NR
See S. Grigoriev, *The Diaghilev Ballet, 1909–1929* (London 1953; Harmondsworth 1960); V. D. Tikhomirov, *Artist, Ballet master, Teacher* (Moscow 1971)

Volkova, Vera, b. St Petersburg, 1904(?); d. Copenhagen, 1975. Russian dancer and teacher. Studied at Akim Volynsky's S. in St Petersburg with Maria Romanovna (mother of ULANOVA) where she learned the VAGANOVA method which she later brought to the West. Left Russia in the early 1920s for China, where she danced with George Goncharov, a former colleague from St Petersburg who later joined her in London. There she met and m. the English painter Hugh Williams. On arrival in England she started teaching privately in 1943 and when she opened her studio at 48 West St in London's West End it became a mecca for dancers. Volkova had a particularly eloquent vocabulary and a gift for awakening artistry in her pupils. Her teaching gave FONTEYN new confidence and expressiveness in the 1940s and helped ensure her NY triumph. After a frustrating period at Milan Sc. (1950), Volkova went in 1951, at the invitation of H. LANDER, to the RDB as ballet mistress, later artistic adviser. The rest of her life was spent in Copenhagen although she was greatly in demand all over the world for guest teaching during the summer vacations. She gave the Danish dancers, through her Russian-style teaching, greater breadth of movement and enabled them to dance the international repertory as well as their August BOURNONVILLE inheritance. MC

Voluntaries, ballet, 1 act, ch. TETLEY; mus. POULENC (Concerto for Organ, Strings and Percussion), sc./c. TER-ARUTUNIAN. Stuttgart, Stuttgart B., 22 Dec 1973; dan. HAYDÉE, CRAGUN, KEIL, KLOS. Revived CG, RB, 18 Nov 1976. Created in memory of CRANKO, the ballet, according to Tetley, is conceived as a linked series of voluntaries, by musical definition free-ranging organ or trumpet improvisations often played before, during, or after religious service. MC

Volunteer Guards of Amager, The *see* KING'S VOLUNTEERS OF AMAGER

von Rothbart, the wicked magician in SWAN LAKE

Vsevolozhsky, Ivan Aleksandrovich, b. St Petersburg, 1835; d. St Petersburg, 1909. Russian diplomat, theatre director, and designer. Director of the Russian Imperial Ts 1881–99 during the years of the ballet co.'s greatest triumphs. He wrote the lib. for SLEEPING BEAUTY and had a great influence on M. PETIPA, guiding him towards musicians such as TCHAIKOVSKY and GLAZUNOV (RAYMONDA), and suggesting the new and successful 1895 staging of SWAN LAKE. He engaged the Italians ZUCCHI, BRIANZA, and CECCHETTI, who did much to revive dancing in Russia, and he also designed some 25 ballets. He directed the Imperial Ts as a nobleman, considering it his duty to provide entertainment for the court (which ballet was). He originated the so-called production council, bringing librettist, choreographer, composer, and designer together for discussions in order to achieve a unity of style. MC

Vyroubova, Nina, b. Gurzuf, 1921. Russian-French dancer and teacher. Studied with her mother, EGOROVA, PREOBRAZHENSKA, KNIASEFF, V. GSOVSKY. Debut as soloist in COPPÉLIA (Caen 1937). Appeared in galas and danced with B. des CE 1945–7. Created roles in PETIT's FORAINS, and V. Gsovsky's SYLPHIDE. Engaged as *étoile*, Paris O.; danced in revival of DRAMMA PER MUSICA, created leading roles in LIFAR's *Blanche-Neige* (the Queen), INDES GALANTES, *Obéron*, *Fourberies* (1952), in which she was very funny, *Les Noces Fantastiques* (1955). She brought her great acting gifts and true romanticism to GISELLE and her classic style to M. PETIPA's *Divertissement* in which she danced AURORA. In SUITE EN BLANC she danced an unforgettable 'cigarette variation'. Left the O. 1956 to become *étoile*, DE CUEVAS B., 1956–60, dancing classical roles, and the leading role in *La Chanson de l'Éternelle Tristesse* (1957; ch. Ana Ricarda). It was with Vyroubova in the de Cuevas SLEEPING BEAUTY that NUREYEV made his Western debut after leaving the Kirov B. Guest artist in many countries. She created leading role in *Abraxas* (VAN DIJK) at Hamburg 1965. Appeared in two films directed by Dominique Delouche, *Le Spectre de la Danse* (1960) and *L'Adage* (1965). She now teaches, at the O., in her own school, and at important seminars. Remarkable for her airy lightness, lyricism and romanticism, Vyroubova also possesses a gift for comedy which gave her a range rare among ballerinas. This twofold aspect of her personality merits her a place among the greatest artists of her time. She m. Kniaseff; their son Yura Kniaseff (b. 1951) is a soloist with the NB of Canada. M-FC

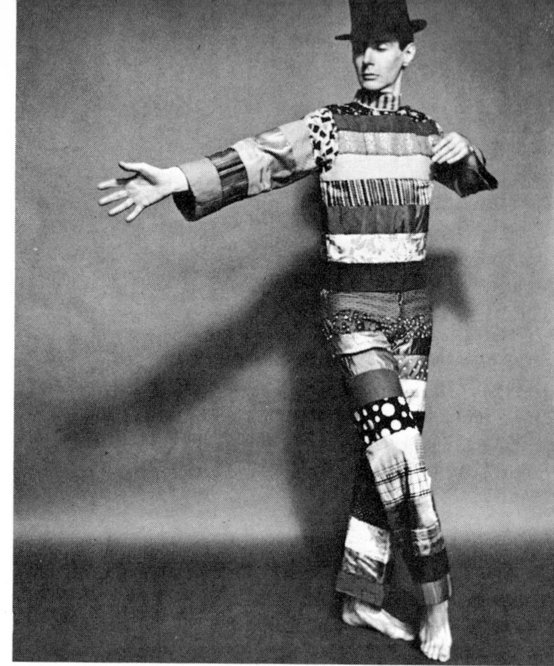

Left: David Wall of the RB dancing in SYMPHONIC VARIATIONS
Above: James Waring

W

Wagoner, (Robert) Dan, b. Springfield, WV, 1932. American dancer and choreographer. Studied in Washington DC with Ethel Butler (modern dance) and Lisa Gardiner and Mary Day (ballet), while serving in US Army. Awarded scholarship at GRAHAM S., danced in her co. 1958–62; with CUNNINGHAM 1959–60; P. TAYLOR 1960–8. Formed his own co., 1969. Works incl. *Duet* (1968; mus. Henry Purcell); *Le Jardin au Monsieur McGregor*, *Brambles* (both 1969); *Westwork* (1970); *Iron Mountain* (1971); *Numbers*, *Changing Your Mind* (both 1972); *Broken Hearted Rag Dance*, *Meets and Bounds*, *A Sad Pavane for These Distracted Times* (all 1973); *Taxi Dances* (1974); *Summer Rambo* (1975); *A Dance for Grace and Elwood* (1976). His choreography is characterized by genial good humour and inventiveness. Several dances have been collaborations with the poet George Montgomery, e.g. a video piece for WGBH-TV, Boston, *George's House* (1975). DV

Walker, David Hatch, b. Edmonton, Alberta 1949. Canadian dancer. Studied at NBS, Toronto, and GRAHAM S., NY. Danced with BR 1968–9, then Graham Dance Co. His roles in the Graham repertory incl. the Revivalist in APPALACHIAN SPRING, the Penitent in *El Penitente*, St Michael in *Seraphic Dialogue*, Orestes in CLYTEMNESTRA, Tiresias in NIGHT JOURNEY, the Minotaur in *Errand into the Maze*. Has choreographed works of his own for independent concerts. He m. ASAKAWA. DV

Wall, David, b. Chiswick, London, 1946. English dancer. Studied RBS (starting with the Saturday morning Junior Associate classes). Joined touring RB 1963; soloist 1964; principal 1966. Encouraged by FIELD, then director of the touring RB, he made rapid progress in both classical and *demi-caractère* roles and was the hero of the touring RB during the Field regime. He is not only a fine dancer but an excellent actor with an engaging personality and equal gifts for romantic and comedy roles. Unrivalled now in DEUX PIGEONS, he is a 'natural' for COLAS, and an ardent ROMEO. His most brilliant creation is Lescaux in MANON. He m. THOROGOOD. MC

Walter, Erich, b. Fürth, 1927. German dancer, choreographer, and director. Pupil of Olympiada Alperova. Danced at Nuremberg 1946–50, Göttingen 1950, Wiesbaden 1951, and was appointed ballet director, Wuppertal 1953. There he established a close relationship with WENDEL; together they made a great reputation for their productions, danced in a neoclassic style, choreography by Walter and with costumes and decor by Wendel. In 1964 appointed director of the ballet, Deutsche O. am Rhein, Düsseldorf, which he has made one of the most important in Germany. GBLW

Waring, James, b. Alameda, CA, 1922; d. New York, 1975. American dancer, choreographer, director, and teacher. Studied in San Francisco and at SAB. First choreography was *Luther Burbank in Santa Rosa*, at HALPRIN-Lathrop Studio T., San Francisco, 1946. Co-founder of Dance Associates, a choreographers' cooperative, NY, 1951. Presented annual concerts in NY with his own co. 1954–69. An influential figure in AVANT-GARDE DANCE both through his works (many dancers who became prominent choreogra-

phers had earlier performing experience in his co.), and his teaching of both technique and composition. Choreographed over 135 works, some of them with designs by contemporary painters, others with costumes designed by himself. He was also an accomplished collagist, and much of his choreography had the character of this medium, with disparate elements brought together in one piece. His ballets were also notable for their musicality, wit, and poetic sense of fantasy and the macabre. His most important works for his own co. incl. DANCES BEFORE THE WALL. Also choreographed *Phantom of the Opera* (1966; mus. John Herbert McDowell), *Northern Lights* (1967; mus. Arnold Schönberg), *Arena* (1967; mus. STRAVINSKY), all for Manhattan Festival B.; *Purple Moment* (1969; mus. popular/ Johann Sebastian Bach), for New England Dance T., revived NDT, 1970; *Spookride* (1969; mus. Chopin/Ezra Sims), for New England Dance T., revived Pennsylvania B., 1970; *Variations on a Landscape* (1971; mus. Schönberg), for NDT; *32 Variations in C Minor* (1973; mus. Ludwig van Beethoven), for COHEN; *Sinfonia Semplice* (1975; mus. Wolfgang Amadeus Mozart), for EGLEVSKY B. Artistic director, New England Dinosaur, 1974–5. DV
See J. Waring, 'Five Essays on Dancing', *Ballet Review*, Vol. 2, No. 1 (New York 1967)

Weaver, John, b. Shrewsbury, 1673; d. Shrewsbury, 1760. English dancing master, innovator, and writer. Worked at Lincoln's Inn Fields, Drury Lane, and other theatres 1702–33. His first ballet-pantomime was *The Tavern Bilkers* (1702). In 1717 he staged LOVES OF MARS AND VENUS. Weaver's ambition was to create entertainments in which (in his own words) 'the tale was carried forward with movement rather than words' and he proceeded to do so in works like *Orpheus and Eurydice* (1718), *Perseus and Andromeda* (1726), and *The Judgment of Paris* (1732). All this was before SALLÉ's arrival in London. Weaver instituted many reforms for which NOVERRE later received credit. As well as making these early *ballets d'action*, he wrote books on dancing and translated from the French Raoul-Auger Feuillet's system of dance notation, *Orchesography* (1706). His other books incl. *An Essay Towards an History of Dancing* (London 1712) and *Anatomical and Mechanical Lectures upon Dancing* (London 1721). Although librettos survive, Weaver's works died with him and there was no ballet master in England able to continue and develop his pioneer work. It was in continental Europe that his ideas eventually came to fruition. MC

Webster, Clara Vestris, b. Bath, 1821, d. London, 1844. English dancer, daughter of Benjamin Webster (of the famous theatrical family) who was a dancer before opening a school in Bath. He had studied with G. VESTRIS, after whom his daughter was named. Clara's debut was at the T. Royal, Bath, 19 May 1830; her first London perf. as a dancer 11 July 1836. Destined to become a leading ballerina of the Romantic era, her life tragically ended when during a perf. of *The Revolt of the Harem* at Drury Lane T. on 14 Dec 1844 her dress caught fire. She died from burns three days later. MC
See Ivor Guest, *Victorian Ballet-Girl* (London 1957)

Wedding Bouquet, A, ballet, 1 act; ch. ASHTON; mus./sc./c. BERNERS; words Gertrude Stein (from *They Must. Be Wedded. To Their Wife*). London, SW, Vic-Wells B., 27 Apr 1937; dan. DE VALOIS, June Brae, FONTEYN, HELPMANN, Mary Honer. A French provincial wedding in the early 1900s. One of Ashton's wittiest ballets, frequently revived. The Stein text was originally sung by a chorus, later (and more effectively) spoken by LAMBERT. DV

Weidman, Charles, b. Lincoln, NE, 1901; d. New York, 1975. American dancer, choreographer, and teacher. Studied at DENISHAWN and with Theodore Koslov. Debut in vaudeville in SHAWN's *Xochitl*, with GRAHAM, 1921. Toured USA, Europe, and the Orient with Denishawn until 1927, when he and HUMPHREY left to form their own school and co., which lasted until 1945. The technique they taught was based on the principle of 'fall and recovery'. Established his own school 1945 and co. 1948, touring extensively. Taught both in California and NY; in his last years he gave weekly concerts at his tiny Expression of Two Arts T., NY, in collaboration with the artist Mikhail Santaro. His dances often dealt with American social themes, sometimes with the strong vein of sardonic humour that characterized Weidman's personality both on stage and off stage. They incl. *The Happy Hypocrite* (1931), *On My Mother's Side* (1940), *Flickers* (1941), *And Daddy Was a Fireman* (1943), *A House Divided* (1945), *Fables For Our Time* (1947).

Also collaborated with Humphrey on NEW DANCE (1935), and *Theatre Piece* (1936), and choreographed musical shows incl. *As Thousands Cheer* (1933), *I'd*

Charles Weidman with HUMPHREY in NEW DANCE

Rather Be Right (1937), *Sing Out, Sweet Land* (1944, also with Humphrey). DV

Welch, Garth, b. Brisbane, 1939. Australian dancer, choreographer, and director. Studied with Phyllis Danaher. BOROVANSKY scholarship 1959. Western TB 1959, guest artist. Borovansky B. 1960, becoming principal dancer. Australian B. Foundation scholarship 1961. DE CUEVAS B. 1961, becoming leading dancer. Australian B. 1962–73, principal dancer. Harkness Foundation grant 1966–7, to study with GRAHAM. B. Victoria 1974, assistant artistic director. A stylish *danseur noble* (ALBRECHT, JEAN DE BRIENNE), effective also in modern dramatic ballets (created The Outsider in *The Display*, ch. HELPMANN). His ballets incl. *Illyria, Othello, Images*. KSW

Wells, Doreen (Marchioness of Londonderry), b. Walthamstow, London, 1937. Studied Bush–Davies S. and gained Solo Seal of RAD. Joined SWTB 1955 and RB at CG 1956, quickly becoming soloist. Principal with the touring section of the RB 1960–70, then divided her time between the two cos. In 1974 retired from dancing to have a son but returned to make guest appearances with LFB, at galas, and on tours abroad with small groups of stars. A dancer of sunny charm and impeccable technique, she danced all the classics and was delightful in ASHTON's FILLE MAL GARDÉE and DEUX PIGEONS. With the touring RB she danced mostly with GABLE and WALL. MC

Wendel, Heinrich, b. Bremen, 1915. German stage designer. Collaborated with WALTER, first in Wuppertal (1953–64) and then in Düsseldorf from 1964. GBLW

West, Elizabeth, b. Alassio, Italy, 1927; d. Switzerland (from a climbing accident near the Matterhorn), 1962. English dancer, choreographer, and visionary whose tenacity against all odds made WESTERN THEATRE B. an exciting co. MC

Western Theatre Ballet. A small English co. formed by WEST and DARRELL to perform works in which 'theatre' played a part as important as dance. West's vision of a regional co. (it was based on Bristol) was accepted by the Arts Council 1969 when it turned the co. into SCOTTISH B. MC

Whims of Cupid and the Ballet Master, The (*Amors og Balletmesterens Luner*), ballet, 1 act, ch./lib. GALEOTTI; mus. Jens Lolle. Copenhagen, RDB, 31 Oct 1786. Since then in the repertory of the RDB, the oldest surviving ballet and always very popular. The present staging uses rather stronger techniques than were known to Galeotti but retains the spirit of the piece. It is a series of *pas de deux* by couples of different nationalities who then retire to a temple of love. The mischievous little Cupid (played by a child from the RDBS) blindfolds them and when they emerge he has craftily paired them wrongly, with disastrous but hilarious complications. Produced Paris O. 1952 by H. LANDER. SKJ

Who Cares?, ballet, ch. BALANCHINE; mus. George Gershwin, orch. Hershy Kay; sc. Jo Mielziner; c. (Barbara) Karinska. NYST, NYCB, 5 Feb 1970; dan. MCBRIDE, Karin von Aroldingen, Marnee Morris, D'AMBOISE. A suite of dances to tunes by Gershwin, such as 'Fascinatin' Rhythm' and 'The Man I Love'. A classical ballet in the style of a Gershwin musical. FM

Widow Simone, the mother of LISE in FILLE MAL GARDÉE

Wigman, Mary [Marie Wiegmann], b. Hanover, 1886; d. W. Berlin, 1973. German dancer, choreographer, and teacher. In 1911, aged 25, she began to study with DALCROZE at Hellerau and from 1913 with LABAN in Munich and Zürich, becoming his assistant. First solo recitals Zürich and Hamburg 1919; in 1920 she opened her own school in Dresden, which became the focus of AUSDRUCKSTANZ. To her school came H. HOLM, GEORGI, Gret Palucca, Margarethe Wallman, KREUTZBERG, TERPIS, and most of the exponents of this style, which spread throughout Central Europe (and to the USA through Holm) and established itself as the dance style of all the German opera houses, only to be ousted by the classical style after World War II.

Wigman danced in London 1928 at a charity matinée and in the USA 1930. Her career as a soloist flourished in the 1920s and 1930s; she gave up dancing 1942. After World War II she had a school in Leipzig; in 1949 she moved to W. Berlin and her school there became the focal point of the Modern Dance in Europe. She choreographed SACRE DU PRINTEMPS 1957; her final creative work was to stage Christoph Willibald Gluck's opera, *Orfeo ed Euridice*, Deutsche O., W. Berlin, 1961. Hers was the greatest influence in Europe of the Modern Dance. GBLW
See Walter Sorell (ed. and tr.), *The Mary Wigman Book, Her Writings* (Middletown, CT, 1976); Mary Wigman (tr. Walter Sorell), *The Language of Dance* (Middletown, CT, 1976)

Wilde [White], Patricia, b. Ottawa, 1928. Canadian dancer. Studied with Gwendolyn Osborne, Ottawa, Dorothie Littlefield, Philadelphia, SAB, NY. Danced with B. International (DE CUEVAS) 1944–5, B. Russe de Monte Carlo 1945–9, guest artist with Metropolitan B. 1949–50, and B. de Paris 1950; joined NYCB 1950, where BALANCHINE choreographed many roles to exploit her strong, brilliant technique. Principal of HARKNESS S. 1965–7. Joined faculty of ABTS 1969, ballet mistress of co. 1970–5. DV

Williams, Dudley, b. New York, 1938. American dancer. Studied ballet with TUDOR, Alfredo Corvino, George Chaffee, modern dance with O'DONNELL,

Mary Wigman in a solo dance *c.* 1937

GRAHAM. Danced in the cos of O'Donnell, 1958–61, MCKAYLE 1960, Graham 1962–6, and AILEY from 1964. A dancer of burning intensity and brilliant technique, he has created roles in most of Ailey's works since 1969, incl. the solo *Love Songs*, choreographed for him in 1972, as well as acting as a ballet master for the co. DV

Williams, Stanley, b. Chappel, England, 1925; grew up in Denmark. Danish dancer and teacher. Studied at RDBS and in Paris, attaining the rank of soloist with the RDB 1949. A strong exponent of the August BOURNONVILLE style and a gifted mime. In 1950 began teaching at the RDBS. In 1960–1 and again 1961–2 was guest teacher with NYCB. Since 1964 on faculty of SAB. MC

Wilson, Robert, b. Waco, TX, 1941. American playwright and director. Studied art and architecture, began teaching body movement and body awareness. His early theatre pieces were based on non-verbal communication; in 1968 presented *Alley Cats* at NY Univ., with himself, MONK, and a cast of 40. Since then he has written and directed *The King of Spain* (1969), incorporated into *The Life and Times of Sigmund Freud* later the same year, *Deafman Glance* (1970), *The Life and Times of Joseph Stalin* (1972), *A Letter for Queen Victoria* (1974), *Einstein on the Beach* (1976, with Philip Glass), *avant-garde* theatre pieces which are a combination of spectacle, music, dance, and non-narrative action. The beholder's sense of objective time is suspended as he surrenders to the hallucinatory feeling the pieces induce. The choreography is usually by Andy de Groat, making use of geometric patterns and repetition, with a great deal of spinning. DV

Wilson, Sallie, b. Fort Worth, TX, 1932. American dancer. Studied with CRASKE and TUDOR. First danced with ABT 1949, and has returned to that co. after periods with the NY Met OB (1950–5) and NYCB, where she created a role in GRAHAM's section of EPISODES (1958–60). Her perf. of the Mazurka in SYLPHIDES is unsurpassed, but she is principally identified with the Tudor repertory, both as interpreter and *régisseuse*, especially PILLAR OF FIRE. DV

Winter, Ethel, b. Wrentham, MA. American dancer, choreographer, and teacher. Graduate of Bennington College, VT. Studied with GRAHAM, joined her co. 1946, danced leading roles incl. Graham's own in *Hérodiade* and *Frontier*. Also has danced many works of her own and in SOKOLOW's *Lyric Suite* (1954), and MASLOW's *The Dybbuk* (1964). DV

Witch Boy, The, ballet, 1 act, ch. J. CARTER; mus. Leonard Salzedo; sc./c. Norman McDowell. Amsterdam, B. der Lage Landen, 24 May 1956; dan. McDowell. Revived Manchester, England, LFB, 27 Nov 1957; dan. GILPIN. The lib. is based on the 'Ballad of Barbara Allen' but with a different ending. A girl falls in love with a witch boy, the villagers, suspicious of his strangeness, kill him but he is immediately reborn. The cycle will be unending. One of Carter's most successful dramatic works. MC

Woizikowski, Leon, b. Warsaw, 1897; d. Warsaw, 1975. Polish dancer, ballet master, and teacher. Studied Warsaw BS and in 1915 joined DIAGHILEV Co. staying until 1929. An outstanding character dancer, his roles incl. PETRUSHKA, the Chief Warrior in PRINCE IGOR, the GOLDEN SLAVE, and also the faun in NIJINSKY's APRÈS-MIDI D'UN FAUNE (which in 1931 he staged and danced for BR). Danced in early seasons of B. Russe de Monte Carlo and from 1935–7 had his own co., Les B. de Léon Woizikowski, which toured Europe. Returned to Poland 1937 and remained in Warsaw throughout World War II. Julian Braunsweg invited him to London to stage *Petrushka* and SCHÉHÉRAZADE for LFB, 1958 and 1960. He continued to work in the West, with MASSINE's B. Europeo 1959, then in Cologne, Bonn, and Antwerp. He returned to Poland shortly before his death. MC

Wooden Prince, The (*A Fából Faragott Királyfi*), ballet, 1 act, ch. Ottó Zöbisch and Ede Brada; mus. BARTÓK (1917); lib. Béla Balázs (1912); sc. Miklós Bánffy. Budapest O., 12 May 1917. Revived in Hungary: Jan Cieplinski (1935), HARANGOZÓ (10 Nov 1939), Ernő Vashegyi (13 Mar 1952), Harangozó (Budapest O., 18 June 1958); ECK (Szeged, B. Sopianae, 25 July 1965; Pécs, 22 Oct 1965); SEREGI (Budapest O., 26 Sept 1970). A fable about a vain princess, a wooden puppet, and the true prince; the theme is basically that happiness has to be earned by endeavour. The libretto leaves wide scope for manifold interpretations. Rechoreographed for film by Seregi 1971, directed Adám Horváth, dan. Róna, Orosz and József Forgách (title role). The score has also been used by many choreographers outside Hungary. GPD

Woolliams, Anne, b. Folkestone, 1926. English dancer, teacher, and ballet mistress. Studied with Judith Espinosa, Volkova, and at the Bush–Davies S. Danced in the film *The Red Shoes* (dir. Michael Powell, 1948). Taught classical ballet 1958–63 at the Folkwang S., Essen. Cranko appointed her ballet mistress, Stuttgart B., 1963, and director of the Stuttgart S. (the John Cranko S.) on its foundation in 1971. On his death (1973) she took over the running of the Stuttgart B. with Dieter Gräfe. Appointed Director of Australian B., 1976. GBLW

Wright, Peter, b. London, 1926. English dancer, choreographer, and director. Studied Jooss, Volkova, and van Praagh. Danced with B. Jooss 1945–6; with Metropolitan B. 1947; soloist SWTB 1949–51; rejoined Jooss 1951–2; then to SWTB 1952, becoming assistant ballet master 1955. Taught at RBS 1957–9. In 1961 to Stuttgart to join Cranko as teacher and ballet master where he choreographed several ballets and staged a production of Giselle (1966) which has since entered the repertories of several cos incl. NB of Canada and the RB. During his stay in Stuttgart he also worked as guest teacher and choreographer with other German cos, and in Norway, Canada, and Israel. In 1970 returned to the RB as Associate Director of the co. and Resident Director of the touring section. Staged Sleeping Beauty in Cologne 1967 and collaborated with Ashton in the RB's 1968 version of the ballet. He m. dancer Sonya Hana. MC

Wright, Rebecca, b. Springfield, OH, 1947. American dancer. Studied with Josephine and Hermene Schwarz in Dayton, OH, and danced in Dayton Civic B. Joined CCJB 1966. A witty and versatile *demi-caractère* dancer, at her most brilliant in Deuce Coupe; her roles also incl. the Little American Girl in Parade, the Ballerina in Petrushka, and Titania in Dream. Left CCJB to join ABT 1975, where her roles incl. the Cowgirl in Rodeo. DV

Wright, Rose Marie, b. Pittston, PA, 1949. American dancer. Studied at school of Pennsylvania B. and danced with that co. In NY studied with NY S. of B. and Margaret Black. Joined Tharp's co. 1968; has danced in most of her works since that time, incl. the original version of Deuce Coupe. A dancer of imposing stature, Wright is capable of feats of incredible virtuosity and speed. Tharp dedicated to her the first NY season of her co., at BAM 1976. DV

Aleksey Yermolayev as Philippe in Flame of Paris

Yacobson, Leonid, b. St Petersburg, 1904; d. Moscow, 1975. Soviet dancer and choreographer. Graduated from Leningrad Choreographic S.; dancer of character and grotesque roles, Leningrad State O. and BT 1926–33. Soloist Bolshoy T. 1933–42. From 1942 choreographer Kirov T. Artistic director and choreographer of his own co., Choreographic Miniatures, 1969–75. Was always seeking new paths in choreography from his first work, Golden Age, produced jointly with Vainonen. Choreographed much in 1930s for Leningrad Choreographic S., notably *Till Eulenspiegel* (1933; mus. Richard Strauss). Interest in *plastique* and free movement led him to collaboration with the I. Duncan Studio, for which choreographed dances 1948. In one of his best-known works, Shurale, he blended classical ballet with Tartar national dance. The epic Spartacus (1956) deliberately abandoned *pointe* work and turn-out, continuing Fokine's precepts. Choreographed *Bedbug* (after Vladimir Mayakovsky's play of the same title, 1962). Created many original programs for his own troupe, incl. *Rodin's Sculptures*, *Exercise XX*, *Ebony Concerto*. Participated in Milan Sc. production of Luigi Nono's opera *Al Gran Sole Carico d'Amore* (*Under the Hot Sun of Love*), 1975. Collaborated with George Cukor in Leningrad on film of *The Blue Bird* starring Plisetskaya and N. Pavlova. Honoured

Art Worker, RSFSR. Two State prizes. He m. Irina Gensler, Kirov character soloist. NR
See G. Dobrovolskaya, *Leonid Yacobson* (Leningrad 1968)

Yaroslavna, ballet, 3 acts, ch./sc. VINOGRADOV, after the 12th-c. prose epic, *The Lay of Igor's Campaign*; mus. Boris Tishenko; scenic adviser Yuri Lyubimov. Leningrad, Maly O., 30 June 1974; dan. DOLGUSHIN (Igor), Tatiana Fesenko (Yaroslavna). A talented but controversial work presenting Prince Igor's defeat and the fighting among princes in ancient Russia; claimed to be closer to history than Aleksandr Borodin's opera *Prince Igor*. Vinogradov uses modern barefoot dance idiom. The Polovtsi Chief Konchak and his agile warriors are portrayed by women on *pointe*. The text of the epic is sung by a chorus while the ballet takes place. NR
See Dmitri Shostakovich, 'Creation is Search' in *Izvestia* (Moscow, 23 July 1974)

Yermolayev, Aleksey, b. St Petersburg, 1910; d. Moscow, 1975. Soviet dancer, choreographer, and teacher. Three State prizes. Virile and powerful classical dancer and exceptional dance-actor, he exerted a strong influence on the moulding of male dancing in Soviet ballet. Graduated from Leningrad Choreographic S., Kirov B. 1926–30. Significantly, he made his debut in the old ballet *Talisman* (1889; ch. M. PETIPA) as Vayu, God of Wind, who defied the laws of gravity, for he was himself to represent a new wind of change blowing through the academic dance. Notably as BASILIO he invented virtuoso steps, especially of elevation, unknown until then in the conventional classical choreography. Other classical roles: SIEGFRIED, BLUEBIRD, ALBRECHT. Bolshoy T. 1930–53. Created Philippe the Marseillais in FLAME OF PARIS, Tybalt in ROMEO AND JULIET (L. LAVROVSKY; Bolshoy productions), Evgeny (BRONZE HORSEMAN), Severyan (STONE FLOWER – Lavrovsky version), etc. From 1961 leading teacher and coach, Bolshoy B., continuing influence on such dancers as VASILIEV, M. LAVROVSKY, LIEPA, and VLADIMIROV. Taught at Moscow Choreographic S. from 1961, headed it in 1968. Choreographed at Minsk O. *The Nightingale* (1939) and *Burning Hearts* (1954). People's Artist, USSR. NR
See Marina Churova (ed.), *Aleksey Yermolayev* (Moscow 1974) (contains articles by Goleizovsky, Vasiliev, Golubov-Potapov, Slonimsky, etc.)

Yevdokimov, Gleb, b. Moscow, 1923. Russian dancer and teacher. Studied Moscow, Bolshoy S. 1932–41; joined Bolshoy B. on graduation. Roles incl. BLUEBIRD, the *pas de trois* in SWAN LAKE, the *pas de deux* in GISELLE, Nur-Ali in FOUNTAIN OF BAKHCHISARAY, all of which he danced in London 1956, also the Mandoline Dance in L. LAVROVSKY's ROMEO AND JULIET. Retired 1962. Continues to teach students of the Bolshoy S. and dancers of the Bolshoy B. He m. KARELSKAYA. JS

Yevteyeva, Elena, b. Leningrad, 1947. Soviet dancer. Graduated from VAGANOVA S. into Kirov T. 1966. Under guidance of DUDINSKAYA developed into technically excellent and lyrically expressive dancer. Danced Beautiful Maiden in YACOBSON's *Country of Marvels* (1967) and ODETTE-ODILE in SERGEYEV's film of SWAN LAKE. Her GISELLE the same year, ethereal and fragile, was considered one of the best interpretations among young Kirov ballerinas. Created Bird in BELSKY's *Icare*, dances Ophelia in Sergeyev's HAMLET, Shirien (LEGEND OF LOVE), the Girl (LENINGRAD SYMPHONY), Eve (*Creation of the World*, ch. KASATKINA and VASILYOV), Nikia (BAYADÈRE), Medora (CORSAIRE, revised version) with great artistry. Honoured Artist, RSFSR. Silver Medal, Varna, 1970. NR

YM & YWHA (Young Men's and Young Women's Hebrew Association), New York's famous 'Y' on East 92nd Street which since 1937 has been a centre for modern dance and dance theatre. Most of the foremost figures in the dance world have appeared in its Kaufmann Concert Hall and it has sponsored many educational projects. MC

Young Ballet *see* BALANCHINE

Young Man Must Marry, The (*Den Unge Mand Skal Giftes*), ballet, ch. F. FLINDT, after Eugène Ionesco's play *Jacques ou la Soumission*; mus. Per Nørgaard; sc. Jacques Noël. Danish TV, 2 Feb 1965; staged Copenhagen, Royal T., RDB, 15 Oct 1967. A young man who does not want to marry is forced into marriage by his family. They present him with a series of nightmarish brides, each more monstrous than the next, ending with a girl with three heads, who absorbs him completely in her dress. SKJ

Youskevitch, Igor, b. Moscow, 1912. Russian dancer, whose family moved to Belgrade 1920; US citizen 1944. Originally an athlete, he began to study ballet at the age of 20 and became one of the great *danseurs nobles* of his time. Studied in Paris with PREOBRAZHENSKA, danced in the cos of NIJINSKA 1934, and WOIZIKOWSKI 1935–7, B. Russe de Monte Carlo 1938–44 and 1955–7, ABT 1946–55 and 1958–9; B. Alicia ALONSO, 1948 and thereafter. His partnership with Alonso, one of the greatest in modern ballet, began in ABT 1946, and continued until 1959. Now has his own school in NY. DV

Yugoslavia. The principal cos are in Belgrade [Beograd] and Zagreb, with smaller cos in Ljubljana, Maribor, Novi Sad, Sarajevo, Skopje, and Split. Zagreb had a professional co. directed by Otokar Bartik in 1894 but in the two principal cities ballet was not firmly established until 1921. In that year the Moscow-born and Bolshoy-trained Margarita Froman (1890–1970) and her brother Max were engaged in Zagreb and began to mount ballets from the Russian classical and DIAGHILEV repertories.

Margarita Froman remained a major influence until she left Yugoslavia for the USA in the early 1950s. She staged the first Yugoslav ballet, *The Gingerbread Heart* (mus. Krešimir Baranovič) in Zagreb, 17 June 1924, and in 1927 in Belgrade. Belgrade had a small co. attached to the O. from its opening in 1921. This was enlarged the following year and a school established under Elena Poliakova from Petrograd and Claudia Issachenko who was also principal dancer. Another Belgrade dancer of the period, Natalija Boscovič, subsequently became a soloist with the co. of A. PAVLOVA, the beginning of a trend that persisted – innumerable Yugoslav dancers and ballet masters made careers elsewhere although ultimately many of them returned to Yugoslavia. Typically, a principal dancer of the 1930s, Ana Roje, became a protégée of LEGAT in London and was an internationally celebrated teacher before rejoining her husband at his famous school in Split. The husband-and-wife team of Pino and Pia Mlakar worked in Germany and Switzerland as well as in Yugoslavia; their daughter Veronika Mlakar danced in the cos of PETIT, ROBBINS, BÉJART, and with ABT. The Mlakars' most popular ballet was *The Devil in the Village* (mus. Fran Lhotka), first staged Zürich, 18 Feb 1935 but soon after revived in Belgrade.

Ballet activity ceased during World War II. The first major production in Belgrade thereafter was Froman's *The Legend of Ohrid* (mus. Stevan Hristić; 28 Nov 1947) based on a Macedonian folk tale; the best known of Yugoslav ballets. An important figure in the postwar years has been PARLIĆ. Before political divergence robbed Yugoslavia of the benefits of Soviet teaching and choreography, several Soviet ballets entered the repertories in both Zagreb and Belgrade where, notably, L. LAVROVSKY staged his GISELLE in the 1950s. A recent and unusual staging has been a Balkan version of the Romeo and Juliet story based on Turkish-Serbian family conflicts, choreographed for the Novi Sad co. by Franjo Horvat, *Stamena* (7 May 1976; mus. Leo Peraki).

Among Yugoslav dancers who have achieved international renown are SLAVENSKA, MISKOVITCH, Vassili Sulich, Milko Sparemblek, and the Moscow-born but Belgrade-educated YOUSKEVITCH. The Belgrade co. has toured most widely incl. Edinburgh Fest. 1951; the Zagreb co. appeared in London 1955. MC

Yuriko [Yuriko Kikuchi], b. San Jose, CA, 1920. American dancer of Japanese parentage. Educated Japan, toured with Konami Ishii Dance Co. of Tokyo, 1930–7. Joined GRAHAM Dance Co. 1944; remained until the early 1960s, creating many roles for Graham incl. the Moon in *Canticle for Innocent Comedians*, Iphigenia in CLYTEMNESTRA, etc. Began to give concerts of her own work in 1949. Danced in the Broadway musical *The King and I* (1951–4; ch. ROBBINS) and in the film version (1955). Teaches at Graham S. and has assisted in revivals of her works. DV

Z

Zajlich, Piotr, b. Warsaw, 1884; d. Warsaw, 1948. Polish dancer, choreographer, and teacher. Soloist and choreographer of A. PAVLOVA's co. 1912–14. Dancer and director, Warsaw B., 1917–34. A versatile dancer; danced ALBRECHT, FRANZ, Amoûn (*Cléopâtre*), GOLDEN SLAVE; created the Devil in PAN TWARDOWSKI and other roles in Polish works. As choreographer, he revived classical works, and prepared first Polish versions of many DIAGHILEV ballets, e.g. SCHÉHÉRAZADE, PRINCE IGOR, PETRUSHKA, OISEAU DE FEU. He also created many original Polish ballets, incl. *Pan Twardowski.* Director, Warsaw BS, 1917–34, 1937–8; the teacher of JASIŃSKI and SHABELEVSKY. Also danced under the name of Shouvalov. JPU

Zakharov, Rostislav, b. Astrakhan, 1907. Soviet choreographer. Graduated from Leningrad Choreographic S. 1926, class of PONOMARYOV. Soloist, Kharkov O. 1936–9. From 1929 started choreographing small pieces; at the same time entered *régisseurs'* faculty, Leningrad T. Inst., under the celebrated director Serge Radlov, by whom he was greatly influenced. He chose T. Inst. because at that time there was no institution of higher education for choreographers, but Radlov understood the importance of expressive movement. Also in the early 1930s, Soviet choreographers were seeking for psychological deepening of ballet's expressive means through *rapprochement* with dramatic theatre. Accepted into Kirov T. 1932, started producing dances in operas. His FOUNTAIN OF BAKHCHISARAY signified a reform in Soviet ballet, since Zakharov applied Konstantin Stanislavsky's method in preparatory work with dancers, probing the inner content of characters. With his *régisseur*'s experience and knowledge, Zakharov created dramatic culminations in each act, suggested by the construction of the libretto. Even the apparently purely mime character GIREY remains one of the most powerful, three-dimensional figures in Soviet ballet. ULANOVA's creation of Maria both provided the ballet with its ideal heroine and served as the first vehicle for the discovery of her outstanding lyrical-dramatic talents.

His next ballet, LOST ILLUSIONS, failed to reach the same logical development of choreographic action. Coralie's dramatic dance in the finale of Act II created on and for Ulanova provided the only exception. Nevertheless even in this short-lived ballet he created rounded characters, which definitely led to the further progress of the Kirov dancers, teaching them how to live a role.

Chief choreographer and opera director, Bolshoy T. 1936–56, where he created PRISONER OF THE CAUCASUS, TARAS BULBA, CINDERELLA, *Mistress*

Rostislav Zakharov's ballet FOUNTAIN OF BAKHCHISARAY, as danced by the Bolshoy B., with KONDRATIEVA as Maria and LAPAURI as Khan Girey

into Maid (after Aleksandr Pushkin's story), also new dances for the revival of GORSKY's DON QUIXOTE, and productions of entire operas and dances in them (Mikhail Glinka's *Ruslan and Lyudmila*, etc.). At Kirov T. choreographed BRONZE HORSEMAN. Headed Moscow Choreographic S. 1946–9. Founder member of GITIS Ballet Faculty; from 1946 has held the chair of Choreography, from 1951 Professor, Choreographers' Faculty, where he heads the course. Published *Iskusstvo Baletmeistera* (*The Choreographer's Art*; Moscow 1959), a new edition, *Notes by a Choreographer* (Moscow 1976); working on *Composition of Dance*. People's Artist, USSR. Professor, Doctor of Science (Arts). NR
See his own books and N. Roslavleva, 'How a Soviet Ballet is Made' in Mary Clarke and Clement Crisp, *Making a Ballet* (London 1975); N. Roslavleva, 'Stanislavski and the Ballet' in *Dance Perspectives*, No. 23 (New York 1965)

Zambelli, Carlotta, b. Milan, 1875; d. Milan, 1968. Italian ballerina and teacher; dominated the Paris O. in a career of over 60 years. Studied at the Milan Sc. BS, under Cesare Coppini. Debut Paris O. 1894, quickly gaining recognition and becoming the principal *étoile* on Rosita Mauri's retirement in 1898. Her style was marked by a brilliant technique – the product of her Milanese training – and qualities of vivacity and sparkle. Her career was centred almost exclusively at the Paris O., although she did make a guest visit to St Petersburg (1901). Among her many creations at the O. were the leading roles in Joseph Hansen's *La Ronde des Saisons* (1905), STAATS's *Javotte* (1909). She also appeared in the standard classics of the O. repertory, e.g. COPPÉLIA, SYLVIA. She never danced GISELLE at the O., but it was one of her roles during her visit to St Petersburg. She officially retired as a dancer in 1930. Her career as a teacher had begun in 1920, when she succeeded Mauri as *professeur de la classe de perfectionnement* at the OBS. She taught there, and also privately, consolidating the Italian dominance that went back to the mid-19th c. Her method had similarities with the CECCHETTI method, since both derived from the method taught at the Milan Sc. BS. Retired 1956. Palmes Académiques 1906; Médaille de la Reconnaissance Française 1920; the first person to enter the Légion d'Honneur for her services to dancing (she was made *Chevalier* in 1926 and *Officier* in 1956). IG
See Ivor Guest, *Carlotta Zambelli* (Paris 1969)

Zarema, the 'other woman' in FOUNTAIN OF BAKHCHISARAY

Zhdanov, Yuri, b. Moscow, 1925. Soviet dancer and choreographer. Graduated from Moscow Choreographic S. 1944, class of Nikolay Tarasov. *Premier danseur*, Bolshoy B., from 1951, dancing classical roles and Evgeny (BRONZE HORSEMAN), Ma Lie-Chen (*Red Flower*; *see* RED POPPY). Nobility of manner, assured partnering, and lyrical-dramatic expressiveness enabled him to become ULANOVA's partner, dancing L. LAVROVSKY's ROMEO many times, also in the film. Partnered STRUCHKOVA, PLISETSKAYA. Danced in Bolshoy B. for 25 years but in that period graduated from Choreographers' Faculty, GITIS. From 1971 has headed State Ensemble of Classical B. (founded by MOISEYEV), choreographed there *Francesca da Rimini* (mus. TCHAIKOVSKY) among other works. Toured with this co. in Italy, Netherlands, W. Germany, etc. Constantly replenishes repertoire, inviting young choreographers. A good painter; he is a member of the Union of Soviet Painters. People's Artist, RSFSR. NR
See Yuri Zhdanov, 'The Heroism of Our Days in Dance' in *Soviet Culture* (Moscow, 29 May 1973); *Po Ispanii* (*In Spain*; Moscow 1970), travel notes and many drawings

Virginia Zucchi as she appeared in *Brahma* in St Petersburg, in which the 'tremendous magnetic force' of her acting made such an impression upon BENOIS, then a boy of 15, that it made him, and later his colleagues, aware of the artistic and dramatic potential of ballet

Ziggurat, modern dance work, 1 act, ch. TETLEY; mus. Karlheinz Stockhausen; sc./c. N. BAYLIS; projections Alan Cunliffe. London, Jeannetta Cochrane T., BR, 20 Nov 1967. Tetley's first created work for BR. The overthrow of a god and resulting chaos. A co. work in powerful dance imagery. MC

Zobeide, the favourite wife of the Shah in SCHÉHÉRAZADE

Zorina, Vera [Eva Brigitta Hartwig], b. Berlin, 1917, of Norwegian parentage; US citizen 1943. Dancer and actress. She m. (1) BALANCHINE, (2) Goddard Lieberson. Studied in Germany with EDOUARDOVA, later with V. GSOVSKY, RAMBERT, LEGAT. Danced in Max Reinhardt's *A Midsummer Night's Dream* (Berlin 1929 and Oxford 1933), and in his *Tales of Hoffmann* (1931). Played opposite DOLIN in the play *Ballerina* (London 1933). Joined DE BASIL's B. Russe de Monte Carlo 1933, changing her name to Zorina 1934. Left 1936; appeared in London production of the musical comedy *On Your Toes* (1937), on Broadway in *I Married an Angel* (1938), and *Louisiana Purchase* (1940), and in the films *Goldwyn Follies* (1937), *On Your Toes* (1939), *I Was an Adventuress* (1940), etc., ch. Balanchine. Guest artist with ABT 1942–4, in Balanchine's *Errante* and APOLLO, etc. In more recent years has specialized in narrating such works as STRAVINSKY's *Perséphone*, Arthur Honegger's *Jeanne d'Arc au Bûcher*, etc. DV

Zubkovskaya, Inna, b. Moscow, 1923. Russian dancer. Studied Moscow Bolshoy S., graduating 1941. Evacuated to Perm 1941, joined Kirov B., where roles incl. ODETTE-ODILE, Nikia (BAYADÈRE), KITRI, and the LILAC FAIRY . Created roles of PHRYGIA, Mekhmene-Banu (LEGEND OF LOVE). She m. dancer Svyatoslav Kuznetsov. People's Artist, RSFSR. JS

Zucchi, Virginia, b. Parma, 1849; d. Nice, 1930. Italian ballerina, especially famous for influence on Russian ballet. Received her early training in Milan. Began to dance professionally 1864 at minor theatres in Italy. Her first important engagement was at the T. Regio, Turin, 1867–8, but her reputation really began at Padua 1873. In 1874 she first danced at the Sc., Milan, where later she appeared in MANZOTTI's *Rolla* (1875) and Amilcare Ponchielli's opera *La Gioconda* (1876). She danced in Berlin, 1876–9, making her debut in FILLE MAL GARDÉE, and at CG, London, during the opera seasons of 1878 and 1879. She danced in a revival of EXCELSIOR, 1883.

In 1885 she first went to Russia, where she was engaged to dance at Kin Grust, one of the pleasure gardens of St Petersburg. Ballet in Russia was at a low ebb, and she stirred such enthusiasm that the Imperial Ts engaged her for the season of 1885–6. She made her debut at the Bolshoy T. (the ballet did not move to the Maryinsky T. until a year later) in

FILLE DU PHARAON, and as a result of her appearances the season's receipts doubled. For the next few years her career was centred on Russia. She danced for the Imperial Ts in St Petersburg 1886–7 and 1887–8, in a repertory incl. *La Fille Mal Gardée,* ESMERALDA, and *The King's Command*, and the opera *Fenella* (in the mimed title role). She danced with her own co., Moscow 1888, making a deep impression on Konstantin Stanislavsky, and in St Petersburg, 1889 and 1892. She was the first of many Italian ballerinas who adorned Russian ballet toward the end of the 19th c. In the last years of her career she danced in Nice 1889–90, and Monte Carlo 1893–6, and occasionally appeared at the T. dal Verme, Milan. She also produced the Venusberg scene in Richard Wagner's *Tannhäuser* at the Bayreuth Fest., at the Sc., Milan, 1891, and at the Paris O., 1895. Last appearance Milan 1898.

She was one of the most famous theatrical celebrities of her time: the young KSHESSINSKAYA and many dancers were inspired by her art, and she awakened a love for ballet in BENOIS and others who played important parts in the DIAGHILEV period. IG *See* Ivor Guest, *The Divine Virginia* (New York 1977)

Züllig, Hans, b. Rorschach, 1914. Swiss dancer, choreographer, and teacher. Pupil of JOOSS and LEEDER in Essen and at Dartington Hall, Devon; soloist, B. Jooss 1935–47. Soloist, SWTB, 1948–9; danced in Essen and Zürich until 1954. Taught, Essen Folkwang S. 1954–6; later danced in Düsseldorf. Taught in Chile 1956–61, then returned to Essen. From 1969 head of the Dance Section, Folkwang S. Choreographed *Le Bosquet* for B. Jooss (1945). GBLW

Zviagina, Susanna, b. Moscow, 1908. Russian dancer. Studied Moscow Bolshoy S. with E. GERDT and GUSEV, graduating 1927. Joined Bolshoy B.; soloist 1937, in character roles such as the Spanish Dance in SWAN LAKE. Appeared in London 1956, 1960; NY 1959. Honoured Artist, USSR. JS

Hans Züllig (centre) as the Young Man, with Noelle de Mosa and dancers of the B. JOOSS in BIG CITY, a production of the mid-1930s

Glossary of Technical Terms

NOTE: Technical terms are described as simply as possible; however, some observations on correct execution have been included so that the reader may get an idea of what to look for in this respect and so develop a critical eye. The terms are taken from the classical ballet terminology but many of them apply to contemporary techniques. For a description of GRAHAM TECHNIQUE see that entry and the note that follows. Readers who wish for more detailed description are referred to the manuals listed in the Bibliography. DV

adage, adagio. In classical ballet the PAS *de deux* usually consists of four sections: an opening adagio in which the man supports the woman in turns and balances, followed by a solo VARIATION for each of them, and concluded by a fast CODA in which they again dance together. By extension the word adagio is often used to describe the technique of PARTNERING. In class, the word adagio is used to denote a long sequence of exercises in slow tempo, either at the BARRE or in the centre, to develop the dancers' strength in sustaining extensions, balances, etc.

ailes de pigeon (also known as *temps de pistolet*). A large beaten step (*see* BATTERIE) in which the legs, extended to front or back, change two or three times; similar to a double CABRIOLE, but with the feet crossing rather than simply beating together, e.g. in the man's VARIATION in the BLUEBIRD *pas de deux*.

air, en l'. Literally 'in the air'. May be used of steps performed with the working leg raised off the floor, e.g. ROND DE JAMBE *en l'air*, or of jumping steps, e.g. TOUR EN L'AIR

allegro. That part of a ballet class comprised of fast turning or jumping, especially beaten, steps. Usually follows the ADAGIO.

arabesque. A position in which the dancer stands on one leg, straight or bent, with the other extended to the back. There are various kinds of arabesques, numbered in the CECCHETTI system according to the way the arms are arranged and whether or not the supporting leg is bent (the numbering in the VAGANOVA system is different). The body is held upright, except in arabesque *allongée*, when it is almost parallel to the floor, and in arabesque *penchée*, when the dancer leans forward and raises the leg higher to follow the line of the body. The arm extended to the front should be at eye level.

arqué. Bow-legged, the opposite of JARRETÉ

assemblé. A jumping step in which the dancer brushes one leg up and out to the front, side, or back, at the same time springing off the other, and brings the legs together in fifth POSITION before landing. (A common error is to bring the feet together only at the moment of landing, but the essential thing is that the legs are brought together in the air.) *See* BRISÉ.

attitude. A position originally derived from Giovanni de Bologna's statue of Mercury, in which the dancer stands on one leg, straight or bent, with the other extended to the front or back with the knee and the corresponding arm raised. Western dancers are taught that the knee of the working leg should be higher than the foot, but in Soviet ballet this rule is not observed.

balancé. A step in which the dancer sways from side to side, usually in waltz time.

ballabile. A group dance usually for the CORPS DE BALLET.

ballerina. Literally 'female dancer', but usually used of one who dances leading roles. Hence prima ballerina, first dancer.

ballet blanc. Literally 'white ballet': applied to ballets like GISELLE Act II or SYLPHIDE in which the female dancers wear white dresses and portray supernatural beings. *See* TUTU.

ballet d'action. Narrative ballet. The term was current in the 18th and early 19th c.; rarely used in contemporary ballet. *See* ANGIOLINI, HILVERDING, NOVERRE, VIGANÒ, WEAVER.

ballet master or **mistress.** Before the word choreographer was used in its contemporary sense, the ballet master was responsible for arranging ballets. Nowadays, the term more usually denotes the person who rehearses ballets created by someone else and also performs certain administrative duties such as drawing up rehearsal schedules; casting, especially of minor roles, is often the province of the ballet master. In continental Europe, however, the ballet master is usually still expected to choreograph a considerable part of the repertory.

ballon. Literally 'bounce'. The quality of smooth, springing ascent and descent in jumping steps, achieved primarily by the pliant use of the feet.

ballonné, pas. A step in which the working leg is extended to front, side, or back and finishes touching the knee or ankle of the supporting leg. This is done either with a jump or a RELEVÉ.

ballotté, pas. A jumping step in which the legs are drawn up beneath the body; one leg is then extended to front or back as the dancer lands on the other foot, the whole done with a rocking motion. Usually executed in a series.

barre. The wooden bar that runs around the wall of the ballet studio at waist height, and which the dancer holds on to during the first part of class – also usually referred to as the barre. Its purpose is to help the dancer find or adjust his balance, and should not be used as a crutch to maintain balance, in an incorrect position.

basque, pas de. A step in which the dancer makes a circular movement with one leg, to front or back, and steps on to it, bringing the other foot forward or back through first POSITION and closing the feet together in fifth position. May also be performed with a slight jump (*sauté*).

basque, saut de. A jumping step in which the working leg is thrown out to the side and the foot of the other is drawn up to the knee of the working leg as the body turns in the air, landing in that position.

battement. A generic term to describe various movements of the leg made with a beating motion. They are performed at the BARRE in systematic progression to exercise all the muscles of the leg.
battement tendu: the leg is extended to the front, side, and back with the toe resting on the floor, to stretch the foot (in modern dance, these are often called 'brushes').
battement tendu jeté (also called *glissé* or *dégagé*): a similar movement with the toe leaving the floor very slightly.
battement frappé: the leg is extended to the front, side, and back from a position in which the working foot is held *sur le*

COU-DE-PIED of the supporting leg; executed in a sharply accented rhythm, the ball of the working foot strikes the floor as the leg extends, until the toe is either touching the floor or slightly raised off it.
petit battement sur le cou-de-pied: the working foot rests on the *cou-de-pied* of the supporting leg and beats from back to front, or from front to back, in accented or even rhythm. When done in series without changing, at a fast tempo, they are called *serrés*.
battement fondu: the foot of the working leg is extended to point at the front, side, or back from a position in which the foot is pointed in front or back of the supporting ankle; both knees are bent at the beginning and straighten simultaneously.
battement fondu développé: a similar movement with the working leg raised in the air.
grand battement jeté: the working leg is raised to front, side, and back, attaining waist level or higher without bending the knee or altering the alignment of the hips (in modern dance, leg lifts). *See* PLACING. Often called simply *grand battement*.
grand battement développé: from fifth POSITION the foot of the working leg is drawn up to the knee of the supporting leg and then extended to front, side, or back, until the leg is straight. Usually an ADAGIO movement but may also be done fast.

batterie. A generic term referring to steps in which the feet beat together or cross in the air, either as an embellishment to add brilliance to ASSEMBLÉS, JETÉS, SISSONNES, etc., or as the essential characteristic of the step, as in ENTRECHATS or BRISÉS.

beaten steps *see* BATTERIE

bourrée, pas de. A linking step in which the weight is transferred from one foot to the other in three movements. In its simplest form, the step is as follows: starting in fifth POSITION with the right foot front, DEMI-PLIÉ on right foot lifting left foot behind right ankle; step on to left foot on half-toe, open right foot, to second position on half-toe; descend on to left foot, demi-plié with right foot behind left ankle. There are many varieties of *pas de bourrée: en avant* (forward), *en arrière* (backward), *dessous* (over), *dessus* (under), *en tournant* (turning), and with or without changing the feet. *Pas de bourrée chaîné* or *couru* is a series of small even steps on point which give the impression that the dancer is gliding across the surface of the stage, e.g. in the entrance of the Queen of the Wilis in GISELLE.

brisé, pas. Literally 'broken step'. A small travelling ASSEMBLÉ embellished with a beat. May be performed to the side, front, or back.
Brisé volé: a series of *brisés* to front and back, landing on one foot, giving the impression that the dancer is skimming over the surface of the floor; e.g. as performed by the male dancer at the beginning of the CODA of the BLUEBIRD *pas de deux*.

brushes *see* BATTEMENT *tendu*

cabriole. A jumping step in which the dancer raises the working leg to front, side, or back, jumps off the supporting leg and brings it up to beat beneath the other. In a double or triple cabriole the legs beat together two or three times.

changement de pieds. The dancer jumps in fifth POSITION, straightening the legs in the air and changing the feet before landing. *See* ENTRECHAT.

Attitude. Giovanni de Bologna's statue of Mercury

character dancing. Dancing derived from folk or national dances, such as the Mazurka, Czárdás, and Spanish and Neopolitan Dances in SWAN LAKE, Act III. A character dancer is one who specializes in this kind of number or in the portrayal of character through dancing: examples of dancers who have excelled in both genres are LAZOWSKI and GRANT.

chassé, pas. A linking step in which the dancer slides one foot forward, backward, or to the side, bringing the other foot up to it in fifth POSITION and continuing into the next movement. May also be done turning.

chat, pas de. Literally 'cat's step'. A light jumping step in which first one foot, then the other, is drawn up beneath the dancer's body before landing again in fifth POSITION.

cheval, pas de. Literally 'horse's step'. As the name suggests, the dancer paws the ground with one foot.

ciseaux, pas. Literally 'scissors step'. A jumping step in which the legs open wide, either to the side or to front and back, starting and ending in fifth POSITION. Also called *écart en l'air*.

coda. The final section of a PAS *de deux*, during which the dancers may have brief solo passages as well as dancing together to a fast tempo. *See* ADAGIO.

corps de ballet. The ensemble of dancers in a ballet co. who appear in support of the soloists. The term may also be applied to the co. as a whole, e.g. at the Paris O.

coryphée. A dancer (of either sex) who has moved out of the *corps de ballet* to dance minor solo roles.

cou-de-pied. Literally, the 'neck of the foot'. The part of the leg between the base of the calf and the ankle. When one foot is *sur le cou-de-pied* of the other leg, it is correctly 'wrapped' around it, i.e. the foot maintains its TURN-OUT, with the heel forward and the toes stretched back.

coupé. Literally 'cut'. Transferring the weight by picking up one foot and putting down the other, either simply from COU-DE-PIED to *cou-de-pied*, or as a preparation for another step, e.g. ASSEMBLÉ, BALLONNÉ, JETÉ. A series of *jetés en tournant* joined by *coupés* interspersed with CHASSÉS, also done with a turn, and performed in a circle around the stage, is sometimes called *tour de reins* ('turn of the lower back').

croisé. Literally 'crossed'. A position of the body in which the dancer turns obliquely to the audience so that when the leg nearest to the audience is raised in front (*croisé devant*), or the leg furthest from the audience is raised in back (*croisé derrière*), it crosses the supporting leg. *See* EFFACÉ, ÉPAULEMENT.

danseur noble. A dancer in the noble classical style, interpreter of such roles as ALBRECHT, SIEGFRIED etc.

défilé. A parade of all the members of a co., disposed according to their place in the hierarchy. A regular event at the Paris O.

demi-caractère. A style of dancing that has elements of CHARACTER DANCING but remains within the classical technique; examples of *demi-caractère* roles are SWANILDA and the BLUE SKATER.

demi-plié. A half-bend of the knee, preparation and conclusion of all jumping steps and turns.

développé. *See* under BATTEMENT

divertissement. A section of a ballet consisting of dances that have no connection with the plot, e.g. the fairytale dances in SLEEPING BEAUTY, Act III, the 'Peasant' *pas de deux* in GISELLE, Act I. Also used to denote a plotless ballet such as RENDEZVOUS.

double work *see* PARTNERING

écarté. Literally 'spread apart'. A position of the body in which the dancer turns obliquely to the audience and opens the working leg, that closest to the audience, to the side, either on or off the floor.

écart en l'air *see* CISEAUX, PAS

échappé. Literally 'escaped'. A step in which the dancer, starting from fifth POSITION, either springs onto the toes or jumps, finishing with the feet open either to the side (second position) or to front and back (fourth position).

effacé. A position of the body in which the dancer turns slightly away from the audience: the working leg is that furthest from the audience. This is what distinguishes it from CROISÉ: the *croisé* position is closed in its effect and the *effacé* open, though the relationship of the working leg to the body is not changed. *See* also ÉPAULEMENT.

elevation. The ability to jump high into the air and give the appearance of remaining suspended at the apex of the jump.

emboîté, pas. Literally 'boxed' or 'enclosed'. Usually performed in series, interlocking steps in which the feet cross one in front of the other, either on toe or in small jumps (when they may also be performed turning).

enchaînement. A combination of steps into a dance phrase, either in class or as part of a ballet.

entrechat. A vertical jump in fifth POSITION, with the feet changing in the air, twice (*entrechat quatre*), three times (*entrechat six*), four times (*entrechat huit*), and, exceptionally, five times (*entrechat dix*). The term *entrechat deux* is rarely used: when the feet beat once and change this is called *changement battu* or *royale*. In all of these the dancer returns to fifth position. In *entrechat trois, cinq*, and *sept* the dancer lands on one foot with the other touching the supporting leg after one, two, or three beats. A clearly executed beat is made with the calves rather than just the heels.

épaulement. Literally 'shouldering'. The slight turning of the shoulders, CROISÉ or EFFACÉ, in relation to the head and legs (the head turns to look over whichever shoulder is turned forward) distinguishes the classic style, particularly of the Italian, Russian, and British Schools. In the old French and the Danish Schools it is rarely used.

équilibre. Balance – the ability to keep the body in balance while moving, or to hold a pose on one foot.

étoile. Literally 'star'. The highest rank a dancer may hold in the Paris OB.

fouetté. Literally 'whipped'. A turning step, usually done in a series, in which the working leg whips out to the side in a ROND DE JAMBE and then in to the knee as the dancer turns on the supporting leg, rising on to the point at each revolution. The 32 *fouettés* performed by ODILE in SWAN LAKE Act III are a supposed touchstone of female virtuosity.

fouetté sauté, a jumping step with no relation to the above: the dancer raises one leg in front of his body and then turns away from it as he jumps off the other leg, landing in ARABESQUE. This may be done with a beat, as, for example, in a CABRIOLE.

gargouillade. Described by RAMBERT as 'you gargle with your feet'. A jump similar to a *pas de* CHAT in which each leg performs a ROND DE JAMBE in the course of the jump. Sometimes called *rond de jambe doublé*.

glissade. A linking step in which the dancer moves to the side, front, or back from fifth POSITION to fifth or fourth position; the important moment of transition in which the feet are fully stretched is often skimped.

jarreté. Knock-kneed, the opposite of ARQUÉ.

jeté. Literally 'thrown'. A jump from one foot on to the other. There are many kinds of *jeté* for which the nomenclature varies in the different METHODS OF TRAINING; in simple terms, a *jeté* may be small, landing with one foot *sur le* COU-DE-PIED, or large, landing in a position such as ARABESQUE or ATTITUDE; they may travel forward, backward, or to the side; they may be beaten (*battu*) or done with a turn (*en tournant*), as in the *grand jeté en tournant*, sometimes called *entrelacé* (frequently, and incorrectly, *tour jeté*), in which the dancer throws up the right leg, springing off the left, turns in the air and lands on the right foot with the left leg extended in arabesque. *See* also BATTEMENT.

leotard. A one-piece garment covering the entire torso, with or without sleeves, worn with tights for practice or, in many contemporary ballets, as a stage costume. Originally designed by the French acrobat Jules Léotard (1830–70), who also invented the flying trapeze.

line. The harmonious disposition of arms, leg, and head in relation to the body. Many dancers distort line in the effort to achieve a high extension, by over-arching the back or tilting the hips out of correct alignment. *See* PLACING.

maître or **maîtresse de ballet** *see* BALLET MASTER OR MISTRESS

manège. The circular path within the stage area in which a series of turning steps is performed. Term originally associated with the circus, particularly equestrian acts.

methods of training. Ballet technique was first codified in France in the 17th and 18th centuries – hence the use of French in most technical terms. As ballet developed into an autonomous theatrical form and was introduced into other countries, Italy, Denmark, Russia, and more recently Britain and the USA all contributed indigenous elements to the technique. BLASIS's *The Code of Terpsichore* (wr. 1828, pub. 1830), which incorporated and enlarged upon his earlier *Elementary Treatise upon the Theory and Practice of the Art of Dancing* (1820), established principles that still govern the academic technique of classical ballet in spite of the increase in virtuosity since that time. The training systems most widely in use today are the Italian (CECCHETTI), the Russian (taught in the West by graduates of the Imperial S. and their pupils, definitively codified in Soviet Russia by VAGANOVA), the Danish (August BOURNONVILLE), and the British (RAD and RBS). Although these systems vary in such matters as nomenclature, order of exercises, and minor details of execution, the basic principles remain the same. There are of course many teachers who have evolved a personal way of teaching, usually by combining elements of these different systems.

mime. In the BALLETS D'ACTION of the 18th c., narrative was conveyed in terms of gesture or mime. The alternation of such sequences and passages of pure dancing continued in the ballets of the Romantic period (mid-19th c.) and the classic ballets of M. PETIPA and others (late 19th c.). A sign language consisting of gestures, some easily intelligible, others seemingly arbitrary, was evolved (derived from the mime of the *commedia dell'arte* and hence of even more ancient origin). This language is often called 'conventional mime', and may be seen in SWAN LAKE, for instance, when ODETTE tells SIEGFRIED the story of her enchantment by VON ROTHBART, or SLEEPING BEAUTY, in the scene of CARABOSSE's curse and the LILAC FAIRY's modification of it. Such passages are often omitted, abbreviated, or replaced by dancing because the mime is unintelligible to the uninitiated spectator, but such an arrangement destroys an essential balance between the balletic equivalents of recitative and aria.

One of FOKINE's key reforms was the replacement of conventional mime (which he used occasionally for a specific stylistic purpose, as in CARNAVAL) by the 'mimetic of the whole body'. Following this principle, many modern choreographers, among them TUDOR and ROBBINS, have used colloquial gesture as an element in their ballets.

movements in dancing. Dance movement may be divided into seven general categories: *plier* (to bend), *étendre* (to stretch), *relever* (to rise), *sauter* (to jump), *élancer* (to dart), *glisser* (to slide), *tourner* (to turn).

partnering. Also known as double work or ADAGIO. The technique of support of one dancer, usually female, by another, usually male, in turns, lifts, balances, etc. A good partner is one who displays the ballerina to best advantage and conceals the effort used in supporting her: the ability to do so depends as much on his sensitivity to her balance and rhythm as on his physical strength. The term 'cavalier' often used to describe the male partner indicates the kind of gallantry that is an essential element in partnering, just as *porteur* rather contemptuously suggested the subservient position into which the male dancer declined in the second half of the 19th c. Among contemporary dancers, examples of fine partners are DOWELL and NAGY. *See* also PAS *de deux*.

pas. Literally 'step'. The descriptive names of ballet steps often include the word *pas*, or sometimes *temps* (literally 'time'), as in *pas de* CHAT or *temps de* POISSON (in some the word is more often understood than actually used, as in BALLONNÉ). *Pas* is also used in the sense of 'dance', as in *pas de deux*, *pas de trois*, *pas de quatre* (dances for two, three, four people), etc., or as in *pas de l'ombre* (dance of the shadow) from ONDINE or *pas des patineurs* (dance of the skaters). *Pas d'action* signifies a sequence in a ballet in which the narrative is carried forward by means of dancing, as in the so-called Rose Adagio in Act I of SLEEPING BEAUTY.

piqué. Literally 'pricked'. Describes any movement in which the dancer steps directly on to the toe, or half-toe, without bending the knee of the working leg, e.g. *tours piqués*, piqué turns.

pirouette. A complete turn of the body performed on one leg; the working leg may be placed with the foot *sur le* COU-DE-PIED or drawn up to the knee of the supporting leg, or extended in second POSITION (this is a *pirouette à la seconde*), ATTITUDE, or ARABESQUE.

placing. Contrary to popular belief, ballet need not be 'unnatural', apart from the pelvic TURN-OUT. A correct and natural placing or alignment of the head and neck, spine, hips, and legs facilitates the execution of ballet movements and lessens the danger of injury. The back should not be over-arched, the pelvis tilted neither forward nor back, but the torso must be pulled up through the front of the hips and the chest held free and open. To allow for easy movement in any direction and balance without strain, the dancer's weight rests lightly on the ball of the foot, rather than on the heels. This basic placing should be maintained throughout the execution of all movements; for instance, it is both incorrect and ugly to increase the height of an extension to the side or back by means of tilting the hips out of their correct alignment or over-arching the back.

plastique. Soft plastic movements, full of contrasts and clear lines but freer in style than the strict classical technique. Usually refers to dances performed in soft shoes or barefoot.

plié. A bending. The first exercises done in every class to loosen muscles, the foundation of the dancer's technique. The dancer stands erect at the barre and slowly bends the knees, keeping them in line with the turned-out feet. A full *plié* brings the buttocks as near to the heels as is physically possible without disrupting the balance of weight. *Pliés* are practised in all five POSITIONS: in the first, third and fifth, the heels are raised to achieve full *plié*; in second and fourth positions the heels remain on the ground. Nearly every step begins and ends in *plié*; it gives impetus to a jump and 'cushions' a soft landing, making it safe and graceful. Every dancer 'warms up' before a performance by careful practice of *pliés*.

pointe. The tip of the toe. Women, and infrequently men, dance *sur les pointes* in blocked shoes; this is often referred to as 'full point'; 'half-point' and 'three-quarter point' are used when the dancer stands with the toes spread flat on the floor and the rest of the foot raised (RELEVÉ) from the metatarsal joint. Ballet is sometimes derisively referred to as 'toe dancing', though this is by no means an indispensable element. Dancers were first unmistakably depicted on *pointe* in prints dated 1821, but the technique had been gradually developed over the previous decade, and made possible the depiction of the supernatural beings, sylphs and wilis and péris, of the Romantic ballet. By the end of the 19th c. feats of virtuoso point work such as the 32 FOUETTÉS and sustained ÉQUILIBRES were an indispensable part of the ballerina's equipment.

poisson. Literally 'fish'. A position in which the dancer's back is arched, head lifted, and legs pulled back with the feet crossed in fifth POSITION, fully pointed. A jump in this position is called *temps de poisson*. When the ballerina is caught or lifted in this position by her partner it is called *pas poisson* or, more usually, fish dive.

port de bras. Literally 'carriage of the arms'. Used in this sense, and also to denote exercises designed to develop this often neglected aspect of the dancer's art. For instance, when a dancer, at the BARRE, bends the whole torso forward and then arches it back, this exercise is called *port de bras* even though its correct execution involves the entire body. There are positions of the arms just as there are positions of the feet; the numbering of them varies according to the METHOD OF TRAINING. The quality of *port de bras* is a good index of a dancer's musicality.

positions. There are five basic positions of the feet in which all steps in classic ballet begin and end, with corresponding positions of the arms (*see* PORT DE BRAS). It is assumed that in all these positions the legs are turned out from the pelvis: *first position*: heels touching, feet in a straight line; *second position*: feet apart in a straight line; *third position*: one foot in front of the other, the heel against the instep – now rarely used; *fourth position*: feet apart, one in front of the other, either opposite first (*ouverte*) or opposite fifth (*croisée*); *fifth position*: one foot in front of the other, the heel against the joint of the big toe. The numbers of the open positions, second and fourth, are also used when the legs are raised to the side, and to the front or back, respectively.

prima ballerina assoluta. A distinction conferred upon KSHESSINSKA to place her above all other dancers of the Imperial Russian Ballet. In her case, the title gave real power. Seldom used today.

rake of the stage. Many stages, especially in Europe, are raked or slanted down towards the footlights.

régisseur. The nearest equivalent in English is stage manager or director; GRIGORIEV, in the DIAGHILEV and DE BASIL companies, performed that function as well as rehearsing the ballets. Nowadays when the term is used it is more likely to cover the latter function only – hence, to have a similar meaning to BALLET MASTER – and the stage manager is a separate individual whose province is the supervision of lighting cues, scene changes, curtain calls, etc.

relevé, a 'lifted' step; the raising of the body on to half or full POINTE. An abridgment of the stricter term *temps relevé*.

répétiteur (Fr. 'rehearser'). A dancer, usually a senior or retired member of a co., who teaches new dancers their roles in the existing repertory, and is generally responsible for the standard of performance, especially that of the *corps de ballet*.

révérence. A bow or curtsey.

rond de jambe. Literally 'circle of the leg'. May be performed on the ground (*à terre*) or in the air (*en l'air*), inwards (*en dedans*) or outwards (*en dehors*), jumping (*sauté*), or turning (as a component of the FOUETTÉ). *Rond de jambe doublé*: *see* GARGOUILLADE.

rosin. A by-product of turpentine, used by dancers in powdered form on their shoes to prevent slipping.

sissonne. A jump from both feet on to one foot with the working leg either going straight to the COU-DE-PIED (which may also be executed with a turn), or opening to the side, front, or back in a scissorlike motion, with or without changing the feet. May be performed with a beat.

spotting. In turning, the dancer avoids dizziness and adds sharpness to the PIROUETTE by fixing his eyes on a point in front of him; as the body turns, the focus remains on that spot until the last moment and snaps back to it as soon as possible. A dancer who is on perfect balance may increase the number of turns by simply repeating this action (used to comic effect by THARP in her choreography for BARYSHNIKOV in *Push Comes to Shove*).

temps de pistolet *see* AILES DE PIGEON

temps de poisson *see* under POISSON

temps relevé *see* RELEVÉ

terre à terre. Close to the ground. Used of steps like GLISSADE in which the dancers' feet leave the floor only enough to point them fully, as opposed to steps of ELEVATION. Also used of dancers who lack the latter quality, such as ELSSLER and ZUCCHI.

tights. A close-fitting garment covering the dancer's body from waist to feet, worn both in class and on the stage. Called in French *maillot*, after the costumier at the Paris O. in the early 19th c. who is credited with their invention.

'toe dancing' *see* POINTE

tour de reins *see* COUPÉ

tour en l'air. A turn in the air, executed as the dancer jumps with the body held vertically straight. Male dancers are expected to perform double *tours en l'air*, and many are capable of triples. The feat is rarely performed by women. MARKOVA did it at the end of the Polka in FAÇADE.

tournant, en. Literally 'turning'. Many steps may be performed, either singly or in series, while the dancer makes a revolution of the body or describes a circle on the floor.

travesti, en. A female dancer dressed as a man, or a male dressed as a woman, is *en travesti*. In the late 19th c., and well into the 20th, roles such as FRANZ were performed *en travesti* at the Paris O.; many comedy roles such as the Headmistress in GRADUATION BALL and WIDOW SIMONE are also done *en travesti* (this latter kind of impersonation is of ancient theatrical origin). In the USA there are now two all-male *travesti* ballet cos, the Trockadero Gloxinia B. and Les Ballets Trockadero de Monte Carlo (the name indicates a keen sense of ballet history), devoted to affectionate and often devastating parody of balletic conventions, both classic and contemporary.

turn-out. French: *en dehors*. As ballet technique increased in virtuosity in the late 18th and early 19th c., a 180-degree turn-out of the legs from hips (or the closest possible approximation) became essential for speed, flexibility, and the ability to move in any direction.

tutu. Ballet skirt. The calf-length tarlatan skirt worn by M. TAGLIONI in SYLPHIDE was the prototype for the ballerina's costume in Romantic ballets. As ballerinas acquired greater virtuosity in the last two decades of the 19th c., the skirt was shortened, first to just above the knee and then to the present style in which it projects straight out at hip level, with many layers of ruffles beneath. The term *tutu* is actually a slang word referring to the latter part of the costume, or rather to the part of the anatomy it conceals.

variation. Solo dance. *See* ADAGIO.

warm-up. Exercises performed by a dancer to prepare the muscles for the exertion of rehearsal or performance. Usually consists of BARRE exercises, though many dancers add stretches and other movements of their own devising.

Bibliography

Histories and reference books

Recommended books for further study are given at the end of many articles. There are, however, several that cover a much wider span and they are listed below. Some books mentioned are out of print but should be available through public libraries and dance collections. An enormous bibliography of materials relating to dance is to be found in the *Dictionary Catalogue of the Dance Collection, The New York Public Library, Library and Museum of the Performing Arts at Lincoln Center, New York* (1974). Another useful bibliography is given in the catalogue for *Ballet: An Exhibition of Books, MSS, Playbills, Prints etc, illustrating the development of the art from its origins until modern times*, organized by Ivor Guest at the National Book League, London W1, 7 Nov 1957 to 4 Jan 1958.

Beaumont, Cyril, *Complete Book of Ballets* (London 1937, 1951; New York 1938, 1949). A monumental survey of the most important ballets from Dauberval to Lichine, listed under the names of their choreographers, omitting only Bournonville.

—— *Supplement to the Complete Book of Ballets* (London 1942, 1952). Bournonville is represented by three ballets; more information about Didelot and important corrections to the *Complete Book*. Both the *Complete Book* and the *Supplement* include Soviet ballets. Beaumont is particularly good at describing complicated plots of the 19th-century repertory.

—— *Ballets of Today* (London 1954). The second supplement to the *Complete Book*.

—— *Ballets Past and Present* (London 1955). The third supplement to the *Complete Book*.

Brinson, Peter, *Background to European Ballet: A Notebook from its Archives* (Leiden 1966). Good on source materials in national collections.

Brinson, Peter, and Crisp, Clement, *Ballet for All* (London 1970; Newton Abbot 1971). The best guide to the ballets in the repertory today; good on dates and historical material on the 19th century.

Brinson, Peter and van Praagh, Peggy, *The Choreographic Art* (London and New York 1963).

Clarke, Mary and Crisp, Clement, *Ballet: An Illustrated History* (London and New York 1973). Complementary to *The Dancer's Heritage*.

Cohen, Selma Jeanne (ed.), *Dance as a Theatre Art: Source Readings in Dance History from 1581 to the Present* (New York 1974).

Guest, Ivor, *The Dancer's Heritage* (London 1960, 1970; New York 1961). A compact history and chronology.

Haskell, Arnold L. (ed.), *The Ballet Annual: A Record and Year Book of the Ballet*; 18 issues, 1947–63 (London and New York).

Kirstein, Lincoln, *The Book of the Dance* (New York 1935; under the title *Dance*, New York 1969). A detailed history from myth and ritual and the Greek theatre to the emergence of the American classical ballet school.

—— *Movement and Metaphor* (New York 1970; London 1971). A superbly illustrated history of ballet through four centuries. There are introductory sections on the component parts of ballet and the history is then traced through fifty seminal works.

McDonagh, Don, *The Complete Guide to Modern Dance* (New York 1976).

Aleksandr Gorsky's version of *Don Quixote*, Moscow, Bolshoy T., 1900

Mason, Francis (ed.), *Balanchine's Complete Stories of the Great Ballets* (New York 1954, 1968). Contains stories of the ballets and also some interesting comments by Balanchine on his own works and a detailed chronology. Updated and revised as *Balanchine's Book of Ballet* (New York 1977).

Lillian Moore, *Artists of the Dance* (New York 1938, 1969). The story told in a series of essays on great dancers from Camargo to Graham.

Some standard reference books are:

Baril, Jacques, *Dictionnaire de la Danse* (Paris 1964).

Chujoy, Anatole, and Manchester, P. W., *The Dance Encyclopedia* (New York 1967). Contains some long articles as well as factual entries; illustrated.

Koegler, Horst, *Friedrichs Ballettlexikon von A-Z* (Velber bei Hannover 1972).

—— *The Concise Oxford Dictionary of Ballet* (New York and London 1977).

E. Y. Surits, *Vse o Balete* (*All About Ballet*) (Moscow and Leningrad 1966).

Wilson, G. B. L., *A Dictionary of Ballet* (London 1957, 1974).

There are also entries on ballets, as well as plays, films, and operas, in the ten-volume *Enciclopedia dello Spettacolo* (Rome 1954–62, supplement 1966).

Technical Manuals

Beaumont, Cyril, and Idzikowski, Stanislas, *A Manual of the Theory and Practice of Classical Theatrical Dancing* (*Méthode Cecchetti*) (London 1922, with a preface by Maestro Enrico Cecchetti; New York 1975).

Beaumont, Cyril, and Craske, Margaret, *The Theory and Practice of Allegro in Classical Ballet* (*Cecchetti Method*) (London 1930).

Craske, Margaret, and Derra de Moroda, Friderica, *The Theory and Practice of Advanced Allegro in Classical Ballet* (*Cecchetti Method*) (London 1956). These three books cover the precepts of Cecchetti's basic exercises.

Grant, Gail, *Technical Manual and Dictionary of Classical Ballet* (New York 1950; paperback New York 1967).

Kersley, Leo, and Sinclair, Janet, *A Dictionary of Ballet Terms* (London 1952; third edition 1973). A useful guide for the layman.

Kirstein, Lincoln; Stuart, Muriel; Dyer, Carlus; and Balanchine, George, *The Classic Ballet, Basic Technique and Terminology* (New York 1952; London 1953). A manual with a short historical survey by Kirstein, a preface by Balanchine, and superb drawings by Dyer. The authors are all associated with the School of American Ballet.
Vaganova, Agrippina, *Fundamentals of the Classic Dance* (*Russian Ballet Technique*). First English translation by Anatole Chujoy (New York 1946; London 1948 as *Basic Principles of Classical Ballet*; New York, paperback, 1969, incorporating all the material from the fourth Russian edition).

Periodicals

Three that are defunct are important. In the USA, *Dance Index*, under various editors but guided principally by Lincoln Kirstein, appeared in 56 issues between Vol. 1 No. 1 (Jan 1942) and Vol. VIII, Nos 7–8 (1948). In 1971 the entire series was published in New York with a cumulative index. Rich in historic and reference material. Also *Dance Perspectives*, a series of quarterly paperbacks founded in 1958 by Al Pischl to continue the work of *Dance Index*. Bought 1965 by Selma Jeanne Cohen (who edited it until its demise in 1976).

In Britain, Richard Buckle's magazine *Ballet* contained historical articles as well as providing a lively view of the contemporary scene. Two numbers were published before World War II. No. 1 being dated July–Aug 1939; publication was resumed 1946. The last issue was Vol. XII, No. 10, dated Oct 1952. There were 77 issues in all; complete sets are rare but worth tracking down.

Existing periodicals include:
In Great Britain, *The Dancing Times*, established 1910; an illustrated monthly which also covered ballroom dancing until 1956, when this section was transferred to a new publication, *The Ballroom Dancing Times*.
Dance and Dancers, established 1950; an illustrated monthly.

In the USA *Ballet Review*, an occasional journal; a stimulating antidote to much 'Establishment' writing.
Dance Magazine, a monthly journal.
Dance News, a monthly newspaper.

In France, *Les Saisons de la Danse* (Paris), a monthly journal.

In Germany, *Das Tanzarchiv* (Hamburg and Cologne), a monthly journal.

Two annuals of note are:
Dance World (New York), established 1966.
Ballett (Velber bei Hannover), established 1965.

Acknowledgments and Notes on Illustrations

The producers of this book wish to thank all the contributors and others who suggested sources of information and illustrations, also all those who are named in the following list of acknowledgments. Every effort has been made to trace the primary sources of illustrations; in the few cases where it has not been possible, the producers wish to apologize if the acknowledgment proves to be inadequate; in no case is this intentional, and if any owner of copyright who has remained untraced will communicate with the producers a reasonable fee will be paid and the required acknowledgment made in future editions of the book. The producers are particularly indebted to Sukey Bullard, Marianne Dumartheray and Vicki Robinson.

Colour photographs

57 The Tate Gallery, London
58–9 Bibliothèque de l'Opéra, Paris. Photo: Françoise Foliot
60 Victoria and Albert Museum, London. Photo: Derrick Witty
109 From *Ballets Russes: The Memoirs of Nicolas Legat*, Methuen & Co., London, 1939; courtesy Madame A. Legat-Pinnes. Photo: Derrick Witty
110–11 Private Collection. Photo: Derrick Witty
112 Photo: Archives de Documentation Photographique Cauboue, Paris
161 Photo: Giraudon, Paris
162–3 Victoria and Albert Museum, London. Photos: Derrick Witty
164 Photo: Anthony Crickmay
213 Photo: Erio Piccagliani, Milan
214–15 Radio Times Hulton Picture Library
216 Photo: Anthony Crickmay
265 Photo: Houston Rogers
266–7 Photo: Reg Wilson
268 Photo: Anthony Crickmay
317 Photo: Anthony Crickmay
318–19 Alwin Nikolais Dance Theater, New York
320 The Cunningham Dance Foundation, Inc., New York. Photo: Jack Mitchell

Monochrome photographs

12 Photo: Martha Swope
13 Photo: Martha Swope
14 Photo: Rosemary Winckley
17 a. Mansell Collection, London
b. Photo: W. H. Stephen
c. Photo: Louis Melançon
20 a. Photo: Martha Swope
b. The Times
21 Radio Times Hulton Picture Library, London
24 a. Photo: J. W. Debenham Collection, Theatre Museum, London
b. Syndication International Ltd, London
27 a. Commonwealth Institute Theatre, London. Photo: Fredericka Davis
b. High Commission for India
28 Camera Press, London
30 Radio Times Hulton Picture Library, London
34 The Trisha Brown Dance Company. Photo: Lois Greenfield
35 Photo: Babette Margolte
38 Photo: Serge Lido
39 Radio Times Hulton Picture Library, London
40 Photo: Martha Swope
41 New York City Ballet
43 a. Archives de Documentation Photographique Cauboue, Paris
b. Photo: Roger Wood
44 Karen Bowen
45 a. Radio Times Hulton Picture Library, London
b. Ballet Rambert. Photo: Anthony Crickmay
46 Col. W. de Basil's Ballets Russes; Private Collection
48 Photo: Eileen Darbey
49 Photo: Ira L. Hill's Studio; Private Collection

50 Photo: Gordon Anthony Collection, Theatre Museum, London
51 a. Royal Ballet, Covent Garden. Photo: Anthony Crickmay
b. American Ballet Theatre. Photo: Martha Swope
52 Batsheva Dance Company. Photo: Jaacov Agor
53 Photo: Donald Southern
54 Royal Danish Ballet. Photo: John R. Johnsen
55 Photo: Erio Piccagliani, Milan
61 a. Novosti Press Agency, London
b. Royal Ballet, Covent Garden. Photo: Zoe Dominic
62 Novosti Press Agency, London
64 The Times
66 Lincoln Center Dance Collection, New York
68 Radio Times Hulton Picture Library, London
69 Photo: Houston Rogers
73 The Times
76 a. The Cunningham Dance Foundation Inc., New York. Photo: Jack Mitchell
b. Photo: Fred Fehl
78 The Wallace Collection, London
81 a. Photo: Roger Wood
b. Photo: Edward Mandinian
83 Novosti Press Agency, London
85 Photo: Houston Rogers
86 Courtesy Wadsworth Atheneum, Hartford, Connecticut
87 Col. W. de Basil's Ballets Russes; Private Collection
89 a. Novosti Press Agency, London
b. Photo: Donald Southern
90–91 Novosti Press Agency, London
92 EMI Film Distributors Ltd. Photo: National Film Archive, London
95 London Festival Ballet. Photo: Shuhei Iwamoto
96 Private Collection
97 a. Photo: Zoe Dominic
b. Photo: Anthony Crickmay
99 The Cunningham Dance Foundation Inc. Photo: Richard Rutledge
100 a. Private Collection
b. Private Collection
101 Dr. Jaromir Svoboda/Art Centrum, Prague
103 a. Language of Dance Library
b. Israeli Music Institute
c. Language of Dance Library
d. Rudolf Benesh
105 Photo: Anthony Crickmay
106 Radio Times Hulton Picture Library, London
107 Mansell Collection, London. Photo: E. O. Hoppé
115 a. Mansell Collection, London
b. Royal Danish Ballet. Photo: John R. Johnsen
118 Archives de Documentation Photographique Cauboue, Paris
121 a. Private Collection
b. Private Collection
125 a. Photo: Gordon Anthony Collection, Theatre Museum, London
b. Royal Ballet, Covent Garden. Photo: Leslie E. Spatt
128 Lincoln Center Dance Collection, New York
130 Photo: Anthony Crickmay
132 Lincoln Center Dance Collection, New York
133 Victoria and Albert Museum, London
134 Royal Danish Ballet. Photo: John R. Johnsen
136 Bild Amerika-Dienst
137 Mansell Collection, London. Photo: E. O. Hoppé
139 Novosti Press Agency, London
141 a. United Artists Television. Photo: National Film Archive, London
b. J. Arthur Rank Organisation
143 Photo: Fred Fehl
147 Private Collection
149 Photo: F. Mydtskov, Copenhagen
150 Novosti Press Agency, London
151 Radio Times Hulton Picture Library, London
153 Photo: Mike Davis
154 Photo: Houston Rogers
158 Photo: Paul Hansen
159 Photo: Martha Swope
166 a. American Ballet Theatre Foundation. Photo: Martha Swope
b. Anglo-Scottish Pictures and Stereo Techniques
171 Photo: Dan Kramer
172 a. Claus S. Hurok
b. New York City Ballet
173 Photo: Gordon Anthony Collection, Theatre Museum, London
174 Photo: Roy Round
175 Photo: Anthony Crickmay
176 Frankel and Dame International, Radio City Music Hall, New York
179 Lincoln Center Dance Collection, New York. Photo: Barbara Morgan
182 a. Photo: Roger Wood
b. Photo: Houston Rogers
187 Royal Danish Ballet. Photo: John R. Johnsen
188 a. Photo: Lipnitski, Paris
b. Private Collection
192 Photo: Anthony Crickmay
193 Photo: Bassano Ltd.
194 Photo: F. Mydtskov, Copenhagen
198 Victor Hochhauser
200 Bibliothèque de l'Opéra, Paris. Photo: Bulloz
201 Radio Times Hulton Picture Library, London
207 Novosti Press Agency, London
210 Col. W. de Basil's Ballets Russes; Private Collection
212 Lincoln Center Dance Collection, New York
217 Private Collection
219 Photo: Anthony Crickmay
220 Private Collection. Photo: Lenare
221 The Ballet Caravan
222 Photo: Anthony Crickmay
224 Photo: Zoe Dominic
225 Photo: Anthony Crickmay
226 Photo: Anthony Crickmay
228 Photo: Houston Rogers
229 Photo: Gordon Anthony Collection, Theatre Museum, London
230 Photo: Gordon Anthony Collection, Theatre Museum, London
234 Pathé Cinema (Societé Nouvelle), Paris
235 Interfoto MTI, Budapest
237 Novosti Press Agency, London
238 Royal Ballet, Covent Garden. Photo: Leslie E. Spatt
239 Photo: Anthony Crickmay
240 Radio Times Hulton Picture Library, London
241 Photo: James D. O'Callaghan
243 a. Photo: Angus McBean

b. Adelphi Theatre, London
247 Photo: G. B. L. Wilson
248 Photo: Anthony Crickmay
249 Photo: Houston Rogers
251 New York City Ballet. Photo: Martha Swope
252 Private Collection
253 Martha Graham Dance Company
254 Mansell Collection, London. Photo: E. O. Hoppé and Bert
255 Photo: Houston Rogers
258 a. Photo: Zoe Dominic
b. Private Collection
259 Mansell Collection, London
260 Royal Opera House Archives, Covent Garden. Photo: Roger Wood
261 Bibliothèque Nationale, Paris
262 Photo: Martha Swope
270 Photo: Studio Lipnitski, Paris
271 a. Photo: E. Richardson
b. Victoria and Albert Museum, London
272 The London Museum
276 Photo: Roger Wood
278 a. Lincoln Center Dance Collection New York. Photo: Baron de Meyer
b. Photo: Gordon Anthony Collection, Theatre Museum, London
280 Photo: John Blomfield
286 Topix, London
290 Photo: Mike Humphrey
293 Photo Peggy Leder
294 Private Collection
296 Photo: Reg Wilson
300 Novosti Press Agency, London
302 Photo: Paul Wilson
306 Photo: Martha Swope
307 Photo: Anthony Crickmay
309 a. Novosti Press Agency, London
b. Photo: Anthony Crickmay
311 Photo: Frank Sharman
314 Photo: Gordon Anthony Collection, Theatre Museum, London
321 Novosti Press Agency, London
322 Photo: Studio Lipnitski, Paris
328 The Australian Ballet
331 New York City Ballet
332 MGM Films Ltd
333 The Paul Taylor Dance Foundation Inc., New York
335 NBC TV. Photo: Fred Hermansky
337 Minnesota Daily
339 S. Hurok. Photo: Maurice Seymour
340 The Times
341 Bouchard, New York
342 Photo: Houston Rogers
343 Photo: Gordon Anthony Collection, Theatre Museum, London
344 Private Collection
346 a. Collection Parmenia Migel
b. Collection Parmenia Migel
c. Lincoln Center Dance Collection, New York
349 a. and b. Private Collection
350 Private Collection
352 Photo: Houston Rogers
354 Victoria and Albert Museum, London
355 Photo: Martha Swope
358 a. Photo: Anthony Crickmay
b. James Waring Dance Foundation
359 Private Collection
361 Ullstein, Berlin
362 Novosti Press Agency, London
365 Novosti Press Agency, London
366 Ivor Guest
367 Ballets Jooss
369 Private Collection
373 Novosti Press Agency, London